February 1993
Volume 7
Number 5

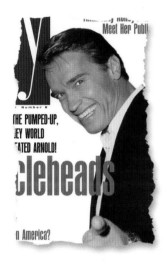

June 1991
Volume 5
Number 8

December 1986
Volume 1
Number 3

August 1992
Volume 6
Number 9

November 1991
Volume 6
Number 2

SPY was a fun-house mirror held up to the excesses and absurdities of its day. Yellow-tied Wall Streeters–turned–inside-traders, scene-makers from Manhattan's Upper East Side and the newly named TriBeCa to L.A.'s west side, Reagan II and Bush 41, Julian Schnabel and Jean-Michel Basquiat, Michael Ovitz, Liz Smith, and Donald Trump were reflected in *Spy*'s pages as the mummified boulevardiers, socialite war criminals, beaver-faced moguls, tigress survivors, and, of course, short-fingered vulgarians they were. During its relatively brief existence *Spy* was, as *Time* magazine put it, an "upscale switchblade [of] good humor and bad manners."

—from Spy *The Funny Years*

June 1991
Volume 5
Number 8

March 1991
Volume 5
Number 5

...of hawks and

April 1988
Volume 2
Number 6

History by

George Kalogerakis

Edited with an

Introduction and Annotations by

Graydon Carter

and Kurt Andersen

Foreword by

Tom Phillips

Designed by

Alexander Isley Inc.

MELCHER MEDIA

miramax books

HYPERION

NEW YORK

The Funny Years

By Tom Phillips
Publisher and Cofounder

Spy was no accident.

BACK IN JANUARY 1985, Kurt Andersen and Graydon Carter crafted notes to each other describing their vision for this new magazine, and that vision was as bold and fearless and culture-changing as the magazine would prove to be.

Some excerpts from Graydon's January 10, 1985, note:

In style, Spy *will be witty, bright, the very life of the party.* Spy *will crackle with smartness and sophistication. Its comments will be saucy, its manner that of the flaneur, a dandy boulevardier with the mind of an atom-smasher....*Spy *will confound social conventions while at the same time pay tribute to them. By day,* Spy *will investigate the great commercial machines that fuel the city, the behind the scenes stories in art, literature, journalism, broadcasting, theatre, fashion, banking, business, show business and the law. By night,* Spy *will dress up for a night on the town to seek out the stories at Manhattan's cabarets, night clubs, theatres, restaurants and after-hour haunts.* Spy *will be a spectator to and a commentator on the passing parade of life in the city.*

...A hundred years from now, the graduate student sifting through the racks at the New-York Historical Society will, with relish, throw himself upon old copies of Spy *to get a feeling for what it was to be young and smart and living in New York in the eighties.*

...Within its pages, Spy *will mark a return to sophisticated satire in think magazines. Not parody, but satire.* Spy *will revive the venerable institution of the magazine gossip column— that is, in the British sense of gossip—not just a ramble of names but meaningful news within New York's societies....*

Irreverence will be our byword, sophistication our creed. Spy *will be above reproach, beyond criticism and, in the eyes of its enemies, beneath contempt.* Spy *will ferret out and expose the fakes, the fakirs, the pompous and the poltroons.* Spy*'s only reverence will be to great, funny, insightful writing.* Spy *will drip with invective as it goes after the villains who clutter the minds of clear thinking people.*

And from Kurt's January 21, 1985, response:

Spy will be bought and read and liked for its hip, clear-eyed sensibility, by readers who share its very smart, youngish New Yorker's outlook on the world and the times. It will be thoughtful and fun-loving both, tasteful but eccentric, brash but civilized, fond of bourgeois creature comforts and skeptical of acquisitive excess. There is nothing in the world that Spy *won't know something about, many things it is amused by, and plenty of things it doesn't approve of, from goofy Avenue C performance art to the maître d' at Ernie's.* Spy *has fierce biases and blind spots and enthusiasms, but they follow no ideological pattern.* Spy *respects and likes Mario Cuomo enormously, for instance, but it would not hesitate to lampoon his sanctimoniousness;* Spy *thinks Ed Koch is a small-minded crank, but the magazine's attitude toward him would be a joshing one, more or less, rather than grim-eyed leftist jeremiads.*

Magazines today tend not to have a distinct sensibility at all, either because articulating a vision is beyond their editorial means or because they are timid, afraid that piquancy will drive away readers. New York *magazine had a clear, confident world view for its first few years, before the magazine became a slave to fashion rather than a commentator on it, wandering off and getting lost amid the boutique racks.* The New Yorker, *even in its enervated, calcified condition, still has a clear sensibility, but it no longer has any vigor; it is cozy and safe and lovely, but almost never compelling.*

Among Spy's *specialties will be a kind of literate sensationalism. The magazine will be almost thoroughly irreverent, often funny and studded with inside information. The magazine will epitomize the energized, slightly hysterical grandeur of the city, its small, exquisite serendipities and grand gestures.*

HUBRIS? PERHAPS. But at least a handful of people found that vision compelling from the outset. I was one of them.

Graydon, Kurt, and I met up for the first time in April 1985, at the suggestion of Kurt's wife, Anne Kreamer. Anne was a true believer—in *Spy*, in her husband, in friends like me—and a forceful personality. And she insisted that this idea was too good to sit idle. I was enlisted as the business partner. But more

important, since I'd had the bug to start a company since college, I was to be the entrepreneurial catalyst.

Three is a good number when it comes to kids in a family or friends on an outing. Three tends to take the pressure off of any one relationship. But three partners in an enterprise is a tricky proposition. When we met for the first time, we decided then and there, over a two-hour lunch, that we were going to do this. But in the seventeen months leading up to the first issue of *Spy*, there were lots of machinations, lots of flare-ups, lots of moments of doubt. The amazing thing is that with the first issue in October 1986, our threesome and the little enterprise we'd created hit stride immediately—even if the magazine itself was still not fully formed—and proceeded to function with a stunning lack of friction.

Building a business around a cultural phenomenon was not easy, but it sure was fun.

We borrowed some money from friends and family, took offices in the historic Puck Building, and started hiring a staff. We initiated fortnightly writers' lunches at a hole-in-the-wall café/bar in Little Italy and began assembling a group of talented contributors. We tried to find investors, and asked everyone from arbitrageur Ivan Boesky to publisher Martin Peretz to *National Lampoon* cofounder Henry Beard, finally scraping together start-up money from a band of generous, blue chip benefactors (and, unlike Boesky, no known felons). In fact, we didn't pull together the funding to really make a go of the venture until after the second issue, when Steven Schragis—who found us, oddly, through CBS chairman Larry Tisch's then right-hand man, Jay Kriegel—wrote a big check.

The prelude to publication was an anxious time, and it made our debut all the more thrilling. By the time the first issue hit the stands, the editors had been stewing on the idea for almost two years. They were all piss and vinegar about how American media had grown stale and predictable and coddling. This magazine would be the antidote, they hoped, the "literate sensationalism" to break through that decade's journalistic malaise. And I, the media naïf in search of a 15- (or 50-) step detailed operating plan for a new enterprise (not some visionaries' conceptual panacea), woke up every morning for that year and a half with a Dylanesque whine in my head asking, "But what does that *meeee*-an?"

Maybe they knew all along. Not all of us would or could admit at the time that the first issue, and even more the second through seventh issues, did not quite live up to the vision. But we hung on. And Kurt and Graydon—and the rest of the editorial founders—did enough things differently and enough things well to earn a degree of the press hype that greeted the magazine from the outset.

And then with the "Little Men" story in June 1987, *Spy* had its breakthrough. We established a way of looking at the world that was skewed and true at the same time—and, by the way, hilarious and ridiculous and acidic and irresponsible in only the most morally justifiable way. And then Graydon's famously Proustian columns and Kurt's endlessly inventive, rhythmic opening essays gained new weight. *Spy* became the new "paper of record" for people who really understood media and urban life and the cultural milieu.

This, then, is what those rambling lunches in Little Italy had been anticipating—a platform for journalistic discourse that was simultaneously above and below the accepted standards of the day. For the next few years, that editorial team could do little wrong. They took chances and repeatedly and brilliantly hit a chord. And the genius at the center of that brilliance was Kurt and Graydon and their astoundingly fertile relationship as coeditors.

My wife, the writer Ellen Hopkins—who had a high regard for the coeditors' wives and their marriages—used to say that Graydon and Kurt were the great loves of each other's lives. Nothing weird or anything. They were the Lennon and McCartney of publishing, the Nichols and May, the Woodward and Bernstein. It was often noted that they finished each other's sentences. Well, that was because they had effectively created a new language, a fearless and funny shared perspective on things—*all* things. Made it tough to do three-way interviews, something we were asked to do every other day during the early months, and something I learned to avoid, partly for my own protection (no one was immune!) and partly to get a word in edgewise.

Spy was never a normal magazine. There was momentum, lots of momentum, but no pacing, no formula. Conceiving and editing the magazine was really hard. Who ever heard of a monthly of modest means claiming turf akin to the paper of record? Our little cadre of fans breathlessly anticipated every issue, and wrote us hysterical letters when their copies arrived a day later than the magazine appeared on the newsstands. And in June 1988, about the time Condé Nast owner S. I. Newhouse, Jr., approached us to try to buy the minority stake of our largest investor, Steven Schragis, Kurt and Graydon started to talk about the risk of

burnout. *Spy* was wildly inventive every month, and that was a blessing—to our readers, to our advertisers, to our internal esprit de corps—and a curse. How to maintain? How to live up to ever-escalating expectations? We're not big, we're not rich, and, increasingly, we've said our piece.

One of the things that still amazes me 15 years later is that *Spy* continued to get better. One man's view, and about this there is no consensus, but the November 1989 issue, which featured an infiltration/investigation of the aging Republican boys' camp Bohemian Grove [see page 198], a series of ultra-condensed Mamet plays entitled *Speed-the-Play* [see page 192], and a complete commemorative "reproduction" of a 1964 issue of *Spy* (perhaps the most fully realized *Spy* feature of all time—see page 160), was our best ever. Then a bunch of things conspired against us. We finally put the magazine up for sale, we went from publishing 10 times a year to 12 (my idea, *ugh*), our principal advertisers were feeling the heat of an encroaching recession, Paul Marciano pulled Guess jeans advertising after being offended by a piece we did on Fairchild's Michael Coady (who, later, when we were both Disney executives, told me he'd forgiven me—*me?!*). The magazine was eventually sold, and then sold again, and then shut down.

Kurt and I—while we were both running Internet media businesses in the late '90s—later used to share a thought that *Spy* was the first popular execution of interactive media. *Spy* in the Internet age would have thrived in a way that the magazine never could. But, fact is, I love that stack of magazines that captured the culture of the era. Ultimately, print is more seductive and enduring—if less shareable—than bits and bytes.

Time threatens to dim the impact of *Spy* in its prime. The population of people who remember *Spy* firsthand is not exactly dying off, but 20 years after our debut, they are becoming dispersed, forgetful, perhaps even fickle. That's why I'm grateful for this book, as I am for my partnership with two brilliant editors and a team of creative folks who changed media in America.

> *Spy was never a normal magazine. There was momentum, lots of momentum, but no pacing, no formula. Conceiving and editing the magazine was really hard.*

We didn't start *Spy* in order to become the sorts of people the magazine specialized in teasing and satirizing, but that's pretty much the way it's worked out.

Back then, we almost certainly would have contrived nasty epithets for two no-longer-angry, no-longer-young men with comfortable professional lives, like the nicknames we habitually and sometimes obsessively bestowed on others—"bosomy dirty-book writer," "short-fingered vulgarian," and "churlish dwarf billionaire" come to mind. And speaking of ironies, what is one to make of an anthology and self-flattering history of a magazine that savaged both Disney and Miramax being published by Miramax Books, a subsidiary of The Walt Disney Company? That one *can* have one's cake and eat it? That in America, all cultural subversiveness is eventually co-opted? That life is a cabaret, old chum? Take your pick.

We sincerely want to welcome you to this history-cum-anthology—which back then we might well have called a "Super-Special 20th Anniversary Commemorative Ultra-Poignant Keepsake Edition." Creating *Spy* was insanely fun—an amazing, exhilarating, and gratifying (as well as terrifying and fatiguing) adventure. This book is intended to be a distillation and something of an explanation of what the fun was all about. We hope to show that you didn't have to be there to enjoy *Spy*. (Besides, some people who *were* there—like Graydon's adorable mother, for instance—didn't even get it at the time. Or so she later said.) Alas, one volume permits us to include only a fraction of the splendid work that ran in *Spy*. But in any event, Spy *The Funny Years* is for both the generationally self-obsessed people who loved or hated the magazine in real time and the younger generation whose own searing childhood memories of the JFK assassination derive from the last 10 minutes of the 1983 NBC miniseries starring Martin Sheen and Blair Brown.

Not to sound too geezery, but things were very different 20 years ago, when we launched *Spy*. The state-of-the-art PC was one one-thousandth as powerful as any run-of-the-mill modern laptop, and cost more than $7,000 in today's dollars. There was no Web, and therefore no Google or email. No cell phones. Long distance still cost a fortune. Fax machines were novelties. There was no Photoshop or Quark, no real digital design. And most of us lived in wooden shanties heated with dried dung and illuminated by lard lamps, rode in horse-drawn omnibuses to the office, and harvested our own oyster suppers in the Hudson River shallows.

There *was* humor and especially parody before *Spy*, of course,

but there was precious little in the way of nonfiction satire or irony in print. The *MAD* of our childhoods and the *National Lampoon* of our youths were filled with nearly nothing but exuberant fictions. There was no *Daily Show*, no bottomless sea of 24/7 Web mischief-making, essentially no reporting or commentary on awesomely powerful cultural institutions such as *The New York Times* and Creative Artists Agency, no E! Entertainment Network or mainstream tabloid weeklies pumping out a flood of snarky celebrity news and gossip. (And the British word *snarky* was all but unknown here, perhaps because the impulse and sensibility it describes—a skeptical, ironic take on the celebrated and putatively important—hadn't yet become ubiquitous and automatic in America.)

When we were imagining *Spy*, we decided that the magazine had to be fact-based, that a story had to be well reported. And it had to be amusing. It wasn't easy to find journalists who were both good reporters and funny in print. In *The New Yorker*'s "Talk of the Town" and *The Washington Post*'s Style section, on the front page of *The Wall Street Journal* and occasionally in the *Times*, there were witty pieces that sounded like smart journalists talking. But they were rare. And the people who could pull that off—writers like Maureen Dowd at the *Times* and Sally Quinn at the *Post* and Ian Frazier at *The New Yorker*—were stars, and we couldn't afford them.

There was humor and especially parody before Spy, *but there was precious little in the way of nonfiction satire or irony. There was no* Daily Show, *no bottomless sea of 24/7 Web mischief-making.*

We were not great reporters ourselves, but we had been keeping our eyes and ears open for a decade as journalists in New York, so we just sort of…knew stuff. If we could establish a new, coherent, consistent voice for the magazine early on, our staff and contributors would at first mimic it and then make some dialect of it their own. That voice, improvised as we went along, was a hash of H. L. Mencken and A. J. Liebling and Wolcott Gibbs from the '20s, '30s, and '40s; parody-*Time*-ese of the '40s and '50s; New Journalism of the '60s and '70s; *Private Eye*, the scabrous (and much jokier) British fortnightly; and the ways we just happened to write. Our first editors, the phenomenally talented Susan Morrison (from *Vanity Fair*) and George Kalogerakis (from some primitive, long-forgotten beta version of the online *New York Times*), picked up and embellished the riff, and others followed.

The magazine's journalistic, literary, and graphic styles kept evolving, but all were based on the essential facts that we didn't have much money and didn't quite know what we were doing—both of those a plus, we have since decided, when it comes to starting something that intends to be fresh and unique. We had pathetically thin Rolodexes, next to no "access." We never produced a "dummy" issue. We didn't have a national distributor when we started. Because we could afford professional photo shoots only for the covers, inside we made a virtue of using goofy and anachronistic free photographs. We never did demographic studies or reader surveys. We never, ever used the term *brand* to describe the magazine. We didn't realize you could borrow clothes from fashion designers for photo shoots. Stupidity was the mother of invention, and at least a godmother of integrity as well.

> *What we always tried earnestly to do,*
> *though, was to be* discriminating
> *in our meanness, to whack people*
> *and things* deserving *of being whacked*
> *at the time, and to administer the correct*
> *severity of whacking in each instance.*
> *(We did not always succeed.)*

Because we tended to produce every issue as if it were our last, we crammed more and more into each one, squeezing in this chart or that sidebar by making the type smaller, and smaller, and still smaller. We were in a hurry. We wanted to have as much fun as we possibly could with our weird, noisy, beautiful little runaway train before it derailed or ran out of steam. Even before we launched, there was a dinner during which the principals—according to the recollection of at least one of them—discussed the idea of running the magazine full-throttle for five years and then shutting it down.

Ah, but the paradoxes of ostensibly visionary leadership: It was also important to convey to the staff that we had *every* confidence that this was *the* magazine for us for our lifetimes. And, therefore, for them. *Spy* did start breaking even at the end of our third year, but a recession (the kinder, gentler George H.W. Bush recession)

promptly ended our very brief era of profitability. And although we intended *Spy* to be a real business (parents and old friends were among the investors), our desire to make an awesome magazine was always stronger than our desire to make money, so as revenues rose, budgets tended to follow right behind. The screenwriter Larry Doyle, who worked for *Spy* as an editor and writer, says that the magazine was "a $120 million art movie." He overstates the budget by 20- or 40-fold, but he's got a point.

Spy was considered mean, especially by people whom we…were mean about. What we always tried earnestly to do, though, was to be *discriminating* in our meanness, to whack people and things *deserving* of being whacked at the time, and to administer the correct severity of whacking in each instance. (We did not always succeed.) For better or worse, the editors of *Spy*, unlike editors of most magazines, were held responsible for every word in every issue. Each of us was only able to pass the buck—*Kurt does all the mean things*; *No, Graydon does all the mean things*—to the other. In our post-*Spy* days, we have never apologized to anybody written about in *Spy*, and we've even worked with a few of them. Graydon was at a book party at Elaine's one night in the '90s and spotted two of *Spy*'s most mercilessly covered early targets, the former *Times* executive editor A. M. Rosenthal and his wife, Shirley Lord—a novelist whom the magazine *always* referred to as the "bosomy dirty-book writer." When they walked up and pleasantly said hello, the former editor of *Spy* thought to himself, *They've got a lot more class than I do*. And thicker skins.

Our only advice to anyone still stinging from an unkind mention in *Spy* is to try to remember something specific the magazine said about *anyone else*—apart from the Trumps and Shirley Lord, of course. The thing is, you probably can't. And those other people can't remember one thing written about *you*, either—unless of course, you happen to be Shirley Lord or a Trump.

---

*It would be unseemly of us to toot our own horn any more on this count. But we're happy to pass the instrument on to others for further tooting. "We're all *Spy* now," a journalist wrote on *mediabistro.com* a few years ago. "Consider: Is there a general-interest magazine today that couldn't find a place for *Spy*'s signature features, like 'Separated at Birth,' or 'Logrolling in Our Time'? Is there a magazine whose opening pages don't use flippant icons and mismatched type to catch the eye? It's hard to prowl the newsstand today without seeing the influence of Kurt Andersen and Graydon Carter's stinging tone or

If you worked at *Spy*, you can't help seeing its memes everywhere these days, in print, on the Internet, on television. And *Spy*'s editorial spores and sensibility live on not only in obvious heirs like *The Onion* and *The Daily Show* but in publications from *Entertainment Weekly* to *Maxim* to *Time* and the *Times* itself, and on cable channels like VH1 and Nickelodeon and shows like *Punk'd*.* Not long ago, the magazine played a part in a very funny exchange on *The Simpsons*—Lisa informed a disappointed hillbilly that *Spy* was no longer publishing—which pleased us hugely and really put us in solid with our children.

Producing this book—that is, allowing George Kalogerakis to do most of the hard work to produce this book—has sent us on a sort of Ghost of Christmas Past return trip to the *Spy* years. And obliged us to stop and consider our, um, er, you know, achievement and legacy. We decided we're proud of what we and our hundreds of colleagues (see pages 300–301) managed to do—amazed by it, really. And happy to have this core sample and chronicle.

Pretty much everyone who worked at *Spy* now inhabits the worlds the magazine criticized from the outside. Both of us have been called sellouts for moving on to more or less conventional careers—mostly by people in their thirties. To which we generally respond: *Look, you're the age we were when we started* Spy— *if you think it was so great, go out and invent your own weird, mean, noisy, beautiful, original thing*. There are reasons neither of us has sought to re-create *Spy*. First, doing so would put us squarely in the category of one-trick ponies, or, in *Spy*ese, "coasters." Second, a magazine like *Spy* must be fueled by a certain youthful, callow recklessness and even anger. And if you're in your fifties and still that reckless and angry, you don't need to start a magazine—you need therapy.

Alex Isley's highly layered page designs, or both. The women's magazine *Jane*, from its bumptious attitude to its checkerboard of typefaces, often comes off as a feminized version of *Spy*....Even the celeb-besotted *Us Weekly* has a rakish feature called 'Fashion Police,' in which comedians and designers rip on celebs' red-carpet attire.... When Jonathan Alter and Mickey Kaus came up with *Newsweek*'s 'Conventional Wisdom Watch'—to cover the horse race of the 1988 presidential election—Alter was told, 'There's no room for irony in a newsweekly.'" Things have changed. —Eds.

1

"Sing, Sing, Sing (With a Swing)"

What *Is* It? Oh, Well, Um, It's Just Sort of a Lifestyle Magazine, Mostly about New York

Come on, it'll be an adventure.
—Graydon Carter, 1986

THE THING IS—*the thing is*—it really was a blast.

We could, for appearances' sake, pretend that it wasn't—pretend that in fact it was a stress-filled grind, rendered charming only by the passage of time. Or that as experiences go it was perfectly okay but unremarkable: "*Spy,* right, yeah—that was kind of interesting."

But none of that would ring true. It wouldn't *be* true.

During its relatively brief existence (particularly during The Funny Years; not so much during The Years That Followed the Funny Years), *Spy* was, as *Time* magazine put it back then, an "upscale switchblade [of] good humor and bad manners." Launched in 1986 by a handful of like-minded, restless malcontents, the magazine was a virtually instant and notorious success. In the space of a couple of years, *Spy* had (arguably) rewritten the rules of magazine journalism, (definitely) offended a lot of people, (perhaps) delighted a few more, produced a best-selling book and

a couple of prime-time TV specials, won an important federal court case in the name of parody, hosted some of the swellest parties of that era in New York (and one in Hollywood), and had still found time to coax two of the richest men in the world into cashing 13-cent checks.

Spy was a fun-house mirror held up to the excesses and absurdities of its day. Yellow-tied Wall Streeters–turned–inside-traders, scene-makers from Manhattan's Upper East Side and the newly named TriBeCa to L.A.'s west side, Reagan II and Bush 41, Julian Schnabel and Jean-Michel Basquiat, Michael Ovitz, Liz Smith, and Donald Trump, and the rest of a sometimes grisly but always entertaining cast of characters were reflected in *Spy*'s pages as the mummified boulevardiers, socialite war criminals, beaver-faced moguls, tigress survivors, and, of course, short-fingered vulgarians they were.

The *Spy* adventure—and to anyone who worked there during its heyday, the whole enterprise carried the whiff of mission—was intense and somewhat terrifying, conducted from the first at warp-speed. The magazine, as well as some of the people involved

Opposite:
***Spy*'s messenger–writer-at-large Walter Monheit en route to his last delivery of the day.**

GREETINGS FROM SPY

in it, would inevitably experience a burnout. As the early '90s verged on the mid-'90s, it would become all too evident that The Funny Years no longer lay ahead. But the price, whatever form it took, was one we were all willing to pay.

The ringleaders for this unlikely escapade were Kurt Andersen, a midwestern polymath with a penchant for breaking his arm and a talent for computing large numbers in his head that was every bit as impressive as his literary skills; Graydon Carter, another gifted writer and editor—part Sergeant Bilko, part Oscar Jaffe, all Canadian, with a preternatural gift for winning at arcade games—whose sense of style was so highly developed that, had the satirical-magazine thing not worked out, he might have plausibly gone into interior decorating or haberdashery; and Tom Phillips, a smart, handsome, civilized pinch fist who left Wall Street to spend his days reminding his two partners that magazine start-ups operated on money as well as ideas, and whose job description as publisher included giving the staff free haircuts—a touching attempt to compensate with shears and combs for *Spy*'s shortcomings in the area of salaries and benefits. Tom's haircuts, at least, were generous and competitive.

The three of them were, it seems now, remarkably young.*

I was hired in early 1986 to help launch the magazine, one of two deputy editors (along with Susan Morrison). *Spy* existed then primarily as a logo and some stationery. True, there was a lease

---

*Not all *that* young, actually. All three of us were in our thirties—one of us in his *mid*-thirties. The two editors were old enough to make serious mischief and young enough to be willing to make it. —Eds.

---

on an office, a top-floor loft in the still-under-renovation Puck Building at Houston and Lafayette streets in lower Manhattan.* But the space was devoid of furniture, computers, in fact of anything that suggested "office"—including people, unless you counted the building's construction workers, who tended to drift through doing urgent, noisy things with their chisels and ladders and drills. The initial entry in a journal I kept about the magazine begins:

June 9, 1986. First day at Spy. *Got dust all over me.*

Not exactly Pepys—or Warhol, for that matter. It lacks the former's obsession with "drawing up a new form of Contract with the Victualler," and the latter's obsession with Halston and Bianca and taxi receipts. Still, it was a beginning.

SPY HAD REALLY STARTED five years earlier and about 50 blocks uptown. Kurt, then 26, had been writing for the broadcast personality Gene Shalit, had just published a humor book called *The Real Thing,* and had begun working as a writer in the Nation section of *Time.* (*Time* boasted a remarkable crop of young journalists. In 1981 in the Nation section were also Jim Kelly, Walter Isaacson, Steve Smith, and Evan Thomas; Richard Stengel, Alessandra Stanley, and Maureen Dowd would soon join them; Frank Rich, Michiko Kakutani, and James Atlas had just left the magazine, and John Podhoretz was a researcher.†) One

---

*It was the Puck Building built in 1885 to house *Puck*, the great satirical magazine of its day. When we discovered we could rent space there, it seemed like kismet, an absolutely providential confirmation of our destiny. Also, the rent was less than $2,000 a month.

†Kelly became the managing editor of *Time* (and now of Time Inc.), succeeding Isaacson, who became the head of CNN and the Aspen Institute; Smith became editor of *U.S. News and World Report*; Thomas is an author and *Newsweek* editor and writer; Stengel was coauthor of Nelson Mandela's autobiography and recently succeeded Kelly at *Time*; Rich is a *New York Times* columnist; Kakutani is the Pulitzer Prize–winning chief book critic for the *Times*; Atlas is a book publisher and author; Stanley and Dowd are television critic and Pulitzer Prize–winning op-ed columnist, respectively, at the *Times*; and Podhoretz is a columnist at the *New York Post*. —Eds.

day another colleague, a 31-year-old stranger from the People section, popped his head into Kurt's office and said, "I read your book—I loved it!"

"Which is a good way to meet anybody," Kurt observes.

"I had read his book and thought it was extraordinary, especially for somebody that age," Graydon says now. "Then we met again at a dinner, and I came away thinking, *I have a feeling this guy's going to be my friend.*"

They did grow close—Kurt became godfather to Graydon's first child, Graydon later became godfather to one of Kurt's, and the two families for a time shared a very damp, very tiny Connecticut summer house. Sometime in 1984, their conversations began to turn away from the doings at *Time* and *Life* to another magazine. One that didn't yet exist.

"It wasn't, 'Let's start a magazine'—and I think we benefited from the fact that there was none of that purposefulness about it," says Kurt. "It was, 'A magazine that did *this* and didn't do *this* would be so great.' That conversation continued for a year or so, until it coalesced and became more refined. And we began to get a little more serious about it."

Jim Kelly knew them both from *Time*—he and Graydon were best friends. "I thought the idea was never going anywhere, because it was a lot more fun to talk about these things over lunch than to actually get anything produced," he says. "And also because Graydon, in the first lunch I ever had with him, in September of 1978, had said, 'Wouldn't it be great to create a magazine like the original *New Yorker*, and you could call it *Spy?*' From *The Philadelphia Story*, of course." *The New Yorker* of the 1920s and '30s, Kelly points out, was sassy and satirical—a different animal from what came after.

"I had the name before I even had a thought of a magazine," Graydon admits, adding that its roots actually predated *The Philadelphia Story*. "It was from the illustrations in the old *Vanity Fair* by the illustrator who called himself Spy—now there's an irony. I loved the fact that it had three letters, so the letters could be large. I'd had a magazine in Canada called *The Canadian Review*, and to get all those letters across the cover—the type was so tiny."

"Graydon had basically left Canada when that magazine had failed," continues Kelly. "So to have first heard about his new magazine idea in 1978 and still be hearing about it in the mid-'80s—I mean, I didn't even absorb whether it was a good idea or not, I just assumed it wasn't going to go anywhere. Also, I didn't

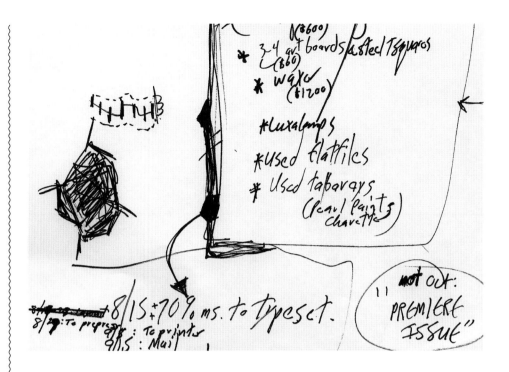

How to make a magazine: Kurt Andersen's to-do list for getting *Spy* and its art department off the ground

think getting a business plan together and selling it to someone was something that would play to their strengths."

Indeed, their strengths lay elsewhere. Kurt and Graydon were by now devoting most of their extracurricular time and energy—and money—to Missile Command and Gravitar, video-arcade games.

"*Spy* was founded not at the Algonquin Hotel* or anything romantic like that, but at Playland, the old arcade over on Broadway in Times Square," says Graydon. "Gravitar is really a skill-set game," he continues. "It is so hard. Even now, every once in a while I'll be in some far-flung corner of the world—in an airport in Rio or something—and I'll see a Gravitar game. And I just want to drop my bags and go and play it again."

By 1985 the pair's on-and-off magazine dialogue (and possibly their supply of quarters) had exhausted itself. "The topic [of starting a magazine] had run its course as a reason to have expense-account lunches that *Time* paid for," says Kurt. "We needed to find out if this were possible to do as a real thing."

---

*In fact, we did have at least one evening of cocktails at the Algonquin while we were dreaming up the magazine, during which Kurt noticed that a bartender there happened to be the doppelgänger of the last Shah of Iran—and thus Separated at Birth? was born. —Eds.

Even now, SPY's writers are sneaking around and scribbling away at scores of knock-your-socks-off feature stories. The Second-Home Homeless. Hunting Small Game in Central Park. New York's Least-Read Columnists. How to be Famous. Bad Philanthropies. The Selective SPY Police Blotter. The SPY Guide to Romans à Clef. Jerk Detectors. How to Marry a Millionaire. Night Clubs by Day. The SPY Celebrity Make-Over Fund. A Field Guide to New York Pests. Review of Reviewers. Weird Coming Events. An Illustrated History of the Rug. Gossip Column Scorecard. The SPY Guide to Terribly Correct Pronunciation. The Ten Stupidest New Yorkers. A SPY Viewer's Guide to the Jerry Lewis Telethon. And our regular monthly column on The Times. Don't miss the fun.

The Facts Speak For Themselves ↘

	SPY	New York	New Yorker	Village Voice
Funny	YES	NO	Rarely	NO
Stylish	YES	Occasionally	NO	NO
Provocative	YES	NO	NO	Predictably
Five part series about grain	NO	NO	YES	NO
Dull, cranky political harangues	NO	NO	NO	YES
Article about caterers in every issue	NO	YES	NO	NO
Annual subscription price	Under $20	$33	$32	$33

The notorious winter 1985–86 direct-mail appeal for charter subscribers: It was fresh and funny, it got a remarkable response, and, after the first issue arrived, the cancellations went through the roof.

THE PUCK BUILDING
295 LAFAYETTE STREET
NEW YORK NY 10012

S P Y

Dear New Yorker:

Isn't New York wonderful? Isn't New York awful? Don't you hate New York? Don't you love New York?

Don't you wish New York had a magazine as playful and stylish and hard-headed and bristling with energy as the city itself?

Beginning in October, it will.

SPY is the funny, fearless, fast-paced magazine for smart New Yorkers. SPY is not just a new publication. It is a whole new kind of intelligent metropolitan magazine. SPY is polished and satirical, sophisticated yet mischievous, well-dressed but slightly ill-mannered, literate, urbane--and just a little dangerous.

"I knew Tom Phillips in college, so I introduced Kurt and Tom," says Anne Kreamer, Kurt's wife and later *Spy*'s advertising sales and marketing director. "Tom was kind of miserable—he'd done the Stanford MBA thing and the investment banking thing [at Rothschild, Inc.], and it was a great opportunity for him to shift gears. And he had the financial rigor and experience and language to put together that stuff—to go out and raise the money—that Kurt and Graydon clearly didn't."

"I was desperately looking for a company to start," says Tom, who, although an obsessive reader of *Rolling Stone*, *Time*, and *Esquire*, had given no thought to becoming a magazine publisher. That changed when he met Graydon and Kurt on April 25, 1985, over a two-hour lunch at a now-vanished Indian place around the corner from the Time & Life Building. "I thought they were brilliant, fun, interesting. They had a very sophisticated enthusiasm, totally infectious. I just listened to them banter back and forth with this idea and thought, *Wow, this is incredible*. We decided then and there that we were going to do this. We said the words."

"THE OTHER GREAT ESSENTIAL that Tom brought," Kurt says, "was that he forced us to write things down: 'Okay, let's start writing a prospectus that describes what this magazine would be.' Graydon and I, by ourselves, might well have never pushed each other to bring it to the next level of reality."

That's the story Kurt and Graydon have always told—that the jump-start to what became *Spy* occurred when Tom ordered them to sit down and write out a hundred story ideas. Although Tom eventually did suggest this, he notes that "it was hardly a brilliant stroke of mine, it was just something I heard at a *Folio* magazine-publishing conference." The really significant motivation kicked in just weeks after that initial lunch.

"We had a little retreat in Tyringham, Massachusetts,"* Tom says. "Graydon and Cynthia, and Kurt and Anne, and me—

*We wrote the editorial plan at the Shaker settlement in Tyringham, at a house owned by Betty and George Kramer, Graydon's then-wife's de facto godmother and her husband. Betty's first husband's father, Hawley Truax, had been the first president of *The New Yorker* and used to have Wolcott, Kaufman, and the like up frequently. And George had been an original investor in *New York* magazine. So writing the plan there, in a library stuffed with volumes by *New Yorker* contributors and editors, seemed felicitous. —Eds.

'the gay partner,' they called me. How long I took that shit from them, because I was single, thin, and neat!* And I announced to Kurt and Graydon, 'That's it, I'm out of Rothschild.' They said, '*What*? You quit your *job*?' At the time, they made the explicit point, 'Well, you sort of forced our hand here. You mean we're actually doing this? We're not just going to talk about it?'"

So they started on their Hundred Ideas. "Kurt and I sat there for a long time, lunch hour after lunch hour at the Time Inc. cafeteria, with nothing," Graydon remembers. "But then Kurt had an idea for…I think it was 'Things Found in the East River in the Last Year,' and it was like breaking the code."

> *"I announced to Kurt and Graydon, 'That's it, I'm out of Rothschild.' They said, 'What? You quit your job?'"*

As a contrarian challenge, they set one rule for themselves: to find an approach that stood entirely apart from contemporary magazines in substance and style. For instance, there would be no reviews. But there would be a monthly review of the reviewers, and, maybe, "Things Found in the East River."

Read today, the *Spy* business plan, written in 1985, shows how clearly they knew what they wanted—at least by the time they were ready to shop it around. The long and casual gestation period had produced an unintended bonus: *Spy* might have been conceived as a lark, but its markings, habitat, song, behavior, and range were in place before it ever left the nest.

"It wasn't like we had this deadline date with investors, or a particular commercial mandate to fulfill," Kurt says. "The wine had time to ferment. And then, once we had an actual MBA-business guy as part of the thing—a smart outsider—we had another six months to shape it. So it grew organically. I have looked back at that prospectus, and I think it is about as close to what we did as a thing like that can be."

The story ideas they wrote down show that the hypothetical *Spy* was both topical ("Sale of the Century," an idea that was never executed, proposed a fund-raising drive "in which readers will send us $3 for a prospective square inch of a Trump Tower condominium,

*Back then all of us were thin. Tom, however, had buff, epicene good looks. Plus, he was not merely "neat" but indispensably *fussy* about lists and folders and phone calls and administrative tasks. —Eds.

SPY

THE PUCK BUILDING
295 LAFAYETTE STREET
NEW YORK, NEW YORK 10012
212/925-5509

Spy lunch

June 17th; 12:30 pm.

Mare Chiaro.

Graydon Carter ✓
Kurt Andersen ✓
Tom Phillips ✓
George Kalogerakis ✓
David Michaelis ✓
Gil Schwartz ✓
~~*Frank Rich*~~
Walter Isaacson ✓
~~*Lynn Hirschberg*~~
Paulina Porizkova
Ed Cohen ✓
Mimi Kramer ✓
Wm. A. Henry III ✓

Tony Hendra.
Nell Tisch ✓
Susan Morrison ✓

Graydon's handwritten list of guests for one of the early *Spy* lunches at Mare Chiaro, a bar that came by its wise-guy atmosphere honestly. Deciding what to tip could be stressful; Kurt once suggested leaving a few bullets.

which, when it is finally purchased, we promise to donate to Gus Hall, the elderly president of the U.S. Communist Party") and unapologetically New York–centric. From the business plan:

And New York? The city had never seemed so welcoming—and so vulnerable—to all manner of arrivistes.

Passing allusions to New York places and personalities and trends and events will be instantly understood by Spy's readers; no special editorial provisions will be made for readers who happen to live elsewhere.... New York is still America's imperial city, still a city of superheated vanity and ambition—and thus a place thick with subjects for Spy.... Now more than ever, people in this city are indulging in what John Updike calls "the true New Yorker's secret belief that people living anywhere else have to be kidding."

AND WHAT EXACTLY WAS THE CITY—and the *world*—*Spy* was about to enter? Ronald Reagan had been president for five years, Ed Koch mayor for eight; greed, it was said, was good, and the streets were slick with new money; the Lower East Side and downtown in general had just become hegemonically hip; the fashion for cocaine was still going strong; women liked their shoulder pads big and their hair bigger; they wore Reeboks to work, carrying their pumps; an alarming number of men wore suspenders, and their ties were yellow and/or skinny; on the radio, it was "How Will I Know" and "Papa Don't Preach," Run-DMC and the Bangles; on MTV, Dire Straits and Robert Palmer, and in the clubs the dB's and Suzanne Vega; the stock market crash was still a year away, the Mets were World Series–bound, and everyone watched *Moonlighting*.

And New York? The city had never seemed so welcoming— and so vulnerable—to all manner of *arrivistes*.

When Susan Morrison first met Graydon, she described to him a cocktail party she'd attended for the international writers' organization PEN at the huge, baroque apartment of the dicey financier Saul Steinberg and his wife, Gayfryd, and how "all the literary people were completely confused when they got there because they thought it was Saul Steinberg the *New Yorker* artist, and all these South American writers were thinking, *This is the way* cartoonists *live in America?* It was a wonderful, hilarious clash of two worlds, and it was so perfectly '80s that the grotesque Steinbergs had moved in on literary New York and bagged it that way," she remembers. "Graydon told me later that it completely captured what he wanted to do with the magazine, and why that moment was so ideal."

"When we said, 'Let's do it,' we only knew that it had to be about New York, and it had to be funny," says Graydon. "The other important thing was that it *had* to work, because there were no other jobs at the end of this."

"Honestly, I don't remember thinking, *Oh, what will we do after this is over?*" Kurt says. "I was only 31. I didn't have children to support. Another job would come along. Although with *Spy*, there was the sense that in order to do it correctly, we had to burn a lot of bridges. And that might not be the cleverest way to plan for one's professional future."

AND SO, BY THE FALL OF 1985, a covert start-up, consisting of two moonlighting employees and a nice-looking but

```
S P Y
MASTER STORY LIST

LAST EDIT: 8/28/86
BY:  SM




     T H E   F R O N T   O F   T H E   B O O K
     -------------------------------------------

          -----------NAKED CITY-----------

                  WEIRD COMING EVENTS
             By George Kalogerakis and staff

          THE ILLUSTRATED HISTORY OF NEW YORK
                   By James Pendergrast

                      THE FINE PRINT
   The highlights, culled from the public record but unreported
  elsewhere, of the metropolitan month's most interesting bits of
   information about well-known people's private lives: co-op
  sales, expanded details of health code violations, famous folks
   with gun permits and pooper-scoop scofflaw records, divorces,
   interesting law suits, names of people denied residency in co-
   ops (E.R.), which millionaire paid the least in taxes (E.R.),
   rich people in rent-controlled apartments, etc. Celebrities who
                collect unemployment insurance

             By Jamie Malanowski and Ann C. Mathers

                         THE TIMES
       A monthly gossip column about the Times. Possible bits:
     following up on quotes (Jim Kelly), backtracking a Wm. Geist
     column (E.R.), job performance reports on the five Sulzberger
            grandchildren who work at the Times.
                         By Atticus

                       MEET THE PRESS
    Edited transcripts of local TV "news personalities" on subjects
       within their so-called realms of expertise. Storm Field on
       quantum mechanics, Joel Siegel on Truffaut's legacy, Ernie
     Anastos in Islamic fundamentalism, Spencer Christian on farm
     subsidy programs. Other sources for this feature: Ray Kerrison,
     James Brady, Roland Smith, Kaitie Tong, Irv Gerkovsky, Charalyne
       Connie Chung, Mark Goodman, Sue Simmons Jack Cafferty.
             By Eric Kaplan, Will Dana, Hanna Rubin

                   GOSSIP COLUMN SCORECARD
```

Pre-publication, *Spy* existed primarily as a constantly circulating, endlessly updatable, purely theoretical story list (one page, of many, at left). Some of these ideas actually saw the light of day; others, mercifully, didn't.

unauthorized visitor who convened with them daily was humming in the corridors of the Time & Life Building, where Graydon was now writing for *Life* and Kurt was *Time*'s architecture and design critic.

"I don't know how we got away with it," says Graydon. "I wouldn't get into work till 11 a.m. But Tom would come in at 9. He had one of those early Macintoshes, and he'd sit there in my office running spreadsheets. We'd use their WATS line—a fancy service that allowed unlimited long-distance use. And we used their printing facilities for the business plan."

"The security system at Time-Life was not what it is now," notes Tom, who showed up at someone else's job so regularly that before long the guards would just wave good morning to him. "I used to work in Kurt's and Graydon's offices when they weren't there. And Graydon was almost never there."

Graydon and Kurt didn't leave those jobs until the spring and summer of '86, respectively, but Tom had time on his hands to puzzle out his new trade. "I didn't know *bubkis* about magazine publishing, so a lot of that year I was learning how to be a publisher," he says. "I was going around meeting with printers and list-brokers and distribution guys. And I worked every connection I could."

The trio met a pair of Italian graphic artists named—they think—Fausto and Carlo, neither of whom spoke much English. There was no money to produce an actual dummy issue, but the three partners paid Possibly Fausto and Possibly Carlo to design a few sample covers and a junk-mail promotional piece, and started looking around for some rich guys with senses of humor—that is, visionary investors with significant seed-round capital. It was late 1985, during the first frenzy of the bull market that would define the country for the rest of the century. *Spy*, even as a concept, was already crouched at just the right angle to bite the hand that was about to feed it.

It had not occurred to the founders that they were planning this magazine for anyone other than themselves, their friends, and people like themselves and their friends. They had gathered only the scantest data, had conducted no research, and met with no sales or marketing consultants. "And we almost never had to say that to potential investors," says Kurt. "They weren't interested in studies—just the idea."

"If a prospective investor said yes, and agreed to give us money," says Graydon, "they picked up the tab for lunch to celebrate. And if they said no, they felt so bad that they picked up the tab as a consolation prize. We had no money, no real dummy. Just a manifesto and a rough business plan."

"Well, we did have a few layouts," says Kurt. (The designer Stephen Doyle, then of Drenttel Doyle Partners, had been recruited to create the look of the magazine.) "But almost nobody ever asked to *see* them."

"There's a chapter in *Spy*'s business plan about how the magazine was going to look," remembers Doyle, "and it's all about 20th-century dedication to typography—basically because there was no budget to buy any artwork. Graydon, who occasionally wore spats back then, had a very formal idea of what *Spy* was going to look like.

"We designed the prototype for, like, $2,000," Doyle continues. "Six months of work! Plus we sometimes went along with them on their presentations, anything to make it seem more legitimate."

Of the three partners, Kurt was the least experienced and least comfortable with the idea of selling, and he remembers that cap-in-hand phase as "horrendous."

"Tom was really the advance man on that," he says. "It was just difficult, temperamentally, for me."

"He hated asking for money," says Tom, "so it's ironic that he was responsible for the biggest number of investors. I had a bunch of little guys at the outset, Stanford Business School friends. And my father put in a chunk." (Tom Phillips Sr. was then the head of Raytheon.) "So that got us off the ground. But then Kurt had these friends who had inherited wealth. He just said, 'I'm doing this,' and they all decided, 'I'll put in $50,000.'"

"In retrospect, it was incredibly easy," says Kurt. "I would say close to 70 percent of the people we went to invested."

One who didn't was Jann Wenner, but he did suggest that the magazine publish a column not about "the press," but specifically and relentlessly about *The New York Times*.

Whether by chance or by design—probably a little of both— the founders had lucked out. A lot of people were feeling flush and not disinclined to throw a modest bit of money into an interesting-sounding venture. And with potential investors who were also baby boomers, there was another button the *Spy* idea pushed: the one wired to any surviving anti-establishment impulses.

"They were adults, but they were trying to figure out how to accommodate their lingering anti-establishment sensibilities,

THE NEW YORK MONTHLY OCTOBER 1986 $2.25

SPY

BRATS
NEW YORK'S 10 MOST
**SPOILED
CHILDREN**

OUR REGULAR COLUMN ON
THE TIMES

NIGHT CLUBS BY DAY

**CELEBRITY
LOOKALIKES**

THE SPY HOW-TO-PARTY TALK THIS FALL

Issue Zero:
A *Spy* cover
mocked up
for investors and
direct mail

SUMMARY

SPY is a smart and stylish satirical monthly about the people and institutions that make metropolitan life wonderful and appalling -- a funny, topical, splendidly-written magazine for grown-up New Yorkers. The sensibility is distinct: intelligent, venturesome and energetic, playful, skeptical and worldly, polished but still a bit edgy, hip and yet suspicious of hip, always happy to stir up a little trouble. There is almost nothing in the world and absolutely nothing in New York that **SPY** doesn't know about and have an original opinion on -- from the pecking order among Avenue C performance artists to the peculiar rituals of lunch at the Council on Foreign Relations. **SPY** will be well-connected but a little wild-eyed, a bemused New York insider with a wicked streak. **SPY** is entertainment of a very high order: it will make smart people smile, and it will make them talk.

From the *Spy* business plan, 1985

and I think *Spy* became one of the ways that could be embodied," Kurt says. "Just as the *Letterman* show, which had gone on the air four years before we started, was embodying that same sensibility. So we were very lucky to catch two waves—the post-'60s ironic mood *and* the go-go financial mood."

STEVEN SCHRAGIS, THEN 30, was working in his family real estate business but yearned to get into the media world. "I just didn't want to be converting rental buildings to co-ops over and over," he says. "So I spoke to probably 20 different people who had opportunities to invest in ideas. Every one of them thought their plan was going to be tremendously successful and was going to launch just what the world needed. And then I came across one plan where I actually agreed with that sentiment." The intermediary between Schragis and the three people peddling this particular idea was the smart, savvy New York politico and then–TV executive Jay Kriegel.

"I honestly, immediately thought, *This is great, this could work*," Schragis says. "I was very anxious to become part of it."

This is how the business plan positioned *Spy* in the market:

No existing publication expressly serves Spy's *editorial and demographic niche. The so-called "think" magazines are stuffy and calcified, unwilling to swing. For most readers they lack urgency. Nor do upscale men's magazines, service-oriented and increasingly homogenized, have urgency or real punch. Humor publications tend to be adolescent and unfunny—irrelevant, in a word. Fashion magazines publish the same sweet, gushy chatter issue after issue.*

"WE WERE SO STUPID," Graydon says. "You look around and you realize: How many stand-alone magazines are there out there? None. Unless they're nonprofit, like *The Nation*."

Nevertheless, Schragis remembers, "I thought, *These people know what they're doing*. I bought into it totally after one meeting. Only as the years have gone by have I realized what a hundred-to-one shot that was."

Most of *Spy*'s investors—a blue-chip, family-fortune-heavy group that eventually numbered more than two dozen and included heirs to Safeway, Coca-Cola, Merrill Lynch, Tesco Supermarkets, Cummins Engine, Pulitzer publishing, *The Washington Post,* and *The New Yorker*, as well as the founder of Conagra and partners in the elite New York law firm Paul, Weiss, Rifkind, Wharton & Garrison—were in for amounts ranging from $10,000 to $100,000 apiece. The total investment—eventually—was $2.8 million. Through the years, the magazine would continue its flirtation with well-known fortunes. S. I. Newhouse Jr., who with his brother Donald, was head of the family's newspaper, magazine, book, and cable empire, made an approach to buy a minority stake of *Spy* in 1988. In 1991, two Europeans—the advertising mogul Charles Saatchi and the Simca car heir Jean Pigozzi—actually did. And when they sold it, in 1994, it was to a Colman's Mustard scion. But for the first four and a half years of *Spy*'s existence the three founders controlled it completely, there was no majority shareholder, and the magazine was beholden to no one backer. "We didn't have to second-guess or explain anything we wanted to do," Kurt says, "not to an owner, or, 'Oh, God, what's this going to do for advertising?' The purity of the conception and business arrangement of the magazine kind of spoiled us all. It made you loath to settle for crap later."

By early 1986, the three partners had raised enough money to send out to a small test group of potential subscribers a direct-mail package that presented the magazine's case so inventively that people who received it still talk about it. (It also served inadvertently as a staff-recruitment device: I first heard about *Spy* when the packet arrived by chance in my mailbox; I knew instantly that I had to work there.) Two magazines, *New York* and *Rolling Stone,* were each intrigued enough to publish a paragraph on the fledgling venture. But that, along with a few hundred austere black posters pasted up around town ("Smart. Fun. Funny. Fearless. *Spy*") and brief mentions in *The Washington Post*, *Adweek* and *The New York Times*, was the extent of the advance promotion.

> *For some time now,* Life *writer E. Graydon Carter and* Time *architecture critic Kurt Andersen have been among the ranks of those yearning for an irreverent publication on the order of Britain's naughty* Private Eye *or "*The New Yorker *as it was during its first 10 years...the real* New Yorker, *when it was talkier and funnier," as Andersen puts it.*
> —*The Washington Post*, February 13, 1986

> *The publisher will be Tom Phillips, an investment banker who is attempting to raise $1.25 million to bankroll the magazine ...Carter and Andersen, who are aiming for a circulation of 50,000, hope to have their first issue out in October.*
> —*New York*, February 17, 1986

TO DO THAT, THEY WOULD NEED A STAFF. And, let's see, maybe some pencils. What else? What do magazines have? A flat surface...something....

"We were just completely half-assed and, as it turned out, incredibly lucky," says Kurt. "We went ahead and hired everybody and rented the place and started doing it even though we hadn't actually gotten checks from the investors. We didn't close our money till a month before the first issue. We were all, in every way—career-wise, financially—out on a very long limb."

On the brink of publishing, the partners had raised a grand total of $140,000 from eight limited partners, with the biggest amount coming from Tom's father. (And they wouldn't complete their first close—for an additional $970,000—until August, as the first issue was about to go to press.) "We were running on fumes," says Tom. In June 1986, the newly minted non-editorial staff—Tom's hires—consisted of a wacky, sometimes brusque receptionist named Pamela Keogh (one of two *Spy* receptionists who later became best-selling authors) and three comely, not-vastly-experienced ad-sales reps, one of whom was the girlfriend of Graydon's stockbroker. There was no art staff until later in the summer; Stephen Doyle was still the art director of record.

Then there was Editorial.

Eric Kaplan, still a teenager, could not have known that he was

The *Times* says hello—and goodbye—to *Spy*.

just months away from becoming a minor celebrity in New York (and to *Spy* readers everywhere) as the magazine's extravagantly naive interviewer/mascot. Before long, probably around the time he reported being recognized on the street "by a couple of society women," we would take the precaution of having him trademarked—it's entirely possible that *Spy* still owns the branding rights to Eric—but back then he was a sweet, withdrawn, barely socialized undergraduate looking for a summer internship. At a *Harvard Lampoon* gathering in Cambridge, he was introduced to Graydon and to Kurt, a *Lampoon* alumnus.

"One of the things I had to do for that dinner was buy a used tuxedo, and it was too long," Kaplan remembers, "so I folded up the pant legs and stapled them. And that got Kurt's attention, I guess, as someone he might want to work with."

> *"Graydon looked at me and said, 'The telephones smell like Brut.'"*

Kaplan, who was living in his mother's attic in Flatbush, was offered a stipend of $50 a week. "My model for summer jobs was my brother, who'd been a typist in a temp pool. I was a very fast typist, so I knew I could make $12 an hour," he says. "I brought this up to Graydon, and he said, 'Yes, and you can make $15 an hour digging graves.'" Kaplan reported for work.

That was one.

Susan Morrison had met Kurt through a mutual friend, the writer Lawrence O'Donnell, and she had once assigned him a freelance piece at *Vanity Fair*, where she was an assistant editor.

"He knew I was pretty miserable, because it was the early part of the Tina Brown era, when the magazine was mostly socialite nonsense," she says. "So he called me up and said, 'Look, we're starting this neat magazine, you should really meet my partner Graydon.'" Morrison suggested a drink at the Grand Hyatt, the bronze-mirrored monstrosity next to Grand Central. "It was a block away from work, and I thought it would be campy," she explains. "So I went over, and Graydon was already sitting there, looking *horrified*—just the fact that he'd had to go *into* that hotel…I knew this was an immediate strike against me, and said something like, 'I'm sorry we had to meet here.' And he looked at me and said, *'The telephones all smell like Brut.'"*

BUT MORRISON HAD HIT IT OFF with them—as did I, that same winter of 1985–86. My entrée? The stationery I was using at the time. Curious about the magazine, I had looked up Graydon's address in the phone book and dropped him a note on "Drones Club" letterhead; it turned out he, too, was a huge P. G. Wodehouse fan, and he called. Although I didn't meet Morrison till we started at our jobs, for both of us, as winter turned into spring, it was a matter of staying in touch with Graydon and Kurt until they got their money and their act together (or at least enough of each) and could officially tempt us with low-ball offers and the promise of zero job security. They finally did, Graydon phoning me at work and urging, "Come on, come on, it'll be an adventure!" So I abandoned a steady position in the nascent new-media wing of *The New York Times* and took the plunge. Any hesitation was strictly for show. I knew that *Spy* was the place for me, and I would have cleaned the floors just to be involved. Fortunately, before long there would be Eric Kaplan™ to wield that mop, and I got hired as an editor, along with Morrison.

"I remember thinking, *This sounds cool, but of course it will fail*," says Morrison, now articles editor of *The New Yorker*. "They were so amateursville,* and it seemed so unlikely that it would turn out to be anything. But I thought it would be really, really fun, and I just liked those guys so much."

Given the careers so many of the people who worked at *Spy* went on to, one might suspect the bosses had a golden touch—possibly even a cogent philosophy—when it came to hiring.

Not really.

"We were out to do a funny journalistic magazine rather than a humor magazine, and therefore, especially in the early days, we hired people who had journalistic qualifications and seemed funny," Kurt says. "But we certainly had no conscious HR strategy. We were incredibly lucky that, you know, you weren't a junkie and Susan wasn't an embezzler. I think what we did throughout *Spy*, to a phenomenally successful degree, was hire people of goodwill, who weren't assholes. Smart, talented people who were fairly well put together mentally, and basically cheerful."

Or, as Graydon puts it, "Just people who wouldn't annoy us, overly."

So the team was in place. Now what?

"I remember getting there, literally the first day, and thinking, *What have I done, I've made a horrible mistake*," says Morrison. "Walking into that space, you just felt like, *Oh, Lord*."

---

*A phrase we introduced her to, as it happens. —Eds.

The editors and publishers of SPY, the mischievous new New York monthly, invite you to join them in celebration of the first issue. Nine o'clock the evening of October first in the ballroom of The Puck Bldg. 295 Lafayette Street at Houston. Black Tie. RSVP 925-5385

The fine print: an invite to (and the accompanying magnifier for) *Spy*'**s launch party, October 1, 1986**

There was…nothing, pretty much nothing. Some thrift-shop desks and chairs,* a couple of phones (but just one line), a typewriter and a very few primitive PCs scattered around among the soaring, 2,000-square-foot loft. I parked myself at a desk at the loft's far end, a few feet from what would have been Graydon's corner office, had it been an actual office. At some distance along the wall of windows from him was Kurt, in his own imaginary office, and then, moving still nearer the front door, Tom in his, with all his available wall space soon taken up by a temporary mural of spies (Tom was dating an artist). Morrison was off at more or less a right angle to me—kind of over *there* somewhere. Staring at one another, distributed around the emptiness—the space was arranged like a regular office except with virtually everything removed—we felt as if we were *miming* a business enterprise.

The loft, furthermore, was unspeakably hot: on the top floor of a nine-story building, no A/C, summer in New York. For several weeks, construction paper covered the floor; it was like working in a giant parakeet cage. Workmen wandered in all day long to drill holes or fire nail guns unexpectedly behind us. Other workmen communicated with them in Polish through the scratchy emergency PA system ("*Wojtek! Wojtek!*"), usually when we'd just placed or taken an important call. A few writers we knew stopped by early on for a look. Guy Martin did—

---

*Much of the furniture we did have—'40s, wooden—had been donated by the man who owned and renovated the Puck Building, and much of SoHo, for that matter, a designer named Peter Gee. —Eds.

he agreed to contribute all the same—and he remembers a water-filled polyurethane tarp hanging from the ceiling above where the new two-person art department was, and Kurt and Graydon trying to pass off the sagging eyesore as something "edgy." Meanwhile, Graydon smoked at his desk, blithely tossing lit cigarettes out the window. It's telling that his most vivid recollection of the summer he finally saw his dream magazine take shape is "the hellishness of the jackhammers, and the no-air-conditioning, and the dust."

To keep coolish, I stashed a cheap folding fan I'd lifted from a Chinese restaurant in my desk drawer, and it stayed with me, like a talisman, for the five and a half years I worked at *Spy*. Eventually, a summer or two later, we did acquire air conditioners—vibrating, noisy, window-mounted, and pretty much ineffective.

Temples throbbing, we'd take breaks by wandering the halls of the nearly empty Puck Building—elegant, massive, a century old, with a gilded life-size sculpture of Puck himself, holding a pen, over the door. The roof had wonderful views in all directions—an excellent vantage point for watching the choreography of the squeegee guys down on Houston Street, as well as for monitoring Keith Haring's comings and goings from his Pop Shop just across Lafayette Street. And, with its relative privacy, the roof would become the site of many editorial meetings, arguments, hirings, and—though the parapet was dangerously low and slight—one firing.

Back inside, it was less bucolic. Jackets were hung on fuse boxes or stray nails. Story ideas were written on index cards and

taped to the wall; when visitors came by, we would discreetly cover them up with newspapers (the index cards—seldom the visitors). We'd send out for lunch to the Four Points deli, where individual cigarettes were also available for purchase; or, living far less dangerously, to the diner Buffa's, a staff favorite (immortalized that same year in Jonathan Demme's *Something Wild*). We'd also send out for photocopies—at the beginning, we had no copier of our own.

We were *always* there. What were we doing, exactly?

"It didn't even seem clear to me for a while that we were actually going to get an issue out," Morrison recalls. "There were just days and days of having meetings and printing out lists of ideas, and then refining those lists, and then having lists of writers' names attached to the other lists, but nothing actually *happening*. I remember how exciting it was when we finally got people on the phone, got people to come in. But even then you had the sense that the writers felt as we did: *This is a phantom magazine, this is not even going to happen.*"

> *There are stirrings of new life on the top floor of the Puck Building,*
> *that venerable red-brick pile on West Houston Street...*
> —Phil Dougherty in *The New York Times*, June 27, 1986

WHEN THE *TIMES*'S HUGELY RESPECTED, old-school advertising columnist suddenly called to say he wanted to come by, we instructed all our friends to phone us repeatedly during the hour or so he was going to be there (*Yes, Mr. Dougherty, as you can see the phones are just ringing off the hook!*). And, the day before, a brooding Eric Kaplan had been dragooned into mopping the entire loft. Graydon encouraged the intern's unhappy labors by standing

Tom, Graydon, and Kurt in *Spy's* first office, complete with very '80s crumpled-copper sconces

nearby and singing "Ol' Man River" to him in a slow baritone.

Dougherty's write-up (published under the headline "*Spy*, a New Magazine For the City") raised our profile and our hopes a notch. It would be *Spy's* last mention in the *Times* for many, many years. The paper of record ignored us until it was able to report *Spy's* sale in 1991 and, in 1998, its demise. But we are getting ahead of ourselves, and, as we shall see, there were reasons for the oversight.

> *The magazine world is in a tizzy, all atwitter over the coming new kid on the block called* Spy, *which bows in October.... When* Spy *tossed a midsummer mixer recently at the Saint disco, most of the guests on hand seemed to have come out to do some spying themselves.* **Spalding Gray**, **Roy Blount Jr.**, **Mark** *and* **Steve O'Donnell**, *and curious editors from* Vanity Fair, New York, Manhattan Inc., Esquire, *and* The New York Times *were busy trying to sniff out what will be in* Spy's *first issue. It was said that* New York's **Ed Kosner** *had passed his invite on to one of his top editors, scrawling in the margin, "Go scope this party out and find out what they're up to." Kosner already had sent a warning to* Spy's *editors saying they should keep "hands off" his stable of writers, and* **Tina Brown** *is said to have circulated a similar memo at* Vanity Fair *calling for tightened security.*
>
> —Liz Smith in *The Daily News*, August 5, 1986

ONE OF MY JOURNAL ENTRIES from that same week suggests that those editors oughtn't to have had much to worry about. "Panic setting in," I wrote. "We must send the first issue to the printer in three weeks. *What* issue? Manuscripts still being edited—still being *written*—and Tom is trying to close the financing.

Graydon strolls the office reading copy and cheerfully repeating, 'Not too shabby, not too shabby...'"

Still, something was starting to come together. Paul Rudnick, an early and frequent *Spy* contributor, remembers stopping by the Puck Building "when the offices were kind of two folding chairs and cardboard boxes, and talking to Susan behind a card table. I remember how giddy and appealing everyone was, and certainly immediately wanted to sign on, because they were talking such a good game and because they had such distinct personalities. Which was rare—that it didn't seem corporate, and that the attitude was to make as much trouble as possible."

We put wire baskets along some mismatched tables we'd lined up, and into them we'd toss manuscripts and floppy disks. (Our arcane system of copy flow occasionally involved a detour to a kiosk at the northwest corner of 79th and Broadway—six miles uptown; that newsstand was near the subway entrance Graydon and I both used, so we'd sometimes rely on its bemused but accommodating proprietor as a floppy-disk drop-off and pickup spot.) The tables were at some point cleared off so we could lay out the first issue—on paper, by hand. The core staff had by now been augmented by a few hired guns. There were freelance copy editors, headed up by the peerless Joanne Gruber, who got her job by sending a fan letter to Kurt several years earlier, and whose career at *Spy* would outlast everyone else's; within a year she was managing editor and even before that was the unofficial moral compass of the magazine. There were freelance fact-checkers, for whose benefit (and for our own) we briefly borrowed a consultant from *The New Yorker*, Anne Mortimer-Maddox, to lecture and advise. Among those checkers was our first chief of research, Lisa Lampugnale, your average decked-out-heavy-metal-head-next-door, like many of us game but only modestly experienced. (Years later, as the name-tweaked Lisa Lampanelli, she became a big comedy success—the standup circuit's "Queen of Mean," a Friars Roast regular, and a star of *The Aristocrats*.) We hired an editorial assistant to input stories, without having first ascertained that he could type; he couldn't, but he would work for $50 a week. There was an art director, Mark Michaelson, who lasted half an issue (but went on to art-direct *New York*, *Newsweek*, *Entertainment Weekly*, and *Radar*). Stephen Doyle and his associates stepped in to fill that void until we could find a permanent replacement. "At night, after our day jobs, we'd come down and do *Spy*," remembers Doyle.

The stress, for all of us, was running in a dead heat with whatever *frisson* we were getting from creating a magazine. "They just pushed us so hard, so late, for so little money and for so long," says Doyle. "I was quitting smoking then, and one day I had a tantrum—I tore a layout in half and threw it across the room, and Graydon looked at me and said, 'Do you want a cigarette? Do you *want* a cigarette? *Can I just give you a cigarette?*'"

Nell Scovell (then married to Tom Tisch, son of tobacco-hotel-broadcasting mogul Laurence Tisch) was the first staff writer hired at *Spy*. "Tom Phillips targeted my husband as a potential investor and sent along the prospectus," she recalls. "I read it and got very excited. I had been a sports writer for *The Boston Globe*, but I hadn't broken into the New York market. *Spy* seemed like a perfect fit. My husband declined to invest but told the *Spy* folks that he would offer them 'my most precious possession—my wife.' We were divorced before the November issue came out.

"I'm sure Kurt and Graydon only met with me because they were hoping to raise cash," continues Scovell.* "Still, I came equipped with 10 story ideas, plus they knew I'd work for cheap. They offered me the job of staff writer at $100 a week. I was thrilled. I had worked on an 'alternative newspaper' in high school and *Spy* had a remarkably similar feel."

As Labor Day approached, everyone was laboring ninety-hour weeks to assemble *Spy* no. 1.

> *The respectable, the privileged and the socially prominent in New York may wish to take cover.... *Spy*, however, appears at a time when there is no shortage of magazines about New York City life. By last count, *Spy *will be the fourteenth city magazine.*
> —*Crain's New York Business*, August 18, 1986

"THERE ARE VARIOUS PERIODS in New York where anyone who's got any excess cash opens a restaurant," says Paul Rudnick. "But during the *Spy* era those people started magazines. And there's a real graveyard: *Egg, 7 Days, Manhattan Inc., Fame, Details* in its earlier form. And *Wigwag*! That one felt like a magazine exclusively aimed at dead librarians."

It wasn't just available cash that accounted for the period's multiple launches. As with the art world around the same time

---

*Not true. —Eds.**

and the rock music scene in the mid-'70s, there was a sort of yearning for something new and disruptive.

"The magazine world lags six or eight years behind the culture," says Guy Martin, who was an *Esquire* contributor at the time. "So the magazine world in the mid-'80s was spiritually and intellectually about 1978. *Rolling Stone* in the '70s and early '80s brought two things to the table: big fiction, with Tom Wolfe, and Hunter Thompson. That was it, in the environment of magazines. *The Atlantic* was slowly dying, *The New Yorker* was way asleep."

Not to draw too simplistic a parallel between *Spy* and, say, punk rock, but the magazine world in 1986 was fat and happy and badly in need of shaking up. And while we were hardly punks in the Johnny Rotten sense, that's exactly how we must have seemed to the big shots *Spy* was about to take on.

> *But is Madison Avenue laughing along with *Spy*? It is if you ask {Tom} Phillips. The first issue closed with 24 pages of advertising from both national and regional advertisers such as Guess Jeans, Absolut Vodka, Piper Heidsieck, Celine, and Café Luxembourg.*
> —*Adweek*, August 25, 1986

THE FIRST ISSUE—three months in the making, or two years, or (by Jim Kelly's reckoning) eight years—*did* close, though a little later than *Adweek* reported, and with 26 pages of advertising. We sent it to the printer on September 10, and the editors celebrated with what I noted in my journal as a "liquid, silly lunch...No business was discussed."

> SPY *BOOSTER BACKING OUT: Ivan Boesky has had second thoughts about $400,000 that *Spy* magazine expected him to invest. One source close to *Spy* editor Graydon Carter says the arbitrageur decided against a deal "because he was nervous about becoming the focus of insider-trading investigations and wanted to pull back on his commitments."...A Boesky spokesman said, "We looked into investing in *Spy*, but we never made a commitment. So the question of why we didn't invest is academic."*
> —*New York*, September 15, 1986

The magazine world in 1986 was fat and happy and badly in need of shaking up.

THAT WAS A BULLET that missed us. Ivan Boesky was indeed almost a *Spy* investor—a major one, brought in by his good friend, then–*New Republic* owner Martin Peretz. But Boesky pulled out suddenly and mysteriously just scant weeks before he began cooperating with federal prosecutors in the case that would eventually convict Drexel Burnham junk-bond banker Mike Milken, the corrupt-capitalism poster boy of his era. Instead of becoming a limited partner in *Spy*, Boesky would soon be regularly covered in its pages.

> *Spy*'s *opening-night gala at the Puck Building {October 1st} is a hot ticket even if some of us can't read the super-small print invite with the 'spy'-glass provided. I am told it reads 'Black tie,' but I think that means 'bulletproof vest.'*
> —Liz Smith in the *Daily News*, September 26, 1986

WE GOT COPIES OF ISSUE NO. 1—unbound, hand-cut and -assembled—on September 22. I wrote in my journal that, going through its pages, "we don't know what to make of it. We do know that we need to brace ourselves for next Wednesday, when it reaches the newsstands." That first issue carried many of the features for which *Spy* would become famous: The Fine Print (with its health-code-violation reports, transcriptions of mobsters talking, letters urging pardons for famous felons, details of juicy lawsuits, entertainers' bizarre contract demands, and more); The Liz Smith Tote Board (the frequency-ranked tally of names the *gossipeuse* mentioned in her column); Party Poop (a photo chronicle of New York nightlife consisting of paparazzi shots no one else would run); Review of Reviewers; and, on the last page, the magical-realist utopianism of New, Improved New York—a sort of poor man's Bruce McCall (who consistently resisted Graydon's entreaties to draw for the magazine). The cover was a shot of Chris Elliott strenuously looking like an ur-yuppie, next to the cover line "JERKS! The Ten Most Embarrassing New Yorkers."

The writers David Owen and Ann Hodgman, early *Spy* contributors (and husband and wife), fought over their copy. "I couldn't believe how much we loved it," Owen says. "If one of us would for a second put it down, the other one would grab it. It was hard to explain to other people, mainly I guess to non–New Yorkers but also to people who didn't have that…*whatever* that worldview is."

"I think we hit our stride pretty fast," Graydon says. "If you go back and look at that first issue, it was kind of there. I mean, the magazine's DNA five years later was not appreciably different."

The week we published, I rode the subway uptown from work with Tom Phillips, who lived in the same neighborhood. The publisher was bouncing. Newsstand sales were great, he said. And that first direct-mail foray from the previous winter, which had gone out to 30,000 people and had got a healthy 8 percent response? Well, now our first issue was finally on its way to them. "We already have 11,000 subscribers!" Tom enthused.

Most of them, it seemed, came to our launch party.

Though a few of the *Spy* staff almost didn't make it. An hour before the party began, a bunch of us were in the alley behind the Puck Building, being photographed for a "Crime Spree" piece for the second issue. The idea was that Eric Kaplan would violate a series of antiquated, little-known New York City statutes prohibiting certain activities, including "Fortune Telling" and "Jostling." We had just persuaded some actual NYPD officers to frisk us for the cameras (for having recklessly "assembled wearing masks") when a real-life mugger tore past us and the police gave chase. Kaplan decided to follow the cops, and he disappeared up Lafayette Street, a "25 CENTS A THROW" cardboard sign from an earlier crime still flapping around his neck.

Kaplan eventually got to the party, as did Robert Altman, Andy Warhol, Liz Smith, Malcolm Forbes, either Boy George or a Boy George impersonator (back then, it mattered which), and 600 other nicely turned-out New York writers, editors, and media types. The Puck Ballroom was unadorned, but needed little—it was a beautiful space.

"The black-tie thing was my idea, for the simple reason that we didn't have any money to decorate the place," says Graydon. "But if you put men in black tie, and women in fancy dresses, there's your decoration. As a result, everybody looked great. And it had this sort of Victorian thing, with the palm fronds. Square bar in the center, an all-girl swing band…."

The first number—by Graydon's decree—was Benny Goodman's "Sing, Sing, Sing (With a Swing)," *Spy*'s unofficial theme until we perverted "My Way" a few years later (with ever-changing custom lyrics by Joanne Gruber). There were life-size cutouts of William Shawn, Tina Brown, and Ed Kosner—then the editors of *The New Yorker*, *Vanity Fair*, and *New York*—with which guests could be photographed, and lined up to do so.

The only ominous note, Tom Phillips remembers, was sounded

by one of his heroes—Altman, of all people. Tom found himself at the party's end in conversation with the great director, then 61 and in his own deep career trough. "People had left, the band had stopped playing, the bar was closed, and he was still there," Tom says. "And Altman said to me, 'You know, this is going to end badly. It's nice now, but it's not going to last.'"

Coverage of the party rivaled coverage of the magazine itself. "They'd already warned me I'd 'stand out in a bad way' if I didn't come in black tie—as if there's such a thing as standing out in a bad way," wrote Michael Musto in *The Village Voice*, adding, "the premiere issue knocks down practically everybody the media's taken great pains to build up."

In the *Daily News*, William Norwich wrote: "Because the premiere issue of the satirical monthly has distressed Gotham's most vainglorious publicity seekers, I expected the bash wouldn't be terribly well-subscribed. Not the case at all. It was like a sunny deb party for longhairs, and all the kids were there…"

Spy was from the start an extremely social undertaking—not just the annual Puck party every October (even after the magazine had abandoned the Puck for Union Square), but also the regular writers' lunches at Mare Chiaro on Mulberry Street, the raucous "closing" dinners with the entire staff after each issue shipped, and the madly debauched staff-only Christmas bashes, in which Graydon ordinarily played a *faux*-lascivious Santa—this in an era before magazine "holiday parties" were common or "hostile sexual environment" an employment-law term of art.*

> *Magazine junkies are having a field day this week with the new* Spy, *on the stands at last. Fears from Park to Fifth Avenue have been confirmed. The guys who publish this mag are going to be mean and lowdown. Their party at the Puck Building brought out a glamorous swingy mix of beautiful young people…. May they live, prosper, and plague the people who count.*
> —Liz Smith in *the Daily News*, October 5, 1986

---

*Around the time we started talking about the magazine, we were also talking not very seriously about starting a club, like London's Groucho, and en route to lunch and the video arcade, we would eye second-floor Times Square dives covetously. *Spy* subsumed that club-making impulse, and in some real way all of the passionate readers were our nonresident members. —Eds.

Spy went interactive in its debut issue with Penn & Teller's charmingly low-tech computer card trick, which featured a special phone number and an "electronic on-off flow chart"—whatever that was. October 1986

The Duchess of Windsor was wrong. Even when her weight dropped to 87 pounds, resulting in hemorrhaging ulcers, she clung with bony hands to a pillow bearing her famous motto. Some call this class. We call it extremism. As NELL SCOVELL *discovered, the evidence suggests that indeed, you can be*

too rich

In New York there is an inverse relationship between a woman's dress size and the size of her apartment. A size 2 gets a 14-room apartment. A size 14 gets a two-room apartment. This phenomenon is counterintuitive, since the larger woman would seem to need more space. But need has nothing to do with it.

Rubenesque heft on a woman used to be a sure sign of wealth, as only the rich could afford to eat well. At Le Cirque these days, the ladies who lunch play with their $28 prix fixe meals and come out thinner than they went in. Miraculously, even those who like to eat *seem not to gain weight*. (In fact, one moneyed scarecrow donates her soiled couture castoffs to the Metropolitan Museum's Costume Institute. Soiled, says an Institute source, not with sweat or champagne, but with vomit.)

Such emaciation is worth nothing if it is not flaunted: diamond chokers clasp chicken necks, Chanel chains bind boyish hips, emeralds droop from shriveled earlobes. And doesn't it seem that the more the wife diets, the more the husband balloons? (It's all those power breakfasts—a necessary part of fulfilling the "too rich" half of the aphorism.) Evenings, the couples march off to black-tie affairs looking like Olive Oyl and Bluto.

Still, self-deprivation can pay off. Look at Nancy Reagan and Princess Diana. But the line between elegance and anorexia is, well—oh, all right—extremely thin. Which of these women cross it? Decide for yourself.

ANNE BASS
Smoking through dinner and taking ballet class every day help keep five-foot-six-inch Anne Bass in a size 4. If she had been staying at 98 pounds for her husband, oil millionaire Sid Bass, her labors were futile. Last fall he ran off with another skinny, Mercedes Kellogg. But he need never worry about confusing them in the dark. "Mrs. Kellogg has more curve than Mrs. Bass," says Boaz Mazor, of Oscar de la Renta. "Mrs. Bass has very nice legs and large shoulders, but she is very flat. Frankly, Mrs. Bass has no bust at all."

Still, Anne Bass might wind up with as much as $400 million from her pending divorce settlement (and the continued company of dancer turned walker Peter Martins).

MERCEDES KELLOGG

"You listen to your body and it tells you the things you want," says Mercedes Kellogg, Sid Bass's new squeeze and the estranged wife of former ambassador Francis Kellogg. "If you're craving meat, you need the blood." Though five feet six and three-quarters inches tall and 110 pounds, Kellogg maintains that she has never dieted. "I smoke, I drink, I eat," she says. "I used to weigh 125 pounds, but it was puppy fat. I lost the weight by moving houses." A size 4 or 6, Kellogg says, "I have tried everything in exercise, but it does not agree with me."

Financially, Kellogg is a questionable starter on this list, but partisans say she's bound to make the move from Park to Fifth with her new steady.

NAN KEMPNER

At five feet nine inches, Nan Kempner, wife of Loeb Partners Corporation chairman Tom Kempner, is the tallest size 4 on the list. Still, she says, "I am *faux maigre*—I look thinner than I am." Unlike most of the rapaciously scrawny, Kempner does not weigh herself obsessively. "The last time I weighed myself, I was under 115—but I was wearing a big fur coat and shoes at the time." She claims she doesn't starve herself, either. "She eats like a horse," says Glenn Bernbaum, owner of Mortimer's. Kempner does, however, have an aversion to sweetbreads and oysters. "The last time I ate an oyster, I was three years old—they're ugly, slimy, icky-poo," she says. "Other than that, I'll eat anything and anyone."

BROOKE HAYWARD

Despite Brooke Hayward's efforts to affect a matronly look, enshrouding her thin hips and flat chest in earth-mother draperies, her chicken neck tells all. The five-foot-seven-inch Broadway brat wears a size 6 and weighs between 108 and 110 pounds. "I don't like the look of very thin women, especially past the age of 45," she says. Hayward is 49 and attributes her weedy figure to genetics, not willpower. "I don't diet at all. I eat three meals a day," she says. "What's more, to be really hideous, I don't exercise at all." Hayward's best-selling 1977 autobiography, *Haywire*, was turned into a miniseries, and husband Peter Duchin pulls in $5 million a year from his dance band business.

& too thin

Writer Nell Scovell: "I felt that the piece should be built around reporting and, fortunately, it was early enough in the magazine's history that you could get people to speak on the record.

"'The last time I weighed myself, I was under 115— but I was wearing a big fur coat and shoes at the time,' Nan Kempner told me on the phone. It was everything I'd hoped for." (continued on next page)

HELEN GURLEY BROWN

"I weigh 105 and I'm five feet four inches tall," says *Cosmopolitan* editor Helen Gurley Brown. But sometimes fat people consumed with jealousy try to thwart her dieting efforts. "One aggravated hostess put chocolate chips in my Sanka out in the kitchen one day, then gleefully told me what she had done after I drank. Bitch!" wrote Brown in *Having It All*. These saboteurs "can't stand that you have the discipline to do what you did. If you weigh less than they do, they want you to gain," she said recently. The wife of film producer David (*Jaws*) Brown and a resident of the Beresford, she admits that staying a size 2 is hard work. "I'm always feeling guilty or hungry—one or the other."

MARY TYLER MOORE

Remember how cute 'n' curvy Laura Petrie looked in her stretch pants? Today those pants would billow. At five feet seven inches, Mary Tyler Moore wears a size 6, although her publicist says she "lost a lot of weight" filming her 1986 smash, *Just Between Friends*. In the movie she aerobicized maniacally, looking like a stick of beef jerky in a leotard (*inset*). Moore, a diabetic, avoids sugar and goes to ballet class every day. As part owner and chairman of MTM Productions, Moore is worth about $30 million.

NANCY KISSINGER *(left)* Nearly six feet tall and a size 8, Nancy Kissinger looks as if she's been stretched on a rack, with special attention lavished on the arms (*inset*). Her secret? A lethal regimen of Coke and cigarettes. As for exercise, Kissinger has been known to go a few rounds at an airport now and then. Henry's company, Kissinger Associates, reportedly grosses $4 million a year—enough to keep her in Coke, Virginia Slims and a Riverhouse co-op.

ANNETTE REED *(right)* The wispy five-foot-five-and-a-half-inch, 98-pound Annette Reed slips easily into a size 2, but it wasn't always that way. "I used to be enormous," Reed says of her teen years, when she bloated to 150 pounds. Strangely, though her waist now measures an ethereal 21.5 inches and her back is topographically indistinguishable from her chest (*inset*), old feeding habits endure. "No wheat germ for me," she says. "I love candy bars and Coca-Cola." Reed lives in a suite at the Carlyle to be near her boyfriend, bald designer Oscar de la Renta, but she doesn't have to worry about the hotel bill (rates start at $10,700 per month). *Forbes* estimates that Reed, her four sisters and her mother, Jane Engelhard, are worth over $365 million, thanks to the late mineral magnate Charles Engelhard Jr., the prototype for Ian Fleming's Auric Goldfinger.

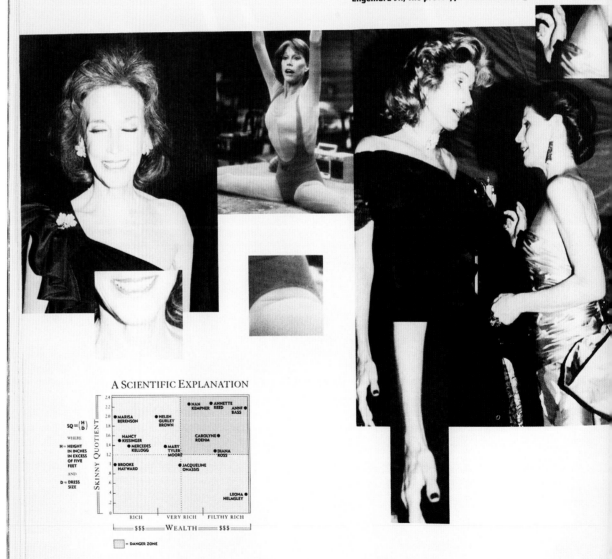

A SCIENTIFIC EXPLANATION

$$SQ = \left(\frac{H}{D}\right)$$

WHERE

H = HEIGHT IN INCHES IN EXCESS OF FIVE FEET

AND

D = DRESS SIZE

SKINNY QUOTIENT (vertical axis: .2 to 2.4)

- MARISA BERENSON
- HELEN GURLEY BROWN
- NAN KEMPNER
- ANNETTE REED
- ANNE BASS
- NANCY KISSINGER
- MERCEDES KELLOGG
- CAROLYNE ROEHM
- MARY TYLER MOORE
- DIANA ROSS
- BROOKE HAYWARD
- JACQUELINE ONASSIS
- LEONA HELMSLEY

RICH   VERY RICH   FILTHY RICH

$$$ ═══ WEALTH ═══ $$$

☐ = DANGER ZONE

CAROLYNE ROEHM

Carolyne Roehm is all angles: nose, chin, shoulders and elbows all jut like sharpened steel. And yet Roehm's chest is strangely flat. At five feet nine and a half inches, she weighs 120 pounds and wears a size 6. Her husband, Henry Kravis, the leveraged-buyout specialist, is worth at least $180 million; they have bought a $5.5 million Park Avenue apartment and a $1.43 million Renoir. Kravis—perhaps threatened with a sharp hipbone—also staked his wife millions when she launched her own couture line.

DIANA ROSS

Diana Ross's hunger for fame has clearly overwhelmed her hunger for food. Her vital statistics: five feet three and a half inches tall; size 2/4; seven-year, $20 million RCA recording contract, which she supplements with Motown royalties and $300,000-a-week appearances in Las Vegas and Atlantic City. Onstage, Ross wears skintight costumes—a major change from the 1960s, when she used to pad her hips and bosom. Her nose has also gotten noticeably, surgically thinner since then.

MARISA BERENSON

Large (five feet eight inches tall) and lean (less than 115 pounds), ex-model Marisa Berenson wears a size 4 and avoids sidewalk grates. The granddaughter of Elsa Schiaparelli, grandniece of Bernard Berenson, daughter of Robert L. Berenson and estranged wife of Trump lawyer and publicity hound Richard Golub, she now claims to be pursuing a film career in Europe. Like Helen Gurley Brown and Annette Reed, Berenson nicely exemplifies the super-svelte "chicken wing syndrome."

JACQUELINE ONASSIS

Although five foot six and a size 6, Onassis has a penchant for long-sleeved gowns that nearly excluded her from this list. But her bony hands give her away (inset). Perhaps she should return to wearing the little white gloves that she popularized as first lady. A slavish exerciser, Onassis jogs every day and rides nearly every weekend. She lives on Fifth Avenue and is estimated to be worth $25 million, despite her tiny salary as an editor at Doubleday. Sister Lee Radziwill, who is even slimmer than Onassis, would have made the list had she not taken a public relations job at Giorgio Armani. Apparently she needed the money.

"Getting Nan helped me get others—Mercedes Kellogg (now Bass) and Brooke Hayward. Boaz Mazor, who worked for Oscar de la Renta, was invaluable, filling in dress sizes for the women who wouldn't speak to me.

"A few months later, Tom Wolfe coined the phrase 'social X-rays' in *Bonfire of the Vanities*."

$16.95), and is in spirit similar to th
passage that ran in this space last June
Since no one in New York had heretofor
ever actually *read* one of Lord's dirty book
—the two that she has written are out o
print—all across town there was voice
astonishment at how *dirty* a dirty-bool
writer the bosomy dirty-book writer is.

Among interested parties, the questio
at hand is not just, How does the woma
know of such things?, but even more press
ing, What sort of deviant calisthenics i
Shirley requesting of her husband, forme
executive editor and incurable romanti
Abe "I'm Writing as Bad as I Can

2

"The Piece Is Great, We Just Have to *Spy*-ify It a Little"

Writing, and Rewriting, for *Spy*

We operated as authors, in a certain way, rather than editors.
—KURT ANDERSEN

IN 1986, READERS OF AMERICAN periodicals were familiar with the entirely fictional humor of the declining *National Lampoon*; the genteel, often arcane, modern *New Yorker* kind; and the Russell Baker–Art Buchwald topical-jokes-and-opinion kind. But they had virtually no experience at all with tough, satirical journalism in which reporting and humor were bound together.

Spy's tone was in place from the start, a little bit of Americanized *Private Eye*, some updated 1930s *New Yorker*, a lot Graydon, and a lot Kurt. Other influences were detectable—H. L. Mencken, Tom Wolfe, P. G. Wodehouse—yet it still felt original: arch, prickly, mean, funny, surprising, insider-y yet retaining the perspective of a crank outsider. "Smart, fun, funny, fearless" was the poster slogan, but it also really was the mission statement in a nutshell. *Spy* was that nicely turned-out yet somehow disconcerting figure jeering rudely—whoa, possibly *threateningly*—from across the street.

Paul Goldberger, dean of the Parsons School of Design, who was then *The New York Times*'s architecture critic, remembers it as a combination of "brilliant, sharp insight and adolescent fuck-you-ness."

"Nothing like this existed," says Kurt. "We had it in our heads what we wanted, but you couldn't say, 'Oh, it's like this, it's like that.' It really took some months of having the magazine out there to show writers what it was we had in mind. And I remember, three months, six months in, writers and editors saying to me, 'Oh, *now* I see what you were talking about.'"

The authorial approach also served the skeletal business plan: Eager, unproven writers with potential cost a lot less than established writers with agents. A few big names appeared in *Spy*— the writer Roy Blount Jr., the magicians Penn & Teller—but not many and (except for Blount, who contributed a brilliant puns-and-anagrams-style crossword puzzle for years) not often.* Rather,

---

*The first writers Graydon called about writing for *Spy* were Christopher Hitchens and Lloyd Grove. Both gave him the brushoff. —Eds.

Opposite: "A strong house tone": here, an especially poignant passage from *Spy*'s monthly column on *The New York Times*, November 1988.

Spy became a finishing school for big-name writers of the future.

Some aspects of the *Spy* style might sound a little hardworking, two decades on, and our trademark kitchen-sink approach to features—multiple sidebars and charts and photos and illustrations and graphs and pseudoscientific equations and the like, to go along with the standard 4,000-to-6,000-word piece—required patience: Every page was packed with reporting, research, sensibility, takes, jokes. "The level of concentration that we had....We'd write these deks [the usually brief précis that introduce an article] that were, like, 200 words," says Bruce Handy, an early contributor who as a *Spy* editor did much to shape the look and sound of the magazine. Probably, too, we overdid the italics (though it has to be said that back then, in the media world, *the gimmick did seem fresh*). But our compulsive use of certain recherché words and phrases—among them *preternatural, vulgarian, manqué, cheesy, swanky, appalling, editrix, naïf, super-, über-, a-go-go, faux*—amused us, and that was ever the main criterion for running anything in *Spy*, whether it be a cover-package extravaganza or a Party Poop caption. Also, we were conducting an informal experiment: We wanted to see whether we could shoehorn any of those words into the lingo.

Apparently we could.

Spy*'s pervasive influence now extends from* Rolling Stone, *which recently referred to "faux naïf magician Doug Henning,"* to Entertainment Weekly, *which just noted the "earnest faux naïf way" of a band called Ed's Redeeming Qualities, to the* Dayton Daily News, *whose movie critic a few months ago described a world that "has been taken over by short-fingered vulgarians." The time seemed ripe to quantify all this pervasive influence, so we ran a NEXIS search {drawing on the same sources for each tally}....*

	1986	1990
Uses of faux:	244	515
of vulgarian:	17	45
of preternatural:	19	35

—*Spy*, May 1991

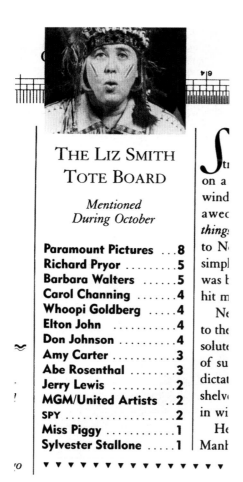

THE LIZ SMITH
TOTE BOARD

*Mentioned
During October*

Paramount Pictures	...8
Richard Pryor	5
Barbara Walters	5
Carol Channing	4
Whoopi Goldberg	4
Elton John	4
Don Johnson	4
Amy Carter	3
Abe Rosenthal	3
Jerry Lewis	2
MGM/United Artists	..2
SPY	2
Miss Piggy	1
Sylvester Stallone	1

December 1986

MOST OF THE STORY IDEAS were generated at editorial meetings, and a number were drawn from that original list worked up by Kurt and Graydon. Others were harvested wherever *Spy* staff happened to be spending their off-hours. But some great material came in over the transom, and freelance contributions ranging from Naked City squibs to full-blown features appeared frequently in the magazine over the years—a lot of those, it must be admitted, pretty thoroughly worked-over.

"It was the most intensely edited magazine I'd ever been involved in, which was one of the things that was so fun about it," says Susan Morrison.

Tad Friend, who started writing for *Spy* in 1986 and later did a stint as an editor, describes "a strong house tone that varied from Kurt playing lead violin"—the dazzling, unsigned Great Expectations editorial that led off each issue*—to the sometimes absurdly reader-interactive From the *Spy* Mailroom column (also unsigned, but which I can now confess to having written for the first five years).

---

*Beginning in 1992, these were written by Larry Doyle. —Eds.

SITUATION TRAGEDY

*b*etween 1960 and 1972 millions of American television viewers enjoyed the antics of the Douglas family on *My Three Sons*. Fred MacMurray played Steve Douglas, a widower and the apparently devoted father of three boys. But over the years, it now seems clear, the specter of death continued to stalk the star-crossed Douglas clan—with no acknowledgment ever made by the preternaturally composed dad. Recent films such as *Blue Velvet* have exposed the maggots hiding beneath the rock of America's TV suburbia. In that context, those old *My Three Sons* episodes take on a disturbing aspect. Everywhere there are hints of foul goings-on just outside the eye of the camera, just beyond that invisible fourth wall.

Fred MacMurray rose to fame on the strength of motion pictures such as *Double Indemnity—films noirs* that explored the rictus behind the neighborly smile, the skull beneath the middle-class skin. Perhaps when MacMurray's advisers were choosing a TV vehicle for the fading movie star in the late 1950s, they deliberately picked a scenario with an underlying tension, a hint of muffled screams beneath the laugh track.

Through its 12 seasons *My Three Sons* told the story of a suburban family whose members disappeared with alarming regularity. Steve Douglas's stated alibis for his vanishing family made little sense, should certainly have piqued the interest of local police, and may help explain why the Douglas family abruptly quit "Bryant Park" for North Hollywood at the start of the 1966–67 season.

An examination of the evidence suggests that Steve Douglas was a murderer who eliminated members of his family as they became conscious of his misdeeds. By the time the series left the air, only Chip, the youngest and stupidest of the original three sons, was left to witness Dad's death spree.

THE DISAPPEARED OF *MY THREE SONS*

(1) **MRS. STEVE DOUGLAS.** When we first meet the family, in 1960, Steve Douglas is a putative widower raising sons Mike, Robbie and Chip with the help of an old man named Bub, allegedly the boys' maternal grandfather. Although Chip is hardly more than a toddler, no mention is ever made of the late Mrs. Douglas, beyond the fact that her untimely death leaves her husband free to date.

(2) **BUB.** In 1964 the jolly grandfather, perhaps beginning to suspect that his daughter's death several years earlier was no accident, suddenly disappears. Dad tells the boys that Bub has gone to "visit his mother in Ireland" and will be back soon. It seems dubious that Bub, a man in his seventies, could have a living mother, but the trusting sons fall for it. In that same episode a mysterious seaman arrives at the Douglas home. Dad convinces the boys this rough character is their "Uncle Charley," who will stick around to help out until Bub comes home. Eight years later, Bub has not returned.

(3) **MIKE.** Eventually the eldest son reaches an age at which he might begin to question his father. Thus, a year after Bub vanishes, Mike disappears. First Dad tells Robbie and Chip that Mike has gone on a honeymoon—and then he announces that Mike has "moved east." Mike never returns.

(4 & 5) **ERNIE'S PARENTS.** Down one son, Steve Douglas begins to take a special interest in Chip's little pal Ernie, who has been hanging around the Douglas home for a couple of seasons. When Ernie is orphaned, Steve generously offers to adopt the little boy. No mention is ever made of how Ernie's parents met their premature death, but it is not long after this that the Douglas clan flees their midwestern home for California. (An even more bizarre note: though it had been established that Chip and Ernie were in the same grammar school class, once Ernie becomes the new third son, Dad claims Ernie is younger than Chip and forces Ernie to go back several grades at his new school.)

(6) **ROBBIE.** In California, Robbie marries a college friend and promptly seeds her with triplets. Robbie, still a teenager, cannot afford to provide for his spawn. Dad invites Robbie, Katie and the triplets to live under his roof. Two years later, Robbie is gone—though the pretty Katie continues to live with her missing husband's father. Visitors are told that Robbie is "away on a business trip"—though when the series leaves the air, Robbie is still gone.

We can only wonder how long it was after the series ended its run that lunkhead Chip or ditz Ernie finally asked Dad one question too many and joined Mom, Bub, Mike and Robbie on the long vacation "to visit Bub's mother" "on business" "back east."

—Bill Flanagan

The first
of several
over-the-transom
contributions
from Bill
Flanagan, later
an MTV executive
and novelist.
October 1987

Vice President George Bush tells a funny to an appreciative golfing buddy.

BY DREW FRIEDMAN

▼ ▼

(continued)

MRS. FIELDS COOKIES
233 Broadway, at Park Row
*This Mrs. Fields likewise had
neither a valid operating permit
nor a food protection certificate.
Inspectors found cartons stored
directly on the floor, creating
conditions conducive to
"harborage." Sure enough,
mouse excreta was found. At the
second inspection, the paperwork
problems had been put in order,
but again cartons were found on
the floor. And the inspectors
again found mouse excreta,
which they described as "old."*

MRS. FIELDS COOKIES
2086 Broadway, at 72nd Street
*At both inspections, Mrs. Fields
was found to lack a valid
operating permit and a food
protection certificate. The
establishment also had holes in
the wall behind the oven, stock
stored directly on the floor and
mouse excreta.*

MRS. FIELDS COOKIES
2891 Broadway, at 113th Street
*On the first inspection, Mrs.
Fields lacked an operating
permit, a food protection*

June 1987

"But it was *Spy*—you could tell what it was," Friend continues. "Because we'd be rewriting something, and then Graydon and Kurt would both be top-editing it, so it ended up having certain hallmarks. It was often a matter of rewriting the first paragraph pretty heavily—then you could shunt people into the story, from a certain perspective, and the rest of it could all be the same, with an occasional joke here and there. You just had to get the right, wised-up tone in the first 'graf. And in the last 'graf, too—you got your last tattoo of kicks in."

Friend, now a writer for *The New Yorker*, remembers that when James Wolcott took on *Spy* in *Vanity Fair* in April 1988 ("You never feel that [*Spy*] will ever showcase anyone remotely resembling a *writer*, as *The New Yorker* and *The Atlantic* have. Its contributors *do* fly in formation, their put-ons as glibly formatted as David Letterman's"), the criticism "bugged the hell out of me, but there was something to it, because it is true that we didn't have individual voices."* (It all evened out. Just before that column appeared, Wolcott sent us an order form and a check for $25.98 for two *Spy* T-shirts. Extra large.)

Larry Doyle, a writer and editor at *Spy* in 1992 and 1993 and now a successful screenwriter, agrees that the magazine had

---

*This was true of many of the features, but not entirely—Handy, Rudnick, Jim Collins, Phil Weiss, and John Lombardi, for instance, among the regular long-form contributors, all had distinctive voices largely untouched by us. And ditto for the columnists, such as Owen, Hodgman, James Grant, Luc Sante, Henry Alford, Joe Queenan, Ellis Weiner, and the pseudonymous Celia Brady. —Eds.

against the
ric,

of Alphabet
s accused of
horized
bers and of
r verification
sponse, the
hen "the
red, he was
ation, his
half, and
·, a 75-year-
ts responsible
use he
om workers
eve the
nd assistant."
d guilty and

against the
Lady Star
sland
nspector
b and found
to worker
adge;
n't verified
rested party;
he premises
as a shortage
l for the sale
e was an
jackpots;
n
rs. The
d $425.

ernment and a grand
jury firmly believe they
are. That's all.

Martin A. Siegel
Kidder, Peabody & Company

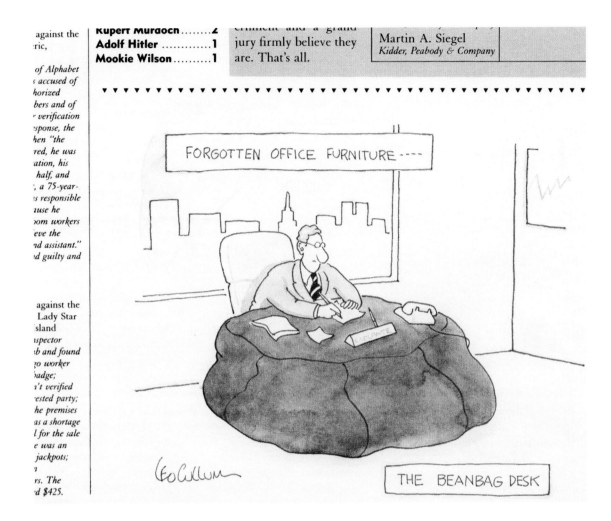

FORGOTTEN OFFICE FURNITURE ----

THE BEANBAG DESK

April 1987

"probably the most severe editing hands in the business," but adds that this was a necessity, as many contributors were far stronger reporters than writers.

"You had to learn a whole new style of dealing with writers," says Morrison. "Because people would hand in their copy, and you'd say thanks, but then nine times out of ten you were giving these pieces personality transplants. You really imposed a completely different voice—put in a lot of mean things, a lot of funny adjectives. Writers' *jaws* dropped. Every editor has lines—I used to say, 'We had to *Spy*-ify it.' Because especially with the first couple of issues, you bounced the thing back, and people were just dumbstruck. They'd never had anything like this happen to them.

"For the kids, I think it was a learning experience," continues Morrison. "It was always a little harder when you were rewriting somebody who was more of a grown-up journalist."

One freelancer—a more mainstream magazine writer than *Spy* tended to publish—was stunned when I sent him the edit of a feature he'd done. It was unrecognizable; his reporting had been excellent, but the tone wasn't remotely *Spy*'s, so we'd rewritten the piece from top to bottom. After the initial shock, he relaxed—no doubt fixing his mind firmly on the high three figures we were paying him—and called me back. "No, okay, it's great, it's funny," he said. "But I don't know what you guys are smoking over there." (Camels. And—for the record—only Graydon was.)

"You got edited a lot, but you learned how to *write*," says Elissa Schappell, a reporter at the magazine in the late '80s and early '90s and now a prominent fiction writer and contributor to *Vanity Fair*. "I remember Graydon sitting me down and saying, 'Your writing

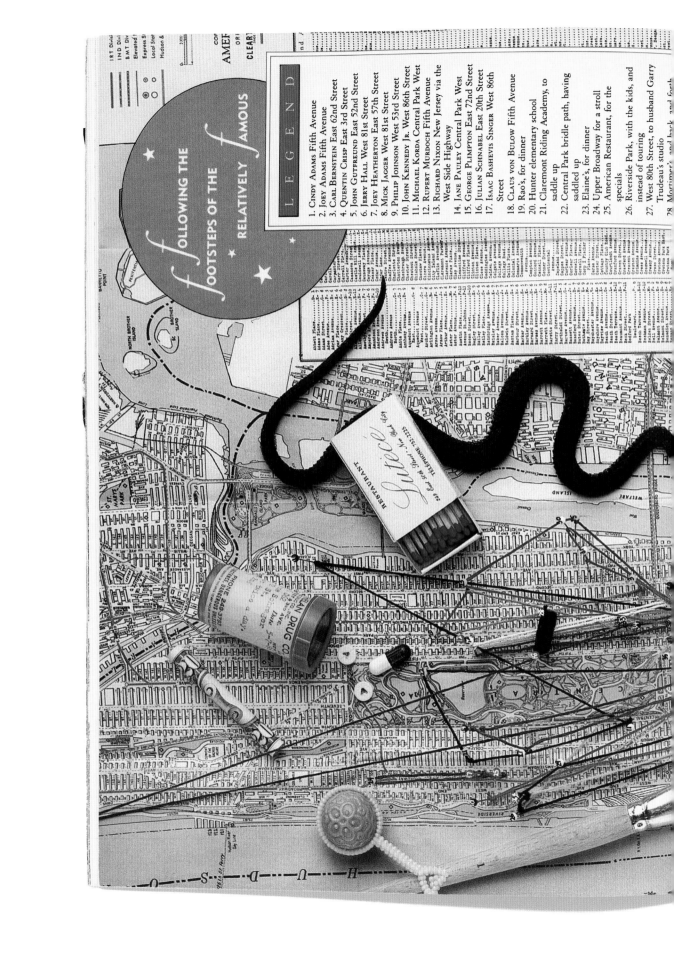

Spy's maps were generally a good deal more readable, though everyone agreed this one *looked* great. November 1986

is like a beautiful car—what good is it if it can't get you across town?' The younger staff would joke about it. You'd write your piece, and you'd get it back and it would be, 'That conjunction? That's mine. And that one there, that's mine, too. That whole sentence? *Mine.*' But it was exciting, the idea that you could be a journalist but also have this big voice—it was a revelation."

"The 'Ivanarama' cover story made my career," says Jonathan Van Meter of his one piece for *Spy.* "Which is sort of bittersweet, because I had so little to do with how funny the piece actually turned out. The *Spy* editing process was kind of like those *Extreme Makeover* shows; you barely recognized the ugly thing you turned in once the editors had their way with it, but you didn't really mind. I've always felt a little guilty taking credit for that piece."

Even Bruce Handy would occasionally get rewritten. "Sometimes Kurt would sort of drop in a whole paragraph," says Handy, who went on to be a writer and editor for *Vanity Fair.*

"I know some people have heavy-handed-editing stories, but I never had a problem with that," says David Owen. "I thought the voice of the magazine was actually one of its strengths."

"I found it to be a pleasure," says contributor Phil Weiss. "I found it to be very light hands in term of the editing, but my style worked for them right then. It was a writer's book in some ways, surprisingly."

"It really was the only magazine where I was allowed to do

NEW IMPROVED NEW YORK

BL'KER

Illustration by David Dircks

IT'S A WONDERFUL LIFE

underground in our New, Improved New York. This Christmas Eve, when last-minute shoppers step aboard the Lexington Avenue Holiday Express, they will find the air filled with the sweet smells of baking—and there to greet them, the kindliest old gent in all of Manhattan. Although the train runs just one day a year, no detail has been overlooked, from the burnished cherry wainscot to the piped-in Brian Eno music. So, weary subway traveler, brush the snow off your fedora and loosen your muffler for a few soothing stops. Michael, the subway concierge (and, he claims, a great-grandson of Horace Greeley), will attend you with a glass of port or a mug of his special eggnog. ✈

exactly what I wanted," says Ann Hodgman, who parlayed her outré *Spy* Eating column (her most famous one, "No Wonder They Call Me a Bitch," was about taste-testing dog food) into a more conventional career as a food writer and author.

"Kurt's editorial suggestions could be scarily perspicacious," remembers the author Henry Alford, who started his career as a reporter at *Spy*. "He once handed me back a galley of a story I'd written, saying, 'Never curb your tendency to aphorize.' I loved that. That was my mantra for a few years."

It was also an appreciative audience, one that you could count on to save your neck whenever inspiration failed.

"Kurt would say 'This is good' or 'This is great,' but he wouldn't give you that whole Barnum & Bailey thing that Graydon would," says Tad Friend. "With one profile I wrote, Graydon said, 'This is too even-handed; it's too lapidary. It needs to be Tad-ified—it needs to be 20 percent tougher.' So I Tad-ified it and turned it back in. And Graydon looked at it and came over and said, 'This is now a fine piece of hatchetry.'"

(As with much of the discourse around the *Spy* offices, the familiar *-ify* marching orders from Graydon and Kurt—joke-ify, sidebar-ify, the more general *Spy*-ify—were simultaneously ironic and dead serious. When I was about to start doing another regular, pseudonymous column to go along with the signed and unsigned things I was already writing, Kurt and Graydon urged me to try to concoct a drastically different tone: They just wanted to guard, Kurt said soberly, against "the creeping Kalogerakisification of *Spy*.")

Friend's first editing assignment for *Spy* was a column by the enthusiastically social playboy/writer Taki Theodoracopulos, who for a time contributed "10021," about the uptown society scene. (The enthusiastically social writer/playboy Melik Kaylan handled *Spy*'s downtown society companion column, "10012.") Friend remembers Graydon telling him, "Now, remember, this is *Taki*," as he handed over the manuscript. "Which I took to mean that every word needed to be rewritten," he says. "But it turned out he meant, 'Treat him with kid gloves.'"

For most of us, handing in a piece of writing at *Spy* was more fraught than any editorial experience before or since. The bar was very high—it was a tough audience, and you wanted every

JOE NERVOUS IN ITALY:

I'M AMAZED MORE GUYS DON'T WEAR COATS THIS WAY BACK HOME. IT FEELS SO RIGHT.

THE MAKE-OVER

August 1990

sentence to sparkle—but it was also an appreciative audience, one that you could count on to save your neck whenever inspiration failed. As Bruce Handy says, "I really did trust all of them. You knew you weren't going to end up with egg on your face."

"*The New Yorker* and *Time* in the '20s and '30s and '40s were different, but in my lifetime up until *Spy*, almost all magazines were purely aggregations of individual writers' voices," says Kurt. "The idea of *editors* really using a magazine assertively, institutionally—*This is our creation*—it's hard to think of other journalistic magazines that did that. You could argue it had its bad aspects, too. But it was something new and exciting at the time. We were taking real responsibility for the whole voice of the magazine—like composers as well as conductors."

It's *Okay*

There are three titanic hoaxes, a cultural triad no

to

IT'S OKAY TO HATE POETRY

human has ever enjoyed for even a millisecond:

Hate

IT'S OKAY TO HATE OPERA

poetry, opera and ballet. Each claims a massive,

High

IT'S OKAY TO HATE BALLET

often hysteric following, each rakes in substantial

Culture

moneys, each has an obscenely enduring history.

**A RUDE MANIFESTO
BY PAUL RUDNICK**

AND EACH REMAINS A WHOLE AND UTTER FRAUD, A DIABOLIC PUNISHMENT, AN ALL-DEVOURING LIE. THESE ITEMS ARE, IF NOT DISTINCTLY EVIL, AT BEST CON JOBS ON A GALACTIC SCALE.

POETRY: SMALL AND FEY. Poetry is simply poor punctuation. A poem is a thought unworthy of a paragraph, random words tossed on the page, literary lint. Poems are Laura Ashley prints for the mind, unicorn dung. They possess none of the time-honored virtues of fine literature: you can't curl up with a nice trashy poem. Poems are rarely adapted as miniseries. Your parents would never forbid you to bring that Jackie Collins *poem* into the house; a volume of Millay seldom falls open to the good parts. People never bicker over who should play Tiresias in "The Waste Land," Valerie Bertinelli or Pam Dawber.

Why are poems composed, or perpetrated? To break up the page in *The New Yorker*. Without poetry Ann Beattie would smush into the cartoons, and the eight parts on ice-making would hurtle against the windbreaker ads. Without poetry high school girls in corduroy jumpers and black leotards might have to make some friends. Emily Dickinson never left her cottage in Amherst, and with just cause: no one asked her to. *Don't invite Emily, she might recite one of her* things. Scholars swear that Shakespeare didn't exist, that his verse was penned by Ben Jonson or Marlowe (under a pseudonym, so they wouldn't be blamed). Has anyone ever got lucky after pulling, "Hey, babe, read any good poems lately?"

As with all operas and ballets, all poems are identical. If you must, skim two lines of any poem, shudder and know the truth. That's right, they all mention "love's fragrant bower." And silvery snowflakes and autumn's pungent grief and echoing silence and little cat feet. You never have to read another; like the actors in *Platoon*, you have tasted hell and survived.

OPERA: BIG AND EMBARRASSING. Opera is eons more loathsome than poetry; with opera, you've paid a lot of money and you're physically trapped. You're stuck sitting there while ungainly genetic mutants bay at the walls. An operatic soprano is not a talent, it is a threat. An opera is a simple tale rendered in pain, in wails demanding medical attention, not bravos. Operatic scores are not music. Music lasts three and a half minutes, requires the presence of three sultry black women and has a picture of Madonna on it. Songs are not about cruel fate, the gods or immortal passion; songs are about how mean your parents are, how hot something is and what you intend to do with your fine love thang. Singers do not continue to sing after they

---

FUNDING HIGHBROW HOAXES

. . . .

HOW MUCH MONEY (THAT COULD HAVE BEEN SPENT ON HOSTESS SNO-BALLS, *TIGER BEAT* AND HOLIDAY ON ICE) DID YOU, THE AMERICAN TAXPAYER, LAVISH ON OUTMODED FORMS OF CULTURAL TEDIUM? *In 1986–87 the New York State Council on the Arts spent $1,611,400 on opera, $1,697,500 on ballet and $261,500 on poetry and small literary presses. The National Endowment for the Arts spent $8.9 million on ballet (and dance in general), $8.08 million on opera (and musical theater) and $4.7 million on poetic and literary causes.*

---

have been stabbed, only after they have overdosed. Singers can be the King, the Boss, the Chairman of the Board, but they cannot be the Dame. If Joan Sutherland were a true artist, she'd be Kooley Joan Ad-Rock, she'd be illin'. If opera had value, it would be in the front bins at Tower Records. If opera had purpose, K-Tel would release two eight-track cartridges, check or money order only, of *Renata Tebaldi—Party Sounds.*

Why, then, the hordes of seemingly worshipful devotees, the slavering for Domingo, Pavarotti and other nuclear accidents? These clutching fans, these howling acolytes, all these people are paid off, a claque. The opera legends and their relatives disburse handsome sums; every Verdi recording includes a coupon for a full rebate. This is the only plausible conclusion; no one would experience opera voluntarily. Opera may well be a fundamentalist plot to discredit gay men. (Don't buy the smoke screen—real homosexuals like *Gypsy*.)

BALLET: TOO, TOO TEDIOUS.

Ballet may well be the most fiendish scam, as it dangles sex, teasing the unwary into infinite evenings of rotting swans and plotless stumbling. Excluding words and featuring occasionally soothing tunes, dance has the potential of being ideal moron fodder, attractive flesh paraded for our dining pleasure. But nay. The bodies are anorexic, crowned with chinless pinheads; the crotches are airbrushed, neutered in nylon. Dancers twirl and hop and pose; they avoid sex, preferring metaphor, floppy tulle and buckets of eye shadow. For most of us, movement is handy: sturdy legs can trot you to Macy's, a Stallone sequel, the corner newsstand. In ballet, movement appears both difficult and dull; standing *en pointe* is of interest only if the Mallomars are on the top shelf.

Dancers are likened to athletes, but organized sports are also a hoax, with the minor entertainment dividend of watching Olympic track stars trip. Dancers are athletes minus the good stuff—the endorsements, the urinalysis, the scratching (if Baryshnikov or Farrell ever reached down and hefted, the evening might begin). If Makarova were gifted, she'd be on *Solid Gold* in a Lurex G-string, humping the floor to Bon Jovi. She'd be at Radio City, tapping out the glory of Easter. And didn't you study *Breakin' 2*, O mighty Balanchine—why doesn't Gelsey spin on her head? (Although after reading *Dancing on My Grave*, I'm certain she has.)

Some insist that ballet exists as a girlhood phase, easing the transit from horses to bulimia. But ballet was concocted, of course, to discipline children. At Christmastime toddlers fidget, lusting for toys and treats. To calm the rumpus, parents wield a grisly stick—"If you don't behave, we're all going to *Nutcracker*." And if that doesn't work, it's *Giselle* or Tudor or—despite federal ordinances—the Ballet Folklorico, or any piece involving tambourines, a virgin and the pepper harvest.

Civilization is founded on hoaxes, on false fun, on educational playthings. Torch the concert halls, nuke the toe shoes, shred anything in pentameter—who'll notice? Subdivide La Scala into a multiplex, ban the Bolshoi—only art museums are allowed, as they provide gift shops. All that should remain of High Art is T-shirts, mugs and calendars. Stop faking cultural orgasm—go watch TV! ◗

HOW TO AVOID POETRY, OPERA AND BALLET

Avoid formal education after tenth grade
Avoid girls with waist-length hair
Avoid the classical annex of Tower Records
Avoid anyone with a PBS tote bag
Avoid England, France and Italy

WHAT BALLET DANCERS DO ON A DAY OFF

Go over wills of elderly admirers
Clean out shoulder bag
Rinse tights, or sell them to elderly admirers
Stretch
Smoke
Buy suede clothing
Kiss small pet dog until it smothers
Have sex with Peter Martins

WHAT OPERA SINGERS DO ON A DAY OFF

Make cookbook deal with Doubleday
Sing guest aria on Johnny Carson, bore millions
Call spouse in foreign country
Develop sore throat
Appear at White House Gershwin gala
Eat to keep strength up
Record "Ave Maria," "Hava Nagila" and "Memory"

WHAT A POETESS WANTS FOR HER BIRTHDAY

More potpourri
More Janis Ian albums
Barrettes
More Yardley English Lavender eye shadow
Lifetime subscription to *Cat Fancy* magazine
No more war
New clogs

ANTIDOTES

For *Tannhäuser*: Pee-wee's Playhouse
For *The Sleeping Beauty*: Dance Fever
For Ovid: crack

WHAT TO DO IF YOU LOVE SOMEONE WHO HAS A BOX AT THE MET, A SUBSCRIPTION TO ABT OR A SUBSCRIPTION TO *THE SEWANEE REVIEW*

Attend the ballet, but keep asking, "How come them chicks ain't got no jugs?"
Attend *La Bohème*; bring your dog
Kill them—shooting anyone in a MOSTLY MOZART T-shirt is only a misdemeanor

GOOD THINGS ABOUT BALLET

Short pieces
Gelsey having her earlobes snipped off
The hippo ballerinas in *Fantasia*
Dancers chewing gum onstage
Vicious 15-year-olds
Elderly Russian dance teachers with gold-tipped canes, swatting dancers' ankles
Grisly photographs of dancers' bare feet, à la Amnesty International
Gelsey hailing a cab in leg warmers and sable

GOOD THINGS ABOUT OPERA

Meals during intermissions
Joan Sutherland's jaw
Charles Ludlam as Callas
Death scenes, with singing
Bugs Bunny dressed as Brunhilde
A Night at the Opera
Riots following last-minute diva cancellations
Curtain-call fistfights
Mad scenes, with bad wigs

CAREERS FOR BALLET DANCERS AFTER AGE 25

Freelance swizzle stick
Solid Gold dancer
Chorus boy behind Shirley MacLaine, with hazard pay for getting hit with loose skin

THANKS, POETRY, OPERA AND BALLET, FOR:

Leslie Browne's film career
White Nights
The Bell Jar
The Turning Point
Yes, Giorgio
Mario Lanza
Nijinsky
"Trees"
Rod McKuen ◗

Cons
fitne
but,
tripl
York
cise
Luxu
cate
that
priv
exc

BEST OF BLURB-O-MAT

"Graydon once told me he'd shared a cab with Walter after Blurb-o-Mat had carried his byline and photo for some months," says editor Joanne Gruber. "Along the way he asked Walter whether he thought the feature was funny. Walter smiled at him vaguely. 'Have you ever read it, Walter? It has your name on it!' Walter smiled, shrugged, and said, 'Can't read everything.'"

BLURB-O-MAT
Capsule Movie Reviews by Eric Kaplan™,
the Movie Publicist's Friend

DEAD POETS SOCIETY, starring Robin Williams (Touchstone)
    Eric Kaplan says, **"Read Oscar's lips: 'Bring me Robin Williams. . . . Now!'"**

June 1989

AFTER DARK, MY SWEET, starring Bruce Dern, Rachel Ward, Jason Patric (Avenue) ღღღღ
    Walter Monheit says, **"Hallelujah! Bruce puts on a Dern good show, but ooof! — my sweet Ward!"**

What the monocles mean: ღღღ — *excellent;* ღღღღ — *indisputably a classic*

July 1990

BLURB-O-MAT
Capsule Movie Reviews by Walter "Dateline: The Copa" Monheit™,
the Movie Publicist's Friend

[Editors' note: By resounding popular decree, Walter Monheit™ has been reinstated as SPY's movie critic–at–large. Of the 41 readers who cast Monheit Plugola Scandal referendum ballots, 36 voted in Monheit's favor, 4 sought his ouster, and 1 was disqualified for voting twice. (A 42nd, particularly bothersome reader sent in a blank ballot accompanied by a request for "more info.") Monheit is back! — chastened, he says, but ready to rumba.]

THE MARRYING MAN, starring Kim Basinger, Alec Baldwin (Buena Vista) ღღღღ
    Walter Monheit says, **"Do you, Oscar, take Kim and Alec to be your *laughfully* wedded partners in sultry screendom, till death do you ooof!?"**

THE SILENCE OF THE LAMBS, starring Jodie Foster, Anthony Hopkins, Scott Glenn (Orion) ღღღღ

March 1991

GLEAMING THE CUBE, starring Christian Slater, Steven Bauer (Twentieth Century Fox)
    Eric Kaplan says, **"Bauer—rhymes with star power!"**

C.H.U.D. II (Vestron)   *Eric Kaplan says,* **"Pure C.H.U.D. excitement—better than the original!"**

November 1988

SONY

BLURB-O-MAT
Capsule Movie Reviews by Walter "Dateline: The Copa" Monheit™,
the Movie Publicist's Friend — Special Product-Placement Edition

GREEN CARD, starring Andie MacDowell, Gerard Depardieu (Touchstone)ღღღღ
    Walter Monheit says, **"A Franco-American™ feast fortified with exta ooof! Andie can perform a naturalization act on me any day!"**

SCREWFACE, starring Steven Seagal (20th Century Fox)ღღღ
    Walter Monheit says, **"For a True Value™ in entertainment hardware, just say-*Gal*! And hey, what's that in Steve's hand? A Phillips™-head? No—it's Oscar's head!"**

October 1990

BLURB-O-MAT
Capsule Movie Reviews by Eric Kaplan®,
the Movie Publicist's Friend

HOT TO TROT, starring Bob Goldthwait, Virginia Madsen, Don the talking horse (Warner Bros.)
    Eric Kaplan says, **"Trot, don't walk, to see this one!"**

June 1988

MR. FROST, starring Jeff Goldblum, Alan Bates (SVS)ღღღ
    Walter Monheit says, **"Jeff's *Big Chill* has turned to *Frost*—and Oscar's warming to him like Thinsulate™!"**

What the monocles mean: ღღღ – *excellent;* ღღღღ – *indisputably a classic*

3

Not Too Shabby at All

Deeper into the '80s: "*Spy* Was Like Trollope—You Opened It Up

and There It Was, on a Plate"

What can I say, it was fun. It's not like we didn't have egos.
—TOM PHILLIPS

THERE WAS NO TIME TO REFLECT on the months and years that had led to the first issue, or even on that issue itself. Another one was past due, and then another, and then another.... *Spy* would publish 10 times a year during most of its run, usually with double issues for the advertising-sparse months of January/February and July/August, 101 issues in all.* Everything—from enlarging our editorial purview to expanding the staff to fine-tuning the design to learning how to sell ads—was being done on the run.

Meanwhile, the founders had been encouraged by the results of that little direct-mail piece.

"We sent out that premiere issue, and with it the bills," says Tom.

"And the fulfillment house kept saying, 'We're getting a lot of activity here!'" Graydon says. "We were very excited, it looked

---

*For the record, we produced 70 issues, our successors, 31. —Eds.

like subscriptions were pouring in. But what it was, as it turned out, was something in the neighborhood of 3,000 *cancellations*. Because whatever they thought this magazine was going to be—*The New Yorker*, or the *Voice*, or *New York*—it wasn't any of them. That was a tough moment. I remember just saying, *Holy fuck!*"

"It was devastating," remembers Tom. "By all rights we should have said, 'That's it, this isn't going to work.'"

Circulation and advertising declined precipitously through the first three issues. "We basically refused to accept that it might not be working," Tom says. Plus, he adds, there *were* some good signs: "Newsstand was positive. [Steve] Schragis came along—he put in about $230,000 around the time of the second issue." And those readers for whom *Spy* was a revelation and a delight also discovered it through word of mouth. After those first few issues, circulation grew rapidly and steadily. And *Spy*, unlike practically every other magazine on earth, did not—clearly could not—rely on direct mail to build its readership.

Over the course of the early issues, more of *Spy*'s signature features were introduced: Luc Sante's true-crime column; Letters

Opposite:
"Witty, natty, and not taken lightly"—Tom Phillips, Kurt Andersen, and Graydon Carter, shot by longtime *Spy* photographer Chris Callis for *GQ*, August 1988

HOLIDAY SUPER BOWL: CHRISTMAS VS. CHANUKAH *By Jonathan Dellheim*

	Christmas	Chanukah
Celebrants	Christians	Jews
Date	December 25	No set date
Time Span	One eve and one day, preceded by a two-month warning period	Eight days no one remembers until stores are closed and it's too late to buy candles
Greeting	"Merry Christmas"	"You look thin—have you lost weight?"
Star of . . .	Bethlehem	David
Miracle	Virgin conceived	One day's oil burned for eight days
Possible Explanation	Low morals	High octane
Main Character (Real)	Jesus Christ—the Lew Lehrman of the first century. (Both switched careers in midlife, both had a message people ignored and both converted from Judaism to Christianity. Unlike Lehrman, however, Jesus rose from the dead)	Judah Maccabee, the only Jew since David to win a fight
Main Character (Fictional)	Santa Claus	God
Symbols	Christmas tree, wreaths, mistletoe and cheap-looking plastic Nativity scenes	Menorah, Chanukah bush and cheap-looking plastic dreidels
Official Drink	Eggnog (335 calories per cup)	Dr. Brown's diet cream soda (under 20 calories per cup)
Backup Singers	Bing Crosby, Perry Como, Andy Williams, Mel Torme, Jose Feliciano, Alvin and the Chipmunks and newcomer Bruce Springsteen	The cantor
Best Ritual	Fighting about what kind of Christmas tree to get	Fighting about what color candles to use
Official Gift (Good Parents)	Puppy or a ten-speed bicycle	Puppy and a twelve-speed bicycle
Official Gift (Bad Parents)	Bible	Bible, key ring, shoelaces, soap, socks, box of tissues, underwear, subscription to *Scientific American*
Commercial Backer	Macy's	Zabar's deli counter
Advantages	Quick religious service, great food, great music, lots of presents and the opportunity to wear red and green	Two Florida vacations in December
Disadvantages	Expensive to get gifts for everyone—perhaps the reason many Jews have amassed large fortunes, while Christians lag behind	Difficult to spell, hard to pronounce. Can only be considered a good holiday when compared with Yom Kippur. Will never give Christmas a run without some hit tunes, several cute reindeerlike animals and a color scheme
Overall	A biggie, though in strict theological terms it does not hold a candle to the day that Christ rose from the dead	Chanukah is the time Jews ask themselves whether they have exhibited the valor of the Maccabees. It is the time Jews recommit themselves to the defense of their faith. It is the time Jews intensify their religious observance. It is the time Jews secretly wish they could celebrate Christmas. ◗

December 1986

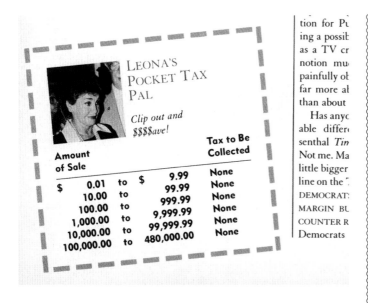

LEONA'S POCKET TAX PAL

Clip out and $$$$ave!

Amount of Sale			Tax to Be Collected
$ 0.01	to	$ 9.99	None
10.00	to	99.99	None
100.00	to	999.99	None
1,000.00	to	9,999.99	None
10,000.00	to	99,999.99	None
100,000.00	to	480,000.00	None

February 1987

to the Editor of *The New Yorker* (which didn't publish them in those days); the *Times* column, which debuted in February 1987—the same issue that featured an assembled-by-hand, never-before-published-anywhere *New Yorker* masthead. ("Most of us had to admit that we didn't know exactly what our coworkers did for a living," one anonymous *New Yorker* reporter wrote us. "Our office manager was forced to draw up a new list of employees just to keep up with your information.") There were one-shots like "Christmas vs. Chanukah" (an early example of the endlessly influential and imitated *Spy* chart), and "Leona [Helmsley]'s Pocket Tax Pal," inspired by the hotelier/harridan's income-tax problems.

Separated at Birth?, which we all thought was silly fun but turned into the magazine's single best-known feature, would debut in the third *Spy* (December 1986) with three lookalike pairs, including Meryl Streep and Mike Nichols. And, farther down the line, the May 1987 issue would contain the debut of The Usual Suspects, *Spy*'s gossip column (impossible for a monthly today, given the long lead times, but difficult even then). One of the first items, which pretty much set the tone, read: "Ferret-eyed snitch **IVAN BOESKY** has three limousines to convey him from his tacky, expensive Westchester estate to his suite of expensive, tacky offices at 650 Fifth Avenue. Two-thirds of the motorcade is bogus—decoys, presumably, so that hit-men, finked-on former colleagues and flower-vending Moonies won't know which one contains the disgraced arbitrageur."

In New York, especially at certain newsstands—the one in the lobby of the old Condé Nast Building on Madison Avenue, for instance—*Spy* would sell out the day it hit the street. And the press was starting to notice.

> *The esteemed Bill Cosby, currently the most popular father figure on television, has become so successful he's now an inviting target, and sure enough, the November issue of* Spy *magazine, that upstart New York humor mag, has volunteered to toss the first stones.*
> —*Los Angeles Herald-Examiner*, November 12, 1986,
> regarding "Some of the Nicer Things About Cosby,"
> by David Handelman, November 1986

> *One New Yorker, who missed a bus to an important meeting because he was chuckling over the magazine, said, "It's like a* MAD *magazine for adults"—a description the editors do not take exception to.*
> —*The Boston Globe*, November 27, 1986

> Spy *is funny and well-written.... It is, however, the snottiest, most negative publication currently on the stands.*
> —*Details*, December 1986

> *I forgive you.*
> —Oprah Winfrey, in a letter to *Spy* (published here in its
> entirety), after *Spy*'s profile of her ("It Came from Chicago,"
> by Bill Zehme, December 1986)

THAT DECEMBER, THE NEWSWEEKLY *Insight* published a roundup of new magazines: "Probably the best of the new breed is a satiric little monthly called *Spy*....It's slick and it's mean. You know it's slick because the voluptuous darling of the fashion world, model Paulina Porizkova, graces the November cover, and she doesn't come cheap. You know it's mean because the magazine calls Governor Mario M. Cuomo's son Andrew 'Ratface Andy' and describes him like this: 'He is not a hood. He is just an ordinary 28-year-old Manhattan lawyer who, *sheerly because of his legal skills, and not because he is the son of the governor*, has attracted casino operator Donald Trump and other major New York developers as clients.'"

...ED AT BIRTH?

...and Louise Fletcher?

...and Eve Arden?

...and Jim Bouton?

...and Ellen Barkin?

LETTERS TO THE EDITOR OF *THE NEW YORKER*

DEAR MR. SHAWN,

I don't suppose you expected to see a letter from one of your own employees, but there's something that's been bothering me for some time now. Why the colored column on the left of every cover? What does it mean? And if it doesn't serve any purpose, why do we do it?

Anonymous *New Yorker* employee
New York

The border, we claim, is not on every cover. Sometimes, we add helpfully, the artist will include the border on the illustration itself. In short, we acknowledge, we don't know what it means, and when we do it, we don't know why.

DEAR MR. SHAWN,

The report by Philip B. in the November 3 Talk of the Town made some discerning points I'd like to support. He admires the Feelies because they wear cool clothes, including "basketball sneakers"; he can't stand bands that wear "tasteless" gear, including "high-top sneakers."

I know just what he means. I love groups that wear sweaters, but I hate ones that wear those woolly pullover things with no buttons on the front.

Mark Lasswell
New York

DEAR MR. SHAWN,

The New Yorker has never, in its 62 years of existence, published a list of its staff members. Every other publication in the world does. Why not you? Don't readers have a right to know who produces the magazine? I'm all for tradition and mystery and saving paper, but isn't it about time you printed a masthead?

Henry Possett
New York

Well . . . all right. Turn the page.

SPY *welcomes letters to the editor of* The New Yorker. *Address letters to "Dear Mister Shawn," c/o* SPY, *The Puck Building, 295 Lafayette Street, New York, N.Y. 10012.* ❧

SIGN LANGUAGE

...d "enjoy" these actual snippets "of" ...ge.

...S BELOW-COST "PRICE"
...44th Street and Third Avenue
"DIFFERENCE!"
...tore, 31st Street and Third Avenue
...WE WILL "CLOSE" THIS
...
...RNITURE"
...NISH "RECORDS"
...Shop, 27th Street and Third Avenue
...PRICES ON WINES; "SUPER" SALE
...nt Liquors, 24th Street and Third

...N.Y.P.D. RECRUITS
...op, 20th Street and Third Avenue
...R AND "COLD SODA"
...SO
...li, 20th Street and Third Avenue

FRESH "SALADS" MADE TO ORDER
—*Arnold's Deli, 18th Street and Third Avenue*

SPECIAL—"2" EGGS WITH HOME FRIES, COFFEE, $2.50
—*East Twelve St. Deli, 12th Street and Third Avenue*

Webster's Ninth New Collegiate Dictionary says quotation marks can be used to enclose the following: direct quotations; words or phrases borrowed from others; words used in a special way; slang words being introduced into formal writing; and titles of things.

At NYU's Linguistics Department, a receptionist said, "That's really a matter for the English Department. It sounds like a prescriptive problem; we're more theoretical."

Brian Culver, who teaches English at NYU, said, "My only explanation would be that people use [quotation marks] pretty freely these days—as a title or to bring attention to something."

The manager at the Karl Ehmer Deli said, "A part-time worker made the sign for me." —*Peter Finch*

THE NEW YORKER

EDITOR William Shawn

MANAGING EDITOR, FICTION Charles McGrath MANAGING EDITOR, FACT John Bennet
SENIOR FICTION EDITOR Roger Angell POETRY EDITOR Howard Moss
FICTION EDITORS Linda Asher, Gwyneth Cravens, Frances Kiernan, Daniel Menaker, Alice Quinn
EXECUTIVE EDITOR Barbara Solonche
FACT EDITORS Gardner Botsford[1], Charles Patrick Crow, Nancy Franklin, William Knapp, Sara Lippincott, Derek Morgan, Susan Moritz
ART EDITOR Lee Lorenz
BOOKS EDITOR Edith Oliver FICTION EDITOR EMERITUS William Maxwell
NEWSBREAK EDITORS Burton Bernstein, Dorothy L. Guth

HEAD COPY EDITOR Eleanor Gould Packard COPY EDITORS Lu Burke, Ann Goldstein, Elizabeth Macklin, Elizabeth Pearson-Griffiths, Marcia Van Meter
HEAD FACT CHECKER Martin J. Baron FACT CHECKERS Peter Canby, Harold Espen, Julie Gray, Christopher A. Kenny, Anne Mortimer-Maddox, Michelle Preston, Richard Sacks, Robert Walsh
HEAD LIBRARIAN Helen Stark LIBRARY Cindy Prentis Frenkel, Christopher Shay
HEAD COLLATOR Edward Stringham COLLATING Katherine Daly Egan, Mary Hawthorne
FOUNDRY (PROOF) READERS Lindsley C. Cameron, Tony Powell
COPY DESK Mary Jane Norris, Michael Rubiner
HEAD OF MAKEUP John M. Murphy MAKEUP John Broderick, John P. Brooks, William Fitzgerald, Patrick Keogh, Bernard McAteer, Victor Webb
PRODUCTION John Gardella, Tony Genduso, Gene Reynolds, Sam Spoto

LIBEL STAFF Joseph Cooper, Milton Greenstein[2]
HEAD OF PERMISSIONS Jillian Frisch HEAD OF MESSENGERS Bruce Diones MAINTENANCE MANAGER John O'Brien
OFFICE MANAGER Sheila McGrath[3]

"A ISSUE" EDITOR Nancy Ramsey
ASSISTANTS TO MR. SHAWN Elizabeth Morgan, Mary Painter, Laurie Witkin
EDITORIAL ASSISTANTS Fabia D'Arienzo, Anne Hall, Karen Kaminsky, Judith E. Mellecker, Alice Truax
HEAD OF "GOINGS ON ABOUT TOWN" Jane Olds Dienstfrey
"GOINGS ON ABOUT TOWN" STAFF John Edwards, Joan Mannion, Sally Ann Mock, Susan Thomsen, Andrea E. Welch
LETTERS DEPARTMENT Buffie Hughes[4]

WRITERS Renata Adler, Charles Dwight Allen, Jervis Anderson, Anthony Bailey, John Bainbridge, Whitney Balliett, Bill Barich, Donald Barthelme, Frederick Barthelme, Ann Beattie, Burton Bernstein, Jeremy Bernstein, Bruce Bliven Jr., Naomi Bliven, Jane Boutwell[5], Paul Brodeur, John Brooks, Henry S. F. Cooper Jr., Arlene Croce, Peter De Vries, Elizabeth Drew, Vickie Karp Dym, Deborah Eisenberg, Frances FitzGerald, Kennedy Fraser, Ian Frazier[5], Mavis Gallant, Veronica Geng, Brendan Gill, Penelope Gilliatt, Emily Hahn, Philip Hamburger, Lis Harris, Robert Henderson, Anthony Hiss[5], Edith Iglauer, Gerald Jonas, Pauline Kael, E. J. Kahn Jr., Garrison Keillor, Mary D. Rudd Kierstead, Jamaica Kincaid, Eugene Kinkead, Jane Kramer, James Lardner, Susan Lardner[5], Andrea Lee, Suzannah Lessard, Andy Logan, Robert MacMillan, Janet Malcolm, Bobbie Ann Mason, Bruce McCall, Bill McKibben[5], Faith McNulty, John McPhee, Ved Mehta, Stanley Mieses, Joseph Mitchell, Lewis Mumford, Alice Munro, William Murray, John Newhouse, Edith Oliver, Mollie Panter-Downes, William Pfaff, David Plante, Andrew Porter, Alastair Reid, Lillian Ross, Berton Roueché, Helen Ruttencutter, J. D. Salinger[6], Jonathan Schell[5], Fred C. Shapiro, Robert Shaplen, Susan Sheehan, Alex Shoumatoff, Mark Singer[5], Julia M. Smith, George Steiner, Calvin Tomkins, Calvin Trillin, George W. S. Trow Jr., John Updike, Helen Vendler, Douglas Watt, William Wertenbaker, Lawrence Weschler[5], Wallace M. White Jr., Thomas Whiteside, Alec Wilkinson, Herbert Warren Wind, Cynthia Zarin

ARTISTS Charles Addams, Laura Jean Allen, Thomas B. Allen, David Annesley, Ed Arno, José Aruego, Niculae Asciu, T. K. Atherton, Nancy Balliett, Perry Barlow, Charles Barsotti, Ross Bateup, R. O. Blechman, Simon Bond, George Booth, Mark Boxer, Robin Dee Brickman, Anne Burgess, Lawrence A. Burke, Shelly Canton, Sir Hugh Casson, Robert Censoni, Roz Chast, Tom Cheney, David Christianson, Richard Cline, John Corcoran, Michael Crawford, Leo Cullum, Andrzej Czeczot, Whitney Darrow Jr., Raymond Davidson, Susan Davis, Chon Day, Robert Day, Richard Decker, Eldon Dedini, Paul Degen, Liza Donnelly, Boris Drucker, Jerry Dumas, Edna Eicke, Alden Erikson, Graham Falk, Joseph Farris, Michael Ffolkes, Ed Fisher, Douglas Florian, Jean-Michel Folon, Dana Fradon, Frederick Franck, André François, Edward Frascino, Bernard Fuchs, Tom Funk, Mort Gerberg, Arthur Getz, Louis S. Glanzman, Heidi Goennel, Herbert Goldberg, Bud Grace, James Graves, Sam Gross, Robert Beverly Hale, William Hamilton, Malcolm Hancock, J. B. Handelsman, Consuelo Eames Hanks, Sidney Harris, Richard Edes Harrison, René Henderiks, Donald Higgens, David Hockney, Syd Hoff, Brad Holland, Albert Hubbell, Carlita Hunt, Stan Hunt, Rea Irvin[7], C. S. H. Jhabvala, Lonni Sue Johnson, John Jonik, Zoran Jovanović, Ilonka Karasz, Nurit Karlin, Jeff Kaufman, Gilbert Kerlin, Edward Koren, Anatol Kovarsky, Robert Kraus, David Langdon, Bill Lee, Stuart Leeds, Pierre Le-Tan, Arnie Levin, Peter Lippman, Lee Lorenz, Joseph Low, Kenneth Mahood, Robert Mankoff, Charles E. Martin, Henry Martin, Michael Maslin, Richard McCallister, C. Taggart McVicker, Roland Michaud, Mario Micossi, Eugène Mihaesco, Warren Miller, Robert Minter, Joseph Mirachi, Louis Mitelberg, Frank Modell, James Mulligan, Roxie Munro, Lou Myers, Merle Nacht, Louis Nitka, John Norment, William O'Brian, Richard Oldden, Jenni Oliver, Everett Opie, W. B. Park, Virgil Partch, David Pascal, Bruce Petty, Zelio Alves Pinto, Peter Porges, David Preston, George Price, Abel Quezada, Donald Reilly, Mischa Richter, Cliff Roberts, Charles Rodrigues, Al Ross, Marisabina Russo, William Sakren, Charles Sauers, Brian Savage, Charles Saxon, Jim Schmalzried, Bernard Schoenbaum, Ronald Searle, J. J. Sempé, Judith Shahn, Vahan Shirvanian, Burt Silverman, Gretchen Dow Simpson, Smilby, Claude Smith, Ton Smits, Leslie Starke, William Steig, Saul Steinberg, Peter Steiner, Mick Stevens, James Stevenson, Jean-Claude Suarès, Beatrice Szanton, Anthony Taber, Robert Tallon, Richard Taylor, Jack Tippit, Barney Tobey, Mike Twohy, Iris Van Rynbach, Dean Vietor, William Von Riegen, Noel Watson, Robert Weber, Barbara Westman, Gahan Wilson, Rowland B. Wilson, Bernard Wiseman, Michael Witte, Bill Woodman, Roz Zanengo, Jack Ziegler

THE NEW YORKER is published weekly by The New Yorker Magazine Inc., 25 West 43rd Street, New York, N.Y. 10036.

[1] Retired, but still edits his wife, Janet Malcolm, as well as Roger Angell and Berton Roueché
[2] Retired, but back in harness lately
[3] Head of "Pond," the typing pool named after its longtime chief, Harriet Walden
[4] They may not print them, but they do answer them
[5] Regular Talk of the Town writers
[6] Late with story
[7] Died in 1972, but his famous drawing is still pressed into service each year for the February anniversary-issue cover

❧

"Letters to the Editor of *The New Yorker*," an occasional feature, and the *New Yorker* masthead, an unprecedented look at who made that magazine, February 1987

This half-page took a staff member almost a half-year to put together.

In fact, Paulina did come cheap: None of our cover models—not Porizkova, not Carol Alt, both then at their career peaks—ever got paid. The only cover models who did were the trained show-business rodents that posed with Alt for "Rat City!" in May 1988.

In keeping with its insider/outsider dynamic, *Spy* would often recruit celebrities—ideally, cool and intriguing ones—to appear on its posterlike covers: among them Carrie Fisher, Tracey Ullman, Chevy Chase (this was the '80s, remember), Bernadette Peters, Elvis Costello, Sandra Bernhard, Winona Ryder, Monty Python's Graham Chapman, Peter Falk, Jamie Lee Curtis, Gene Siskel and Roger Ebert, Michael Keaton, Sharon Stone, Mike Myers and Bart Simpson, as well as campy old-timers like Wayne Newton, Milton Berle, and Joan Rivers. With the exception of the 1992 issue featuring a profile of Wayne Newton, the issues for which the celebrities fronted carried not one word of journalism about them; they were purely performers. "The model was sort of *Saturday Night Live*," Graydon says, "where you have the Not Ready for Prime Time Players but you get a famous guest host and that's who was on the cover." Kurt adds: "The effect was to make it like, 'Oh, yeah, they may be strange and scary, but, hey—that's a famous person, this must be a *real magazine.*'"

After *Spy* picked up some steam, it became easier to get certain kinds of people to agree to pose, but it could also work the other way. For our "WASPmania!" cover (August 1987), after ur-WASP Spalding Gray had backed out, we went to the other conceptual extreme and asked New York's mayor, Ed Koch, to pose in a riding outfit, complete with crop. Remarkably, he agreed. Susan Morrison went down to City Hall to measure him—"including his inseam," she says.

"But Koch must have gotten his first look at the magazine as he was being driven to the shoot," says art director Alex Isley, because the mayoral motorcade made a U-turn. Stood-up and in no position to squander booked photo studio time, the magazine had photographer Chris Callis—who was by some stroke of luck roughly of Kochian dimensions—dress and pose for his own photo (see page 117).

Gag covers of satirical magazines were much trickier propositions in the prehistoric '80s. The kind of photo manipulation that can now be done at home by a middle-schooler waiting for his iPod to load didn't exist. So *Spy* resorted to expensive, state-of-the-art Scitexed (the very word!) covers, the first of which was an image of Teddy Kennedy being splashed, in an allusion to Chappaquiddick,

The rat wrangler and the final, 100 percent unretouched May 1988 cover

with a bucket of water ("Kennedy Bashing!," November 1987). The verisimilitude was remarkable and *Spy* went on to do many of them, enlisting staff members as body-doubles.

At the very beginning it wasn't a matter of *Who should we get?* but *Who can we get?* After Chris Elliott, Paulina (who popped up again, in another outfit, a few issues later as our April '87 cover-girl simply because we already had the image), and deb-of-the-moment Cornelia Guest ("Brats"), for our fourth cover, "Scary New York" (January/February 1987), Morrison and I lobbied for Buster Poindexter, David Johansen's then-still-new lounge-lizard alter ego. Graydon briefly agitated for a "Freeloading Brits" cover, but was outvoted, three to one (*Spy* was shockingly democratic). Johansen stopped by the Puck loft to pick up Morrison, wearing a tuxedo and dangling a six-pack of Miller Lite languorously over his shoulder—Morrison later confided that it felt, in the best way, like prom night. At the conclusion of the shoot, which was outdoors on a bitterly cold evening near the Hudson River, Johansen/Poindexter gallantly put Morrison into a taxi—"The lady gets the foist cab"—shut the door, then turned to me with a grin and said, "Wanna get a belt?"

The only cover models who ever got paid were the trained rats.

SPY'S INSTANT SUCCESS nearly destroyed it. "The magazine was intended to be platformed, like a quality movie," Graydon says. "You know, start in New York, build toward L.A., and then

"My Usual, Highly Visible Booth, Please, Ona"

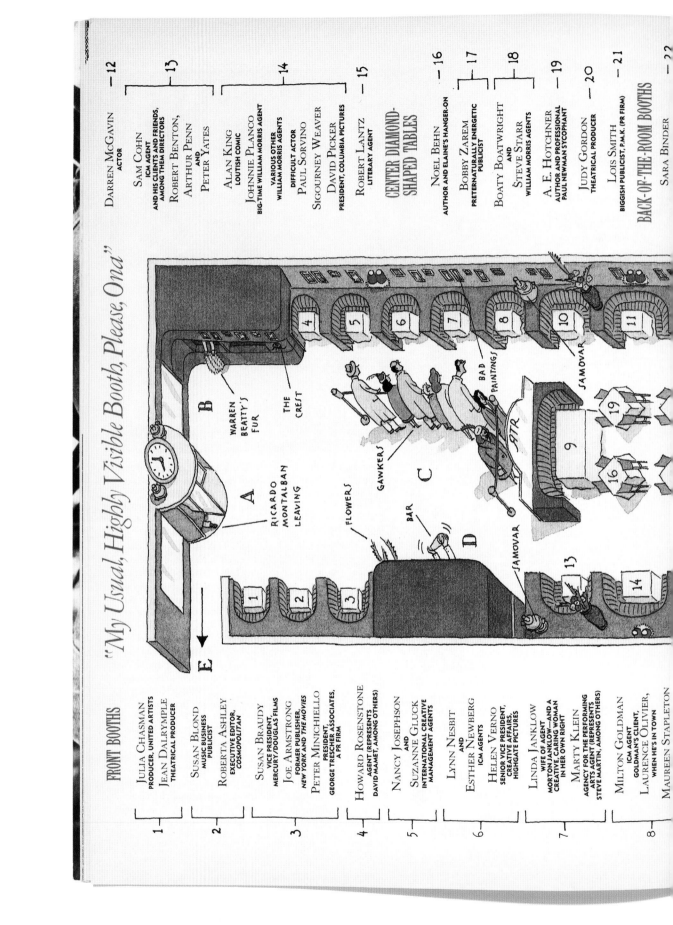

FRONT BOOTHS

1.
- JULIA CHASMAN, PRODUCER, UNITED ARTISTS
- JEAN DALRYMPLE, THEATRICAL PRODUCER

2.
- SUSAN BLOND, MUSIC BUSINESS PUBLICIST
- ROBERTA ASHLEY, EXECUTIVE EDITOR, *COSMOPOLITAN*

3.
- SUSAN BRAUDY, VICE PRESIDENT, MERCURY/DOUGLAS FILMS
- JOE ARMSTRONG, FORMER PUBLISHER, *NEW YORK* AND *THE MOVIES*
- PETER MINICHIELLO, PRESIDENT, GEORGE TRESCHER ASSOCIATES, A PR FIRM

4.
- HOWARD ROSENSTONE, AGENT (REPRESENTS DAVID MAMET, AMONG OTHERS)

5.
- NANCY JOSEPHSON AND SUZANNE GLUCK, INTERNATIONAL CREATIVE MANAGEMENT AGENTS

6.
- LYNN NESBIT AND ESTHER NEWBERG, ICM AGENTS
- HELEN VERNO, SENIOR VICE PRESIDENT, CREATIVE AFFAIRS, HIGHGATE PICTURES
- LINDA JANKLOW, WIFE OF AGENT MORTON JANKLOW AND A CREATIVE CARING WOMAN IN HER OWN RIGHT

7.
- MARTY KLEIN, AGENCY FOR THE PERFORMING ARTS AGENT (REPRESENTS STEVE MARTIN, AMONG OTHERS)

8.
- MILTON GOLDMAN, ICM AGENT, GOLDMAN'S CLIENT, LAURENCE OLIVIER, WHEN HE'S IN TOWN
- MAUREEN STAPLETON

12.
- DARREN McGAVIN, ACTOR

13.
- SAM COHN, ICM AGENT AND HIS CLIENTS AND FRIENDS, AMONG THEM DIRECTORS ROBERT BENTON, ARTHUR PENN AND PETER YATES

14.
- ALAN KING, LOUTISH COMIC
- JOHNNIE PLANCO, BIG-TIME WILLIAM MORRIS AGENT
- VARIOUS OTHER WILLIAM MORRIS AGENTS
- DIFFICULT ACTOR PAUL SORVINO
- SIGOURNEY WEAVER
- DAVID PICKER, PRESIDENT, COLUMBIA PICTURES

15.
- ROBERT LANTZ, LITERARY AGENT

CENTER DIAMOND-SHAPED TABLES

16.
- NOEL BEHN, AUTHOR AND ELAINE'S HANGER-ON

17.
- BOBBY ZAREM, PRETERNATURALLY ENERGETIC PUBLICIST

18.
- BOATY BOATWRIGHT AND STEVE STARR, WILLIAM MORRIS AGENTS

19.
- A. E. HOTCHNER, AUTHOR AND PROFESSIONAL PAUL NEWMAN SYCOPHANT

20.
- JUDY GORDON, THEATRICAL PRODUCER

21.
- LOIS SMITH, BIGGISH PUBLICIST, P.M.K. (PR FIRM)

BACK-OF-THE-ROOM BOOTHS

22.
- SARA BINDER

SEMI-IMPORTANT BACK-OF-THE-ROOM — 23

"PELMENY CLUB" OF THE EPONYMOUS, VILE-TASTING BEEF AND VEAL DUMPLINGS ON MENU; MEETS ON WEDNESDAYS; IF YOU DROP BY, YOU HAVE TO TELL A JOKE. ONE CAN ONLY IMAGINE THE FUN.

MEMBERS INCLUDE SCREENWRITER **ANDREW BERGMAN**,

ALLITERATIVE TV CRITIC **JOEL SIEGEL**,

DIDACTIC *U.S. NEWS* WRITER **MICHAEL KRAMER**,

ADMAN **JERRY DELLA FEMINA**, — 24

ABC NEWS CORRESPONDENT **JEFF GREENFIELD** AND **GERRY IMBER**, "PLASTIC SURGEON TO THE STARS"

UNEMBARRASSING BOOTH FREQUENTED BY AGENTS FROM ICM AND APA — 24

DIANE SOKOLOW — 25 FILM PRODUCER

LONG TABLE ("STEPPES") — 27
FREQUENTED LARGELY BY NON-SHOW-BUSINESS PEOPLE, WHO IN A GROUP LOOK LIKE THEY ARE HAVING AN OFFICE GOING-AWAY PARTY

BACK-OF-THE-ROOM TABLES ("SIBERIA") — 28 29 30 31

NAVIGATIONAL LANDMARKS
A. FRONT REVOLVING DOOR
B. COAT CHECKROOM
C. ROPED-IN HOLDING PEN FOR NONFAMOUS
D. BAR
E. STAIRWAY TO GULAG

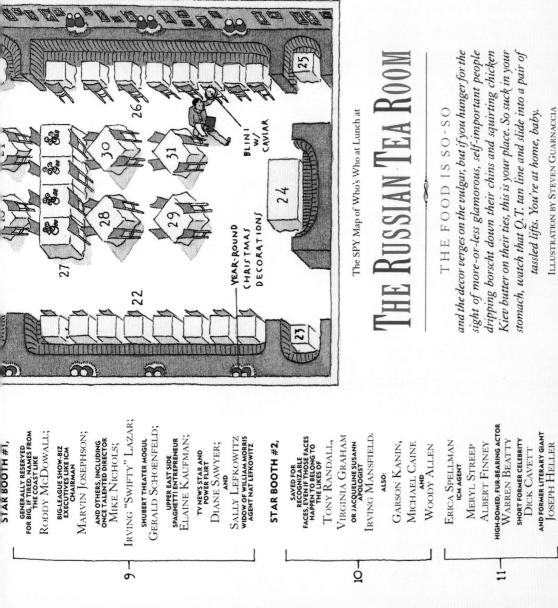

The SPY Map of Who's Who at Lunch at

THE RUSSIAN TEA ROOM

THE FOOD IS SO-SO

and the decor verges on the vulgar; but if you hunger for the sight of more-or-less glamorous, self-important people dripping borscht down their chins and squirting chicken Kiev butter on their ties, this is your place. So suck in your stomach, watch that Q.T. tan line and slide into a pair of tassled lifts. You're at home, baby.

ILLUSTRATION BY STEVEN GUARNACCIA

BLINI W/ CAVIAR

YEAR-ROUND CHRISTMAS DECORATIONS

STAR BOOTH #1, — 9

GENERALLY RESERVED FOR BIG, IF TIRED, NAMES FROM THE COAST LIKE **RODDY MCDOWALL**;

BIG-LEAGUE SHOW-BIZ EXECUTIVES LIKE ICM CHAIRMAN **MARVIN JOSEPHSON**;

AND OTHERS, INCLUDING ONCE TALENTED DIRECTOR **MIKE NICHOLS**;

IRVING "SWIFTY" LAZAR;

SHUBERT THEATER MOGUL **GERALD SCHOENFELD**;

UPPER EAST SIDE SPAGHETTI ENTREPRENEUR **ELAINE KAUFMAN**;

TV NEWS STAR AND POWER FLIRT **DIANE SAWYER**; AND **SALLY LEFKOWITZ** WIDOW OF WILLIAM MORRIS AGENT NAT LEFKOWITZ

STAR BOOTH #2, — 10

SAVED FOR RECOGNIZABLE FACES, EVEN IF THOSE FACES HAPPEN TO BELONG TO THE LIKES OF **TONY RANDALL**, **VIRGINIA GRAHAM** OR JACQUELINE SUSANN APOLOGIST **IRVING MANSFIELD**.

ALSO: **GARSON KANIN**, **MICHAEL CAINE** AND **WOODY ALLEN**

— 11

ERICA SPELLMAN ICM AGENT

MERYL STREEP

ALBERT FINNEY

HIGH-DOMED, FUR-BEARING ACTOR **WARREN BEATTY**

SHORT FORMER CELEBRITY **DICK CAVETT**

AND FORMER LITERARY GIANT **JOSEPH HELLER**

slowly roll out across the rest of the country. But it just went haywire, the issues were selling out."

"Distributors in Texas and Illinois would call us up out of the blue, asking us to let them sell it," Kurt remembers.

Writers, printing costs, salaries…these things had to be paid more or less up front. Then, a month or two or three later, the money would come in from advertising and sales. "It was that gap that almost caused us to run out of money," says Graydon. "We had to print and distribute so many more copies than we'd planned."

But in the summer of 1987, after *Spy* had proven itself for half a year, Steven Schragis put up more than a million dollars in addition to his initial investment, which saved the day. The new investment also made him a general partner along with the three founders, and got him (eventually) a nominal title on the masthead. But it didn't buy the editorial involvement he'd craved. "I was looking to play a role, I wasn't looking for a blind investment," he says now. "In retrospect, I was naive and should have crafted it more carefully. Sometimes you do things and you think, *It will all work out fine.* And a lot of it did. Some of it didn't."

TO: KA, EGC, SM
FROM: GK
…#6. When a story is dropped, added or moved as we prepare an issue, please tell me directly. I don't want to hear about it from Edward the elevator operator.
—Interoffice memo, December 31, 1986

APART FROM THE DISMAL EVIDENCE that we were working on New Year's Eve, it's also clear that we desperately needed a managing editor, someone to make the trains run on time. During *Spy*'s first year, I played that role by default, but in a place where the M.O. was utter chaos (sorry, *unfettered creativity*) and two of the people you were trying to keep in line signed your checks, that made for a complex job—as a series of real, for the most part exceptionally effective, *Spy* managing editors would discover over the years.

But at least we were hiring, filling in some of the gaps. That winter the office hummed along a little louder than before. At the Christmas dinner there were place settings for 28. (Two long tables, hence four heads: Kurt, Graydon, Tom, and—obviously—18-year-old Eric Kaplan.) No speeches, no toasts, just a nice vibe

to it all. We'd somehow put together four issues; *Spy was* a real magazine.

Susan (calling out): "Graydon? Why did you give me these photos of French napkins?" Kurt (instantly, from his office): "It's his way of saying he loves you."
—Journal entry, February 1987

"BECAUSE EVERYONE WAS SO YOUNG, people were not burdened by more mature responsibilities at that point," says Paul Rudnick. "They could afford to work for *Spy*. There wasn't that sense of 'I'm going for a job interview'—it was more like joining a gang. And there was a level of absolute snobbery involved: 'We're *Spy*, so we're better.' It had a charm to it."

Then and later, *Spy* drew talented misfits; it was a self-selecting pool, because if you wanted to work there, it was, presumably, because you *got it*. Bob Mack, who started as a fact-checker in 1987 and eventually became a reporter (and later started a magazine for the Beastie Boys), believes that "the ones who came *after* had at least been reading *Spy*, so the magazine started attracting smarter kids."

"I was older than most of the people when I started there," says Jamie Malanowski, a *Spy* mainstay and a contributor as writer and/or editor to almost every issue (and now the managing editor of *Playboy*). "I was already 33, and had not done much, and I was feeling that if I was going to make anything out of this writing, I had to do it here and now. So I brought a lot of anxiety of my own. But after a while, you realized that this was like a great basketball team, you were winning games together. Someone else's success was a good thing, even if it somehow made you uneasy."*

Bruce Handy, who was freelancing after a stint at *Vogue*, wrote a short, desperate note to "Susan Morrissey" ("I'm a writer. I'm sick of interviewing self-serving hacks for a living. I'm enclosing clips") and was immediately given an assignment. Henry Alford was a

---

*Jamie had been suggested by the PR man John Scanlon. Graydon met him at a bar on the West Side and they had a few drinks. He was funny, had a good grasp of politics and popular culture, and he clinched the deal by saying he would make a good editor because he had "a lead ass"—meaning he would just sit there and get the job done. And he did. —Eds.

casting assistant in the film business when he started mailing short pieces to *Spy* blindly; they were odd, lapidary exercises, and they were fall-down funny.

"I changed professions and became a writer because of *Spy*," says Alford. "One day I decided to ask Susan if there were any job openings. The phrase 'dream come true' is not inapplicable." (Alford was hired as a reporter in 1988.) "The first time I met Susan and Graydon," he remembers, "she was wearing a hairband, and he mentioned *The Times* of London twice: I felt thoroughly out-WASPed."*

"One of the biggest first impressions I got was that everyone was sophisticated—and good-looking," says the good-looking David Kamp, who started as an intern in 1987, later became a senior writer and editor, and eventually went on to *Vanity Fair*. "It sounds superficial, but it had a bearing on the way the whole place operated. Humor traditionally is the province of trolls—it especially was in the '70s and '80s—and the sophistication of *Spy* appealed to me. It really was like stepping back a bit into Frank Crowninshield and Robert Benchley and Dorothy Parker and P. G. Wodehouse. It was the elegance of the language— the language was *so* careful at *Spy*—and the design, but also the people. Even the Puck Building was elegant."

Elegance was the Puck's strong suit. (That and the fact that, as the building filled up with photography and film studios, we might bump into almost anybody roaming the halls— Isabella Rossellini, John Cleese, Miles Davis. Early on, Davis, during a video shoot, created a bright, bold mural on the wall just outside *Spy*'s front door; it lasted a few months before the building's management obliterated it one weekend with paint buckets and rollers.) But the heating and cooling advances of the twentieth century were entirely absent; the overheated building of the summer dog days was, in winter, a chilly, seemingly unheatable space; the extra bodies helped only a little. "The first day I walked into the place, it was early, and no one on the editorial staff was around," says Adam Dolgins, hired in 1987 as a promotions assistant (he stayed at *Spy* longer

---

*But the misapprehension that we were rich New York preppies always rankled us: The two founding editors and Susan Morrison were all products of provincial middle-class families and public-school educations. Our only original non-WASP editor, Kalogerakis, was, in fact, a New York preppie. —Eds.

than almost anyone, and was marketing manager by the time he left; he went on to be a producer for MTV). "Caldwell Davis [an ad-sales rep] was hunched down wearing this trapper's hat of his and just peering out—he looked like some colonial-era character like Ben Franklin, or some frontiersman. It was *freezing*."

It probably didn't help that Graydon was partial to opening his window in mid-winter, scooping up ammunition from his sill, and instigating indoor snowball fights. Or that one receptionist misplaced *Spy*'s Con Ed bills, causing the power to be turned off.

"We were paying minimum wage," says Geoff Reiss, who spent seven years at *Spy* in the marketing/production end.

"There wasn't that sense of 'I'm going for a job interview'—it was more like joining a gang."

"So we had the screwiest succession of people coming in and being messengers and receptionists." (Reiss was perhaps *Spy*'s steadiest, as well as craftiest, staff member; after he'd interviewed for the job, and the door shut behind him, Graydon turned to Tom and Kurt and said, "He's either incredibly normal or he's Ted Bundy." Reiss is also remembered fondly for his largesse with petty cash: He had a drawer stuffed with bills and liked to pull it open and say, "Take some money, take some money." He is now a senior vice president at ESPN.)

And the screwiest publisher! "Did you ever get one of Tom's haircuts?" Reiss asks. "On one of my first days there, before I knew he cut hair, I overheard [a female ad salesperson] ask him for 'a quick bang job.' I thought, *This place is stranger than I imagined*."

AMONG THE RECEPTIONISTS, there was the well-read Michael Lipscomb, he of the fingerless gloves and *faux*-British accent. He looked like an African prince, and he was unflappable, as one had to be at *Spy*. Once, a friend of editor Joanne Gruber's who enjoyed using assumed names phoned and identified himself as the long-dead "David Ben-Gurion."

"David Ben-Gurion, the founder of the state of Israel and its first prime minister?" Lipscomb inquired.

"That's right."

A pause, then:

"Please hold....Joanne, David Ben-Gurion on line three."

Other receptionists included Hank Rosenfeld, a standup comic

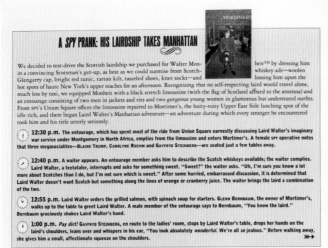

who once appeared on a *Spy* cover as a gangster; Liz Tuccillo, who went on to become a producer of *Sex and the City* and coauthor of the best-seller *He's Just Not That Into You*; Pamela Clarke Keogh, who was fired and later became a best-selling biographer; and, briefly, Nicki Gostin, now *Newsweek's* photo editor, who was also fired, because no one could understand her Australian accent—and, having begged to stay on in *some* capacity, became photo researcher and took over the Separated at Birth? franchise.

Spy's messengers made *Spy's* receptionists look like actuaries.

"Remember Robin?" asks Reiss. "Robin had gender-identification issues. I remember his deepest wish was that at the *Spy* anniversary parties he'd get to be a cigarette girl. We had Victor, a gentleman from Mexico who once set the

couch on fire when he fell asleep with a cigarette. We had one messenger who stole the payroll, so nobody got paid for a week. We had others who lost their travel money playing three-card monte. Others stole office supplies and were silly enough to be caught selling them on the sidewalk two blocks away. And we had Walter."

Walter Monheit, easily *Spy's* best-known belowstairs employee (he would probably surpass even Eric Kaplan—check the Q Scores), was sent to us by paparazza Marina Garnier. He had retired from his job as a bank messenger and, as Reiss puts it, "was looking for a few extra bucks." A dapper, elderly roué, he would come into the office during the late afternoon, make a few runs, and then head out for the bright lights. Monheit was a party fixture, on any given night capable of outlasting people a third his age in a frantic, oxygen-depleting tour of clubs, restaurants, and sundry openings. He held an apparently irresistible charm for the ladies, and at one point was assumed to be, by more than a few fellow nightcrawlers, *Spy's* publisher, not its messenger. He was our Larry "Bud" Melman (of *Letterman* fame—another *Spy* coverboy), only mustachioed, better dressed, and, with his thick middle-European accent, all but incomprehensible. By the time *Spy* started running the movie-reviewing Blurb-o-Mat under Monheit™'s name and monacled, be-ascoted photo, the magazine had trademarked him too. He also hit his marks nicely for one of the great *Spy* pranks when, as "Laird Monheit," he successfully infiltrated the Upper East Side ladies-who-lunch crowd. Impersonating Scottish royalty came as easily to Walter as balancing shot glasses on his head while performing the limbo; it was his consort at the swank café Mortimer's, *Spy's* Aimée Bell, whose heart was racing in fear that day as she introduced him to Gayfryd Steinberg, Carolyn Roehm, Molly Wilmot, and others of their extremely fancy ilk. ("You remember *the Laird*." "Ohhh! The Laird!")

We were shocked, well into The Monheit Years, to run across an old issue of *Newsweek* with photo coverage of Sly Stone's 1974 wedding at a concert at Madison Square Garden: There in front was Walter, doing the limbo. We were equally shocked to discover, just recently, that he had been only about 60 when he worked at *Spy*—he had seemed much older—and that he was a Holocaust survivor.

(Monheit retired after *Spy*, and at press time was looking forward to his 80th birthday. He lives in Bensonhurst with his cat,

Precious. "I don't get around much anymore," he says. "Well, last night I went to Marquee. Nothing special was going on. I did some dancing, and I danced with a candle on my head for a while, but that's it.")

EVEN WITHOUT MONHEIT, the cast of characters in the pages of *Spy* was, if anything, rich (in more ways than one). Some—including, when the magazine started covering him and Hollywood in 1987, Michael Ovitz—were unknown to the general public, including our readers. The truth is, we scarcely knew who some of them were, either. But by chronicling their escapades in issue after issue, *Spy* turned them into something approximating flesh-and-blood characters who blundered through our serialized-nonfiction-novel-of-a-magazine every month.*

When I mention to the *Spy*-influenced *Los Angeles Times* columnist Joel Stein, who was a teenager in New Jersey when the magazine was in its prime, that he must not have known who half the names in it were, he replies, "I *still* don't know."

"All those people only exist to me in *Spy*," he continues. "Writing for my high-school newspaper and making jokes about Mike Ovitz, I couldn't tell you, outside of the *Spy* definition, who these people were. I just knew that Ovitz was a powerful Hollywood trope that I could throw in." Stein admits that he eventually chose his agent—Amanda "Binky" Urban of ICM—in part because "she was Binky Urban *from* Spy *magazine*. When I was 16, she was one of the 10 most interesting people in the world. Binky Urban, Mike Ovitz, Michael Eisner, the people from the *Times*—[son and father publishers] Pinch and Punch [Sulzberger]—those were important and famous people. And they met at Mortons somewhere in my mind, with Celia Brady.

"When I moved to New York, years later, I was at some art gallery opening and I saw Walter Monheit. I walked over to him. 'Excuse me, are you Walter Monheit?' 'Why, yes, I am.' That was a very exciting moment."

---

*Years later, Graydon got a very nice note from Oscar-winning screenwriter and director Steve Gaghan, who said that he had grown up in Kentucky and that getting *Spy* in the mail each month reminded him that there was a whole other world out there. It's pretty much how we felt when we were kids and a new issue of *MAD* or *National Lampoon* would appear. —Eds.

OUR GOLDDIGGER HALL OF FAME

PAMELA DIGBY

MARRIED

RANDOLPH CHURCHILL
son of Winston
LELAND HAYWARD
agent–producer
AVERELL HARRIMAN
Union Pacific scion

BROOKE RUSSELL

MARRIED

DRYDEN KUSER
millionaire-distillery buff
BUDDIE MARSHALL
investor
VINCENT ASTOR
Hudson Bay Company heir

BARBARA "BABE" CUSHING

MARRIED

STANLEY MORTIMER JR.
sportsman–investor
WILLIAM S. PALEY
CBS founder

(CONTINUED)

BETSEY CUSHING

MARRIED

JAMES ROOSEVELT
son of Franklin
J. H. "JOCK" WHITNEY
venture capitalist

MARY "MINNIE" CUSHING

MARRIED

VINCENT ASTOR
Hudson Bay Company heir
JAMES FOSBURGH
portrait painter

CARROLL McDANIEL

MARRIED

MARQUIS DE PORTAGO
oily ne'er-do-well
RICHARD PISTELL
businessman
MILTON PETRIE
mass-market retailer

JACQUELINE BOUVIER

MARRIED

JOHN F. KENNEDY
womanizing president
ARISTOTLE ONASSIS
repulsive dead Greek

Our Golddigger Hall of Fame, from "How to Marry a Millionaire," September 1987

An

Advertising

Case

Study

My survey of feminist reactions to Newport cigarette ads was probably not very scientific, and the sample audience was rather small — two — but the results are nevertheless significant: fully 50 percent of those queried consider Newport's advertising campaign outstandingly twisted. ➤ First I delivered a batch of the Newport ads to Gloria Steinem. When I suggested that certain dark mis-

TAKE ME, HURT ME, SMOKE ME

ognystic themes turned up again and again in the ads, Steinem looked blank. Then I sent a set to Betty Friedan. She called the next day with her own evaluation. "These ads," Friedan said, "are absolutely per- **BY JOHN LEO** verse." ➤ There you go. ➤ With Newport ads, either you see it right away or you don't. And we're not talking subliminal seduction, genitalia in ice cubes or anything nutty like that. We're talking sexual combat disguised as play. ➤ The advertisements, which began appearing in the mid-1970s, have become one of the most ambitious (more than $80 million spent on magazine advertising alone during the last decade) and successful cigarette campaigns in recent history. The early ads featured almost amateurish photos of people sitting around smoking and laughing. The cigarettes eventually disappeared from the ads, the photography improved dramatically and the pictures began to show vigorous baby-boomers engaged in outdoorsy shenanigans — all with a trademark undercurrent of sexual tension. Newport sales started rising 15 to 25 percent annually. (They increased by $170 million from 1975 to 1979 alone.) In fact, the campaign helped turn around the foundering corporate fortunes of Lorillard, the tobacco company that makes Newport and which is owned by CBS president Laurence Tisch and his brother Preston. ➤ Why are the ads so successful? Postfeminist resentment. About half the photos depict women who seem to be off-balance and menaced, or at least the target of berserk male energy. A man stands in the middle of a swimming pool, spinning a fully dressed woman around on his shoulders. A woman sits inside a large bell, her hands to her ears; her boyfriend, who is laughing, has apparently just rung the bell. ➤ In Newport's sexual wars, men get pushed around, too. During a miniature-golf game, a giggling woman tees up her ball on the mouth of a supine male. ➤ For some reason, the Lorillard people seem intensely interested in mock fellatio. Newport women tend to suck on icicles, drink from hoses whenever they can and open their mouths as tiny white snowflakes, water spray or feathers from pillow fights drift their way. ➤ How does Lorillard get away with retailing sexual animosity? Part of the trouble is that anyone who claims to see cryptic sexual messages in ads is apt to be relegated to the Frederic Wertham–Wilson Bryan Key lunacy fringe. Wertham, you will remember, was the fellow who kept seeing sexual parts turn up in comic books, including triangles of pubic hair slyly hidden in Tarzan's shoulder. Wilson Key detected the word *sex* faintly imprinted almost everywhere in the magazine world, from Ritz crackers ads to a *Time* cover on Vietnam. The Newport campaign is nothing that loony or complicated. ➤ One of the people who used to shoot the ads for Lorillard is Joel Meyerowitz, the reputable fine-art photographer. When contacted about the Newport photographs, he seemed more embarrassed about being caught doing commercial work than about being tagged as the perpetrator of softcore sex and violence. Like the brand manager and art director of the campaign, who were also contacted, Meyerowitz implied that the campaign had been intended solely to depict rollicking, wholesome activities of fun-loving couples. ➤ *Sure.*

◄ MOST WOMEN WHO DRINK FROM garden hoses usually do not do so when a man's nose is three inches away and the water is shooting out at 100 pounds per square inch. The water speed suggests danger. Clearly, the poor woman has some unmet oral needs, or she would have given up Newports and power hoses by now. The hunched, too-close position of the male in an oral-sex photo is the standard soft-core-porn way of suggesting that sex is forced.

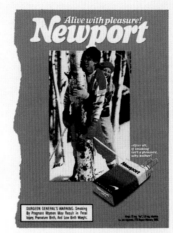

▲ IN THE PAST YEAR NEWPORT ADS have been killing off more males than females. Does research show that female smokers want more symbolically dead males, or is it simply a fair-minded attempt to even the body count? People who ski rapidly into trees tend to be maimed. The sex-and-death theme is carried by the odd phallic demibranch sticking out from the tree.

▼ THIS MALE IS SURPRISING AND DE- lighting the female by plunging his hands into her pumpkin. Pumpkin-plunging occurs frequently in the Newport universe.

▲ THIS MAN IS EMITTING A SYM- bolic scream, the only sensible thing to do when a woman symbolically stomps on your private parts while you are unwisely spread-eagled halfway up a tree.

▲ SUGGESTIONS OF ORAL SEX ARE ho-hum in fashion and advertising, but orgasmic fellatio scenes are still puzzlingly rare. Here a devoted girlfriend opens wide, apparently happy to have his machine go off at roughly the level of his crotch and her mouth. Obviously a trouper, she tries to catch as many of his precious bodily gum balls as she can.

August 1988

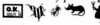

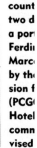

Spy-ifying the public record, from The Fine Print; top, October 1986; right, March 1987

Baltimore's City Paper *publishes a nationwide poll of media people's favorite magazines:* Spy *is tied for 9th, and ranks first among their own picks. Genuine joy around the office.*

—Journal entry, April 3, 1987

"GENUINE JOY"? YIKES. But we must have still been feeling like scrappy longshots. Sure, we had no trouble casually keel-hauling New York's ruling class, but at just six months of age, learning that we were big in Baltimore (according to a paper owned by Russ Smith, who later ran his weekly *New York Press* out of our old Puck Building loft) was reason to uncork the champagne, or at least pop open some Manhattan Specials.

Kurt says that, at the time, he thought we really nailed it with the September 1987 issue, which included a long profile of George Steinbrenner, James Traub's cover story on Mob lawyers, and Nell Scovell's "Golddiggers of 1987: How to Marry a Millionaire." There was also a tiny, over-the-transom Naked City short sent in by someone called Fleming Meeks—now the editor of *Smart Money*—which staff and readers alike embraced, "Elvis's Weight on the Planets." This was nothing but a brief list: "Elvis on Mercury, 97 pounds. Elvis on Venus, 232 pounds." It got pinned up in office cubicles around the city, Jay Leno read it when he guest-hosted *The Tonight Show*, Screamin' Jay Hawkins discussed it in Jim Jarmusch's *Mystery Train*, and it still has a healthy afterlife on the Internet. You simply never know.

"I really felt like it had coalesced, and we knew what we were doing," Kurt says of that issue. "Which is why I've said ever since that it takes a year for any new magazine to really hit its stride."

The next issue introduced The *Spy* 100 ("Our Annual Census of the Most Annoying, Alarming and Appalling People, Places and Things"), which would appear, with ever-more-complicated ranking formulas, every October. Other reader favorites like the Blurb-o-Mat (breathless, ad-ready testimonials for new movies), Logrolling in Our Time (the monthly celebration of promotional cronyism in book-blurb-writing), The *Spy* List (the, um, utterly, utterly random list of names that was essentially a libel-resistant blind item in the form of a puzzle), and the whimsical Ten Years Ago in *Spy* were all slipped into the mix around this time.

So was Private Lives of Public Enemies, a monthly Drew Friedman cartoon. *Spy* would end up publishing some terrific cartoonists and illustrators over the years, including Al Hirschfeld, Ronald Searle, Danny Shanahan, Michael Crawford, Robert Risko, Gary Panter, Steve Brodner, Gahan Wilson, Steven Guarnaccia, and Barry Blitt. Matt Groening drew Bart Simpson for our "*Spy for Kids*" cover in February 1991.

There were two possible explanations for the high head count at the first-anniversary party Spy *magazine tossed for itself at its downtown Manhattan office building a few weeks back: an open bar and fear. Show up, smile, and stay on* Spy's *sunny side, and maybe you won't appear in some future issue, pinned down photographically on the "Party Poop" page and identified, with the magazine's characteristic cheekiness, as a "mummified boulevardier" or "beaver-faced mogul." Since its debut issue last October,* Spy *has honed its unique editorial combination of good humor and bad manners into an upscale switchblade that has nearly doubled in circulation.*

    —*Time*, October 1987

"*SPY* WAS A SCARY REVELATION when I first saw it," says the artist Barbara Kruger, "a potent mix of bravery, truth-telling, and spite—a breath of poisonous air. I read it every month with absolute joy, and sadness. You just wondered, *Where are they coming from?*"

Well, from insecurity, suggests writer Ann Hodgman. "You couldn't put out that kind of magazine—you couldn't do that kind of writing—without being insecure," she says. "People who are basically secure and confident *just don't care* about where other people stand in the pecking order, or who's toppled from his perch, or who seems to be successful but really isn't. Or at least they pretend not to care. Even *Spy*'s little features, like translating the Chinese characters on restaurant signs, speak of a basic feeling that nothing can be relied on except one's own ability to seek out falsehood in one's environment. What seems so striking about *Spy* in retrospect is the tension between the obvious insecurity and the fact that everyone working there was actually *extraordinarily* talented. You don't usually get a mix like that."

"You were thumbing your nose at the whole city and at the same time getting enormous attention and credit," says Bruce Handy. "And everybody you knew, everybody you wanted to read you, was reading it."

"You did sort of drop everything and start reading it," says Paul Goldberger. "There was no Internet, nothing appeared online, so the arrival of a printed copy of anything was a *moment*—and *Spy* was an important moment."

"There was no coverage of the media, to speak of, in the newspapers," Kurt points out. "And that helped us, because as much attention as we were getting, we were able to open up out of town, a little bit—even though we were opening up in the center of town. We didn't have to deal with weekly items about this or that in *The New York Observer*, or daily in Gawker or *mediabistro.com* or Romenesko. It would be totally different today, because of this frenzied mediasphere of newspapers and the Internet. So both as a kind of precursor to that—which it was—and in the sense of being free from that scrutiny—which we were—we benefited."

The three founders were becoming minor celebrities. They were savvy about promoting *Spy*, though they really didn't need to do much. Susan Mulcahy, who edited Page Six at the *New York Post* and then was a gossip columnist for *Newsday* during *Spy*'s early years, would sometimes get calls from Tom or Graydon tipping her off to upcoming stories in the magazine. On the other hand, she says, "I used to go to lunch with Graydon once in a while, but we'd never discuss *Spy*—we'd always talk about Barbara Pym." Gradually, for Mulcahy and others, the *Spy* founders themselves became item-worthy, "like when Kurt was going to join the Century Association, and meanwhile his magazine had trashed everybody who belonged to it."

"I don't think any of us really got too big for our britches," Kurt says. "Once it got really going, I mean, maybe you get a few more invitations, and Graydon could go to Nell's or something. But we didn't have the Metallica problem—too many groupies, too much money, all that kind of stuff."

    "I don't read it."
        —*Abe Rosenthal, executive editor of* The New York Times

    "I don't read it."
        —*Marvin Siegel, culture editor of the* Times

    "I honestly don't read it."
        —*Ed Klein, editor-in-chief of the* Times Magazine

    —From a 1988 feature on *Spy* in *GQ*

ELVIS'S WEIGHT ON THE PLANETS

*t*en years after his death, Elvis's fame has assumed not just global but galactic proportions, as last month's anniversary festivities demonstrated. Here's how the King weighs in around the universe as we know it:

Elvis on Mercury	97 pounds
Elvis on Venus	232 pounds
Elvis on Earth	255 pounds
Elvis on Mars	97 pounds
Elvis on Jupiter	648 pounds
Elvis on Saturn	275 pounds
Elvis on Uranus	232 pounds
Elvis on Neptune	303 pounds
Elvis on Pluto	13 pounds
Elvis on the moon	43 pounds
Elvis on the sun	7,140 pounds

—*Fleming Meeks*

September 1987

Bush wins. Call a halt to this senseless tragedy now—before it's too late.

CRIME REPORT:
HOMICIDE-FREE DAYS
According to the Police Department, there were five days in 1987, none on weekends, when no murders were committed in New York City: March 16, March 19, July 1, October 2 and December 26. There were eight such days in 1986. ❂

34 **SPY** AUGUST 1988

From
The Fine Print,
August 1988

SETS & SUBSETS
(No. 2 in a series)

—*Robert Hutter*

October 1987

"Mr. Gelb is not interested in discussing Spy *magazine," a woman in Arthur Gelb's office said politely the other day.* Spy *magazine, on the other hand, is very much interested in discussing Mr. Gelb, the managing editor of* The New York Times. *In the April edition of its regular column about the* Times, Spy *took out after Gelb, giving voice to longstanding mutterings in the culture world. This was, mind you, in the "Nice Issue." It was a typically perverse move for* Spy, *which in 18 months has established a national reputation for elegant meanness, seen circulation rise from 25,000 to 65,000 and been nominated for a National Magazine Award. And it instantly bumped the magazine's 'The* Times' *column several notches up on the list of must-read material in media circles—{but} what a shame that* Spy *doesn't reach the executive floor of the* Times *building. "I've never heard anybody make a reference to* Spy *magazine on this floor," Director of Editorial Development Seymour Topping, a former managing editor,*

says with elaborate disinterest. Staffers around the third-floor newsroom are apparently more curious. Photocopiers work overtime on the day the column appears.

—Bill Barol in *Newsweek*, April 25, 1988

ALL THOSE YEARS PRE–JAYSON BLAIR, it was unheard of for anyone to know inside details of the all-powerful *Times*, or, if you cared about its future editorial treatment of you or your work, to criticize it. *Spy*'s (pseudonymous) account each month of the inner and sometimes outer workings of the paper of record and its editors was a hit with readers in the media and the arts—and especially with the rank and file at the *Times*—but clearly not with the *Times* brass. (When word came back to us about how furiously the *Times* column was being photocopied there, we were delighted, but not so much that we didn't explore the possibility of printing that page of each issue on copier-proof paper stock.)

1957 Sartre abandons Sneakers in a cardboard box on the *métro*.

— *Henry Alford*

GENERAL CONTEST

John S.P. Walker

June 1989

THE SPY LIST
(first in a series)

Milton Berle
Gary Cooper
Sonny Corleone
Willem Dafoe
Anthony
Haden-Guest
Don Johnson
Levon Helm
George S. Kaufman
Henry Kissinger
Toulouse Lautrec
Roddy McDowall
David Metcalfe
Armando Orsini
Tony Peck
Robert Plant
Iggy Pop
David Lee Roth
Secretariat
James Woods

March 1988

Goldberger, who was the *Times*'s architecture critic and later culture editor, remembers the column's impact at the paper. "There was utter fascination and complete paranoia all wrapped up together," he says. "The higher up you were, the less likely you were to admit to reading it. But I suspect they all did."

"The guy who was the PR person for *The New York Times* was the most lovely, polite, professional person," remembers Mulcahy. "I was always calling him and asking, 'Is Max Frankel dyeing his hair?' and 'Does Punch Sulzberger have a gun in his drawer?'"

"Running the *Times* column," Kurt says, "and the *Times* as a result never running anything on us, even as we were becoming this institution to reckon with, probably allowed us to keep indie cred longer than we deserved."

That October, however, the *Times* quietly expanded its restaurant health-code-violation coverage, which had been a mere listing, in apparent emulation of *Spy*'s let's-quote-the-official-report-in-all-its-horror approach (though the *Times* didn't go as far as awarding tiny rat icons, our version of Gault Millau's toques). Even without the rodent graphics, it was as close to an acknowledgment of *Spy* as the magazine was likely to get from the paper—until the following spring, when we learned that they had assigned a major piece on us.

A reporter from the Times, *Steven Erlanger, spent hours interviewing Kurt and Graydon separately. I've never seen either so nervous (before) or drained (after). Their feeling is that it's going to be a hatchet job.*

—Journal entry, April 6, 1988

THE STORY NEVER RAN, and the rumors were that the *Times* pooh-bahs had deemed it too kind to *Spy*. Erlanger, later the *Times*'s culture editor and now the *Times*'s Jerusalem bureau chief, describes what happened.

"It all became overplayed partly because of the question of

THE SPY 100 EQUATION:

$$\text{SCORE} = \frac{L^2}{4} + \frac{[\text{MAX}(2 \times S, M) \times M + (7 \times A)]}{\sqrt{F} + 3} + B$$

where

L = Inherent Loathsomeness
S = Spy Mentions
M = Misdeeds
A = Spy Audit
F = Mitigating Factors
B = Bonus Points

From
The Spy 100,
October 1987

David Kamp:
"Marissa Rothkopf
and I were interns
for The *Spy*
100 in the
summer of '87.
So Graydon says,
'Okay, we're
going to sneak
you guys into
the morgue
in the Time & Life
Building.' And
even though he
was doing nothing
technically
wrong—his ID was
still valid—he was
so nervous. Spy
was already
getting a lot
of attention, and
his former
colleagues were
seeing him and
saying, 'Graydon,
congratulations,
seeing a lot of
press about you.'

1 Ivan Boesky

1986 rank 41
Inherent loathsomeness (1–10) 10
Number of SPY issues mentioned in 7
Mitigating factors (1–10): None 0
Misdeeds (1–10): Caught participating in insider trading on an egregious scale; paid $100 million to the SEC, pleaded guilty to a felony count; tapped his phone while talking with his partners in crime and squealed on everyone he could think of; then, *coincidentally*, just before sentencing, took up Talmudic studies 10
SPY audit (1–5): His settlement was the largest in history, but the consensus is that he retains perhaps $100 million 5
Bonus points (1–10): Wife's name is Seema 7
Score **90.33**

2 Ronald Reagan

1986 rank 4
Inherent loathsomeness (1–10) 10
Number of SPY issues mentioned in 10
Mitigating factors (1–10): Didn't resign (meant to but forgot), thereby sparing us President Bush *and* giving our slow-on-the-uptake nation a chance to see Reagan for what he is; glanced at a few short memos; waved a lot; proved informative as a sort of living cadaver and anatomy lesson 1
Misdeeds (1–10): Didn't resign; drifted more obviously into intellectual oblivion; Reykjavík, Bork, the Iran-contra affair . . . and so on 10
SPY audit (1–5): Earns $200,000 a year for an eight-hour work week and *seasons* of vacation 4
Bonus points (1–10): Deft, savvy foreign policy .8
Score **90.00**

3 Donald Trump

1986 rank 1
Inherent loathsomeness (1–10) 10
Number of SPY issues mentioned in 10
Mitigating factors (1–10): Offered to pay for funeral of child killed by bear; feuded with Ed Koch; completed Wollman Rink; didn't run for office 3
Misdeeds (1–10): Still pushing for the abhorrent Television City; reaped enormous publicity from fuss surrounding child's zoo death, Koch feud and rink reconstruction; didn't promise he'd *never* run for office 10
SPY audit (1–5): Made $30 million in four months speculating in Bally Industries stock 4
Bonus points (1–10): Played himself on TV miniseries *I'll Take Manhattan* 8
Score **81.18**

4 Corporate Lying

1986 rank 17
Inherent loathsomeness (1–10) 9
Number of SPY issues mentioned in 7
Mitigating factors (1–10) 3
Misdeeds (1–10) 9
SPY audit (1–5)
Bonus points (1–10) 5
Score **59.27**

Promises from management at CBS and Cap Cities that there would be no layoffs—then, after layoffs, that cutbacks in the network news divisions won't hurt quality; CBS describing the desperate overhaul of its new, odious *Morning Program* format as fine tuning; Audi announcing plans to rename the Audi 5000 sedan (the death car) but making no announcement about fixing the problem; the Beech-Nut Nutrition Corporation, its president and a VP of manufacturing pleading not guilty to a 470-count indictment charging, among other things, that the company knowingly sold apple juice that contained little, if any, apple juice (this after New York agriculture officials had fined the firm $250,000 in 1984 for selling 5 million bottles of mislabeled juice); and Chrysler rolling back odometers on used cars sold as new. On the other hand, the "liar" campaign for Isuzu was a smash success. *Meli meli, kiki bobo.*

5 Dennis Levine

1986 rank 3
Inherent loathsomeness (1–10) 9
Number of SPY issues mentioned in 8
Mitigating factors (1–10): Didn't want to be the only one profiting from insider trading, so he brought some friends in on the ring; finked on Ivan Boesky; definitely not a man of the "Just say no" generation ..5
Misdeeds (1–10): When it was suggested to him that he might curtail his insider trading, he said he hadn't made enough yet 8
SPY audit (1–5): What "not enough" means: in five years (1980–85) he worked $170,000 into $12.6 million 5
Bonus points (1–10): Used mother's maiden name (Diamond) as password for his Swiss bank account 7
Score **58.38**

6 Peter Holm & Joan Collins

1986 rank 55
Inherent loathsomeness (1–10) 8
Number of SPY issues mentioned in 1
Mitigating factors (1–10): None 0
Misdeeds (1–10): Holm, Collins's ex-manager and sex toy, said in asking support from her, "While our income and expenses may seem extraordinary to the average person . . . it is our normal way of life, and is typical of those depicted in the television series *Lifestyles of the Rich and Famous*, on which we have been featured several times" 8
SPY audit (1–5): Holm asked for $2.6 million ...5
Bonus points (1–10): He also asked for $80,000 a month, including $12,000 for clothing and accessories and $6,000 for entertainment 9
Score **58.00**

7 George Steinbrenner

1986 rank 11
Inherent loathsomeness (1–10) 10
Number of SPY issues mentioned in 4
Mitigating factors (1–10): Unifies New Yorkers in one grand, focused loathing 2
Misdeeds (1–10): The deal that put most games on pay TV; his threat to move the team to the Meadowlands; calling his accountant "a young black boy"; his failure to sign Jack Morris; his denial that collusion with other owners was part of that decision; his public flogging of Lou Piniella 10
SPY audit (1–5): La Coupe will give you a Steinbrenner 'do for between $40 and $50 2
Bonus points (1–10): Hank, his son and heir, is said to be a chip off the old block 6
Score **56.83**

8 Edwin Meese

1986 rank 15
Inherent loathsomeness (1–10) 9
Number of SPY issues mentioned in 2
Mitigating factors (1–10): Showed endearing lack of guile in entrusting life savings to a former encyclopedia salesman; helped minority-run South Bronx contractor get $32 million Army deal ..2
Misdeeds (1–10): The salesman was financial adviser to the contractor, and Meese had stock in minority-run Wedtech Corp.; waited a week to safeguard Iran-contra documents while shredders purred ..9
SPY audit (1–5): Made $45,857 on a $50,662 initial investment in Wedtech 4
Bonus points (1–10): Despite testifying to the contrary, can't recall meetings with Ollie North 8
Score **52.94**

9 Ruination of Times Square

1986 rank 33
Inherent loathsomeness (1–10) 9
Number of SPY issues mentioned in 1
Mitigating factors (1–10): One more reason not to go to Times Square on New Year's Eve 3
Misdeeds (1–10): One developer is demolishing the USO Center to build a high rise; another is razing Leighton's Haberdashers and the Strand Theater for an office tower; others are tearing down other human-scale vestiges for charmless monoliths 9
SPY audit (1–5): Price of one building has increased 33% over past two years 4
Bonus points (1–10): Michael Lazar, former city official and major Times Square speculator-developer, indicted in corruption scandal 8
Score **51.28**

10 Bernhard Goetz

1986 rank 2
Inherent loathsomeness (1–10) 8
Number of SPY issues mentioned in 4
Mitigating factors (1–10): America now understands that the typical Manhattanite is an unsociable hothead geek, not a café-hopping bon vivant 1
Misdeeds (1–10): Goetz was more concerned with his electrical gizmos than with his trial; jury acquitted him on all but a weapons charge; *Time* and *Newsweek* scoured files for instances of a black shooting white aggressors and being acquitted 9
SPY audit (1–5): With $5—what he was allegedly asked for—he could have avoided the subway 4
Bonus points (1–10): Restored luster to his escorts, the self-aggrandizing Guardian Angels 8
Score **51.25**

11 Leona Helmsley

1986 rank **18**
Inherent loathsomeness (1–10) **9**
Number of SPY issues mentioned in **5**
Mitigating factors (1–10): Tax scam tactics provided work for jewelry store and postal employees involved in mailing empty boxes out-of-state ...**4**
Misdeeds (1–10): Avoided paying taxes on half a million dollars' worth of jewelry purchases; using phony invoices, allegedly charged millions of dollars in renovations on her 28-room Greenwich mansion to various Manhattan business properties ...**8**
SPY audit (1–5): $38,662—what the state lost ..**5**
Bonus points (1–10): The porcine "Queen" once had a bill rewritten to include her Connecticut address, thereby saving $4 in sales tax **7**
Score **50.25**

12 Pat Robertson

1986 rank **63**
Inherent loathsomeness (1–10) **8**
Number of SPY issues mentioned in **4**
Mitigating factors (1–10): None **0**
Misdeeds (1–10): Now campaigning to collect 3 million signatures of people who say they want him to run—as if it were *their* idea; sued Rep. Paul McCloskey for saying that during the Korean War Robertson's father, a senator, got Pat transferred to a noncombat unit, "Casual Company" **7**
SPY audit (1–5): Likely Christian Broadcasting Network shortfall: $21 million through March **3**
Bonus points (1–10): Hired a hack TV journalist to pretend to interview McCloskey for broadcast—then used some of the information in his lawsuit ..**8**
Score **49.67**

13 Mort Zuckerman

1986 rank **46**
Inherent loathsomeness (1–10) **7**
Number of SPY issues mentioned in **6**
Mitigating factors (1–10): Has subsidized *The Atlantic* for the last five years **3**
Misdeeds (1–10): Used real estate losses to avoid paying federal income taxes; sued *The Atlantic's* former owners; treated Nicholas Daniloff's incarceration as a marathon photo opportunity; plans to build a huge skyscraper on Columbus Circle **9**
SPY audit (1–5): Billed *The Atlantic* $7,000 for the use of his $8.5 million apartment **4**
Bonus points (1–10): Masquerades as a journalist by writing an unread column in *U.S. News* and pitching in the Sag Harbor softball game **8**
Score **48.99**

14 Roy Cohn

1986 rank **8**
Inherent loathsomeness (1–10) **10**
Number of SPY issues mentioned in **5**
Mitigating factors (1–10): Actually had character witnesses during disbarment hearings **3**
Misdeeds (1–10): Even if you could libel the dead, it would be hard to libel a lawyer disbarred for "dishonesty, fraud, deceit, and misrepresentation." He died last year, but his sharklike visage still hangs over New York's power community **8**
SPY audit (1–5): Died with a $1.5 billion suit against him pending; owed the IRS $7 million..**4**
Bonus points (1–10): His cousin wrote a *Vanity Fair* piece about Cohn's last days, revealing primarily that Cohn had two llamas and that one died **1**
Score **48.82**

15 Andrea Dworkin

1986 rank ....**--**
Inherent loathsomeness (1–10) **8**
Number of SPY issues mentioned in **0**
Mitigating factors (1–10) **2**
Misdeeds (1–10) **9**
SPY audit (1–5) **4**
Bonus points (1–10) **7**
Score **47.69**

In *Intercourse*, Dworkin writes, "Intercourse is the pure, sterile, formal expression of men's contempt for women." This year she published *two* books that argued against sex on the grounds that through sex men conquer women, who willingly collude, fools that they are; the only sympathetic man in her novel, *Ice and Fire*, is impotent and "has too much respect for women" to threaten them with an erection.

Coitus is the punishment for exhibiting oneself: for being afraid to be happy in private, alone. Coitus is the punishment for needing a human witness. I write. Solitude is my witness.

Coitus is the punishment for the happiness of being. Solitude is the end of punishment. I write. I publish.

Coitus is punishment. I write down everything I know, over some years. I publish. I have become a feminist, not the fun kind. Coitus is punishment, I say. It is hard to publish. I am a feminist, not the fun kind. Life gets hard. Coitus is not the only punishment. I write. I love solitude: or slowly, I would die. I do not die.

Coitus is punishment. I am a feminist, not the fun kind. —from *Ice and Fire*

16 Alfonse D'Amato

1986 rank **20**
Inherent loathsomeness (1–10) **7**
Number of SPY issues mentioned in **3**
Mitigating factors (1–10): None **0**
Misdeeds (1–10): Traveled to upper Manhattan in disguise and under police protection to buy crack. He didn't need the costume—even when he's in a suit, no one would take him for a senator **7**
SPY audit (1–5): In 1986 he raised $6,523,394 (fifth most of any senator), spent $8,104,587 (third most)—yet, somehow, after the campaign he still had $652,971 left **5**
Bonus points (1–10): What irony: New York is represented in the U.S. Senate by a lisping, frog-eyed machine pol, and New Jersey by Bill Bradley ...**7**
Score **47.25**

17 Racism in Baseball

1986 rank **92**
Inherent loathsomeness (1–10) **10**
Number of SPY issues mentioned in **1**
Mitigating factors (1–10): Black sociologist Harry Edwards hired to agitate for improvement **5**
Misdeeds (1–10): In the year dedicated to Jackie Robinson's memory, Dodger general manager Al Campanis said blacks lacked the "necessities" to manage; he was fired, baseball flogged itself, some blacks joined front offices—none were hired as managers; see No. 7, George Steinbrenner **8**
SPY audit (1–5): Edwards hired Campanis as his assistant (for an undisclosed salary) **3**
Bonus points (1–10): *Times* article about declining black attendance at games confuses the issue ...**6**
Score **47.23**

18 George Bush

1986 rank **13**
Inherent loathsomeness (1–10) **8**
Number of SPY issues mentioned in **8**
Mitigating factors (1–10): Not president.........**3**
Misdeeds (1–10): A wanker and a toady—20 years in public life and *there's nothing there*; he either agreed with the diversion of money to the contras or wasn't asked; with Reagan, you wonder if Casey or Poindexter told him—with Bush, you wonder if they even had his number in their Rolodexes **6**
SPY audit (1–5): Has raised over $10 million for (doomed) presidential campaign **4**
Bonus points (1–10): "I don't find Mr. Bush to be a source of ridicule walking the streets of New Hampshire," said his Northeast coordinator **5**
Score **47.20**

19 Tammy Faye Bakker

1986 rank ....**--**
Inherent loathsomeness (1–10) **8**
Number of SPY issues mentioned in **3**
Mitigating factors (1–10): Foresight (named her LP *Enough Is Enough*) and breeding (asked and received God's permission before using cosmetics) **1**
Misdeeds (1–10): Burst into tears for the cameras in front of her Tega Cay house; burst into tears during an interview aboard Melvin Belli's yacht; burst into tears on TV while begging for money; acquired 14 furs **8**
SPY audit (1–5): She and Jim drew $1.6 million in salary and compensation from PTL last year **5**
Bonus points (1–10): On a shopping spree, was heard to say, "Oh, my shoppin' demons are hoppin' " ...**6**
Score **46.75**

20 Ed Koch

1986 rank **24**
Inherent loathsomeness (1–10) **8**
Number of SPY issues mentioned in **7**
Mitigating factors (1–10): Called Donald Trump "piggy, piggy, piggy" **5**
Misdeeds (1–10): By suffering a stroke, nearly betrayed New York by allowing Andy Stein to get perilously close to becoming mayor; members of his corrupt administration continue to get caught; insisted that Mother Teresa accept a cheesecake ...**7**
SPY audit (1–5): $600—approximate monthly revenue lost by Parma restaurant, a favorite of the prediet Koch and his pals **3**
Bonus points (1–10): Wasted his last, best chance for a rebound by not appearing on SPY cover **7**
Score **45.73**

"And beads of sweat were forming. We get to the library and he shows us around—'Here's the inanimate subject files, here's the fucking whatever files, here's the photocopier,' and so on. And thereafter I was given Kurt's Time-Life ID, and Marissa was given Graydon's—she had a sort of flapper, wedge cut, which I guess from a distance wasn't a world of difference from Graydon's hairstyle. We were trained to flash them very quickly. We never got caught. That was our research library."

butut of his 100 free albums and an accounting of subsequent sales. No date has been set.

FAMOUS LONG AGO
As we all know, fame is fickle; there's no business like show business; and the bigger they are, the harder they fall. These easy truths in mind, we begin our semiregular survey of recent, less-than-boffo box office grosses. The following concerts took place in late February and early March:

LEON RUSSELL and EDGAR WINTER, *Sarasota*
582 ticket buyers, $5,820 gross

PAUL REVERE AND THE RAIDERS, *Sarasota*
400 ticket buyers, $5,000 gross

VANILLA FUDGE and RARE EARTH, *East St. Louis*
326 ticket buyers, $4,418 gross

FOGHAT, *Austin*
633 ticket buyers, $3,798 gross

BADFINGER, *St. Louis*
435 ticket buyers $3,684 gross

SPORTS UPDATE
After pleading guilty in April to child-molestation charges, Dallas placekicker Rafael Septien became the third current or former Cowboy to be convicted of deviant-sex charges. This is believed to be an NFL record. Former receiver Lance Rentzel (indecent exposure) and former linebacker Hollywood Henderson (sexual assault of a quadriplegic at gunpoint) are the other members of Coach Tom Landry's pervert squad. ◗

who [*Spy's Times* columnist J. J.] Hunsecker was, so everything got wrapped up with some of the attacks on the *Times*—which frankly these days seem quite pale," he says. "And I was asked to do a piece about *Spy*. I felt a little bit like it could be a poisoned chalice, because feelings were quite high. I talked to [*Private Eye's*] Richard Ingrams, I talked to Tina Brown, I talked to a lot of people. I do remember asking Kurt and Graydon, who insisted that everything was fact-checked, how they fact-checked the allegation that [the wife of a senior *Times* man] had had an affair with Joseph Heller."

(Cynthia Cotts, *Spy's* research chief in the late '80s, would have "long, long conversations" with *Spy's* lawyer, David Korzenik, on the sourcing for the *Times* column and Celia Brady's equally scurrilous and must-read Hollywood column. "These were always sensitive pieces," she says. "I often only had a general description of who the sources were and how they were in a position to know.")

Erlanger filed the piece and was called into the office of Max Frankel, then executive editor at the *Times*. The story, it seems, had "become one of these little *issues*—people went over it, there was some tension about it," Erlanger says.

"Max said that they'd decided not to run it. I was very amused by that. I said I knew it was a good piece, and that I was sure he had good reasons for not running it, and that I didn't really want to know what those were," he remembers. "He seemed very relieved."

And the gist of the *Times's* great unpublished *Spy* story?

"That Graydon and Kurt had both come, if you like, from the provinces, to take New York by storm and conquer it," Erlanger says. "And they had done so. And they're both very clever people, and their careers have gone on to show all that—as have others' from *Spy*. But, in this American way, there was this overestimation of New York. *Spy* was deeply in love with New York, and made a goddess out of New York, and that was the method by which the editors made their splash and paved their way. That was the one thought of the piece."

Erlanger says he was "a happy reader" of *Spy*, and that the magazine was "a very good publishing story, but it hit certain high people at the *Times*, and I think they took it too much to heart. People weren't used to that kind of thing. Now, I mean, it's kind of like, 'Duck, and let the shit fly.'"

Spy's failure to win a National Magazine Award for General Excellence in our circulation category also helped us prolong

My Brilliant Career

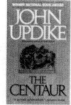

"Updike at his ... best." —THE WASHINGTON POST on *The Centaur.* "Updike's finest novel." —THE WASHINGTON POST on *Of the Farm.* "Updike at his best." —TIME on *The Music School.* "[Updike's] best ... book." —THE NEW YORK TIMES Book Review on *Bech: A Book.* "Updike's best book." —THE DALLAS MORNING NEWS on *Rabbit Redux.* "One of Updike's finest ... " —THE

CHARLOTTE OBSERVER on *A Month of Sundays.* "It is, quite simply, Updike's best novel yet." — NEWSWEEK on *Marry Me.* "Updike at his best." —THE WALL STREET JOURNAL on *Problems.* "Unquestionably Up- dike's finest novel." — THE BOSTON GLOBE on *Rabbit Is Rich.* "Updike keeps getting

better." —THE PHILADELPHIA INQUIRER on *Bech Is Back.* "[Updike's] best in years." — SAN FRANCISCO CHRONICLE on *The Witches of Eastwick.* — Howard Kaplan

▼ ▼

March 1988

our outsider status. We were nominated for the award in 1988, lost to *The Sciences,* and repaired to Milano's bar on Houston Street to sort out how we felt about that—like, wouldn't winning have been worse, in a way?* There, accompanied by Sinatra on the jukebox, Graydon ad-libbed the first of several versions of "*Spy* Way," after which we went back to work. (*Spy* was nominated again for general excellence for its '92 issues, and Bruce Handy's '88 feature on postmodernism was also a finalist [see pages 118–21].)

"*Spy* took the approach that the world, the New York world in particular, was small and full of little communities, and that one could parse it out and have the sense of there being a kind of neighborhood gossip or echo in each of those," says Melik Kaylan, an early contributor. "And by having a kind of prurient,

---

*No. —Eds.

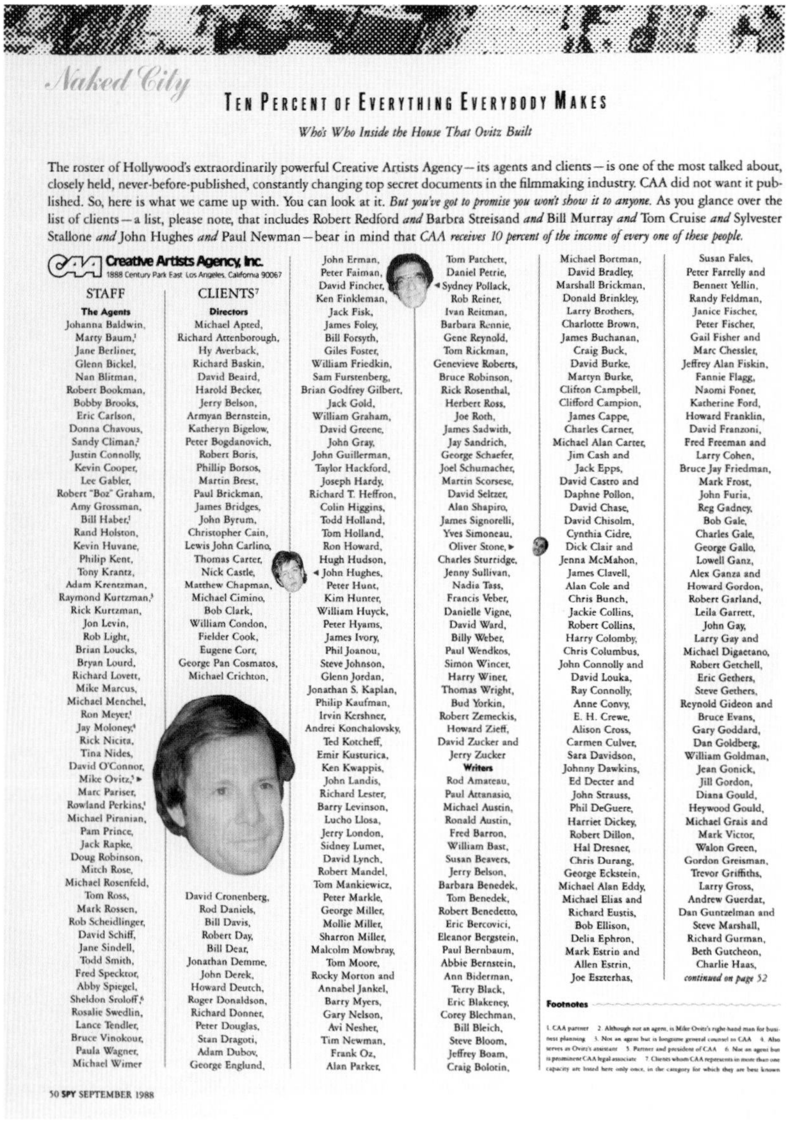

Naked City

Ten Percent of Everything Everybody Makes

Who's Who Inside the House That Ovitz Built

The roster of Hollywood's extraordinarily powerful Creative Artists Agency—its agents and clients—is one of the most talked about, closely held, never-before-published, constantly changing top secret documents in the filmmaking industry. CAA did not want it published. So, here is what we came up with. You can look at it. *But you've got to promise you won't show it to anyone.* As you glance over the list of clients—a list, please note, that includes Robert Redford *and* Barbra Streisand *and* Bill Murray *and* Tom Cruise *and* Sylvester Stallone *and* John Hughes *and* Paul Newman—bear in mind that *CAA receives 10 percent of the income of every one of these people.*

CAA Creative Artists Agency, Inc.
1888 Century Park East Los Angeles, California 90067

STAFF

The Agents

Johanna Baldwin,
Marty Baum,[1]
Jane Berliner,
Glenn Bickel,
Nan Blitman,
Robert Bookman,
Bobby Brooks,
Eric Carlson,
Donna Chavous,
Sandy Climan,[2]
Justin Connolly,
Kevin Cooper,
Lee Gabler,
Robert "Boz" Graham,
Amy Grossman,
Bill Haber,[1]
Rand Holston,
Kevin Huvane,
Philip Kent,
Tony Krantz,
Adam Krentzman,
Raymond Kurtzman,[3]
Rick Kurtzman,
Jon Levin,
Rob Light,
Brian Loucks,
Bryan Lourd,
Richard Lovett,
Mike Marcus,
Michael Menchel,
Ron Meyer,[1]
Jay Moloney,[4]
Rick Nicita,
Tina Nides,
David O'Connor,
Mike Ovitz,[5] ▸
Marc Pariser,
Rowland Perkins,[1]
Michael Piranian,
Pam Prince,
Jack Rapke,
Doug Robinson,
Mitch Rose,
Michael Rosenfeld,
Tom Ross,
Mark Rossen,
Rob Scheidlinger,
David Schiff,
Jane Sindell,
Todd Smith,
Fred Specktor,
Abby Spiegel,
Sheldon Sroloff,[6]
Rosalie Swedlin,
Lance Tendler,
Bruce Vinokour,
Paula Wagner,
Michael Wimer

CLIENTS[7]

Directors

Michael Apted,
Richard Attenborough,
Hy Averback,
Richard Baskin,
David Beaird,
Harold Becker,
Jerry Belson,
Armyan Bernstein,
Katheryn Bigelow,
Peter Bogdanovich,
Robert Boris,
Phillip Borsos,
Martin Brest,
Paul Brickman,
James Bridges,
John Byrum,
Christopher Cain,
Lewis John Carlino,
Thomas Carter,
Nick Castle,
Matthew Chapman,
Michael Cimino,
Bob Clark,
William Condon,
Fielder Cook,
Eugene Corr,
George Pan Cosmatos,
Michael Crichton,
David Cronenberg,
Rod Daniels,
Bill Davis,
Robert Day,
Bill Dear,
Jonathan Demme,
John Derek,
Howard Deutch,
Roger Donaldson,
Richard Donner,
Peter Douglas,
Stan Dragoti,
Adam Dubov,
George Englund,
John Erman,
Peter Faiman,
David Fincher,
Ken Finkleman,
Jack Fisk,
James Foley,
Bill Forsyth,
Giles Foster,
William Friedkin,
Sam Furstenberg,
Brian Godfrey Gilbert,
Jack Gold,
William Graham,
David Greene,
John Gray,
John Guillerman,
Taylor Hackford,
Joseph Hardy,
Richard T. Heffron,
Colin Higgins,
Todd Holland,
Tom Holland,
Ron Howard,
Hugh Hudson,
◂ John Hughes,
Peter Hunt,
Kim Hunter,
William Huyck,
Peter Hyams,
James Ivory,
Phil Joanou,
Steve Johnson,
Glenn Jordan,
Jonathan S. Kaplan,
Philip Kaufman,
Irvin Kershner,
Andrei Konchalovsky,
Ted Kotcheff,
Emir Kusturica,
Ken Kwappis,
John Landis,
Richard Lester,
Barry Levinson,
Lucho Llosa,
Jerry London,
Sidney Lumet,
David Lynch,
Robert Mandel,
Tom Mankiewicz,
Peter Markle,
George Miller,
Mollie Miller,
Sharron Miller,
Malcolm Mowbray,
Tom Moore,
Rocky Morton and
Annabel Jankel,
Barry Myers,
Gary Nelson,
Avi Nesher,
Tim Newman,
Frank Oz,
Alan Parker,
Tom Patchett,
Daniel Petrie,
◂ Sydney Pollack,
Rob Reiner,
Ivan Reitman,
Barbara Rennie,
Gene Reynold,
Tom Rickman,
Genevieve Roberts,
Bruce Robinson,
Rick Rosenthal,
Herbert Ross,
Joe Roth,
James Sadwith,
Jay Sandrich,
George Schaefer,
Joel Schumacher,
Martin Scorsese,
David Seltzer,
Alan Shapiro,
James Signorelli,
Yves Simoneau,
Oliver Stone, ▸
Charles Sturridge,
Jenny Sullivan,
Nadia Tass,
Francis Veber,
Danielle Vigne,
David Ward,
Billy Weber,
Paul Wendkos,
Simon Wincer,
Harry Winer,
Thomas Wright,
Bud Yorkin,
Robert Zemeckis,
Howard Zieff,
David Zucker and
Jerry Zucker

Writers

Rod Amateau,
Paul Attanasio,
Michael Austin,
Ronald Austin,
Fred Barron,
William Bast,
Susan Beavers,
Jerry Belson,
Barbara Benedek,
Tom Benedek,
Robert Benedetto,
Eric Bercovici,
Eleanor Bergstein,
Paul Bernbaum,
Abbie Bernstein,
Ann Biderman,
Terry Black,
Eric Blakeney,
Corey Blechman,
Bill Bleich,
Steve Bloom,
Jeffrey Boam,
Craig Bolotin,
Michael Bortman,
David Bradley,
Marshall Brickman,
Donald Brinkley,
Larry Brothers,
Charlotte Brown,
James Buchanan,
Craig Buck,
David Burke,
Martyn Burke,
Clifton Campbell,
Clifford Campion,
James Cappe,
Charles Carner,
Michael Alan Carter,
Jim Cash and
Jack Epps,
David Castro and
Daphne Pollon,
David Chase,
David Chisolm,
Cynthia Cidre,
Dick Clair and
Jenna McMahon,
James Clavell,
Alan Cole and
Chris Bunch,
Jackie Collins,
Robert Collins,
Harry Colomby,
Chris Columbus,
John Connolly and
David Louka,
Ray Connolly,
Anne Convy,
E. H. Crewe,
Alison Cross,
Carmen Culver,
Sara Davidson,
Johnny Dawkins,
Ed Decter and
John Strauss,
Phil DeGuere,
Harriet Dickey,
Robert Dillon,
Hal Dresner,
Chris Durang,
George Eckstein,
Michael Alan Eddy,
Michael Elias and
Richard Eustis,
Bob Ellison,
Delia Ephron,
Mark Estrin and
Allen Estrin,
Joe Eszterhas,
Susan Fales,
Peter Farrelly and
Bennett Yellin,
Randy Feldman,
Janice Fischer,
Peter Fischer,
Gail Fisher and
Marc Chessler,
Jeffrey Alan Fiskin,
Fannie Flagg,
Naomi Foner,
Katherine Ford,
Howard Franklin,
David Franzoni,
Fred Freeman and
Larry Cohen,
Bruce Jay Friedman,
Mark Frost,
John Furia,
Reg Gadney,
Bob Gale,
Charles Gale,
George Gallo,
Lowell Ganz,
Alex Ganza and
Howard Gordon,
Robert Garland,
Leila Garrett,
John Gay,
Larry Gay and
Michael Digaetano,
Robert Getchell,
Eric Gethers,
Steve Gethers,
Reynold Gideon and
Bruce Evans,
Gary Goddard,
Dan Goldberg,
William Goldman,
Jean Gonick,
Jill Gordon,
Diana Gould,
Heywood Gould,
Michael Grais and
Mark Victor,
Walon Green,
Gordon Greisman,
Trevor Griffiths,
Larry Gross,
Andrew Guerdat,
Dan Guntzelman and
Steve Marshall,
Richard Gurman,
Beth Gutcheon,
Charlie Haas,
continued on page 52

Footnotes

1. CAA partner 2. Although not an agent, is Mike Ovitz's right-hand man for business planning 3. Not an agent but is longtime general counsel to CAA 4. Also serves as Ovitz's assistant 5. Partner and president of CAA 6. Not an agent but is prominent CAA legal associate 7. Clients whom CAA represents in more than one capacity are listed here only once, in the category for which they are best known

50 SPY SEPTEMBER 1988

...And Still More Proof That CAA Runs Hollywood

Naked City

Who's Who, Part Two

Bob Harling,
Hal Harris,
Susan Harris,
Jim Hart,
Patrick Hasburgh,
Hilary Henkin,
Marshall Herskovitz,
Julie Hickson,
R. Lance Hill,
Janis Hirsch,
Allison Hock,
Savage Steve Holland,
Jean Holloway,
Willard Huyck and
Gloria Katz,
Jeremy Iacone,
Neal Israel,
Georgia Jeffries,
Sue Jett,
Robert L. Joseph,
Danny Kallis,
Robert Mark Kamen,
Jack Kaplan,
Mark Kasdan,
Allan Katz,
Tim Kazurinsky,
William Kerby,
Stephen King,
George Kirgo,
Julie Kirgo and
Diana Kirgo,
Robert Klane,
Richard Kletter,
Ron Koslow,
John Kostmayer,
Wendy Kout,
Richard Kramer,
Aaron Latham,
John Leekley,
Michael Leeson,
Alan Leicht,
Jerrold Leichtling and
Arlene Sarner,
William Link,
Bob Littell,
Walter Lockwood,
Joseph Loeb and
Matthew Weisman,
Jerry Ludwig,
Adrian Malone,
Babaloo Mandel,
Andrew Marin,
Brad Markowitz and
Bryce Zabel,
Richard Matheson,
Richard C. Matheson,
Robert McCullough,
Rex McGee,
Carol McKeand,
Nigel McKeand,
Ian McKewan,
Menna Meyjes,
Gene Miller,
Jim Moloney,
Donovan Moore,
John Mortimer, ▸
Ray Morton and
Timothy Williams,
Pat Nardo,
Stephen Nathan and
Paul Price,
Marc Norman,
Barry Oringer,
Paul Owen and
David Hanson,
Doug Palau,
Robert Palm,
Gail Parent,
David Parker,
Heidi Perlman,
Charlie Peters,
Harley Peyton,
Anna Hamilton Phelan,
Dean Pitchford,
Jean-Yves Pitoun,
Robert Pollock and
Eileen Pollock,
Daryl Ponicsan,
Duane Poole,
Thomas Pope,
Ruth Prawar-Jhabvala,
Jeffrey Price and
Peter Seaman,
Greg Pruss,
Charlie Purpura,
Harold Ramis,
Susan Rice,
David Rintels,
Mike Robe,
June Roberts,
Sally Robinson,
Al Rogers,
Henry Rosenbaum,
Mark Rosner,
Gary Ross,
George Rubino,
Paul Rudnick,
Al Ruggerio,
Chris Ruppenthal,
David Sacks and
Rob LaZebnick,
Ezra Sacks,
Robin Schiff,
Arnold Schulman,
Roger Schulman and
David Cohen,
Lorenzo Semple Jr.,
David Shaber,
Geoffrey Sherman,
Ronald Shusett,
Sterling Silliphant,
Stu Silver,
Lane Slate,
Robert Smigel,
Ed Solomon,
Frank South,
Anne Spielberg,
Nancy Steen and
Neil Thompson,
Norman Steinberg,
Leslie Stevens,
Fred Mustard Stewart,
Wesley Strick,
Steve Sunshine and
Madeline Sunshine,
Tom Swale,
Scott Swanton,
Tom Szollosi,
Joan Taylor,
Ken Taylor,
Joan Tewkesbury,
Camille Thomasson,
John Tinker,
Sandy Veith,
◂ Gore Vidal,
Ed Weinberger,
Colin Welland,
John Wells,
Gina Wendkos,
Alan Timothy Williamson,
Andrew Wolk,
Tracy Keenan Wynn,
Anthony Yerkovich,
Robert Young

Actors

Suzy Amis,
Terry Anderson,
Ann-Margret,
Rosanna Arquette,
Dan Aykroyd,
Mikhail Baryshnikov,
Kim Basinger,
Jim Belushi,
Tom Berenger,
Powers Booth,
Beau Bridges,
Wilford Brimley,
Matthew Broderick,
Pierce Brosnan,
Bryan Brown,
Ellen Burstyn,
Dyan Cannon,
Kim Cattrall,
Richard Chamberlain,
Chevy Chase,
Cher,
Rae Dawn Chong,
Jill Clayburgh,
Glenn Close,
Sean Connery,
Courtney Cox,
Richard Crenna,
Tom Cruise,
Tim Curry,
Jane Curtin,
Valerie Curtin,
Jamie Lee Curtis,
Willem Dafoe,
Ted Danson,
Rebecca DeMornay,
Robert De Niro,
Bo Derek,
Bruce Dern,
Danny De Vito,
Matt Dillon,
Kirk Douglas,
Michael Douglas,
Robert Downey Jr.,
Sam Elliott,
Emilio Estevez,
Farrah Fawcett,
Barbara Feldon,
Sally Field,
Jane Fonda,
Bonnie Franklin,
Zach Galligan,
Teri Garr,
Cynthia Gibb,
Whoopi Goldberg,
Lou Gossett,
Kim Greist,
Amy Gross,
Gene Hackman,
Goldie Hawn,
Mariel Hemingway,
Barbara Hershey,
Charlton Heston,
Arthur Hill,
Gregory Hines,
Dustin Hoffman,
Dennis Hopper,
C. Thomas Howell,
Tom Hulce,
Lauren Hutton,
Kate Jackson,
Julie Kavner,
Michael Keaton,
Val Kilmer,
Perry King,
Kevin Kline,
◂ Jessica Lange,
Ray Liotta,
John Lithgow,
Robert Loggia,
John Lovett,
Dolph Lundgren,
Karl Malden,
Penny Marshall,
Kevin Meaney,
Bette Midler,
Demi Moore,
Bill Murray, ▸
Judd Nelson,
George Newborn,
◂ Paul Newman,
Michael O'Keefe,
Al Pacino,
Jason Patrick,
Sean Penn,
Rhea Perlman,
William Petersen,
Sidney Poitier,
Gilda Radner,
Robert Redford,
Ann Reinking,
◂ Burt Reynolds,
Jason Robards,
Susan St. James,
Jack Scalia,
Diana Scarwid,
Kyra Sedgwick,
Steve Seagal,
Jane Seymour,
Craig Sheffer,
Martin Short,
Elisabeth Shue,
Lori Singer,
Sissy Spacek,
Sylvester Stallone,
Pamela Stephenson
Eric Stoltz,
Sharon Stone,
Madeleine Stowe,
Barbra Streisand,
Donald Sutherland,
Marlo Thomas,
Lea Thompson,
Jon Voight,
Christopher Walken,
Rachel Ward,
Lesley Ann Warren,
Julie Waters,
Peter Weller,
Gene Wilder,
John Wildman,
Robin Williams,
Debra Winger,[8]
James Woods,
Sean Young

Performers

Gregory Abbott,
AC/DC,
The Adventurers,
Herb Alpert,
America,
Harry Anderson,
Jimmy Barnes,
Big Pig,
Michael Bolton,
Jackson Browne,
The Call,
George Carlin,
Peter Cetera,
Eric Clapton,
Cock Robin,
Crosby, Stills and Nash,
Cruzados,
Martha Davis,
Neil Diamond,
Dio,
D'Molls,
Dream Academy,
John Eddie,
Fire Town,
Fleetwood Mac,
Flesh for LuLu,
John Fogerty,
Hall & Oates,
Herbie Hancock,
Deborah Harry,
Corey Hart,
Hipsway,
Bruce Hornsby
and the Range,
House of Freaks,
Hunters & Collectors,
Hurrah!,
◂ Michael Jackson,
Magic Johnson,
Kings of the Sun,
The Kinks,
KISS,
Loverboy,
Madonna, ▸
Christine McVie,
John Cougar Mellencamp,
Midnight Oil,
Joni Mitchell,
Graham Nash,
Roy Orbison,
Northern Pikes,
Graham Parker,
Dolly Parton,
Joe Piscopo,
Iggy Pop,
◂ Prince,
Dan Reed Network,
Paul Reiser,
Robbie Robertson,
Scritti Politti,
Sheila E,
Patty Smyth,
Rick Springfield,
Starship,
Jermaine Stewart,
Rod Stewart,
Stephen Stills,
Supertramp,
'til tuesday,
Danny Wilson,
ZZ Top

Composers[9]

Wally Bardarou,
Jellybean Benitez,
Tony Berg,
Carter Burwell,
Michel Colombier,
Michael Convertino,
Brian Eno,
Harold Faltermyer,
Bryan Ferry,
Berlin Game,
◂ Philip Glass,
Herbie Hancock,
Mark Isham,
Joe Jackson,
Jimmy Jam
and Terry Lewis,
Pat Leonard,
Steve Levine,
David Mansfield,
Johnny Marr,
William Ovis,
Dean Pitchford,
Phillippe Sarde,
Lalo Schifrin,
Joseph Vitarelli,
Narada Michael Walden

Footnotes

8. Represented independently by Rick Nicita 9. Though some composers are not primarily known as such, this is the capacity in which CAA represents them

52 SPY SEPTEMBER 1988

Laying Ovitz bare: a painstakingly assembled CAA client list, September 1988

ad hominem interest in people, and showing them up publicly, *Spy* in some way made the world even smaller."

"It was like Trollope," says Guy Martin. "You opened it up and there it was, on a plate. Except it was being told to you in a bar by a really smart guy—it was talked out. Alex Heard's piece on going to dinner with Nixon in New Jersey [October 1986]? I thought it was illegal to publish that stuff!"

"I think that some of the magazine editorial establishment was not just worried that we were going to make fun of them," Kurt says, "but that we were working harder, inventing new ways to do a magazine. At the time, a member of that establishment actually told me that *Spy*'s energy and labor-intensiveness and risk-taking made him feel like a complacent hack."

"The information-rich stuff that was being churned out by *Spy*'s small staff, on a monthly basis!" says Martin. "I remember [*New England Monthly* founding editor] Dan Okrent picking up a copy and saying, 'How do they get people to do all this work?'"

It looks especially remarkable from our current Google-mad vantage point. Stories were written and edited on PCs, but that was the absolute limit of computerization. There were no databases or email. But Kurt and Graydon both came from Time Inc., where the research facilities were extensive, and they couldn't help wanting to re-create the same deep, virtually scientific density of information in *Spy*—even if it sometimes meant sneaking interns with borrowed IDs into the Time Inc. library uptown, back when Time Inc. had a library.

"*Spy* was just fucking hilarious," says Terry McDonell, then a former *Newsweek* editor starting up a magazine called *SMART*, now the editor of *Sports Illustrated*. "I was mocked in it occasionally, which was always sort of thrilling because it raised your status. I thought it was so smart, and the graphics were funny and cool— I thought it was right on."

"I can tell you that *Esquire* was fucking terrified of *Spy*," says Martin, then a regular contributor to both magazines. "The map *Spy* ran of [*Esquire* editor Lee] Eisenberg's office bathroom? He actually accused me of telling them. It wasn't just that they were bad boys—the accuracy level was very high. People, even if they were being attacked, had to watch: for the information itself."

Not just editors noticed.

"Your worst fear was to get the issue and find yourself in it," Ron Meyer, a Creative Artists Agency founding partner and now chairman of Universal Pictures, said recently. "And when you found yourself in it, it was slightly painful but definitely funny. The problem was that you never knew it was coming, and there was always a germ of truth to what was said. [*Spy* was] rough on all of us, but clearly CAA was a consistent target, and Mike Ovitz, my partner."

The roster of Hollywood's extraordinarily powerful Creative Artists Agency—its agents and clients—is one of the most talked about, closely held, never-before-published, constantly changing top secret documents in the filmmaking industry. CAA did not want it published. So, here is what we came up with. You can look at it. But you've got to promise you won't show it to anyone.
—*Spy*, September 1988

"Who is Celia Brady and why is she saying all those terrible things about Hollywood?" —The Los Angeles Times

IT WAS JUST TWO PAGES, and nothing but a painstakingly researched and comprehensive list of names that took a year to compile—but the impact in Hollywood was unbelievable. Until *Spy* published the list, not even the agents on it knew the full extent of their agency's client roster, and major stars had no idea who else their agents represented. CAA head Michael Ovitz was then all-powerful but largely unknown outside show business. No longer.

What added to the shock of such scoops was...well, the shock. "The magazine was fact-checked as closely as humanly possible without contacting the subject—so people couldn't brace themselves," Graydon says.

Graydon and Kurt had a source or two for the CAA list, and as it happened, so did the reporter they assigned the story to, Rachel Urquhart.

One of the sources, who had apparently seen *All the President's Men,* told Urquhart: *I won't give you any names—but if you'd like to read me any names you have, I'll make a sound to indicate any that are wrong.* "So I would read these names slowly into the phone, to almost total silence," she remembers. "It was really tense."

Ovitz recently told Kurt, "When you published our client list, that was the biggest coup of all time. I really thought it was

BEST OF THE INDUSTRY

Spy's scabrous Industry column, by the pseudonymous Celia Brady, was must-read—or at least must-have-summarized—for Hollywood executives. "I don't know that I'd use the word 'fun' to describe the experience," says "Celia" today. "Knocking out a column like that once a month was work. Luckily, Hollywood never let me down with any lack of outrageous material."

THE MOUTH THAT BORED: THE LAST DAYS OF THE JACK VALENTI FLACKATHON?

Hit the Road, Jack: The flurry of late-summer telephone calls between Lew Wasserman (the ancient overlord of MCA/Universal), Barry Diller (the overlord of Fox), Michael Eisner (the overlord of Disney) and Mike Ovitz (the overlord) concerned a potential problem that lay just over the horizon. It had to do with movies and their putative effects on real life. This worried them: the big-budget movies of the summer (*Total Recall, Robocop 2, Die Harder, Another 48 Hrs.*) and the most celebrated of the $1-million-plus scripts sold recently (*The Last Boy Scout, The Ticking Man, Basic Instinct*) were all of the hyperviolent action-fantasy variety. This worried them, too: Detroit is a postapocalyptic armed camp, novelty murderers terrorize New York, teenagers in the Midwest kill friends for fun. In the movies, more and more, people are using sexy automatic weapons against one another with horrifying nonchalance. In real life, more and more, people are using sexy automatic weapons against one another with horrifying nonchalance. "Our message," one studio executive fretted out loud, "is that life is cheap." Whether or not there is a connection between special-effects homicide and the real thing, the current worry in Hollywood is that someone like Jesse Helms will start believing there is one, which might lead to some really senseless, really tragic violence — terminated projects and fired executives.

Sitting in the middle of all this is the

Meanwhile, over at Orion, home of the ever-diminishing profit, it seems that Woody Allen, heretofore one of the studio's major assets — he is referred to there as an "annuity"—is unhappy. When Woody's contract came up for renegotiation last January, Orion apparently wasn't forthcoming enough with cash. Woody traditionally receives about $1 million for writing and directing his movies, with penalties built in if he goes over budget. (Sidney "That's a Take" Lumet has a similar deal in his contracts, except he gets to keep the difference when he comes in *under* budget, an arrangement that may have caused him to put some of his movies together too quickly—see *Garbo Talks*. And what would you rather have: one more take with Dustin Hoffman, say, or another grove of trees for the house in East Hampton?) Of course, in Woody's case, what he gets in return for this relatively small sum of money (Oliver Stone, the conscience of our generation, gets $4 million per picture for the same duties) is complete creative control over scripts,

casting, advertising and final cut. The problem, however, is that Woody needs more money. The most visible recluse in New York lives, despite his rumpledness, a high-priced existence. What with the Rolls, Mia's digs on Central Park West, their young son and Mia's eight other children, the $8,000-a-month maintenance he pays on his Fifth Avenue co-op, and the tab at Elio's, anyone would have trouble making ends meet on $1 million a year.

When Orion balked at giving him an increase in salary, Woody tried to set up a deal for himself with Jeff "Sparky" Katzenberg at Disney. Sparky agreed to make the deal with Woody, but with a few minor provisos: no creative control over scripts, mutual discussions on casting (a Katzenberg specialty), no say in advertising and no final cut. When Woody blanched (*the man's a national treasure, after all*), Katzenberg pointed out that not one of Woody's recent films had earned back its money (*Hannah and Her Sisters* in 1986, which followed five money losers, was the last profitable one) and furthermore that Disney's *New York Stories*, one segment of which Woody directed, had cost the studio $18 million and grossed only $12 million. Woody, needless to say, is back at Orion, except that he did agree to perform in Paul Mazursky's new film for Touchstone, *Scenes from a Shopping Mall*, with Bette Midler. For $3 million.

But back to Medavoy. When he

July 1990

between the two. The score so far: Tom Patchett (creator of *ALF*) from Brillstein to CAA; Jay Tarses (creator of *Molly Dodd* and *"Slap" Maxwell*) from CAA to Brillstein; Dan Aykroyd to CAA; Richard Dreyfuss to Brillstein. Jim Belushi, a CAA client, is still on the fence. Brillstein has sworn vengeance and has told at least one talent agent that he wants to bury CAA. And the talent agency is not exactly encouraging its stable of stars to make deals with Lorimar.

Although Ovitz is arguably the most powerful man in Hollywood just now, he is not a studio head. Ovitz and Jeff Berg, his counterpart at International Creative Man...

THE FEUD BETWEEN SUPERAGENT Mike "the Manipulator" Ovitz and super-hyphenate (manager–producer–studio head) Bernie Brillstein continues unabated this month. Brillstein is chairman and chief executive officer of Lorimar Film and Entertainment. He is also the manager of Lorne Michaels and Jim Henson and the producer of the movies *Dragnet* and *Ghostbusters*, as well as of *ALF*, *The Days and Nights of Molly Dodd*, *It's Garry Shandling's Show* and *The "Slap" Maxwell Story* on television. (Brillsteinophiles will additionally recall his role as best supporting manager, to John Belushi, in Bob Woodward's *Wired*.) The ball-shaped, fatherly Brillstein tangled with Ovitz and his enormously powerful talent agency, Creative Artists Agency (CAA), over their mutual client, Dan Aykroyd. (California state law prohibits managers from also acting as talent agents, which explains the corepresentation of Aykroyd. The fee structure varies, but most managers charge 15 percent of a client's gross earnings, with an additional 10 percent to the agent—although in many instances the agent serves in name only, at a much lower fee paid and negotiated by the manager.) It seems that Aykroyd complained to driven, personality-free Ovitz that Brillstein, busy with his own studio and production deals, wasn't paying enough attention to Aykroyd's career, and that Ovitz suggested firing him. Aykroyd did. Not surprisingly, Brillstein evidently felt betrayed by Ovitz, especially since he purports that he, Brillstein, "made" CAA the success it has become during the last decade. Another source of conflict was all those cute little *ALF* dolls, and whether CAA would share in the large licensing fees. Brillstein's and Ovitz's clients have been forced to choose

THE INDUSTRY

summer — will be hard-pressed to see profits anytime soon.)

Trims and Ends: If you're seeing a lot of Brian Grazer in the press these days, it's because the slender producer was recently heard screaming at his public-relations hirelings that he's sick of being overshadowed by his partner in Imagine Films, the estimable Ron Howard, and was particularly miffed at being left off *Premiere*'s list of the 100 most powerful people in Hollywood. He has told friends he's going to kill somebody if he doesn't make it next year....I loved the party to rededicate Warner Bros. Studios. I loved the Busby

September 1990

Tori. Tori. Tori: Aaron Spelling — the man who once likened the television business to *Death of a Salesman* by saying, "We are all Willy Lomans in this business. We make our trips to the networks and tell them an idea, and they either buy it or turn it down"— has recently been exhibiting behavior typical of an altogether *different* type of family drama, one more in keeping with the glamorous sop he himself produces. It seems that Spelling is a father with a heart so big that he has set aside a handsome portion of the eighteen acres that his 65,000-square-foot Holmby Hills house spreads across for his daughter, Tori, so that when she grows up her heart, body and furniture will always belong to daddy.

Generous to a fault, Spelling has also taken to shoehorning Tori's name into various production contracts that land on his desk. Furthermore, as if oblivious to the fact that this is the first time in 25 years that he has no series on the air — and to the layoffs in his company — Spelling recently had to be talked out of giving the young actress a Rolls-Royce for her sixteenth birthday. Yes, a seeming extravagance — but then again, given that Spelling furnishes his wife, Candy, a Los Angeles beauty with the complex-

ion of a lovingly burnished turd, with $10,000 a night in gambling funds whenever they go to Las Vegas, his gift of a Rolls would simply have been the sign of a man who knows how to treat *all* his girls right.

Image Is Everything: If you were Nor-

October 1989

March 1988

NO MORE APRIL FOOLS' SHE-NANIGANS FOR US: THE MO-MENT HAS COME TO GROW up, get serious, address the issues of the day carefully, thoughtfully, straightforwardly. We can't just sit back and mock the grotesque and marvel at the bizarre. We must do more than merely tease and chastise. We are privileged members of history's most privileged generation, children of plenty who stopped a war and rededicated a nation to its ideals of tolerance. Enough jokes, enough merrymaking. It's high time that we told the world not just what repels and astounds us, but what we are *for*. 🌂 We're thinking. 🌂 All right, here's one: *we are* for *helping sick babies feel better*. Earlier this year, back before the honeymoon was over, back during those several seconds of fondness we felt toward the president, back when he was still new to the White House—indeed, the morning after he had, Reagan-like, got lost there—George Bush arose at 6:00 a.m. to take care of El-lie LeBlond. Ellie LeBlond is his two-year-old granddaughter (one of the little white ones). "Pumped a half a Tylenol into her," Bush said later, making Ellie sound like a finicky chainsaw, "and she's looking good." 🌂 Bush has been doing a lot of things we are for: we are *for* giving Dan Quayle inconsequential make-work, and we are *for* fishing. Casting off a Florida key, the president landed a catfish—pumped a hook into her, and she's looking good—even though it was not what he was after. Bush is a *bonefish* man. When he catches one, he says, he strokes it (afraid so: kindly, gently) before tossing it back. Bush was fishing when some British tourists happened by, and the president of the United States (who had on television just referred to his own wife as "a blimp," and whose spokesman announced, "There are times when he may want to do personal things late at night") suddenly blurted out, "Do you think Margaret Thatcher would like a little bit of this bonefishing action?" This being spring, we are, naturally, *for* U.S. presidents making goofy double entendres about Tory prime ministers. 🐟 The Reagan-Bush administration's

No more April Fools' shenanigans

One of Kurt Andersen's Great Expectations opening essays, April 1989

heroic Oliver North has managed, in the manner of CIA turncoats who know too much, to blackmail the government into backing off from prosecuting him fully. And Bush has been excused from appearing as a witness at North's trial, because, according to a White House official, "presidents just don't testify in court." What *do* presidents do? Well, former presidents

sign several-million-dollar book deals 48 hours after leaving office. (Diverting but trivial best-selling books: we're definitely *for* them.) Former presidents continue to put on ridiculous headgear if photographers are anywhere in the vicinity. And they pull down around $1,000 a minute for delivering after-dinner speeches. More, maybe, if they tour as a double bill with alleged felons and national heroes, a marketing-of-Ronald-Reagan plan that Oliver North recently proposed.

Just as the nation's focus was on Washington and the new administration, another charismatic national hero, Teddy Kennedy, was doing some late-night . . . fact-finding at a bar called American Trash on upper First Avenue. (We are most certainly *for* the hearty but responsible consumption of alcoholic beverages. We are somewhat less enthusiastic about pineapple-juice-based drinks, such as those Kennedy was drinking on upper First Avenue. As for upper First Avenue: probably more against than for.) Anyway, Teddy pumped a half a drink into himself, and he's looking good—pretty good, anyway, until he had a dustup with a fellow high-spirited Irish-American bar patron, who told the senator, *You're no John Kennedy.*

Georgette Mosbacher notwithstanding,

the 1980s are now really, finally over. We're sure of it, with such astonishing images of 1990s-ness cropping up—the lice infestation at the Library of Congress, for example. They called in Dr. Thomas Parker, an emergency library entomologist, to delouse the place, and he delivered his assessment: the lice had attacked *Barron's, The Wall Street Journal* and *Architectural Digest*. Who knew that modern vermin were so calculating, so attuned to the nuances of social mood? We just thank God that Dr. Parker got to Washington before they reached the shelf where the *USA Today*s and Jay McInerney novels are kept.

Ever since a firsthand encounter in 1973, we have been very much *for* killing lice (*memo to Librarian of Congress: Throw out any terry-cloth bathrobes immediately*), by wholesale fumigation if necessary—pump a half a pint of DDT into them, and they're looking good. Poison gas? Government-run exterminations? Speaking of Germany, it is important to reiterate that the West German chemical company Imhausen-Chemie did not—repeat, *did not*—help Libya build its new chemical-weapons factory. "We have nothing to do with this project," said company *Über*executive Jürgen Hippenstiel-Imhausen, his denial sounding somehow familiar, somehow very . . . German. "We don't have the know-how—and we wouldn't do so anyway, because we are a responsible company."

Not to jump to conclusions prematurely, but we just may be seeing early signs of a mid-1940s revival. New German war crimes, Hirohitomania, a flying ace in the White House, not enough sex and last winter's J. Crew clothing catalog. J. Crew is marketing a corduroy jacket as one that "might have been worn by J. Robert Oppenheimer at Los Alamos." Okay, we'll take one of those— and while you're at it, send along one of those very handsome white smocks that might have been worn by Wernher von Braun at Peenemünde.

Don't get us wrong: we're *for* science and technology—especially when it's used to update perfectly good all-American 1940s-era products. The Wm. Wrigley Company just hired Advanced Polymer Systems Inc., whose vice president of re-

search and development is a man named Sergio, to put tiny, flavor-filled *synthetic sponges* into sticks of Doublemint and Juicy Fruit. Advanced Polymer figures that the flavor lasts twice as long, up to 22 minutes. And they say the American Century is over.

First scientists solve the chewing-gum-flavor-extension problem; then, in a flash, they solve the drug problem. Researchers have discovered that a dose of PCP, or angel dust, *protects* brain cells during heart attacks and strokes. In other words, pumped some PCP into her, she's looking good. Does this mean—yikes!—that now we're *for* angel dust?

We thought we were for minority-hiring schemes, especially in Boston. The Boston Fire Department lists 361 minority-group members among its fire fighters. It turns out that at least eleven of those putative blacks and Hispanics, however, may be white people (including twin brothers named Malone) who lied about their race in order to get hired—life imitates *Soul Man*—because in Boston blacks and Hispanics can pass the civil-service exam with lower scores than whites. Each suspected white person is now being required to produce "proof that one has participated as a member of the black community" (*memo to Sammy Davis Jr.: Don't try to become a Boston fireman or policeman*).

Of course, we are *for* policemen, within reason, partly because they face such daily peril on our behalf. Or so we always thought. The following people, according to the new study "Job-Related Deaths in 347 Occupations," are among the many with jobs more dangerous than a cop's: bulldozer operators, flight attendants, metalworkers, roofers, surveyor's helpers, millers, cabdrivers, truck drivers and—more than twice as dangerous—garbage collectors.

So, Bush is not altogether objectionable, angel dust is good for you, affirmative action backfires, cops are wusses. . . . We embark on spring suddenly confused and ambivalent, no longer so sure just what or whom we are for or why. The solution? *Spring*: take off the storm windows, hand over a baby daughter, pump a half a quart of orange juice into us, and we're looking good. ⬧

going to put us out of business. I wanted people to think we were deeper, that we represented everyone. And we didn't! You wouldn't believe the security we had to keep that from getting out. I swear I thought it was going to put us out of business."

Spy's coverage of Hollywood wasn't a one-shot proposition. Celia Brady's pseudonymous, fearless, authoritative, see-you-Monday-night-at-Mortons "Industry" column ran regularly and disruptively. Michael Eisner and Jeffrey Katzenberg at Disney were, along with CAA, the other most frequent (if not obsessive) subjects. And in Hollywood, an industry fueled perhaps more than any other by fear and dissembling, Celia Brady's reporting and truth-telling were nothing short of astonishing.

> *"I wasn't too good at heroes. But we all knew who the villain was: Mike Ovitz."*

Who is Celia Brady and why is she saying all those terrible things about Hollywood?...The question of Brady's identity isn't just a matter of bemused speculation. So caustic has been Brady's pen and so high-placed her victims that one powerful agent is widely rumored to have put a private detective on her trail.

—Michael Cieply, *The Los Angeles Times,* January 4, 1989

SPY CONTRIBUTOR PAUL RUDNICK had started doing some screenwriting around that time and was one of the people suspected of being Celia. "And to this day I have no idea who it was," he says. "There was a theory [in Hollywood] that it changed every month, that there was a committee. But people in Hollywood were *obsessed* with who Celia Brady was and were genuinely hurt and outraged and felt, as only people in Hollywood can, that this should be taken up by Congress. 'How *dare* they...report our salaries?' It got to the point of desperation, especially among the studio people: 'How could *Spy* find out these things?' Certainly none of the trade papers were getting that response.

"In Hollywood, they would read nothing *but* the Celia Brady column," continues Rudnick. "That was a measure of *Spy*'s power: *It forced Hollywood figures to read.*"

Celia's identity remains known to only a few people, and she has never spoken publicly about her time as a *Spy* columnist. She agreed to be interviewed for this book.

CELIA BRADY SPEAKS:
A Spy *The Funny Years* Exclusive

How did you approach the Industry column?
If you heard a rumor in Hollywood, it almost always turned out to be true: what executive was in trouble, what star was on drugs, what producer was throwing ashtrays across the room, and what Bruce Willis was asking for in his perk package. In Hollywood, these things are common knowledge. Everybody talks, everybody gossips. But nobody had ever printed it before.

One of *Spy*'s editors—I don't remember which—said that the key to a column is to create memorable heroes and villains. I wasn't too good at heroes. But we all knew who the villain was: Mike Ovitz. There was something about him and his agency that rubbed me the wrong way. He seemed too eager to prove how powerful he was. He was calling journalists everywhere, all the time, whispering, in some kind of pseudo-secrecy, "Is this a secure line?" I didn't buy—no, I *resented* the mythology he was trying to build up around himself. And I knew too many people who had been crushed by his agency. He seemed like a nasty man with a need to preen, covering it with a false humility. He had no time for anyone who couldn't help him or wasn't higher up on the ladder he was so busy scaling.

What happened when the column started to appear?
It was a like a firestorm. The first column was an assessment of the various studios. Who was going to stay in power, who was going to lose their jobs. No one had seen their names in print like this before. And everyone wanted to know who was behind it.

Was there any fallout at the studios?
I was writing pretty much what "everyone" already knew. It was now just that everyone knew it. I don't think I hastened anyone's losing a job. I certainly didn't paint any saintly producer as a monster. The people I portrayed as such were already monsters. They just found it appalling that someone shed light on their daily operating manner. In Hollywood everyone knows who is awful, who is out of control, who is stupid, who is on drugs, who is acting capriciously. But seeing it in print was another story. I remember one woman (I think she was at CBS theatrical films, RIP) who kept people waiting for hours, and was just a nightmare to work with. Cackling. Screaming. Nasty. When we came along

Writer LYNN SNOWDEN:

Fig. 1

✂ CUT HERE

"Before," from "Busty Like Me: One Woman's True Story," August 1987. "While I was sitting there writing it, Graydon kept walking past my desk whispering, 'Movie of the Week, Movie of the Week,' says Lynn Snowden. "It was a big ha-ha. But when the piece came out, it actually sold as a movie of the week."

"The only way to bridge the gap was to become temporarily bosomy— really bosomy. For two weeks I did everything I normally did, wore everything I normally wore. The only difference was in the Size of My Breasts"

and detailed her working habits, she was furious at the magazine, but it never occurred to her that she shouldn't have been acting like that in the first place.

Was it stressful to do?
As I recall the editors telling me, everyone in New York wanted to know who Celia Brady was. At dinner parties in Los Angeles, the guessing game would immediately begin. I would feign ignorance; I'd nod in agreement when everyone would assume that she had to be operating at the highest levels of the studios, as only that kind of person could have access to that kind of information. What they didn't realize, of course, is that *everyone* had access to bits and pieces of that kind of information, from Chuck of Chuck's Parking to Bernard, the maître d' at Spago. Everyone talked, everyone listened, everyone watched the wheels go around.

Did you ever come close to getting caught?
No, I don't think so. Possibly because the obvious answer—that it could literally have been anyone—escaped them. I could have been an executive, a director, an actor, or a reporter at *Variety*. I remember reading an article in *The Los Angeles Times* where they tried to figure it out, and none of the people they interviewed as possible suspects were even close. For all they knew, I could have been working at the *L.A. Times*. And maybe I was. Or maybe I wasn't.

I do recall being in a social setting with two William Morris agents who wanted to sign Celia Brady. I was most amused when they also began to speculate about the possibility of sleeping with her.

What about the years since—does the name come up often?
Outside of the founding moguls, and a few superstars like Spielberg, nothing, and no one, lasts in Hollywood. With each year, the name "Celia Brady" comes up less frequently. This is the way things go out here.

So where was I?

THE MAGAZINE ALSO ENGINEERED the *Spy* Celebrity Pro-Am Ironman Nightlife Decathlon, an annual event with unwitting bon vivant participants. The first year, 1988, it pitted the writer Anthony Haden-Guest against Watergate journalist Carl Bernstein against book-publishing wunderkind Morgan Entrekin (see pages 131–39). *Spy* operatives tailed each one on various nights on the town, taking notes ("1:05 a.m. [Jay] MCINERNEY's car speeds up Sixth Avenue through Greenwich Village. We pull up alongside, and ENTREKIN displays for us his supersophisticated, editing-weary middle finger....1:20 a.m. The check arrives and is mistakenly placed before HADEN-GUEST— his face goes white and sweat forms on his brow....1:30 a.m. His reportorial instincts aroused, BERNSTEIN finishes his drink and escorts his contact outside, pausing to glare at our by now all-too-familiar cherry-red Ford Tempo"), snapping photos, and awarding points (for Hours Logged, Venues Visited, Number of Anonymous Women Seen With, Estimated Cost of Evening, and Desperate Phone Calls Made).

The magazine was seldom in higher gear than during this period, both internally and externally. "*Spy* media blitz," reads an entry from my journal. "Today: *Time*, *Newsweek*, *Washington Post*, *Washington Times*, CNN, *Live at Five*. Expected tomorrow: *Newsday*, *USA Today*, 'Page Six,' *Letterman*...."

"It was a pretty frantic time," says Graydon. "Some of that attention did take away from the actual fun of doing the maga-

"After," from "Busty Like Me." The fake breasts were later reused by Milton Berle when he posed in drag for the cover of *Spy*'s March 1988 issue.

fashion models such as Elle MacPherson, Ashley, Estelle and Paulina Porizkova are enjoying a vogue. Couturiers such as Azzedine Alaïa, Claude Montana, Karl Lagerfeld and Jean-Paul Gaultier have revived the hourglass silhouette with boned corsets, strapless dresses, scooped necklines— clothes engineered to hoist and display breasts.

But despite the alleged and heavily advertised comeback of big breasts, a lawyer on *Donahue* discussed the problem of discrimination against some women because of their large bust size. I realized that all of my girlfriends were small-busted. Was I guilty of prejudice toward busty women? Did I truly believe I was somehow more serious and more interesting *simply because my breasts are small*? And what was there about this subject that had made me start posing earnest rhetorical questions? I wanted to find out for myself: was being busty all glamour, or was it a crippling physical and social burden?

In other words, would it be fun to be really built?

How but by becoming a big-breasted woman could a small-breasted woman hope to learn the truth? The only way I could figure to bridge the gap between us was to become temporarily bosomy—*really bosomy*—and go undercover on the streets of New York. For two weeks last spring, I would do everything I normally did, wear everything I normally wore. The only difference would

be in the Size of My Breasts.

I prepared to walk into a life that looked scary and exciting. With my decision to become a big-busted woman, I realized that I knew nothing of what might indeed be her daily torment, her desire always to shout out, *There's more to me than my breasts. I'm a person, too, you know!*

In other words, *was it going to be fun being really built?*

DAY ONE

WITH THE HELP OF A WOMAN who is in the business of fitting prosthetic breasts, I went from a modest A-cup to a voluptuous D-cup. I opted to have special pockets for the false breasts sewn into my new bra; I'd worried that they would slide out and down my dress when I ran for a bus.

My new breasts resembled teardrop-shaped, very soft beige pillows, with a slightly raised nipple built in. Each was packed in its own box. After leaving the store I walked down Fifth Avenue carrying my breasts in a plain shopping bag. They felt heavy and burdensome after only a few blocks.

I tried them on at home. The transformation was total and startling. The person who stared back at me from the mirror looked like a pinup girl. She had gigantic knockers. Enormous hooters. Bodacious ta-tas. I had never seen this person before. She was me. I was Busty.

"Is it crowded

in there?"

he said.

Did he mean

inside my

jacket?

Or in the gym?

zine. Although I remember the day the Japanese film crew came up to the office, and the whole staff did calisthenics for them." (To something called "Let's Get Satirical," improvised on the spot to the approximate tune of "Let's Get Physical," the 1981 Olivia Newton-John hit.) "But I also remember thinking: *If I was 23 years old and working here, I would think I was the luckiest fucking person in the world.*"

"When *Spy* was first hot, Graydon and I were flown down to Bermuda for the American Magazine Conference," says Kurt.

"Having explained that we had used our *Time* offices, phones, and printing facilities for the planning of the magazine, we declared on one of the panels that 'one thing we're proud of is that we're the only successful new magazine to come out of Time Inc. during the last decade.' This was just after the huge failures of *TV Cable Week* and *Picture Week* and years before *EW* and *InStyle*. The guys who ran Time Inc. at the time were in the audience, and they were just apoplectic."

"If I were them," says Graydon, "I would've been pissed too."

els to the "peninsula" of Labrador. Triangular shape   *rador is not a peninsula."*

The GUEST TOWELS of TURIN

Mark O'Donnell, who contributed cartoons and pieces to *Spy*, is a novelist and, more recently, coauthor of the Broadway musical *Hairspray*. **February 1989**

Naked City

CELESTIAL HINDSIGHT

SPY's Horoscope for Skeptics

*a*nother look at the horoscopes of familiar people on momentous days of their lives.

Subject: BILLY MARTIN
Sign: Taurus (b. 5/16/28)
Date: June 23, 1988
Notable Activity: Got fired for the fifth time from job as Yankee manager
Horoscopes: "You…seem to imagine that partners or associates do not approve or understand. But their opinions are of no importance, for it is only your own long-term happiness that matters now." — Patric Walker, *New York Post*; "Doing sales work can be lucrative; your gift for gab works well." — Joyce Jillson, *Daily News*

Subject: IVAN BOESKY
Sign: Pisces (b. 3/6/37)
Date: March 23, 1988
Notable Activity: Began serving a 36-month jail sentence
Horoscope: "You may well adopt a new and superficially less glamorous mode of getting around: you may find you are walking or bicycling. Anyway, you enjoy a simpler, plainer, and in fact more realistic approach to neighborhood concerns. Your community opens its arms and hugs you, in a way you haven't previously experienced here." — Jane Gaskell, *Town & Country*

Subject: RONALD REAGAN
Sign: Aquarius (b. 2/6/11)
Date: May 31, 1988
Notable Activity: Fell asleep while listening to speech at Moscow summit
Horoscope: "More rest would be good." — Joyce Jillson, *Daily News*

Subject: REV. AL SHARPTON
Sign: Libra (b. 10/3/54)
Date: June 14, 1988
Notable Activity: Suffered credibility reverses as former aide Perry McKinnon declared that Sharpton's allegations regarding Tawana Brawley were "nothing but a pack of lies"
Horoscope: "Expect disruptions in plans and sleepless nights. Your professional qualifications will be put to the test." — Laurie Brady, *Star*   — *George Mannes*

"MR. STALLONE ON THE LINE…"

*h*ollywood's tangled web of telecommunication yields a curious Zeitgeist all its own. The present moment's hierarchy of notoriety and bankability translates neatly into who takes whose calls and how quickly. Using only American Society of Magazine Editors–sanctioned journalistic techniques, SPY attempted to gauge just how hot the man responsible for *Rambo III* still is. A cross section of producers, agents, politicians and fellow actors was called; the moment each was informed, "I have Mr. Stallone on the line," we punched our timer and logged—to the second—how quickly meetings were interrupted, other lines put on hold and transfers to car phones accomplished, as people's people fell over one another to connect our man to theirs.

For any experiment to be scientifically valid, there must be a control group, so we made the same phone call to comparable professionals within the industry with one variation: a change in the superstar for whom we were purportedly placing the call. When the folks who make the magic realized they had the man who sang "It's Nice to Go Trav'ling" in *This Is Elvis* on the line, the cat who put the *rat* in Rat Pack—yes, *Joey Bishop*—the results were…uh, different.

	SLY STALLONE	JOEY BISHOP
AGENTS	Lucy Aceto, William Morris agent. Call-back time (despite her being home ill): 0:28:03	Sue Mengers, William Morris superagent. Call-back time: 0:38:15 (asked, "Can you tell me who he is?")
PRODUCERS	Don Simpson, producer (*Beverly Hills Cop*, *Top Gun*). Call-back time: 0:02:00	Joe Papp, Public Theater producer. Call-back time (as SPY went to press): 89 days
FELLOW STARS	Carrie Fisher, actress. Call-back time: immediately	Bob Hope, TV-special entrepreneur. Call-back time: 0:02:01
STATESMEN	Sonny Bono, mayor of Palm Springs. Call-back time: 0:01:05	Ed Koch, mayor of New York. Call-back time (after a City Hall underling said, "The mayor does want to speak to him"): 0:01:45
RENAISSANCE MEN	Michael Mann, executive producer (*Miami Vice*, *Crime Story*). Call-back time: 0:48:50	Bobby Zarem, preternaturally energetic publicist. Call-back time (as SPY went to press): 89 days
TALK SHOW HOSTS	Geraldo Rivera, greasy, gap-toothed host of *Geraldo*. Call-back time: 0:01:15	Regis Philbin, host of *The Morning Show*. Call-back time: 19:08:30
TALKING HEADS	Charles Redman, State Department spokesman. Call-back time: 1:16:55	Ted Koppel, *Nightline* anchor. Call-back time (as SPY went to press): 89 days
TOTAL CALL-BACK TIME	2 hours, 38 minutes, 8 seconds	267 days, 19 hours, 50 minutes, 31 seconds

—*John Brodie*

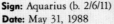

"Mr. Stallone on the line…," an ur-*Spy* prank, September 1988

THE HARDEST PART WAS ADMITTING IT WAS SO DAMN popular. After that it was but a short, opportunistic step to justifying it as a full-length feature—as a cover. ✂ It—the "Separated at Birth?" photo featurette that has appeared in every issue of SPY for the past year—is, we've come to realize, our golden-egg-laying goose, and this month we aim not to strangle but to force-feed it, fatten it up and put it on display. After all, we know enough not to look a gift horse in the mouth. Likewise, we comprehend in toto precisely what our bread and butter is. When the 2-millionth reader approached a member of our staff at a party with the words "You work at SPY? I have a *great* 'Separated at Birth?' for you," we understood all too well that the tide couldn't be turned and public opinion couldn't be—uh-oh! —*flown in the face of*. So we scrapped the substantive, socially significant cover story we had planned and instead filled lots of editorial space normally given over to fine, lapidary prose with photos of—get this—people who look like people other than themselves. It's incredible, but they do. ✂ Historically, "Separated at Birth?" has worked best when the enforced twinning has resonated in ways beyond mere physical appearance. The element of surprise is dear to us. Caspar Weinberger and Jean Cocteau (December 1986) had probably never appeared in the same sentence together, yet there they were, pictured side by side in SPY—instant siblings. The same could be said of the Carson McCullers–Bob Geldof pairing (March 1987), which had the added twist of crossed sexes—as did William Casey–Eleanor Roosevelt (May 1987). Always open to experimentation, we've

Separated at Birth?

even worked with primates (Clint Eastwood and a baboon, March 1987) and Disney characters (Laurence Tisch and a *cartoon* dwarf, Dopey, last month). ✂ That last sentence raises the question of intentions: any subliminal messages, you wonder, in our selections? Mostly it's that we think they look alike. At least, that's our story. ✂ And how was this "Separated at Birth?" extravaganza put together? We could tell you that technicians at the SPY Laboratories fiddled for months with developing fluid and infrared lights and calipers to produce the results before you, or that it was really *you*, the *readers*, without whom we are *nothing*, who made it all possible. But in fact the whole package is, incredibly, the result of an open call for look-alikes. Two remarkable candid photos from a wild, wacky "Separated at Birth?" gala evening are included here: jolly Carl Bernstein and Howdy Doody re-create their joint audition amid a crush of reporters, and pols D'Amato and Cuomo do the mirror scene from *Duck Soup*. ✂ So we are being *not the least bit* condescending when we say we have a feeling you'll enjoy this "Separated at Birth?" feature. One last thing: *all rights reserved*, out there. Unless you look like no one else in the world, we own you. ≫→

The Unabridged Edition

Soon-to-be-post-presidential-candidate Bruce Babbitt

&

Washington Post chairman Katharine Graham?

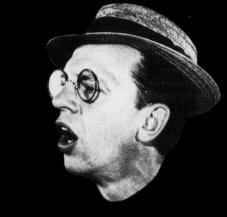

Erstwhile Rolling Stone Mick Jagger

&

Don Knotts as the Incredible Mr. Limpet?

Gorgeous lalapalooza Tammy Faye Bakker

&

an Ewok?

It wasn't just that they looked "alike," of course—it was the eyes, the expression, the angle of the head, and whenever possible some more profound resonance as well.

Photo editor Nicki Gostin: "I'm still good at it. I can look at someone and immediately tell them who they look like. It's like learning the violin, it never goes away."

TV oddity Jim Bakker . . .

and TV oddity
Herve Villechaize?

Pizza Hut spokesman
Rich Hall . . .

and onetime hoofer
Buddy Ebsen?

The Duchess of York . . .

and former *Brady Bunch*
servant Ann B. Davis?

Nose flesh amputee
Marlo Thomas . . .

and former black person
Michael Jackson?

Mrs. Oliver North . . .

and her husband's friend
General Richard Secord?

Iranscam witness
William B. O'Boyle . . .

and Canadian personality
Dan Aykroyd?

In-need-of-a-comeback
Paul McCartney . . .

and weirdly-enjoying-a-
comeback Angela Lansbury?

Jowly has-been novelist
Bret Easton Ellis . . .

and jowly has-been
Richard M. Nixon?

SEPARATED AT BIRTH?

Prodigious writer
John Updike . . .

and litigious writer
Renata Adler?

SPY-loving comedian
Jay Leno . . .

and *Life of Riley* star
William Bendix?

Israeli violinist
Itzhak Perlman . . .

and non-Israeli guitarist
Roy Clark?

Dead comedienne
Totie Fields . . .

and rock vulgarian
Ozzy Osbourne?

Moment by Moment star
Lily Tomlin . . .

and the young John Huston?

Golddigger–arts patroness
Gayfryd Steinberg . . .

and Mormon entertainer
Marie Osmond?

Former Minister of War
Caspar Weinberger . . .

and party girl
Kitty Carlisle Hart?

Actress JoBeth Williams . . .

and billionaire adulterer
Sid Bass?

SEPARATED AT BIRTH?

Steely political footnote
Geraldine Ferraro . . .

and once-important pop star
David Bowie?

Tetchy actor of his gen-
eration Robert De Niro . . .

and tetchy actor of *his*
generation Laurence Olivier?

Yale University president
Benno C. Schmidt Jr. . . .

and Ernie from
My Three Sons?

Current trivia answer
Redd Foxx . . .

and future trivia answer
Robert Bork?

Former comedian
Mel Brooks . . .

and arbitrageur Carl Icahn?

Walter (trusted by 1960s
adults) Cronkite . . .

and Captain (trusted by 1960s
kids) Kangaroo?

Tina Turner . . .

and Edward G. Robinson?

Mullah-Iranian-madman
Sayyed Ali Khamenei . . .

and writer-director-
impregnator Woody Allen?

Choreographer
Martha Graham . . .

and Yerosha, the monkey
cosmonaut?

Widow-comedienne
Joan Rivers . . .

and . . . ?

Demimonde fixture
Carmen d'Alessio . . .

and Dr. Zaius of
Planet of the Apes?

Mets outfielder
Darryl Strawberry . . .

and Dino?

TRIPLETS

SEPARATED

AT BIRTH?

Actor-writer Peter
Ustinov . . .

and furniture designer
Philippe Starck . . .

and crockery destroyer
Julian Schnabel?

Julio Iglesias . . .

and Francesco Scavullo . . .

and the Phantom of the Opera?

Masterful film director Martin Scorsese . . .

and high-strung philosopher Charles Manson?

Emilio Estevez . . .

and Martin Sheen?

Kurt (*Elvis*) Russell . . .

and real killer Charles (*Badlands*) Starkweather?

David Johansen . . .

and Buster Poindexter?

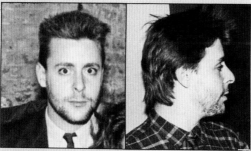

Insufferable punk actor Judd Nelson . . .

Patty (*The Patty Duke Show*) . . .

and Cathy (*The Patty Duke Show*)?

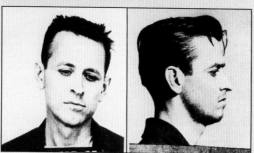

and Martin Luther King Jr. assassin James Earl Ray?

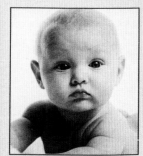

Winston Churchill . . .

and a baby? ③

PHOTO RESEARCH BY AMY STARK   *Research assistants: Susan Buttenwieser, Susan Dudenhoeffer, Blake Eskin, Bob Mack, Julie Mihaly*

BEST OF THE MAIL: PART ONE

Spy's letters pages were intensely interactive. After a while, it felt as if readers were trying out for the Mailroom Column. Several of them, notably Jason de Menil and David Halbfinger (see page 215), got multiple call-backs.

DEAR EDITORS **N**o doubt about it, you all are going to be stuck with a hit on your hands instead of the egg on the face that some were hopefully predicting.
Malcolm S. Forbes,
New York

December 1986

DEAR EDITORS **R**egarding your "New Meese Bombshell" [by Jack Hitt, May]: I strongly object to your description of Judge Robert H. Bork having been rejected for the Supreme Court because of his "racist record in scholarly writings." His writings have never been racist. Indeed, his record is one of solid opposition to racism and discrimination.

The article to which you refer was published in *The New Republic* in 1963 in opposition to the public-accommodations provisions of the Civil Rights Act of 1964, not to the act itself. Nevertheless, in 1973 Bork publicly modified those views.

In your effort to be clever, you have grossly misrepresented the record of a distinguished lawyer, scholar and jurist, and a man without a single ounce of prejudice in his body. You demean your own publication by such comment. It reminded me of an old phrase of political worth—it might help you in the publication field: "You lose ground when you throw mud."
Alan K. Simpson
United States Senate
Washington, D.C.

November 1988

DEAR EDITORS **P**lease cancel this pseudo-tongue-in-cheek, supposedly impish piece of drivel.
Louisa Carol DePaola
Kew Gardens, New York

DEAR EDITORS **I**'m sorry to say that I do not care for your magazine. It is not only overpriced, it is also boring.
Angela T. Pinelli
Hillsborough, New Jersey

February 1987

From the SPY mailroom: In the two and a half years this column has been appearing, no one has ever asked us exactly how it's put together. Well, we'll tell you. First we come up with an opening gimmick; you are enduring one right now. Then we weed out the cards and letters that are obviously nothing more than auditions for publication— wacky requests, irrelevant information, private correspondence, petty complaints; these are what we choose to work with. Finally, we set aside a generous portion of the column for our readers to engage in a wide-ranging debate on what *nubbin* really means.

There are many exceptions to the rule, of course, but this particular column will for the most part follow that pattern. With one special bonus: Bill Cosby has written us.

A William H. Cosby Jr. of Manhattan has returned a recent SPY subscription solicitation sent unwittingly to him— returned it *unopened*, despite the envelope's attention-grabbing promise that a FREE Gorby Lick 'n' Stick Birthmark was inside. Scrawled across the envelope: "NO!!! This is funnier than anything you've done with my name in it. Bill Cosby." By "this," we assume Mr. Cosby means our attempt to sell him a subscription. Of course, of course— he must already *have* one. Are our faces red!

Cos's was not the only Gorby Lick 'n'

January 1990

New York

The Wrong Man

I repudiate the allegation in your September Tammany Hall column that I passed on to reporters "the Dinkins love letters." The facts are— facts which your magazine could have learned had anyone there been journalist enough to speak with me about the allegation—that I was aware of the letters and strongly rejected the idea of using them for campaign purposes. The liberal who delivered the letters to the reporter did so against my will. Several well-known liberals and sons of well-known liberals know that I was against using the letters

and did everything in my power to stop their use.

Your suggestion that I passed on the letters is irresponsible and factually incorrect in every significant respect.
Roger Ailes
New York

Bryn More

"Till Death—or Irreconcilable Differences—Do Us Part" [by Aimée Bell, September] featured one bride from my high school class; one from my college class, with her maid of honor from the same class; and one who was the cousin of our college president. Reading it was sort of like attending a mini-reunion through a one-way mirror. Please run a monthly department about other people I have known.
Marcia Ringel
Class of 1964, Columbia High
School, Maplewood, New Jersey
Class of 1968, Bryn Mawr
College
Ridgewood, New Jersey

December 1991

4

"Don't Be Such a Typesetter— This Is the Way We Do It"

Selling, Producing, Promoting—and Paying for—*Spy*

Spy was not about a standard professional ad sale. I'd make cold calls and say, "I'm from Spy *magazine," and hear, "That an espionage magazine? What the heck is that?"*

—ANNE KREAMER

SPY'S FIRST ISSUE had 26 pages of paid advertising; the second had 13. Anne Kreamer, who had introduced Graydon and (her husband) Kurt to Tom Phillips, had sold *Sesame Street* and other Children's Television Workshop programs internationally. After issue number two she said to Tom, "I don't know whether I can sell advertising or not, but let me see if I can do it." She quit her job to join *Spy*—and did sell, magnificently, by focusing on business owners rather than their ad agencies and by hiring "quirky individuals" rather than professional ad-sales types. Many of the people who sold ads for *Spy* came from outside the business world, and when they left *Spy* they often left business as well. It was an unusual approach—but *Spy* was an unusual sale. Kreamer, *Spy*'s ad sales and later marketing director until she left the magazine in 1990, had her work cut out for her.

"It was incredibly hard. We were all in that tiny little space, two of us at each desk, going out making cold calls and trying to get business for this thing that naturally antagonized every single possible advertising base that we could hope to find," she says. "It was like psychology. 'Which of these editorial pieces would they most get and find amusing?' And we weren't very smart in the beginning. We didn't think about positioning ads against the *Times* column and Separated at Birth? and things like that. But the people who were on the sales staff *loved* the magazine. So the ideas that came out were naturally the ones that were appropriate."

Adam Dolgins, who started in promotion—"and 'circulation,' which involved going around to newsstands and asking them to move *Spy* away from *Soldier of Fortune* and put it next to something else"—also sold ads for a time. "Because I was passionate about *Spy*, I probably *wasn't* the best salesperson," he says. "People either got it, and loved it, and were going to champion it at their particular company—or they didn't. And whenever I ran up against somebody who didn't, I just said fuck it, and left."

Opposite: Rupert Murdoch on the mockup of the May 1987 cover; he did not pose for us.

_f_

THE **F**INE PRINT

by Jamie Malanowski

I LOST IT ON THE BMT

Down in the bowels of the Transit Authority's headquarters in Brooklyn is the TA's Lost Property Unit. Last year something in the neighborhood of 9,171 objects were turned in by conductors, police officers and honest citizens. The Lost Property office tries to contact the owners and holds on to an object for six months in case someone claims it. In 1986 about 2,500 items were returned to their owners.

Among the items currently waiting to be claimed are an organ, a pair of skis, about 10 bicycles, 1 gas mask, 2 artificial legs, an artificial arm, 5 wigs, a pair of crutches, an ax, an Indian saber, an épée, a fuel injector, some rosary beads, approximately 15 pairs of false teeth, 7 canes, 1 Hulk Hogan doll, 1 Cabbage Patch Kid, 1 Cabbage Patch Kid Preemie, a blender, about a dozen tennis rackets, assorted basketballs, several bowling balls, a hair dryer, a sledgehammer, a garden hose, a violin, a guitar, a clarinet, a set of drums, about 15 35mm cameras, an ancient Brownie camera, about 7 beepers, dozens of Walkmans, about 20 TV sets, lots of jewelry, a 1913 Barber U.S. dime valued at $115, a 1912 Liberty Head nickel valued at $145, about 75 watches, a Mark Cross pen, a copy of Songs of the African Veldt _and a moped._

(continued)

Although it was born of necessity and not choice, _Spy_'s communal atmosphere—with editorial and advertising cheek by jowl, not on separate floors as is the case at most magazines—was, as Kreamer sees it, "mind-blowingly great, because whenever a big piece of business would come in, the entire office would actually celebrate. Everybody understood that getting the Guess Jeans advertising meant that writers would get paid."

By the beginning of _Spy_'s second year, advertising had taken off—issues included not just regulars like Absolut and Guess but all manner of liquor, fashion, cigarette, media, entertainment, and electronics ads.

Another _Spy_ innovation, then quasi-taboo at respectable periodicals, was the advertorial, particularly those sponsored by J&B Scotch. "We mocked the brand and created polls and used advertisers to fund editorial ideas that we didn't have the money to do," Kreamer says.

"The advertorials are still just amazing," says Kurt. "You know, 10 years before any _Daily Show_ existed, we were doing funny but real national political polls, using pollsters who became the Clintons' and Bloomberg's pollsters."

The _Spy_/J&B advertorials would never get more attention than they did in December 1987, when a jokey, hypothetical political calendar I had written anonymously and in haste months earlier (it appeared in the November issue) made the off-the-wall prediction that on December 15, Gary Hart, who had already dropped out of the presidential race after his sex scandal, would re-enter the contest. In fact, he did—and, uncannily, on that very date. My colleague Caldwell Davis came over, looked me in the eye, and said, "Okay, I just want to know: _Will I marry, and when?_" The fluke prediction was reported by Peter Jennings on ABC's _World News Tonight,_ and also picked up by NBC and NPR, among others. It was starting to feel as if we couldn't do anything, however meaningless, without causing a stir.

The June issue is lost—Federal Express can't find it.
—Journal entry, May 4, 1987

THE _ONLY_ JUNE ISSUE—that is, the original set of boards—vanished on its way to the printer.

"It was gone, and of course it wasn't simply, 'Let's just print it out again,'" says Adam Dolgins. "It had to all get pasted back up, which seems absurd. How could that be?"

Campaign

1987

October 28 Republican debate (*Firing Line*). Headmaster William F. Buckley Jr. puts them through their paces, whacks knuckles, if gently.

December 1 Democratic and Republican debate (Washington). Candidates form two rows and shake hands while the PA system plays "Getting to Know You."

December 15 Confessed adulterer Gary Hart reenters race "for the good of the nation."

December 21 Confessed adulterer Gary Hart withdraws, saying he wants to spend Christmas with his family.

1988

January 11 Mario Cuomo's coy professions of noncandidacy, a monthly event during 1987, become biweekly.

January 15 Democratic debate

From the "J&B/Spy Campaign Manual,"
November 1987

THE FIRST 20 SENTENCES OF THE VICE PRESIDENT OF THE UNITED STATES'S SPEECH ACCEPTING THE REPUBLICAN NOMINATION FOR PRESIDENT OF THE UNITED STATES

"Thank you. Thank you very, very much. Thank you so much. Thank you so very much. Thank you very, very much. Thank you all. Thank you, ladies and gentlemen. Thank you very, very much. Thank you. Thank you all very much. Thank you so much. Thank you. Thank you, ladies and gentlemen. Thank you very, very much. Thank you. Thank you all very, very much. Thank you. Thank you. Thank you, ladies and gentlemen. Thank you very, very much."

November 1988

"It wasn't on computer," says Alex Isley, *Spy*'s art director for its first two years. "It ended up in Virginia sitting beside some secretary's desk for four or five days. We were already in the middle of re-creating it—we had to remake it from scratch, all the original photos were in that package."

"In so many ways talking about *Spy* is, as Graydon says, like talking about the nineteenth century," says Kurt.

"I remember our typesetter worked in one of those grim offices downtown," says *Spy* production manager Geoff Reiss. "And the guy who ran it and I were arguing over money, because Tom was unhappy with what we were paying—it was like $3,000 an issue—and the guy pulled out this stack of galleys and showed me what it was like to go through five or six passes at a story: 'I don't know if you guys appreciate that this is the hardest thing we do. You keep making all these changes—*nobody* makes all these changes.' And I said, 'Don't be such a typesetter. This is the way our guys do it.'"

At the office, the editorial staff gradually got more computers, though Tom was known to balk on such grounds as *Well, even if we had another computer, there's no table to put it on*. Adam Dolgins

still remembers "the excitement and confusion when the fax machine—the kind with the wet paper—came in. You know, 'How does it work?'"

Equally confusing was the arrival at the office, around the same time, of general partner–cum–"publishing director" Steve Schragis. Schragis was a decent guy, but in the context of *Spy*'s clubby, us-against-them atmosphere, he was an interloper who would have to prove himself in order to have any hope of belonging. And, by his own admission years later, he was inexperienced and a little naive about how exactly that might happen.

He was the largest investor, so he wanted to weigh in on the editorial content of the magazine—anathema at most publications, but especially at one whose very raison d'être was to do exactly as it pleased, without meddling from the money people. Tom, for instance, stayed *way* out of editorial matters.* It didn't help that to accommodate Schragis's occasional visits to the office, a workspace would have to be created for him, so there was

---

*Amazingly, Tom never asked us to pull a punch. He was an absolute enthusiast for the full-bore, hell-bent *Spy* editorial approach. —Eds.

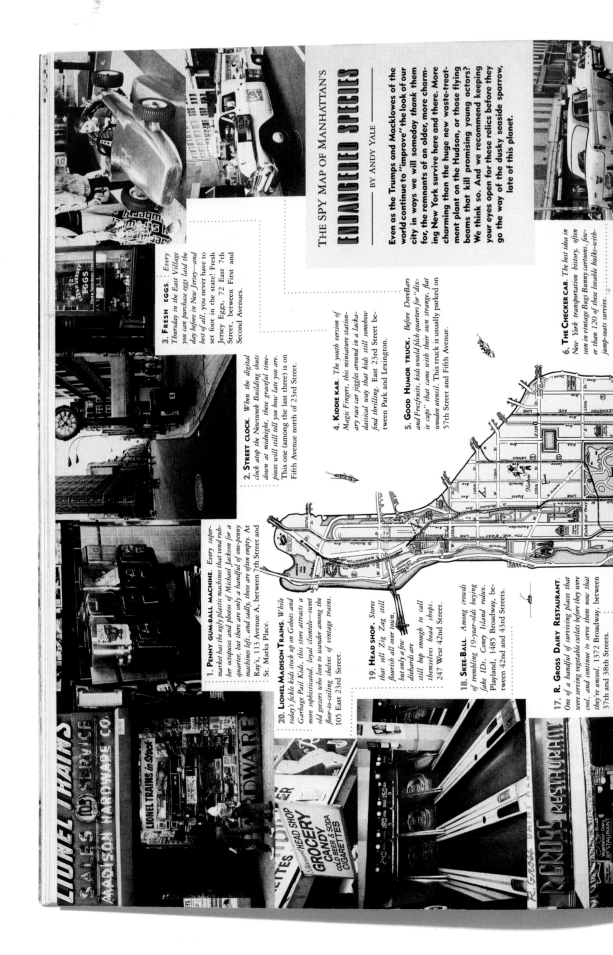

THE SPY MAP OF MANHATTAN'S

ENDANGERED SPECIES

BY ANDY YALE

Even as the Trumps and Macklowes of the world continue to "improve" the look of our city in ways we will someday thank them for, the remnants of an older, more charming New York survive here and there. More charming than the huge new waste-treatment plant on the Hudson, or those flying beams that kill promising young actors? We think so. And we recommend keeping your eyes open for these relics before they go the way of the dusky seaside sparrow, late of this planet.

1. PENNY GUM-BALL MACHINE. Every supermarket has the ugly plastic machines that vend rubber octopuses and photos of Michael Jackson for a quarter, but there are only a handful of one-penny machines left, and sadly, these are often empty. At Ray's, 113 Avenue A, between 7th Street and St. Marks Place.

2. STREET CLOCK. When the digital clock atop the Newsweek Building shuts down at midnight, these graceful timepieces will still tell you how late you are. This one (among the last three) is on Fifth Avenue north of 23rd Street.

3. FRESH EGGS. Every Thursday in the East Village you can purchase eggs laid the day before in New Jersey—and best of all, you never have to set foot in the state! Fresh Jersey Eggs, 72 East 7th Street, between First and Second Avenues.

4. KIDDIE KAR. The youth version of Magic Fingers, this miniature stationary race car jiggles around in a lackadaisical way that kids still somehow find thrilling. East 23rd Street between Park and Lexington.

5. GOOD HUMOR TRUCK. Before DoveBars and Frozfruits, kids would filch quarters for "dixie cups" that came with their own strange, flat wooden utensil. This truck is usually parked on 57th Street and Fifth Avenue.

6. THE CHECKER CAB. The best idea in New York transportation history, often seen in vintage Bugs Bunny cartoons, fewer than 120 of these lovable hulks—with jump-seats survive.

17. R. GROSS DAIRY RESTAURANT. One of a handful of surviving places that were serving vegetable cutlets before they were cool, and continue to serve them now that they're uncool. 1372 Broadway, between 37th and 38th Streets.

18. SKEE-BALL. Among crowds of trembling 19-year-olds buying fake IDs, Coney Island redux. Playland, 1485 Broadway, between 42nd and 43rd Streets.

19. HEAD SHOP. Stores that sell Zig Zag still flourish all over town, but only a few diehards are still hep enough to call themselves bead shops. 247 West 42nd Street.

20. LIONEL MADISON TRAINS. While today's fickle kids stock up on Gobots and Garbage Pail Kids, this store attracts a more sophisticated, loyal clientele—sweet old geezers who love to wander among the floor-to-ceiling shelves of vintage trains. 105 East 23rd Street.

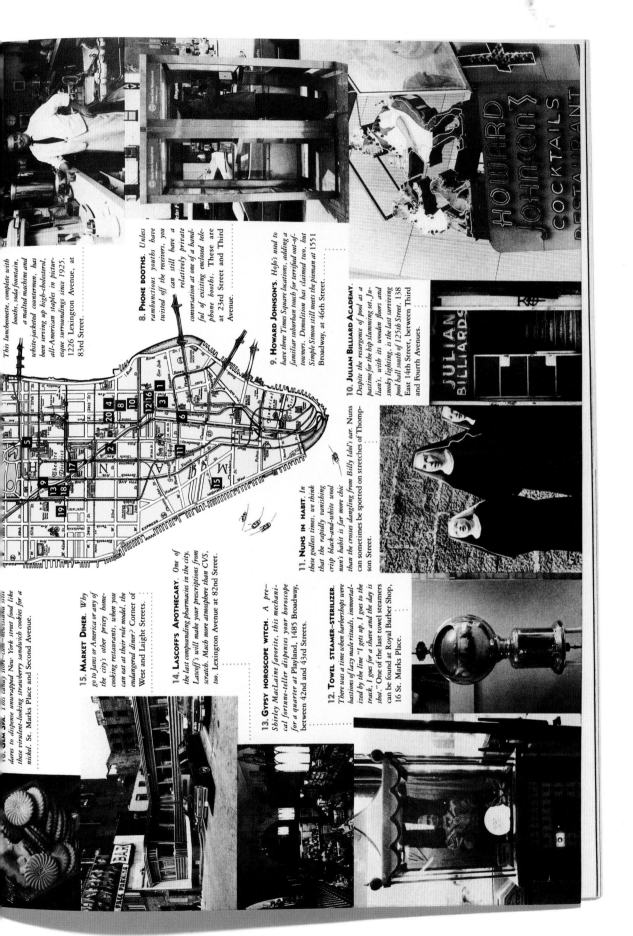

16. SEM SPA. *This candy store—little-known and still dares to dispense unwrapped New York street food like these virulent-looking strawberry sandwich cookies for a nickel. St. Marks Place and Second Avenue.*

This luncheonette, complete with booths, soda fountain, a malted machine and white-jacketed countermen, has been serving up high-cholesterol, all-American staples in picturesque surroundings since 1925. 1226 Lexington Avenue, at 83rd Street.

8. PHONE BOOTHS. *Unless rambunctious youths have twisted off the receivers, you can still have a relatively private conversation at one of a handful of exciting enclosed telephone booths. These are at 23rd Street and Third Avenue.*

9. HOWARD JOHNSON'S. *Hojo's used to have three Times Square locations, adding a familiar suburban touch for terrified out-of-towners. Demolition has claimed two, but Simple Simon still meets the fireman at 1551 Broadway, at 46th Street.*

10. JULIAN BILLIARD ACADEMY. *Despite the resurgence of pool as a pastime for the hip slumming set, Julian's, with its wooden floors and smoky lighting, is the last surviving pool hall south of 125th Street. 138 East 14th Street, between Third and Fourth Avenues.*

11. NUNS IN HABIT. *In these godless times, we think that the rapidly vanishing crisp black-and-white wool nun's habit is far more chic than the crosses dangling from Billy Idol's ear. Nuns can sometimes be spotted on stretches of Thompson Street.*

15. MARKET DINER. *Why go to Jams or America or any of the city's other pricey home-cooking restaurants, when you can eat at their role model, the endangered diner? Corner of West and Laight Streets.*

14. LASCOFF'S APOTHECARY. *One of the last compounding pharmacies in the city, Lascoff's will make your prescriptions from scratch. Much more atmosphere than CVS, too. Lexington Avenue at 82nd Street.*

13. GYPSY HOROSCOPE WITCH. *A pre-Shirley MacLaine favorite, this mechanical fortune-teller dispenses your horoscope for a quarter at Playland, 1485 Broadway, between 42nd and 43rd Streets.*

12. TOWEL STEAMER-STERILIZER. *There was a time when barbershops were bastions of lazy male rituals, immortalized by the line "I gets up, I goes to the track, I goes for a shave and the day is shot." One of the last towel steamers can be found at Royal Barber Shop, 16 St. Marks Place.*

Still standing nineteen years later: 2, 7, 14, 16 (the cookies are gone), September 1987

auᴛomoᴛive indusᴛry.   —Aavantage, December 1, 1989
                                              — Don Steinberg

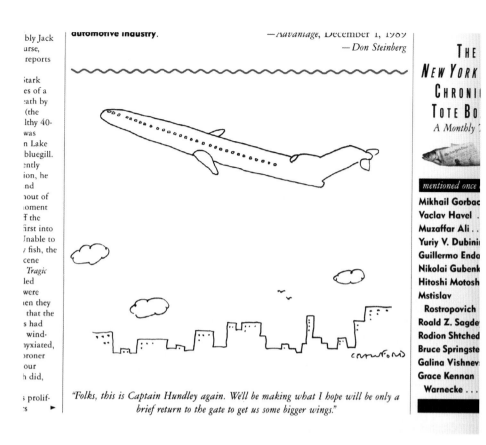

bly Jack
urse,
reports

itark
es of a
ath by
(the
lthy 40-
was
n Lake
bluegill.
ently
ion, he
nd
nout of
noment
f the
iirst into
Unable to
/ fish, the
cene
Tragic
led
were
ien they
that the
s had
wind-
nyxiated,
oroner
our
h did,

s prolif-
's   ►

"Folks, this is Captain Hundley again. We'll be making what I hope will be only a brief return to the gate to get us some bigger wings."

June 1990

more doubling-up of desks, the fact-checking department was moved into the conference room, and meetings were bumped upstairs to the Puck roof in warmer weather, or, on inclement days, to a storage room. Schragis found himself in an impossible situation, and though everyone tried to behave, his presence brought out an institutional cruel streak. "It was like having a stepparent," one colleague remembers. "We were so tightly knit, and then *he* came in."

"I had an informal role," Schragis says now. "I knew something about advertising. I had some leads. I felt I had something to offer as far as what articles, what takes, what way of phrasing things would in fact carry out the mission of the business plan. I had a lot of ideas. I wanted to participate editorially. So if you're participating in editorial, and you're participating in business, and you're a limited partner, you get a bit of a mess."

"My first real sense of Schragis was when we did the 'Nazi Hunt' story," says Susan Morrison, referring to Phil Weiss's account of Rupert Murdoch's screwball pursuit of Josef Mengele in South

America in the pages of the *New York Post.* (Weiss, who did several splendid features for *Spy,* including a profile of then–U.S. Attorney Rudolph Giuliani called "The Toughest Weenie in America" and a classic undercover piece on California's secretive Bohemian Grove [see pages 198–214], calls the May 1987 Mengele story his favorite.) Morrison continues: "I was so proud of it, so happy with it, and Alex Isley had designed a beautiful cover with the headline 'Nazis! Nazis! Nazis!'—it was like *The Producers.* And I remember Steve coming in and literally stamping his feet like a six-year-old: 'We can't do this! The Holocaust!' So we went with 'Nazi Hunt!' instead." (Though we were tempted by Eric Kaplan's coverline suggestion: *POST* BIG TO MENGY: PHONE HOME!)

"It was the first time at *Spy* where someone said, *You can't do this,*" says Morrison. "It was an important development—nobody knew how to respond. And we caved. It was horrible."

Around that time Kaplan wrote a joke involving the rock promoter Don Kirschner and the Banana Splits and, he remembers, "Steve said, 'I don't think you should compare Don Kirschner to the Banana Splits.' And somebody said to me, 'This guy just gave millions of dollars to the magazine, and all he's getting out of it is being able to say to people like you that Don Kirschner is different from the Banana Splits.'"

Schragis also wanted to go to editorial meetings but, somehow, the meetings would always get rescheduled. "It's hard, I see that more now than I did then," he says. "'Cause meetings tend to get called, 'Okay, let's get together in an hour.' So very often I was there Monday, and I wished I'd been there the following Friday."

"It was really uncomfortable," remembers Geoff Reiss. "Steve was on salary on a par with what Kurt and Graydon and Tom were getting paid, as the 'publishing director.' One day Tom wasn't around and I needed Kurt to sign Steve's check, and it was the tensest moment I ever had with Kurt. He basically said, 'Don't ever ask me to sign this again.' Tom did a really good job of keeping Steve at arm's length from those guys."

Schragis is diplomatic about it all today. "At times I was frustrated by Graydon, at times I was frustrated by Kurt," he allows. "But other times they were quite gracious to me."

The bottom line is, well, the bottom line: *Spy* would not have survived its early years without Schragis's investment. For that, and for his undeniable enthusiasm for the magazine, he was a crucial part of the *Spy* mix.

**Mockup (above)
and final cover,
May 1987**

**Pulling
people's levers:
"Participating
Plutocracy,"
from
The Fine Print,
November 1987**

f THE *F*INE PRINT E x t r a !   *Naked City*

PARTICIPATORY PLUTOCRACY: HOW OFTEN THE RICH AND FAMOUS VOTE

Voting is a right routinely denied much of the world's population, but here in America, the franchise can be enjoyed by every citizen over 18. Of course, not everyone exercises that right, including many of those to whom the American way of life has been kindest. Herewith, a sample of prominent New Yorkers who are registered to vote—and a ten-year record of their attendance at the polls.*

NAME	PARTY	NUMBER OF ELECTIONS ELIGIBLE TO VOTE IN	NUMBER VOTED IN	PERCENTAGE	NAME	PARTY	NUMBER OF ELECTIONS ELIGIBLE TO VOTE IN	NUMBER VOTED IN	PERCENTAGE
Victor Navasky	Democrat	14	14	100	Arthur O. Sulzberger Jr.	Democrat	12	6	50.0
Lillian Ross	—	9	9	100	I. M. Pei	—	6	3	50.0
Arthur Schlesinger Jr.	Democrat	8	8	100	Susan Sarandon	Democrat	6	3	50.0
Jimmy Breslin	Democrat	5	5	100	Jules Feiffer	Democrat	13	6	46.3
Griffin Dunne	Democrat	2	2	100	Steven Ross,	Democrat	13	6	46.3
John Brademas	Democrat	9	8	88.9	Warner Communications				
Osborn Elliott	—	9	8	88.9	Nora Ephron	Democrat	11	5	45.5
John V. Lindsay	Democrat	9	8	88.9	Harry Helmsley	Republican	12	5	41.6
Anne Ford Scarborough	—	9	8	88.9	James Atlas,	Democrat	5	2	40.0
John Guare,	Democrat	16	14	87.5	author				
playwright					Marshall Brickman	Democrat	5	2	40.0
Patricia Lawford	Democrat	8	7	87.5	Dustin Hoffman	Democrat	5	2	40.0
Vartan Gregorian,	Democrat	5	4	80.0	Richard Avedon	—	3	1	33.3
N.Y. Public Library					William Hurt	—	3	1	33.3
Tom Brokaw	—	9	7	77.8	Susan Seidelman	—	3	1	33.3
Jerome Robbins	—	9	7	77.8	Raul Julia	—	6	2	33.3
Louis Auchincloss	Republican	12	9	75.0	Elie Wiesel	Liberal	6	2	33.3
Joey Adams	—	8	6	75.0	Alice Mason,	Democrat	12	4	33.3
Sydney Gruson	Democrat	15	11	73.3	realtor				
Jill Krementz	Democrat	20	14	70.0	Anne Jackson	Democrat	19	5	26.3
Arthur Liman	Democrat	20	14	70.0	Stephen Sondheim	Democrat	12	3	25.0
Kurt Vonnegut	Democrat	20	14	70.0	Ed Kosner,	Democrat	14	3	21.4
Frank Rich	Democrat	13	9	69.2	editor				
Eli Wallach	—	9	6	66.7	Carly Simon	Democrat	5	1	20.0
Jerome Zipkin,	—	9	6	66.7	Treat Williams	Democrat	5	1	20.0
rich hanger-on					Hal Prince	Democrat	10	2	20.0
Vincent Canby	Democrat	6	4	66.7	George Plimpton	Democrat	20	4	20.0
David Halberstam	—	6	4	66.7	Diane Keaton	Democrat	11	2	18.2
Paul Goldberger,	Democrat	11	7	63.6	Isaac Stern	Democrat	11	2	18.2
architecture critic					Wallace Shawn	Democrat	12	2	16.7
Thomas Hoving	Republican	8	5	62.5	Itzhak Perlman	Democrat	13	2	15.4
Pete Peterson,	Republican	8	5	62.5	Mortimer Zuckerman	Democrat	7	1	14.3
banker					Sydney Biddle Barrows	Republican	1	0	0
Frances FitzGerald,	Democrat	20	12	60.0	Rupert Murdoch	—	1	0	0
author					Billie Joan King	—	3	0	0
Cindy Adams	Republican	12	7	58.3	Woody Allen	Democrat	4	0	0
Joan Ganz Cooney,	Democrat	12	7	58.3	Roy Scheider	Democrat	4	0	0
TV executive					Herb Schmertz,	Democrat	4	0	0
Al Franken	Democrat	19	11	57.8	corporate PR man				
Harry Belafonte	Democrat	14	8	57.1	Barbara Howar	Democrat	5	0	0

Of the 68 people listed, 49 were eligible to vote in the last two mayoral elections. Fifteen of those missed either the 1981 or 1985 mayoral election, and 28 missed both—further evidence that Mayor Koch rules less with the support than with the numb consent of the people.

Voters can be suspended from the rolls because of nonparticipation. Harry Helmsley has been suspended and reinstated once, George Plimpton twice. Plimpton, in fact, has voted only five times since 1972.

The nine naturalized citizens on the list—Stern, Perlman, Zuckerman, Murdoch, Wiesel, Pei, Gregorian, Gruson and Brickman—have a combined voting record of 39 percent (27 out of 69).

Rupert Murdoch registered under his given and less despotic name, Keith. As a result of spy's inquiry, a Board of Elections supervisor noted that Murdoch had failed to supply the ID number found on his naturalization papers, and the supervisor said he would notify Murdoch that his right to vote would be suspended until his documents were provided.

Woody Allen, Pete Peterson and Joan Ganz Cooney typed their registration forms. All others were filled out by hand.

Griffin Dunne took the trouble to vote by absentee ballot in the 1986 gubernatorial election. Jerry Zipkin absentee-voted in 1984, presumably for pal Nancy's husband, who has proved, appropriately, to be an absentee president.

Among the Timesmen on the list, Arthur Ochs Sulzberger has the poorest record—although his attendance has been perfect in general elections, he has skipped all primaries.

—*J.M.*

*Information taken from active records maintained by Board of Elections. Longtime voters may have portions of their records in storage. We used records from between 1976 and 1986. We did not count judicial elections, special elections, community school board elections or bond issue votes. Voters are currently removed from the rolls if they've missed voting for four consecutive years; previously, voters would be removed after two. If people have moved outside of Manhattan, they could be legally voting at their new residences, but they would still be regarded as eligible but not voting until removed from the rolls.

It's compact. It's synthetic. It's very qui

It's hard but may be rubbery to the touc

It's black or white or gray or silver.

It was designed by Germans or Italian

 or people who wish they were Germa

or Italian.

It's probably electronic, maybe digital.

It didn't exist when we were children.

Its quality is high – higher than we nee

It's not a necessity. It needs explainin

 *It was*

not cheap.

We felt a little silly and excited buying

We feel a little guilty and proud showing it of

IT'S YUPPIE

by Bruce Handy

PORN

And we can't help ourselves.

II YOU TAKE AN ACT of fellatio out of context by photographing it, then publish the photo in a magazine with a title like *Swallow My Leader* and sell it from the back rack of a dingy little newsstand, you invest the original act of fellatio with a lurid power it might not otherwise have had. Lacking any hint of the byplay of personalities, the picture becomes a mere symbol, a lightning rod for the cravings of its beholder.

That's pornography—the objectification of bodies.

Now imagine a teapot. It's been designed by a postmodern architect with a household name (well, in the *right* households). Handcrafted from the finest metals, it retails for $100 in hushed, spacious stores with industrial shelving and salesboys who style themselves after Edwardian fops. The teapot gleams. Its form reveals a charming playfulness, balanced by its underlying architectonic sobriety—*Hey, kind of like my personality,* you might wishfully think, gazing upon it. Or you might sigh and daydream . . . *TriBeCa, 5,000 square feet, a Fischl on the wall.* . . .

OUR LUST FOR FANTASY GADGETRY HAS ITS ROOTS IN 1950s AND 1960s CHILDHOODS— X-RAY SPEX, *MAN FROM U.N.C.L.E.* RADIOS AND PELLET GUNS

This teapot is no longer about boiling water. It's about being able to pay a lot of money for a teapot. It's a teapot that, once in your possession, reflects your obvious good taste. It's a teapot that seemingly shouts for all the world to hear, "Praise be to the god of *objets* that I am owned by someone with as developed a sense of style as YOUR NAME HERE."

Thrusting off the yoke of its original, dreary context as a utensil—sad cousin to tongs and strainers—the postmod teapot becomes instead a symbol, a lightning rod for the economic and class aspirations of its owner.

That's yuppie pornography—the objectification of objects.

HOW TO KNOW IT WHEN YOU SEE IT

Twenty Questions to Ask About an Object

Yuppie porn comes, of course, in a dizzying array of shapes, sizes and strains— hard-core and soft-core, nerd and Euro, high tech and *objet*, jock and preppy. But what if the expensive object under consideration is *not* yuppie porn at all? What if it's merely overpriced? Don't scoff: plutonium is expensive, but it isn't yuppie porn. How to tell the difference? Ask yourself the following questions. If the answer to any three is "yes," you're looking at yuppie porn and you may proceed accordingly.

I
Will the simple fact of owning it make me feel morally superior, even though it's not a book or a record?

II
Does it do something that at one point in my life never occurred to me needed to be done?

III
Is it not sold in Montana and the Southern Hemisphere?

IV
Did it win an award from Italians?

V
Is it imported?

VI
Is it imported from a northern European country or from northern Italy?

VII
Does it convert yen into deutsche marks?

VIII
Would Steve Jobs own it?

IX
Would David Byrne own it?

X
Is it in MoMA's design collection?

XI
Does it involve halogen?

XII
Would I look sharp if I used it and a cordless phone at the same time?

XIII
Is there no chance that my parents would own it?

XIV
If ten years ago I had time-traveled ten years into the future and seen myself buying it now, would I have been embarrassed?

XV
Do I want it because—oh, I don't know, because I just want to *go for it*?

XVI
Although it's really expensive, would it be out of place at Graceland?

XVII
Will I soon be bored with it except when my friends come over and I pretend that I use it all the time and it's really fun?

XVIII
Will it disconcert my cats?

XIX
Is it both advertised and mocked in SPY?

XX
Is it a climate-controlling air filter— humidifier?

—*B.H.*

GOD KNOWS

WE'VE ALL

FELT THOSE

EXQUISITE LITTLE

PANGS WHEN

CONFRONTED

WITH A

COMPACT-DISC

PLAYER

For the first time, conspicuous consumption is not vulgar.

Our lust for cool gadgetry has its roots in childhoods in the 1950s and '60s. And it is no coincidence that the magic high tech we yearned for back then—X-Ray Spex, James Bond's tricky devices, Napoleon Solo's *Man From U.N.C.L.E.* radios and pellet guns, the Minox miniature camera your friend's older brother had—all had sexual associations. For where was early yuppie porn show-cased and lovingly described? In *Playboy*, of course, alongside references to Hef's motorized circular bed and giant hi-fi sets.

Back then, adolescents of all ages swore up and down that they bought *Playboy* "for the *articles*—really." Today we buy yuppie porn not because of its low-down thrill, *no*, but because "it's so well designed and so well made." Sure.

On urban boulevards, and now even in suburban malls, the yuppie-porn stores prosper, their showrooms full of over-wrought luxuries, uptight leisure wares, appliances with variously inane and arcane applications. You've seen these stores: The Sharper Image, Hammacher Schlemmer, D. F. Sanders & Company, Dot Zero, S.E.E. Ltd. Maybe you've passed by and—just for one weak-kneed moment—thought about going in. Maybe you're an occasional customer. Maybe you get . . . *their catalogs*. No one is immune. Even tweedy Judge Bork look-alikes who sneer at the nouveau riche–ness of much yuppie porn get all gooey when strolling through the Museum of Modern Art's design collection—it gets you excited *and it's good for you too*. And God knows we've all felt those exquisite little pangs, that telltale, vaguely eroticized covetousness, when confronted with a compact-disc player.

Yeah, what's wrong with having nice things? challenges a chorus of bobbed, be-bowed, business-suited young women named Jennifer. At its most innocuous, yuppie pornography involves a keen, heightened level of appreciation, consumerism raised to a kind of art form (just as baseball is kind of like alfresco dance, and tractor pulls are kind of like agrarian opera). It's the idea that good design can be an expression of *you!*—a nearly King Jamesian creed in the hands of such essential yuppie-porn texts as *Metropolitan Home* and *House & Garden*. See my Krups espresso maker? I bought it! It's mine! Look at its Euro-

---

WHEN IS A STORE NOT A STORE?

YUPPIE-PORNOGRAPHY EMPORIUMS—are they stores, or are they something much more insidious? Just as the Puritans bound alleged witches and

plunged them into icy New England ponds to see whether or not they would drown, so did we seek the truth by using a simple test—how yuppie-porn mongers answered the following question: **What kind of a store are you?** Straight answers were not forthcoming. Judge the results for yourself.

A2Z

South Street Seaport

"We sell gadgets, all different **unique** items."

Brookstone Company

South Street Seaport and Herald Center

"We sell **unique** items."

Dapy

431 West Broadway

"A lot of fun products, **high-tech** items—it's very **unusual**. You have to see it to believe it."

SOINTU

20 East 69th Street

"We're a **design** store. **Decorative** accessories."

Hammacher Schlemmer

147 East 57th Street

"**Certain** gifts and appliances and electronics."

Museum Store The Museum of Modern Art

11 West 53rd Street

"We sell **design** things, **modern** stuff. Corkscrews that have a **modern design**."

THE SHARPER IMAGE

South Street Seaport

"We're a new **high-tech** product-type store. And also some **unusual** items."

D.F. SANDERS & CO.

386 West Broadway and 952 Madison Avenue

"Home furnishing, industrial **design**. "

STAR MAGIC

743 Broadway and 275 Amsterdam Avenue

"**Space-age** gift store. Crystals, books, **unique** stuff."

CONTROL GROUP

JIMMY'S HARDWARE

926 Columbus Avenue

"We're a hardware store. We sell hardware."

Herald Square

"What? We're a department store. Why do you ask?"

—*B.H.*

Design, *like* erotica,

can be a euphemism.

At its worst, yuppie pornography

is as exploitative and

programmatic as the real thing.

It knows what tempts you.

---

styling, we and the Jennifers implore, thinking we're baring our souls when we're simply making a scene, no different, really, from a hammy movie star returning to Off-Broadway for some Shakespeare. Self-flattering, perhaps, but harmless.

Design, like *erotica*, can be a euphemism. At its worst, yuppie pornography is as exploitative and programmatic as the real thing. It knows what tempts you. Like skin magazines, with their garter belts and stockings, yuppie porn features its own fetishistic trappings. Molded white plastic. Sleek, black matte finishes. Rubbery gray Flextel coatings. Chrome. Anodized aluminum. Digital readouts, and still more digital readouts—indeed, controls of cockpit complexity. Power surfaces, they fuel power fantasies.

Perhaps yuppie porn is an inevitable result of the rise of the affluent, self-indulgent generation that gives it its name. After all, smut nearly entered the cultural mainstream during the early-1970s heyday of the sexual revolution (ask anybody between the ages of 35 and 50 with highbrow pretensions whether they ever waited in line to see *Deep Throat* or *Behind the Green Door* or *Emmanuelle*; they did). And just as the first well-crafted aboveground smut was Scandinavian (*I Am Curious {Yellow}*), so were the prototypical yuppie-porn objects (Braun, BMW) imported from northern Europe. Today, as sex becomes a strictly procreative endeavor, with ancillary applications as an advertising tool, Americans are turning their appetites toward money and power—the very appetites the yuppie-pornographers prey on. Your typical professional male making 85 grand a year who buys himself a personal paper shredder (Hammacher Schlemmer, $229.50)

YOUR TYPICAL PROFESSIONAL MALE DOESN'T BUY A PERSONAL PAPER SHREDDER BECAUSE LAWRENCE WALSH HAS JUST SUBPOENAED HIS SHOPPING LIST. HE BUYS IT BECAUSE *IT* TURNS HIM ON

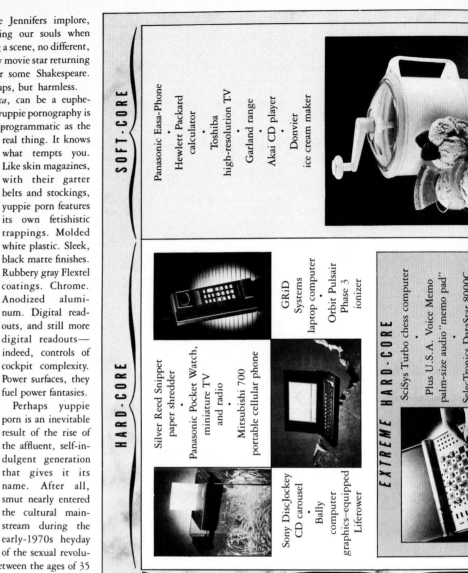

SOFT-CORE

Panasonic Easa-Phone
Hewlett Packard calculator
Toshiba high-resolution TV
Garland range
Akai CD player
Donvier ice cream maker

HARD-CORE

Silver Reed Snippet paper shredder
Panasonic Pocket Watch, miniature TV and radio
Mitsubishi 700 portable cellular phone
GRiD Systems laptop computer
Orbit Pulsair Phase 3 ionizer
Sony DiscJockey CD carousel
Bally computer graphics-equipped Liferower

EXTREME HARD-CORE

SciSys Turbo chess computer
Plus U.S.A. Voice Memo palm-size audio "memo pad"
SelecTronics DataStar 8000C

NERD

THE YUPPIE PORNOGRAPHY HALL OF FAME

A Connoisseur's Guide

Back in the 1960s and early '70s, technology and demographics and design converged to put the first, primitive precursors of yuppie porn into homes in Cambridge and Manhattan, Evanston and Westwood: Color TV. Remote-con-

SPY DECEMBER 1987

Bionaire
ultrasonic
humidifier
·
Zenith
camcorder
·
Huri-Huri
weeding knife

Saab 900
Turbo
·
MontBlanc pen
·
Braun juicer

Krups
coffee maker
·
Braun
coffee grinder
·
Alvar Aalto vase
·
Graves teapot

danMark
telephones
·
Braun calculator

Braun shaver
·
See-through
Swatch

Wüsthof Dreizack
knives
·
Barbour raincoat
·
Pirelli flooring

Quotrek portable
stock-quotation device
·
Sharp Travel Partner
world time clock, alarm,
calendar, currency converter
and calculator

Lamy
pens
·
Tizio
lamp
·
[ixi:z]
rubberized
accessories

Artemide
halogen hanging lamp
·
Halliburton aluminum briefcase
·
Stainless-steel
Sub-Zero refrigerator

Epson Elite 100 Plus
portable electronic typewriter
·
Range Rover
·
Alpine car stereo

Calphalon
cookware
·
Bang & Olufsen
turntable

ADS receiver
·
Hafler amplifier

EURO·STYLE

Tone phones. Luxo lamps, then track lighting and dimmer switches. Digital watches. Pocket calculators. Bucket seats, tachometers on the dashboard.

The stuff was still American, the colors a bit off. Everything was still *large* and sheet-metal clunky. But it was heading straight for the eighties.

Nowadays, with second- and third-generation yuppie porn, and yuppie-porn stores in every city, we need finer distinctions. There is hard-core yuppie porn (excess technology, a sense of *power*, everything to extremes) and soft-core yuppie porn (more allusive, playful). There are the devices that feed on a native American nerdishness and those that appeal to Euro-cool pretensions. There are, in short, items of yuppie porn for every conceivable taste.

doesn't buy it because Lawrence Walsh has just subpoenaed his shopping list. He doesn't buy a car espresso maker (Dapy, $65) because he wants to sip cappuccino as he zips along the Cross Bronx Expressway. He doesn't buy a Swiss army knife–style pocket office tool (The Sharper Image, $32) because he never knows when or where he's going to have to punch holes in an important document or staple two of them together (that's what the minimum wage is for). He buys these things because *they turn him on*. He may be an aesthetic retard, but to him, personal paper shredders are "sexy." *Sexy*: it is no coincidence that in the 1980s the word is more often and easily used to describe *things*, and always things that have nothing to do with sex.

There's hard-core yuppie porn and there's soft-core (*see box, pages 66–67*). High-tech design-dripping gizmos so state-of-the-art, so overspecialized, as to go beyond utility into the realm of pure exhilarating *thing*ness—that's the hardest-core stuff: rotating-tuft toothbrushes, phone wiretap detectors, "the ultimate precision yo-yo" (The Sharper Image, $39) made from "two ounces of aircraft aluminum, machined to exact tolerances."

Soft-core yuppie porn is more suggestive, more dependent on vicarious associations with the life-styles of the moneyed and despotic: the very briefcase "favored by Andrew Carnegie," bowls and silverware that a sleek family of Italian Fascists might have used.

Ask the employees of yuppie-pornography mills what kind of store they work for (a housewares store? an electronics store? a gift store?) and invariably they pause, uncomprehending, then blurt out buzzwords, most often *unusual* and *unique* (*see box, page 65*). It's like listening to a Reagan press conference. Which is not to imply that yuppie-pornographers are doddering cheeseheads—it's just that

IT IS NO COINCIDENCE THAT THE WORD *SEXY* IS MOSTLY USED TO DESCRIBE *THINGS*, AND ALWAYS THINGS THAT HAVE NOTHING TO DO WITH SEX

YUPPIE PORNOGRAPHY VS. THE REAL THING: A FIELD TEST

Why The Sharper Image Is Better Than Show World

THE SHARPER IMAGE (SOUTH STREET SEAPORT)	SHOW WORLD (42ND STREET AND EIGHTH AVENUE)
▶ Up-to-the-minute, high-tech interior; odorless	✶ Mirror balls; cloying smell of ammonia mixed with air freshener
▶ Employees wear sharp-looking business suits (blue blazers and red ties on weekends)	✶ Employees wear motley, ill-considered underwear ensembles
▶ Sample products are hands-on	✶ Naked women are behind Plexiglas
▶ Free, continuous videotapes show attractive, cheerful models demonstrating safe products	✶ A 25-cent token gets you 60 seconds' worth of videotapes showing unattractive, cheerless models demonstrating unsafe sex
▶ Sales staff helpful to visiting writers: "Hi. My name is Steve. Can I help you with anything?"	✶ Sales staff unhelpful to visiting writers: "Yo! The magazines aren't for reading."

Why Show World Is Better Than The Sharper Image

THE SHARPER IMAGE	SHOW WORLD
▶ No private booths	✶ Private booths

—B.H.

Smart?
Fun?
Funny?
Fearless?

IN S P Y,

THE BEST IS YET

TO COME.

Future Features Include
**JUST WHO CAUSED
THE CRASH OF '87?**
CANADIANS IN OUR MIDST:
THREAT OR MENACE?
BRATS IN LOVE:
THE RON AND CLAUDIA STORY
A GUIDE TO POSTMODERN
EVERYTHING
**WHAT THE LADIES WEAR AT THE
NEW YORK ATHLETIC CLUB**
MAHABHARATAMANIA
**HOW TO STAY FAMOUS
AFTER THE FACT**
A BRIEF HISTORY OF
WHITE RAP MUSIC
EMBARRASSING WEALTH
Plus:
THE *NICE* ISSUE

"What kind of store are you?" doesn't quite make sense to them because, unlike stores in the sense that our parents or *The World Book Encyclopedia* understands them, yuppie-porn emporiums are defined not by functional specialty but by fantasy. "People are surprised," a D. F. Sanders & Company clerk told me, "when the stuff actually works."

"WE'RE SELLING Lacking convenient, Yellow
TEMPTATION," Pages–style handles,
the yuppie-pornog-
raphers try to distin-
SAYS ONE guish themselves
from one another
MERCHANDISER. with the desperate,
straight-faced pom-
posity of, say, Albert
"THE MORE YOU Gore, Richard Gep-
hardt or Bruce Bab-
HAVE, THE MORE bitt. Brookstone
claims to offer the
classiest products,
YOU'RE TEMPTED The Price of His
Toys the newest,
A2Z and Ham-
TO WANT" macher Schlemmer
the best. But they're only as different as *Playboy*, *Penthouse* and *Hot Blonde Teasers*, offering variations on the same theme.

The most semiotically aware yuppie-pornographer is the San Francisco–based The Sharper Image, whose very name hints at a sophisticated self-consciousness. The total Sharper Image environment is even more cleverly conceived: it pretends it's a television newsroom. The identically suited or blazered sales staff operates from a raised cash-register station that faithfully re-creates the desk-as-command-module aesthetic of local TV news teams. The gray walls, smoothly lit, sport the giant cordu-roy grooves and crimson highlights so redolent of modern TV journalism. Deco-rously arranged about the "set," the prod-ucts themselves come on like a bevy of Michele Marshes and Chuck Scarbor-oughs—eye candy with authority.

The founder and president of The Sharper Image, 38-year-old Richard Thal-heimer, whose aggressively smiling face graces every catalog, has set himself up as the Hefner of his empire. "He sees himself as the model consumer," explains a spokeswoman. And indeed, Thalheimer is as much a living prophet of the *In Search of Excellence* life-style as Hef is of the more old-fashionedly sybaritic. His Marin

County mansion is reported to be a verita-ble yuppie-porn shrine, crammed with shiny exercise equipment and very serious-looking telephones.

The latest development is the advent of the "Toys for Adults Show," a traveling retail bazaar founded in 1983 that now in-cludes ten cities on its tour (it stopped in at the Javits Center last month). "Toys for Adults" aims to be a colossus, the ulti-mate, the Times Square of yuppie porn, and it features not only the usual catalog gewgaws but such big-ticket whoppers as $45,000 luxury mobile homes and $60,000 Lamborghinis. At its Hartford, Connecticut, show bankers were on hand to make loans to the smitten yet strapped, as were financial consultants, who told you how to restructure your holdings so as to make payments on a $20,000 mink jump-suit. "We're selling *temptation*," coos a "Toys for Adults" spokeswoman with a Tolstoyan understanding of human na-ture. "The more you have, the more you're tempted to want."

Like The Sharper Image's Thalheimer, Gary Kirschner, the founder of "Toys," is a man who mirrors the yearnings of his constituents. "I like looking at Ferraris," he says. "I think most people like looking at Ferraris." Granted. But where does he draw the line? Is there ever a consumer good he finds . . . *excessive?*

"Naturally, we try to be very selective," he responds. "To me, a fur coat that turns into a flight jacket is ridiculous. Besides, my wife isn't into furs—you know, the animal thing," he adds in a whisper. "But there are people out there to whom that will appeal. As long as an item's not ridic-ulous to the point of being stupid . . ."

But philosophic quibbles aside, Kirschner has a point. Yuppie pornogra-phy, like color pictures of genitalia, exists because people want it. Kirschner, Thal-heimer and their ilk aren't corrupting anybody; the fact is, the yuppie-porn aes-thetic, like illiteracy and Haägen-Dazs, runs rampant throughout America. Any-where upscale surface flash is an end in it-self, there's yuppie porn: *American Gigolo* and *Power* and *RoboCop* are yuppie-porn movies; *New York Woman* and *L.A. Style* are yuppie-porn magazines; Vintage Con-temporaries are yuppie-porn books; Gary Hart and Joe Biden were yuppie-porn can-didates; surrogate motherhood and lipo-suction are yuppie-porn biology; *this* is yuppie-porn thought. ⑤

Inclu
● Ove
● Cha
● An

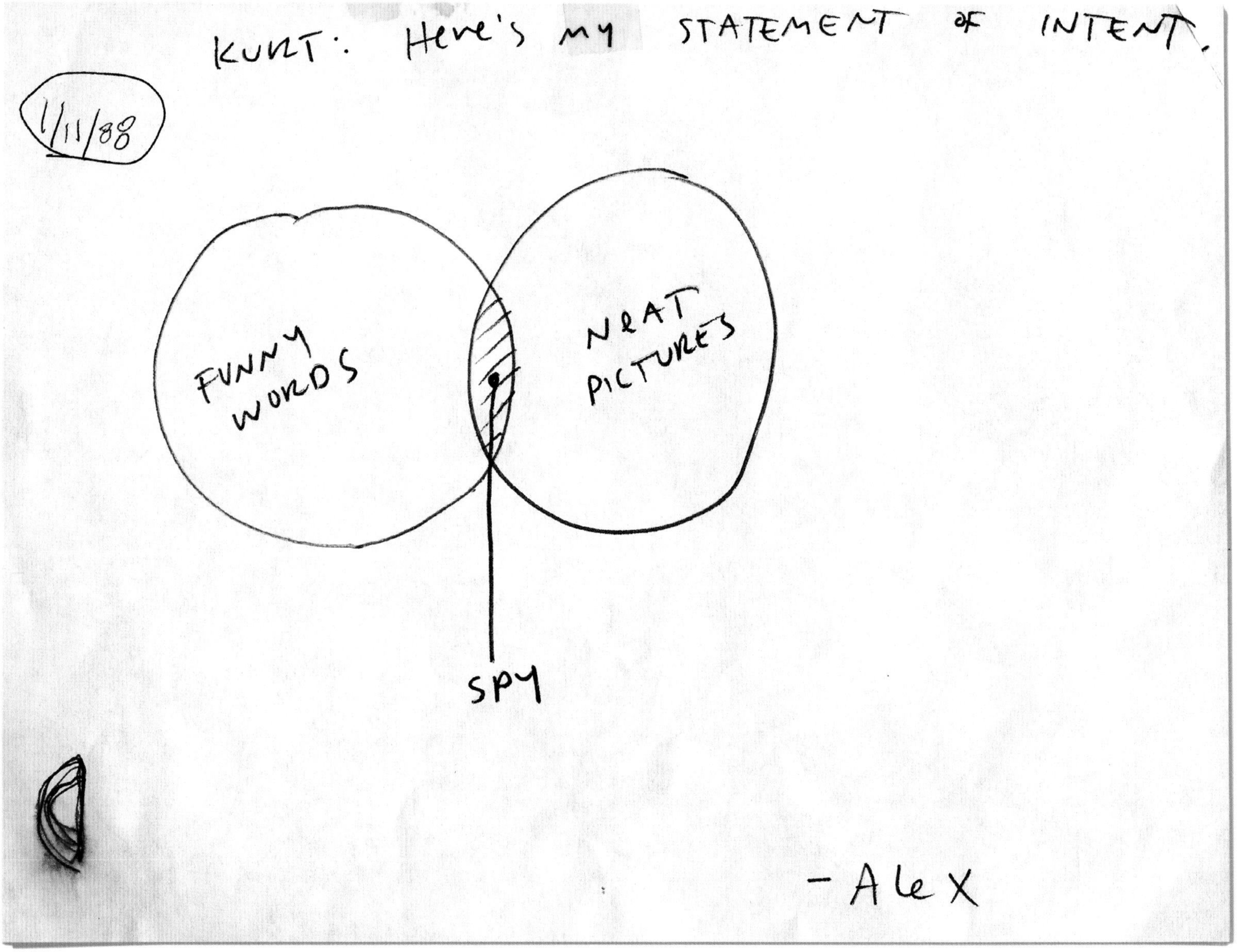

KURT: Here's my STATEMENT of INTENT.

1/11/88

FUNNY WORDS

NEAT PICTURES

SPY

— Alex

5

"If You Get Close, It's Funny": Designing *Spy*

And, by the Way, the Type Wasn't Actually, Technically, All *That* Small. Really.

I'd always get upset when the headline would be changed at the last minute. Then again, how often in your life do you get to design a story called "Arrivederci, Sleazeball"?
—ALEX ISLEY

WHATEVER *SPY*'S IMPACT AND INFLUENCE, it had as much to do with style as it did with substance. The early sample covers and pages mocked up by those Italians—Possibly Fausto and Possibly Carlo—in 1985 bore little resemblance to the magazine that was eventually published; the basic blueprint was created by Stephen Doyle and advanced by *Spy*'s series of art directors—most notably Alexander Isley (1987–88, and also the designer of this book), but also B. W. Honeycutt (1988–91) and Christiaan Kuypers (1991–93). The fact that Doyle and Isley both worked for Tibor Kalman's mischievous design firm M&Co. put some bits of Kalman's DNA into *Spy*. While *Spy*'s look was tweaked several times, its essential aesthetic was there in the first issue and in the last.

"We had already developed the vocabulary of the magazine with those prototype boards," says Doyle. "Naked City [*Spy*'s front of the book] was great, because you could really mess around with it—the grid was based on a bible from 1519 or something. *Spy* had so many unexpected antecedents. It was a real melting pot of graphic ideas."

Honeycutt, who died in 1994, gave the magazine's hey-we're-rich-and-national boom years an appropriately bigger, slicker look. Same as Isley, he was an easygoing, gentlemanly North Carolinian—though Honeycutt was additionally a former child preacher and choirboy who, it was rumored, had been banished from the flock for sleeping with the minister's daughter *and* son.

"The design was brilliant in part because it foreshadowed where design was going," says Paul Goldberger, specifically citing the Internet and "all the funny connections" one makes on it—an intricate construction that existed in more primitive form in every issue of *Spy*.

"*Spy*'s design prefigured the Web in terms of the multiple entry points and levels of information," says Steve Heller, the graphic design critic and historian. "But what ultimately makes

**Opposite:
Alex Isley's essay
on what Spy
should be.**

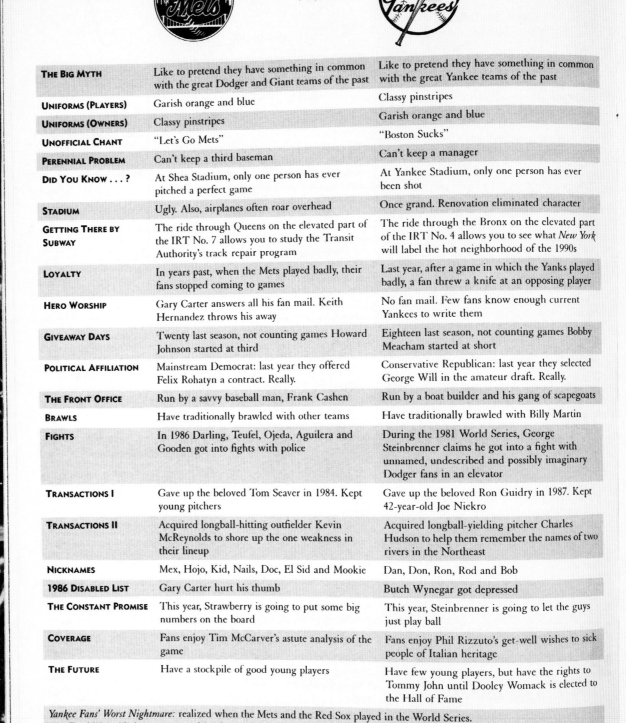

Mets VS. **Yankees**

	Mets	Yankees
THE BIG MYTH	Like to pretend they have something in common with the great Dodger and Giant teams of the past	Like to pretend they have something in common with the great Yankee teams of the past
UNIFORMS (PLAYERS)	Garish orange and blue	Classy pinstripes
UNIFORMS (OWNERS)	Classy pinstripes	Garish orange and blue
UNOFFICIAL CHANT	"Let's Go Mets"	"Boston Sucks"
PERENNIAL PROBLEM	Can't keep a third baseman	Can't keep a manager
DID YOU KNOW . . . ?	At Shea Stadium, only one person has ever pitched a perfect game	At Yankee Stadium, only one person has ever been shot
STADIUM	Ugly. Also, airplanes often roar overhead	Once grand. Renovation eliminated character
GETTING THERE BY SUBWAY	The ride through Queens on the elevated part of the IRT No. 7 allows you to study the Transit Authority's track repair program	The ride through the Bronx on the elevated part of the IRT No. 4 allows you to see what *New York* will label the hot neighborhood of the 1990s
LOYALTY	In years past, when the Mets played badly, their fans stopped coming to games	Last year, after a game in which the Yanks played badly, a fan threw a knife at an opposing player
HERO WORSHIP	Gary Carter answers all his fan mail. Keith Hernandez throws his away	No fan mail. Few fans know enough current Yankees to write them
GIVEAWAY DAYS	Twenty last season, not counting games Howard Johnson started at third	Eighteen last season, not counting games Bobby Meacham started at short
POLITICAL AFFILIATION	Mainstream Democrat: last year they offered Felix Rohatyn a contract. Really.	Conservative Republican: last year they selected George Will in the amateur draft. Really.
THE FRONT OFFICE	Run by a savvy baseball man, Frank Cashen	Run by a boat builder and his gang of scapegoats
BRAWLS	Have traditionally brawled with other teams	Have traditionally brawled with Billy Martin
FIGHTS	In 1986 Darling, Teufel, Ojeda, Aguilera and Gooden got into fights with police	During the 1981 World Series, George Steinbrenner claims he got into a fight with unnamed, undescribed and possibly imaginary Dodger fans in an elevator
TRANSACTIONS I	Gave up the beloved Tom Seaver in 1984. Kept young pitchers	Gave up the beloved Ron Guidry in 1987. Kept 42-year-old Joe Niekro
TRANSACTIONS II	Acquired longball-hitting outfielder Kevin McReynolds to shore up the one weakness in their lineup	Acquired longball-yielding pitcher Charles Hudson to help them remember the names of two rivers in the Northeast
NICKNAMES	Mex, Hojo, Kid, Nails, Doc, El Sid and Mookie	Dan, Don, Ron, Rod and Bob
1986 DISABLED LIST	Gary Carter hurt his thumb	Butch Wynegar got depressed
THE CONSTANT PROMISE	This year, Strawberry is going to put some big numbers on the board	This year, Steinbrenner is going to let the guys just play ball
COVERAGE	Fans enjoy Tim McCarver's astute analysis of the game	Fans enjoy Phil Rizzuto's get-well wishes to sick people of Italian heritage
THE FUTURE	Have a stockpile of good young players	Have few young players, but have the rights to Tommy John until Dooley Womack is elected to the Hall of Fame

Yankee Fans' Worst Nightmare: realized when the Mets and the Red Sox played in the World Series.
Met Fans' Worst Nightmare: averted (perhaps) when airport security found the loaded derringer in Carlene Pearson's purse.

—*Jamie Malanowski*

April 1987

The original cover idea for the 1988 April Fools "Nice Issue" was to feature Donald Trump (well, a photo of a model with Trump's head retouched in), pointing out what a great guy he was. The reader would then open the issue to find a second cover using the identical picture with the addition of a long red tail. Unfortunately, the ad sales guys loved the idea of having two covers as well, and proceeded to sell ads on both inside front covers, thereby giving premium placement to two advertisers. So much for the "tail" idea. We ended up still using a two-cover approach—when opened, the cover lines, logo, and bar code all collapsed as the cover boy went sprawling. It can now be revealed that the tuxedoed body double for Donald Trump was Kurt, who stayed in Trumpian character throughout the photo shoot.

Spy memorable, and missed, was its sense of humor eloquently expressed through its graphic presentation. Wit, satire, and more than a hint of sarcasm abound. Nothing, especially in print, has replaced it."

Joe Clark, a *Spy* obsessive from Canada who maintains an unofficial website (*www.fawny.ca/spy*) devoted to the magazine, notes that "the sheer viciousness and the fabulous typography of *Spy* are what really killed me. *Spy* did not need an explanation, even in Toronto. The magazine was for curmudgeons. Curmudgeons are frustrated idealists. That was *Spy*."

"To the extent that I sometimes run across issues, it's still really fresh, even knowing that so many of the things *Spy* pioneered have been ripped off, used, misused, badly used by so many other publications," says *Time*'s Jim Kelly. "It was a very data-rich magazine, and thanks partially to blogs today, and the Web, you can lead such a data-rich life. And that's something that *Spy* really, really loved and immersed itself in. It was a real trove every month."

"*Spy* was such a wisecracking little brother; it had to come into the room dressed like a grown-up," Stephen Doyle says. "So it slipped in, in a disguise of confidence and gentility. The serif type, the letter spacing, all this twentieth-century publishing history that went into it gave the authority it needed to be as sarcastic as it was."

And yet: "I always had a feeling that *Spy* was nothing like what Graydon had intended it to look like," says Isley. "He had this vision of it being *The American Mercury*—very elegant, caps and small caps."

"I *had* sort of envisioned it as a magazine more of type than of any kind of illustration, where the type was the star," says Graydon. "My original idea was even to take a computer and have the alphabet redrawn—have four different versions of every letter, so each one is ever so slightly different. And then you design a computer system, a program, to do the type, where it'll choose those four A's, say, in random order. So that it would look like hot type, rather than computer-generated type? It was more like an Addison & Steele sort of magazine."

Isley started in January 1987—just in time to put together the March issue, the magazine's fifth. More than anyone, he would be responsible for *Spy*'s groundbreaking design. He was 25.

"I was real nervous, not having ever been at a publication," he remembers. "When I first met Kurt and Graydon, I said, 'Well,

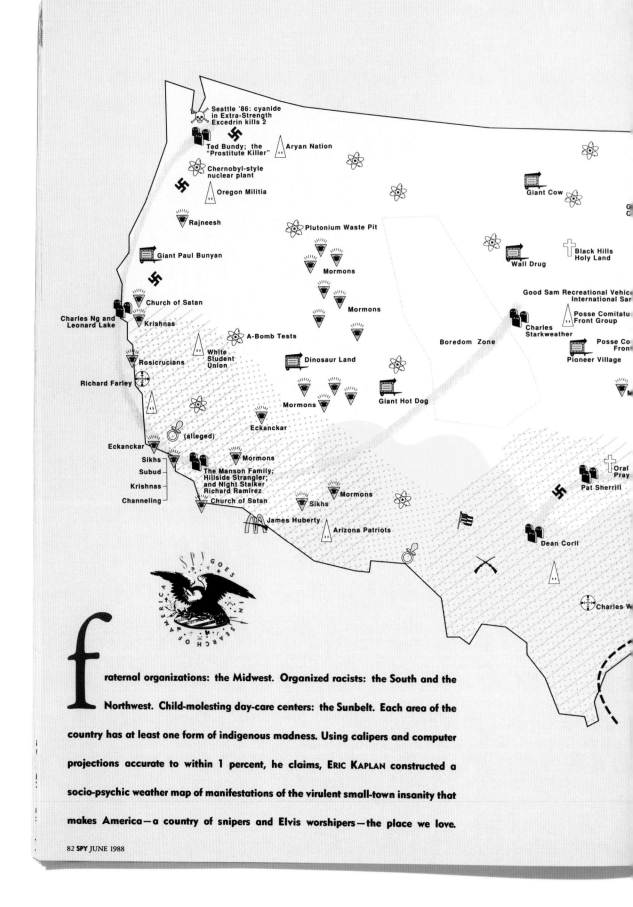

Seattle '86: cyanide in Extra-Strength Excedrin kills 2

Ted Bundy; the "Prostitute Killer"

Aryan Nation

Chernobyl-style nuclear plant

Oregon Militia

Rajneesh

Plutonium Waste Pit

Giant Cow

Giant Paul Bunyan

Black Hills Holy Land

Wall Drug

Mormons

Church of Satan

Good Sam Recreational Vehicle International Sar

Charles Ng and Leonard Lake

Krishnas

Mormons

Posse Comitatu Front Group

Charles Starkweather

Boredom Zone

Posse Co Front

Rosicrucians

White Student Union

A-Bomb Tests

Dinosaur Land

Pioneer Village

Richard Farley

Mormons

Giant Hot Dog

Eckanckar

(alleged)

Eckanckar

Eckanckar

Sikhs

Mormons

Oral Pray

Subud

The Manson Family; Hillside Strangler; and Night Stalker Richard Ramirez

Mormons

Pat Sherrill

Krishnas

Channeling

Church of Satan

Sikhs

James Huberty

Arizona Patriots

Dean Corll

Charles W

fraternal organizations: the Midwest. Organized racists: the South and the Northwest. Child-molesting day-care centers: the Sunbelt. Each area of the country has at least one form of indigenous madness. Using calipers and computer projections accurate to within 1 percent, he claims, ERIC KAPLAN constructed a socio-psychic weather map of manifestations of the virulent small-town insanity that makes America — a country of snipers and Elvis worshipers — the place we love.

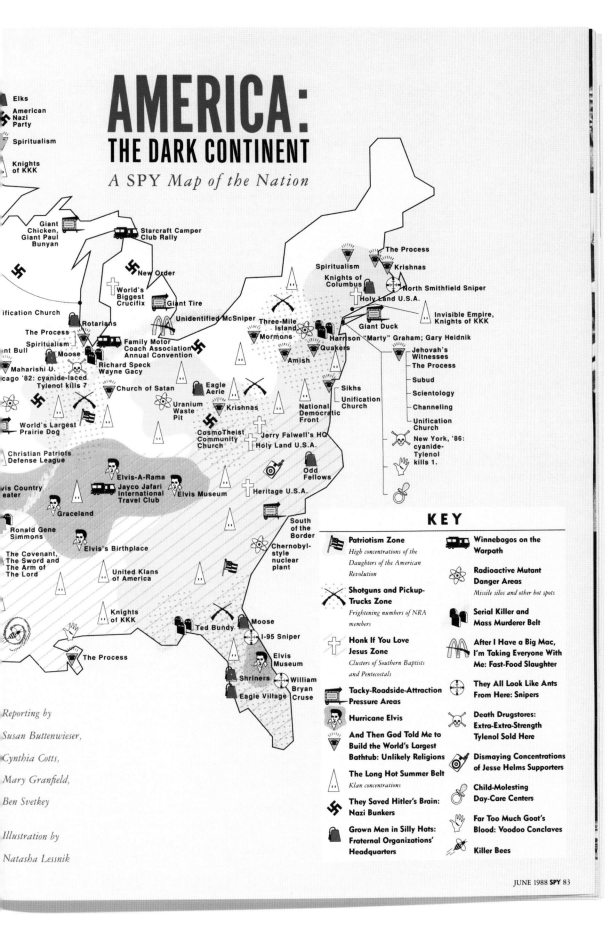

AMERICA:
THE DARK CONTINENT
A SPY *Map of the Nation*

Elks
American Nazi Party
Spiritualism
Knights of KKK

Giant Chicken, Giant Paul Bunyan
Starcraft Camper Club Rally
New Order
World's Biggest Crucifix
Giant Tire
ification Church
Rotarians
Unidentified McSniper
The Process
Spiritualism
nt Bull
Moose
Family Motor Coach Association Annual Convention
Maharishi U.
cago '82: cyanide-laced Tylenol kills 7
Richard Speck Wayne Gacy
Church of Satan
Eagle Aerie
Uranium Waste Pit
Krishnas
World's Largest Prairie Dog
Christian Patriots Defense League
CosmoTheist Community Church
Jerry Falwell's HQ
Holy Land U.S.A.
vis Country eater
Elvis-A-Rama
Jayco Jafari International Travel Club
Elvis Museum
Graceland
Ronald Gene Simmons
Elvis's Birthplace
The Covenant, The Sword and The Arm of The Lord
United Klans of America
Knights of KKK
Ted Bundy
Moose
I-95 Sniper
The Process
Shriners
Eagle Village
Elvis Museum
William Bryan Cruse

The Process
Spiritualism
Knights of Columbus
Holy Land U.S.A.
Krishnas
North Smithfield Sniper
Three-Mile Island
Mormons
Giant Duck
Invisible Empire, Knights of KKK
Quakers
Amish
Harrison "Marty" Graham; Gary Heidnik
Jehovah's Witnesses
The Process
Subud
Sikhs
Unification Church
Scientology
National Democratic Front
Channeling
Unification Church
New York, '86: cyanide-Tylenol kills 1.
Odd Fellows
Heritage U.S.A.
South of the Border
Chernobyl-style nuclear plant

Reporting by

Susan Buttenwieser,

Cynthia Cotts,

Mary Granfield,

Ben Svetkey

Illustration by

Natasha Lessnik

KEY

🏴 **Patriotism Zone**
High concentrations of the Daughters of the American Revolution

⚔️ **Shotguns and Pickup-Trucks Zone**
Frightening numbers of NRA members

✝️ **Honk If You Love Jesus Zone**
Clusters of Southern Baptists and Pentecostals

🚐 **Tacky-Roadside-Attraction Pressure Areas**

Hurricane Elvis

🔺 **And Then God Told Me to Build the World's Largest Bathtub: Unlikely Religions**

🔺 **The Long Hot Summer Belt**
Klan concentrations

卐 **They Saved Hitler's Brain: Nazi Bunkers**

🎒 **Grown Men in Silly Hats: Fraternal Organizations' Headquarters**

🚐 **Winnebagos on the Warpath**

⚛️ **Radioactive Mutant Danger Areas**
Missile silos and other hot spots

🎒 **Serial Killer and Mass Murderer Belt**

After I Have a Big Mac, I'm Taking Everyone With Me: Fast-Food Slaughter

🎯 **They All Look Like Ants From Here: Snipers**

☠️ **Death Drugstores: Extra-Extra-Strength Tylenol Sold Here**

⊚ **Dismaying Concentrations of Jesse Helms Supporters**

💍 **Child-Molesting Day-Care Centers**

✋ **Far Too Much Goat's Blood: Voodoo Conclaves**

🐝 **Killer Bees**

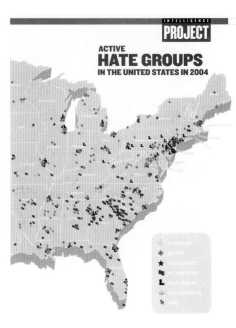

INTELLIGENCE
PROJECT

ACTIVE
HATE GROUPS
IN THE UNITED STATES IN 2004

If *Spy*'s (since-imitated, see above) attempt to come to terms with the real America triggers vague associations with, say, the electoral map of certain recent presidential elections, we're not going to argue.
June 1988

I've never worked on a magazine.' And Kurt said, 'That's okay, I've never put one out, either.' And we laughed and shook hands and that was it." In no time he was logging 350-hour months: "It was just crazy. And we were understaffed—it was usually me and two other people. But it was my chance to have my name on a masthead."

Isley's influences were *MAD* magazine (he calls *MAD*'s invitation, years later, to design its 40th-anniversary anthology "the high point of my life"); Robert Best's *New York*; *National Lampoon* ("because it wasn't designed to look like a humor magazine, and the idea of something funny in a straight package was really interesting to me"); and, "of course, the George Lois covers for *Esquire*."

But he also drew inspiration from a range of other sources, like old Montgomery Ward catalogs and the Yellow Pages. Naturally, he had to entertain, channel, and accommodate the not-always-identical wishes of the two coeditors. And *two* editors, he'd announced as a condition of his taking the job, would be enough: "I said, 'I will only answer to you.' That was a good thing, because everyone was so eager and interested and passionate about *Spy*, it would have been hard to have too many people commenting."

"After about six or eight months of them giving me meticulous descriptions about what every story should look like, they just started to say, 'Do an Alex thing.'"

The rest of us were barred from his fiefdom. "People would pull manuscripts away, or they'd want to see layouts," says Isley. "The designers had strict instructions not to let any editors open up the flat-files to look at stories. There were standing orders not to let Susan *in the area*."

Outsiders were even less welcome. I remember rushing over to intervene once when Isley found himself cornered by an irate contributor who'd turned up and started yelling about a digitally manipulated picture we'd run of Ronald Reagan in trunks, because it showed too much chest hair, "and *everyone* knows Reagan doesn't have *any* chest hair." But viewed from a safe distance, the Isley art department was a jolly inner sanctum, especially when James Brown went on full-blast late at night.

"Graydon always knew what he liked, and Kurt always knew what he didn't like," Isley remembers. "Graydon loved making it look elegant. Kurt hated bullshit, prima donna stuff. Between

the two you had to reconcile that. But they would speak to me in a unified voice—it would have been a disaster otherwise. And after about six or eight months of them giving me meticulous descriptions about what every story should look like, they just started to say, 'Do an Alex thing.' I'm not sure what it *meant*, but it was nice."

Isley insisted that his design staff had to read every piece before working on it: "I was really obnoxious. I'd say, 'What is this about? *You didn't read it, did you?* You can't design it!' I used to read the manuscripts and laugh out loud. I'd think, *Why do I need to even bother to design this?* We had to cut Jamie Malanowski's 'Yankees vs. Mets' piece in half. I still regret that, twenty years later—it was so good, the stuff we cut."

While *Spy* did *seem* visually busy—the occasional contributor Patricia Marx describes it as "the first magazine that catered to the attention-deficit-disordered"—Isley makes the point that there wasn't really as much commotion in the design as there appeared to be.

"To me it's really low-tech," he says. "Design people often fall into the same traps. If it's for kids, you make it look like it's a video screen. If it's for something funny, you put things at wacky angles—you're telegraphing jokes. But people are smarter than that. I think you could argue that in designing *Spy*, we overcompensated. It was funny and aggressive, but pretty straight. There were three typefaces that we used—two, really—but you could make it look like there was more going on. I remember Kurt told me, 'I don't want *Spy* to be for browsers, I want it to be for readers.' So if you read closely, you're rewarded. From a distance it doesn't look like anything, but if you get close, it's funny."

"Everything was some kind of neat little gizmo," says Susan Morrison, referring not just to graphic aspects of the magazine but also to the party invitations, promotional mailings, business cards, and other *Spy* paraphernalia the art department produced, which freely made use of tiny magnifying glasses, cut-out dolls, golf tees, finger puppets, sunglasses, matchbooks, paste-on tattoos, watercolor kits, and so forth.

"A lot of the grammar of our magazine had to do with publications like *Highlights for Children*, things from our youth," Morrison continues. "It was right around the time of *Pee-wee's Playhouse* and Nick at Nite—and we had a lot of retro graphics, like Clip 'n' Save and tote boards and O-Matics and all the little

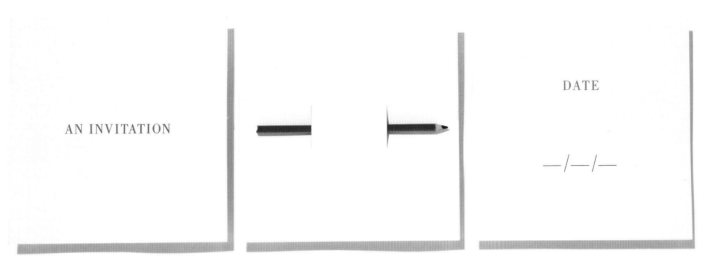

AN INVITATION — — DATE —/—/—

Invitation to a *Spy* J&B Scotch party. The recipient would get an envelope containing a phone number to call. Date, time, and place would be on a recording. The beauty of this approach was that you could use the same invitation more than once. But we didn't.

REMY MARTIN & *SPY* MAGAZINE

Pop-up invitation for the *Spy*-sponsored opening of the opera *Nixon in China* at the Brooklyn Academy of Music. Nixon's people would not let us use a photo of his head. The hands were funnier, anyway.

In association with

Brooklyn Academy of Music

and China Grill

NIXON IN CHINA

Gorbachev birthmark tattoo, November 1989

NOW *YOU* CAN LOOK JUST LIKE GORBY!

❶ Put on boxy gray suit, white shirt and tie; expose and lightly moisten right side of forehead.

❷ Correctly position, then firmly press official birthmark decal against right side of forehead.

❸ Remove decal; greet astonished passersby.

OFFICIAL S P Y LIFE-SIZE RUB-ON MIKHAIL GORBACHEV BIRTHMARK DECAL

Illustrations by Ben Chase

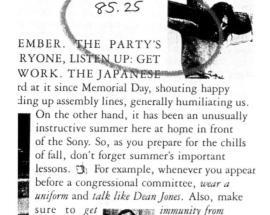

interactive things we did. It's amazing, when you look at the *Spy* layouts, how many of them are like board games. We all had a similar aesthetic. I think it's no accident that all of us are people who go crazy at flea markets and buy weird little things from the '30s. It's a nostalgic way of looking at the world. It was also our way of subverting how serious and dry journalism had become."

But perhaps the greatest influence on Isley was *Spy*'s lack of money. "Design is knowing what the problem is and trying to solve it," he says. "In *Spy*'s case the problem was that it was a magazine that didn't have a lot of money, and had too many words." Some signature design flourishes—the floating silhouetted heads, the tiny iconic images, the corny stock photography—were budget-driven solutions. The photo of Liz Smith in war paint and headdress that for years graced The Liz Smith Tote Board, for instance, was chosen because it was free—it had come in a press kit for a benefit.

"It's just like editorially, where'd they'd use the same description time and time again, like 'churlish dwarf billionaire'—if it was anything about money or greed, we'd use the same little illustration of a stack of money," Isley says. "Whenever it was something about writers, we'd use that photo of the old typewriter—which I'd bought on Astor Place for $20 and then shot."

"I ended up doing a lot of the drawings and photos myself because we couldn't afford anything else," he continues. "I remember haggling over the cost of knock-outs"—detailed masking of parts of a photo's background—"the things you take for granted at regular magazines. There was one big fight, over a little hand holding a pencil, and I wanted to knock out the white, which would have cost an extra $16—the arguments about that! I felt so passionately that it had to be white. And I remember Tom saying, 'No! No way! *Sixteen dollars?!*' I was so upset, and so young, I really wanted to make each issue *perfect*."

Isley still has copies of *Spy* covered, page after marked-up page, with evidence of Tom's disbelief at the astronomical film-prep charges being visited upon the well-crunched budget. "$14.27!," Tom would write plaintively. Elsewhere, his righteous publisher's indignation painful to witness, a simple, accusatory "$32" would be scrawled. "On each page of each issue I'd write a prep cost—to the dollar, to the cent," Tom admits, somewhat sheepishly. "Very Proustian cost-accounting. But I had to learn what a magazine really cost to produce."

"We'd fight about that kind of stuff, every penny," says Isley. "Then you'd look at *Esquire*, and they'd paid $700 for a spot illustration—$700 was our art budget for *the whole issue*."

```
GOOD COPY    DISTR; ED RES1 RES2 ART LEGAL

SLUG: cover.hed
STORY: cover heds/august
EDITOR: gc & ka
WRITER: gc & ka
SECTION: cover
DATE: 5.29
..................................................
WASPmania!
That Desperate Yearning for All Things Clubby and Cozy and Old

Pop Tarts: Fawn, Dawn & Jessica

It's Okay to Hate Opera

Busty Like Me

Busty Like Her A SPY Experiment

Busty Like Me A True Story
```

Cover copy

**Cover concept
sketches**

A COVER STORY

Spy's approach to covers was to take a (more or less) well-known person and photograph him or her to illustrate a story within the issue. Through some fortunate connection we were able to get New York mayor Ed Koch to pose for the cover of the "WASPMania!" issue. We could not believe our luck. Koch had long been one of *Spy*'s targets; the only catch was that the mayor would only be able to pose for 30 minutes on a Saturday morning, several days after the rest of the issue had gone to the printer.

The printer was literally holding the presses. We waited in the studio on the appointed Saturday, and waited. And waited. And finally got a call saying that the mayor had changed his mind. We were out of time and knew we couldn't leave without a cover. Who could model? All eyes first turned to Graydon ("No fucking way!"), and then to Alex, who was photographed in the riding outfit, with the plan to retouch Koch's head onto his body. We all felt that this would not come across as particularly plausible, however. Fortunately, our photographer, Chris Callis, had a face that was deemed un-WASPy enough. Thanks to sheer desperation, the photographer ended up gracing the cover of the issue.

Cover models

Cover

Postmodern
Graphics

Postmodern
ARCHITECTURE

A S P.y Guide

**The Rise
and Fall
of a Great
American
Buzzword**

POSTMODERN
Furniture

Postmodern
DECORATION

by Bruce Handy

*Post-
modern*
CLOTHING

The word *postmodern* used to mean something, in much the same way that *prehistory*, say, means things that happened in the epoch before history was invented, or that *canine* means "of dogs." *Postmodern* started life as a critical term. First in architecture, then in painting and dance, it referred to works that consciously rebelled against modernist style, often by paying homage to the once-shunned styles and genres of the past. ▶ To college professors and *Artforum* editors it still means that. To rock critics and slick-magazine-caption writers and wraithlike people standing around the lobby at the Brooklyn Academy of Music — well, it's hard to pin down what *postmodern* means to them. It can mean anything that's sort of old

Post~modern **THEATER**

POST~MODERN *Food*

POSTMODERN **Television**

POSTMODERN **MU-SIC**

POSTMODERN **ART**

Post~modern **FICTION**

April 1988

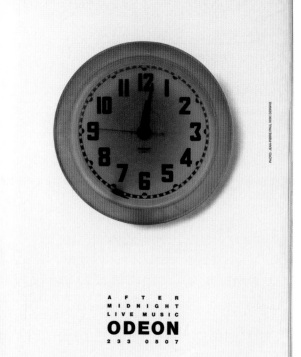

AFTER
MIDNIGHT
LIVE MUSIC
ODEON
233 0507

MONDAY   TUESDAY   WEDNESDAY

We think we know postmodernism when we see it. Does it contain a novel within a novel that has the same title as the novel? Is it painted on broken china? Are you listening to it at BAM? For a building, is it funny?

---

but sort of new, a little bit ironic, or kind of self-conscious—like movies that steal bits from old movies, or photographs of the photographer. It's used in reference to creative endeavors that never had a modernist movement to begin with—art forms such as music videos, rap songs and panty hose design. It's culturespeak, shorthand for *Stuff That's Cool in 1988*. It's the postmodern (you know what we mean) version of *groovy*, except that using it makes you sound smart.

Figuring out why any given pundit considers any given work postmodern can be

It's culturespeak, short for Stuff That's Cool in 1988. It's the current version of groovy— except that using it makes you sound smart.

as exasperating and elusive as conceptualizing six-dimensional spheres or trying to sense your own brain. *Moonlighting*, for example, has been called a postmodern

TV show because it constantly calls attention to the fact that—*duh*—that's what it is…*a TV show*. Well, okay. But isn't that kind of art-about-artiness a quintessentially *modernist* attribute? But isn't modernism yet another historical style that postmodernists can now pillage? But didn't George Burns and Ernie Kovacs do this stuff and do it better 30 years ago? But isn't that the postmodern message: *It's been done?*

Okay. Give the brain a rest. We've done the work for you. After months of intensive research and half-baked discussion, what we've learned is this: basically, post-

modernism is whatever you want it to be, if you *want it had enough.*

Perhaps because of this, *postmodern*, like an aging hack, has less and less to do with

any kind of art; it's evolved into the sort of buzzword that people tack onto sentences when they're trying to sound more educated than they fear they really are, not unlike the way *gestalt* was used in the 1970s, or *science* in the Dark Ages. Now we read about postmodern politicians grappling with postmodern economies while postmodern talk shows discuss postmodern sex. *What does any of this mean?* We have a hunch that such usages are intended to convey some kind of vague, bemused approbation, as if *postmodern* were a rough synonym for "of the wacky times in which we live." But we're not positive.

We've always wanted to have an era to call our own but felt that *the Reagan Years* came off sounding like a slide show at the Republican National Convention. The Late Postmodern Era—now, *that* sounds romantic, like waking up in bed with Zelda Fitzgerald and calling your hangover the Jazz Age. Confusing? Only if you brood about it. Let's just wade on into the glamorous bog we call postmodernism. And let's bring along some zippy charts and graphs and lists and disjointed commentary. Why? Because postmodern magazine articles are like that.

THE GREENING OF POSTMODERNISM: READINGS

There once was a time when postmodernism could be daunting. Consider the following bit of feverish academic hairsplitting by critic Irving Sandler, from the fall/winter 1980 issue of *Art Journal*.

"Post-modernism needs to be dealt with in the same manner as modernism, that is, as either exclusive or inclusive. The definition of exclusive post-modernism depends on a conception of exclusive modernism. Exclusive postmodernism wants to invert exclusive modernism and, in the process, destroy it; it is *parricidal.* Inclusive post-modernism is merely the latest stage of inclusive modernism, that is, modernism that encompasses post-modernism. Thus, both exclusive post-modernism and pluralism are opposed to exclusive modernism. But pluralism is broader than exclusive post-modernism, since it views art as open in every direction, including that of exclusive modernism."

Tough sledding, huh? Compare that with the punchy, kicky criticism typical of this, the Late Postmodern Era:

"Fad hatting for fall by the Postmodern milliner [Sherry] Vigdor."—photo caption, *Elle*,

November 1986 (And how does a hat designer get to be postmodern? "She's not above stealing ideas from Saturday-morning cartoons: A flapped cap woven with leather is called 'Wascal' in homage to Elmer Fudd.")

"The Postmodern parka? Après-ski gone party with semiprecious metallic parkas for p.m." —another photo caption, *Elle*, November 1986

"People are learning how to appreciate the discomfort that a lot of postmodernists deal with,' [artist Sherrie] Levine said. 'The ideas that people started talking about 10 years ago in this country are now common knowledge.'"—Andy Grundberg, "When Outs Are In, What's Up?," *The New York Times*, July 26, 1987

"The photographs [in Tama Janowitz's *A Cannibal in Manhattan*] are dumb—in the intentional, postmodern manner—but they're more fun than the bloated text on either side of them."—Terrence Rafferty, "Advertisements for Themselves," *The New Yorker*, October 26, 1987

"Senator Simon had previously endeared himself to me by announcing early in the cam-

paign, 'I'm not a neo-anything,' thereby putting down both neoconservatives and neoliberals (actually, Simon is a post-modern neoliberal, which means 'old-fashioned New Dealer')." —William Safire, On Language, *The New York Times Magazine*, November 8, 1987

"More than self-indulgent posturing, *Walker* is a postmodern repetition (fueled by Joe Strummer's tasty pastiche of salsa, Ennio Morricone, and Mexican ballads). It's *The Wild Bunch* scaled down for the contra war."—J. Hoberman, "Hell Is for Heroes," *The Village Voice*, December 8, 1987

POSTMOD SEX—headline in *The Village Voice Literary Supplement*, December 8, 1987

"Jacqueline Schnabel's few feet ten inches of compact curves and nonstop legs might have been custom-made for the erotic tailoring of Azzedine Alaïa… Her own artist husband also admires Alaïa's work, although, like any good husband in a postmodernist age, he occasionally, she says, wants to see her in something 'more plain, from the fifties.'"—Ben Brantley, "Alaïa Alliance," *Vanity Fair*, December 1987 p

---

"Andrew Humm, spokesman for the Coalition of Lesbian and Gay Rights, confronting the postmod Joe Pine [referring to Morton Downey Jr.] at their December 9 taping."—photo caption, *The Village Voice*, December 29, 1987

"Where will rap end up? Where most postmodern American products end up: highly packaged, regulated, distributed, circulated

and consumed."—Cornel West, quoted by Greg Tate in "Hiphop Nation: It's Like This Y'All," *The Village Voice*, January 19, 1987

"By chance…I picked up G. K. Chesterton's set of stories, *The Club of Queer Trades*, which, although published in 1905, anticipates the problem of the postmodern American service

economy… By way of postmodern, entrepreneurial example, I can think of at least four minor enterprises likely to become…major industries."—Lewis Lapham, "After Keynes," *Harper's*, January 1988

"[Los Angeles pastry chef Michel Richard] has taken inspiration from the postmodern fantasies all along the fashionable strip of Melrose

Avenue, where his restaurant is situated." —Corby Kummer, "Buying the Scene," *The Atlantic*, January 1988

One crisp morning in 1984, did some fellow look up from the sports pages and quip, "Cubs versus Padres…hey, it's postmodern baseball!"

What do these people mean? We aren't sure. More to the point, *they* aren't sure. And just to make *sure* they aren't, we've tried to track down some of the writers quoted above in

order to discuss the postmodern question.

Elle editors were unwilling to explain why the ski parkas were postmodern. "We're busy," complained a spokeswoman.

More forthrightly, Terrence Rafferty admitted that he was unsure exactly "how or why" the intentional dumbness of the photos in Janowitz's book reflected a postmodern influence. "But it does seem to me characteristic [of postmodernism]," he added.

"Mr. Safire hasn't really addressed himself to the question," said Safire's *New York Times* assistant in response to our request for an interview regarding Paul Simon's postmodernism. "You can read about it in his column if it becomes timely."

"It has become kind of vague and catchall, hasn't it?" replied Ben Brantley when asked about his reference to the postmodern age. "The quote [from Schnabel] got distorted at the end—it's a reference to a Bardot sort of thing."

Lapham explained his use of the word *postmodern* to modify *economy:* "It was just by way of analogy. It's just a phrase, a term of art. As I understand it, postmodern art is largely minimalist. Right?" Well …*no.*

REAL-LIFE POSTMODERN STUFF: WHERE IS IT? WHAT IS IT?

This being the Late Postmodern Era, it follows that we must be surrounded by postmodern artifacts, heaps of them. *But which ones are they?*

Why, here we are now at an East Village art gallery. Look at that sculpture of Jackie Kennedy in her bloodstained, Dallas death-day ensemble—*and a video monitor showing cartoons where her face should be!* Sure, it's hip. But is it postmodern, or just exuberantly tasteless?

We think we know postmodernism when we see it—yes, the Jackie sculpture looks pretty PoMo to us—but perhaps the question is best tackled on a case-by-case basis. After scouring the worlds of fashion and art on both coasts, we have compiled a list of concrete, easy-to-recognize criteria.

ARCHITECTURE:
► Does the building have pilasters or pediments or the same color scheme as the 1984 Summer Olympics?
► Is it a cube with a peaked roof?
► Does it look like something futuristic—as conceived by Sir Christopher Wren?
► For a building, is it funny?
► Is it funny but not a Las Vegas hotel or a fast-food stand in Los Angeles?
► Is it easy to like?

MUSIC:
► Does the piece make use of old TV themes or of Malcolm X speeches?
► Does it sound like a combination of Philip Glass and Richard Wagner, or Ornette Coleman and Ennio Morricone?
► Are you listening to it at BAM?
► Is it easier to like than Milton Babbitt but harder than Tchaikovsky?

PAINTING:
► Does the work combine naked figures and old advertising characters in a cryptic, arbitrary manner?
► Is it painted on broken china?
► Does the gallery owner call it *neo*-anything?
► Is it a photocopy?
► Do you look at it and say, "My 23-year-old could do that"?

TELEVISION:
► Do the characters talk to the camera sometimes?
► Does the program have a "look"?
► Does it remind you of an old TV show, only it's insincere and has better production values?

INTERIOR DESIGN:
► Does the room sport suspiciously well

placed water stains, rust marks and peeling paint?
► Was it designed by Daryl Hannah's character in *Wall Street?*
► Is there more than one piece of furniture in the room with spheres or other geometric shapes for legs?
► Would you really want to live there?

LITERATURE:
► Does the text contain shopping lists, menus and/or recipes?
► Does it contain a novel within a novel that has the same title as the novel?
► Does the cover feature a bunch of little geometric shapes and a quote from Robert Coover?
► Does it remind you of Céline, if Céline had drunk a lot of Tab and watched a lot of TV?
► Is it easy to hate?

GRAPHIC DESIGN:
► Is it like MTV?
► Do the layouts look like this one?

CUISINE:
► Does it look like graphic design?
► Is it carpaccio?
► Does it have a purplish element?
► Is it slightly bitter—or extremely sweet?

MOVIES:
► Does it remind you of an old movie, only it's set in a postapocalyptic wasteland?
► Does it remind you of an old TV show, only it's insincere and has better production values, and it's longer?

FASHION:
► Is the garment modular?
► Does it remind you of an old Chanel dress, only it's ironic and has worse production values?
► Did the designer do a Rose's lime juice ad?
► Did *Elle* magazine *say* it was postmodern?
► Would you feel foolish wearing it outside New York or Los Angeles?

THEATER AND PERFORMANCE ART:
► Are there video monitors, working or not, onstage?
► Does it seem like a parody of something, only without jokes?
► Have any of the performers been signed for Susan Seidelman's next film?
► Is it easier than old-fashioned performance art to like, but just as easy to fall asleep during?

FROM POMO TO NOMO: A TIME LINE

The Late Postmodern Era, like vertebrates, didn't just happen; it evolved. Here's how. But first a humble note: if all recorded history were laid out the length of Broadway, the Late Postmodern Era would take up as much space as the guy selling used Sunday papers in front of Zabar's.

March 1978: Philip Johnson's AT&T Building with decorative Chippendale top announced; average New Yorker hears about postmodernism for the first time.

1949: The phrase *postmodern* is coined by J. Hudnut in *Architecture and the Spirit of Man.*

September 1962: *The Jetsons* premieres.

1962–65: Robert Venturi goes to Las Vegas, convinces himself he likes fake-Roman buildings and kitschy signs, writes *Complexity and Contradiction in Architecture,* bible of postmodern architecture.

1964: Susan Sontag decides that if somebody as smart as Susan Sontag is amused by pop culture dreck, it must be okay; publishes the essay "Notes on 'Camp.'"

Early 1970s: Baby-boom intelligentsia, in order to justify years spent watching *The Jetsons* and *Batman,* starts thinking of those wasted years as cultural-history research.

1977: Architectural historian Charles Jencks publishes *The Language of Post-*

Modern Architecture, using the word *postmodern* so many times that he is given credit for coining it; average architect hears about postmodernism for the first time.

August 1, 1981, 12:01 a.m.: MTV debuts; vulnerable American youths are first exposed to self-conscious, cinema gimmicks; *MTV-esque* becomes awkward adjective.

October 1982: After his wildly multicolored Portland Building opens in Portland, Oregon, Michael Graves is the figure around which the public's interest in postmodernism has coalesced in *New York Times Magazine* profile.

March 1982: *The Atomic Café* is released; worrying about the Bomb becomes trendy, partly as 1950s nostalgia, partly as yearning for destruction-free, Jetsonian future.

December 1983: AT&T Building is finished; having no choice, New Yorkers get used to it.

makes for cool tape loop two weeks later at Danceteria.

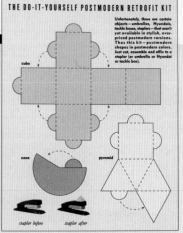

THE DO-IT-YOURSELF POSTMODERN RETROFIT KIT

Unfortunately, there are certain objects—umbrellas, Hyundais, tackle boxes, staplers—that aren't yet available in stylish, overpriced postmodern versions. Thus this kit—postmodern shapes in postmodern colors. Just cut, assemble and affix to a stapler (or umbrella or Hyundai or tackle box).

cube

cone   pyramid

stapler before   stapler after

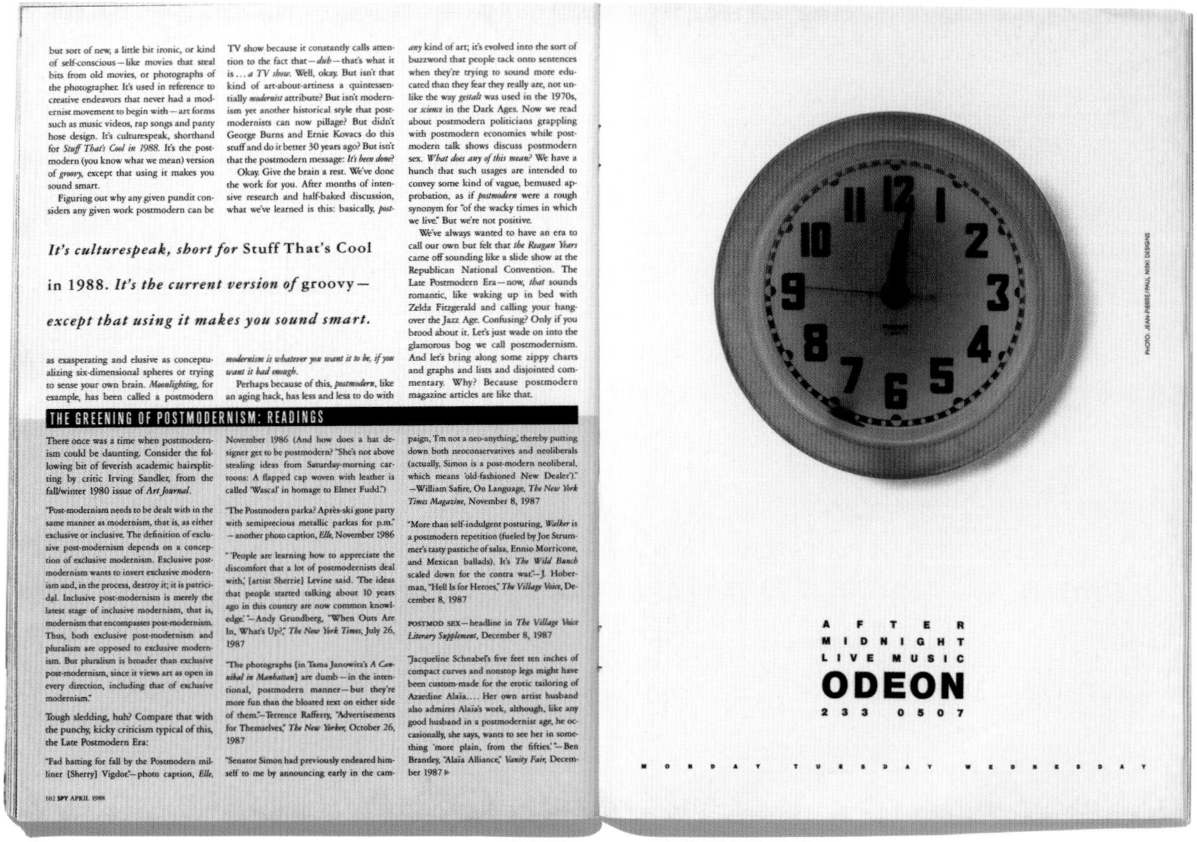

September 1984: *Miami Vice*, the MTV-esque *Dragnet*, debuts on NBC.
March 1985: *Moonlighting*, the self-conscious *Thin Man*, debuts on ABC.
1985: Coca-Cola becomes New Coke and Coca-Cola Classic, betraying corporate awareness of country's newfound passion for mucking around with archetypes.
1985: The Philip Morris Company sponsors the Brooklyn Academy of Music's NEXT WAVE Festival; postmodernism attains cultural status of tennis tournaments, Jesse Helms and other tobacco-industry-supported entities.
1985: Michael Graves designs addition to the Whitney Museum of American Art, is accused of trashing original, modernist building—the first popular stirrings of the Late 1980s Postmodern Backlash.
1986: Rumors surface that Chevy Chase, the postmodern Bob Hope, will star in a feature film version of *The Jetsons*.
September 1986: *Pee-wee's Playhouse*, *Captain Kangaroo* with an ontological migraine, debuts on CBS; kids who have never heard of Pinky Lee or Howdy Doody or Soupy Sales, *kids who weren't even alive in the 1970s*, are treated to a show about the history of children's television.
November 1986: November issue of *Elle* combines the adjective *postmodern* with the words *ski* and *parka*, indicating the meaninglessness of the former and the desirability of the latter.
December 1986: British *Vogue* accuses SPY of employing a "mad post-modernist art director."
March 1987: *Max Headroom*, the self-conscious, MTV-esque *Mod Squad*, debuts on ABC; Max Headroom becomes spokesman for New Coke; "Catch the Wave" slogan eerily reminiscent of BAM's NEXT WAVE Festival.
September 1987: Retrospective on postmodernism opens at IBM Gallery, a few dozen yards from Philip Johnson's AT&T Building; causes no stir whatsoever.
February 1988: *Metropolitan Home*, the greatest popular proselytizer for postmodernism, abandons the cause, takes up motto "No Mo Po Mo."
September 1988 (projected): Coca-Cola introduces New Coke Classic with Michael Graves–designed can; inaugurates "Catch the NEXT WAVE" BAM tie-in with Robert Wilson/Philip Glass opera based on early *Max Headroom* shows; does a six-page spread featuring models in pop-top pilasters.

Postmodern photography has nothing to do with postmodern fiction. To people in the theater, *postmodern* means something entirely different from what it means to architects, and it means something quite different again in Hollywood. When you think about it, just what *do* Cindy Sherman, Kathy Acker, Twyla Tharp, Michael Graves and Bruce Willis have in common? Well, nothing, nothing at all, really, except they're all . . . sort of . . . you know—*postmodern*.

WHO'S WHO, WHAT'S WHAT

A POSTMODERN CATALOG

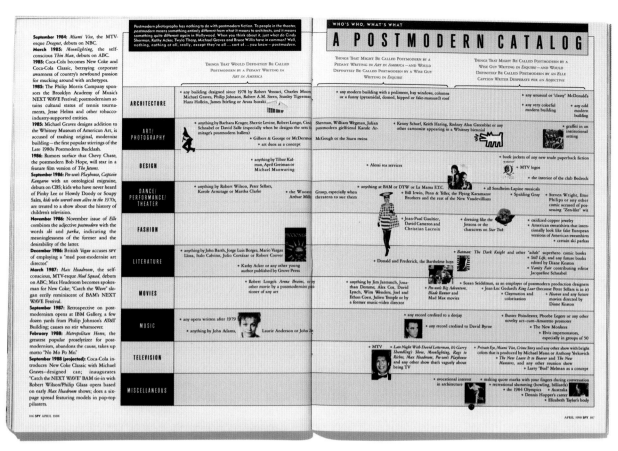

	Things That Would Definitely Be Called Postmodern by a Pedant Writing in *Art in America*	Things That Might Be Called Postmodern by a Pedant Writing in *Art in America*—and Would Definitely Be Called Postmodern by a Wise Guy Writing in *Esquire*	Things That Might Be Called Postmodern by a Wise Guy Writing in *Esquire*—and Would Definitely Be Called Postmodern by an *Elle* Caption Writer Desperate for an Adjective
ARCHITECTURE	• any building designed since 1978 by Robert Venturi, Charles Moore, Michael Graves, Philip Johnson, Robert A.M. Stern, Stanley Tigerman, Hans Hollein, James Stirling or Arata Isozaki	• any modern building with a pediment, bay windows, columns or a funny (pyramidal, domed, hipped or fake-mansard) roof	• any unusual or "classy" McDonald's • any very colorful modern building • any odd modern building
ART/ PHOTOGRAPHY	• anything by Barbara Kruger, Sherrie Levine, Robert Longo, Cindy Sherman, William Wegman, Julian Schnabel or David Salle (especially when he designs the sets for postmodern girlfriend Karole Armitage's postmodern ballets) • Gilbert & George or McDermott & McGough or the Starn twins • art duos as a concept	• Kenny Scharf, Keith Haring, Rodney Alan Greenblat or any other cartoonist appearing in a Whitney biennial	• graffiti in an institutional setting
DESIGN	• anything by Tibor Kalman, April Greiman or Michael Manwaring	• Alessi tea services	• book jackets of any new trade paperback fiction • MTV logos • the interior of the club Bedrock
DANCE/ PERFORMANCE/ THEATER	• anything by Robert Wilson, Peter Sellars, Karole Armitage or Martha Clarke • the Wooster Group, especially when Arthur Miller threatens to sue them	• anything at BAM or DTW or La Mama E.T.C. • Bill Irwin, Penn & Teller, the Flying Karamazov Brothers and the rest of the New Vaudevillians	• all Sondheim-Lapine musicals • Spalding Gray • Steven Wright, Emo Philips or any other comic accused of possessing "Zen-like" wit
FASHION		• Jean-Paul Gaultier, David Cameron and Christian Lacroix	• dressing like the Jetsons or the characters on *Star Trek* • oxidized-copper jewelry • American sweatshirts that intentionally look like fake European versions of American sweatshirts • certain ski parkas
LITERATURE	• anything by John Barth, Jorge Luis Borges, Mario Vargas Llosa, Italo Calvino, Julio Cortázar or Robert Coover • Kathy Acker or any other young author published by Grove Press	• Donald and Frederick, the Barthelme boys	• *Batman: The Dark Knight* and other "adult" superhero comic books • *Still Life*, and any future books edited by Diane Keaton • *Vanity Fair* contributing editor Jacqueline Schnabel
MOVIES	• Robert Longo's *Arena Brains*, or any other movie by a postmodernist practitioner of any art	• anything by Jim Jarmusch, Jonathan Demme, Alex Cox, David Lynch, Wim Wenders, Joel and Ethan Coen, Julien Temple or by a former music-video director • *Pee-wee's Big Adventure*, *Blade Runner* and Mad Max movies	• Susan Seidelman, as an employer of postmodern production designers • Jean-Luc Godard's *King Lear* (because Peter Sellars is in it) • Claymation and colorization • *Heaven* and any future movies directed by Diane Keaton
MUSIC	• any opera written after 1979 • anything by John Adams, Laurie Anderson or John Z	• any record credited to a deejay • any record credited to David Byrne	• Buster Poindexter, Phoebe Legere or any other novelty act–cum–Amaretto promoter • The New Monkees • Elvis impersonators, especially in groups of 50
TELEVISION		• MTV • *Late Night With David Letterman*, *It's Garry Shandling's Show*, *Moonlighting*, *Rags to Riches*, *Max Headroom*, *Pee-wee's Playhouse* and any other show that's vaguely about being TV	• *Private Eye*, *Miami Vice*, *Crime Story* and any other show with bright colors that is produced by Michael Mann or Anthony Yerkovich • *The New Leave It to Beaver* and *The New Munsters*, and any other reunion show • Larry "Bud" Melman as a concept
MISCELLANEOUS		• avocational interest in architecture	• making quote marks with your fingers during conversation • recreational slumming (bowling, billiards) • the 1984 Olympics • Australia • Dennis Hopper's career • Elizabeth Taylor's body

106 SPY APRIL 1988

APRIL 1988 SPY 107

IN SEARCH OF THE POSTMODERN MOMENT

Sometime in the mid-1980s, Early Postmodernism became Late Postmodernism. The question is, exactly when? Just as paleontologists can date the extinction of the dinosaurs by picking through sedimentary rock, we hoped to find the beginning of the Late Postmodern Era by dissecting the corpus of recent periodical literature.

As we studied our data, two incidents looked to be possible signposts for the shift: the October 1982 *Times Magazine* profile of Michael Graves and the November 1986 issue of *Elle*, with the postmodern hats and ski parkas—the apotheosis of Late Postmodern blather. Somewhere between the dates of these two publications, we theorized, lay the hypothetical Postmodern Moment, the very instant when even taffeta-mad fashion editors began to bandy the word *postmodern* about as if it were *charm* or *now*.

Calculating quickly, we discovered that the midpoint between fall 1982 and fall 1986 was fall 1984. Was this the Postmodern Moment? A look at that autumn's events shows that it was indeed a time when stylish pastiche and cannibalization of the past were most definitely in vogue. Consider:

- Armageddon surfaces as a campaign issue
- Trivial Pursuit craze
- Cubs make playoffs
- *Miami Vice* premieres
- Paul McCartney releases a rerecorded "Yesterday" for *Give My Regards to Broad Street*
- *Time* cover stories on AMERICA'S UPBEAT MOOD and MINDING OUR MANNERS AGAIN
- Haute-pizza craze
- VCRs are hottest Christmas gift
- Preparations for the 50th anniversary of Muzak
- Compilation of *TeeVee Toons*, Vol. I
- Stephen Sprouse shows retro-sixties fashions
- Baby Fae gets baboon heart

That's not all. With the help of a computer search through the Nexis data bank, in which every article from most of the important American newspapers (including *The New York Times*, *The Washington Post* and *The Los Angeles Times*) is cataloged, we turned up myriad *postmodern* citations—our textual equivalent of fossilized stegosaurus droppings.

year	number of postmodern articles
1980	21
1981	50
1982	83
1983	60
1984	116
1985	138
1986	197
1987	247

Looks like a regular *postmodernism* epidemic, doesn't it? Note the false peak of 1982, when 83 *postmodernism* articles—*a new story every 4.4 days*—appeared in the popular press. The next year, only 60 stories appeared, and it seemed that the craze was subsiding. But then came 1984, and the rest is history.

So, on a crisp morning in October 1984, did some reasonably literate, reasonably trendy fellow—an advertising copywriter, say—look up from the sports pages and quip, "Cubs versus Padres . . . *hey*—it's like a postmodern World Series," thereby ushering in the profligate Late Postmodern Era? Probably. But we may never know for sure.

YABBA-DABBA-DOODADS

POSTMODERNISM AND THE HANNA-BARBERA CONNECTION

There's a simple way to tell the tyros from the fogies: whereas early postmodernists looked back many centuries, to classical architecture, Renaissance painting and Romantic music, late postmodernists look back many television seasons to the days of Hanna-Barbera Productions's cheesily animated cartoons.

	Early postmodernists	Late postmodernists
Literature	Julio Cortázar (*Hopscotch*)	David Leavitt (*Family Dancing*): characters in his stories are always saying things like "Ern, let's watch 'The Flintstones.'"
Music	John Adams (*Shaker Loops*, composition for septet)	M.C. Shan: he created a rap song called "Jane, Stop This Crazy Thing" by rerecording George Jetson's final-credit howl
Art	Julian Schnabel	Kenny Scharf: he uses Elroy Jetson as a leitmotiv in his paintings
Film	Hans-Jürgen Syberberg (*Our Hitler*)	John Hughes: his *Planes, Trains and Automobiles* featured a sing-along of *The Flintstones'* theme song
Architecture	Michael Graves	Alan Buchsbaum: his restoration of the Nevele Hotel lobby looks like it was influenced by watching too many episodes of *The Jetsons*
Nightclubs	Palladium's Michael Todd Room	Bedrock: this new club pays homage to *The Flintstones'* hometown, featuring spray-paint portraits of major cast members
Food	Duck sausage pizza with goat cheese	Fruity and Cocoa Pebbles: the only breakfast cereal endorsed by Fred Flintstone and Barney Rubble
Television	*Miami Vice*	*The Flintstone Kids*: a prequel to *The Flintstones*

TOMORROW'S POSTMODERNISM TODAY

Someday, probably not too far in the future—April 30, 1989, just to be daringly specific about it—your mother will mention the cute postmodern ottoman she's thinking about buying for the den, thereby providing the coda to *postmodern*'s reign as the lexicographic hot young thing.

Then what? What kind of Marilyn Monroe will Madonna be if she's no longer the postmodern Marilyn Monroe?

The *deconstructed* Marilyn Monroe.

And what does *deconstruction* mean? We could read deconstructionist critic Jacques Derrida and then sweat bullets trying to explain the concept in clear, clever prose. Or we could let you suss it out for yourself—figuring that any decent definition of *deconstruction* has, at this point, a half-life of six months or less, and that, sooner rather than later, you'll be able to read about it in *Elle*. We say, let the handbag-and-belt editors wrestle with it.

108 SPY APRIL 1988

NAKED CITY $400

FINE PRINT   public info   Ann Mathews   J Malanowski   GK   ~~200~~ 7/3 ~~2~~ ~~15-Jul~~ 1 Aug.
[police blotter] → [coming events]   GK   TK   1/3   1 Aug/ 20 Aug.
[THE TIMES] ← $600   800 1/3
                                                                ~~1,000~~ 2.5 15-Aug
MEET THE PRESS   Hanna Rubin   GK   400   1/3 7-Jul
     $100 —   Will Dana
                                    Eric Kaplan

ILLUSTRATED HISTORY OF NY $250   J Pendergrast   GK   1/3 1²Jul
~~MISCELLANEOUS~~   Oval Office/West Side Pier M Shnayerson GK 300 1/4 15-Jul
SHORTS   ~~Sam Roberts~~ Joan Kaufman   1/4

          Roach Control   J Malanowski   GK   300   1/4 15-Jul
          Liars' Poker   Nell Tisch   GK   300   1/4 15-Jul
      /   Reagan ~~press release~~ In house KA   1/4 15-Jul
          Bob Greene's rugs   GC; Jim Kelly GK   300   1/4 15-Jul
          Liz Smith scorecard   Eric Kaplan   GK   1/4 15-Aug
          Pigeons for sale   Allen Kurzweil SM   300   15-Jul
          Tina Brown's T-shirts   ~~staff~~   short   15-Jul
          ~~Helpfulness update   Patty Marx   GK   300   15-Jul~~
          Barber to the bald   Patty Marx   GK   300   15-Jul
          Warhol's nutrition hints Maura Moynihan   15-Jul
      ~~Moynihan on NYC (?)~~   15-Jul
  $100   VIP rooms   Joe Dolce   GK   15-Aug
  $100   Posh condo names   Jim Reginato   GK   300   15-Jul
         (Corporate challenge fashions Jim Reginato GK   15-Aug)
         Funny court cases   Nell Tisch   GK   300   15-Jul
         Pampered pets   Nell Tisch   GK   300   15-Jul

CLIP 'N SAVE   Guide to Correct Pronunciation staff or   GC ~~2,400~~ 2/8 15-Jul
         $50   romans a clef

ALL WASHED UP   Keith Haring   Ted Friend ~~Mira Stout~~   KA 1,000 1 25-Jul
         $400   ~~Fran Lebowitz~~

                                    Phil Weiss
NEWS OF THE WORLD   Urinalysis   Rinker Buck   KA   1560 ~~3,200~~ 1   10 Aug.
                                    Lynn Hirschberg

DOCUDRAMA Hollywood on Houston / casting call   staff   KA   800   1/4   15 Aug

SPY for the defense   staff   1/3 p. 15 Aug.

• animal sacrifice
• Joe Dolce/ grey organi
• Handelman in
- Kastor / books in

~~Naked City~~

H. club

(weddings)

1

6

"What Are You Going to Do, Buy More Earrings?"

A Few Words (at, Sure, a Shockingly Low Rate, but Someday You'll Realize That This Was the Best Job You Ever Had) about *Spy* and Money

Spy looks terrific, and it gets better every month.... My only complaint has to do with the way Spy treats its writers.... I'm sure it's tempting to hang on to those fees for as long as you possibly can.... Because your lead time is what it is, you are always at least two months behind in paying up.... There's an endless supply of first-time freelancers who are so happy to see their names in print that they don't care if they ever get paid. But you can't fill a magazine forever with the work of eager volunteers.

—LETTER FROM DAVID OWEN
TO TOM PHILLIPS, AUGUST 26, 1988

OH, CAN'T WE, NOW?

"I was upset about how chintzy *Spy* was to writers, not only how low the rate was but how incredibly slowly you got paid," explains Owen, an author and *New Yorker* writer. "I remember feeling sort of grumpy at those writers' lunches at Mare Chiaro. All these people were doing all this work to get the magazine going, and then we got *lunch*. It seemed like a typical freelance-writer rip-off, where you'd be paid with food and drink and feel incredibly grateful for it. I've always marveled at how easily a writer will be suckered by a lunch."

(Sometimes it took more than a lunch: Rick Stengel was suckered into writing—or rather, *invited by Kurt to contribute*—a piece for *Spy* in exchange for an Armani tuxedo. Stengel still has the suit.)

Owen, his own will apparently weakened by the catered *tortellini bolognese*, offered up several great *Spy* ideas at those lunches, including Letters to the Editor of *The New Yorker* and Ten Years Ago in *Spy*. He had written for Michael Kinsley at *Harper's* in the early '80s, an experience he likens to *Spy* (i.e., smart magazine, no money), with one difference. "You didn't feel quite as screwed at *Harper's*, because there was no sense that this was going to be a bonanza for anybody, the way there was at *Spy*," he says. "At *Spy*, when it was the media darling of the world, it looked like those guys were going to get very rich from it. So it was very satisfying later when it seemed like they had waited too long."

For Owen, the memory of his pals' pathetic inability to sell out

Opposite: A portion of Susan Morrison's story list for the first issue. Note the generous fees.

Ronald Reagan,
president

POP-UP
PROUST

CRAWFORD

18 **SPY** AUGUST 1987

adoptio
Connec
Compr
offices
16 The
second
Challe:
Central
boundl
New Y
Runner
year im
qualific
Chief I
Officer

March 1989

August 1987

remains a sustaining one. "All these stories would have a *much* more bitter edge if it had worked out for them financially," he says, laughing. "Then the 10 cents a word would have seemed sort of poisonous."

Indeed, the list of contributors and their fees from—by way of example—the December '86 issue is, even if you factor in inflation, a sobering document. Owen's piece that month, a droll roundup of trade magazines, brought him $125—assuming he got the check—but even more shocking is what we paid Paul Rudnick for his "Brats" cover story, a chart-sidebar-and-"listification"-festooned feature: $750. At those rates, no wonder he soon went Hollywood.

But Rudnick takes a generous view of *Spy*'s thriftiness. "I always had the feeling that *Spy* wanted to be very successful and hugely influential and discussed, but that while they would have been delighted to make pots of money, that wasn't an actual part of the equation," he says. "There are certain worlds—theater is another one—where you know nobody's going to make a killing, so everyone's there because they really want to be, and because they think it will be a huge amount of fun. And *Spy* definitely had that aura."

Spy's frugality extended, naturally, to its full-time staff. My journal from those years contains many grisly accounts of negotiations for raises that, in the end, translated to hard-won pennies a day, and virtually every former colleague I interviewed took little time coming around to the money issue.

"As an intern at *Spy* I made $50 a week," says Michael Hainey, who started there in 1989. "When they promoted me to a staff position, I went up to $10,500 a year. Graydon would repeat to us over and over, 'This is the best job you're ever going to have, one day you're going to look back on this....' And a lot of times you hear that kind of thing and you know it's bullshit. But you knew that he was right."

One early *Spy* intern was David Kamp, who, once he was out of Brown University, was hired full-time: $12,500 a year. "It was the biggest thing in the world when I got a raise to $17,500, and Graydon took me to a sushi lunch that day and said, 'David, I know this *seems* like a lot of money, but I'm going to tell you something: The more fucking money you make, the more fucking money you'll need.'"

Lorraine Cademartori, who eventually became managing editor

of *Spy*, was hired as a production editor in 1989. "I'd moved up from Texas and was working at a book publisher and was bored silly," she says. "I met with Kurt and B. W. Honeycutt. That day, B. W. was in full, odd, intimidating mode: ripped T-shirt, spiky hair, the earring—such a sweet guy, an angel to work with, but he scared the hell out of me that first time. I got hired, and on the subway, after I had negotiated my absurdly low salary, I literally was crying, I was so happy. I was already making nothing—this was just a little bit less than nothing."

"I felt like I deserved more money at one point," remembers Lisa Lampugnale, *Spy*'s first chief of research. "So there's Graydon, in those fucking ties and the best outfits ever, and I go in and say, 'I want more money.' And he's like, 'Oh, you don't need more *money*. What are you going to do, buy more earrings?' (I had a lot of funky, big jewelry then—I had to do *something*, I was the Fat Chick. Nowadays you can't say that to a chick on the job. Actually, I don't think you could back then, either.) I go, 'Dude, I *really* need the extra money.' And he did make it work out. But oh my God, he was a talker and a half."

(Only once did I see Graydon literally speechless. In 1988, we included Jamie Lee Curtis on a particularly invasive *Spy* List, and one morning soon after she strode into the *Spy* offices unannounced, found Graydon at his desk, gave him a big smile, said, "I just wanted to tell you that I really love the *Spy* Lists"—and walked out. He never even had a chance to react.)

"I remember how busted the whole thing was," says Pamela Keogh, *Spy*'s first receptionist. "One of my jobs was to do Graydon's expense account. And he needed, like, $40 from his cab receipts, and he *really* wanted that money." Keogh was there only about half a year. "I was actually fired, by Tom Phillips. But he said, 'Don't worry, you can just tell everyone we ran out of money!'"

"These guys didn't pay themselves very well; they didn't pay anybody very well," says Geoff Reiss. "At my interview I was lectured by Graydon on how fortunate I was to be offered $9,000. 'Do you have *any* idea how many people would like this job?' It was intimidating."

It was not a trust-fund staff. Yes, New York was more affordable then; a nice two-bedroom in the East Village could be had for $700. But Graydon in particular was also a mensch about getting freelance assignments for the younger employees at places where he had some pull. "He was very generous," says Elissa Schappell. "He would say, 'Are you interested in this? You need

to learn to do this.' And he would show you how to write a profile: 'You're going to open with this, you're going to go into that....'") Additionally, Kurt and Graydon and Tom all felt strongly about promoting from within, so there was a feeling that if you worked hard you'd do well, and if you had ideas they'd be listened to.

Plus, there were perks, perks that went beyond the cheap black sneakers with the *Spy* logo and the advertising-bartered Aeroflot jackets foisted on the staff as Christmas gifts (also known as bonuses): *Spy*'s barter arrangements—meals for ads—with restaurant advertisers were "the essence of the job," says Walter Kirn, who during his brief tenure as an editor managed to eat countless free dinners, bringing along as many grunt-level staffers as he could.

If barter wasn't possible, the opportunity for unofficial freeloading often was. "It sustained a lot of the younger people," says Rob Spillman, then a *Spy* fact-checker. "When the Puck Building was doing all those glam events—Letterman's fifth-anniversary party, whatever—we'd all go downstairs and sneak in."

"TOM HAD A TREMENDOUS EFFECT on the overall culture of the business side," says Geoff Reiss. "He so personalized every element of the business that people withheld negative news that he could have had a role in helping to fix. It was as if you were telling your dad that you just wrecked your car. 'Noooo...Oh, noooo.' He just got so emotionally involved with this stuff.

"And he had an incredible mastery of the details of the business," Reiss goes on. "There was that green metal file cabinet near his desk with, like, a hundred drawers in it? Only he knew exactly what was in each drawer, and he'd pull one out and there's a month-old printing bill in there, and he wants to talk about $3.50 hand strips that were needed to close the pages. 'They billed us for 843 of these strips! I don't know how it could have been more than 790.' He was on *everything*."

"My conversations with Tom Phillips could be a running gag in a sitcom," says writer-editor Jamie Malanowski. "Even though I was owed more money, Tom was perpetually pulling in numbers and telling me, no, in fact I owed *them* money. It was like a company store! It was never a satisfactory conversation. But it was funny."

Malanowski was part of the Gang of Four, a participant in the Great Staff Writers' Revolt of July 29, 1987. The episode was a

that would still annoy their parents, found satisfaction in an excess of problems, chief among them learning to live monogamously. People of the Van, by contrast, sought a reasonable facsimile of promiscuity that would not preclude Thanksgiving dinner. In practice this meant *Hustler* and Plato's Retreat.

It was a time of surpassing sexual excess. How do we know? Because the sexual titans of the 1970s have become the television talk show guests of the 1980s. Indeed, were it not for an unlimited supply of repentant seventies reprobates—incestuous parents, snuff-porn directors, political *belles de nuit*, pedophiles and so on—Donahue, Oprah, Geraldo and the rest would be out of business.

Speaking of Phil Donahue, a key subset of seventies men reacting to the women's movement were those who simply accepted both unconditionally. This was male feminism, the best-known proponents of which were Alan Alda, John Irving and Donahue. It is worth noting that despite (or because of) their feeling-giving-sharing capitulation, male feminists felt the need to maintain a macho image—Alda as Hawkeye the combat physician, Irving by frequently wrestling with his sons and/or bears, Donahue by scuffling with right-wing nuts at airports.

From My Lai to Me: the human potential movement

It must now be clear that the seventies were characterized not just by a taste for problems but by an endearing conviction that *all problems have solutions.* The human potential movement—catering almost exclusively to Recovering Radicals—took as its unifying principle the notion that just as *you* were the problem, *you* were the solution. Vague though this premise may seem in the 1980s, it sounded pretty cogent to people who only a year or two earlier had felt that intergalactic rock consciousness was The Answer.

The various forms of therapy that guided Recovering Radicals on their journey from Me-the-Problem to Me-the-Solution were, like everything else in the seventies, exotic, even baroque. Forget mom-and-pop Freudianism. Instead, people paid for applications of est, Transcendental Meditation, Sensory Deprivation, rebirthing, assertiveness training and rolfing; of Reichian therapy, of Janovian therapy, of Arica therapy, of Esalen therapy, and of countless pseudoreligious *isms*, both imported (Moonie-ism, 14-year-old-perfect-masterism, Sufism, Taoism, various Buddhisms, yoga) and domestic (Jesus freakism, Carlos Castaneda-ism and Satanism).

The loonbar systems and pseudocreeds of the 1970s—forerunners of the present New Age—were successful for many reasons. They fulfilled a taste for self-obsession conditioned by years of drug abuse. They fulfilled a taste for conspiracy conditioned by years of drug paranoia. They soothed

THE MISSING LINKS

HOW AMERICA GOT FROM *FATHER KNOWS BEST* TO UNIVERSAL GOURMET LIFE-STYLE

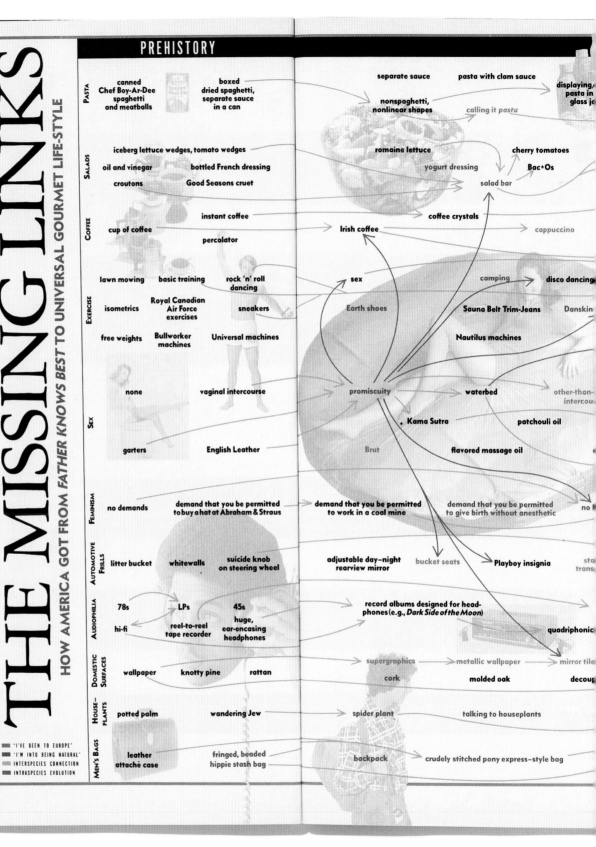

PREHISTORY

■ "I'VE BEEN TO EUROPE"
■ "I'M INTO BEING NATURAL"
▨ INTERSPECIES CONNECTION
■ INTRASPECIES EVOLUTION

PASTA	canned Chef Boy-Ar-Dee spaghetti and meatballs	boxed dried spaghetti, separate sauce in a can		separate sauce / nonspaghetti, nonlinear shapes	pasta with clam sauce / calling it *pasta*	displaying pasta in glass ja...
SALADS	iceberg lettuce wedges, tomato wedges / oil and vinegar / croutons	bottled French dressing / Good Seasons cruet	romaine lettuce	yogurt dressing	cherry tomatoes / Bac•Os / salad bar	
COFFEE	cup of coffee	instant coffee / percolator	Irish coffee	coffee crystals	cappuccino	
EXERCISE	lawn mowing / isometrics / free weights	basic training / Royal Canadian Air Force exercises / Bullworker machines	rock 'n' roll dancing / sneakers / Universal machines	sex / Earth shoes	camping / Sauna Belt Trim-Jeans / Nautilus machines	disco dancing / Danskin
SEX	none / garters	vaginal intercourse / English Leather	promiscuity / Brut	Kama Sutra	waterbed / patchouli oil / flavored massage oil	other-than-intercou...
FEMINISM	no demands	demand that you be permitted to buy a hat at Abraham & Straus	demand that you be permitted to work in a coal mine	demand that you be permitted to give birth without anesthetic		no ...
AUTOMOTIVE FRILLS	litter bucket	whitewalls / suicide knob on steering wheel	adjustable day–night rearview mirror	bucket seats	Playboy insignia	sta... trans...
AUDIOPHILIA	78s / hi-fi	LPs / reel-to-reel tape recorder	45s / huge, ear-encasing headphones	record albums designed for head-phones (e.g., *Dark Side of the Moon*)		quadriphonic
DOMESTIC SURFACES	wallpaper	knotty pine / cork	rattan	supergraphics	metallic wallpaper / molded oak	mirror tile / decou...
HOUSE-PLANTS	potted palm	wandering Jew	spider plant	talking to houseplants		
MEN'S BAGS	leather attaché case	fringed, beaded hippie stash bag	backpack	crudely stitched pony express–style bag		

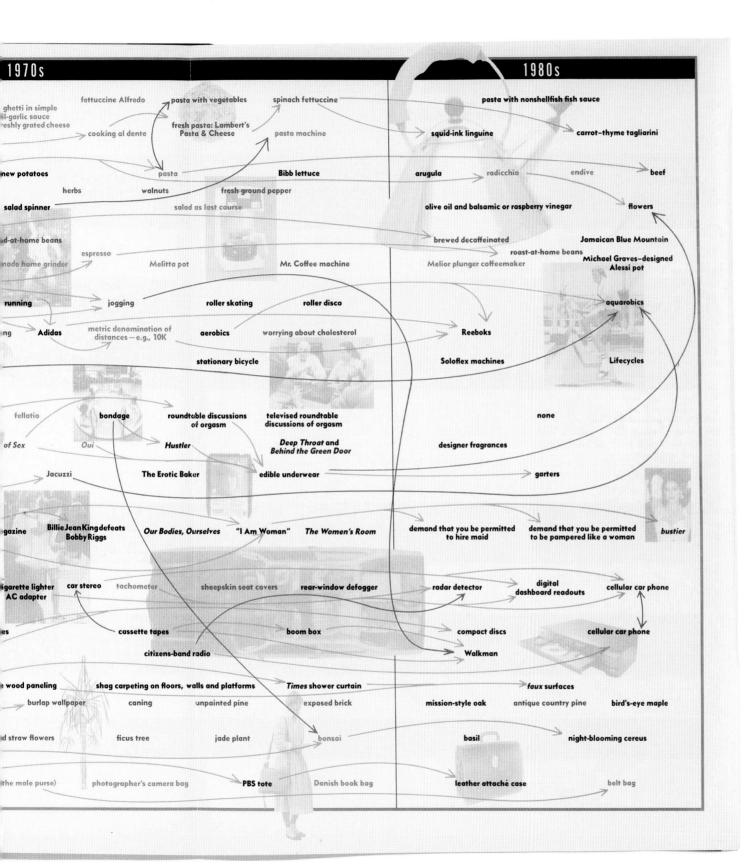

ghetti in simple
il-garlic sauce
reshly grated cheese

fettuccine Alfredo   pasta with vegetables   spinach fettuccine   pasta with nonshellfish fish sauce

fresh pasta: Lambert's
Pasta & Cheese

cooking al dente   pasta machine   squid-ink linguine   carrot–thyme tagliarini

new potatoes   pasta   Bibb lettuce   arugula   radicchio   endive   beef

herbs   walnuts   fresh ground pepper

salad spinner   salad as last course   olive oil and balsamic or raspberry vinegar   flowers

d-at-home beans   brewed decaffeinated   Jamaican Blue Mountain

espresso   roast-at-home beans

made home grinder   Melitta pot   Mr. Coffee machine   Melior plunger coffeemaker   Michael Graves–designed Alessi pot

running   jogging   roller skating   roller disco   aquarobics

ng   Adidas   metric denomination of distances—e.g., 10K   aerobics   worrying about cholesterol   Reeboks

stationary bicycle   Soloflex machines   Lifecycles

fellatio   bondage   roundtable discussions of orgasm   televised roundtable discussions of orgasm   none

of Sex   Oui   Hustler   Deep Throat and Behind the Green Door   designer fragrances

Jacuzzi   The Erotic Baker   edible underwear   garters

gazine   Billie Jean King defeats Bobby Riggs   Our Bodies, Ourselves   "I Am Woman"   The Women's Room   demand that you be permitted to hire maid   demand that you be permitted to be pampered like a woman   bustier

igarette lighter
AC adapter   car stereo   tachometer   sheepskin seat covers   rear-window defogger   radar detector   digital dashboard readouts   cellular car phone

es   cassette tapes   boom box   compact discs   cellular car phone

citizens-band radio   Walkman

wood paneling   shag carpeting on floors, walls and platforms   Times shower curtain   faux surfaces

burlap wallpaper   caning   unpainted pine   exposed brick   mission-style oak   antique country pine   bird's-eye maple

d straw flowers   ficus tree   jade plant   bonsai   basil   night-blooming cereus

(the male purse)   photographer's camera bag   PBS tote   Danish book bag   leather attaché case   belt bag

Giving the '70s a cultural context, from "The 1970s: A Dynamite *Spy* Boogie-Down Celebration of the Most Embarrassing Decade of the Twentieth Century," December 1988.

THE FEUD CHAIN

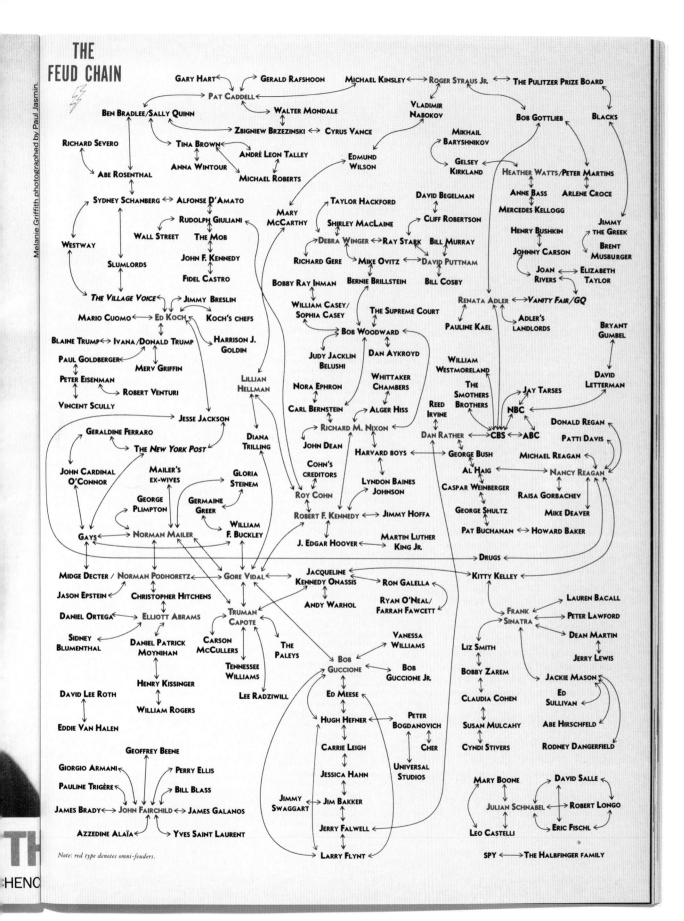

Melanie Griffith photographed by Paul Jasmin.

Note: red type denotes omni-feuders.

From "Feuds!,"
November 1988

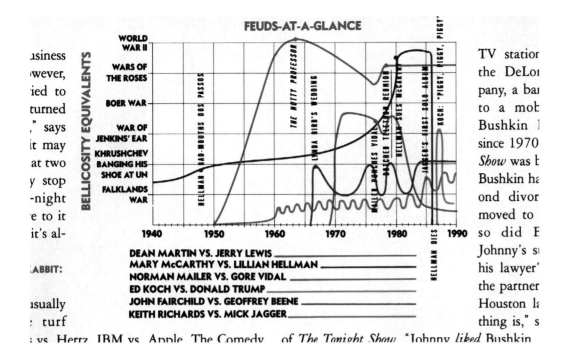

FEUDS-AT-A-GLANCE

BELLICOSITY EQUIVALENTS

WORLD WAR II — WARS OF THE ROSES — BOER WAR — WAR OF JENKINS' EAR — KHRUSHCHEV BANGING HIS SHOE AT UN — FALKLANDS WAR

1940 1950 1960 1970 1980 1990

DEAN MARTIN VS. JERRY LEWIS _____
MARY McCARTHY VS. LILLIAN HELLMAN _____
NORMAN MAILER VS. GORE VIDAL _____
ED KOCH VS. DONALD TRUMP _____
JOHN FAIRCHILD VS. GEOFFREY BEENE _____
KEITH RICHARDS VS. MICK JAGGER _____

Further clarification, from "Feuds!," November 1988

usiness
wever,
ied to
turned
," says
it may
at two
y stop
-night
e to it
it's al-

.ABBIT:

usually
: turf

: vs. Hertz. IBM vs. Apple. The Comedy

TV statior
the DeLoi
pany, a bai
to a mot
Bushkin I
since 1970
Show was k
Bushkin ha
ond divor
moved to
so did E
Johnny's s
his lawyer'
the partner
Houston la
thing is," s

of *The Tonight Show*. "Johnny *liked* Bushkin

watershed moment in the early history of *Spy*.

"*Spy* was incredibly cheap, obviously, and my original contract was for forty cents a word," says Tad Friend, another of the magazine's four staff writers at the time. "Then, two months into it, they *cut* me. Because I was making so much money—$180 a month—they made it forty cents a word up to 2,500 words, and *thirty cents* a word thereafter. And I was outraged." The outrage was channeled into what he now calls, his eyes flashing (well, not really, but it sounds good) at the memory nearly two decades later, "the unionization of July 1987."*

"Nell Scovell and I were being paid $5,200 a year," says Lynn Snowden (now Pickett). (When Graydon had offered to hire Snowden for $100 a week and she asked whether she'd be allowed to freelance, Graydon laughed and said, "I think you're going to *have* to.") "Nell and I would sometimes get an idea and then go, 'You know what? Not for a hundred a week. I'm not doing that. Too ambitious.' One day the four of us were in the

---

*Thirty and forty cents per word sounds low, but this was 1987. In constant dollars—all right, constant pennies—the equivalent word rates today would be fifty-five to seventy cents. Okay, the rates were pretty low. —Eds.

conference room throwing around ideas, and Nell made the not-for-a-hundred-a-week comment.' And Jamie said, '*What?*' Because he thought, *If you guys are only getting* that, *it's going to be impossible for* us *to get any more money.* They felt it would be in their best interests if we were getting the same as they were, and then we could *all* ask for more."

"As close as I felt to Kurt and Graydon, there was also a feeling that we were widgets, a little bit, in their view—and I was better treated probably than some other people," says Friend. "When we sat down and compared, I was embarrassed because I was making, I think by a significant amount, more than the others. They shrewdly made me the ringleader. We wrote this letter and all signed it, with four or five different points, which basically boiled down to 'MORE MONEY.'" The letter, even though it did not result in excommunication, came to be known around the office as *The Ninety-five Theses*, after Martin Luther. "And I gave it to Graydon and he did one of his pop-eyed responses, and sat me down and gave me the *M*A*S*H* speech. Which he gave to everyone else, too."

"It got very personal very quickly," says Snowden. "I was scarred by that—*now* I'm hearing I'm not even worth the $5,200! But there was one pretty funny moment. I was stammering out how I was getting a lot more freelance work and feeling appreciated more elsewhere, and how I'd like to feel a little of that at *Spy*. And Graydon took out a piece of paper and wrote down some things and slid it over to me. He said, 'What's that?' I looked at it: 'Gary Burghoff, McLean Stevenson, Larry Linville.' I said, 'Actors who were on *M*A*S*H*?' And he said, 'Actors who *left* *M*A*S*H* and were *never heard from again*.'"

"It was totally divide and conquer," remembers Friend. "'You shouldn't be lumping yourself in with them! If you leave *Spy* now, you're going to be like Larry Linville and Gary Burghoff and McLean Stevenson, the guys who left because they thought they could make it big elsewhere'—I think Graydon said specifically that I was going to be Larry Linville—'but the *reason* for their success was *M*A*S*H*. And *Spy* is the reason you writ-

ers have any credibility in this city at all. And…well, we want to switch you over to do more editing anyway.' And that's what happened. And I got paid a little more. I don't know how it worked out for the other people."

"The night before, I'd written down all the stories I'd done or contributed to," says Scovell. "Graydon regarded the list, took a beat, then sat up straight. 'We'll work something out,' he said."

"They cut separate deals with each of us," says Snowden. "Graydon also made it clear that he worked at *Time* all those years and never, ever discussed salary with coworkers. I was very young, I didn't know. It was a lesson. I remember Jamie coming out of his interrogation looking shaken, ashen."

As for Graydon, he spent the rest of that day in his office, contentedly humming "The Internationale."

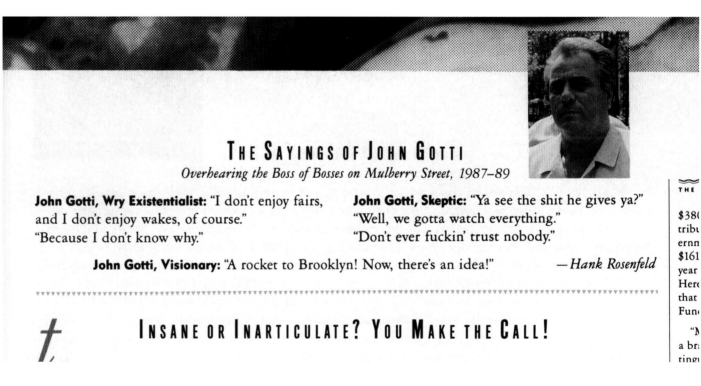

THE SAYINGS OF JOHN GOTTI
Overhearing the Boss of Bosses on Mulberry Street, 1987–89

John Gotti, Wry Existentialist: "I don't enjoy fairs, and I don't enjoy wakes, of course."
"Because I don't know why."

John Gotti, Skeptic: "Ya see the shit he gives ya?"
"Well, we gotta watch everything."
"Don't ever fuckin' trust nobody."

John Gotti, Visionary: "A rocket to Brooklyn! Now, there's an idea!"

—*Hank Rosenfeld*

INSANE OR INARTICULATE? YOU MAKE THE CALL!

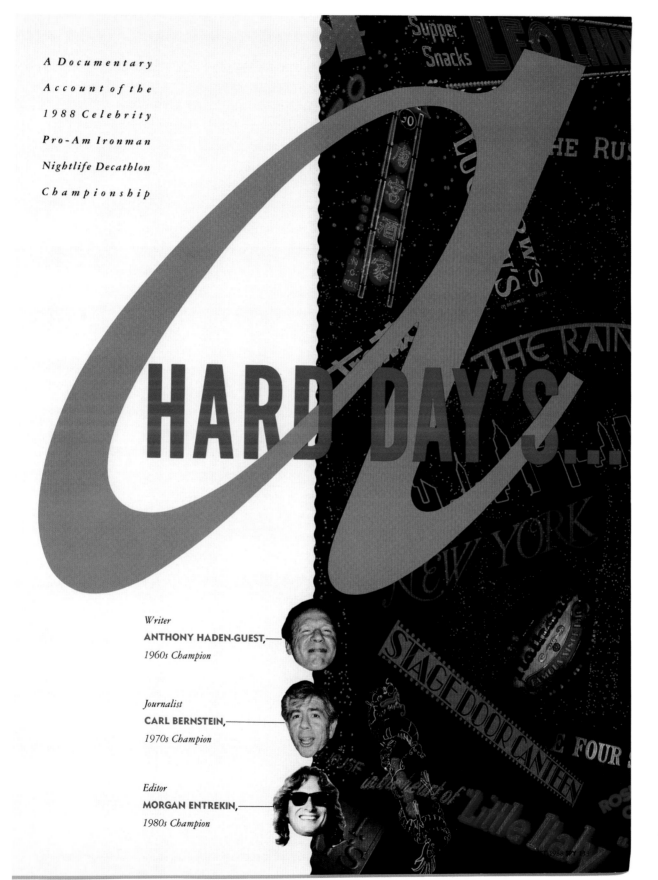

*A Documentary
Account of the
1988 Celebrity
Pro-Am Ironman
Nightlife Decathlon
Championship*

HARD DAY'S...

Writer
ANTHONY HADEN-GUEST,
1960s Champion

Journalist
CARL BERNSTEIN,
1970s Champion

Editor
MORGAN ENTREKIN,
1980s Champion

August 1988

For many of us, the glory days — a happy era of multiple-stop nights on the town, individual hangovers merging into one, periodic paternity suits, misplaced panty hose — seem positively Pleistocene: it's been a while. Indeed, in the decades-long Ironman competition to choose the hardiest night crawler, that test of conversational dexterity, relentless drinking, sexual ruthlessness and the mysterious something that is perhaps best described as an imperviousness to appearing ridiculous in the eyes of sensible adults, we at SPY are — unashamedly — also-rans. Other souls, made of sterner stuff, have also been winnowed from the competition in the years since Studio 54 closed: where are Dianne Brill, Halston and Andy Warhol now?

A team of experts we impaneled in a booth at Nell's said — with near unanimity — that over the decades the city's standout Nightlife Achievers have been writer Anthony Haden-Guest (1960s champion), author Carl Bernstein (1970s champion) and editor Morgan Entrekin (1980s champion). At least, that's what we think they said. It was kind of hard to hear.

How can these three men behave as they do and still be as productive as they are? Entrekin, after all, has his own office; Haden-Guest writes for magazines every year without fail; and Bernstein has spent half a decade working on an entire book. Or is it precisely *because* they comport themselves with such abandon — experience fueling the creative flame — that they are so professionally impressive?

In any event, these are three *life forces* we're talking about. But only one person can be said to be the true nightlife champion, and we decided to find out who he is. We asked aspiring litterateurs and amateur gumshoes **JOHN BRODIE** and **BOB MACK** to follow in the three titans' footsteps for an evening so that we could judge the performances of Entrekin, Haden-Guest and Bernstein in ten categories (hours spent out, number of celebrities seen, number of drinks drunk, and so forth).

Thus, on randomly chosen evenings this spring — evenings no more nightlife-intensive than any others in the lives of these three men — each competitor was tracked, on foot and by Ford Tempo, from party to nightclub to private liaison, by this determined pair of SPY operatives who sought only knowledge and were willing to record the intimate details of perfect strangers' activities to attain it. To ensure a fair competition, the subjects were unaware, until now, that they were participants in the 1988 Celebrity Pro-Am Ironman Nightlife Decathlon Championship.

The results are before you. Who will win?

ANTHONY HADEN-GUEST

What does Anthony Haden-Guest do? He chaffs, he sparkles, he talks British-charmingly about his upcoming book for Simon & Schuster and about articles he has written for *New York* and *Vanity Fair*, several of them within the last decade.

CARL BERNSTEIN

A man who has been played on film by both Dustin Hoffman (*All the President's Men*) and Jack Nicholson (*Heartburn*) might feel he had the right to take it easy. Not Carl Bernstein. He's out almost every night gathering material for *Disloyal*, the

MORGAN ENTREKIN

The courtly Nashvillean has his own publishing imprint at Atlantic Monthly Press. Though he is widely supposed to have been an inspiration for Jay McInerney's dissolute character Tad Allagash in *Bright Lights, Big City*, Entrekin insists, to anyone

---

Thursday, April 14, 1988

5:35 p.m.: We take up a position outside **HADEN-GUEST**'s blue-and-white **townhouse**, on East 80th Street, somewhat daunted by what appears to be a security guard patrolling a nearby driveway. He turns out to be a parking-lot attendant. After 35 minutes, we determine that **HADEN-GUEST** must be elsewhere, perhaps already regaling his friends with the story of how earlier in the day he served as a superprestigious **honorary race official** at **The Manhattan Yacht Club**'s 1988 Legend Cup race.

6:25 p.m.: Aware that **HADEN-GUEST** is expected at a reception at **Asprey**, the expensive British

---

long-awaited book on his parents and the McCarthy era — another manuscript, as it happens, commissioned by the patient house of Simon & Schuster. Bernstein spends most of his time interviewing people who've never met his parents, *but that's just the kind of admirably thorough reporter he is.*

Monday, April 18, 1988

6:58 p.m.: We park our **Ford Tempo** in front of **The Chrysler Building**'s Lexington Avenue entrance and await the throng expected for *New York* magazine's twentieth-birthday party. The first guest to arrive — two minutes early, in a tuxedo, but without his wife, former top model **Ivana** — is self-who will stop dancing long enough to listen, that he is one of the hardest-working book editors in New York.

Tuesday, March 29, 1988

5:30 p.m.: We arrive at 19 Union Square West, where **ENTREKIN** puts in very full days at **Atlantic Monthly Press**, and park across the street in our inconspicuous cherry-red **Ford Tempo**. It soon becomes clear that this must be one of those very rare days when **ENTREKIN** has left the office early.

6:30 p.m.: We proceed to the **Art Greenwich Theater**, at the corner of Greenwich Avenue and West 12th Street, the location of the star-studded

---

luggage-and-knickknack store in super-tasteful **Trump Tower**, we pilot our **Ford Tempo** to 56th and Fifth and immediately spot legendary 52-inch-high *Esquire* editor **Lee Eisenberg**.

7:00 p.m.: **HADEN-GUEST** arrives in a dinner jacket and with his trademark cowlick tamed, escorting a **matron** whom he deposits along with his coat on a lower floor. While grazing on cheese sticks and champagne, he entertains a circle of lesser celebrities, including superfamous diver **Valerie Taylor**, with a stream of witty banter.

8:05 p.m.: **HADEN-GUEST** leaves **Asprey**, walks north on Fifth Avenue and catches a cab going east

---

effacing city benefactor **Donald Trump**.

7:15 p.m.: By now *Times* columnist **Abe Rosenthal** and his wife, **Shirley Lord**, recording executive **Ahmet Ertegün**, **Katharine Graham**, **Rupert Murdoch**, Senator **Daniel Patrick Moynihan**, **Jerzy Kosinski**, *Times* editor **Warren Hoge**, **Peter Maas**, **Brooke Astor**, and the ubiquitous **Suzy** have all walked through the revolving doors and smiled delightedly to see the inflatable 25-foot-high pink birthday cake topped off — hey, that's nutty! — with a ten-foot-tall teddy bear.

7:52 p.m.: **CARL BERNSTEIN**, looking dapper in a blue suit and white raincoat that complement his luxuriant gray hair, arrives by **cab** at

---

New York premiere of **Bright Lights, Big City**, which **ENTREKIN** is sure to attend.

6:35 p.m.: Seminal artist **Keith Haring** arrives at the theater in a mock letterman jacket with a **female companion**. Hard on their heels are humorist **P. J. O'Rourke**, wearing a pink bow tie and new boating moccasins, and an eclectic array of Hollywood stars: **William Hickey**, **Griffin Dunne**, **Jennifer Beals**, **Lauren Hutton** and **Jodie Foster**. Modest, hardworking journalists **George Plimpton**, **Clay Felker**, **Bob Colacello** and **Gloria Steinem** sweep in, followed by **Carl Bernstein**, who entertains the paparazzi by bellowing, "Don't touch my hair!" when **Ms. Hutton** and her **female companion** try to ruffle his preternaturally stiff **coiffure**.

Reporter John Brodie: "We were so inept. We'd figure things out slowly—like when you're following someone in the city you don't have to drive as fast as you think, because there are always traffic lights. We'd get in trouble when we got too clever. Occasionally I would follow someone from in front of them, which I thought was unobtrusive, but in fact you end up losing them. The real problem was photographs. Now it's so much easier to take long-lens, no-light photos. This was also before the whole tabloidization of everything. It was much more, you know, Peeping Tom."

Haden-Guest demonstrates the latest rhinoplastic techniques at Asprey.

on 57th Street, heading for an exclusive dinner party at real estate middlewoman **Alice Mason**'s.

HADEN-GUEST makes it to Mason's building, at 150 East 72nd Street, before we have time to set up for a photo. We do, however, catch a glimpse of former novelist and Alice Mason regular **Norman Mailer** and his wife, painter **Norris Church Mailer**. Norman hastens into the party, doubtless eager to advise Anthony on refining the narrative schema of his book-in-progress on drug runners in Lebanon (which includes an account of his own kidnapping).

8:30 p.m.: In the next half hour a cavalcade of aging publishing and show business figures cross **Alice Mason**'s entryway, including taut-skinned *New York Observer* impresario **Arthur Carter**, **Helen Gurley Brown** and **David Brown**, **Norman Podhoretz**, and **Aileen**

"Suzy" Mehle, doing more of the footwor for which she has become legend. **HADEN GUEST**'s publisher, Simon & Schuste chairman **Dick Snyder**, puts in an appear ance and alarms our subject by inquirin when Simon & Schuster can expect hi fashionably late book. **HADEN-GUEST** evidently not recognizing Snyder, riposte "And what business is it of yours?"

11:00 p.m.: We prepare for th end of the fete, as it is **Ms Mason**'s practice to expel her fel low social climbers sharply at 11:00 p.m.

11:45 p.m.: Trailing the pack o departing guests, **HADEN-GUEST** says his **goodbyes** with undis guised glee; his night has just begun.

Bernstein sails eagerly into The Chrysler Building. No one notices.

last. **BERNSTEIN** enters the party with light, expectant step, apparently unaware that many of the distinguished guests have long since descended from **The Cloud Club** on the 66th floor and departed in thei **limousines**. Once upstairs, among those **BERNSTEIN** fascinates are **Marilyn Bethany Clay Felker** and **Joe Klein**. **BERNSTEIN** men tions the lecture series on the press tha he gives each summer aboard the **Queen Elizabeth 2** and concludes weightily, "I'm tired of the **Hamptons**." *The New York Times* will report the following day that "Carl Bern stein talked to anyone."

8:52 p.m.: Back downstairs we encounter *New York* cover boy **Jimmy Breslin**, who is at curbside awaiting the arrival of his wife. He tells us

7:00 p.m.: The great conflict of the evening begins when **Jay McInerney** arrives not with his steady date—walking docudrama **Marla Hanson**—but with **Tracy Pollan**, who plays **Michael J. Fox**'s love interest both on and off the screen. **Hanson**, who arrives alone, attempts to slip into the theater unnoticed but is ushered back before the flashbulbs by tactful publicist **Peggy Siegal**. Once inside, **Hanson** joins **ENTREKIN**'s buddy/co-worker **Gary Fisketjon**, who has just had a riveting conversation with generational spokesman **Bret Easton Ellis**.

Palladium operator **Steve Rubell** shows up with another hardworking journalist, **Claudia Cohen**. While **Rubell** runs across the street to fetch **Claudia** a slice of **pizza**, she generously allows the paparazzi ten

minutes to photograph her svelte body (vividly wrapped in a magenta topcoat) and her curiously beautiful face (vividly burnished with orange lipstick).

7:15 p.m.: MORGAN ENTREKIN arrives at last, very fashionably late, accompanied by a squadron of **three blonds** with whom he has perhaps been discussing the textual problems posed by their tag-team translation of **ENTREKIN**'s entire line of books into Swedish.

9:35 p.m.: So that traffic won't be clogged by a caravan of stretch limousines, **Peggy Siegal** has thoughtfully hired a superglamorous **bus** to ferry the celebrities to the trendy **Canal Bar** for dinner following the premiere. An

entourage consisting of **Jay McInerney Gary Fisketjon**, **P. J. O'Rourke** and the sulky **Marla** elects to travel by limousine instead **ENTREKIN** decides not to join **Jay** and **Gary** in reconstituting what **Jay** has rightly called "a galaxy of our own" but rather to escort one of his presumed **translators** to a taxi before reentering the theater and emerg ing with another young blond woman, un doubtedly an **author**. **ENTREKIN**, his bud ding **novelist** and **Carl Bernstein** then take the **bus** and, we may assume, trade wry **aperçus** into man's existential plight, which are, unfortunately, lost to history.

9:50 p.m.: The bus arrives safely at **Canal Bar**, and we watch transfixed as record producer **Jellybean Benitez** bellies up to the bar

Haden-Guest, man of a thousand faces, leaves Alice Mason's disguised as the Phantom of the Opera.

11:50 p.m.: After walking a block east down 72nd Street, **HADEN-GUEST** takes a cab up Third Avenue and turns right on 88th Street.

12:05 a.m.: We press our noses up against the glass of **Elaine's** and stare into the fabled grotto. Apparently still a bit fatigued from the previous night's wrestling match that caused his expulsion from **Au Bar**, an ersatz Nell's that opened in January, **HADEN-GUEST** wants nothing more than to share a quiet drink with a few sophisticated colleagues.

We enter the eatery and sit at the bar, where we can observe the room's thrilling complement of writers, including top editor **G. Barry (Playboy) Golson**, top vocalist

John Henry Kurtz and top story editor **Peter (Equalizer) McCabe**. A charming **lady** in a Nerf-ball orange minidress turns to us and inquires, approximately, "Where do you gentlemen hail from?" When we respond "**California**" and "**Manhattan**," she falls into a companionable silence. **HADEN-GUEST** settles into the seat reserved for him at top scriptwriter **David (Miami Vice) Black**'s regular Thursday-night table.

1:05 a.m.: The gentlemanly **HADEN-GUEST** makes a practice of standing whenever anyone gets up from the table. But in the confines of **Elaine's** he feels he can relax his renowned manners a bit, and he removes his dinner jacket to expose a burgundy-colored **vest** and a supersexy **formfitting undershirt**.

---

that some of the men at the party "like to wear dresses" but declines to be specific. Party animal **Rudolph Giuliani** limbos into the party, where he is greeted with loud cries of "*Ru*-dee! *Ru*-dee!" Freelance racist **Edward Koch** shows up with a very understated **siren** on his limousine and a super-subtle entourage of **bodyguards**.

9:30 p.m.: After never-say-die boulevardiers such as **Barry Diller** and his female date **Lally Weymouth**, **Joni Evans**, **Andy Stein**, and **Cindy** and **Joey Adams** leave, we wonder if **BERNSTEIN** might also have departed, but a check with the security guard confirms that there is only one exit. When we ask a jovial **departing guest** about **BERNSTEIN**'s whereabouts, he replies, "If he's still up

there, then he's behind the bar.... There's hardly anyone left."

10:04 p.m.: Our patience is rewarded when **BERNSTEIN** finally emerges with several **women** and wunderkind **Clay Felker**, who is outfitted in a loden-green hunter's hat.

When one of the women asks **BERNSTEIN** what his plans are for the evening, he says airily, "I'm going home." The statement hangs in the air, and he feels compelled to add, "Well, at least long enough to drop off this damn thing," gesturing toward his **complimentary gift bag**. The bag contains a super-useful **Plexiglas paperweight–cum–envelope holder** and a super-thoughtful **boxed set of all four New York magazine special anniversary issues**.

10:06 p.m.: **Felker** and friends bid adieu to **BERNSTEIN**, who walks downtown half a block and makes a **phone call** from the southwest corner of 42nd and Lexington. He then takes a cab to his **brownstone** apartment, on 62nd Street between Second and Third Avenues.

10:20 p.m.: **BERNSTEIN** leaves his **brownstone**, walks east to Second Avenue, turns right and ducks into a **convenience store** to pick up a **New York Times** before hailing a taxi.

In the cab he puts on his reading glasses and immerses himself in the paper's **Metropolitan News section** as he courses all the way downtown to **Canal Bar**. The story on the party—the story that mentions **BERN-**

Entrekin gets off the bus. Which way to Caesars Palace?

alongside **Tama Janowitz** and helps himself to an assortment of pizzas, cheesecakes and raspberry tarts.

10:30 p.m.: We take up a position outside the restaurant's kitchen door on Spring Street—**ENTREKIN** has been known to leave restaurants through the back to facilitate a speedy return to the office. But on this night, he is apparently working too hard to attempt such a Beatlesque prank.

11:00 p.m.: **Bret Easton Ellis**, tired from bearing the weight of wisdom beyond his years, retires to a cab with his **date**. **George Plimpton**, arm in arm with a young **blond**, strolls toward the romantic **Hudson River**.

11:40 p.m.: Glamorous couple **Claudia Cohen** and **Steve Rubell** depart in her Jaguar. Superglamorous couple **Gloria Steinem** and **Mort Zuckerman** follow in a limousine. **Clay Felker** begins to look for his topcoat and fashionable loden-green hunter's hat.

11:50 p.m.: After searching at least three limos, **Felker** finds his coat and hat.

12:50 a.m.: **Gary Fisketjon** departs for home, but **Carl Bernstein**, **Jay**, **Marla**, **P.J.** and **ENTREKIN** pile into Jay's limousine. We prepare for a chase; having spotted our photographer, **Fisketjon** has apparently told **ENTREKIN** that he is being followed.

Reporter Bob Mack: "When we went out those nights, Graydon said, 'I want you boys to conduct yourselves appropriately out there, because you are ambassadors of *Spy*.'"

1:15 a.m.: **HADEN-GUEST** is not above a little roguish horseplay, and he and his fellows are soon engaged in witty speculation about the color of the **orange-minidress-wearing woman**'s **underwear**. **Peter McCabe** takes it upon himself to solicit a definitive answer from the object of their guesswork. Charmed, she answers, "Fuck you!"

1:20 a.m.: The check arrives at the table and is mistakenly placed before **HADEN-GUEST**, who suddenly appears stricken with a touch of the grippe, or another **writer's affliction**—his face goes white and sweat forms on his brow. He returns to normal when vocalist **John Henry Kurtz** picks up the check.

1:30 a.m.: A number of his companions leave, and **HADEN-GUEST** decides to augment his entourage and atone for **McCabe**'s impropriety by apologizing to the **orange-minidress-wearing woman**. He explains that the shenanigans were prompted by "frank admiration," not mockery, and urges the woman, who reveals that her name is **Judy**, to join him. She does.

1:50 a.m.: **HADEN-GUEST** demonstrates the impressive range of his social skills by alternately praising **Judy**'s home state and mocking her thick New Jersey patois. When she asks, "Do any of youse wanna go to the **China Club**?" he wittily replies, "No, weese don't wanna go to the fuckin' **China Club**."

2:00 a.m.: Owner **Elaine Kaufman** herself comes over to **HADEN-GUEST**'s table and joins the group in a few drinks. Filled with the Dutch courage necessary for the task at hand, **Elaine** asks **HADEN-GUEST** to settle his back tab. He produces **Chemical Bank** stationery and signs it as the piano player plays "Big Spender."

2:45 a.m.: We send **HADEN-GUEST** a **Scotch and water**, which he acknowledges by lifting his glass. After downing his drink, **HADEN-GUEST** comes over and introduces himself; we tell him that we're enormous fans of his work, and he invites us to his table. Once seated, he allows us to buy him a **grappa**—his traditional nightcap.

STEIN's name—won't appear until the next day's morning edition.

10:46 p.m.: **BERNSTEIN** enters **Canal Bar** and settles in at a table with a few friends, including designer **Carolina Herrera** and perennial-escort-of-other-men's-wives **Steve Rubell**. We order a couple of **Bass Ales** at the bar and watch **BERNSTEIN** placidly chew.

Midnight: While **BERNSTEIN** sips a last glass of what appears to be **wine**—forgoing his usual **Moussy**—**Rubell**, **Herrera** and their friends move on.

We finish our beers and head to the car to await **BERNSTEIN**. But he shows no signs of leaving, though he does make

three **phone calls**, using not the ordinary pay phone by the kitchen but the ultra-exclusive **house phone** on the maître d's podium.

12:25 a.m.: **BERNSTEIN** meets a blond **source** and a redheaded **journalism student** at the bar and invites them both back to his booth, where he shares his journalistic **credo** with them. Then, as they watch with shining eyes, **BERNSTEIN** sturdily heads back out into the field to do more reporting.

12:30 a.m.: **BERNSTEIN** walks east on Spring to Hudson Street, where he catches a cab that takes him up to 23rd Street. The cab turns right and stops in front of the **Zig Zag** bar, at

206 West 23rd Street. The instant we park, an ultraglamorous **sanitation truck** obscures our view of **BERNSTEIN**. By the time it moves, he has vanished.

We check **Zig Zag**, upstairs, downstairs, even the bathroom. No **BERNSTEIN**. Nobody at all, in fact. We get back in the car, figuring that he ditched us and made tracks for **M.K. BERNSTEIN** chooses that precise moment to come out of the apartment building at **208 West 23rd Street**, just one door down, escorting a brunet, female **source**.

1:15 a.m.: **BERNSTEIN** begins to interview his **source** at **Zig Zag**'s bar (*You're sure you've never met my parents?*), and we try to snap a few photos through the bar's windowed facade.

1:05 a.m.: **McInerney**'s **car** speeds up Sixth Avenue through **Greenwich Village**. We pull up alongside, and **ENTREKIN** displays for us his supersophisticated, editing-weary **middle finger**. We fall back and have to run a **red light** to catch up with the limo, which has turned on 26th Street and soon turns again onto Fifth Avenue. It pulls up in front of **M.K.**,

Walking—all together, now!—into M.K.

the extraordinarily trendy restaurant and nightclub at 25th and Fifth. The "**wrecking crew**," as this group may well call itself, is soon waved inside.

1:30 a.m.: Inside, **ENTREKIN** sequesters himself at a second-floor table—his office away from the office. He speaks at length with his author **O'Rourke**, undoubtedly offering acute editorial suggestions about the latter's forthcoming collection of travel essays.

The evening's drama, meanwhile, reaches its climax. Having finally corralled **Jay McInerney** in an intimate setting on the stairway between **M.K.**'s first and second floors, **Marla Hanson** complains about his fickle behavior. In dialogue that will, we hope, be immortalized in one of

Jay's forthcoming romans à clef, he says earnestly, "I know, I'm sorry…I know, I'm sorry." She replies earnestly, "Yes, but you didn't have to make me look like a fool." They embrace.

2:30 a.m.: **ENTREKIN** holds court with **O'Rourke**, **Bernstein** and three blond **author-translators** in the club's dining area, transforming it into a modern-day **Algonquin Round Table**.

An **M.K. employee** insists that our paparazzo either check her camera or leave. We leave.

2:40 a.m.: From our position outside the club we see **Bernstein** depart with **Lauren Hutton**. Apparently eager to continue his relentless ques-

Men at Work

ANTHONY HADEN-GUEST

1. **Asprey**
   *Arrived 7:00 p.m.,
   departed 8:05*
2. **Alice Mason's home**
   *Arrived 8:15 p.m.,
   departed 11:45*
3. **Elaine's**
   *Arrived 12:05 a.m.,
   departed 3:45*
4. **Haden-Guest's home**
   Arrived 3:55 a.m.

CARL BERNSTEIN

1. **Chrysler Building**
   *Arrived 7:52 p.m.,
   departed 10:04*
2. **Bernstein's home**
   *Arrived 10:07 p.m.,
   departed 10:20*
3. **Canal Bar**
   *Arrived 10:46 p.m.,
   departed 12:30 a.m.*
4. **Zig Zag**
   *Arrived 12:45 a.m.,
   departed 1:30*
5. **Source's apartment**
   Arrived 1:32 a.m.

MORGAN ENTREKIN

1. **Art Greenwich Theater**
   *Arrived 7:15 p.m.,
   departed 9:35*
2. **Canal Bar**
   *Arrived 9:50 p.m.,
   departed 12:50 a.m.*
3. **M.K.**
   *Arrived 1:30 a.m.,
   departed 3:40*
4. **Nell's**
   *Arrived 3:50 a.m.,
   departed 4:23*
5. **Abingdon Square**
   *Arrived 4:35 a.m.,
   departed, on
   the run, 4:35 (see detail)*
6. **Entrekin's home**
   Arrived 4:36 a.m.

KEY TO DETAIL

—————— Path taken by
Entrekin's cab

- - - - - - Path taken by
SPYmobile

·—·—·—· Path taken, at top
speed, by Entrekin
himself

Reporter Michael Hainey: "When we were doing the special Hamptons edition in 1990, there was a big party one night at Sapore di Mare. The first cell phones had come out, they were like something out of World War II—like shoeboxes with batteries, and the phone sat on top—and you'd plug it into the lighter in your car to charge it. I said to John Brodie, 'I have an idea. Give me the cell phone.' We walk up to the gate where the security guy was. I said, 'I'm Bruce Wasserstein's personal assistant and I have an important call for him on his cell phone.' 'Okay, come on in.' And that's how we got the scene for that story."

3:00 a.m.: He reintroduces us to **Judy**, who has begun to make noises about leaving immediately for the **China Club**, and to a **female editor** from **Fawcett Books**, who seems enamored of him. She notes thoughtfully that Anthony is "the basis for **Peter Fallow**—you know, from *The Bonfire of the Vanities*," and instructs us to "watch him try to get out of paying the bill."

When we tell **HADEN-GUEST** that "we are writers," he expresses sincere concern about how we can afford to live and allows us to buy him another round. He speaks nostalgically of having once read poetry as an opening act for **Jethro Tull**, then imparts two bits of timeless wisdom: "Go to **The World**" and "Listen to the new **Pet Shop Boys** album." Hearing "Chain of Fools" on

the jukebox, **HADEN-GUEST**, 51, gets up and dances with his chair, wiggling his hips in very mod fashion.

3:30 a.m.: The reverie is broken when a member of **HADEN-GUEST**'s circle whom we mistakenly assumed had left, another superfamous **writer**, appears out of the shadows and asks him, "Is that a clip-on bow tie?" In a stunning display of grace under pressure, **HADEN-GUEST** elegantly unties his authentic bow.

This triumph seems to demand celebration, and **HADEN-GUEST**, who has a gift for turning everywhere he goes into a funloving discotheque, convinces **Judy** to dance cheek to cheek with him as the pianist sings "Sugar pie, honey bunch…"

3:45 a.m.: As the lights blink to signal the last call **HADEN-GUEST** decides that "it must be time to either leave or get romantic." Judy is still set on going to the **China Club**, so Anthony waves goodbye to her and draws the **female editor** close.

We diffidently offer them a ride home, which **HADEN-GUEST** accepts with surprising eagerness. As our cramped **Ford Tempo** coasts west on 83rd Street he regales us with anecdotes about the days when he hung out with **Eric Clapton** and **Charlie Watts**. When we reach his **townhouse**, he asks us up for a **glass of wine**, but from the arch of his eyebrow we understand that the offer is perfunctory and that this is one drink he and the **female editor** would prefer to have alone.

Bernstein and his female source outside Zig Zag. Notice the thrillingly unfocused vérité quality of the photograph.

But this tips off the **bartender**, who tips off **BERNSTEIN**.

1:30 a.m.: His reportorial instincts aroused, **BERNSTEIN** finishes his drink and escorts his contact outside, pausing to glare at our by now all-too-familiar cherry-red **Ford Tempo**.

They walk down the street to the **Aristocratic Deli** and buy a pack of **Marlboro Lights**. They then retire to the **source**'s apartment building to resume the interview.

2:15 a.m.: After 45 minutes of uneventful waiting, we realize that **BERNSTEIN** has decided a quiet domestic evening would be a welcome respite from his hectic superjournalist **life**.

tioning for a possible profile of one of America's former top models, America's top journalist attempts to slip into her cab. She prevents this by slamming the door. He hails his own cab.

2:45 a.m.: Because **M.K.** is in a five-story building with large windows on its facade, we are afforded a rare glimpse from the sidewalk of the ultraprofessional **ENTREKIN** hard at work on the mezzanine.

He finds another talented potential **author** and, after only a few moments of what appears to be **contract negotiation**, attempts to whisper some editorial direction into her mouth. "Speak to my agent," she apparently suggests as she shoves him away.

3:40 a.m.: **ENTREKIN** leaves **M.K.** with two more congenial potential **female authors**, one blond and one brunet. We follow **ENTREKIN**'s cab down Seventh Avenue to 14th Street.

3:50 a.m.: **ENTREKIN** strides into yet another office away from the office, **Nell's**, which—although the velvet ropes have been taken in for the evening—is always open to hardworking editors. **ENTREKIN** is accustomed to these 18-hour workdays, but we have to gulp coffee to stay awake as we watch the ultraglamorous **sanitation trucks** pass by.

4:23 a.m.: **ENTREKIN** leaves **Nell's** and escorts his **blond** author to a cab before hailing another for

himself and the **brunet**, who apparently requires further editorial guidance. They head west on 14th Street, and it soon becomes apparent that the street-smart **ENTREKIN** knows he is being followed. He directs the cabdriver to stop at a green light. We stop behind his cab in the far-right lane. When the light turns red, the cab bolts into the intersection and makes a dangerous left turn south onto Hudson Street. We follow, even more dangerously.

The cab abruptly halts at **Abingdon Square**, and **ENTREKIN** gets out and saunters down Bethune Street before beginning a mad sprint down Greenwich toward his house, a block and a half away. The early-morning sunrise seems to reflect faintly off his yellow socks as he races into the distance and disappears for good.

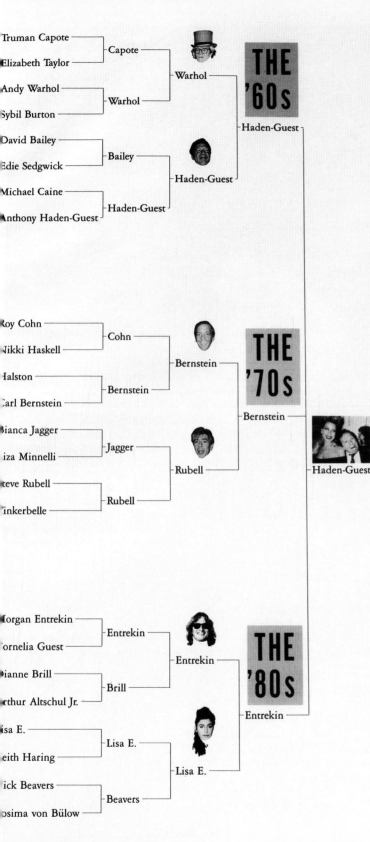

Bracket — THE '60s
- Truman Capote / Elizabeth Taylor → Capote
- Andy Warhol / Sybil Burton → Warhol
- Capote / Warhol → Warhol
- David Bailey / Edie Sedgwick → Bailey
- Michael Caine / Anthony Haden-Guest → Haden-Guest
- Bailey / Haden-Guest → Haden-Guest
- Warhol / Haden-Guest → Haden-Guest

Bracket — THE '70s
- Roy Cohn / Nikki Haskell → Cohn
- Halston / Carl Bernstein → Bernstein
- Cohn / Bernstein → Bernstein
- Bianca Jagger / Liza Minnelli → Jagger
- Steve Rubell / Tinkerbelle → Rubell
- Jagger / Rubell → Rubell
- Bernstein / Rubell → Bernstein

Final: Haden-Guest / Bernstein → Haden-Guest

Bracket — THE '80s
- Morgan Entrekin / Cornelia Guest → Entrekin
- Dianne Brill / Arthur Altschul Jr. → Brill
- Entrekin / Brill → Entrekin
- Lisa E. / Keith Haring → Lisa E.
- Nick Beavers / Cosima von Bülow → Beavers
- Lisa E. / Beavers → Lisa E.
- Entrekin / Lisa E. → Entrekin

THE SCORECARD

Numbers represent points earned unless otherwise noted.

	Morgan Entrekin	Anthony Haden-Guest	Carl Bernstein
Hours logged	9.5 (47.5 points)	8.75 (43.75 points)	6 (30 points)
Venues visited	4 (40 points)	3 (30 points)	3 (30 points)
Number of A-list celebrities seen with	17	12	25
Number of anonymous women seen with	5 (25 points)	5 (25 points)	1 (5 points)
Number of women seen with at end of night	0	1 (10 points)	1 (10 points)
Estimated cost of evening	$65 (5 points)	$10 (60 points)	$36 (34 points)
Blocks traveled	73	48	134
Drinks ostentatiously consumed	6 (30 points)	7 (35 points)	3 (15 points)
Desperate phone calls made	0	0	5
Outstanding achievement	4:30 a.m. jog (50 points)	Danced with his own chair (40 points)	Read in cab without getting carsick (10 points)
Total points	287.50	303.75	298.00

The winner is the old pro, Anthony Haden-Guest, whose glorious thirst and steadfast disinclination to pay for any services put him over the top. But the important thing to remember is that there are no losers here, unless, of course, by *loser* you mean people who didn't win. (Special jeunesse dorée kudos, in passing, to Clay Felker, Aileen "Suzy" Mehle and Steve Rubell, each of whom turned up on two of our three competition evenings.)

In Haden-Guest's honor, for the past few days all the SPY staff has been dreaming of is loosening our bow ties, dancing to Motown records and signing vaguely worded book contracts with Simon & Schuster. This has hampered productivity somewhat, but who cares? Drinks all around! ❥

Ironman Nightlife Decathlete Anthony Haden-Guest: "I have a fugitive memory that I was aware, at some stage, that I was being tailed; I don't think it affected my behavior any. And I still have an Armani jacket I was given, as a prize for winning—with a martini motif." The jacket was, in fact, Valentino.

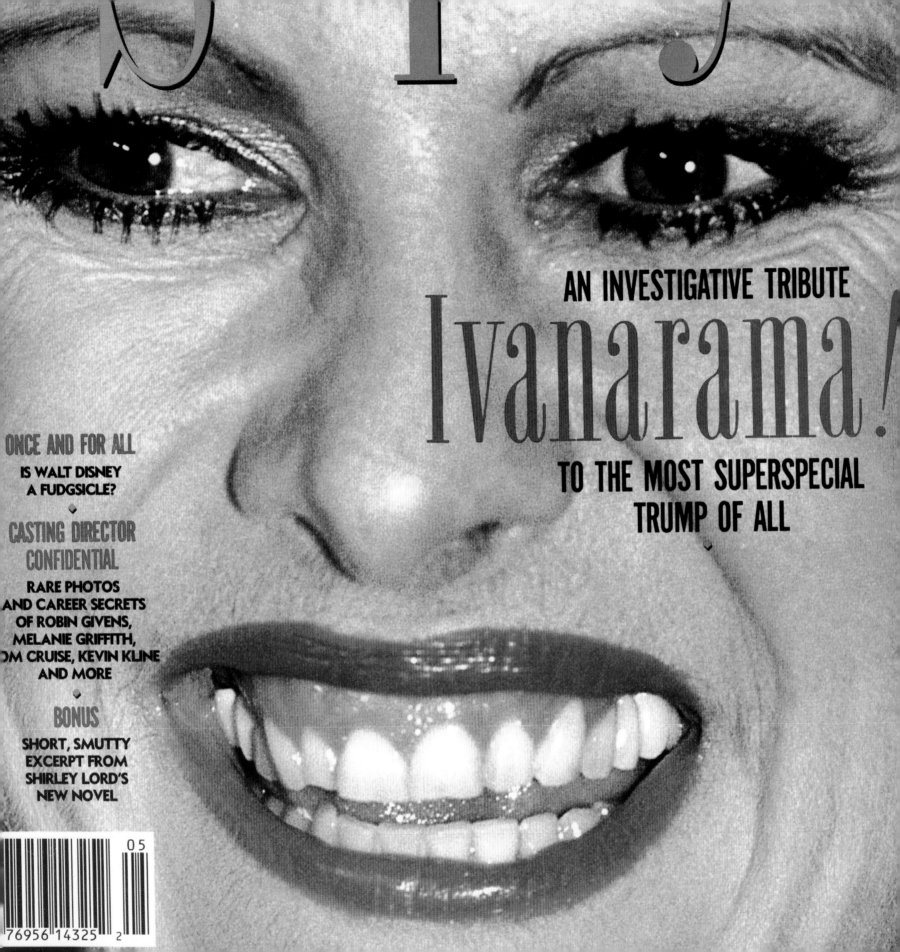

AN INVESTIGATIVE TRIBUTE

Ivanarama!

TO THE MOST SUPERSPECIAL
TRUMP OF ALL

ONCE AND FOR ALL

IS WALT DISNEY
A FUDGSICLE?

•

**CASTING DIRECTOR
CONFIDENTIAL**

RARE PHOTOS
AND CAREER SECRETS
OF ROBIN GIVENS,
MELANIE GRIFFITH,
OM CRUISE, KEVIN KLINE
AND MORE

•

BONUS

SHORT, SMUTTY
EXCERPT FROM
SHIRLEY LORD'S
NEW NOVEL

05

7695614325 2

7

"Oh, and by the Way? Your Father's on Our Cover Next Month, Wearing a Coconut Bra"

Ruined Friendships, Burned Bridges, and the Concept of No Sacred Cows

You always got a reaction when you told people you worked for
Spy. The magazine and its mandate were very loaded. You hoped
for Hip and Funny, you often got Insider-y and Gossip-Bearing
and Vaguely Menacing, and you tried to avoid Meaner Than an
Antique-Shop Cockapoo.

—HENRY ALFORD

IF YOU WORKED AT *SPY*, particularly if you wrote or edited
for *Spy*, you would, when in mufti outside the office, inevitably
bump up against a certain amount of hostility. We all weathered
painfully cooled if not completely ruptured friendships; sooner
or later the magazine would rough up someone you knew, or
someone close to someone you knew. And even though there
probably existed, as Paul Rudnick says, "a weird feeling of affection that *Spy* had for the monsters it was covering," that affection
tended to come wrapped in phrases like "socialite/war criminal"
and "bosomy dirty-book writer."

So maybe a nice, handwritten note wouldn't hurt?

"I probably learned this from Graydon, who's such a terrific

note-writer, but *Spy* forced me to perfect the note written the
week before the issue hit the stands where somebody you know's
father or mother was horribly humiliated," says Susan Morrison.
"I remember writing one to David Kissinger right before
'Bohemian Grove' came out with his father"—the socialite/war
criminal—"on the cover, wearing a coconut bra. You'd never
apologize or distance yourself from it, it was more, 'just to give
you a heads-up that this is coming.'

"I think a lot now about the meanness of *Spy*," Morrison
continues. "It didn't really spring from any malevolence in us. I
remember all through the '80s meeting people and they'd say,
'Wow, you seem so nice.' I think that because so few of us traveled in any of those circles, we didn't know how deeply we did
wound certain people. We were young, for one thing, and we
really saw it from across a social divide; we saw ourselves as being
behind the barricades. I always think about Graydon's roots—
this guy from another country who wants to make it big here,
throwing stones. And I suppose we all had some of that, and
there was safety in numbers."

Opposite:
The May 1989
cover. As Tom
Brokaw said
recently, "I miss
Spy, although
I am not sure
I'd feel the same
way if I were
Ivana Trump."

Some of *Spy*'s victims were gracious enough to turn the other cheek. A few years after her *Spy* List–provoked office visit, for instance, Jamie Lee Curtis gamely posed for our cover. Although, says her half-brother-in-law Anthony Haden-Guest—the writer, bon vivant, and frequent *Spy* whipping boy—"I think being fairly thick-skinned yet not really being *too* happy about it is what made one a perennial target. But it was *fairly* friendly fire. Some of my more humorless acquaintances would say, 'How terrible, how mean of them!' If one is honest, being in the magazine had an effect on one's life. But not necessarily a negative one.

"Oddly enough," continues Haden-Guest, "I saw the Met's *Don Giovanni* last night, where he was dragged down to hell for behavior that was very similar to what we were doing. Instead, *we* got put in *Spy* magazine."

"Didn't Pat Buckley, after a Halloween mask of her face had appeared in the magazine, then allow a *Spy* photographer into her apartment to photograph her dogs?" asks Henry Alford. "*Quel esprit*, Pat! It's like the audience members at Molière's plays who, recognizing themselves as the inspiration for a caricature, would stand up and say, '*C'est moi!*' For a certain kind of person, satire is just another little party thrown in your honor."

On the other hand, after *Spy* called CBS chairman Laurence Tisch a "churlish dwarf billionaire," Graydon got a call from PR man John Scanlon, who was then working for Tisch: "Look, Graydon, you've really gone too far this time. To begin with, Larry is not technically a dwarf." Graydon jotted that down, and in the next issue *Spy* ran a clarification in which a CBS spokesman pointed out that Tisch was not "technically" a dwarf.

"There was a certain amount of anger driving *Spy*—a commonplace observation about comedy, but it was true," says Bruce Handy. "In some way it was like trying to take down your betters. But I was so grateful for a place where you didn't have to tone anything down, you didn't have to be afraid."

Walter Kirn remembers experiencing "cognitive dissonance" because "there was this rap that we were maladapts hiding in a basement shooting spitballs at the people who run the world." In fact he found his colleagues "smart, funny, nice, generous people—but capable of this subversive point of view.

"I didn't see the magazine as mean," Kirn continues. "I didn't understand that New York is all about publicity, and everything that isn't puffery is looked at as assassination. It was hard for me to understand the furor. I thought, *This is funny writing, these things we're ridiculing are so far past needing to be ridiculed.*"

Our calling, as Graydon would remind us periodically, was to "feed the underdog and bite at the ankle of the overdog."

"*Spy*'s targets were the *arrivistes*," says contributor Melik Kaylan. "The Old Money, blue-rinse old ladies would say, 'Oh, I love *Spy*.' Those people are the first to enjoy the discomfiture of their fellow socialites. They could afford to laugh at other people, and they could afford to laugh off anything that was said about them. They were not on the make."

Still, Phil Weiss remembers accurately that in some quarters, "*Spy* was hated. But *Spy* had a sense of values. The magazine made a lot of mistakes, but I think one of the great things is that they weren't afraid to make mistakes. It really *was* mean-spirited, but it was kind of what the '80s deserved."* (Years later, says Aimée Bell, when she and another *Spy* editorial assistant, Matt Tyrnauer, ended up at *Vanity Fair*, "one of our first observations was that at

Editor C[...]

"We are [...]
other c[...]
city." —[...]

"We are [...]
style m[...]
Journal, [...]

"We're [...]
national [...]
Observer, [...]

"It is no[...]
The busi[...]
the same[...]
1990 ▶

September 1990

---

*"Mean-spirited" came to mean, around this time, "really, *really* mean." The most memorable critique of *Spy* for being cruel was a story on page one of *The Wall Street Journal*, of all places. —Eds.

Spy everyone was so mean in print and so nice in person, and at *Vanity Fair*, in those early days, it was the opposite: kiss-ass in print, horrible in person.")

Most regular *Spy* contributors at some point felt uneasiness about something they'd written. For Bruce Handy, it was his 1988 profile of Eric Breindel, the *New York Post* editorial-page editor. Breindel (who died some years later) was a well-connected conservative pundit who had been busted in 1981 for buying heroin (while he was working for the Senate Foreign Relations Committee), had gone through rehab, and was then presiding over an editorial page that railed against second chances and compassionate social policies for the luckless—second chances kind of like the one he had gotten. Rich material for *Spy*, and the magazine came down hard.

"A year or two after the piece came out," Handy says, "I was at a PEN dinner, sitting next to some lady who said, 'I really like *Spy*, but there was one time when I think they crossed the line—the Eric Breindel story.' 'Oh, I wrote that story....' In hindsight maybe the tone was a little harsh, and I think if I wrote it now I would be more empathetic about his drug problems. I remember, though, thinking he was a huge hypocrite."

David Korzenik, the libel lawyer who vetted *Spy* during its whole run, also remembers getting an earful regarding the Breindel piece: "People felt a little bit wounded by its toughness." But, he says, "here is a person who got mercy when he needed it, but was not allowing the same thing to play out for other people. And that seemed to me to be deeply subject to serious criticism, even though I winced at the piece like everybody else. It was cruel, but fair."

"When the magazine became reality instead of just a proposal, it got a little scary," says Steve Schragis. "Deciding who would be the number-one Most Loathsome Person was something the national media was going to report on. Someone who happened to get on the list at number 62 was going to have a wife read it and children read it and would live with it forever. Then there was Eric Breindel. I remember a lot of letters about it, people he was friendly with defending him. This guy was taking it very hard that a national magazine was ridiculing him. I think it was that article that really got to me, and suddenly almost everything in the magazine I was having trouble with."

Schragis, as an investor, was also put in a curious position

Now It Can Be Told How Bad It Feels To Be Done by Spy

* * *

Magazine of Muck and Satire Runs Profiles That Leave Their Subjects Twitching

By Cynthia Crossen
Staff Reporter of THE WALL STREET JOURNAL

Character assassination at the hands of Spy magazine can be a painful death, or it can just be overkill.

Did you know that a well-known executive (not to be named here) actually "ordered a female employee to carry a wine bottle filled with his urine" to someone at a party and that another famous businessman is a "sleazeball" who induces teenage girls to "wear diapers and suck a lollipop"? Do you care? It's in Spy.

The 3½-year-old monthly magazine of humor and muck is sharp, satirical, and funny in small doses. It prints things the respectable press wouldn't scruple to go near, and thus has a niche. It has avid fans among the 133,000 people, who buy it ($2.95 per copy on the newsstand). Although it describes itself as "The New York Monthly," only 28% of its circulation is in New York City, with Los Angeles being its second-largest market. Its owners say it makes money. And what could be wrong with that?

Just Deserts?

It also causes a good deal of pain and suffering to its victims—generally public figures who would have a hard time winning a libel suit even if they could prove that what Spy says about them isn't true. And the truth does hurt sometimes. Since many of those spat at, or mowed down in long profiles, are publicity seekers in the first place, it might be argued that they get from Spy about what they deserve. Still, the magazine is *so* cruel.

Leah Rozen, who wrote a nasty article herself about Norman and Frances Lear, calls Spy's profiles "assassination pieces." Assassination attempts might be a better characterization, as its victims generally live through it. But subjects describe the experience as humiliating, and so traumatic that years later some still can't bring themselves to talk about it, or they do so only on the condition that the muck won't be raked up again. "Everywhere I went, people asked me about the Spy story," says a profile subject, asking anonymity. "It was agony."

Hot Off the Presses

In its March issue, Spy does it again—to Judy Price, the president of New York's Avenue magazine. Less injured is Peter O. Price, her husband, the chairman of Avenue and the publisher of the new daily sports publication, the National. (The paper's national distributor is Dow Jones & Co.) Spy calls the Prices' magazine a "sycophantic wet kiss." And that turns out to be about the nicest thing it has to say about the Prices, their business methods, their social aspirations, their religious practices and their personal appearance. How one looks is very important to Spy.

"It makes you feel dirty," says Mrs. Price. "It's demented, it's a bunch of filth. You have to get up and go to work the next day, but you still feel frustrated because you can't go around telling everyone what the real truth is."

Mr. Price calls the story "brutality without bounds," and says it was all the more remarkable considering that Steven Schragis, a major owner of Spy, had recently spoken to Mr. Price about putting money into Spy.

Mr. Price says that a few months ago Mr. Schragis, when asked, told him that Spy was looking for new investors and considered the Prices "prospects." Mr. Schragis says that Mr. Price brought up the idea of investing, and that he went along, telling Mr. Price he would make sure Mr. Price was at the "top of the list" to receive a prospectus. "It was really just

Please Turn to Page A8, Column 5

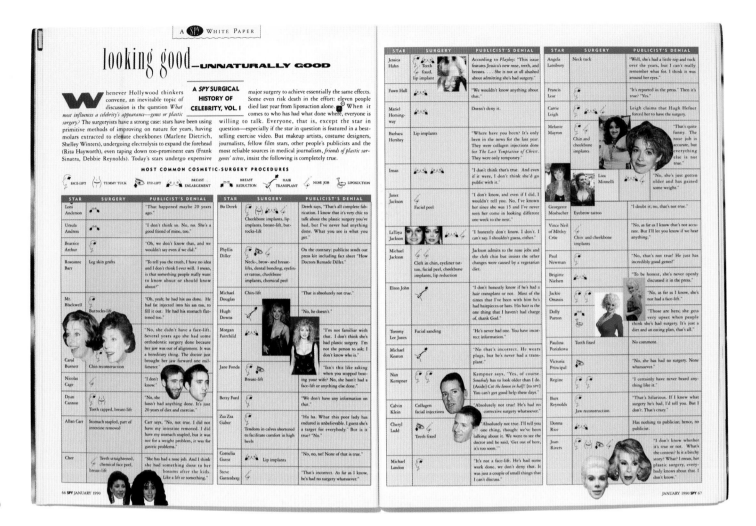

January 1990

because of "all this picking on Trump." The Schragis family knew Trump. In fact, the "Ivanarama!" issue (May 1989) featured, in addition to Jonathan Van Meter's "Investigative Tribute to the Most Superspecial Trump of All," an account of Donald Trump's epistolary excesses vis-à-vis *Spy*—many of the letters were reproduced—including a bizarre episode in which the Schragis family got pulled into the morass.*

"Trump was ripe for criticism and sarcasm, and I knew it was

---

*Schragis's father had bumped into Trump and jokingly said that if Trump advertised in Spy, maybe we'd stop writing all those nasty things about him. Trump went off on a wild writing spree based on that unfortunate but offhand and hardly serious comment. —Eds.

well-written and funny, but he was a real person to me," Schragis says. "And that was awkward, because my family's interests and *Spy* magazine were clashing."

"You can count on one hand the times we went way, way too far," says Graydon. "I always tell people that when you print it out, it looks different from when you were writing it on a computer screen. And once it's in galleys, it looks even more different. It amplifies at each stage. By the time it's in the magazine, it's five times as strong. And it's very hard to realize that when you're doing the first draft."

In our post-*Spy* years, we've all found ourselves meeting people, working with (and for) people, befriending, even dating people whom we—or our magazine—had once carved up in

"Do you not be happy with me as the translator of the books of you?"

December 1987

print. For every dozen gratifying "Oh, I *loved Spy*" encounters, there is an uncomfortable introduction in some office corridor, a combustible dinner party, a long flight seated just across the aisle from a former target.

Sometimes an article or a quote didn't even need to see print to have repercussions—the phone call from *Spy* was enough. "I called Nora Ephron once to get her to comment on suntanning and summer beauty tips," Lynn Snowden remembers, "and she of course saw right through it and was very icy. About three months later there was a short story of hers in *Esquire*, and in it was a really despicable, shallow female character named 'Marilyn Snowden.'"

When Snowden worked on a piece about plastic surgery, some of the reporting was making her uneasy, so she tried to tone it down. "And Tad Friend gave me a lecture: 'You've really got to do this.' Finally I said I'd use a pseudonym."

Spy was filled with pseudonyms: Celia Brady (from the narrator Cecilia Brady in Fitzgerald's *The Last Tycoon*), J. J. Hunsecker (the Walter Winchell character in *The Sweet Smell of Success*), Macaulay Connor (the *Spy* magazine reporter played by Jimmy Stewart in *The Philadelphia Story*), Michèle Bennett (former Haitian dictator "Baby Doc" Duvalier's then-wife), T. S. Lord and Liz Imbrie (the Katharine Hepburn and Ruth Hussey characters in *The Philadelphia Story*), Humphrey Greddon (from Max Beerbohm's Oxford satire *Zuleika Dobson*), Laureen Hobbs (Marlene Whitfield in *Network*), Henry "Dutch" Holland (Alec

Guinness in *The Lavender Hill Mob*), and Ignatz Ratzwizkiwzki (from Preston Sturges's *The Miracle of Morgan's Creek*), to name but a few. We thought it was playful, and only very slightly cowardly. As a result, twenty years later, "Celia Brady" is still a successful player in the movie industry whose colleagues have absolutely no idea about her Scarlet Pimpernel past at *Spy*.

"There was a point where if I asked Kurt not to write about somebody, that would probably intrigue him more—and he'd write about him."

Lisa Birnbach, who worked as an editor at the magazine after Graydon had left, found the take-no-prisoners approach unsettling, perhaps because she was already an adult with a best-seller (*The Official Preppy Handbook*) under her belt when she arrived, and hadn't been on The Long March. "I was definitely impressed to the point of almost awe by the no-sacred-cows position," she says, "and I was astonished by the sangfroid with which Kurt would burn a bridge. I couldn't get over it. And my husband was a movie producer, so it made me really nervous to be there.

"We were once at a very small dinner party in Beverly Hills—four couples—and the Michael Eisners were there," she says. "And I was in the midst of telling my Wayne Newton story"—Birnbach, not yet on staff, had just spent quality time with Newton in Vegas for a *Spy* profile—"and the host is egging me on, so I'm telling about the nun who lived in the house and the flamingos on the property and 'Mr. Presley gave me this' and 'Mr. Sinatra gave me that.' And Eisner says, 'Who are you writing this for?' And the host says, '*Parade*'"—to which Birnbach had also been contributing and which, unlike *Spy*, did not continually eviscerate Eisner. But it quickly surfaced whom the piece was really for. "And Michael Eisner turned his back on me, in his chair," she says. Eisner never spoke to Birnbach again, even though her husband was then producing a film (*Hocus Pocus*) for him.

"It was uncomfortable for me when I'd look at Kurt's desk to see who the next victims would be, and invariably there was someone I knew there," she remembers. "But I was so proud of the magazine, that they weren't like me, that they were bold. There was a point where if I asked Kurt not to write about somebody, that would probably intrigue him more—and he'd write about him."

It's worth noting that some "friends of *Spy*" (literally two or three or four) were never subjected to close scrutiny. And although we covered the doings of the Condé Nast media empire regularly, and Si Newhouse was a subject of small-bore teasing, *Spy* never ran a column on the company.

"We started doing all these media columns," says Susan Morrison, "like The *Times*, The Industry, The Webs"—that was about the TV networks—"and The Trade, the fashion one. And we always wanted to do one called 'The Women,' about Condé Nast. But we never did—for one thing, Graydon was writing for *Vogue*—and that's something I really regret. It was such a ripe time to do it."

There was at least one disappointed reader. "Si once told me," Graydon says, "when we were having dinner in London, 'The thing I always wish you had done, I wish you'd had a Condé Nast column. Then I would have known,' he said with a laugh, 'what was going on here.'"

"BECAUSE OF *SPY'S* POPULARITY, it was actually getting harder and harder to report for it," says Nell Scovell. "Tina Brown offered me a job at *Vanity Fair* for more money than all four *Spy* staff writers were making put together. I'd like to say that when I told the people at *Spy* I was leaving they wished me well, but they didn't. Then, a few months after I left, my ex-husband's name turned up on a *Spy* List of henpecked husbands."* (Scovell went on to a big-time career in television.)

"You could feel so vulnerable there," says Elissa Schappell. "You're with people who are making fun of people for a living. When you leave the room, you don't know who's got your back. And the game is to one-up, so it's not just that someone's going to say, 'Oh, look, her ass looks like two cats fighting in a sack'—there's someone *else* who's going to say, 'No, no, actually it looks like two baboons playing the congas.' 'No, *actually....*' Your ears are on fire walking down the hall. I remember one Christmas they did a staff Separated at Birth?, and I was separated at birth with Tweety Bird, and I thought, *Oh, my God, everyone thinks I look like Tweety Bird! Is Tweety Bird a boy or a girl? Are people confused about my gender? Is it the shape of my head?*"

Graydon never let Morrison forget an early idea she had for a piece based on something she just heard about: the Ringling

---

*We don't know what she's talking about. The Spy Lists were entirely random collections of well-known names. —Eds.

CELESTIAL HINDSIGHT
Special Courtroom Bonanza!

act I sing "There's No
h I believe. That is my
n or sad, I think of that

Subject: WILLIAM HURT
Sign: Pisces (b. 3/20/50)
Date: June 19, 1989
Notable Activity: On first day of trial to determine whether had common-law marriage with Sandra Jennings, denied that they were ever married
Horoscope: "You need to forget about being mild-mannered and self-effacing. When dealing with home, family or career issues, prove how independent…you can be."—Patric Walker, *New York Post*

Subject: REV. AL SHARPTON
Sign: Libra (b. 10/3/54)
Date: June 29, 1989
Notable Activity: Was charged with 67 counts of grand larceny, falsifying business records and scheming to defraud; in courtroom, announced that State Attorney General Robert Abrams, who had brought indictment, was "insane"
Horoscope: "Finances become an issue midweek and arguments develop over extravagant spending."—Laurie Brady, *Star* Magazine

October 1989

The Dorian Gray Syndrome

Didn't they look older ten years ago?

1980 — Phyllis Diller, 70 — 1985

1983 — Barbara Walters, 56 — 1987

1973 — Joan Rivers, 50 — 1986

114 SPY APRIL 1988

**From
"Forever Young,"
April 1988**

Bros. and Barnum & Bailey Circus elephant march through the Queens Midtown Tunnel into Manhattan. "I put down my pencil and said, 'Susan, they do this every year at this time,'" Graydon says. "They even have a name for it—the Elephant Walk. After that, any time she suggested something even faintly obvious or tired, I would wag a finger and say, 'Elephant Walk.'" It drove Morrison crazy.

"*Spy* was the wonderful family we all wished we'd had," says Michael Hainey, who started as an intern and became a full-time reporter. "But like any family, it fucks you up. I think a lot of people spent a lot of money in therapy trying to get over *Spy*, for a long time. Maybe it was inevitable. You had an immensely tal-

ented group of people, and all the neuroses and things that go along with that."

We all had one another's numbers. Yet the rare attempts by others—even though the raw material was there for the taking—to turn the tables on *Spy* through the years, most notably a *New York* magazine cover story and a full-blown parody book called *STY*—were disappointing.* Maybe they needed authentic *Spy*-ification.

***As we dimly recall it, *STY*'s high concept was that all the subjects were pigs with "funny" pseudo-celebrity names. Neither of us remembers even looking through *STY*, let alone reading it, which is sort of weird in retrospect. —Eds.**

"TWO GUYS. ONE BLACK. CIA. BY THE BOOK. THE OTHER, WHITE. LAPD. SLOPPY. MADMAN'S ON THE LOOSE. PLUTONIUM. CITY HELD HOSTAGE. TWO GUYS TEAMED UP. ONLY THEY DON'T GET ALONG, SEE.."

A SPY Guide to Making Hit Movies the Surefire, Scientific

BUDDY•O•MATIC

Way

Thousands of years ago the Greeks determined that there were only a finite number of human conflicts that served as the basis for all drama. If you've been to a movie in the past year, you've probably noticed that Hollywood, in its tireless quest for the new and the fresh, has managed to boil this number down to one: the Buddy Movie. To save producers millions of dollars in development costs and theatergoers the ordeal of actually *watching* the current crop of buddy films, noted cinemalogist BRUCE FEIRSTEIN has devised a remarkable, pioneering and altogether foolproof technique for plotting, writing and casting Buddy Movies — the Buddy-o-Matic. It's easy: just work your way through the 58-step Buddy-o-Matic process, choosing any of the multiple-choice options available at each step, and you'll have yourself a surefire Buddy Movie treatment.

Our story begins in

Los Angeles, [2]	Moscow, [8]
Chicago, [3]	Hollywood, [9]
Detroit, [4]	Boston, [10]
San Francisco, [5]	Miami, [11]
the Pacific	Saigon, [12]
Northwest, [6]	Beverly
New York, [7]	Hills, [13]

where a craze

psychopathic

serial killer [14]	CIA agent [19]
drug dealer [15]	Vietnam vet [20]
arms merchant [16]	Chinese tong lord [21]
Mafia kingpin [17]	pimp [22]
KGB agent [18]	diamond smuggler [23]

is creating all sort

of

havoc and mayhem [24]
civic unrest [25]
trouble for the mayor [26]
embarrassment for the embassy [27]
PR problems for the department [28]

by murdering

young nurses [29]
young models [30]
young hookers [31]
young female MPs [32]

in

particularly

lurid [33]	bloody [37]
vicious [34]	misanthropic [38]
sadistic [35]	titillating [39]
grotesque [36]	

style, and for no apparen

reason.[40] Next, we meet

Richard Dreyfuss, [41]	Mel Gibson, [49]
Nick Nolte, [42]	Judge Reinhold, [50]
Billy Crystal, [43]	Mikhail Baryshnikov, [51]
Jim Belushi, [44]	Sam Elliott, [52]
Mark Harmon, [45]	James Garner, [53]
Dan Aykroyd, [46]	Treat Williams, [54]
Tom Berenger, [47]	somebody named
Willem Dafoe, [48]	Quaid, [55]

wh

1. The origins of the modern-day Buddy Movie (also known as the postheroic drama) are generally ascribed to a 1969 Twentieth Century Fox production, Butch Cassidy and the Sundance Kid, although the archetype had previously been employed by such premodernist comedy teams as Laurel and Hardy and Abbott and Costello, and the latter-day neo-expressionists Martin and Lewis. While scholars of the genre have failed to reach a consensus concerning the archetype's first appearance, most agree that seminal influences on the form have included William Shakespeare's The Two Gentlemen of Verona, the mythical tale "Romulus and Remus," the biblical Cain and Abel story and, of course, the postwar Japanese-American classic King Kong vs. Godzilla.

2. Dragnet (Universal Pictures, 1987); Lethal Weapon (Warner Brothers, 1988).

3. Running Scared (MGM, 1986). The city boasts an especially cooperative film commission to expedite shooting.

4. Beverly Hills Cop (Paramount, 1984).

5. The Presidio (Paramount, 1988); 48 HRS. (Paramount, 1982).

6. Shoot to Kill (Touchstone, 1988) winds up in Vancouver; Stakeout (Touchstone, 1987) takes place in Seattle.

7. Shakedown (Universal, 1988). For northern Manhattan, i.e., Harlem, see Shaft's Big Score! (MGM, 1972) or Uptown Saturday Night (Warner Brothers, 1974).

8. Actually Finland. Moscow does not believe in film commissions; Red Heat (Tri-Star, 1988) and White Nights (Columbia, 1985) were shot elsewhere.

9. Sunset (Tri-Star, 1988).

10. Currently available.

11. Miami Vice (the curr prototypical television budd format setting).

a(n)

down-and-out[56]
by-the-book[57]
recently divorced[58]
soon-to-be-retired[59]
wizened, seen-it-all[60]
no-nonsense[61]
alcoholic[62]
wrapped-too-tight[63]

sergeant[64]
detective[65]
MP[66]
FBI agent[67]
CIA operative[68]
principal dancer[69]

who has just

broken up with his girlfriend[70]
woken up with a hangover[71]
screwed up with the police commissioner[72]
seen his partner get killed[73]
been dumped by his wife[74]

in the

sloppy bachelor's apartment[75]
middle-class two-family house[76]
slick high-tech loft[77]
tasteful suburban home[77a]

e shares with a cutely named

dog[78]
cat[79]
goldfish[80]
hangover[81]
houseplant[82]
gun[83]

somewhere in/outside of

Los Angeles.[2] Moscow.[8]
Chicago.[3] Hollywood.[9]
Detroit.[4] Boston.[10]
San Francisco.[5] Miami.[11]
the Pacific Saigon.[12]
Northwest.[6] Beverly
New York.[7] Hills.[13]

ow, at

military headquarters,[84]
police headquarters,[85]
a diner,[86]
an underground
parking lot,[87]

we meet

head detective[88]
police commissioner[89]
FBI special agent[90]
ex-Marine[91]
CIA bureau chief[92]

Lou Gossett, who

doesn't like[93]
is antagonized by[94]
is fed up with[95]

ichard Dreyfuss[41] Mel Gibson[49]
ick Nolte[42] Judge Reinhold[50]
illy Crystal[43] Mikhail Baryshnikov[51]
m Belushi[44] Sam Elliott[52]
ark Harmon[45] James Garner[53]
an Aykroyd[46] Treat Williams[54]
m Berenger[47] somebody named
illem Dafoe[48] Quaid[55]

but recognizes his

unique crime-fighting ability,[96]
personal involvement in the case,[97]
penchant for screwing things up,[98]

so he teams him

ith

Eddie Murphy[99] Arnold Joe Piscopo[107]
Sidney Poitier[100] Schwarzenegger[103] Peter Weller[108]
Danny Glover[101] Bruce Willis[104] Sean Connery[109]
Gregory Hines[102] Shelley Long[105] Tom Hanks[110]
John Hurt[106]

and gives them

an order[111]
one last chance[112]
a command against
his better instincts[113]

to catch the

rial killer[14] CIA agent[19]
rug dealer[15] Vietnam vet[20]
rms merchant[16] Chinese tong lord[21]
afia kingpin[17] pimp[22]
GB agent[18] diamond smuggler[23]

before the end of

their stakeout.[114]
seven days.[115]
the Tét
Offensive.[116]
the Moscow
Ballet season.[117]
48 hours.[118]
the world.[119]

At first, they

loathe[120]
despise[121]
hate[122]
can't stand[123]
don't trust[124]
ignore[125]
needle[126]

each other.

here one is

white,[127]
neat,[128]
clean,[129]
law-abiding,[130]
methodical,[131]
angry,[132]
racist,[133]
middle-class,[134]
happily
married,[135]
an American,[136]

the other is

black,[137] corner-cutting,[142]
slovenly,[138] ghetto-bred,[143]
a communist,[139] trigger-happy,[144]
street-smart,[140] horny,[145]
impulsive,[141] foulmouthed,[146]

and they don't

en

eat alike.[147]
dress alike.[148]
drive alike.[149]
listen to the
same music.[150]

Nevertheless, they go to a(n)

art gallery[151] blue-collar
war zone[152] strip joint[155]
Moscow Ballet slime-infested bar[156]
premiere[153] brothel[157]
busy pier[154] glitzy disco[158]

oking for clues to catch

James Remar,[159] Willem Dafoe,[163]
Klaus Maria Brandauer,[160] Dabney Coleman,[164]
Gary Busey,[161] Gene Hackman,[165]
Jürgen Prochnow,[162] James Woods,[166]

and in order to prove ➤➤➤

Off Limits (Fox, 1988)
actually shot in
iland. The Republic of
nam does not have a film
mission; until 1986 this
lly meant shooting in the
ippines. However, with the
rture of Ferdinand Marcos
e to Francis Coppola for
calypse Now) and

subsequent political unrest.
Thailand, Malibu and the
Elstree Studios in London have
become the locations of choice
for directors seeking to
duplicate Saigon and its triple-
canopied jungle environs.
13. Beverly Hills Cop II
(Paramount, 1987).
14. 48 HRS., Off Limits.
Shoot to Kill.

15. Red Heat, Beverly Hills
Cop, Running Scared.
16. Beverly Hills Cop II —
but even the most dedicated
buddyphiles have yet to be able
to fully discern the plot.
17. The Pope of Greenwich
Village (MGM, 1984), other
references too numerous to cite.
18. Red Heat (see also note 15).
19. Archaic; mainly used in

1960s Cold War thrillers and
any 1980s Robert Ludlum
miniseries costarring Jaclyn
Smith and Richard
Chamberlain.
20. Generic; mainly used in
conjunction with movies
listed in notes 14, 15, 16, 19.
21. Any film costarring John
Lone.
22. With the greater

sensitivity in the late 1980s
about black stereotypes, the
term young investment
banker may be substituted as
a synonym. For TV-movies-of-
the-week, international
white-slave trader will
achieve the same purpose.
23. Slightly dated — which
may explain why The
Presidio did only middling

business.
24. Dead Heat (New World
Pictures, 1988), Off Limits.
25. Stakeout.
26. 48 HRS.
27. White Nights.
28. Beverly Hills Cop II.
29. Derived from the Roger
Corman-American
International Pictures school of
film, beginning with The

→→ **himself/herself,**

Eddie Murphy [99]	Shelley Long [105]
Sidney Poitier [100]	John Hurt [106]
Danny Glover [101]	Joe Piscopo [107]
Gregory Hines [102]	Peter Weller [108]
Arnold Schwarzenegger [103]	Sean Connery [109]
Bruce Willis [104]	Tom Hanks [110]

gets into a

- fistfight [167]
- gun battle [168]
- car chase [169]

that leads nowhere but

impresses

Dreyfuss. [41]	Harmon. [45]	Gibson. [49]	Garner. [53]
Nolte. [42]	Aykroyd. [46]	Reinhold. [50]	Williams. [54]
Crystal. [43]	Berenger. [47]	Baryshnikov. [51]	somebody named
Belushi. [44]	Dafoe. [48]	Elliott. [52]	Quaid. [55]

[170]

Now things get complicated.

It seems

Richard Dreyfuss [41]	Mel Gibson [49]
Nick Nolte [42]	Judge Reinhold [50]
Billy Crystal [43]	Mikhail Baryshnikov [51]
Jim Belushi [44]	Sam Elliott [52]
Mark Harmon [45]	James Garner [53]
Dan Aykroyd [46]	Treat Williams [54]
Tom Berenger [47]	somebody named
Willem Dafoe [48]	Quaid [55]

has fallen in love with [171]

James Remar's [159]	Willem Dafoe's [163]
Klaus Maria	Dabney Coleman's [164]
Brandauer's [160]	Gene Hackman's [165]
Gary Busey's [161]	James Woods's [166]
Jürgen Prochnow's [162]	

James Remar [159]	Willem Dafoe [163]
Klaus Maria	Dabney Coleman [164]
Brandauer [160]	Gene Hackman [165]
Gary Busey [161]	James Woods [166]
Jürgen Prochnow [162]	

has taken

hostage [171a]

Richard Dreyfuss's [41]	Mel Gibson's [49]
Nick Nolte's [42]	Judge Reinhold's [50]
Billy Crystal's [43]	Mikhail Baryshnikov's [51]
Jim Belushi's [44]	Sam Elliott's [52]
Mark Harmon's [45]	James Garner's [53]
Dan Aykroyd's [46]	Treat Williams's [54]
Tom Berenger's [47]	one of the Quaid
Willem Dafoe's [48]	brothers's [55]

girlfriend,

- Mary Elizabeth Mastrantonio. [172]
- Maria Conchita Alonso. [172, 172a]

And to make matters worse, the pair follows the

killer to a

- bathhouse, [173]
- casino, [174]
- deserted warehouse, [175]
- airplane hangar, [175]
- private shooting range, [176]
- very expensive restaurant/brothel, [177]
- private country club, [178]
- plush Bel Air estate, [179]

where they discover he's not just a crazed psychopathic

serial killer [14]	Vietnam vet [20]
drug dealer [15]	Chinese tong
arms merchant [16]	lord [21]
Mafia kingpin [17]	pimp [22]
KGB agent [18]	diamond
CIA agent [19]	smuggler [23]

but is really killing the

- young nurses [29]
- young models [30]
- young hookers [31]
- young female MPs [32]

as part of his twisted,

- maniacal [180]
- diabolical [180]

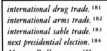

plan to control/destroy the

- international drug trade. [181]
- international arms trade. [182]
- international sable trade. [183]
- next presidential election. [184]
- Moscow Ballet season. [185]
- missing American atomic bomb. [186]
- ozone layer. [187]
- Far Eastern diamond market. [188]
- world and its environs. [189]

Now

- there's no way out. [190]
- the heat is on. [190]
- they're running scared. [190]
- they'll shoot to kill. [190]
- they're off-limits. [190]
- they're on a midnight run. [190]

After a/another

- car chase [191]
- gun battle [191]
- sex scene [191]

with much

- destruction of city property, [191]
- automatic-weapons fire, [191]
- high-speed swerving and sheet-metal carnage, [191]

they run up against

James Remar's [159]	Willem Dafoe's [163]
Klaus Maria Brandauer's [160]	Dabney Coleman's [164]
Gary Busey's [161]	Gene Hackman's [165]
Jürgen Prochnow's [162]	James Woods's [166]

→→

Wild Angels (1966).

30. Ibid.

31. Ibid.; also, Off Limits.

32. The Presidio.

33. Red Heat.

34. 48 HRS.

35. Off Limits.

36. Gorky Park (Orion, 1983).

37. Shoot to Kill.

38. Stakeout.

39. Lethal Weapon.

40. At this point in the story, it is essential that the reason for the killings remain unclear. The killer's motivation (known as the "big secret" or "final plot twist") is always revealed in the last third of the movie — except in the case of James Bond–derived films, in which the "missing American atomic bomb" is always established up front.

41. Stakeout.

42. 48 HRS.

43. Running Scared.

44. Red Heat.

45. The Presidio.

46. Dragnet.

47. Shoot to Kill.

48. Off Limits.

49. Lethal Weapon.

50. Beverly Hills Cop II.

51. White Nights.

52. Shakedown.

53. Sunset.

54. Dead Heat.

55. In the event one of the Quaids is unavailable, Bette Midler may be substituted. (See the Disney/Touchstone female variations on the buddy genre, Outrageous Fortune and Big Business.)

56. Nick Nolte, 48 Hours.

57. Dan Aykroyd, Dragnet.

58. Billy Crystal, Running Scared.

59. Ibid.; also, Brian Dennehy, Gorky Park.

60. Jim Belushi, Red Heat.

61. Tom Berenger, Shoot to Kill; also, Willem Dafoe, Off Limits.

62. Nolte, 48 HRS.

63. Mel Gibson, Lethal Weapon.

64. Ibid.; also, Judge Reinhold, Beverly Hills Cop II.

65. Nick Nolte, Sam Elliott, Mark Harmon, Billy Crystal, Jim Belushi, Dan Aykroyd et al.

66. Willem Dafoe, Off Limits.

67. Sidney Poitier, Shoot to Kill.

68. Currently available.

D
ON

➤ **assistant,** | Richard "Jaws" Kiel, 192 | **who is about to kill either** | Richard Dreyfuss 41 | Dan Aykroyd 46 | Mikhail Baryshnikov 51
Brigitte Nielsen, 192 | | Nick Nolte 42 | Tom Berenger 47 | Sam Elliott 52
| | | Billy Crystal 43 | Willem Dafoe 48 | James Garner 53
| | | Jim Belushi 44 | Mel Gibson 49 | Treat Williams 54
| | | Mark Harmon 45 | Judge Reinhold 50 | somebody named Quaid 55

or | Eddie Murphy 99 | Shelley Long 105 | **but is stopped by either** | Eddie Murphy 193 | Arnold | Joe Piscopo 193
| Sidney Poitier 100 | John Hurt 106 | | Sidney Poitier 193 | Schwarzenegger 193 | Peter Weller 193
| Danny Glover 101 | Joe Piscopo 107 | | Danny Glover 193 | Bruce Willis 193 | Sean Connery 193
| Gregory Hines 102 | Peter Weller 108 | | Gregory Hines 193 | Shelley Long 193 | Tom Hanks 193 | **or**
| Arnold | Sean Connery 109 | | | John Hurt 193 |
| Schwarzenegger 103 | Tom Hanks 110 |
| Bruce Willis 104 |

Richard Dreyfuss. 193 | Dan Aykroyd. 193 | Mikhail Baryshnikov. 193 | **At last, they realize how much they** | like 194
Nick Nolte. 193 | Tom Berenger 193 | Sam Elliott. 193 | | need 194
Billy Crystal. 193 | Willem Dafoe. 193 | James Garner. 193 | | respect 194
Jim Belushi. 193 | Mel Gibson. 193 | Treat Williams. 193
Mark Harmon. 193 | Judge Reinhold. 193 | somebody named Quaid. 193

each other. And with | time running out, 195 | **they use a combination of** | street-smarts | **and**
| the bomb about to explode, 195 | | police know-how
| the ballet curtain about |
| to go up, 195 |

police know-how | **to appropriate a** | cement truck | **and engage in another** | car chase | **through**
street-smarts 196 | | Greyhound bus | | gun battle 197
| | Ferrari Testa Rossa 197

Harlem, 198 | the Third Street tunnel in | | | James Remar 159
the Chicago subway system, 199 | downtown L.A., 204 | | | Klaus Maria
the Moscow park system, 200 | the atrium of a Hyatt hotel, 205 | **where they save** | Mary Elizabeth Mastrantonio, 172 | **kill** | Brandauer 160
an elevated subway line in | the DMZ, 206 | | Maria Conchita Alonso, 172, 172a | | Gary Busey 161
Brooklyn, 201 | Mardi Gras, 207 | | | Jürgen Prochnow 162
the Miami Intracoastal | the Universal Studios Tour, 208 | | | Willem Dafoe 163
Waterway, 202 | the Feast of San Gennaro, 209 | | | Dabney Coleman 164
the Golden Gate Bridge, 203 | any Chinatown, 210 | | | Gene Hackman 165
| | | | James Woods 166

and make Lou Gossett very happy | **— but not before the** | last scene, | **in which**
| | final goodbye,
| | end of the movie,

Richard Dreyfuss 41 | Dan Aykroyd 46 | Mikhail Baryshnikov 51 | | Eddie Murphy 99 | Shelley Long 105 | | bar
Nick Nolte 42 | Tom Berenger 47 | Sam Elliott 52 | | Sidney Poitier 100 | John Hurt 106 | | Porsche
Billy Crystal 43 | Willem Dafoe 48 | James Garner 53 | | Danny Glover 101 | Joe Piscopo 107 | | yacht
Jim Belushi 44 | Mel Gibson 49 | Treat Williams 54 | | Gregory Hines 102 | Peter Weller 108 | | warehouse 211
Mark Harmon 45 | Judge Reinhold 50 | somebody named Quaid 55 | **turns to** | Arnold | Sean Connery 109 | **outside a**
| | | Schwarzenegger 103 | Tom Hanks 110
| | | Bruce Willis 104

and scowls, | "Trust me," | **before driving into** | Los Angeles. 2 | Moscow. 8
| "Can I have my lighter back?" 212 | | Chicago. 3 | Hollywood. 9
| "Do svidaniya," | | Detroit. 4 | Boston. 10
| "You're not of this planet," 213 | | San Francisco. 5 | Miami. 11
| "Can I have my tanning lotion back?" 214 | | the Pacific | Saigon. 12
| | | Northwest. 6 | Beverly Hills. 13
| | | New York. 7 | the sunset. 213

69. Baryshnikov, White Nights.
70. Nolte, 48 HRS.
71. Ibid.
72. Ibid.
73. Ibid.
74. Dreyfuss, Stakeout.
75. Crystal, Nolte, Elliott, Belushi et al.
76. Any picture shot in Queens.
77. Any picture shot in Manhattan.
77a. Lethal Weapon.
78. Known as the Harvey Trait (after the 1950 James Stewart film Harvey), this is considered by screenwriters to be a fast and relatively easy way of giving sympathetic and endearing qualities to an otherwise cardboard character.
79. Ibid.
80. Ibid.
81. Ibid.
82. Reinhold, Beverly Hills Cop II.
83. Ibid.
84. The Presidio.
85. Beverly Hills Cop, Beverly Hills Cop II, Stakeout, Shoot to Kill, 48 HRS., Lethal Weapon, Red Heat et al.
86. A nice change of venue; otherwise, insert "CIA Headquarters."
87. Low-budget films only; the scene can be shot in the parking garage of the hotel where the cast and crew are being housed, or, for pictures made by Universal or Fox, right in the studio's own parking lot. (Note: if the movie is set in Chicago, at least one scene must be placed in the multistoried indoor parking lot at the base of the Marina Towers, the twin-towered circular buildings at the corner of State Street and the Chicago River.)
88. 48 HRS.
89. Beverly Hills Cop II.
90. Shoot to Kill.
91. Out of Bounds (Columbia, 1986).
92. When in doubt, this always works; in British films, substitute "MI5."
93. Beverly Hills Cop II.
94. 48 HRS.
95. Running Scared.
96. Lethal Weapon.
97. Lethal Weapon, 48 HRS., Dead Heat.
98. Shakedown, Beverly

Hills Cop II.
99. 48 HRS.
100. Shoot to Kill.
101. Lethal Weapon.
102. White Nights, Running Scared, Off Limits.
103. Red Heat.
104. Sunset.
105. See note 55.
106. Only in the gay variation on the theme, Partners, costarring Ryan O'Neal and John Hurt (Paramount, 1981).
107. Dead Heat.
108. Shakedown.
109. The Presidio.
110. Dragnet.
111. 48 HRS.
112. Dragnet, among others.
113. Beverly Hills Cop II, Partners, Shoot to Kill.
114. Stakeout.
115. Lethal Weapon.
116. Off Limits.
117. White Nights.
118. 48 HRS.
119. Known as the 007 Gambit, this is used only in James Bond- or Superman-derived films and requires the establishment of the "missing American atomic bomb" just after the unprecedented-wave-of-gratuitous-violence sequence that precedes the opening credits and begins the film. (For further clarification, see note 40.)
120. Sidney Poitier and Tom Berenger in Shoot to Kill.
121. Peter Weller and Sam Elliott in Shakedown.
122. Mikhail Baryshnikov and Gregory Hines in White Nights.
123. Tom Hanks and Dan Aykroyd in Dragnet.
124. Nick Nolte and Eddie Murphy in 48 HRS.
125. Ibid.
126. Richard Dreyfuss and Emilio Estevez in Stakeout.
127. Although listed here for reasons of clarity as single attributes, any combination or mixed usage of these personality traits is acceptable, per the Hope/Crosby rule of mutual antagonism, first cited in the Road to... series (Paramount, beginning 1940) and later perfected in Neil Simon's The Odd Couple (Paramount, 1968). However, in the event a "multiple buddy" format is utilized (known as the Dirty Dozen Formulation or the Platoon Template), each individual character must be given a single, easily recognized quirk/antagonism/stereotype that will put him in constant conflict with other members of his "Buddy Universe."
128. Aykroyd, Dragnet.
129. Estevez, Stakeout.
130. Danny Glover, Lethal Weapon; Belushi, Red Heat; Poitier, Shoot to Kill.
131. Glover, Lethal Weapon.
132. Nolte, 48 HRS.; Gibson, Lethal Weapon; Murphy (all).
133. Murphy (all); Nolte, 48 HRS.
134. Glover, Lethal Weapon; Estevez, Stakeout.
135. Glover, Lethal Weapon.
136. Belushi, Red Heat.
137. Murphy, Hines, Glover, Poitier.
138. Elliott, Shakedown;

Piscopo, Dead Heat.
139. Arnold Schwarzenegger.
140. Murphy, 48 HRS., Beverly Hills Cop.
141. Gibson, Lethal Weapon.
142. Murphy, Piscopo, Schwarzenegger.
143. Murphy, Hines, Glover, Poitier, Schwarzenegger.
144. Gibson, Lethal Weapon.
145. Murphy, 48 Hours; Hanks, Dragnet; Harmon, The Presidio; Hines, Running Scared; Dreyfuss, Stakeout.
146. Murphy, all roles.
147. Dragnet.
148. 48 HRS.

149. Beverly Hills Cop.
150. All of the above.
151. Beverly Hills Cop II.
152. Off Limits.
153. White Nights.
154. Stakeout.
155. Beverly Hills Cop.
156. 48 HRS.
157. Archaic; if scenes of women are necessary, substitute "Playboy Mansion" (Beverly Hills Cop II) or mock-Playboy Mansion (Dragnet) for this entry.
158. A generic nightclub/disco, obligatory for any movie set in Manhattan.
159. 48 HRS.
160. International Espionage films only; he's the European James Woods (see note 166).
161. Lethal Weapon.
162. Beverly Hills Cop II.
163. Although Dafoe enjoyed co-hero status in Off Limits,

he had previously worked the other side of the street in other, lesser-known buddy variations, such as Streets of Fire (Universal, 1984) and Roadhouse 66 (Atlantic Releasing, 1985).
164. Dragnet.
165. Superman-based films only.
166. When in doubt, James Woods is always the perfect crazed psychopathic Vietnam vet/nervous-twitching-homicidal-maniac-with-a-grudge, nothing-left-to-lose, no-regrets, next-time-it's-the-death-penalty/all-purpose, we-

understand-because-of-the-way-he-looks, incorrigible hard-case villain.
167. 48 HRS.
168. Off Limits.
169. Sunset.
170. Among buddy-film cognoscenti, this is referred to as the Obligatory Eddie Murphy Fish-out-of-Water White-Baiting Sequence.
171. Stakeout.
171a. Ibid.; also, Beverly Hills Cop.
172. Although neither of these women have actually appeared here, we all think they have; therefore, they're on the list, and thus probably an inspired choice.
172a. In the event that neither Mary Elizabeth Mastrantonio nor Maria Conchita Alonso is available, Rae Dawn Chong may be substituted.

173. Gorky Park.
174. It can't be too long before Atlantic City establishes a film commission. (It should be noted that all James Bond films have a requisite casino tableau, wherein 007 appears in a white dinner jacket, introduces himself to the villain over a baccarat table by saying "Bond—James Bond" and then proceeds to {a} steal his nemesis's girlfriend and {b} break the bank.)
175. In low-budget films the outside of the soundstage can always be re-dressed to achieve this effect.

176. Beverly Hills Cop II.
177. Sunset, Dragnet, etc., etc.
178. Beverly Hills Cop.
179. Depending on the budget of the film, "plush Bel Air estate" can incorporate all features listed above.
180. A small sociological/semantic insight: before Watergate, all grand schemes were called "diabolical"; after Richard Nixon's resignation in 1974, they all became "maniacal." If you're creating a period-piece Buddy Movie, the correct terminology will help ensure authenticity. (See City Heat, costarring Clint Eastwood and Burt Reynolds {Warner Brothers, 1984}.)
181. Beverly Hills Cop.
182. Beverly Hills Cop II (sort of).
183. Gorky Park.
184. The Manchurian

Candidate (United Artists, 1962).
185. White Nights (sort of).
186. See note 40.
187. When the revised edition of Buddy-o-Matic is issued in 1992, we're sure we'll have an example. Several.
188. The Presidio.
189. See note 165.
190. At some point in the movie, it's always a good idea to have one of the characters say the name of the film—if for no other reason than to act as a convenient segue into the title song, which, of course, will reinforce ticket sales when

the Kenny Loggins–Michael McDonald collaboration becomes a hit on Top 40 drive-time radio.
191. These are all mandatory Buddy Movie scenes. Should a producer find himself running low on funds at this point in the film, he should simply approach one of the studios whose last Buddy Movie failed and ask to buy some of the second unit's extra footage. No one will know the difference.
192. Always think international box-office appeal when casting this role.
193. Actually, it doesn't really matter whose life is saved, as long as some kind of ritualistic death-cheating scene takes place to formalize the all-important "buddy-bonding" process. The modern prototype is the Butch Cassidy cliff-jumping scene.

194. The differences between these three are subtle but nevertheless important; in 48 HRS. they respect but don't need each other; in The Presidio they need but don't like each other; in Lethal Weapon they kind of like each other but don't necessarily respect each other. This may seem specious to you, but to the studio head who decided to spend $10 million making the movie, it made all the difference in the world.
195. In the trade this is known as the ticking clock; it gives the movie a time frame and forces a heightened sense of drama by requiring the buddy team to resolve the problem before the deadline passes.
196. For international pictures in this era of glasnost, the phrases American can-do and Russian brute strength may be substituted according to taste.
197. This is all known as the Rule of Incongruous Transportation. Any vehicle will do, as long as it is completely anomalous. In Beverly Hills Cop II it's a cement truck on Santa Monica Boulevard; in Dragnet, a tank in Bel Air; in Running Scared, a car on the subway tracks. The only exception to this rule takes place in New York City, where nothing seems incongruous.
198. It doesn't matter which, as long as it is bigger, longer, louder and deadlier than the scene described in note 191.
199. Site of climax of Uptown Saturday Night.
200. Running Scared.
201. Reds (Paramount, 1981).
202. The French Connection (Twentieth Century Fox, 1971).
203. Most episodes of Miami Vice.
204. Most Huey Lewis videos.
205. Every nighttime beer commercial.
206. Low-budget films. See note 87.
207. Off Limits.
208. The Louisiana State Film Commission's phone number is (504) 342-8150.
209. Essential in any Mafia/homage-to-Coppola production.
210. 48 HRS. (Just add fog. John Lone is optional.)
211. Using whatever is the most expensive prop or set still standing.
212. 48 HRS.
213. The operative word here is cool. No matter what they say, it must be totally unemotional, completely denying the relationship they've formed. If all else fails, they can always punch each other. (For the perfect realization of this scenario, see the final moments of Rocky II, wherein Rocky Balboa climbs back into the ring with Apollo Creed for a poignant, friendly, man-to-man sparring contest.)
214. Re: the Sunset. No, this is not an homage to John Ford; rather, it is an homage to what should have been the final scene of the most expensive Buddy Comedy of all time—the much-discussed, long-awaited Dustin Hoffman–Warren Beatty Buddy Epic, Ishtar.

TEST-DRIVING THE BUDDY-O-MATIC™

Our story begins in Beverly Hills, where a crazed, psychopathic Vietnam vet (James Woods) is wreaking havoc and mayhem by murdering young nurses in a particularly sadistic style for no apparent reason.

Next we meet Nick Nolte, a soon-to-be-retired detective—who has just seen his partner get killed and has just been dumped by his wife—in the tasteful suburban home he shares with a cute-named dog somewhere in Los Angeles.

Now, at police headquarters, we meet police commissioner Lou Gossett, who doesn't like Nolte but recognizes his unique crime-fighting ability, so he teams him with Shelley Long and gives them a command, against his better instincts, to catch the nurse-murderer before the end of the week.

At first the two partners despise each other. Where one (Nolte) is neat, law-abiding and methodical, the other (Long) is slovenly, corner-cutting and foulmouthed, and they don't even dress alike (Nolte prefers a crisp suit and tie; Long, dungarees and an old flak jacket) or listen to the same music (Nolte, classical; Long, rap). Nevertheless, they go to a blue-collar strip joint looking for clues to catch Woods, and in order to prove herself, Long gets into a gun battle that leads nowhere but impresses Nolte.

Now things get complicated. It seems Nolte has fallen in love with James Woods's girlfriend, Maria Conchita Alonso. And to make matters worse, the two partners follow Woods to a bathhouse, where they discover he's not just a crazy nurse-murderer—that it is all part of his twisted, maniacal plan to destroy the ozone layer.

Now they're running scared. After a car chase with much destruction of city property, automatic-weapons fire, high-speed swerving and sheet-metal carnage, the pair runs up against James Woods's assistant, Brigitte Nielsen; she is about to kill Nolte but is stopped by Long. At last the pair realize how much they respect each other. And with time running out, they use a combination of street smarts and police know-how to appropriate a cement truck and engage in another car chase through the Universal Studios Tour, where they save Maria Conchita Alonso, kill James Woods and make Lou Gossett very happy. But not before the last scene, in which Nolte turns to Long outside a warehouse and scowls, "Can I have my tanning lotion back?" before driving into Los Angeles.

La Jolla, California

DEAR EDITORS Ah, come on guys, Sharpton wears gold jewelry and I don't. ["The New York-Equivalent Map of Los Angeles," September].

Don Simpson
Los Angeles, California

December 1988

We're often asked to explain the elusive appeal of "Separated at Birth?" (on occasion we've tried to explain it without actually having been asked, but now we just drink club soda). We confess we never really understood it ourselves until a letter arrived from Tim Hillson asking permission to use SPY's *Separated at Birth?* book in a Department of Psychology, University of Western Ontario, research project on "the perceived humour value of stimuli." Sounds interesting. Sounds Canadian. Now, just why do the researchers think the photos are funny? "A close physical similarity in the persons in a pair juxtaposed with a large difference between their backgrounds are what we hypothesize would be responsible for at least some of the humorous effect of the pairing." Plausible. But will our participation help mankind? "The research itself will help establish a cognitive-emotional model of humour, which would be of benefit to people in general, as humour has been shown to be a healthy stress mediator." Uncanny! *Almost the exact wording used in the original plan for this magazine.*

October 1989

true nature and reading *Wild Oats*.

I should with more heart cry you some of the same mercy for Eric Breindel ["When Bad Things Happen to Ambitious People," by Bruce Handy, June] if I could recall the smallest indication that his personal comeuppance had taught him the tolerance for others whose sins are meagerer than his own that he makes his living by withholding.

Murray Kempton
New York

We may have exaggerated the extent of Epstein's plagiarism, but his appearance in our little catalog of remarkable recent comebacks, which also included those of Congressman Studds, G.I. Joe and Dwight Gooden, wasn't intended to suggest that Epstein was "undeservedly absolved." Come to think of it, we didn't even mean to suggest that Breindel was undeservedly absolved—only, as you seem to agree, that his subsequent public mean-spiritedness as editorial editor of the New York Post *is weirdly unbecoming.*

September 1988

Another reason: As a criminal investigator for the U.S. Customs Service, I was part of Vice President Bush's highly publicized "drug task force," comprising Customs, the DEA and the Coast Guard. Many times, other federal and state agencies joined in. When a seizure was made, each federal agency submitted a report. This meant each agency took credit for the seizure, so a 400-pound cocaine seizure was reported as at least a 1,200-pound seizure (three-agency minimum participation). The year-end "figures" were impressive, and Bush's program was hyped as very successful.

Ana M. Contreras
Miami, Florida ➤

October 1992

DEAR EDITORS I would like to assure you, after reading your November 27 *Newsday* comments and those by Lewis Grossberger in *7 Days* [December 13], that I am NOT "rattled" by the SPY Tote Board. In fact, I consider it a great compliment to receive so much attention and space from you. I particularly enjoy it because it is like a nonsense game and seems to bear little resemblance to any reality. It is sometimes very amusing. The Tote Board has certainly made me better known than any other kind of exposure I have ever had, and it has given me a new, youthful audience.

You have certainly misunderstood my defense of Abe [Rosenthal] and Shirley [Lord]—much to my amusement. They are merely part of the whole.

Liz Smith
New York
Ah. What?

April 1990

A Thousand Points

The July/August article "1,000 Reasons Not to Vote for George Bush" [by Larry Doyle, David Robb and Joe Conason] is a classic. Years from now, when the Republican Party's Reign of Terror has finished, I will pore over my dusty copy and show it to my grandchildren.

Scott Loughrey
Baltimore, Maryland

October 1992

CHAPTER

8

"Together, We Make One Great Editor"

Kurt and Graydon and the Mom 'n' Pop Operation That Was *Spy*

They were almost like young lovers: They were completely into themselves as a unit, they were so adoring of each other, and they complemented each other so beautifully, that there were times—I'm sure without intending it—when they could shut out the world around them.

—SUSAN MORRISON

"WELL, THERE'S YET *ANOTHER* REASON I didn't think *Spy* was going to work out."

That's Jim Kelly, addressing the deeply unusual arrangement of a magazine's having two coequal top editors. (As the managing editor of Time Inc., and a pal of both Graydon's and Kurt's for a quarter century, he's in a position to comment.) But it did work, and Kelly thinks it had something to do with each having "a good sense of what was important to the other," as well as an understanding that there had to be a compromise of sensibilities.*

"And I think they had, at least for each other, a very good emotional intelligence," Kelly continues. "Also: Instant success helps! There are lots of magazines where you turn around and you say,

'Oh, this is its third year? I've only seen a couple of issues.' *Spy* was a success even before it began." The two editors, says Kelly, were also blessed with excellent and similar senses of humor: "If I didn't know one, I would easily think the other was the funniest person I'd ever met."

But whatever rapport existed between them (and they did indicate to one early interviewer that, combined, they made one great editor), there were still *two* of them.

Susan Morrison recalls that it could be "managerially awkward," in the sense that "it was sort of the way children operate—you show this idea to Mom, you show that idea to Dad—we all instinctively knew what each liked, and you would try to forge the alliance with the one who you knew was going to like that

---

*The synchronicity could take strange turns. Once, Graydon had to check into New York Hospital to have a polyp removed from his cheek. That day, Kurt obligingly fell off his bed (don't ask), broke his shoulder, and ended up in...New York Hospital. We edited the magazine from there. —Eds.

Opposite: Graydon and Kurt in the Puck Building's Ballroom, 1988

particular piece." (It could backfire. One of my journal entries from January 1988: "Still annoyed about Randall Short's piece being cut. Graydon explains that Kurt hated it and killed it. Yesterday, Kurt had told me that it was Graydon who hated and refused to run it.")

They spoke as one when staff writer Paul Simms, wearing his cartoon-editor hat, would show them some of the cartoons he thought were worth running—his 21-year-old sensibility often at odds with his bosses'. "They were always very quick and decisive," says Simms. "As in, 'Oh, *God. Never.* What are you *thinking?*'"

"There were more pluses than minuses," Morrison says, "because there was something about the power-sharing arrangement that never seemed as randomly dictatorial as working for someone who would just say yes or no, and there'd be no appeal, everything done in a vacuum."

The conventional wisdom—that Graydon was the charismatic toastmaster and Kurt the one-person brain trust—runs along these lines:

"Graydon was the cheerleader, the impresario, the energy-provider at *Spy*," says Tony Hendra, who contributed to the magazine and then succeeded Kurt as editor in 1993. "Whereas Kurt was kind of the intellectual nexus of the whole thing." (Graydon had left in 1991; by '93, much of the staff had never even worked with him.) "The people who were devoted to Kurt were *really* devoted to him," says Hendra, "they thought he was the Leonardo da Vinci of humor—as ingenious and surprising and well versed and all that."

The Best Little Hair House   Zorro Hair Theatre — *Eric Ostrander*

May 1988

"Graydon has an unerring instinct for the Achilles' heel," says Guy Martin. "Kurt has always had an absurdist, mathematical bent—'Let's compare Mayor Koch to a ball of hair, or a burning pyre.' He can do three-column figures in his head, it's why there were all the charts and graphs. I think of Kurt as a guy who's completely willing to roll a bomb under a table and watch it blow up. And when you package that anarchic gene with brainpower...."

"Kurt was reputed to be the smartest man in the world, and I basically would ratify that," says Paul Rudnick. "He became like a reference source."

But hewing too close to those reputations is reductive. Kurt and Graydon were both great writers and editors. Each was capable of being inspiring or maddening. It's possible they diverged most markedly in their philosophies regarding the purchase of electronic equipment: Kurt bought quality stuff at regular stores like normal people; Graydon, one of the last people in New York to own and operate a Betamax VCR, was proud of his sixth sense for the can-you-fucking-believe-this bargain.

One December, Graydon, cash-poor and wanting to buy a video camera to shoot home movies of his children, was headed back to the Puck Building after a late lunch. "The snow is falling, I swear," he claims, "and some kid comes out of the shadows and says he has a Sony camcorder and he'll sell it for $125. I said, 'Let me see it.' He says, 'Not here. Bring the money down and I'll show it to you.'" Graydon got the money and met the guy in the alley behind the Puck Building. "I open the box, and there, carefully wrapped, was what I thought was the camcorder with wires sticking out of it and such." Clutching his purchase, Graydon returned to his office, where he—and a small crowd of staff that had gathered—discovered that in fact he had bought a piece of concrete.

Kurt, hearing the sudden howls of laughter, sauntered into Graydon's office, picked up the jagged chunk, and studied it. "So...," he said at length, indicating a faint crevice, "the cassettes go in *here?*"

The next day, the staff quietly took up a collection and presented Graydon with an art-department–designed gift certificate redeemable for $300. "It was right out of O. Henry," Graydon remembers. "I almost wept. And because everyone was paid so horribly, I never collected the money. But somewhere I still have that certificate."

Graydon's credulity was of the free-range variety.

"The time he thought he'd bought a Stradivarius violin at a

flea market in Connecticut?" says David Owen. "I mean, Graydon and his enthusiasms! *'This is going to just change everything. It's going to change our lives.'* Couldn't *believe* he'd found it in New Milford! Bought it for something like $30 or $50 from this *sucker* who hadn't realized what he had. Someone from Sotheby's was going to come up. And then, of course, it turned out it was a phony."

"Graydon was—and remains—a genuine eccentric," says Rudnick, who probably wasn't even aware of the editor's deep-seated fear that employees would "start bringing pets in" to the otherwise laissez-faire *Spy* offices. (Once, someone did. A friend of Kurt's visited with an unleashed dachshund, which promptly crept around the partition into Graydon's office. Graydon let out a terrified whoop, and the dog clacked away across the hardwood floor at high speed. "I thought it was a rat," Graydon explained.)

"I think you need those kinds of people to lead a magazine, or any organization for that matter," Rudnick continues. "Someone who is helplessly himself, and therefore irreplaceable. I remember early on that Graydon had this reputation of raffish mystery, and it was based almost entirely on the fact that he was *Canadian.* That somehow became a euphemism for 'He killed a man in Tangier.' He was up for it, too. There was that sense of someone leading you on a wonderful adventure, right over the waterfall."

"I came to New York in October of '89 for a six-month internship at *Spy*," says Michael Hainey, then almost painfully shy and operating under the assumption that he would soon return to Chicago and start his real career, in PR. "And my first December, that was the infamous Christmas party." (More on that later.) "The drinking started at two in the afternoon, and by five Graydon called me over and said, 'Michael, Michael, Michael'—put his arm around me, said, 'Do you like it here?' I said yeah. 'Good. Want a job?' 'Yeah, I'd love a job.' 'Good, good. You're going to be a star. New York is going to open up for you.' Graydon saw something in people and then grabbed them and told them they could do it." (Hainey, who eventually became deputy editor of *GQ*, never did move back to Chicago.)

At *Spy*, Graydon's office was the one with the photos of the Flatiron Building and of playwright George S. Kaufman smoking a cigarette after he'd won his second Pulitzer Prize, the bust of Canadian prime minister Sir Wilfred Laurier draped with the editor's "default ties," and—one regular visitor insists—croquet balls. Or maybe it was just the *suggestion* of croquet balls. "The surface of his desk was basically the interior of a London gentlemen's club,"

rning workout.
Y DREW FRIEDMAN

April 1989

THE SPY LIST

John Fitzgerald Kennedy
and
Robert Francis Kennedy

Walter Cronkite
and
Frank Sinatra

John Travolta
and
Cornelia Guest

Ronald Reagan
and
Gardner McKay

George Will
and
R. Emmett Tyrrell

Paula Weinstein
and
Tom Hayden

Auberon Waugh
and
Martin Amis

APRIL 19

says Guy Martin. Kurt's office was more minimalist, but no more conventionally officelike. One day I heard Tom Phillips, from inside his office, yell to Anne Kreamer, the marketing director (and Kurt's wife): "Anne! C'mere! I wanna show you something." Immediately Kurt called out: "Anne, if he tries to show you his penis, just walk away."

I remember phoning Kurt in late 1988 to let him know that *Spy* reporter Rachel Urquhart and I were getting married, and apologizing for not being able to tell him in person. "Oh, that's all right," he said, cheerily. "It's much easier for me to be effusive over the phone." Kurt, the man least likely ever to host a Super Bowl party or participate in a fantasy-baseball-league draft, nevertheless could faithfully turn up at a corporate challenge race in Central Park in support of the *Spy* running team—and announce, "I feel like I own a racehorse." Graydon, on the other hand, couldn't look into a sports-equipment bag without seeing a range of glorious

may borrow a page from Krieger's book: Retain public-relations counsel, issue a press release and announce that you have established an educational foundation; call it the Karma Foundation. Announce a new entrepreneurial venture; name it after yourself. Is it necessary to mention in the press release that your leave-taking was not wholly amicable? Must one allude to the firing thing, or to disputes with one's employer over the advisability of one's trading style? Krieger chose to emphasize the constructive elements of his situation:

"Options trading specialist Andrew Krieger announced today he will leave the investment firm of Soros Fund Management on June 30, 1988 to pursue two personal interests, Krieger & Associates Ltd. and the Karma Foundation. . . .

"'Increasingly over the last several months [he was quoted in his own press release as saying] I have been receiving substantial and unsolicited offers from major institutions and individuals that I manage their investment trading portfolios. Simultaneously, I have been studying how I could better manage my own funds and my growing philanthropic objectives. The decision . . . ensures me the time and freedom to accommodate that investor interest and still have a means for participating more actively in various socially responsible endeavors.'"

The release, antedating the restatement of foreign-exchange earnings by Bankers Trust, mentioned the $338 million booked by the firm in last year's fourth quarter. It was an understandable error—if Bankers Trust didn't understand Krieger's positions, Krieger himself, so long gone from the bank, could hardly be expected to know.

In truth, the press release raised as many questions as it answered. If it was true that Krieger wanted to manage money, why was he in such a hurry to leave a place that had so much of it? Why would he freely choose to leave the payroll of a man who is known to pay top dollar for talented traders? Krieger, when reached on the telephone, reiterated, "I was not fired. I resigned." Likewise a Soros spokesman: "It was an amicable parting." Amicable, no doubt. George Soros, risk-taker extraordinaire, is once again able to sleep at night, and Krieger, Bankers Trust trading ace, is able to raise new money for his own fund. "I'm not worried about having sufficient capital," Krieger has said. "I'm concerned that we don't accept too much." Anyway, there will always be lepers. ❥

Where Was PHILIP?

BY MICHAEL SORKIN

"YOU CANNOT NOT KNOW HIStory." —Philip Johnson

"I do not believe in principles, in case you haven't noticed." —Philip Johnson

POLITICS

It seems that *everyone's* an ex-Fascist nowadays. There's Kurt Waldheim, the well-known Austrian ex-Nazi, and Herbert von Karajan, the well-known German ex-Nazi. Then there's Paul de Man, the renowned Yale professor, recently deceased, who, it turns out, wrote pro-Fascist articles for Belgian newspapers during the war. And of course there's always Martin Heidegger, the late philosopher, Nazi Party member and prominent exfriend of the *Führerprinzip*.

These creeps have been getting a lot of print lately, and the question everyone seems to be asking is, what difference does it make? Do we have to reconsider *Blindness and Insight* (De Man) or *Being and Time* (Heidegger) or the UN resolution on Afghanistan (Waldheim) just because their authors might also have abetted the mass extermination of certain unfit persons? And should we expect some kind of apology?

The *Times* gave ample space last summer to the revelations about De Man, but nobody ever seems to ask these questions about that raffish old ex-Fascist Philip Johnson—arts patron, museum trustee, friend of the mighty, dean of American architecture and designer most recently of William Paley's new building to house the Museum of Broadcasting. Of course, it's not exactly as if his work could seem any *more* opportunistic. And, it's true, nobody has produced any pictures of the elegant tastemaker sporting in the Balkans in SS drag. Still, to coin a phrase, *where was Philip?* Let's return to the 1930s, when the young Museum of Modern Art curator had more on his mind than promoting a new architectural style and himself.

In 1934 the beginning of Johnson's political career was heralded by the following four-line headline in the *Times*: TWO FORSAKE ART TO FOUND A PARTY/MUSEUM MODERNISTS PREPARE TO GO TO LOUISIANA AT ONCE TO STUDY HUEY LONG'S WAYS/GRAY SHIRT THEIR SYMBOL/YOUNG HARVARD GRADUATES THINK POLITICS NEEDS MORE 'EMOTION' AND LESS 'INTELLECTUALISM.' What a lark for the self-styled disciples of self-styled American Fascist Lawrence Dennis. "We shall try to develop ourselves," declared Johnson's friend and MoMA colleague Alan Blackburn, "by doing the sort of things that everybody in New York would like to do but never finds time for. We may learn to shoot, fly airplanes and take contemplative walks in the woods."

There was, to be sure, some vagueness about the program of and membership in the new party. "We have no definite political program to offer," declared Blackburn, the party mouthpiece. The two also declined to reveal membership data (an estimated high-water mark was fewer than 150). The one thing that was certain was the choice of shirting. Imagine the conversation when this was decided. *Brown is too . . . seasonal. Black? Like those Italians? Silver? Déclassé! Gray?* Gray! *Wire Turnbull & Asser!*

Tiring rapidly of Louisiana and the Kingfish (whose embrace of the two-man volunteer brain trust from New York City was apparently less than effusive), the pair switched crypto-Fascist demagogues, now sucking up to the revolting anti-Semites and right-wingers William Lemke and Father Charles Coughlin, donating at least $5,000 to their activities. In his book *Demagogues in the Depression*, David Bennett describes the two fellow travelers in 1936: "Johnson and Blackburn . . . appeared at the Coughlin convention, ostensibly representing the 'Youth Division of the NUSJ [National Union for Social Justice—Coughlin's organization].' Although inactive in Union affairs, they were fascinated by radical politics and their financial aid gave them access to party organizers. Later they were to form the quasi-fascistic National Party." Indeed, Johnson, who grew up in Cleveland, even attempted a run at the Ohio state legislature in the mid-1930s. Such an irony: just as the world might have been spared years of carnage if Hitler had only been admitted to architecture school, imagine the architecture that might have been avoided if the electorate had had the prescience to make young Philip a legislator.

As the 1930s progressed Johnson began to sign his name to a variety of articles for the publications of the lunatic fringe, quickening the pace of his pro-German maunderings as world war approached. For instance, in a 1939 issue of *Today's Challenge*, an article titled "Are We a Dying People?" offered the latent master builder's views on the master race. "The United States of America is committing race suicide," he warned. Deploying statistical evidence of the precipitous decline of the "white" race, he rebuked the "philosophy of Individualism and Materialism" as "eugenically bad" for failing to fulfill "the imperatives of racial maintenance."

Then, in a mighty peroration subtitled "The Will to Live," Johnson offered a truly chilling metaphor to describe the way in which this will is to be exercised. "Human will is a part of the biological process," he declared. "Our will . . . interferes constantly in the world of the lower animals. When English sparrows threaten to drive out our songbirds, we shoot the sparrows, rather than letting nature and Darwin take their course. Thus the songbirds, thanks to our will, become the 'fittest' and survive."

This was written in *1939*.

As it turns out, the national origin of those sparrows was not meant entirely metaphorically. Credentialed as European correspondent for Father Coughlin's scurrilous, Jew-baiting paper *Social Justice*, Johnson filed, as war accelerated, a stream of tacitly pro-Nazi dispatches mocking the English. (And his fine aesthete's eye and celebrated wit were fully operational even in the midst of war. "It is said, with how much truth I am unable to say," he wired in a dispatch from the summer of 1939, "that a large London hospital had had to add to its staff because of the increased accidents caused by the 'volunteer' nurses. I can only vouch for the fact that most of these volunteers look very bad indeed in their baggy uniforms; I have heard Paris audiences laugh out loud at them.")

Likewise, his anti-Semitism is filtered through his refined sense of what really matters. Back in Paris, he wrote, "Another serious split in French opinion is that caused by the Jewish question, a problem much aggravated just at present by the multitude of émigrés in Paris. Even I, as a stranger in the city, could not help noticing how much German was being spoken, especially in the better restaurants. Such an influx naturally makes the French wonder, not only about these incoming Jews, but also about their co-religionists who live and work here and call themselves French. The facts that [Léon] Blum and the men around him are Jews, that there are two Jews in the present cabinet, Messrs. Zay and Mandel, and that the Jewish bankers Mannheimer, de Rothschild and Lazard Freres are known to stand behind the present government all complicate the situation." Philip made the danger in this complication clear in another *Social Justice* article, published in July 1939: "Lack of leadership and direction in the [French] State has let the one group get control who always gain power in a nation's time of weakness—the Jews."

The undoubted high point of Philip's career as a journalist came as he accompanied the Nazi blitzkrieg to Poland in September. Arriving in Berlin shortly before the invasion, Johnson crossed into Poland to get the story. In a dispatch in the September 11 edition of *Social Justice*, he found

the Poles "so excited and so worried about the crisis which they feel is at hand, that they arrested me at the border merely for taking pictures." Later he ridiculed the defensive efforts being undertaken by that hapless nation, puny measures that, he related, caused his German pals to roar with laughter when he reported them.

The Polish police weren't the only ones suspicious of Philip's activities at the border. Near Danzig he encountered William Shirer, who describes their meeting in *Berlin Diary*: "Dr. Boehmer, press chief of the Propaganda Ministry in charge of this trip, insisted that I share a double room in the hotel here with Philip Johnson, an American fascist who says he represents Father Coughlin's *Social Justice*. None of us can stand the fellow and suspect he is spying on us for the Nazis. For the last hour in our room here he has been posing as an anti-Nazi and trying to pump me for my attitude. I have given him no more than a few bored grunts." (Johnson responded to this in a 1973 interview in a British architectural journal, saying about Shirer, "[He is] a very irresponsible journalist . . . very third rate writer.")

Meanwhile, back on the Polish beat during the Nazi invasion, Philip proclaimed his "shock" at his first visit to the country of "Chopin, Paderewski and Copernicus." Under the subhead JEWS DOMINATE POLISH SCENE he wrote, "The boundaries of Europe seem to the traveller to [*sic*] the most part arbitrary lines. But here was a real boundary. Once on the Polish side I thought at first that I must be in the region of some awful plague. . . . In the towns there were no shops, no automobiles, no pavements and again no trees. There were not even any Poles to be seen in the streets, only Jews!" Later Philip visited Lodz, "a slum without a city attached to it." It didn't take long to find out who was to blame; it was the 35 percent of the population who happened to be Jewish and who, "dressed in their black robes and black skull-caps and with their long beards . . . seem more like 85 per cent." Philip retained his fine sartorial eye. No gray shirts here.

At the end of 1939 Philip returned to the U.S., where he lectured to the American Fellowship Forum, the Nazi-front group behind *Today's Challenge*. Then, late in 1940, he went back to Harvard to study architecture. In 1943 he was drafted, and he served two years. At the end of the war he resumed his curatorship at MoMA and shortly thereafter began his architectural practice, going on to become the most celebrated designer in America.

And what about some sort of apology? Some version of the Waldheim grovel? There never has been one from Johnson—not publicly, at any rate. However, apology or no, he has been forgiven. When Philip was up for election to MoMA's board of trustees in 1957, someone had the bad taste to mention that the man had spent years as, er . . . a Jew-bashing Fascist. John D. Rockefeller's wife, Blanchette, already a museum trustee, rose to the occasion with suitable noblesse oblige. "Every young man," she said, "should be allowed to make one large mistake." ❥

Nothing awkward: Despite this column, Philip Johnson later cooperated eagerly with *Spy* for a feature story. October 1988

possibilities. "At one [magazine-league] softball game, at his urging," remembers Geoff Reiss, "we managed to have *Rolling Stone* hit a very soft, restricted-flight ball, while we hit some souped-up plastic-core thing that traveled miles. Graydon made sure each half-inning the balls were swapped. We killed them."

"I always felt that Kurt and Graydon were like the sun. We all wanted our orbits to be as close as possible to them," says Jamie Malanowski. "If we'd been older, we'd probably have realized how desperately they needed us. It was enormously flattering when Kurt liked one of your pieces, it really felt like something special. And when Graydon was pleased with something, you never had a better cheerleader.

"It was an education to get to know someone like Graydon," continues Malanowski. "I remember at one meeting, Graydon's sitting there and saying, 'I can tell right now, without looking, which of you is wearing shoes with soft soles and which shoes with hard soles.' It was my first encounter with someone who had that eye for those kinds of details. And you would recognize it in his writing, and you'd begin to try to use some of these visual observations about people in your own writing."

One year when Graydon was named to the International Best-Dressed List, I mentioned it to him—he claimed he hadn't heard—and he asked that "we keep it just between us," then fumbled elaborately with his tie, searching for soup stains.

John Brodie was Graydon's assistant, toiling at a tiny desk in the corner of the editor's office when the Puck space began to overflow with staff. He had the privilege of lending his boss money for cab fare, and of retrieving for him, each morning at the brand-new Dean & DeLuca in SoHo, "one fully leaded cappuccino and a Camel softpack."

There were other perks.

"Graydon would go to cover shoots and say, 'I'm going to get you Jay Leno's autograph,'" Brodie remembers. "And then he would come back with this amazingly personal autograph from Jay Leno—like, 'Keep filin', keep faxin'—Jay.' And I would be, like, 'That is so cool.' I'd put it in a little plastic frame and put it up at my desk. When Milton Berle was on the cover, it was, 'With all my love—Uncle Miltie.' Carol Alt: 'John, you can be *my* editorial assistant anytime,' with a lipstick mark. Finally, when Graydon took me out to lunch and promoted me to reporter, he said, 'By the way, I have to tell you, I did all those autographs myself.'"

THE OTHER TEMPTATIONS OF CHRIST

To sleep in until 11:00 a.m. someday, even though the disciples gather at 8:00 a.m.

To work a miracle for *my own* benefit for a change

To hold my nose in the marketplace when I walk by the beggars

To tether my oxen in the areas by the shops reserved for the infirm

To cast the first stone at an uprising

Not to give Ruth of the Wheatfields a wedding present (*I changed all that water into wine at her engagement party. How much does she expect?*)

To wrap Herod's house some night with papyrus

To get it in writing from God that I am really His son so I don't have these doubts

To destroy all paintings that make me look fat

To invite Caesar to dinner when I know he is busy so I get the credit

To butt in line at the tannery. If I am the Lord, why should I wait? —*Patricia Marx*

November 1988

Perhaps the most common refrain among *Spy* alumni: They were, as editors, unique in making people want to do their best work. "Kurt because you didn't want to disappoint him intellectually, Graydon because you didn't want to let him down," says Michael Hainey. "It was a weird chemistry they put together. You felt such a personal stake in that magazine. And they did an amazing job of running the circus."

"Given the magazine's flair for gossip, I'd always assumed, before I met Kurt and Graydon, that they'd be screaming queens," says Henry Alford. "I was, uh, mistaken."

Still: Their biggest fight *was* about commitment.

At least according to Graydon. Kurt recalls an earlier one, in 1985, before *Spy* had even published. "Tom and Graydon and I were meeting, and I said something—maybe criticized some idea

THE fine PRINT

SILVER LININGS Sure, President Kennedy's assassination was a cataclysmic tragedy that has ripped open a perhaps unhealable wound in the national psyche. And yet, Americans that we are, some of us have found ways to wangle some not inconsiderable dinero from the horrifying event (no doubt a healthy response, as our shrinks would say). {Sick, sick, sick—Ed.}

Publishing ventures have proved particularly rewarding. Already there have been five bestsellers serving up reheated Kennedyana, as well as several works that haven't quite cracked the top ten. Dig our estimates of the cottage-industry profits* that JFK's death has made possible:

Four Days, written by the editors of UPI and American Heritage and published by Simon & Schuster, has sold 2.5 million copies at $2.95 each. That works out to a $272,875 windfall for the publishers and an $885,000 take for the authors, though it's not clear how the royalties were split among the poor wretches who actually put the book together.

A Day in the Life of President Kennedy, written by Jim Bishop, published by Random House, has sold 140,000 copies at $3.95 a copy, thus earning Bishop, the aging hack, $66,360 and his publishers $20,461.

The John F. Kennedys, written by Mark Shaw, published by Farrar, Straus & Giroux, has sold 97,000 copies at $7.50 apiece. Shaw's take works out to $87,300, the publisher's to $26,917.50.

America the Beautiful, *in (continued)*

* How the calculations were made: according to Publishers' Weekly, authors make 12 cents on every dollar of net sales, while publishers earn 3.7 cents.

and featuring the vocal talents of a PHILADELPHIA PARTYGIRL and a certain married NOBEL PRIZE–WINNING CIVIL-RIGHTS LEADER. But you didn't read that here, Clyde.

Roy Cohn

Evil, unconvicted perjurer ROY COHN was consulting with a client not long after his own recent trials. How much, the client wanted to know, would Cohn's fee come to? The lawyer said $10,000, then rubbed his fingers together to suggest that a portion of the money would go toward bribing a judge. After the client left, seemingly satisfied, a colleague took Cohn aside. *Roy,* the long-suffering colleague implored, *it's a no-lose case. You don't have to resort to that kind of stuff.* To which the bullet-headed Stork Club habitué replied, *You think I don't f---ing know that? The point is, the guy wants to* think *he's getting his money's worth. And what he don't know won't hurt him.* ❭

... ONLY IN THE DREAM, RIGHT, THE DISMEMBERED TURNS OUT TO BE ETHEL KENNEDY...

THE DOROTHY KILGALLEN TOTE BOARD

Note: Dorothy Kilgallen was on vacation during part of our tally period. Taking her place during that period was "internationally famous singer" Jane Morgan.

Barry Goldwater	1
The Beatles	
Frank Sinatra	
Fidel Castro	
Liz and Dick	
Cyd Charisse	
Cassius Clay	
Communists	
Robert Goulet	
Abbe Lane	
Ingemar Johansson	
Trini Lopez	
The New Christy Minstrels	
Mamie Van Doren	

POEM:

SOMEONE'S CRYING, LORD

Who are you really
Mr. Plastic Corfam Mr. Madison Avenue Zum Zum
wurstbar man?
If I had a hammer
I'd wake you up.

—Faun Rosenberg

COINCIDENCE? OR...?

Lincoln vs. JFK: A Funny Comparative Chart

ABRAHAM LINCOLN	JOHN F. KENNEDY
Last name contains 7 letters	Last name contains 7 letters
Was elected in 1860	Was elected in 1960
Had a vice president named Johnson	Had a vice president named Johnson
Johnson contains 7 letters	*Johnson* contains 7 letters
Was shot in a theater by an assassin who ran to a warehouse	Was shot from a warehouse by an assassin who ran to a theater
Was advised by his secretary, named Kennedy, not to go to the theater	Was advised by his secretary, named Lincoln, not to go to Dallas
Was married to a high-strung woman	Was married to a string-bean woman
Had a beard	Used beards
"Four score and seven years ago"	Seven scores in four days ❭

up his credentials with the bomb-them-back-to-the-Stone-Age set. **4.** BEATLEMANIA-MANIA. Yes, they're a good combo and we like their songs. But girls, *please!* An

NAKED LUNCHCOUNTER
A Civil-Rights Restaurant Review

"What does the Negro want?" That's the question the pundits and newsweeklies were asking all summer long. We think we have a general idea. But in order to formulate a precise answer, we dispatched our southern correspondent to the Monson Motor Lodge restaurant in St. Augustine, Florida — where Martin Luther King Jr. and his aide Ralph Abernathy, among others, were refused service and arrested during a June sit-in. Our man's report on what the Negroes missed:

Today's blue plate special is fried chicken, mashed potatoes and a choice of turnip greens or creamed corn, all for 50¢. The meal begins promisingly enough, with a dazzlingly sweet iced tea and a wink from the sassy waitress (*Is this blushing flower of white southern womanhood part of the solution or a part of the problem*, I wonder idly), but the chicken itself is greasy, overfried and encased in a uniforma batter tasting largely of cornstarch — a sodden, one-note symphony. A wandering fork provides no respite: the long-in-the-tooth potatoes, laced with nubbins of clustered unmixed insta-flakes, evidently owe their unfortunate life to Betty Crocker. As for the greens, they are, well, *green* — the sole sensory observation it seems incumbent on me to make. What the Negro wants is one thing. What he will get at southern lunch counters, I infer as I pay the bill and leave, is dyspepsia.

—John Kennedy Toole

PRIVATE LIVES OF PUBLIC ENEMIES

White House aide Jack Valenti assists President Johnson with some highly sensitive business.

THE SPY LIST

Lord Buckley

James Coburn

John Coltrane

Adelle Davis

Cary Grant

Aldous Huxley

Christopher Isherwood

John F. Kennedy

Ken Kesey

Arthur Koestler

Robert Lowell

Clare Boothe Luce

Henry Luce

Anaïs Nin

André Previn

THE fine PRINT

the words of John F. Kennedy, compiled by the editors of Country Beautiful *magazine, published by Doubleday, has sold 70,250 copies at $4.95 each, earning those hardworking girls $41,728.50, and $12,866.29 for Doubleday.*

Additionally, the "Harper Memorial Edition" of Profiles in Courage, *published by Harper & Row, sold almost 93,000 copies at $12.50 each. Thus the rather ancient opus earned another, entirely unexpected $43,012.50 or so for the publishers, and roughly another $139,500 that the Kennedy estate would presumably have been happy to do without (and that Ted Sorensen could probably use). Also, excerpts from the Warren Commission report have just been published by Doubleday and McGraw-Hill (Oswald did it — oops!); sales of the book are expected to fall in the 50,000-to-75,000 range.*

(Unfortunately, figures are unavailable for A Tribute to John F. Kennedy, *edited by Pierre Salinger, published by Encyclopedia Britannica and Atheneum; and Bill Adler's* The Kennedy Wit, *published by Citadel Press.)*

Along with tangible profits, many people's careers have received boosts thanks to Oswald's marksmanship. The brilliant performance of Tom Wicker of The New York Times, *writing from Dallas for the newspaper of record — under what was obviously incredible pressure — so impressed his bosses that he is now the Washington bureau chief (see* The Times, *page 7). Similarly, Dan Rather, CBS's slightly wiggy Dallas correspondent, seems to have caught the fancy of his superiors. He may end up with a plummy foreign assignment, perhaps Vietnam. Of course, the biggest promotion, along with a $57,000 raise in pay, went to LBJ.*

(continued)

Among the names we enjoyed putting on the masthead of this hypothetical 1964 version of *Spy* **were Tom Wolfe, Diane Arbus (in the photo department), and Seymour Hersh. We saw Carl Bernstein as an intern, and the publisher and editor-in-chief was, of course, Walter Monheit. November 1989**

we have to put up with the imitators, all those Dreamers and Pacemakers and Rolling Stones and other flashes in the pan? **5.** THAT WORLD'S FAIR OUT IN FLUSHING. ►

that Graydon had or something? And he just blew up and was going to walk out on the whole thing: 'That's just—that's fuckin' *it*! Forget it!' And Tom made peace. But that wasn't a huge low. The magazine didn't exist at that point. It's like when you're living with somebody, and you have a big fight. At least you're not married yet, you know?"

But the one Graydon remembers—which Susan Morrison and I witnessed—came in the midst of working on the first issue in the summer of '86. It had to do with Kurt's continuing to write for *Time*, where he was the architecture critic, contributing a piece a month. "I wanted Kurt to quit," Graydon says. "He was managing to juggle it pretty well, but I guess I wanted him to commit. And I think we went up to the roof, so you kids wouldn't hear." (That's exactly what they did; there was an eruption of angry voices, they hurried out the door and up the stairs, but were soon back—and back to normal.)

Neither is particularly comfortable analyzing their unusual rapport and its effect on the staff, but Kurt gives it a shot:

"I think it was clear to us, half-consciously, from the beginning that we were complementary people. But it really was like a great band, maybe, and we were the frontmen? Something where, let's say, the 10 core players were *so* fully invested in it, every tune, every lyric, every performance, every piece of cover art. And it was kind of amazing."

PRIVATE LIVES

Lee Atwater entertains some friends with a Negro spiritual.

ILLUSTRATION BY DREW FRIEDMAN

May 1989

Shredded Wheat
Kravis; Shredded
Carolyne Roehm
Lewis Rudin; tal
Joseph Flom
Koch and G
Stein: power lav
stadium-name-g
Shea
Koch and G
developer Richar
Koch and D
Stein: American
chairman James
III (individually
Stein, corporately
developer Leonai
Koch and St
Messinger: min
propaganda How
Rubenstein
Goldin and
Messinger: The
Firefighters Asso
Stein and Di
Kennedy brothei
errand boy Steph
condo peddler ar
Trump hireling I
Stein and M
Republican adm
Femina
Goldin and
Messinger: Dor

GET IT WHILE Y
Fame is fleeting,
so than on televi
you're Michael C

SADDAM HUSSEIN: HITLERIAN BRUTE OR AMERICA'S SAVIOR?

(Or Ted Turner's New Best Friend?)

actually *watch the movie.* To hold the subjects' attention, the researchers rigged the TV monitor so that a light flashed every 15 seconds or so. The subjects were instructed to press a button on their chair whenever the light flashed. In the end, Wheeler and Rubin, with the help of those six stalwart volunteers, were able to prove that the devices worked equally well but that the circumferential device was easier to use. (What's the point? Well, the next time you hear Southside Johnny advance the thesis that "it ain't the meat, it's the motion," you'll know that science is working toward a time when that proposition can be tested clinically.)

Some studies achieved more practical results. In 1974 two researchers from Canada, Donald Dutton and Arthur Aron, studied the effects of anxiety on sexual attraction. In one experiment, they paired male subjects with an attractive woman who was part of the research team but was posing as a fellow subject. The researcher in charge then told the men that each would soon get hit with an electrical shock; some were told they'd receive a strong shock, others just a tingle. First, however, they had to answer some written questions, including two about the female subject who was their partner: *How much would you like to ask her out for a date?* and *How much would you like to kiss her?* Dutton and Aron found that a subject who'd been told he would soon get hit with a strong shock was more apt to be attracted to the woman than was a subject who'd been told to expect a tingle.

And some of the studies were more sociological. One researcher found that beer parties, or "keggars," were popular with college students *because they promised an opportunity to meet a member* ▶

Saddam to the rescue...of our beleaguered arms manufacturers?

"The barons of America's military establishment owe a moment of heartfelt silence in thanks to Iraq's Saddam Hussein."
— *Chicago Tribune*

"Along comes a 'rescuer' named Saddam Hussein. Thanks to Iraq's invasion of Kuwait, the US defense industry is back in the saddle."
— *The Christian Science Monitor*

"'You can thank Saddam Hussein for $2 to $3 billion in weapons' spending, [military writer Thomas McNaugher] said." — *Newsday*

...of our beleaguered incumbents?

"The specter of Iraq's Saddam Hussein may help incumbents showing up on TV visiting troops."
— *USA Today*

"Candidates seeking re-election this year were supposed to face voters angry about the savings and loan scandal and uneasy about the economy. Then the Persian Gulf crisis 'knocked everything else off the radar screen,' says Republican strategist Ed Rollins." — *USA Today*

...of East-West relations?

"In time...we may even thank the unscrupulous Saddam Hussein for helping steer the world toward a new era in global equilibrium."
— Timothy Cooper, in a letter to *The Washington Post*

"Officials say the Gulf crisis...could even help to further cement the East-West accord Gorbachev has labored to achieve." — Reuters

"Thanks to Saddam Hussein, Turkey is once more a courted and valued Washington ally."
— *Los Angeles Times*

...of our farmers and oilmen?

"The seizure of Kuwait by Iraqi strongman Saddam Hussein is certain to help the Texas oil economy." — *The Washington Times*

"Thanks to Saddam Hussein, Americans are once again bemoaning their dependence on foreign crude, welcome news for the makers of ethanol."
— *Fortune*

"This year all kinds of things went down: real estate, media, banks, public stocks, private companies, you name it (among major categories, agriculture and oil were strong—thank you, Saddam Hussein)." — *Forbes*

"The long-battered oil service industry is breathing a sigh of relief—thanks to Saddam Hussein." — Reuters Business Report

...of hawks and spooks?

"The American 'hawks' should also be grateful to him."— commentary by Aleksandr Bovin, *Izvestia*

"[Michael Hershman, president of the Fairfax Group, an intelligence and security group] said [that] now, thanks to Saddam Hussein, he is projecting a 50 to 60 percent rise in this year's revenues....CEO Gerard Burke said events in the Persian Gulf will help push Parvus' [another spy and security firm] revenues near the $2-million mark this year. [And] he expects to be busy handling consequent terrorist crises for a few years to come." — *Washington Business Journal*

...of our stove manufacturers?

"Even Saddam Hussein can't help but bring a little warmth to Some American hearts and hearths....Thanks to Hussein, the makers of wood and coal stoves are feeling a boomlet in a business that has seen far more downs than ups in the past decade or so." — UPI

...of the quality of our lives?

"War has become human again, and the world has Saddam Hussein...to thank for it."
— *The Washington Times*

"'I think we should thank Hussein. He's making us a better country.'"
— local biker Half Horse, quoted in *Seattle Times*
— *David Shenk*

the *Irony* EPIDEMIC

HOW CAMP CHANGED FROM LUSH TO LITE,

WHY DAVID LETTERMAN IS A GOD,

OUR FIELD GUIDE TO THE UNWITTINGLY HIP

AND THE FASHIONABLY UNFASHIONABLE,

AND AN INTRODUCTION TO THE

TINY CONVERSATIONAL ART OF AIR QUOTES

BY PAUL RUDNICK AND KURT ANDERSEN

Meet Bob and Betty.
Bob is wearing a

LET YOUR FINGERS DO THE TALKING

How Hand Semaphore
Evolved from Thumbs-Up
Earnestness to
Air-Quotes Irony

1935-44

hibiscusy Hawaiian shirt that he purchased at a "vintage" clothing boutique for approximately six times the garment's original 1952 price. He also carries his lunch in a tackle box and wears a Gumby wristwatch, Converse high-tops and baggy khakis from Banana Republic; at the store, the pants had been stacked in an artfully ruined Indiana Jones–style jeep. Bob describes his look as "Harry Truman mixed with early Jerry Mathers." Bob assumes we know that Mathers played the title role on *Leave It to Beaver.*

Betty wears Capri pants, ballet flats and a man's oversize white shirt, along with a multizippered black-leather motorcycle jacket imprinted with Cyrillic letters. She's "Audrey Hepburn by way of Patty Duke as James Dean's girlfriend waiting on the drag strip." Betty refers to herself as Bob's "old lady." Bob calls himself "Dad." When Bob and Betty describe themselves in these ways, they raise the middle and forefingers of both hands, momentarily forming twitching bunny ears — *air quotes,* the quintessential contemporary gesture that says, *We're not serious.*

Betty and Bob have a child, a two-year-old whom they call "Kitten." The child is probably too young to catch the reference to *Father Knows Best,* even though she sits with her parents when they watch *Nick at Nite,* the cable TV service devoted almost entirely to the quasi-ironic recapitulation of shows from the early 1960s. The invitations to Betty and Bob's wedding were printed with sketches of jitterbugging couples; for their honeymoon they rented a station wagon and drove south, visiting Graceland, Cypress Gardens and the Texas School Book Depository. Betty and Bob buy Fiestaware and Bakelite jewelry and beaded "Injun" belts, as well as souvenirs from the 1964 World's Fair and "atomic" furniture from the fifties — "real Jetsons stuff." Bob has taught the family mutt, Spot, to do the twist. Bob dreams that his animal will one day appear on the "Stupid Pet Tricks" segment of *Late Night With David Letterman.* Bob works in advertising, "like Darrin on *Bewitched.*" Betty is a corporate attorney — "a lawyer from hell," she says. Bob and Betty are fictional, but Bob and Betty are everywhere. Welcome to the wacky, totally awesome, very late-1980s world of heterosexual camp, Camp Lite. This is the era of the permanent smirk, the knowing chuckle, of jokey ambivalence as a way of life. This is the Irony Epidemic.

NO WONDER IT'S COME TO THIS — WE'VE BEEN building up to a mass outbreak for a century. Oscar Wilde was a major celebrity, remember, even in America. There were the Symbolists and Ronald Firbank and Dada — Marcel Duchamp was the Letterman of his generation as much as he was the Schnabel — and Hollywood comedies of the 1930s. It was Cary Grant's ironic swerves that put him over, not his dinner jackets: in *His Girl Friday,* when Grant refers to Bruce Baldwin, played by Ralph Bellamy, he describes him as "that guy who looks like that fella in the movies — Ralph Bellam[y]"

From the 1940s through the 1960s, America ha[d] plenty of everything — big appliances, steady jobs, Crest with fluoride — everything except irony. Bob and Betty's parents, having survived a depression and a world war intact, were perhaps disinclined [to] dress up in outfits amusingly evocative of the Hoover era, or to see the inherent comedy in their new tract houses. Little Bob and little Betty, however, sprawled in front of the Sylvania, gorgin[g] on Hydroxes and doing their social studies homework between *Soupy Sales* and *The George Burns and Gracie Allen Show,* were learning to bite the hands that overfed them, ironists in the making. Instead of war and economic cataclysm, their coming-of-age rituals consisted of signing petitions and taking drugs; more than any previou[s] generation, they have the luxury of making fun, [of] grinning and scoffing, of being ironic. Irony has always been a luxury item, but now, like foreign travel and original art, it is a luxury that millions of people can afford. When you have spent your whole life on Easy Street, you can become Dan Quayle, or you can become part of the Irony Epidemic. Or, if you're of a mind to organize an absolutely nutty George Hamilton Memorial Limbo Competition at the country club, both.

Among the early symptoms of the Irony Epidem[ic] was pop art. Paintings of soup cans, paintings of Elvis, paintings of comic-book panels, sculptures made out of detergent boxes . . . *hey, art isn't serious, it's a hoot!* The allusions were to fifties Hollywood and sixties television, not to Periclean Athens or the eighteenth century; irony was suddenly accessible, irony was fun.

The year for pop art was 1964, the same year Susan Sontag published "Notes on Camp." Sontag's essay was like a thrilling, open-ended mother's excuse note for a whole generation of gifted children: *To Whom It May Concern: Johnny ha[s] my permission to enjoy TV and Jacqueline Susann books.* The most serious woman in America gave h[er] imprimatur to a jolly, perverse sensibility that was back then and in the main, homosexual and male — a sensibility that embraced pop junk — Judy Garland, complicated floral prints, truck-stop waitresses, The Supremes, plastic purses, the tang[o,] whatever — as well as the high-culture obligatories A campy outlook, Sontag announced, permitted refined people to wander happily through an unrefined world: if you can't prevent Miami Beach, you can learn to love it, sort of. During the sixties, irony was camp, camp was irony.

Camp was patented by gay men; camp is a kin[d] of gay soul. Ostracized groups tend to create their own art forms, out of necessity; soul music, with i[ts]

gospel heritage, means something to Aretha Franklin that it cannot possibly mean to Hall and Oates. Old camp obsesses on the brazen, the sophisticated, even the European. Old camp wants to puff a cigarette in an ivory holder while lolling atop a baby grand at the Ritz. Old camp fetishizes self-sacrifice and romantic agony, the scale of emotions usually available only to women, especially women in important wigs.

"Notes on Camp" was still ricocheting around intellectuals' heretofore orderly brains—*Diana! Lionel! We've just gotten back from* Disneyland, *of all places!*—when Robert Venturi wrote his book

*C*AMP LITE DOMESTIC LIFE

"FOOD"
Sno Balls

Oreos

Fizzies

S'Mores

Fluffernutters—or any dessert made from a recipe on the Rice Krispies or Ritz crackers box

Tuna casserole

Jell-O

Cheez Whiz

Pigs-in-blankets

TV dinners

"ADULT LEISURE ACTIVITIES"
Twister

Etch A Sketch

Tee Vee Toons's three-volume set of television theme songs, *Television's Greatest Hits*

Trade paperbacks that detail every episode of *The Honeymooners, The Beverly Hillbillies* or *Gilligan's Island*

Slumber parties, bachelor parties and sock hops

Barbecues

Bowling

Cocktails after work

"CLOTHING"
Ray-Ban Wayfarers

Schott leather jackets

Beaded cashmere sweaters

Madras sports jackets and Bermuda shorts

Oversize "vintage" overcoats

Seamed hosiery

Garter belts

Old prom dresses

Gaudy neckties worn with gabardine shirts and suspenders

Levi's jackets with Elvis or Marilyn hand-painted on the back

Opera gloves

Patent-leather purses

Bright-colored Converse high-tops

"DECOR"
Boomerang-shaped tables

Patterned linoleum

Beanbag chairs

Lava lamps

Black-and-white RCA TVs

Framed pre-1970 *Life* magazine covers

Jukeboxes

—*P.R.*

celebrating Las Vegas, thus pushing architecture off on its own snickery detour. After Venturi (even his name sounded like some kitschy car, an Impala with fins and cruise control), major buildings could look like billboards and motels—as long as they looked that way *ironically.* Or major buildings could have columns and gables and keystones and all kinds of quaint bric-a-brac—as long as the old-fashioned geegaws were applied *ironically.*

Warhol, Sontag, Venturi—then, during the same Big Bang, *Batman* came to TV, demonstrating that ordinary Americans would go for stylized, mock-

bad entertainment. Roy Lichtenstein was prime-time. Camp Lite had arrived.

The larger epidemic of irony, meanwhile, was spreading more slowly. The counterculture was virtually irony-free: for every Firesign Theater record, there were hundreds of Earth Day manifestos, Jane Fonda declarations of solidarity, John Lindsay displays of earnestness, communal suppers of tofu and human placenta.

Just when it became clear that John Lindsay and placenta-eating were not going to transform the world, an irony industry sprang up to fill the void. Bob had subscribed to *National Lampoon* when he was still in high school; for their first date, Bob took Betty to the *Lampoon*'s Off-Broadway show, *Lemmings*; their first purchase as a couple was a color Sony, bought so they could watch *Saturday Night Live.* In a few years, a generation's perpetual frown had become a perpetual smirk.

One minute everything had been deadly earnest. The next minute everything was amusing. Gerald Ford bumping his head was funny. Patty Hearst as a revolutionary bank robber was funny. Jimmy Carter fighting off a rabbit was funny. Even Richard Nixon, once he had been purged, became a laughable character, Oscar the Grouch with underlings. Thanks to Steve Martin and Bill Murray and *SCTV*, schlock comedians and schlock singers were funny—unintentionally so, *ironically* so. The entire malformed, third-rate pop culture universe was, in fact, suddenly a wellspring of unwitting mirth, of "found humor." To get the joke, all you had to do was what you had always done best—*watch a lot of TV*: game shows were funny, cheap late-night commercials were funny, cable (especially public-access cable) was funny, Jack Lord was funny, Marie Osmond was funny, Tom Snyder was funny, Jerry Lewis and his telethon were funny—*and none of them knew it,* which made them all the funnier. Even chunks of nontelevised life—trailer parks, theme parks, the *National Enquirer,* the *New York Post,* morticians' trade magazines—were funny. The Irony Epidemic was just gathering steam when Bob and Betty first started going to certain movies (*Plan 9 from Outer Space,* for instance) *because they were so bad,* and it had achieved its full range when there was a whole subculture devoted to bad movies—bad-film books, bad-film festivals, bad-film scholars (see "Camp Lite Goes to College," page 96).

Camp Lite consists especially of a fetishism for the good-old-days artifacts that the Irony Epidemic has turned up—Ray-Bans and skinny ties, *Sergeant Bilko* and Bermuda shorts. The rise of Camp Lite can be traced to the Hollywood nostalgia productions of the 1970s: *American Graffiti* and *Animal House, Grease* and *Happy Days.* These were the works that portrayed the fifties and early sixties as something to be pined for, something cute and

1967–75

pastel-colored and fun rather than racist and oppressive and un-air-conditioned.

Whereas camp *during* the fifties and sixties emerged from the more passionate, fabled art forms of ballet, opera and Joan Crawford vehicles, Camp Lite is almost purely the spawn of fifties and sixties television, with its bland sitcom chuckles and tiny, comfy dilemmas. Camp Lite is limited to the nonintellectual, to lunch boxes and memories of summer Scout outings. True camp, homo- or heterosexual, lampoons and adores, while Camp Lite reflexively eulogizes and coddles.

Camp can curdle in the benign clutches of 10 million Bobs and Bettys, and in nostalgia junkyards such as *Nick at Nite*. When a minority form is coopted, there is always a loss of dynamic, of nuance. Imagine a Debbie Gibson rendition of "Respect." Consider Bruce Willis's Camp Lite pseudo-Bogie shtick. Camp Lite at its mass-marketed worst — Spuds Mackenzie, Hard Rock Cafes, Willis — has no edge, no gilded layers. Its allusions can become entirely arbitrary. The new Fox science-and-technology TV show, *Beyond Tomorrow*, features human Camp Lite artifacts — Alan Hale Jr., Jo Anne Worley, Mickey Dolenz, Charo — in its commercials *for no particular reason*, a Fox spokesperson says, *just because . . . well, we thought they were cool*. Even in its more wholesome forms, Camp Lite is mere Trivial Pursuit, a matter of lists, of congratulating oneself on remembering,

for instance, all the first names of the Brady Bunch.

The only thing more unnerving than the proliferation of air quotes (*Between my "significant other" and my "career," I sometimes wonder whether going for the "good life" makes sense*) is when they imperceptibly fade away. Camp Lite, after all, began with a genuine ironic impulse — the first few dozen 1980s buildings with columns, the first few hundred times *"They laugh alike, they walk alike, at times they even talk alike"* was sung by young adults late at night, the first few thousand men who buttoned their top shirt buttons. But after a million and then 10 million repetitions, the once ironic gesture begins to lose the perversity that made it interesting in the first place.

In the middle of an Irony Epidemic, nothing stays ironic for very long: in record time, the vogue for sixties fashion (peace symbols, miniskirts, Day-Glo) evolved from a jokey cognoscenti revival to a straight-faced mass-market merchandising phenomenon — has already drifted, for the second time in two decades, toward the dustheap of the passé. From Avenue C to K Mart in five years flat, via *Elle* and MTV — such is the force of Camp Lite. A knowing Bohemian flicker becomes a mindless national bonfire, mock nostalgia turns into the real thing. What starts out as a perverse, essentially ironic appreciation of the detritus of the last several decades — of porkpie hats, *Mr. Ed*, Twister, Led Zeppelin, poodle skirts — very quickly becomes an

CAMP LITE GOES TO COLLEGE

I. "What? Me Study?: A Selective Survey of the Mildly Antiau-thoritarian Thesis Topics of Late-Twentieth-Century University Students"

You're a college student. It's time to choose a topic for your senior paper. You don't want to write about Keats or feudalism like everyone else. You're not about to buy into the whole academically correct establishment thing. Plus, the only primary sources you know really, really well, the only texts in which you have a deep fluency, are old TV sitcoms, game shows, pop music, comic books. Like other ironically inclined contemporaries, you'll write a thesis on pop culture: "The Outsider as Hero of Urban Mythology in *Superfly* and *Shaft*," for instance, or "Elysian Fielders: The Chrono-Spatial Existentialism of Professional Baseball." It's strident

sprezzatura, risk-free scholarship: the text, the footnotes and the title page will look perfectly legitimate to professors and parents, while the topic (camouflaged in academic jargon, as in "Strategies for Heterosexual Interaction in Singles Bars") is a wink to classmates and your own ironic self that you're not really a grade-grubbing weenie.

None of the titles cited in the preceding paragraph is, as far as we know, an actual thesis. Those cataloged below, however — *attention, Allan Bloom!* — are real titles from Amherst, Harvard, Stanford and Yale.

- "The Glory Shall Be a Defense: The 1969 Mets and New York City" (1984)
- "Elvis as Hero of Global Village Culture" (1984)
- "Rebuilding the Dream: Artifice and Authenticity in the American

Shopping Mall" (1985)
- "All My Children: A Literary Study of Soap Operas" (1985)
- "Organized Summer Camping: An Institution of Stability for American Youth in Times of Transition" (1986)
- " 'I Heard It Through the Grapevine': An Exploration of the Motown Sound" (1986)
- "Why Spock Isn't Captain: Control and Self-Determination in *STAR TREK*" (1987)
- "Nostalgia for the 1960s in Popular Culture: The Mythification of the Age of Aquarius" (1988)
- " 'Rhymin' and Stealin' ': The Beastie Boys Phenomenon 1987" (1988)

Gets you thinking, doesn't it? After all, you *have* always thought Scrooge McDuck was an overlooked manifestation of the Jay Gatsby ethos. You can champion the cause of the common man, proving the relevance and value of TV shows and T-shirt slogans by means of pseudo-Derridean deconstruction and favorable comparison with such accepted academic benchmarks as

the Eliot canon and tribal courtship rituals. You can quote both Roland Barthes *and* Larry the dorm janitor (a typical McDuck fan). It's all a slightly more intellectual version of the *But Dad, Jesus had long hair* dinner-table argument. And no matter how hard you work on it, you are still, after all, getting credit for *reading comics*: indeed, you're living the undergraduate dream — obeying authority while giving the impression that you're not the sort of person who obeys authority.

II. "The 'Real' World: Toward an Understanding of the Problem of Postgraduate-Career-Decision Deferral Processes"

You've graduated. Your thesis grader conceded that Huey, Dewey and Louie did resemble, to some extent, a zoomorphic tripartite Nick Carraway. Now what? Get a job? That would be as embarrassingly straightforward as . . . well . . . having written a serious thesis. The alternative? *Live the joke* — graduate school.

automatic, essentially earnest appreciation. As this decade began, postmodern architects and painters were playing around, fun-lovingly "quoting" the taboo past with their cartoony colonnades and corny arches, their human figures and realistic tableaux; before the decade was half over, the postmodernists were proffering their columns and portraits with deadly seriousness. As this decade began, Bob and Betty thought kidney-shaped coffee tables were amusing monstrosities; as the decade ends, Bob and Betty consider them merely stylish. Does anyone think *New Yorker* editor Robert Gottlieb doesn't *really like* plastic purses? The Irony Epidemic has been a way for all kinds of taboo styles to sneak past the tastefulness authorities—*Don't mind us, we're just kidding*—and then, once inside, turn serious. By the end of the Bush administration, Grand Funk Railroad will be on a smash comeback tour.

During the Irony Epidemic, even interesting artists become art directors in anthropologists' clothing, advance men for Camp Lite: in his film *True Stories,* David Byrne cooed over Dust Bowl trailer parks, teased hair and prefab shopping malls as if murmuring, *I must get that pole lamp for my loft!* Directors John Waters, Jonathan Demme and Susan Seidelman, in films such as *Hairspray, Married to the Mob* and *Making Mr. Right,* have also indulged in kitsch glut, piling the screen with hot pink T-Bird convertibles and rustling prom

petticoats to be applauded on their knack for retro chic. The trend toward re-created fifties chromium diners, like Ed Debevic's in Chicago and L.A., or Manhattan's Dine-o-Mats, are pure exercises in overeager Camp Lite merchandising. Dine-o-Mat on Third Avenue and 57th Street teems with where-it's-at youngsters at all hours; the genuine Horn & Hardart Automat (owned by the same corporation as the ersatz Dine-o-Mat), at 42nd and Third, is patronized by a few bums and cops and household workers. Camp Lite produced the Monkees revival, the brand-name-studded pages of Stephen King and Ann Beattie, the return of cigar smoking, white cotton anklets worn with high heels and the concept of Deb of the Year.

Camp Lite does not celebrate *or* savage; it does not get its hands dirty. Camp Lite is about avoidance. Today's irony-stricken yuppie lives in terror of becoming . . . *anything.* Staking a claim can inspire ridicule: *You're a lawyer?* Admitting to marriage, parenthood—to maturity—implies aging, stolidity. If everything is a pose, a sitcom riff, then you're still a kid, just goofing around.

The punk movement, exported to the U.S. during the early years of the Irony Epidemic, became a pretext for a certain kind of Camp Lite artifact—safety-pin jewelry, Astor Place Mohawks, Debbie Harry. And punk was a way for nerds to be cool: a certain fey artlessness and arch egghead lyrics (*My building has every convenience/It's going*

---

ack around 1975, as papers on side diners began appearing in emic journals and spaghetti- ern experts became full profes- American Studies departments ed their attention from the his- ally significant (e.g., Herman ville) to the quaint and the com- place (e.g., Herman Munster). graduate school can be a per- mark-time paradise, scholarship a smirk, the ultimate noncom- al, ironic life-style.

"Going Pro: The Ethnosocio- cal Implications of the Pre- Postdoctoral Self-Justifica- Process"

come to the faculty. You've set- in at your carrel, decorating it Trans Formers and Caesars Pal- postcards. Your office hours are ed on the door, between unin- onally hilarious *National En- er* clippings and Xeroxed pages the 1953 *Boy Scout Handbook.* go to all the grad-student— e air quotes here—"mixers" in ESSO gas pumper's jumpsuit

and an RFK memorial bolo tie. You fancy yourself a human hodgepodge of amusing American trash.

But somewhere along the way, the savvy smirk has become an af- fectionate grin. The implicit irony of studying the Godzilla/Mothra schism or K Mart iconography has been replaced by reverence. You ac- tually start *believing* that Scrooge McDuck can tell us quite a bit about ourselves as Americans.

Eventually you trade in your hand-painted hula-girl tie and Brooklyn Dodgers cap for a tweed jacket and Bean boots—both worn, of course, ironically: once you were Maynard G. Krebs, now you're Professor Lawrence from *Gidget.* In pursuit of tenure, you publish an article in the *Journal of American Culture,* put out by Bowling Green State University and the Popular Culture Association. You flesh out your McDuck thesis (expanding the Meyer Wolfsheim/Gyro Gearloose parallel) and submit it. It's as rele- vant now as it ever was, and it's sure to measure up alongside these actual excerpts from recent issues of the *Journal:*

"REINTERPRETING THE FIFTIES: CHANG- ING VIEWS OF A 'DULL' DECADE" (Sum- mer 1985)—"Put in the context of the 'Happy Days' format, was it a stable, simple era of Richie Cun- ninghams or a fantasy-land popu- lated with Fonzie-like rebels?"

"THE WHIMSEY AND ITS CONTEXTS: A MULTI-CULTURAL MODEL OF MATERIAL CULTURE STUDY" (Spring 1986)— "The model is illustrated by an ex- amination of a distinct type of beaded novelty object made by Tus- carora Iroquois women and mar- keted as a souvenir in the tourist area of Niagara Falls."

" 'THE LOVE BOAT': HIGH ART ON THE HIGH SEAS" (Fall 1983)—"The study includes a surprising list of some other behaviors that were ob- served to be accompanying or inter- rupting viewing: looking out of windows, picking one's nose, scratching . . . smoking, rocking . . . dressing and undressing, posing . . . reciting . . . fighting . . . throwing things . . . mimicking or answering the TV . . . picking up objects . . . pacing, asking questions about the

TV, teasing and hair combing were among some of these behaviors. This extensive list is cited because it reveals the complexity of television viewing behavior."

"THE 'MCDONALDIZATION' OF SOCIETY" (Spring 1983)

"THE VENEREAL CONFRONTS THE VENERABLE: 'PLAYBOY' ON CHRISTMAS" (Winter 1984)—"The costume's white beard has fallen round her neck to cover the front of her bo- som; her buttocks stick out from the costume's waistband."

"CALIFORNIA GIRLS AND THE AMERICAN EDEN" (Winter 1984)

"COMIC BOOK LUDDITE: THE SAGA OF 'MAGNUS, ROBOT FIGHTER' " (Spring/ Summer 1984)—"As a comic book, *Magnus, Robot Fighter* falls into that amorphous category known as 'pop- ular culture,' part of the literature of the masses, the vernacular reading of the common folk. Because of this, comic books have only recently become the subject of serious schol- arly inquiry."   —*Paul Simms*

to make life easy for me) became, in the case of Talking Heads, ironic rock, Sondheim for kids. Dylan had made alienation stylish, but now it chuckled instead of whined. As the Irony Epidemic kicked into high gear Sid Vicious, a bona fide angry young punk, recorded, sniggeringly, "My Way." And today even rap music, the quintessential underclass form, incorporates snatches of the *I Dream of Jeannie* theme; who says Camp Lite is lily-white?

Victims of the Irony Epidemic do not dread commitment — they fear uncoolness. When Bob wears his garish shirts or his black-rimmed nerd glasses, he implicitly announces, *I am aware enough to appreciate the squareness of this shirt and these glasses; I don't like them — I get them.* When Betty dons her thrift shop Holly Golightly strapless, she wears it as a costume, so she can't be accused of becoming her mother. Bob and Betty idolize Letterman; because he keeps things goofy and light, there's no danger of embarrassment. Letterman is enormously talented, of course, but he can become the hipster's Perry Como. Letterman, as the avatar of Camp Lite, as Mr. Ambivalence, is usually thrown by anything truly, weirdly campy. Pee-wee Herman makes him uncomfortable, as does Sandra Bernhard. Pee-wee and Bernhard possess the heedless risk of true camp. They toy with gender, with anguish and dementia.

CAMP LITE	TRUE CAMP
• Watching a videocassette of *One Million Years B.C.*, starring Raquel Welch as a cavewoman	• Working out to Raquel's exercise video and wondering if Tahnee, Raquel's daughter, is a happy girl
• Having a cookout, wearing madras Bermudas and playing Beach Boys tapes	• Attending the trial of a particularly baroque serial killer
• Giving someone a copy of Jackie Collins's *Hollywood Wives* as a joke gift	• Buying a gown from The Dynasty Collection and wearing Forever Krystle toilet water
• Ritual group viewings of *Lifestyles of the Rich and Famous*	• Watching only those *Lifestyles* segments that feature Donna Mills behind the Iron Curtain
• Attending the Warhol auction	• Attending the Warhol funeral

Letterman is far happier around people like Larry "Bud" Melman, his proprietary piece of flesh-and-blood found humor — targets, curious oafs, threatless.

Camp Lite tends to focus on the mild, the rural or suburban, and the male. Witness Letterman's fixation on small-town news items, on animal acts and the lad who nurtured the largest okra in Iowa. Camp Lite yearns for childhood in a wheat field, adolescence on the beach at Rincón; Dad at the barbecue is God. Camp Lite, at worst, is a cocktail party that descends into group renditions of the theme from *The Flintstones* and critical debates about whether Gilligan ever got off the island.

The Reagan years have been Camp Lite incarnate, the great winking downside of the Irony Epidemic.

By seeing Reagan as a joke, as Mr. Magoo or Don DeFore's dim Mr. B from *Hazel*, young America denatured him. No one had to dwell on the ugliness of his policies if he was treated as a cartoon, sleepily wed to Cruella De Vil. Voting Republican has become a pose rather than a sin.

Air quotes abound nowadays. Air quotes eliminate responsibility for one's actions, one's choices. Bob tells co-workers with a grin that he's got to get home to — raise hands, insert air quotes here — *the little woman*, or to *the wife and kids*, as if his family didn't really exist, as if he's still "a wild and crazy guy." Betty tells friends she's "ultra–Type A" and, with air quotes, "a yuppie madwoman," so they won't imagine she actually enjoys her 12-hour days at the firm.

Air quotes undermine any real art. The paintings of David Salle, endlessly and almost purely referential, *Moonlighting*, even *Who Framed Roger Rabbit* — all of them are Xeroxed clip jobs, Cliffs Notes on fondly remembered original works of the past. Real art and regular hobbies you can happily experience in solitude. But given the choice, who would play miniature golf or go to a Cindy Sherman show *alone*? Art in the age of air quotes requires a fellow smirker, someone else smart enough to get it. Irony is a group sport. A certain sort of postgraduate boy can go with other postgraduate boys to the Baby Doll Lounge to watch strippers and enjoy the shows ironically; alone, he would consider himself pathetic.

Camp Lite uses irony as an anesthetic, an escape route. It is a breed of timidity, a reluctance to rock the yacht. Camp Lite can redeem itself, by cultivating some danger, some bracing recklessness, some of the alienating weirdness that spawned it. Otherwise, Camp Lite will remain a smug reflex, a painless roost for guys 'n' gals without imagination or real spunk, a mask for easy condescension — "I *love* Joe Franklin."

The place of Joe Franklin may be a benchmark for the remarkable sweep of the Irony Epidemic, circa 1989. Franklin now *knows* he has become an object of jokes, a piece of found humor. He even claims to be complicit in the process. "Look, my friend," Franklin told the *Times*, "Billy Crystal, he's doing a satire on a satire. I'm putting on the whole world! I'm tongue-in-cheeking every moment of my life." Nor is he the only one: Tab Hunter appeared in a John Waters movie, Frankie Avalon and Annette Funicello made the Camp Lite *Back to the Beach* in 1987, Robert Goulet was in both *Beetlejuice* and *Scrooged*, Zsa Zsa Gabor and Charo flounced around on Pee-wee's CBS special last Christmas, Vanna White suggests she *understands* she's just a Pet Rock with blond hair and breasts. When the kitsch starts talking back — *Look, I know I'm schlock, I know I'm a joke* — it's almost enough to make a person turn earnest. **ᗺ**

Air quotes undermine any real art. The paintings of David Salle, endlessly and almost purely referential, Moonlighting, *even* Who Framed Roger Rabbit — *all of them are Xeroxed clip jobs, Cliffs Notes on fondly remembered original works of the past.*

BEST OF LOGROLLING IN OUR TIME: Heroic, Bartleby-like work on the part of Howard Kaplan, who produced these on a monthly basis without the help of the Internet. The phrase and concept of "logrolling" became part of the cultural patois.

LOGROLLING IN OUR TIME

"Burroughs's visionary power, his comic genius, and his unerring ability to crack the codes that make up the life of this century are undiminished."
—J. G. Ballard on William Burroughs's *The Western Lands*

"Head and shoulders above his fellow writers." —Burroughs on Ballard's *Crash*

"Her work demands our attention."
—David Leavitt on Mary Robison's *An Amateur's Guide to the Night*

"Intoxicating, sublime." —Robison on Leavitt's *Equal Affections*

"A work of truth and beauty—beautifully imagined, beautifully written, beautiful to read." —George Garrett on Mary Lee Settle's *Prisons*

"Congratulations are too mild for this triumphant procession of a book."
—Settle on Garrett's *The Succession*

—Howard Kaplan

June 1989

LOGROLLING IN OUR TIME

"Our greatest living historical novelist."
—Anthony Burgess on Gore Vidal's *Lincoln*

"There is no other writer like him."
—Vidal on Burgess's *Little Wilson and Big God*

"Reading Madison Smartt Bell is like watching a juggler do it with 200 apples, 500 oranges, and a couple of newborn kittens."
—Carolyn Chute on Madison Smartt Bell's *Waiting for the End of the World*

"Quite possibly the only truly original stylist this last ten or fifteen years has produced."
—Bell on Chute's *Letourneau's Used Auto Parts*

"We await new Jenkins novels like children anticipating Christmas morning."
—Bob Greene on Dan Jenkins's *Dead Solid Perfect*

"I would go almost anywhere to read a Bob Greene column."
—Jenkins on Greene's *Cheeseburgers*

—Howard Kaplan

September 1989

LOGROLLING IN OUR TIME

"Cheever continues to do what the best fiction has always done: give us back our humanity, enhanced."
—John Updike on John Cheever's *Falconer*

"Superb—the most important American novel I've read in years." —Cheever on Updike's *Rabbit Is Rich*

"Remarkable ... Powerful ... Mesmerizing ... Lyrical" —Susan Cheever on Paul Theroux's *O-Zone*

"A terrific novel about the way we live now." —Theroux on Cheever's *Doctors and Women*

"A beautiful book, and worthy of those mountains he is among."
—Paul Theroux on Peter Matthiessen's *The Snow Leopard*

"Sharp-eyed, honest, and exceptionally well-written."
—Matthiessen on Theroux's *The Old Patagonian Express*

"A feat of imaginative breadth ... which lifts fiction high. The whole landscape is the brighter for it."
—George Steiner on Anthony Burgess's *Earthly Powers*

"A work of literature ... an astonishing book." —Burgess on Steiner's *The Portage to San Cristóbal of A.H.*

"He is, to say the least, a mature and wise writer." —Anthony Burgess on Robertson Davies's *The Manticore*

"A delight to read." —Davies on Burgess's *Little Wilson and Big God*

—Howard Kaplan

May 1988

LOGROLLING IN OUR TIME

"Richard Ford's sportswriter is a bird rare in life and nearly extinct in fiction—a decent man."
—Tobias Wolff on Richard Ford's *The Sportswriter*

"This is a wonderful book...[by] one of this country's very finest writers, working at the top of his talent."
—Ford on Wolff's *This Boy's Life*

October 1989

LOGROLLING IN OUR TIME

"Anyone who takes himself seriously as a reader should have this funny book."
—Andy Rooney on Russell Baker's *The Rescue of Miss Yaskell*

"The only truly funny man on television."
—Baker on Rooney's *A Few Minutes with Andy Rooney*

"A huge novel in every sense of the word—scope, achievement, heart. May it flourish!" —Margaret Atwood on Marge Piercy's *Gone to Soldiers*

"An arresting triumph of the imagination that should pique the curiosity of male readers and must necessarily be of consuming interest to every woman now alive."
—Piercy on Atwood's *The Handmaid's Tale*

"Greene is still sound in wind and limb...and still brilliantly clear-sighted."
—Paul Theroux on Graham Greene's *Getting to Know the General*

"In the fine old tradition of travel for fun and adventure...compulsive reading."
—Greene on Theroux's *The Great Railway Bazaar*

—Howard Kaplan

October 1988

March 16, 1989

Mr. Graydon Carter
SPY
The Puck Building
295 Lafayette Street
New York, N.Y. 10012

Dear Graydon,

   As per your letter of March 9, I am
surprised that you do not know who called me
from SPY Magazine. Your curiosity will be
satisfied in court (although, hopefully, that
will not be necessary).

                              Sincerely,

                              Donald J. Trump

CHAPTER

9

"That Might Be Funny in Your World, But It Isn't Funny in Mine"

Why *Spy* Had No Intention of Ever Seeing You in Court

I remember Graydon calling a meeting and announcing that the magazine had just gotten new libel insurance, and he wanted to try it out. And so everyone tried to think of someone we could taunt.

—PAUL RUDNICK

THE FIRST THING that Lisa Lampugnale, *Spy*'s first chief of research, remembers fact-checking was a map of mafiosos' residences and hangouts (see page 174). With growing alarm, she realized that many of them were right near the Puck Building, which was on the edge of what could then still legitimately be called Little Italy. "And two weeks later I'm walking near the offices and fucking John Gotti walks by," she says. "And I think it's because of the Mob addresses map and I'm gonna get killed!" The Gambinos' Ravenite Social Club was only a couple of blocks away on Mulberry Street, and Gotti, then neither incarcerated nor dead, was a common sight in the neighborhood. Lampugnale, an Italian-American, did change her name when she became a standup comic, but that's probably just a coincidence.

Spy heard from a great many lawyers over the years, and the editors' collection of threatening letters from Donald Trump is considered the largest currently in private hands. We also cherish one from Gore Vidal, dated November 7, 1988—two wonderful pages taking issue with our treatment of him in our November 1988 "Feuds" cover story by Lynn Hirschberg. *Spy* called him "litigious," and he threatened to sue over that characterization. Vidal's letter begins, "Get your act together, Spies…" and concludes, "See you in Federal Court. Have a nice pre-trial deposition." (See page 215.)

But (with one exception) *Spy* was never sued.* And we rarely needed to publish corrections. Here's an early one we're not proud of:

I read Spy *because I want to be with-it. I must confess that I was a little surprised when I read in your December issue that my last name is pronounced ain-JELL, when all my life I've*

*****Spy** was **never** sued while we were running it. —Eds.**

One of many, many mash notes we received from Donald Trump during 1988 and '89. Over the course of a year, he offered up his then-wife Ivana for an interview; expressed dismay later on that we were doing a story on her; accused (falsely and hilariously) the father of one of our investors of extortion; cautioned us against "liable"; and announced, in one of his letters, "I don't want to make [this] public"— before talking about it to various papers, magazines, and television news programs.

**Map to the
Mob's homes,
October 1986**

been pronouncing it AIN-juhl....Obviously, I've been wrong all this time, and so has everybody else in my family. Thanks for straightening us out.

—Letter from Roger Angell, *New Yorker* writer and editor

Spy is pleased to have saved Mr. Angell and his family any further embarrassment. The editors regret, however, their error concerning...

—*Spy's* response, March 1987

THERE WERE A NUMBER OF REASONS for *Spy's* clean record, but the main one was a sincere and strenuous striving for accuracy: in addition to multiple fact-checkers, the magazine hired the redoubtable attorney David Korzenik to vet every single word of *Spy,* save those in the first issue. His earnest (lawyerly) respect for the magazine's mission and his sense of humor (alas, also lawyerly) were treasured by all. *Spy's* fact-checkers even took to saving and displaying Korzenik's most memorable pronouncements, including the one that gives this chapter its title.

"When I first was approached to do this," Korzenik says, "I really thought it was going to be a different magazine; I thought it would benefit from the law, which is generous to parody and humor. But when I started getting copy, it really wasn't that. It was also an investigative-journalism magazine, serious reporting that was very factual. It made jokes about the things that it had uncovered, but it wasn't in its essence light humor."

So Korzenik made a decision not to factor a "humor discount" into his analysis of *Spy* material. "It probably made my job much more involved," he says, and it forced him to think, *What's our support for this, how do we have this, what's our sourcing? If we're challenged on this, how are we going to demonstrate that and either scare off a claim or defeat a claim?*

Korzenik says that colleagues who knew about his work for *Spy* were respectful. "Their assumption was that you're going through a minefield, that you weren't spending a lot of time saying, 'Well, this *could* be defamatory,' because it just *was*," he says, laughing. "Not only was it defamatory, but we were doing it in a way that was designed to freak somebody out, to really nail them. We were really shaking the beehives."

Dear Sir: Your reference to me as a "legendary Lothario among the PSAT set" of course explicitly calls me a child molester. As you

THE WORLD CHAMPIONSHIP

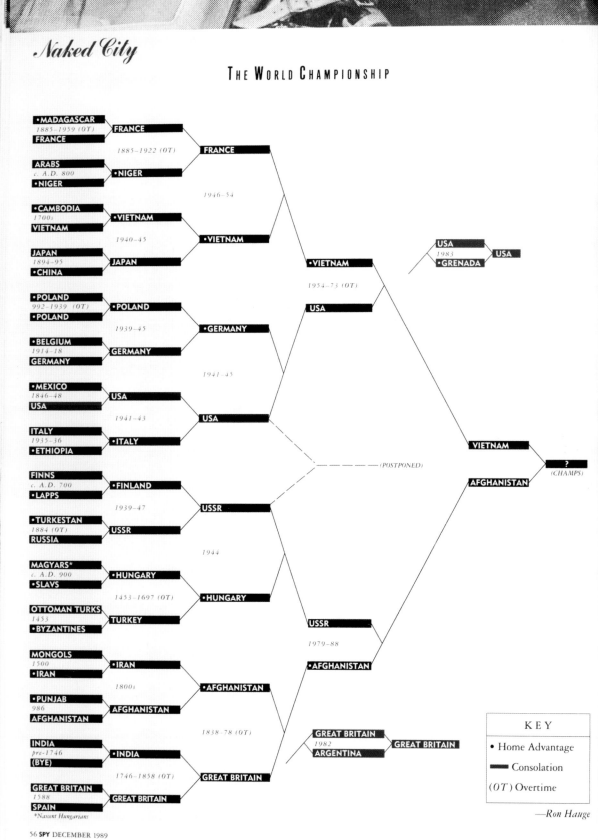

- **MADAGASCAR**
  1885–1959 (OT)
- **FRANCE** → **FRANCE**
  1885–1922 (OT) → **FRANCE**
- **ARABS**
  c. A.D. 800
- **•NIGER** → **•NIGER**

1946–54

- **•CAMBODIA**
  1700s
- **VIETNAM** → **•VIETNAM**
  1940–45 → **•VIETNAM**
- **JAPAN**
  1894–95 → **JAPAN**
- **•CHINA**

→ **•VIETNAM**
1954–73 (OT)

USA — *1983* **•GRENADA** → **USA**

- **•POLAND**
  992–1939 (OT)
- **•POLAND** → **•POLAND**
  1939–45 → **•GERMANY**
- **•BELGIUM**
  1914–18
- **GERMANY** → **GERMANY**

1941–45

→ **USA**

- **•MEXICO**
  1846–48
- **USA** → **USA**
  1941–43 → **USA**
- **ITALY**
  1935–36
- **•ETHIOPIA** → **•ITALY**

(POSTPONED)

- **FINNS**
  c. A.D. 700
- **•LAPPS** → **•FINLAND**
  1939–47 → **USSR**
- **•TURKESTAN**
  1884 (OT)
- **RUSSIA** → **USSR**

1944

- **MAGYARS***
  c. A.D. 900
- **•SLAVS** → **•HUNGARY**
  1453–1697 (OT) → **•HUNGARY**
- **OTTOMAN TURKS**
  1453
- **•BYZANTINES** → **TURKEY**

→ **USSR**
1979–88

VIETNAM

AFGHANISTAN

?
(CHAMPS)

- **MONGOLS**
  1500
- **•IRAN** → **•IRAN**
  1800s → **•AFGHANISTAN**
- **•PUNJAB**
  986
- **AFGHANISTAN** → **AFGHANISTAN**

→ **•AFGHANISTAN**

- **INDIA**
  pre-1746
- **(BYE)** → **•INDIA**
  1746–1858 (OT) → **GREAT BRITAIN**
- **GREAT BRITAIN**
  1588
- **SPAIN** → **GREAT BRITAIN**

1838–78 (OT)

GREAT BRITAIN
1982
ARGENTINA → **GREAT BRITAIN**

*Nascent Hungarians

KEY
- • Home Advantage
- ▬ Consolation
- *(OT)* Overtime

—Ron Hauge

Legal ★ALL★STARS

FLOYD ABRAMS
FIRST-AMENDMENT LAWYER

FLOYD ABRAMS #2
FIRST-AMENDMENT LAWYER

BORN: 7-9-36, NEW YORK, N.Y. **HT:** 5'10" **WT:** 175 LBS.
ENDORSES CHECKS: RIGHTHANDED **NICKNAME:** LADDIE **EDUCATION:** CORNELL, YALE LAW SCHOOL

CAREER	HIGHLIGHTS
Associate at Cahill Gordon & Reindel, 1963–70; partner, 1970–present Visiting lecturer at Yale Law School, 1974–80, 1987 Visiting lecturer at Columbia Graduate School of Journalism, 1980 Visiting lecturer at Columbia Law School, 1981–85	Co-counsel for *The New York Times* before the Supreme Court in the Pentagon Papers case in 1971. Recently lost a libel case for NBC in which Wayne Newton was awarded $19.2 million.

STATISTICS
WON-LOST RECORD IN SUPREME COURT ORAL ARGUMENTS: 5-3 ANNUAL BILLABLE HOURS: 2,350
BILLING RATE: $275 AN HOUR ANNUAL COMPENSATION: $1 MILLION (ESTIMATED)

TALKIN' LAW ABRAMS WAS THE FIRST STUDENT IN CORNELL'S HISTORY TO WIN PUBLIC-SPEAKING CONTESTS THREE YEARS IN A ROW.

Legal ★ALL★STARS

DAVID BOIES
CORPORATE LITIGATOR

DAVID BOIES #7
CORPORATE LITIGATOR

BORN: 3-11-41, SYCAMORE, ILL. **HT:** 5'11" **WT:** 175 LBS.
ENDORSES CHECKS: RIGHTHANDED **NICKNAME:** NO NICKNAME (DOESN'T EVEN LIKE TO BE CALLED DAVE) **EDUCATION:** UNIVERSITY OF REDLANDS, NORTHWESTERN UNIVERSITY, YALE LAW SCHOOL

CAREER	HIGHLIGHTS
Associate at Cravath, Swaine & Moore, 1966–72; partner, 1973–present Chief counsel to the Senate Antitrust Subcommittee, 1977–78 Chief counsel to the Senate Judiciary Committee, 1978–79	As lead attorney for CBS, Boies successfully defended the company against libel charges made by General Westmoreland in 1984 and 1985. Currently lead attorney for Texaco in its ongoing struggle to overturn the $8.5 billion judgment in favor of Pennzoil.

STATISTICS
TRIAL WON-LOST PERCENTAGE SINCE 1980: 13-1 BILLABLE HOURS: 2,500
BILLING RATE: $300 AN HOUR ANNUAL COMPENSATION: $1 MILLION

TALKIN' LAW EVERY YEAR BOIES, WHO HAS BEEN MARRIED THREE TIMES, TAKES SOME OF HIS SIX CHILDREN ON A CROSS-COUNTRY JEEP TRIP.

Two trading cards from our "Legal All-Stars" series (with perforated edges facilitating quick removal for swapping or flipping), included in May 1987. We also did a famous-chefs edition. We probably should have done more.

Dear Mr. Stein: Tom Phillips has asked me to respond to your letter of August 21 regarding an item about you in the September issue of Spy. *Your reaction is understandable, considering the generally negative tone of the item and its context. As for the phrase "legendary Lothario among the PSAT set," no one at* Spy *contrived this to suggest that you are a child molester. {We're sure} that you're not. The allusion is to the many teenage girls who have, by your own account, made romantic overtures to you because of your influence in the film industry. We have read {your memoir}* Hollywood Days, Hollywood Nights *and remember your portraits of Marcie and Traci and Sonya and Angie vividly…. Interest in rather young women is clearly a leitmotif in your work…. Please accept* Spy's *apologies for any misunderstanding.*

—Letter from research chief Cynthia Cotts to Ben Stein,
September 6, 1988

AFTER LEAVING *SPY*, Cotts amended her résumé with a new skill: "mollifying [potential] litigants."

That summer of 1988 was especially stressful for the fact-checkers, Cotts remembers, because the magazine had grown to the degree where it was now perfect-bound (with a flat, book-like spine, as opposed to folded and stapled) and the number of editorial pages had doubled: twice as many facts to check.

Spy's succession of research chiefs had the difficult job of making certain that the often unruly opinions and highly tendentious accounts presented in the magazine were accurate and defensible and, if at all possible, still funny.

"It was a somewhat Sisyphean task," says Cotts, who'd had serious training as a fact-checker and had worked at *The Village Voice* (where she later became the paper's press columnist) and *Vanity Fair*. "*Spy* at its best presented a slanted and enchanted version of history. A certain amount of fact-checking could put a high sheen on a story, but to *thoroughly* fact-check a *Spy* narrative would be to strip it of its charm. To be a really aggressive fact-checker can be annoying to the editors and writers. It's not the most popular job."

Spy's fact-checkers had an especially tall order, for all kinds of reasons. Sometimes it was just hard to keep a straight face on the telephone: "Are his fingers really short?" "Can you confirm that your husband wears a toupee?" And the research chiefs had to not only supervise the checkers (and correspond with Ben Stein) but act as liaisons between Korzenik and the editors. This could sometimes result in marathon, four- or five-hour phone sessions with the lawyer, and running battles with editors.

"The research people were really intelligent; they understood the legal issues," says Korzenik. "I would sometimes ask [Cotts's successor] Carrie Weiner, 'How do we know this?' And she would say, archly, 'Oh, it's a *known fact.*' By which she clearly meant, 'We don't really have anything yet, and unless we do we're not going to run this.'"

ALTHOUGH *SPY* HAD LIBEL INSURANCE, Korzenik says that most of the saber-rattling wasn't about money: "People were looking to bust the story up, if they could. The one thing I've always felt proud of, throughout the whole twelve years, is we never paid a penny to anybody, either in court or out."

"I think Graydon and Kurt and Tom didn't really believe that *Spy* would be a target for anyone," says Carrie Weiner. "Donald Trump would always send those threatening letters on very thick card stock, with his signature and an embossed seal, but Graydon would just post them outside his office. I think they were really delighted every time Trump would write to us."*

"I would work with the research people on the first round, and then I'd start to go up the line with the writer and the editor," Korzenik says. "And if there were still open issues, we'd try to resolve them with Kurt or Graydon. One time I told Graydon I wanted to get certain adjustments on a story, to get us into a little more of a safe harbor. And he kind of listened to my pitch, and said, 'What are you going to do if I don't change this?' For a second I was just kind of...." Korzenik shakes his head in disbelief. "I finally said, 'I don't know, Graydon, I think I'll probably call your parents.' He liked

---

*Completely and absolutely delighted. It was like talking to the TV during *Looney Tunes* and having Daffy Duck reply. And our general lack of concern about litigation, slightly bizarre in hindsight, was closer to semi-youthful blitheness than self-conscious fearlessness, but was in any case necessary to the success of the project. —Eds.

that, and he made the change."

Korzenik applauds the tone set by Kurt and Graydon, in terms of backing their writers and their sources. "There was a sense of confidence: 'You're good writers, you're bright, you can go out and get the stuff, we're behind you, we're going to support this,'" he says. "And Susan Morrison was out there in the world, people knew that if you told her this, she's going to run with it, she's not afraid. That was the sense that all these editors conveyed: If you have something, we're going to move on it.

"It was a young crowd," he adds. "Not all older, seasoned writers. But intelligent. My feeling about legal protection is, the better the writing, the safer you are. When people write well, they don't write with confused and ambiguous sentences. And the writers at *Spy* were *very* good writers."

"Donald Trump would always send those threatening letters on very thick card stock, with an embossed seal, but Graydon would just post them outside his office."

TO: EDITORS
FROM: CARRIE, ON
BEHALF OF DAVID KORZENIK
RE: LEGAL CONCERNS ABOUT TKs
{"to come," the universal journalistic placeholder}

...David worries that, if we are taken to court, prejudicial phrasing {in drafts of stories} of TKs would get us into trouble as evidence of malice and would thereby make it easier for someone to win a libel judgment against us. In one recent example, we said something like, "Among David Duke's accomplishments are EGREGIOUS RACIST THING TK, EGREGIOUS THING TK, and EGREGIOUS RACIST THING TK." Although we know that Duke has done some egregious racist things but we're not quite sure of the details yet, we should keep that backwards approach to ourselves as much as possible. From a legal standpoint it looks much better for us to seem to have the details first and to form our opinions of Duke afterwards....
—Memo from Carrie Weiner, 1989

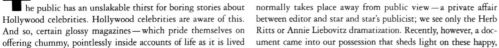

FLATTERY WILL GET YOU TEN PAGES . . . MAYBE

The Tina Brown–Mike Ovitz Correspondence

The public has an unslakable thirst for boring stories about Hollywood celebrities. Hollywood celebrities are aware of this. And so, certain glossy magazines—which pride themselves on offering chummy, pointlessly inside accounts of life as it is lived by the stars (journalist has lunch with star, journalist goes shopping with star, journalist wipes star's nose after a teary confession, they bond)—have found themselves over a barrel: in order to win the stars' necessary cooperation, the magazines have been obliged to cede editorial control to the very people on whom they are supposed to be reporting. Actors and actresses and other famous people—untrained people who may not have gone to journalism school or even worked for their school newspapers!—get to choose the writers who will attend to their musings, the photographers who will immortalize their features, and even, more and more often, the musings and photos that eventually see print.

As appalling as this is, it is no secret. But the process itself

Brown *Ovitz*

normally takes place away from public view—a private affair between editor and star and star's publicist; we see only the Herb Ritts or Annie Liebovitz dramatization. Recently, however, a document came into our possession that sheds light on these happy, cooperative doings in the world of journalism–cum–public relations.

The document is a letter from *Vanity Fair's* editor in chief, Tina Brown, to Mike Ovitz, founder and president of the immensely successful Creative Artists Agency—a man frequently called, by SPY and others, the most powerful in Hollywood (due to both the incredible breadth of talent his agency represents and his eagerness to throw his weight around). While Brown doesn't entirely give away her franchise here, she does demonstrate some of the lengths to which even a powerful and relatively serious journalist will go to get her story. (The letter is unedited. Any unusual syntax, punctuation or spelling is Brown's own.)

[1]In fact, around this time writer Nancy Collins was to have interviewed Ovitz for an unconsummated profile in *New York*. Ovitz, notoriously secretive, has never granted the sort of in-depth interview Brown begs him for in this letter.

[2]Rupert Murdoch's *Premiere* competes with *Vanity Fair*, of course, and Brown's husband, Harry Evans, was famously sacked as the editor of the London *Times* by Murdoch.

[3]Ovitz had recently hired New York publicist Howard J. Rubinstein to improve CAA's press and give it a higher profile on Wall Street, the ultimate source of *serious* Hollywood money and power.

[4]"Packaging," a common television practice that CAA pioneered for the movies, involves putting together a film's creative team—stars, writer, director—from one's roster of clients and then selling the entire "package," in all-or-nothing form, to a studio. Brown's choice of words in expressing distaste for the term is highly evocative: *crass* and especially *downmarket* are buzzwords that Brown falls back on (synonyms, frequently, for *poor, fat, unattractive* or *too ethnic*) when dismissing article ideas, people, restaurants and the like. A sample usage: "Kill the Oprah profile—she's just too *downmarket*."

December 19, 1988

Dear Mike:

I was surprised to hear from a friend who works there that you are on the point of "breaking your silence to the press in Premiere," probably to Nancy Collins.[1] I felt sure this could not be true, since it would be rather like Marlon Brando choosing "Falcon Crest" as a vehicle for a comeback.[2] I hope that is not Mr. Rubenstein's advice.[3] If it is, you should fire him. However, on the basis that the above is not true, then I thought I should lay out a little more clearly what Vanity Fair would do if you decided the time was right to cooperate with a major profile.

As I see it, the world has a very limited and unsophisticated grasp of what an "agent" does, particularly when that agent is you. Right now, the most hackneyed prevailing perception of you is as a "packager," a term which has a connotation of crassness that has little to do with what you actually achieve on a daily basis.[4] It seems to me that a better term for your role in the life of Hollywood would be a *catalyst*: activating creativity by a gifted sense of talent, material, timing and taste, plus, of course, extraordinary business acumen in putting it all together.[5] Probably no one since Thalberg has seeded so many creative partnerships or brought so many movies to the screen.[6]

In addition to what you personally achieve, you have, in a

[5]Brown's flattery of Ovitz is well taken—to the extent one can argue that agents have become the auteurs of modern Hollywood; whether this has led to better movies is another question. Brown is more unquestionably on target about Ovitz's "extraordinary business acumen": besides the multiple 10 percents CAA collects from its clients' salaries on a packaged film, the agency is said occasionally to extract what one person familiar with the process delicately calls "side agreements" or "consulting fees"—extra moneys paid by a film's producers to CAA for, in essence, delivering the project in the first place. This is the sort of thing that in another era the antitrust division of the Justice Department might have sued to stop. CAA also pioneered the practice of forcing movie studios to give stars their own development deals, which rarely result in finished movies but enable an agency to collect commissions from actors who would otherwise be idle.

[6]Irving Thalberg is perhaps the *only* genuinely liked studio executive in Hollywood history. Having served as MGM's head of production between 1924 and his death in 1936, he brought to the screen such films as *Greed, Grand Hotel, A Night at the Opera* and *The Thin Man*. Some of the films Ovitz is *generally* credited with bringing to the screen are *Ghostbusters, Legal Eagles, Ghostbusters II* and *Rain Man*.

[7]Brown employs a generous verb—*inspired*—to describe Ovitz's managerial techniques, which have produced a regimented, fear-driven corporate culture and have been well chronicled in these pages. Perhaps the most famous expression of CAA culture is Ovitz's alleged threat to defecting screenwriter Joe Eszterhas last year that "my foot soldiers who go up and down Wilshire Boulevard each day will blow your brains out."

very short number of years, created a consu culture. In an entirely ego driven business the people who work for you into putting t client's needs before their own competitive part, gives CAA its unique speed, efficienc corps and is, incidentally, the source of all seeks to discredit it. The aura of leadership discomforts rivals who like to think that al

These are some of the reasons we want to piece in Vanity Fair that will become the d of other journalists as well as readers.

To dramatize the CAA story successfully, need very good access to you and the peopl you. We would also need you to green ligh clients to cooperate in a way that would no Which brings me to my final point. Arnie the notion that I might write this profile m that is very hard for me to do.[9] Although s could be done in New York City, to undert reporting and research, run a staff of 42 an page magazine every month, takes an enor other major obsession, my 3 year old son. I school in January and needs me to be with impossible for me to come to Los Angeles reporting I believe is necessary, until Vanit Man Ray Exhibit with the Getty in March

So what I'd like to suggest is that you th Jesse Kornbluth coming out in January to the lines I've laid out, knowing that I wou it and shaping it every step of the way. Jess writing talent to do this piece, he is sophis and knowledgeably well disposed toward C person of the highest integrity.[11]

The alternative of waiting for me seems, You are right to feel this is the moment to ten page VF profile would have phenomen 700,000 readers include everyone who cou plus the opinion formers across the board. demographic phenomenon.[12] In the last tv following people have either written or tol cover to cover: Henry Kissinger, Brooke A Ben Bradlee, Don Simpson, John Le Carré, Newman, Louis Malle, Calvin Klein, Phili Geffen, Mike Wallace, the U.S. Ambassad

[8]A reference to Arnie Glimcher, owner of the Pace Gallery in New York. He is Ovitz's art dealer and friend and served as an art-world consultant on *Legal Eagles*, for which he received an associate-producer credit; Brown is apparently using Glimcher as a go-between with Ovitz. (Here's a nice bit of networking: Brown knows Glimcher through literary agent Morton Janklow, with whom she is friends thanks largely to Janklow's daughter, Angela, whom—despite her lack of appraisable editorial talent—Brown had presciently hired as an editorial assistant three years before writing this letter.) Since *Legal Eagles*, Glimcher has become a full-fledged film producer (most notably of *Gorillas in the Mist*—which was featured in *Vanity Fair's* October 1988 issue), with Ovitz's encouragement and help. In this he *may* serve as something of a role model for Brown (see below).

[9]Intriguingly, Brown passes up the chance to point out that during her four and a half years (at the time) of editing the magazine, she had deemed only three other subjects worthy of her byline. Perhaps this is because one of them was David Puttnam, a nemesis of Ovitz's during Puttnam's tenure as chairman of Columbia Pictures; the others were socialite Gayfryd Steinberg, who subsequently befriended Brown, and Princess Diana, who didn't.

[10]Brown erroneously refers to a party *Vanity Fair* sponsored not at the Getty Museum in Malibu but at the Museum of Contemporary Art in downtown Los Angeles — the first of the magazine's splashy forays into Hollywood society.

[11]With the obvious exception of Bob Colacello, Jesse Kornbluth is perhaps the…*most agreeable* of all *Vanity Fair* regulars; at the time of Brown's writing, he had recently executed credulous profiles of Sigourney Weaver and Jodie Foster, and in the very issue then on the stands Kornbluth had a story on Ovitz's good friend and client Barry Levinson, director of *Rain Man* (a CAA package). Also, Kornbluth is himself a screenwriter — his first produced work is a docudrama on Leona and Harry Helmsley, to air this fall on ABC — and is thus, as Brown notes, "knowledgeably well disposed toward CAA." Indeed, this must be something of an under-statement, given that Kornbluth is aware the agency controls the lion's share of important motion picture talent.

[12]More specifically, only 33 percent of *Vanity Fair* readers have graduat-ed from college (another 34.4 per-cent didn't even attend one), and their median household income is a not-really-all-that-upmarket $38,556 (figures are for 1989).

[13]It's no coincidence that these peo-ple read the magazine, if not cover to cover, at least avidly. Out of the impressive gaggle of 17 names Brown drops, all but the two rela-tive nobodies, Mrs. Barnet Newman and the ambassador to the Phil-ippines (Nicholas Platt) have been spotlighted, for the most part flat-teringly, in her magazine. In addi-tion, Lumet, Malle, Klein, Mos-bacher and Trump have had their wives and/or children featured (in August 1986 the magazine ran a harsh review of a novel by Sally Quinn, who is married to Ben Bradlee). It's also no coincidence that Brown is in a position to speak with these people on the subject of their leisure-time reading. As readers of *Mirabella* will remember, it was Liz Smith who advised the British-born Brown that if she wanted to succeed socially and professionally in Ameri-ca, she would have to make nice with the powers that be in the pages of her magazine, which she has tended to do. And which is, of course, the subtext of this letter.

There are actually two ambitions at play here. Brown has made no secret of her boredom with maga-zine editing, and colleagues are con-vinced of her desire to produce films

Robert Mosbacher and Donald Trump. In fact, everyone from Arafat to Bernie Brillstein![13]

I don't think any other publication today can offer such a readership, least of all a fan mag like Premiere.[14]

Can we discuss this the moment the strains of auld lang syne have faded?[15]

Best,

Tina Brown

(her father, in fact, was a producer of British B-movies). Not only is she fawning over an important, news-worthy subject for her magazine, but Ovitz represents a potential entrée for her into the movie business. As for him, despite his power in Holly-wood, he has, by many accounts, grown bored with the inherently undistinguished role of agent; he is said to aspire to a more creative, more conventionally respected role in the film community — producer or studio head. With her canny paean to his "creativity," "gifted sense of talent" and "taste," plus the compar-ison to Thalberg, Brown plays to precisely these longings.

[14]What could be more "downmar-ket" than a fan mag? In fact, *Premiere* counts among its readers a larger fraction of people who attended col-lege and more members of the "pro-fessional/managerial" class than does *Vanity Fair*, according to demograph-ic figures for 1989.

[15]Brown means after the New Year. As it happened, Ovitz didn't agree to the profile — a surprising, even admirable act of forbearance given that Brown had done everything short of signing an ironclad contract

to guarantee the profile would have been an epochal piece of puffery. (Not long after Brown wrote Ovitz, he was the subject of largely positive stories in both *Time* and *The New York Times Magazine* but gave both publications only the most cursory cooperation.)

Regardless, Brown and Ovitz have developed a warmly symbiotic rela-tionship since this letter was writ-ten. For starters, seven CAA clients were on the covers of 1989's 12 *Van-ity Fair*s — not that there is anything sinister in this, just that it shows how much the magazine has to offer even the most powerful man in Hol-lywood. More unusual is Brown's recent habit of sending Ovitz copies of entertainment-related stories before publication so that, we may fairly assume, he can draw her attention to any material he finds inconvenient. Meanwhile, he has thrown her a series of intimate din-ner parties featuring important Hollywood personages, and in Cul-ver City this past spring he helped deliver a star-studded crowd to the *Vanity Fair*–sponsored benefit for Phoenix House — all of which has done much to boost the Los Angeles profiles of both *Vanity Fair* and its savvy editor. ❧

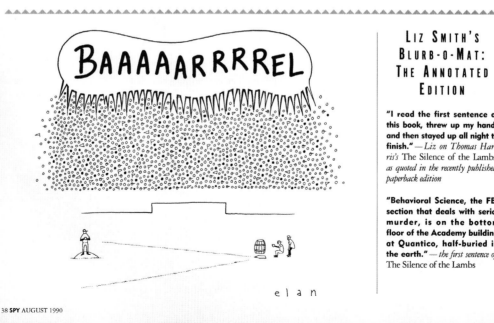

elan

LIZ SMITH'S BLURB-O-MAT: THE ANNOTATED EDITION

"I read the first sentence of this book, threw up my hands and then stayed up all night to finish." — *Liz on Thomas Har-ris's* The Silence of the Lambs, *as quoted in the recently published paperback edition*

"Behavioral Science, the FBI section that deals with serial murder, is on the bottom floor of the Academy building at Quantico, half-buried in the earth." — *the first sentence of* The Silence of the Lambs

Tina Brown's leaked importunings to Michael Ovitz to sit for a profile, when she was editor of *Vanity Fair* and he was King of Hollywood: "You have inspired the people who work for you," she wrote. "The aura of leadership you give out discomforts rivals." Reaction at *Vanity Fair* went well beyond discomfort. August 1990

"I TRIED TO GET PEOPLE AS NEAR to the edge as they could go," says Korzenik, meaning near to but *back* from the edge. "There were close calls at times. But Graydon and Kurt understood that they couldn't afford to hit a rock. There were moments that were tense, but overall people had a good sense of humor. Susan would really edit people, but that would give me confidence—she'd say, 'This is what I know, this is what I've got, I should be able to say this'—she'd put it across to you."

Gentlemen: On page 24 of your December 1987 [see page 237] issue you published an item relating to an alleged relationship between Mr. J. D. Salinger and Ms. Catherine Oxenberg and a purported trip to California by Mr. Salinger to see her. As Mr. Salinger's attorney I have been requested to advise you that there is no truth whatsoever to these allegations....
—Letter from R. Andrew Boose of Kay Collyer & Boose,
December 15, 1987

Most of the legal threats were pre-publication—"people know you're writing, they know you're on them, and they go bananas—and their lawyers reflect that anxiety," says Korzenik.

Attention: Thomas L. Phillips Jr., Publisher
RE: Richard Gere

Gentlemen:
This office represents the above named.
I am informed of your intention to cause publication of an illustration and article involving Mr. Gere.
While it is not our objective to impinge on your First Amendment rights under the federal Constitution, we are compelled to bring the following to your attention.
Investigation will confirm the falsity of the intended publication....
—From a letter from Allan A. Sigel of Sigel & Boothe,
Los Angeles, May 9, 1990

THE "ILLUSTRATION AND ARTICLE" in question never existed. True, there might have been a casual office conversation about actors and rodents, followed by a casual phone conversation on the same topic with colleagues on the West Coast, but the arrival of that fax within hours was nevertheless impressive.

ıch time did North or his wife, Betsy, spend
; his pockets?   —*Joe Mastrianni*

ν pointers.
ᴅʀᴇᴡ Fʀɪᴇᴅᴍᴀɴ

July 1989

THE SPY LIST

Bill Blass

Bob Crane

Lemuel Gulliver

John F. Kennedy

Jerzy Kosinski

T. E. Lawrence

Robert Mapplethorpe

O

Sean Penn

Snidely Whiplash

apparently tied
crime and the su
MCA internal a
pressure seems to
brought in part
Conductor" Scia
an underboss of
crime family of
At the same tim
began receiving
advance notices
people in organi
to the project. G
Bacow conclude
opposition came
"Jimmy Blue Ey
octogenarian lie
Genovese crime j
been close to La
was the situatic
Giaquinto and
Sciandra was in
end, the situatic
apparently thro
tion of a powerf
⁎16. On July
about 11:16 a.
[*called*] GIAQU
spoke about wl
be their meetin
SCIANDRA on J
at the Bistro G
BACOW indicat
GIAQUINTO ha
advantage of in
'The Bistro
restaurant in E
⁎17. It is th
affiant that thi
and the meetin
BACOW, GIAQU
SCIANDRA . . .
MCA/Univer
which was crit

There was another preemptive lawyerly strike—this time regarding something *Spy* was actually working on—involving Steven Seagal in 1993, after the founding editorial team had left the magazine.

"They sued us before I wrote a word," says John Connolly. "What happened was, Seagal came up to Jean Pigozzi—and Pigozzi's a pretty big boy—and started jabbing his finger in his chest: 'I'm gonna get you, I'm gonna get your magazine,' and so on." Connolly, formerly an NYPD detective, was *Spy*'s tough-talking star muckraker, and Pigozzi was *Spy*'s new owner, with Charles Saatchi, as of 1991. Seagal was—this is a while ago—a big Hollywood action star and a creation of Michael Ovitz. The story involved Hollywood power brokers and restaurants in Brooklyn and the kinds of contracts not normally associated with magazine work.

Seagal had heard that Connolly was in Los Angeles interviewing people for a story about him, and sued for slander—sued one of Connolly's sources and also Connolly, for having repeated the alleged slander in the form of questions to other sources. "They figured that would cause us to back off," Korzenik says. "But it made us tighten the whole thing up. We went through maybe eight different drafts until it was *built* for litigation. Then they added *Spy* to the lawsuit. And we printed all their threats! They'd send us letters denying stuff that we weren't even *writing* about, and we printed them.

"One day Connolly was on the phone with me," Korzenik continues. "And he keeps saying, 'Yes, counselor. *No*, counselor,' which is basically the way police officers talk to lawyers when they're really not happy. He's clearly thinking that I'm going to give the piece a legal haircut. But John really reported his stuff well. Maybe it was because he had been a detective. He understood the evidentiary weight of what he was delivering."

Pigozzi, though new to the game, stood his ground and backed his magazine. The piece ("Man of Dishonor") ran in the July/August 1993 issue.

As the case proceeded, Connolly learned about a separate lawsuit between Seagal and a garage attendant who claimed that Seagal had assaulted him. Seagal had countersued for defamation. Connolly met with the garage attendant's lawyer, cleverly loading him with questions about *Spy*'s case and *Spy*'s article. Seagal's lawyer objected—but the magistrate ruled that Seagal had to answer the questions, Seagal took the Fifth on one, then chose to drop the countersuit—and stop the interrogation. (The assault claim was ultimately settled.)

Months later, Seagal withdrew his case against *Spy* and Connolly; no money was paid him.

But let's conclude this chapter with an adventure in fact-checking that won't require mass applications to the Federal Witness Protection Program. *Spy*'s longest and most nitpicky correction followed a June 1989 column about the well-known photographer (and occasional recording artist) Lynn Goldsmith. *Spy*'s clarification went into whether Goldsmith tried to slip a tape of one of her songs into Soviet first lady Raisa Gorbachev's pocket (she did not), whether she owned the rights to certain photos of Keith Richards (she did), and a few other minor matters.

Missing in the correction's published form were the last two sentences, crossed out of the final draft. They read: "Finally, Ms. Goldsmith claims that she does not scream 'Give it to me!' during her photo shoots. Rather, she says, 'I *want* it. I *want* it.'"

PRIVATE LIVES OF PUBLIC ENEMIES

First Lady Nancy Reagan begins preparations for leaving the White House.
ILLUSTRATION BY DREW FRIEDMAN

December 1988

LIFE
IMITATES
ART

The S P Y Collection:

 People We Confuse With

Paintings and Sculpture,

 Paintings and Sculpture

We Confuse With People

...henever we think of Sammy ...vis Jr., which is often, we ...k of the singer, the dancer, ... entertainer. We think of ...y and Frank and the big ...ms in Vegas and Nixon and ...da Lovelace. We think of ...ndy Man." And we think of ...ism.

...hat's right. *Cubism.*

...And to be perfectly honest ...ut it, whenever we look at ...ain Picassos, we think of ...my.

...t may be an unintended by-...duct of an art-history lec-...e that Rosamond Bernier ...e years ago—back in the ...s when . . . why, it was still ...ving's Met. Whatever the ...se, we can't help seeing ...t art everywhere we look. A ...ace at the New York *Daily* ...s tells us that it is not Liz ...th writing the gossip col-...n but a Willem de Kooning ...vas come to heavily air-...shed photographic life. ...h Richards (English, b. ...2) goes on tour and we ...k of the terrifying Expres-...ist faces of Egon Schiele ...strian, 1890–1918). And

to us, the hellish canvases of Hieronymous Bosch teem with all manner of Roy Cohns (American, 1927–86).

In every case, it isn't so much that *these* people look exactly like *those* paintings. If that were so, we would simply have presented you with a series of cheap analogies: Frank Zappa and Leon Redbone as Van Dycks, Katharine Hepburn as *Nude Descending a Staircase,* Buddy Holly and the Big Bopper as . . . well . . . a Jackson Pollock. (Did we mention that some of the cheap analogies would also have been in questionable taste?) And we could have stretched things a bit to include works of contemporary architecture, so many of which look like De Chiricos with tax abatements (although Peter Allen, it must be said, reminds us of certain Helmut Jahn buildings). On the other hand, that affinity is half deliberate on the part of the architects (and possibly even in Peter Allen's case). Similarly, Henry Geldzahler seems to have leapt to life from a Hockney painting only be-

cause Hockney has painted him. And just because Sarah Brightman describes her hair as Pre-Raphaelite doesn't mean we'll run a publicity shot of her next to a color plate of a Rossetti.

No, what we've gathered here in this pioneering art-historical monograph are not look-alikes. Rather, the people in our gallery *profoundly suggest* the work of a certain painter or sculptor or school. And—we know this could be a little alarming to those who take their art seriously—vice versa. How utterly remarkable that Diego Velázquez, applying his rich brush strokes in seventeenth-century Madrid, could have captured the essence, the very soul, of Herve Villechaize; and yet he has. Uncannily, their names are similar, too.

Having such a peculiarly trained eye is a curse as well as a blessing. It's now impossible for us to look at a Brancusi without thinking of a Grimaldi—specifically, of Princess Stephanie and then, in rapid succession, of whether *she* was actu-

ally driving, of the young Grace Kelly, of Gary Cooper and *High Noon* and the melody to "Do Not Forsake Me," which subsequently lodges itself in our heads for the next two days as if on a maddening internal tape loop. When this starts to happen, museums and galleries become dangerous, strictly off-limits. As are, by the same token, any celebrity-clogged venues. (When the two types of danger spots converge, as at last fall's sale of French Impressionists at Sotheby's, *forget it*—that night we asked Degas's *Danseuses Russes* for its autograph and came very close to bidding $3.2 million for Gayfryd Steinberg.)

In the pages ahead, suffer us our appreciation, and appreciate our suffering as we catalog the well-known late-twentieth-century people who look like art and the art that looks like well-known late-twentieth-century people. If nothing else, it should give you a whole new appreciation for the surface dynamism and iconographic subtleties of Shelley Duvall.

March 1989

It's Deliberately Elongated at the Top

How can it be that such glamorous, high-profile and *alive!* celebrities summon forth the oeuvre of so weltschmerzy and comparatively obscure an Expressionist as **Egon Schiele** (1890–1918)? Nouveau intellectual actress **Daryl Hannah** (b. 1960) uses

her attenuated, highly descriptive limbs. Sleeping-with-fashion-models rock musicians **Ric Ocasek** (probably younger than Bill Wyman) and **Keith Richards**

(b. 1943) are left to use their haggard Lost Generation faces. Ocasek came by his Schielisms genetically, while Richards achieved his through years and years of too much fun, plus one picture (*Hail! Hail! Rock 'n' Roll*) with Chuck Berry.

Pumping and selling iron —
that's just one of the things
Umberto Boccioni (1882–
1916), the Italian Futurist, and
Arnold Schwarzenegger (b.
1947), the Austrian Reaganite,
have in common. Here's
another: although it was
completed in 1913, Boccioni's
*Unique Forms of Continuity in
Space*, some scholars now
believe, was conceived as a
sculptural ode to the dynamism
of last Christmas's comedy laff-
riot, *Twins*.

UISITE SOLIDITY
no surprise that Colombian
er **Fernando Botero**
932), vein-clotted
lomerateur **Saul Steinberg**
939) and spooky matricide
uée **Sukhreet Gabel**
949) are contemporaries.

Although Steinberg remains
tethered to his wife's side in
Manhattan, and although
Gabel doesn't get out much,
either, now that the Myerson
trial is over, who can deny their
influence on Botero's work,
and/or vice versa? *Dancing in

Colombia* (oil on canvas, 1980)
boasts a playful cameo
appearance by Steinberg (there,
on the far left — does painting
Steinberg qualify Botero as a
landscapist?). And there's
Gabel (note the virtually
expressionist gestures —

preternaturally red hair,
overstuffed-rag-doll face). And
there, finally, is Steinberg
himself, looking as though he's
being squeezed out of the top
of a tuxedo-shaped oil-paint
tube. No preoccupation with
form *here*!

SHE DIDN'T EVEN NAME HER
RANCE *GUERNICA*
e is no question that
ma **Picasso** (b. 1949) has
nteresting provenance. And
's disquieting that the
tieth-century painter she
es so insistently is not her
r, Pablo, the misogynist
st, but his second-drawer
emporary, **Fernand Léger**
1–1955). Go figure.
ract figure.

PERFECT REPLICAS
Critics who suspect that pop
artist **Roy Lichtenstein**'s
(b. 1923) comic-strip characters
don't resemble living, breathing
human beings any more closely
than does your average Paul
Klee will find all the proof they
require in plasticman New
York *Daily News* publisher
Jim Hoge (b. 1935) and
plasticwoman **Vanna White**
(b. 1957). Only the thought
bubbles are missing.

Giotto, Duccio, Giuliani, Streep...In the work of these four, one can always depend on life, texture, piety, impeccable renditions of sundry world speech patterns, and major indictments.

BEYOND THE LIMITS OF FORM AND FEMININITY

Woman and Bicycle, you say? That's no bicycle, that's **Carol Channing**. Only the wild brushstrokes of **Willem de Kooning** (b. 1904) could capture so splendidly the exuberant vigor, not to say syntactical imbalance, of such merry, cackling ladies-about-town as Channing (b. 1921), **Liz Smith** (b. circa 1928), **Bubbles Rothermere** (b. 1934) and **Aileen "Suzy" Mehle** (b. 1924 — that's A.D.). And only De Kooning's drawing, with its haunting teeth-in-a-windstorm effects, could do justice to this group.

CHICKS NOUVEAUX

There's certainly a case to be made that author–study-in-black-and-white **Tama Janowitz** (b. 1956) has taken an **Aubrey Beardsley** (1872–98) drawing as one of her spiritual/aesthetic mentors. But it takes two really *great* decorative artists to bridge the gap between *The Yellow Book* and Jack La Lanne television ads — Beardsley (sinful, decadent) and **Cher** (game, uninhibited). Forget about the sort of technical problems only time travel can solve: Cher (b.1946) is a walking, talking pen-and-ink drawing at every award ceremony she attends, and the influence of her fevered post–Bob Mackie dressmakers on Beardsley's illustrations of Salome and Lysistrata is undeniable. Do we have to add that an Oscar figured prominently in both their careers?

TROMPE L'OY!

Once seen, the overripe, grotesque faces painted by **James Ensor** (1860–1949) are not forgotten: smiling yet hideous, they terrify even as they would be jolly. The same might be said about the expressionist comedy of **Jackie Mason** (b. 1931), the expressionist eyeliner of **Louise Nevelson** (1900–88) and the expressionist ersatz-personality of **Ronald Reagan** (b. 1911).

FREE-THROW MONUMENTALISM

This is either the best starting five since the 1970 Knicks or the beginnings of a nice little gallery off Spring Street. **Manute Bol** (b. 1962), by the way, may pull down about $400,000 a year from the Warriors, but one piece from the *Walking Man* series brought $7.65 million at Christie's in London last November, a new auction record for **Alberto Giacometti** (1901–66), the Bob Cousy of figurative twentieth-century sculpture. Way to go, 'Berto!

QUASI-STARRY NIGHT

Certain questions arise. Does **Linda Hunt** (b. 1945) eat potatoes? Would **Vincent van Gogh** (1853–90) have painted so many self-portraits if he'd known that a century later they would end up looking like publicity stills for *Platoon* and *The Last Temptation of Christ*? Meanwhile, contemporary postimpressionism buffs debate the restoration of *Lust for Life*, with **Willem Dafoe** (b. 1955) as Vincent — and Harvey Keitel as Paul!

REPELLENT WAIFS

Schmroadway — we can catch **Liza Minnelli** (b. 1946) on
and in strip-mall bad-art stores across the country any
courtesy of American master **Walter Keane** (b. 1921).
rly **Goldie Hawn** (b. 1945) on the right (ca. 1968)
adiates black-velvet-painting bathos.

OYL ON CANVAS

The ovoid faces and elongated
bodies of **Amedeo Modigliani**
(1884–1920) enjoy a revival in
the form of actress–cable
producer **Shelley Duvall** (b.
1949), proving that it's but a
shortish leap across media —
and decades — from the statement of *Bambina Con Trecce*
(1916) to the statement of
Faerie Tale Theatre (ongoing).
Promising pupils in the school
of Duvall: designer **Carolyne
Roehm** (neck) and novelist
Joyce Carol Oates (eyes).

DUTCH UNCLES

It's a pity **Frans Hals** (ca.
1581–1666) worked in
Holland in the seventeenth
century instead of at Elaine's or
Spago on a Tuesday. Get the
florid, gouty countenances of
hyperbolic publicist **Bobby
Zarem** (b. 1936), hyperbolic
producer **Bernie Brillstein**
(b. 1931), hyperbolic actor
Ernest Borgnine (b. 1917) and
hyperbolic comedian **Sam
Kinison** (b. 1953) together in
one room, and you might as
well call it *Frans Hals Live!*
and sell tickets.

MORE IS MOORE

The softly rounded sculptures
of **Henry Moore** (1898–1986)
are well known: *Busty Figure*;
Reclining Woman; *Nude*; *Bronze
Woman*; *Fatgirl With Purse*.
Whoa! *Fatgirl With —?* Look
again: sensuous outlines and
material-celebrating contours,
yes, but not bronze — rubber. In
other words, "fashion designer"
Dianne Brill (b. circa 1950).
Also pictured here: actress
Toukie Smith (b. mid-
twentieth century), a Robert De
Niro paramour, impersonates a
Moore at Pier 92, where it is
hoped she will remain until
July, when she embarks on an
18-month tobacco-company-
sponsored tour that will see her
similarly placed in various
embassy gardens, university
quadrangles and meadows.

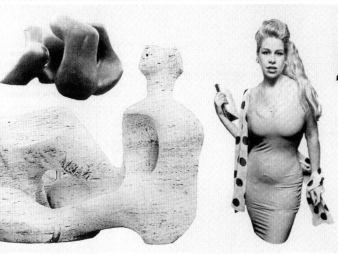

TWO VIRGINS

**Giotto, Duccio, Giuliani,
Streep** . . . devotional artists all:
the first two (Tuscan and
Sienese schools, respectively) to
God and the perpetuation of
the Byzantine style; the third
(NYU School of Law) to the
Press Conference; and the
fourth (Yale School of Drama)
to the Show-Off-y Role. In the
work of these four, one can
always depend on life, texture,
piety, impeccable renditions of
sundry world speech patterns,
and major indictments. 𝔰𝔭

10

"You'll Feel Better If You Look Natty"

In Between the Parties, Somehow, We Managed to Put Out a Magazine

What I most remember about Spy *is what I wore to one of the parties—the first and only time I've ever worn a strapless dress. It was so glamorous. You never thought that living in New York was really going to be like that.*

—PATRICIA MARX

EVEN BY THE STANDARDS OF THE '80s, *Spy* was a party magazine, and a convivial place during daylight hours as well. The office bred many affairs, several marriages, a couple of divorces, umpteen kids, and dozens of lasting friendships. "You would call people that you'd just spent the week working with to hang out on a Saturday," remembers John Brodie. Today there's still an annual dinner—hosted by Aimée Bell and David Kamp (one of those *Spy* marriages) and paid for by Graydon, for two dozen of the magazine's former editorial assistants and assorted friends—every December in Greenwich Village. And the spawn of various *Spy* couples are probably right now plotting to shake up school projects with disrespectful epithets about the faculty, and bold, innovative (if frustratingly hard to read) construction-paper design.

Some of *Spy*'s after-hours activities were clean and healthful: Kurt and Anne hosted an annual picnic at their cottage upstate, at which friendly games of badminton, softball, and horseshoes were about as wild as things got; the *Spy* running team actually won a national championship one year; and the softball team, led by long-ball hitter Graydon, enjoyed pounding magazines in the Central Park league—often without cheating.

There was also, in November 1989 at Lincoln Center, a wonderful single performance (to benefit the AIDS charity Broadway Cares) of *Speed-the-Play*, David Ives's parody of David Mamet's oeuvre, which *Spy* had just published (see pages 192–93). Every play was distilled to mere minutes and seconds. The cast featured A-list Mametians like Joe Mantegna, Felicity Huffman, and William H. Macy, and Mamet's favorite stage director, Gregory Mosher, directed; the audience included the Kinks' Ray Davies, writer Harold Brodkey, and Mr. Mamet himself. But *Spy* could even turn an evening of theater into a debauch: Each act of *Speed-the-Play* lasted no more than a few minutes, whereas the several

**Opposite:
E. Graydon Santa
informing the
staff who's been
naughty and
who's been very
naughty indeed,
December 1989**

intermissions, with wide-open bar, went on and on.

Most of the fun and games happened indoors, generally lasted late into the night, and frequently involved stingers or sidecars or whatever the blue drink of the month was. There were the requisite promotional parties with advertisers, but the really disgraceful behavior seemed to fall into three main categories of bacchanal: the monthly closing dinner; the staff Christmas party; and the October anniversary gala. A few indiscreet recollections follow. And any *Spy* offspring reading this should stop right about now.

"The closing dinner every month—having seen now the way most magazines run, I don't think I realized at the time how unusual and great that was," says Carrie Weiner. "Because for one evening every month, everybody was sitting at the same table. And although there was a hierarchy, it wasn't like you never got to talk to the guy in charge."

Elissa Schappell remembers one dinner with "people spitting drinks in each other's faces and knocking over tables." That might or might not have been the same dinner at which Lynn Snowden demonstrated how she could put her entire fist in her mouth. But the gatherings did provide some (very) informal face time with the principals. At a dinner at a West Broadway restaurant with "everyone pretty drunk as usual," Tad Friend recalls being the recipient of one of Graydon's "endearing take-you-under-his-wing speeches, with everyone grinning but me shifting in my seat. It was about how I was 80 percent a great writer, but the other 20 percent was too naive. 'You have to have a six-year plan! You have to learn

that New York is based on *false heat*; that's the part of the puzzle you haven't appreciated, and once you've learned that, your pieces will be *shorter* and *tighter*. Six-year plan! Write more about business, learn how the city really works, the tick-tock of the inside mechanisms.'

"Then he arm-wrestled me, and pinned me, had a couple more drinks, and launched into part two of his speech, which was all about how I was young, and that I prided myself on being a young, hot writer, but there was always someone younger and hotter who'd come along, that Eric Kaplan was going to be much bigger than any of us at this table someday [Kaplan did become a successful TV writer/producer] and I should get used to that. He said, 'I have to face the fact that Kurt is a much better writer than I am—but I'm a better editor than he is.'

"Part three of the speech," continues Friend, "after another round of arm-wrestling and some more stingers, was about hangover prevention. It was a four-step approach: one, coat your stomach before going out, with four aspirins and milk; two, when you wake up the next morning, raw egg and Worcestershire sauce, whipped. Visine for the eyes. Extra-close shave—double shave—then wear a bow tie, because 'you'll feel better if you look natty.'"

That recipe would have come in handy at what was by far the most notorious of the staff parties, held in 1989 in some townhouse on a West Village street that we can't recall, at an Italian restaurant no one can think of the name of, which in any case didn't remain open very long after we'd got done with it.

In this temperate new age, a recounting sounds more like the late '20s than the late '80s. Elissa Schappell's husband, Rob Spillman, an occasional researcher for the magazine (and now editor of the literary quarterly *Tin House*, which he and Schappell cofounded), arrived on the quiet block a little late, though not too; it couldn't have been much past nine. He opened the front door and found himself peering into what looked like the ninth circle of hell, a noisy, roiling mass of humanity: We had long since reached the edge of the precipice, and marched right over it.

One male staffer, it soon became clear, was disappearing into dark corners at regular intervals with a series of female colleagues. Another had removed almost all of his clothing, doubtless to achieve greater mobility while handling the karaoke mike. "He wouldn't let it go," Spillman remembers. "He would hit people if they came up and tried to take it." E. Graydon Santa was in full regalia, but kept tipping over on his stool. (Each year, every staff member would come up and sit on his lap to receive presents, insults, and *faux*-lewd remarks.*) It was Christiaan Kuypers's turn, and no sooner had he perched there than the inebriated Santa told him, through his bad false beard, "Mrs. Claus talks a little too much about how attractive you are." Sections of what might once have been a longish conga line were snaking their separate, truncated ways among the revelers, many of whom appeared, for no apparent reason, to be screaming and standing on

---

*Graydon sort of based his Santa on Bob Hope's wolfish turns in the *Road* pictures. —Eds.

chairs. The restaurant's staff had evidently seen the writing on the wall (perhaps literally) and retreated to higher ground. Spillman took it all in and thought, *Oh, my God. Where is my wife?*

"The problem," Schappell explains, "was we started drinking during the early afternoon at the office. We were dispatched to get 'pre-party cocktails.' Susan's desk was the bar. It was like, 'Why not!' The afternoon cocktail bell had gone off." The karaoke machine, which Morrison had bought for $99, and which likewise did not survive the evening, only made matters worse.

Joanne Gruber was one of the few sober people in the place. "Santa/Graydon was singing to the tune of 'Chicago,' but the lyrics were mostly about all of us," she remembers. "Walter Kirn also sang 'Chicago,' and many other hits, but no one heard because his mike wasn't attached to the karaoke machine. While all the other pandemonium was happening, he was crooning with his eyes closed and the most satisfied smile on his face— like, *I'm wowing them, I'm killing them, nobody's even trying to get the mike from me!* With the mike that *was* plugged in, Tom Phillips both sang and danced 'Kung Fu Fighting' for us.* Graydon decided he no longer wanted to be Santa Claus and went into a

---

*One of the first times we met with **Tom** to discuss *Spy*, before we had agreed to make him our partner, he showed us photographs of himself dressed in drag for a business school production of *The Rocky Horror Picture Show*. He was very, very proud of those pictures, which we found charming, although maybe not in precisely the way he intended. —Eds.

Party Poop, from far left: Gary Fisketjon, Morgan Entrekin, and Jay McInerney; ex-Duke John Schneider and friend; Christie Brinkley and Billy Joel, all at Spy's party at The Tunnel, January 1987; Tama Janowitz and the late Al Lewis at Spy's Separated at Birth? party, December 1987

LET'S PUT ON OUR <u>OWN</u> SHOW!

The Complete David Mamet-in-a-Can Broadway Sets and Players

1. Fold back side and bottom flaps of stage.
2. Cut sets out of magazine page and curve them so that the tabs fit inside the slots.

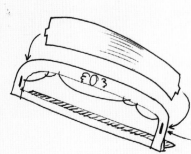

1. Bend flaps back and join together at slots to form a ring.
2. Slip finished puppet over desired finger.
3. Shake finger to indicate dialogue.

SPEED-THE-PLOW

Performance time: 50 seconds

ACT I

Gould's Hollywood office. Morning.

FOX: Gould, you're the new head of production at this studio and I'm an unsuccessful independent producer, and you owe me a favor.

GOULD: That's right, Fox.

FOX: I've discovered this trashy script. Will you take it to the head of the studio and make me rich, Gould?

GOULD: Yes I will, Fox. At ten o'clock tomorrow morning.

FOX: Thank you, Gould.

GOULD: I'm a whore.

FOX: I'm a whore, too. Who's your sexy new secretary?

GOULD: She's just a temp, Fox.

FOX: I'll bet you $500 you can't get her into bed.

GOULD: It's a bet. (*Into intercom*) Karen, would you come in here, please? (KAREN *enters.*) Karen, will you read this book about cosmic bullshit and come to my apartment tonight to report on it?

KAREN: Yes, sir.

CURTAIN

ACT II

Gould's apartment. That night.

GOULD: Did you read the book, Karen?

ILLUSTRATIONS BY BARRY BLITT

THE MAMET PLAYERS

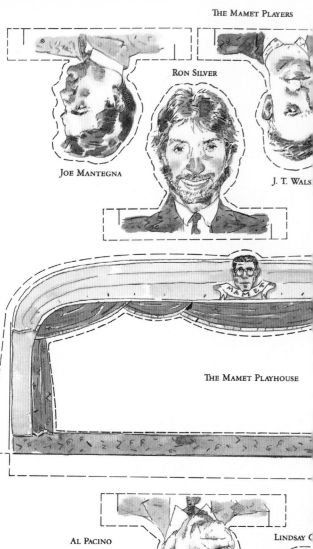

RON SILVER

JOE MANTEGNA

J. T. WALS

THE MAMET PLAYHOUSE

AL PACINO

LINDSAY C

ROBERT PROSKY

KAREN: Yes, and I think it's brilliant and that Mr. Fox's script is trash.
GOULD: But I'm just a whore.
KAREN: I think that you're a very sensitive man.
GOULD: At last, a woman who understands me!

CURTAIN

ACT III

Gould's office. Next morning, just before 10:00 a.m.

GOULD: I'm not going to recommend your script to the head of the studio, Fox. I'm going to recommend the book about cosmic bullshit instead.
FOX: You're only doing this because Karen went to bed with you, Gould.
GOULD: Gee, maybe you're right, Fox. (*Into intercom*) Karen, would you come in here, please? (KAREN *enters.*) Karen, you're fired. (KAREN *exits.*)
FOX: She's a whore.
GOULD: She's a whore.
FOX: And life is good.

CURTAIN

GLENGARRY GLEN ROSS
Performance time: 57 seconds

ACT I

Scene 1. A booth at a Chinese restaurant.
WILLIAMSON: Levene, you're a failure.
LEVENE: Forty, fifty, sixty years ago I was the best goddamn hustler of swampland in the history of the real estate scams! (*Long pause.*) Now, I happen to need some leads so that I can win a Cadillac as top salesman of the month. And you're my boss. So, Williamson?
WILLIAMSON: You can't have any leads.
LEVENE: Oh, *please*, John, *please?*

Scene 2. Another booth at the restaurant.
MOSS: Aaronow.
AARONOW: *Duhh.*
MOSS: Somebody should steal the leads from the real estate office.
AARONOW: *Duhh.*
MOSS: I mean you and me, Aaronow. Tonight.
   (AARONOW *thinks.*)
AARONOW: But wouldn't that be illegal?

Scene 3. Another booth.

ROMA: What is the meaning of life?
POTENTIAL CUSTOMER: I don't know.
ROMA: Me neither. Would you like to buy some real estate?

CURTAIN

ACT II

The real estate office. The place has been ransacked.
WILLIAMSON: Aaronow, someone broke into the office last night and stole the leads.
AARONOW: *Duhh.*
WILLIAMSON: Was it you?
AARONOW: *Duhh.*
   (ROMA *enters.*)
ROMA: Gracious heavens. The office has been ransacked?
WILLIAMSON: Yes. Was it you, Roma?
ROMA: Fuck you, John.
   (LEVENE *enters.*)

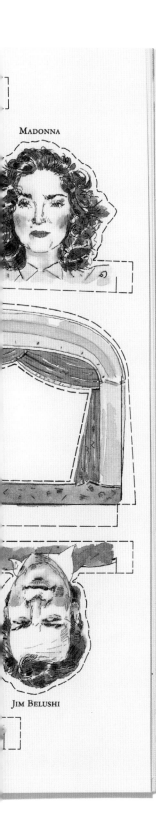

MADONNA

JIM BELUSHI

Selections—later performed at Lincoln Center— from playwright David Ives's parody of David Mamet. Printed on heavy paper, this could be cut out and made into a home finger-puppet theater. November 1989

BEST OF PARTY POOP

Spy's most childish monthly feature. "Once I started to look at contact sheets, I realized that the most entertaining and revealing photos are the ones that don't even get printed up," says editor Susan Morrison. "The best pictures suggested combustive little narratives, and we supplied those stories." After some coaxing, the photographers, chiefly Patrick McMullan and Marina Garnier, were on board. "Only *Spy* was poking high-society with a stick," continues Morrison. "The downtown scene was becoming a snooty mirror-image of uptown. Dianne Brill was just a subterranean doppelgänger of Pat Buckley."

After Kermit the Frog, the remarkable new Dianne Brill balloon was the big hit of Macy's Thanksgiving Day Parade.

February 19

NOT NECESSARILY A GOOD IDEA
A carful of happy, excited children shipped in to play with Michael Jackson.

June 1992

IN the course of a completely legal meeting with completely respectable business associates, John Gotti ogles a sophisticated European beauty at Regine's.

October 1987

PILLARS OF SOCIETY Wee entertainer Sammy ◀Davis Jr. and wee etymological curiosity and agent Swifty Lazar▶ look hopelessly out of scale, even on tippytoes, nestled beneath the towering hulks of, respectively, Carol Alt and Nancy Kissinger.

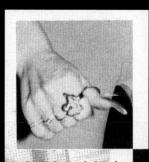

Dolly Parton's hand leaving Nell's

February 1989

▶ If superdweeb Rudolph Giuliani ever hopes to be mayor, he will have to learn, as Ed Koch has, to unbutton his jacket before allowing someone (like Tony Lo-Bianco) to hoist his arm skyward in a gesture of victory.

June 1989

AVAST, ME MATEYS Lauren Hutton as pirate; as woman with patch on her forehead

January 1993

*A*t Howard Stern's WXRK studio, an eager Jessica Hahn is held down by her lawyer-handler.

December 1987

TAKING PRECAUTIONS Bill Clinton never speaks in a space that is not equipped with a visible fire extinguisher and a perfectly proportioned miniature person hovering nearby to operate it.

▲ Presidential candidate Al Haig, evidently saying a little prayer that no one is taking his picture with fellow comedian Phyllis Diller.

December 1987

August 1992

Good Vibrations, or Something Who knew that teeny overleveraged businessman Henry "Stumpy" Kravis had so much soul?

June 1991

photograph of fatgirl Dianne Brill, chatting here with Reinaldo Herrera, a rich South American whom *Vanity Fair* calls its special projects editor, at Anita Sarko's Palladium pajama party.

...er (above), and ...ext to Tatiana ...es chastity on ...Associations ... Lollobrigida

November 1986

rican belief
e junk food
igh-quality
vill be bet-
a pamphlet
t *Food Reci-*
tzer, a lady
Michigan,
days break-
f fast-food
ewives can
home that
they came
: franchise. Finally, we referred to
y William Poundstone, the para-
d, who tells readers what Shriners
l lodge doors, what song lyrics say if

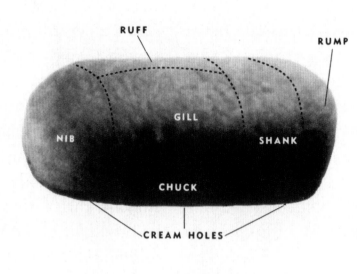

FIG. 25
NON-USDA-APPROVED TWINKIE CUTS

of Twink
with thei
somethi
cheerful
sticky tu
nicely in
hand lik
terfinger.
are hewn
cake, seer
by comp
things tha
eat them
slither apart in your hand. When
to plop out on your sleeves and d
chin, you long for a trim authenti
way it glides tidily into an open m

closet to change, but only got the top half of his outfit off and then fell out, half-dressed."

SANTA WAS ULTIMATELY HEADED NORTH, of course—to the Upper West Side—and so was his Manhattan-born elfin assistant, John Brodie.

"Snow was falling," Brodie remembers. "So there was this perfect West Village tableau of an older, rouged-up, drunk gentleman in a Santa Claus suit and a young fellow walking arm in arm into the Christopher Street subway station. There were just no cabs, and we figured it would be easier to take the 1 train. And I'm sitting on those wooden benches in the subway next to this disheveled Santa thinking, *If friends of my parents were to walk by and see me right now....*"

The huge, annual, quasi-public parties, those black-tie affairs in the Puck Ballroom, ran for six years, through the fifth-anniversary iteration in 1991. And it was that one at which Penn Jillette ate fire and Wayne Newton performed "*Spy* Way" ("The record shows / We've thrown the blows / And thrown them *Spy* way!"). These were anything but sedate, but since they were also the public face of the magazine, the staff generally made some effort to contain itself—or at least limit the structural damage. One thing was indisputable: The anniversary parties were a hot ticket, the annual big-production showstopper of a ferociously social outfit.

"I started at *Spy* in the summer of '92," says Larissa MacFarquhar. (She was Kurt's assistant and has gone on to become a *New Yorker* staff writer.) "And I would hear tales of these fantastic parties and the fun everyone used to have and how gleeful the office was. I did feel that I'd missed the heyday."

BEFORE, IT WAS JUST FRIGHTENING

to ride the subway, but in our *New, Improved New York it's frightening* and fun. *The IRT* Tornado, *the fastest and most daredevilish of the Transit Authority's five shortcut roller-coaster shuttle trains, thunders and screeches from 53rd and Madison to Times Square in 16 seconds flat—including the extra 1.5 seconds for the loop-the-loop through Rockefeller Center. The new above-ground track sections were designed and constructed by New York City high school shop students. On the Tornado and the other shortcut trains, the problem of punks riding between cars pretty well takes care of itself; delays due to switching problems or track fires are a thing of the dark, subterranean past—and when the doors accidentally open at 75 mph, 560 feet up, the thrills get* really *chilling.* ✺

ILLUSTRATION BY DAVID DIRCKS

New, Improved New York, April 1987. Note the three founders' Hitchcock-like cameos.

November 1989

bInside ohemian Grove

BY PHILIP WEISS

MY THREE WEEKS OF MALE BONDING AND FUNNY COCKTAILS WITH HENRY KISSINGER, WILLIAM F. BUCKLEY, HENRY KRAVIS AND RONALD REAGAN AT THE MOST EXCLUSIVE FRAT PARTY ON EARTH

MONTE RIO IS A DEPRESSED NORTHERN CALIFORNIA TOWN OF 900 where the forest is so thick that some streetlights stay on all day long. Its only landmark is a kick-ass bar called the Pink Elephant, but a half-mile or so away from "the Pink," in the middle of a redwood grove, there is, strangely enough, a bank of 16 pay telephones. In midsummer the phones are often crowded. On July 21 of this year Henry Kissinger sat at one of them, chuffing loudly to someone — Sunshine, he called her, and Sweetie — about the pleasant distractions of his vacation in the forest.

"We had jazz concert," Kissinger said. "We had rope trick. This morning we went bird-watching."

Proudly Kissinger reeled off the names of some of his fellow campers: "Nick Brady and his brother is here." Brady is the U.S. Treasury Secretary. "Tom Johnson is here."

The then-publisher of the *Los Angeles Times*, who had copies of his newspaper shipped up every day. "That Indian is here. Bajpai." Shankar Bajpai, former ambassador to the U.S. "Today they had a Russian."

The Russian was the physicist Roald Sagdeyev, a member of the Soviet Supreme Council of People's Deputies, who had given a speech to Kissinger and many other powerful men too. George Shultz, the former secretary of State, wearing hiking boots, had listened while sitting under a tree. Kissinger had lolled on the ground, distributing mown grass clippings across his white shirt, being careful not to set his elbow on one of the cigar butts squashed in the grass, and joking with a wiry, nut-brown companion.

The woman on the line now asked about the friend.

"Oh, Rocard is having a *ball*."

Kissinger was sharing his turtleneck with Rocard, for nights amid the redwoods grew surprisingly cool. The two of them were camping in Mandalay, the most exclusive bunksite in the encampment, the one on the hill with the tiny cable car that carries visitors up to the compound. Meanwhile,

I. P. Daley: an old-timer enjoying his most hallowed Bohemian right

THE PRIESTS

WORE BRIGHT RED, BLUE AND ORANGE HOODED ROBES THAT MIGHT HAVE BEEN DESIGNED FOR THE KU KLUX KLAN BY MARIMEKKO

Kissinger had been offering Rocard advice: "I told him, 'Do anything you want, hide in the bushes—just don't let them see you.'"

Rocard was Michel Rocard, the prime minister of France, and this was a secret trip. No one was supposed to know he was peering up at ospreys and turkey vultures and hearing Soviet speakers along with former American secretaries of State and the present secretary of the Treasury. And David Rockefeller too. And Dwayne Andreas, the chairman of Archer-Daniels-Midland. Merv Griffin. Walter Cronkite.

No one was supposed to know that Rocard himself would be speaking the next day down at the lake, under the green speakers' parasol. As orange dragonflies coupled dazzlingly over the water, as bullfrogs sounded, Rocard would lean forward and say, "Because you are such an astonishing group of men, I can speak privately."

It was a devilishly charming thing to say, calculated to flatter the men of the Bohemian Grove.

Every summer for more than a century, all-male Bohemian Club of San Francisco led a retreat into a redwood forest 70 mi north of the city, four and a quarter squa miles of rugged, majestic terrain that membe consider sacred. The religion they consecrate right-wing, laissez-faire and quintessentia western, with some Druid tree worship throv in for fun. The often bizarre rites have elevat what was once a provincial club for San Fra ciscans embarrassed by the rude manners of t Wild West into the most exclusive club in United States, with 2,300 members drawn fro the whole of the American esta lishment and a waiting list years long.

In the first 50 years of the clu existence the Bohemian Gro was comparatively accessible outsiders, but in the 1930s, as tl club gained influence and its re woods provided a haven f Republican presidents, it gre quite secretive about its ritua and membership—you won't ev find the Grove on public map This has been especially true the last ten years as Bohemi stunning roster has waxed ev more statusy, as Kissinger ar Rockefeller and Nick Brady ha joined, drawing the attention left-wing protesters, scholars elites, and reporters. The encam ment has become the prima watering hole for Republica administration officials, defense contractoi press barons, old-line Hollywood figures, estal lishment intellectuals and a handful of Germa speaking men in lederhosen. What the Bois Boulogne was to the ancien régime, the Grove to America's power class. Ronald Reagan ar George Bush are members. So are Gerald For and Richard Nixon—though club directors a said to be miffed at Nixon, a longtime Boh mian Grover who's still listed as sleeping Cave Man, one of the Grove's 119 curiously ar sometimes appropriately named camps.

Today the Grove is stocked with Reaganite Former Defense secretary Caspar W. Wei berger, former attorney general William Frenc Smith and former Transportation secretai Drew Lewis are all members. At the encam ment last July, Al Haig was there, along wit three other former secretaries of State: Ki singer, Shultz and William P. Rogers (Rogers a a guest of former national security adviser W liam P. Clark's). James A. Baker III, the curre secretary of State, is also a member, but h couldn't make it this year. The right-wing Hoover Institution at Stanford attended in full force and brought along the president of Washington's Heritage Foundation. William F. Buckley Jr. and Malcolm Forbes held court. Big business shows up: Thomas Watson Jr. of IBM, billionaire John Kluge of Metromedia. Former Bank of America chairman Samuel Armacost brought IBM chairman John F. Akers, Bechtel chairman S. D. Bechtel Jr. brought Amoco chairman Richard Morrow. Noted and hoary writers and personalities are members: Herman Wouk, Art Linkletter, Fred Travalena. Scenting power, press lords skip in from all over the country. Joe Albritton, former owner of *The Washington Star*; Charles E. Scripps and Jack Howard of the 21-paper Scripps Howard newspaper chain; Otto Silha of Cowles Media; the McClatchys of the McClatchy chain; and David Gergen of *U.S. News & World Report* all obey the Bohemian command of keeping the goings-on from their readers.

Every spring for many years now, Bohemian Club presidents have formally summoned such men to the Grove with great effusion:

"*Brother Bohemians: The Sun is Once Again in the Clutches of the Lion, and the encircling season bids us to the forest — there to celebrate... the awful mysteries!*"

"*Bohemians come! Find home again in the Grove! Burn CARE and hurl his ashes, whirling, from our blade!*"

"*Come out Bohemians! come out and play, come with all the buoyant impetuous rush of youth!*"

And this year, when president George Elliott wrote, more drably, "*Around campfires large and small, warm hospitality awaits you. Of course you must be with us,*" I heard his summons, too.

It was a good time to visit the Grove. The country was still steeped in the aw-shucks authoritarianism of the Reagan years, and if there is any place to study the culture of our ruling class, it is here among the Grove's benevolent, string-tie aristocracy. Also, it seemed possible that Ronald Reagan himself might make a triumphant return to his longtime camp, Owl's Nest. While president he had avoided the Grove, a custom Nixon cemented in 1971 when he canceled a speech planned for the lakeside in the secret encampment after the press insisted on covering it.

For me, the trick was getting in. A guest card was out of the question: club bylaws have stated that a member-sponsor's application "shall be in writing and shall contain full information for the guidance of the Board in determining the merits and qualifications of the proposed guest." No, Section 8, Article VIII was too fine a screen for me. And my attempts to get a job as a waiter or a valet in one of the camps failed. (The only

There the establishment boys are: roughing it in 1941

book entirely devoted to Grove life, *The Greatest Men's Party on Earth*, was written in 1974 by John van der Zee, a San Francisco writer who got in for four days as a waiter.)

In the end I entered

by stealth. Students of the Grove had warned that security was too good; they'd sniff me out quickly. I might last three hours before they put me in the Santa Rosa jail for trespassing. Lowell Bergman, a producer with *60 Minutes* who used to hunt rabbits in the nearby hills, remembered a fire road leading into the site near the Guerneville waste-treatment plant but said they'd spot me sneaking in. Others mentioned barbed wire and electronic monitoring devices at places where the Grove abuts Monte Rio, and helicopters patrolling the "ridge roads" that traverse the 1,000-foot hills and form the Grove's perimeter. One day I drove up to the front gate and got a daunting glimpse of what looked like the Grove sheriff, a barrel-like figure in a Smokey the Bear hat. A Berlin-ish set of checkpoints seemed to stretch

What would Smokey say? At the annual Cremation of Care, grown men dress as Druids and the outside world goes up in smoke.

out behind him.

But by then I'd made my connection. My driver was Mary Moore, an Earth Mother type with long silvery-blond hair who is the most active member of a distinctly Californian left-wing group called the Bohemian Grove Action Network. Moore agreed to help me get in, providing me with a sort of underground railroad. She put at my service a mountain guide who demanded only that I keep the methods he devised for me confidential. He had a keen geographical sense and a girlfriend who described a plan to seed magic crystals at the Grove gates to make them open of their own accord so that Native American drummers could walk in.

We didn't do it that way, but it turned out that Grove security isn't quite what it's reputed to be. Reporters seeking to write about the Grove had rarely been inside, and then usually for only a few hours at a time, but I was determined to have a good, long look, so I took care to blend. I outfitted myself in conservative recreational wear — a pressed plaid shirt, Perma-Prest chinos, Top-Siders, a sport jacket — I always carried a drink, and I made it a point to have that morning's *Wall Street Journal* or *New York Times* under my arm when I surfaced (though television is against the rules, newspapers are sold at the Grove Civic Center). Thus equipped, I came and went on 7 days dur-

Lawyer David Korzenik: "They didn't tell me about this one until they were already going in. 'Cause obviously it's a total trespass. A trespass claim could be made, and he'd be fined—he'd have a misdemeanor. Then there's theft of services—he was drinking cocktails, sleeping there, whatever. But these guys are so secretive, they didn't really want to have any lawsuits. Their likelihood of suing over a story like that is very low."

Writer Phil Weiss: "It was really easy to do. An idiot could have done it, and I was that idiot." (continued on next page)

ing the 16-day encampment, openly trespassing in what is regarded as an impermeable enclave and which the press routinely refers to as a heavily guarded area. Though I regularly violated Grove rule 20 ("Members and guests shall sign the register when arriving at or departing from the Grove"), I was never stopped or questioned. (Another rule forbade cameras outside one's own camp. I waited till my last day to bring one in.) Indeed, I was able to enjoy most pleasures of the Grove, notably the speeches, songs, elaborate drag shows, endless toasts, prebreakfast gin fizzes, round-the-clock "Nembutals" and other drinks—though I didn't sleep in any of the camps or swim naked with like-minded Bohemians in the Russian River at night.

My imposture included misrepresenting myself in conversation with other campers, and my story kept changing as I learned more about how life inside was organized. I said I was a guest of Bromley camp, where unsortable visitors end up. At 33, I was one of the youngest Bohemians, but I was welcome almost as a policy matter. "We looked around and saw we were becoming an old-men's club," a member said, explaining recent efforts to recruit fresh blood. Being from New York was fine; the Grove limits retreat guests to out-of-staters (though clamoring by well-connected Californians to visit the forest has resulted in the rise of the June "Spring Jinks" weekend). I used my real name. No one inside acted suspicious, but paranoia about the Grove seemed justified, and I brought along my own version of cyanide: Interol, a tranquilizer used by actors to counteract stage fright. One day a member asked if I was related to a Bohemian named Jack Weiss. "No, but I've heard a lot about him and I'd like to meet him." "You can't," he said. "He's dead." After that I began working a dead West Coast relative's promise to have me out to the Grove one summer into a shaggy-dog story about my invitation.

In this way I managed to drop in on the principal events of

Heigh-ho, heigh-ho: the Bohemia-bound Secretarial pool

the encampment, right up to the final Saturday, July 29, 12:30 p.m., when I attended a Lakeside Talk whose giver was, intriguingly, the only one not identified in the program of events. "Speaker: To Be Announced," it said, raising the question of what dignitary might be thought more important than Prime Minister Rocard, who was listed as the speaker on the middle Saturday.

My first full-strength dose of Bohemian culture took place two weeks earlier, the first Saturday night, when after a long day in the Grove I took a seat on the grassy lakeside among 1,500 other men for the encampment's famously surreal opening ritual. As the magic hour of 9:15 approached, a helicopter from a network newsmagazine circled frantically far above the darkened forest, searching out a spectacle lit at that point only by

the hundreds of cigars whose smokers had ignited them in defiance of the California Forest Service's posted warnings. My neighbor suggested that someone ought to "shoot the fucker down," flashing the press hatred that prevails in Bohemia.

"My friends don't understand this," a pudgy 35-year-old in front of me confided to his companion. "I know that if they could see it, they would see how terrific it is. It's like great sex...."

The world's most exclusive enchanted f[...]

It was the sort of analogy I was to hear often in the nearly [...] hours I spent inside the Grove. The friend and I leaned clo[...]

"It's *more* than it's cracked up to be. You can't describe it," [...] explained. Then everyone hushed as a column of hooded [...] ures carrying torches emerged solemnly from the woods [...] yards away, bearing a corpse down to the water.

YOU KNOW YOU ARE INSIDE THE BOHEMIAN GROVE WHEN Y[...] come down a trail in the woods and hear piano music fr[...] amid a group of tents and then round a bend to see a man w[...] a beer in one hand and his penis in the other, urinating into [...] bushes. This is the most gloried-in ritual of the encampme[...] the freedom of powerful men to pee wherever they like, a ri[...] the club has invoked when trying to fight government anti-s[...] discrimination efforts and one curtailed only when it comes [...]

KISSINGER a few popular redwoods just outside the D[...] ing Circle. Tacked to one of these haples[...]

OFFERED FRENCH PRI[...]

postprandial trees is a sign conveying the fairy-dust mixt[...] of boyishness and courtliness that envelops the encampme[...] GENTLEMEN PLEASE! NO PEE PEE HERE!

Everything in the encampment is sheltered by redwoods, wh[...] admit hazy shafts of sunlight, and every camp has a more or l[...] constant campfire sending a soft column of smoke into the tre[...] The walled camps are generally about 100 feet wide and stre[...] back up the hillside, with wooden platforms on which memb[...] set up tents. Bohemians sleep on cots in these tents, or, in [...] richer camps, in redwood cabins. The camps are decora[...] with wooden or stone sculptures of owls, the Grove symbol. Me[...] bers wash up in dormitory-style bathrooms and eat breakf[...] and dinner collectively in the Dining Circle, a splendid outd[...] arena with fresh wood chips covering the ground and only [...]

sky above. It never rains when the encam[...] ment is on.

During the day, idleness is encourag[...] There are few rules, the most famous one [...] ing "Weaving Spiders Come Not Here"—[...] other words, don't do business in the Gro[...] The rule is widely ignored. Another, [...]

ten rule is that everyone drink—and that yone drink all the time. This rule is strictly ered to. "His method was to seize a large e bucket, throw a hunk of ice into it, pour veral bottles of gin and a half a bottle of verth, and slosh it all around," goes one Grove pe. The traditional 7:00 a.m. gin fizzes ed in bed by camp valets set the e. Throughout the skeet-shooting, domino-playing and the museum s, right up through the "afterglows" follow each evening's entertaint, everyone is perpetually numbed loose, but a clubbish decorum pres just the same. No one throws up. y and then, though, a Bohemian down in the ferns and passes out. he sense that you are inside an acclub is heightened by all the furings that could not survive a wet on outdoors: the stuffed lion on of Jungle; the red lanterns in the s behind Dragons at night, which to the haunting atmosphere; the atings of camels, pelicans and ed women that are hung outside; soft couch in the doorway of Woof; everywhere pianos that, when the impment is over, go back to the o warehouse near the front gate. re's a feeling of both great privilege rusticity. Bohemians talk about hing it, but at a privy in the woods the river, there is a constantly wed supply of paper toilet-seat rs. And the sand at the Russian

Then the beer brewer himself came out to sing: "Mandalay," the song based on the Kipling poem. He was a goateed giant with massive shoulders and a beer gut. Rudyard Kipling, romantic colonialist and exponent of the masculine spirit, is, naturally, one of the Grove's heroes, and "Mandalay" is a triumphant white-

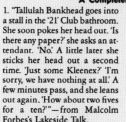

BA-DUM-BUM: THE LIGHTER SIDE OF POWER-MONGERING

A Completely Authentic 1989 Bohemian Grove Joke Book

1. "Tallulah Bankhead goes into a stall in the '21' Club bathroom. She soon pokes her head out. 'Is there any paper?' she asks an attendant. 'No.' A little later she sticks her head out a second time. 'Just some Kleenex?' 'I'm sorry, we have nothing at all.' A few minutes pass, and she leans out again. 'How about two fives for a ten?'"—from Malcolm Forbes's Lakeside Talk.

2. "My wife was talking to a friend of hers the other day who says, 'You know what they say about oysters being an aphrodisiac? It's not true.' 'How do you know that?' 'Well, we went out to dinner last night and my husband ordered a dozen oysters. Only five worked'"—Ibid.

3. A Bohemian at dinner holds up a wine bottle filled with a yellowish liquid and reads the label in puzzlement: "*Château du pissoir*"—from the Owl Hoots cartoons at the Camp Fire Circle.

4. "You're as young as the woman you feel"—from the Low Jinks theatrical performance.

5. A Bohemian cuts out a photograph of a woman's crotch from a skin magazine and carefully tapes it to the cover of *Cockpit*, a magazine for private-aircraft fanciers that's popular among many corporate members. He leaves the magazine on a table in the campground. All day Bohemians grab the magazine to look inside, where they find only pictures of leather jackets and airplanes—a Bohemian prank recounted at the Grove beach.

6. "A man stumbles home early one morning. His angry wife yanks open the door and he lurches onto the floor. Getting up, he says, 'I think I'll skip my prepared remarks and take your questions now'"—from Associated Press president Louis Boccardi's Lakeside Talk.

7. "A ten-year-old boy is fornicating with his nine-year-old sister. 'Gee, you're almost as good as Ma,' he says. 'Really?' she says. 'That's what Pa says'"—Bohemian rib-tickler told at Land's End camp.

8. "Take care when you unsheath your sword—it can pierce a young lady's…heart"—advice from one character to another in the Grove play.

9. "The gravity on Jupiter is extremely strong. It's kind of like the lady in the play with the big boobs—she has to crawl out onstage!"—from a museum talk by Wally Schirra, the former astronaut, or, as he put it, "smart-ass-tronaut."

10. Two Vassar women run into one another in New York during the Depression. Their families have suffered terrible reverses. "It's gotten so bad I've taken to the streets, I'm practicing the world's oldest profession," says one. "Oh my God," says the other. "Before I did that I'd dip into capital"—Forbes.

11. "A lot of years have been going by for me. You know, there are three things that begin to happen as the years pile up. First, you begin to forget things. [*Pause.*] I can't remember the other two"—from Ronald Reagan's Lakeside Talk. —P.W.

ISTER MICHEL ROCARD ADVICE: "DO ANYTHING YOU WANT, HIDE IN THE BUSHES—JUST DON'T LET THEM SEE YOU"

r beach is traversed by coconut-fiber mats rich figured squares cut from the carpets in "City Club," the five-story brick Bohemian ding in downtown San Francisco.

ll day long there is music in the Grove, and ight in some camps there are programs of rtainment: comics, singers, actors. Any Bohen is welcome at such events. One afternoon, instance, the Valhalla deck was crowded men drinking Valhalla's home-brewed beer listening to singers. They sang from a small e in front of a redwood on which was hung amed nineteenth-century engraving. The e was permeated by a kind of Nazi kitsch k Forest imagery, and the setting seemed Wagnerian—though the music was somes undercut by the soft drumming of ting urine off the edge of the porch, where the drinkers went one after the other. The 's railing posed a dilemma. It was set at ch level, so you had to sort of crouch.

man's-burden song. The brewer finished tearily, his arms high above his head, fists clenched: "*Take me back to Mandalay-ah.*"

Amid wild applause one man removed a heavily chewed cigar to say, "If that don't send a chill up your spine, you ain't a Bohemian."

His friend, a man in a yellow brocade vest, agreed. "He really put the balls into it."

"Yep, Big Daddy's in town."

ONE REASON FOR THE BOHEMIAN CLUB'S POOR public relations is the name it gave to the yearly opening ceremony: The Cremation of Care. The cremation is intended to put the busy men of the club at ease and banish the stress of the outside world, but it arouses critics of the encampment because they interpret it to mean that Bohemians literally don't care about the outside world. Cremation of care, they fear, means the death of caring. Demonstrations outside the Grove a few years back often centered around

"Now, you should never tell an editor anything, because they're just going to want more. I was going to the phone booth to call Susan Morrison and she was immediately upping the ante: 'Who's there? Who can you meet?' Kissinger was behind me in the telephone line at that time. Graydon insisted that I go meet Reagan. He was the one who gave me the line about 'Tell him that you named your son after him.'"

the "Resurrection of Care."

The cremation took place at the man-made lake that is the center of a lot of Grove social activity. At 9:15 a procession of priests carrying the crypt of Dull Care came out of the trees on the east side, along the Grove's chief thoroughfare, River Road. They wore bright red, blue and orange hooded robes that might have been designed for the Ku Klux Klan by Marimekko. When they reached the water, they extinguished their torches.

At this point some hamadryads and another priest or two appeared at the base of the main owl shrine, a 40-foot-tall, moss-covered statue of stone and steel at the south end of the lake, and sang songs about Care. They told of how a man's heart is divided between "reality" and "fantasy," how it is necessary to escape to another world of fellowship among men. Vaguely homosexual undertones suffused this spectacle, as they do much of ritualized life in the Grove. The main priest wore a pink-and-green satin costume, while a hamadryad appeared before a redwood in a gold spangled bodysuit dripping with rhinestones. They spoke of "fairy unguents" that would free men to pursue warm fellowship, and I was reminded of something Herman Wouk wrote about the Grove: "Men can decently love each other; they always have, but women never quite understand."

Then the crypt of Care was poled slowly down the lake by a black-robed figure in a black gondola, accompanied by a great deal of special-effects smoke. Just as the priests set out to torch the crypt, a red light appeared high in a redwood and large speakers in the forest amplified the cackling voice of Care: "Fools! When will ye learn that me ye cannot slay? Year after year ye burn me in this Grove....But when again ye turn your feet toward the marketplace, am I not waiting for you, as of old?"

With that, Care spat upon the fires, extinguishing them. The priests turned in desperation to the owl. "O thou, great symbol of all mortal wisdom, Owl of Bohemia...grant us thy counsel!"

Every year there are new wrinkles on the cremation ceremony. The big improvement this year was to project a sort of hologram onto the owl's face so that its beak seemed to move. Also, it was Walter Cronkite

IN THE END I ENTERED BY STEALTH. STUDENTS OF THE GROVE HAD WARNED T

talking. (Cronkite camps in Hill Billies along with George H.W. Bush, William F. Buckley Jr. and former astronaut and ex–Eastern Air Lines chairman Frank Borman.) Cronkite, as the owl, said that the only way Care could be cremated was to use fire from the Lamp of Fellowship before him, an "eternal" gas flame that burns day and night while the encampment is on.

That did it. Care went up in blazes. Around me the men ex-

ploded in huzzahs. Fireworks went off at the lakeside, a brass band in peppermint-striped jackets and straw boa came out of the woods playing "There'll Be a Hot Time in Old Town Tonight."

The sudden appearance of men in striped jackets sh what a bouillabaisse of traditions the Grove is. Bohemian (literature is pious on this score. It boasts that the Crematio Care ceremony derives from Druid rites, medieval Chris liturgy, the Book of Common Prayer, Shakespearean dr and nineteenth-century American lodge rites.

Early Bohemians were hungry for exaltation and grabbe to any tradition they could find to dignify their exile in the gar West. The club was founded in 1872, just three years a the transcontinental railroad was completed, by a grou newspapermen and artists who plainly felt social anx about their surroundings. Early club menus offered dollec western dishes such as "boiled striped bass au vin blanc" "café noir." The club's "men of talent" (i.e., artists and writ included writers of a populist bent: Mark Twain, Bret Ha Henry M. Stanley. Bohemian Jack London was a socialist; hemian Henry George, a radical reformer.

But the club's newspapermen were also socially ambiti aiming to chronicle California's rise in the and sciences. *Bohemian*, they agreed in their e annals, didn't mean an unwashed shirt and poe it signified London, the beau monde, men of e nence whose purses were always open to th friends. By such standards, San Francisco b nessmen surely looked crude.

Just the same, the club needed such "me use" to support their activities, and inevitably businessmen took over. Prohibition dealt a de ly blow to the club's democratic leanings by closing the cer Grove bar. Social activity became decentralized, relocate individual camps, and less egalitarian, a trend that contin during the Depression, when rich camps got even richer. M bers poured money into capital improvements for the Grove if it were the haven to which they could flee during the rev tion. (By 1925, according to one account, most of the Gro 2,800 acres had been purchased for the sum of $99,500.) dy Roosevelt had been a member. Franklin Roosevelt was and by the 1930s the Grove had become clannishly conse tive. Will Rogers is said to have been denied membership cause he once made a joke about the Grove.

The Bohemian Club's waiting list, which had first appea in the Coolidge years, grew to ridiculous lengths. I was told if a Californian is not admitted before he is 30, he can des of membership unless he achieves commercial or polit prominence. Many older men die waiting. And members

Hello Muddah, hello Fadduh: the Grove is one super-deluxe sleep-away camp for fat adolescents you won't see advertised in The New York Times Magazine.

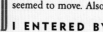

OVER THE RIVER AND THROUGH THE WOODS

A Guide to Right-Wing Fantasia

BOHEMIAN GROVE
CAMPS, FACILITIES AND ROADS
SONOMA CO., CALIFORNIA

SCALE IN FEET

0 100 200 400 600 800

SURVEYED BY W.S.W.KEW, 1956

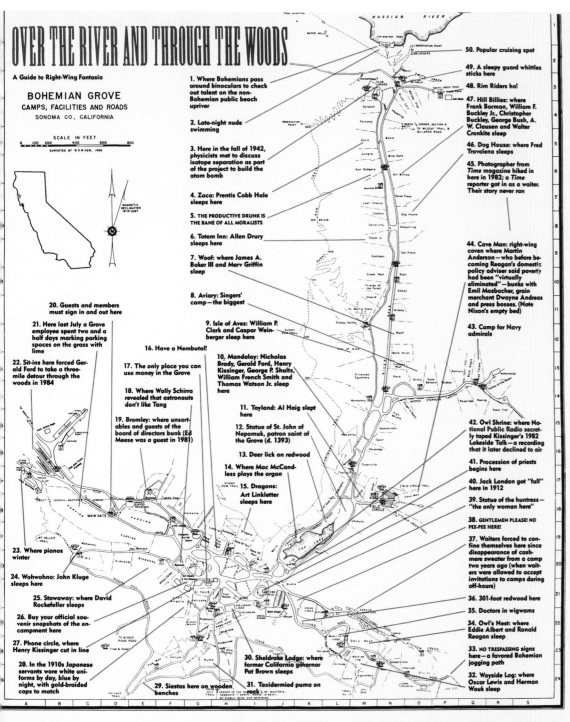

1. Where Bohemians pass around binoculars to check out talent on the non-Bohemian public beach upriver

2. Late-night nude swimming

3. Here in the fall of 1942, physicists met to discuss isotope separation as part of the project to build the atom bomb

4. Zaca: Prentis Cobb Hale sleeps here

5. THE PRODUCTIVE DRUNK IS THE BANE OF ALL MORALISTS

6. Totem Inn: Allen Drury sleeps here

7. Woof: where James A. Baker III and Merv Griffin sleep

8. Aviary: Singers' camp—the biggest

9. Isle of Aves: William P. Clark and Caspar Weinberger sleep here

10. Mandalay: Nicholas Brady, Gerald Ford, Henry Kissinger, George P. Shultz, William French Smith and Thomas Watson Jr. sleep here

11. Toyland: Al Haig slept here

12. Statue of St. John of Nepomuk, patron saint of the Grove (d. 1393)

13. Deer lick on redwood

14. Where Mac McCandless plays the organ

15. Dragons: Art Linkletter sleeps here

16. Have a Nembutal!

17. The only place you can use money in the Grove

18. Where Wally Schirra revealed that astronauts don't like Tang

19. Bromley: where unsortables and guests of the board of directors bunk (Ed Meese was a guest in 1981)

20. Guests and members must sign in and out here

21. Here last July a Grove employee spent two and a half days marking parking spaces on the grass with lime

22. Sit-ins here forced Gerald Ford to take a three-mile detour through the woods in 1984

23. Where pianos winter

24. Wohwohno: John Kluge sleeps here

25. Stowaway: where David Rockefeller sleeps

26. Buy your official souvenir snapshots of the encampment here

27. Phone circle, where Henry Kissinger cut in line

28. In the 1910s Japanese servants wore white uniforms by day, blue by night, with gold-braided caps to match

29. Siestas here on wooden benches

30. Sheldrake Lodge: where former California governor Pat Brown sleeps

31. Taxidermied puma on rock

32. Wayside Log: where Oscar Lewis and Herman Wouk sleep

33. NO TRESPASSING signs here—a favored Bohemian jogging path

34. Owl's Nest: where Eddie Albert and Ronald Reagan sleep

35. Doctors in wigwams

36. 301-foot redwood here

37. Waiters forced to confine themselves here since disappearance of cashmere sweater from a camp two years ago (when waiters were allowed to accept invitations to camps during off-hours)

38. GENTLEMEN PLEASE! NO PEE-PEE HERE!

39. Statue of the huntress—"the only woman here"

40. Jack London got "full" here in 1912

41. Procession of priests begins here

42. Owl Shrine: where National Public Radio secretly taped Kissinger's 1982 Lakeside Talk—a recording that it later declined to air

43. Camp for Navy admirals

44. Cave Man: right-wing coven where Martin Anderson—who before becoming Reagan's domestic policy adviser said poverty had been "virtually eliminated"—bunks with Emil Mosbacher, grain merchant Dwayne Andreas and press bosses. (Note Nixon's empty bed)

45. Photographer from Time magazine hiked in here in 1982; a Time reporter got in as a waiter. Their story never ran

46. Dog House: where Fred Travalena sleeps

47. Hill Billies: where Frank Borman, William F. Buckley Jr., Christopher Buckley, George Bush, A. W. Clausen and Walter Cronkite sleep

48. Rim Riders ho!

49. A sleepy guard whittles sticks here

50. Popular cruising spot

...mes dear. The initiation fee for regular voting membership is said to be $8,500, and dues are ...t at more than $2,000 a year. Because the reg-...r members require entertainment, "men of ...lent" pay greatly reduced fees. On Wouk's ...ptance, for instance, he was put to work writ-... a history of the club.

...The encampment became controversial in the early Reagan years when reporters, still suffering the hangover of Carter populism, questioned club executive appointees about the club's sexist practices.

The Grove's keenest adversary is Mary Moore, who lives in a countercultural shantytown in nearby Occidental. Moore was the 1953 San Luis Obispo County Fiesta queen, but by 1980 she

I WAS ABLE

TO ENJOY MOST PLEASURES OF THE GROVE— THE SONGS, ELABORATE DRAG SHOWS, PREBREAKFAST GIN FIZZES AND ROUND-THE-CLOCK "NEMBU-TALS"—THOUGH

had become, she says, a "woman-identified woman," and the Grove's thunderous maleness and what she calls its "closedness" disturbed her. Of course, just about anybody could hate the Grove. With its dense concentration of extravagant war- and money-mongers, it's an easy object of protest, and 72 left-wing groups eventually joined Moore to form the Bohemian Grove Action Network.

For a while, in the early 1980s, Moore and BGAN thought they might actually liberate the redwoods. In 1984 folksinging demonstrators tried to quarantine the Bohemians inside the Grove because they were so dangerous to the outside world. Fifty people were arrested. Summer after summer BGAN stoked Grove conspiracy theories by getting hold of the guest list. In 1981, for instance, Dan Rostenkowski, Ed Meese and former president of CBS News Van Gordon Sauter attended (Sauter as the guest of former California governor Edmund "Pat" Brown—Jerry's father). Meese, by the way, is about the only major Reaganite who didn't end up as a member.

In its obsession with the encampment, BGAN has unwittingly taken on Bohemian

Campfire of the vanities: recumbent Bohemians like to sleep it off ⸱ the redwood benches of the central Camp Fire Circle.

and limos around to get to the gate had disa⸱ peared. The Grove was still there.

When I got to Monte Rio, only a couple signs of protest remained. Moore's answerin⸱ machine message asking friends not to call h⸱ at her vintage-clothing store in the town of S⸱ bastopol included a denunciation of the Crem⸱ tion of Care. And inside the Grove the guest l⸱ was well guarded. It was posted in a locked gla⸱ case during the day, and was removed eve⸱

I DIDN'T SWIM NAKED WITH LIKE-MINDED BOHEMIANS IN THE RUSSIAN RIVER AT NIGH⸱

traits, becoming a kooky mirror image of the Grove. It wove spidery webs of string across Bohemian Avenue to block the way in. It urged its followers to form "Boho Clubs" to study members so they could be "held accountable by the American People" for participating "in the maintenance of the process of plutocratic patriarchy which threatens the planet Earth with omnicide from the nuclear menace." When BGAN resurrected Care, it chanted its own hymns:

On a day much like this five score years ago
The first hideous fire was lit in Monte Rio
And sweet Care was banished from this lovely land,
And Bohemians revelled upon their shifting sand.

But by 1985 BGAN's energies were ebbing. The media's anti-elitist mood, never all that ferocious, was spent. The reporters that Mary Moore had helped spirit into the Grove for hours at a time had come out with vague,

Kawabunga! Bohemians in skivvies hear a speech, 1950

watered-down versions of what went on, or their news organizations had suppressed the accounts. By 1988 the gauntlet of hippies and solarheads and woman-identified women whom the Bohemians had been forced to maneuver their Jags

night. This was about the highest security I sa⸱ inside.

"I'M ADMITTING FOR THE FIRST TIME IN M⸱ life having no willpower," a man was saying ⸱ his wife on one of the public phones. He look⸱ bewildered and hung over, and I figured Boh⸱ mians were warmly and mysteriously saying ⸱ him what they were saying to me: "I can tell th⸱ is your first Grove."

It was just past noon on Sunday, the mid⸱ weekend at the encampment—the busie⸱ weekend, with attendance approaching 2,2⸱ men. The most dignified had arrived. On t⸱ River Road you heard some small business ta⸱

"David Jr.'s going into the family busine⸱ now."

"He's got a scruffy beard."

"Yes, he looks radical, but he doesn't talk li⸱ one."

"Abby, now, she's the one who raised her fist⸱ graduation? Had a red fist painted on the ba⸱ of her gown."

Of course. The Rockefellers.

"Where was that? Radcliffe?"

"You know, they've got a lot of liberal facul⸱

"They're always on the periphery ⸱ radicalism."

"My son was in Santiago, and David sent h⸱ letters of introduction to seven leading bank⸱ in seven countries."

It was in the phone circle that Henry Kissinger alienated some brother Bohemians on the middle weekend. Wandering into the clearing, he announced to the air, "I have to make two phone calls."

At lakeside the grass was crowded for the day's talk. Under the green parasol stood General John Chain, commander of the Strategic Air Command, who spoke of the country's desperate need for the Stealth B-2 bomber. "I am a warrior and that is how I come to you today," he said. "I need the B-2."

The important men come out for the Lakeside Talks, and each speaker seems to assume that his audience can actually do something about the issues raised—which, of course, it can. On the first weekend, for instance, Associated Press president Louis Boccardi, addressing his listeners as men of "power and rank," gave them more details than he said he was willing to give his readers about the plight of Terry Anderson, the Middle East correspondent held hostage since 1985. It was a transparent plea for help.

Other Lakeside speaking is more indulgent. Here Nicholas Brady examined the history of the Jockey Club. Here William Buckley described how he had sat at his desk and cried upon learning of Whittaker Chambers's death. Here Henry Kissinger made a bathroom pun on the name of his friend Lee Kuan Yew, who was in attendance—the sort of joke that the people of Singapore, whom Lee rules with such authoritarian zeal, are not free to make in public. The speeches are presented as off-the-record—one of the absurdities of Grove life, given that they are open to several thousand people. As the Soviet Sagdeyev said in his speech, "There is no *glasnost* here."

After General Chain's talk, the usual quiet business chatter went on. "Your secretary, I got to tell you, she's 110 percent," a dark-haired man said to an older fellow.

Three other men discussed a friend of theirs who had [left] early that morning for New York. One of them seemed [puz]zled—the friend wasn't the sort to get going at 7:45, he no[ted].

"It was a free ride," the other friend explained. "Bill Sim[on] had room on his plane."

"Simon doesn't know he doesn't have money."

They all got a big kick out of this. Simon was Treasury se[cre]tary in the Ford administration and today is a major savi[ngs] and loan conglomerateur, active in takeovers. It would se[em] that this year's encampment was useful to him. Two weeks la[ter] he plunged into Sir James Goldsmith's battle to take [over] B.A.T. Industries PLC of England, a deal that could give Sim[on] a toehold in Europe. He was surely influenced by Pr[ime] Minister Rocard's Saturday-aftern[oon] Lakeside Talk, in which he dangled [the] most sanguine business expectati[ons] of the new European order [see "[The] Case of the Disappearing Prime M[in]ister."]

In 1982 reporters followed Germ[an] chancellor Helmut Schmidt to [the] Grove gates, and the front page of [the] *Christian Science Monitor* termed [the] Grove "the West's hidden summit." T[his] year Rocard's visit went unreported[. A] week after the encampment, a Wa[sh]ington correspondent for a Fre[nch] paper insisted to me that the last ti[me] the prime minister had visited the [U.S.] was a year and a half ago.

"One of the contemporary my[ths] about the Bohemian Club is that it [is a] gathering and decision-making p[lace] for national and international 'po[wer] brokers,'" the club's then-president s[aid] in 1980. In fact, the encampment [has] always had political significan[ce.] Richard Nixon, Barry Goldwater [and] Nelson Rockefeller all stopped in [as] they geared up for their respec[tive] presidential campaigns. Politicians say there is no place [like] the Grove to help get a campaign rolling. No wonder this ye[ar's] guest list included the two biggest congressional bagmen [of] recent years: Representative Tony Coelho, former chairma[n of] the House Democratic Campaign Committee, and Represen[ta]tive Guy Vander Jagt, his counterpart on the Republican c[om]mittee. These men were interested in something more t[han] pseudo-Druidic rituals.

The club says it serves as a "refuge" from the strivings of [the] marketplace, and though it's true that actual deal-makin[g is] discouraged, I heard business being done on all sides. The [pay] phones were a hub of activity. "Owner slash developer," a m[an] dictated to his secretary one morning. On the blackboard n[ear] the bootblack stand there were phone messages for corpor[ate] raider Henry Kravis and Bloomingdale's chairman Ma[rvin] Traub. That day as I sat writing a letter (actually my notes) [in] the Civic Center, a one-story building in which various ame[ni]ties (Grove stationery, laundry facilities) are available to Bo[he-]

THE CASE OF THE DISAPPEARING PRIME MINISTER

What France's Michel Rocard Said on His (Secret) Summer Vacation

The people and press of France thought their crafty prime minister, Michel Rocard, was on his boat off the coast of Brittany during the last two weeks of July this year. But thanks to an invitation from his pal Henry Kissinger, Rocard had been smuggled into the Grove—and not just to party with the guys, but also to talk openly and honestly before his fellow campers. (Whether highly placed aides arranged pillows under the covers of his bed back home is unclear.) His speech has, to date, gone entirely unreported.

Prime Minister Rocard began his July 22 talk at the Grove lakeside with a clumsy miscalculation—"There is no press here"—but from that point on it was all Gallic charm. Hundreds of miles from AP stringers and *Le Monde* reporters, he whispered secrets, he punctured allies. The speech was remarkable not so much for its content as for its candor and tone.

Of the Europeans' goal to eliminate trade barriers in 1992, Rocard confided dramatically, "We are building a nation. The world is rich with multilingual nations." Within ten years, he said, Europe will have a unified currency. Only Margaret Thatcher will resist, but "as always," he added, "she will get on the train when it is leaving the station."

In Europe, Rocard has a reputation as a right-wing socialist. Among the Bohemians he was chummy. The Americans and the French, he said, have a special alliance in leading the way to disarmament, while Thatcher is "defiant"; she cannot be counted on. Rocard also considered the Germans hopeless. They suffer what the prime minister called "the German disease"—fear of fighting on their own soil, making them partial to nuclear arms.

To the subject of business matters, Rocard brought a Bohemian zeal. Government-subsidized farming, he said, is "hypocrisy!" The farms aren't efficient but governments back

Michel Rocard

them because of the political consequences of opposing them. "Ridiculous," he said, then tilted forward in a delightful gesture of conspiracy. "Let me tell you a secret. We too are fed up with subsidizing farmers. We too want to get out of this silly system." The only way out, he whispered, is a private, "gentleman's agreement" involving agricultural trade. At lakeside there was an approving murmur. For the gentleman's agreement is the stock-in-trade of Bohemia.   —*P.W.*

ans, I overheard a large fellow in cranberry-
lored shorts on the phone, bragging to some-
e back at the office. "I got slightly
ebriated—slightly!—*heavily* inebriated with
e president of the Portland Opera last night.
aid we might have a deal for him. They're go-
g to have Pavarotti there in November. I said
en we got back we'd talk about it."

It was in the phone circle that Henry Kis-
nger alienated some brother Bohemians on
e middle weekend. Wandering into the clear-
g, he announced to the air, "I have to make
o phone calls." A man finished his call, and
issinger, ignoring a half-dozen men in line,
ok the booth and proceeded to retail to a
man, evidently his wife, the Russian speak-
s joke about the KGB's interrogation of a CIA
ent.(The CIA agent denies involvement first in
alamitous ship disaster, then in Chernobyl."So
what are you responsible
for?" the KGB asks him.

A HELICOPTER

FROM A NETWORK NEWSMAGAZINE CIRCLED FRANTICALLY FAR ABOVE

our agricultural policy.") The woman on the
e evidently objected to the joke, for Kissinger
id, revealing a dovish streak, "Maybe the
GB *did* write it, but it is not a sign of strength."
Kissinger's crusty performance was not ap-
eciated by the men he'd cut in front of in line.
ne Bohemian, a patrician fellow with silver
ir, wheeled in rage, saying, "I'll be god-
mned." Cutting in line is distinctly un-
hemian behavior.

Everywhere you hear what is Bohemian and
at isn't Bohemian. One night I wandered
o Fore Peak camp and got a lecture from a
an named Hugh about Bohemian values as
ey concerned Fore Peak's famous drink, a
ixture of hot rum and hot chocolate. Many
ars ago a doctor called it a Nembutal, and the
me stuck, so much so that one Fore Peak
mper wears a stethoscope and a white lab
at with DR. NEMBUTAL stitched on it. Hugh
id that an old college friend came to stay in
hemia and took over the mixing of the
nks. He persisted in putting in too much
m to see how many guys would pass out.
"Hey, knock it off, this is Bohemia," Hugh had
to tell him. He never in-
vited the chum back.

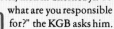

A tenet of Grove life
is noncompetitive egali-
tarianism: all men are
equal here. But in fact,
class and status differ-
ences among camps are
pronounced. Just as you
have to be sponsored for
membership, you have to

be sponsored for a camp. The screens get pretty
fine. Nonetheless, the ideal of equality is com-
forting. Among other things, it permits alcoholic failures to feel equal for a few days with
their workaholic cousins. Since everyone is supposed to kick back and forget work, it's the
fuckup's annual revenge. At Sundodgers there is
a motto on the mantel: THE PRODUCTIVE
DRUNK IS THE BANE OF ALL MORALISTS. It tells
the productive they can drink, it tells the
drunks they're productive.

A HIGH POINT OF THE MIDDLE WEEKEND WAS
the performance of The Low Jinks, the Grove's
elaborate musical-comedy show. Over the years
the Jinks has become the leading entertainment
at the encampment, surpassing the mannered
and ponderous Grove Play, which is performed
the next weekend. The Jinks is vigorously low-
brow. It takes place on the Field Circle stage,
which is wedged in between two camps, Pink
Onion (notable for its pink sheets) and Cave
Man (notable for big-deal right-wingers and a
plaque commemorating Herbert Hoover).

The Field Circle seats are steeply canted; sitting in one feels like being inside a megaphone.
The mood was American and bellicose. For a
good half hour the band warmed up the audience, playing the fight songs of many California
colleges and the armed services and culminat-
ing with "The Star-Spangled Banner." Individual melted into group, but what a group:
George Shultz was seated below me, and word
in the camp was that a year and $75,000 or so
had been spent for a production that would be
seen just once, just by them. I felt like a mem-

THE DARKENED

FOREST, MY

NEIGHBOR

SUGGESTED,

"SHOOT THE

FUCKER DOWN"

*That's the
way it is:
the 40-foot-
tall Great
Owl of
Bohemia
lip-synched
Walter
Cronkite in
this year's
Cremation
of Care.*

THE MAN

PEELED OFF THE MASK TO REVEAL THAT HE REALLY WAS KISSINGER, AND HE SAID IN HIS FAMILIAR GRAVELLY ACCENT, "I AM

ber of the greatest nation ever, the greatest gender ever, the greatest generation ever. At such times—at many such times, among strong leaders, deep in the forest—the Grove takes on a certain Germanic *übermenschlich* feeling.

This year's Jinks was called *Sculpture Culture*, and the humor was not just lame but circa-1950s college follies lame. Rex Greed, an effeminate gallery owner who sells toilets ("a counterpoint of mass and void"), tries to convince artist Jason Jones Jr. that his future lies in sculptures composed of garbage. When a character describes modern art as "the talentless being sold by the unprincipled to the bewildered," the crowd's roar seemed to contain the grief of hundreds of businessmen who have shelled out

Calling Alfred E. Neuman: the ultrasophisticated poster for this year's Low Jinks revue, which cost about $75,000 to produce once

his capital"). One day in the Gr[ove] I tipped a camp valet and he offe[red] some unsolicited informati[on.] Hookers came to a certain bar [in] Monte Rio at ten each night, [he] said. It was the same bar-lod[ge/] motel where the local police had [ar]rested a man for pandering a [few] years back. The bust came right [af]ter a Lakeside Talk by Willi[am] Webster, then the FBI direc[tor,] and the timing suggested it was his doing. [But] the charges were dropped, and the man is [re]membered fondly in the Grove. A Bohemi[an] I overheard on the beach one day said that [the] man's genius had been in keeping vacation[ing] families in the motel ignorant of the other bu[si]ness going on there. "Now, that's good mana[ge]ment," he declared, capturing the robust laiss[ez]

HERE BECAUSE I HAVE ALWAYS BEEN CONVINCED THAT THE LOW JINX IS THE ULTIMATE APHRODISIAC

for headquarters art they do not understand.

The girls were all played by men, and every time they appeared—their chunky legs and flashed buttocks highly visible through tight support hose—the crowd went wild. After one character called the secretaries in the show "heifers," the audience couldn't resist breaking into "moos" every time they came back onstage. But the biggest crowd pleaser was Bubbles Boobenheim, a showgirl turned patroness who rubbed her prosthetic behind against the elevator doors at stage left. The doors were used repeatedly for wrong-floor gags. For example, at one point a Little League team came out that included Bohemians Bob Lurie and Peter O'Malley, the real-life owners of the San Francisco Giants and the Los Angeles Dodgers, in uniform.

When one character, a PR executive, expressed a desire to make his mistress an honest woman, she objected, reminding him of an old Bohemian saying: "If it floats or flies or fools around, don't buy it, rent it." The scene brought to mind the reputation for prostitution that hangs around the Grove. From time to time law enforcement has tried unsuccessfully to bring cases against local procurers, and the Bohemian Grove Action Network circulates testimonials by a former paid mistress of a club member ("I only saw him troubled by one thing," she wrote. "He bought [an apple juice concern] for one million dollars and…he was fearful he would have to dip into

The iconography of the Grove

faire spirit of the Grove.

The sexism and racism of the Jinks were o[f a] peculiar sort. Black jokes are out because the[re] are a handful of black members—though o[ne] day near the Civic Center I did hear a group [of] old-timers trying to imitate Jesse Jackson. As [for] Jews, old membership lists suggest that th[ey] have taken a very small part in the club for [de]cades. That leaves women and Hispanics as t[he] gets for jokes—such as the one about Bubble[s's] protégé Raoul, who painted Puerto Rican fla[gs] on the backs of cockroaches.

The Jinks jokes about women were straig[ht] out of an old jokebook. "My father said if y[ou] have a choice between an angry woman an[d a] rabid dog, take the dog," Jason Jones Jr. sa[id.] "It's already got a fur coat and the license i[s a] lot cheaper." And Rex Greed said, "The o[nly] difference between rape and rapture is sal[es]manship." The sensibility of the Grove recalls [an] era before the surgeon general's report on smo[k]ing, before the death of God and duty, befo[re] the advent of cholesterol and Sandra D[ay] O'Connor (whose husband, John, bunks in Pe[li]cans). The mood is reminiscent of high scho[ol.] There's no end to the pee-pee and penis jok[es,] suggesting that these men, advanced in so ma[ny] other ways, were emotionally arrested someti[me] during adolescence.

The most striking prop in The Low Jinks w[as] a sculpture of a female torso whose breasts a[nd] buttocks had both been attached to the front, [an] improvement that looked vaguely hostile. A[nd] all the talk about male fellowship often soun[ded] just like a college freshman's version of [NO] GUЯLS ALLOWED, an institutional escape fro[m] women, from their demands, aggressions a[nd] vapors. At certain times of year women a[re] owed to enter the Grove — but only under "chaperonage," according to a 1980 statement by the club president. *Chaperon*—for adult women. It's another Bohemian wee-wee word, mething you haven't heard since you were 14.

The club's nemesis here is the state of California, which eps chipping away at the Grove's maleness, lately threatening take away its liquor license and its tax-exempt status because discriminates against women. The state has established a achhead at the Grove's front office, a hundred yards outside main gate, where, under legal pressure, seven women have en employed. Inside the Grove there is a feeling of mournful vitability about the day women will join encampment. Bohemians talk about w much it will muddle things. "It would ew everything up, excuse the pun," said old-timer sipping a drink by the river. here'd be a lot more preening and peacock- than there already is," a big gay Bohe- an told me. Members have cited their vilege to walk about in "various states of dress." And former California governor Brown has said publicly, many times, t the presence of women would keep Bo- mians from enjoying their hallowed free- m to pee.

The peeing is ceaseless and more than a le exhibitionistic. Everyone talks about it. hemian reminiscences describe such bi- re initiation rites as escorting new mem- rs to the redwood at which one of the nders "did his morning ablutions." The vl Hoots, poster-size cartoons tacked up h day near the Camp Fire Circle, are filled h pissing pictures. One featured a spuri- s design for a commemorative stamp of b member U.S. Postmaster General An- ny Frank relieving himself on a redwood. Are you going to show it?" I heard a 50-ish hemian, the "captain" of Pow Wow camp, out one day as young George went to pee off the deck.

'Most of it. At least six inches."

'Now, don't be modest, George."

A screen door creaked on a little house farther up the hill, d a Bohemian named Richard poked his head out, emerging m his siesta.

'Do it counterclockwise, Dickie, that's best," the captain led out.

'Oh, I've had my hand off it for two minutes now," Rich- ard protested.

and some woman-identified- the world's only establishment drag queens

"There's a lot of wasted time."

This dick-fussing often manifests itself as that starkest of male nostal- gias, the hankering for the punctual erections of boyhood. According to 1979 figures, the average age of Bohemians is 55. Impotence is on many people's minds. The poster outside Monkey Block advertising this year's Grove play, *Pompeii*, fea-

Anti-Bohemian activist Mary Moore, a woman-identified-woman dedicated to liberating the redwoods from man-identified-men . . .

tured a gigantic erection under a toga. The set for the play in- cluded a wall inscription in Latin meaning "Always hard." One day I was at the Grove beach when a Bohemian discovered that a friend's sunscreen was supposed to impede aging.

"You got it too late."

The owner of the lotion sighed. "Well, I should give up put- ting it on my face and arms and spray it on my prick — see if that'll do any good."

Bohemian discourse is full of oblique organ worship as well. There's all the redwood talk. Bohemians rhapsodize endlessly about towering shafts and the inspiration they give men. I LOVE THIS TREE AS THE MOST SOUND, UPRIGHT AND STATELY REDWOOD IN THE GROVE. LET MY FRIENDS REMEMBER ME BY IT WHEN I AM GONE, reads a plaque left by a Bohemian at the base of a 301-footer.

Other references aren't so subtle. Late in The Low Jinks the elevator doors opened and a man came out wearing a rubber Henry Kissinger mask. He had a dumpy body a lot like Kissinger's. A "heifer" asked him why he was there. The man peeled off the mask to reveal that he really was Kissinger, and he said in his familiar gravelly accent, "I am here because I have always been con- vinced that The Low Jinks is the ultimate aphrodisiac."

THE ENCAMPMENT GOT EVEN LOOSER AS the third and last weekend approached. The fairy unguents were wearing off; after two weeks the place stopped looking so magical and began to seem as ordinary as a tree- house. The nonfamous hard-core Bohemians were more in evidence now, men who wore owls in various forms — owl belt buckles, brass owl bolo ties, denim shirts embroi- dered with owls. Wooziness was pervasive. At his Lakeside Talk, Malcolm Forbes said that Khrushchev knows the Soviets "are in over their heads," and even as the name Gorbachev was murmured throughout the audience, Forbes rambled on, dotty and heedless, 25 years out-of-date.

At Faraway a guy beckoned me into the camp to enjoy "a little orange juice." It tasted like lighter fluid sprinkled with mint flakes.

"What's in this?"

"Oh, just a little orange juice," the host repeated, smiling.

"What do you call this?" I asked another Farawayer.

"I call it dangerous," he said and told of how a dropped cigar had once ignited a batch.

The men of Faraway had captured the rearranged-woman's- torso sculpture from The Low Jinks and now displayed it against a wall, having wedged a fern leaf in "her" crack. Mean- while, the tacked-up Owl Hoots drawings dubbed the sculp- ture the "statue of Piece" and pictured a Bohemian comment- ing that she would be "fun to dance with." Several of the Hoots jokes were at the expense of the homeless. One cartoon had a camper at Bromley turning away a filthy guy with a bag of cans.

ALL PLAY AND NO WORK

Even Back in the Real World, One Former President Kicks Back and Relaxes

Nicholas Brady missed putting the finishing touches on Mexico's new debt-reduction plan. French prime minister Michel Rocard skipped out on a big post-Bastille-bicentennial mess in Paris. Malcolm Forbes missed out on some of the superexciting buzz about *Egg*, his odd new life-style magazine. Henry Kravis was away while his former partner Jerome Kohlberg prepared to sue him for breach of contract. What did Ronald Reagan miss while he was wandering the northern California woods with tipsy, overweight guys in lederhosen? SPY obtained a copy of the former president's schedule for one day this year, complete with doodles. His routine, as we suspected, is every bit as hectic and momentous as it was when he put in his standard 11:00-to-3:00 days in the Oval Office.

❶ Reagan works in a luxurious top-floor suite in the Century City office tower that was taken over by German terrorists in *Die Hard*. Maintenance man Horatio Rameriz has taken it upon himself to roll out a blue carpet for his building's most famous tenant to walk on as he travels to and from his limousine each day. "He's a big fan of the former president," explains Reagan spokesman Mark Weinberg. "Horatio paid for the carpet, and he cares for it."

❷ The former president familiarizes himself with the day's script.

❸ Yep, the pen works.

❹ Having completed and crossed off each laborious duty in his hectic morning schedule, Reagan turns his attention to lunch.

❺ If he's not napping now, you're

not holding a magazine.

❻ Given that the Reagans' wedding anniversary is coming up on March 4, it would seem to be a valiant effort to figure out exactly how many years it's been, anyway. Unfortunately, since the marriage took place in 1952, the answer Reagan comes up with is wrong.

❼ Ralph Bookman, Reagan's allergist—the man who administers, as the former president puts it, "my sneeze shots."

❽ Beverly Hills barber Harry Drucker, who says he has been cutting Reagan's hair exactly the same way for nearly half a century, sees him at least twice a month. He describes the former president's coiffure as "a traditional haircut, a conservative haircut. It isn't," he points out helpfully, "a hippie-type haircut."
— *Paul Slansky*

THE SCHEDULE OF
PRESIDENT RONALD REAGAN

Tuesday, February 28, 1989

Time	Activity	Location
9:45 am	Depart for Office	Residence
9:55 am	Arrive at Office ❶	Fox Plaza
10:00 am (30 min)	Staff Time ❷	Office
10:30 am (5 min)	Taping for Robert Schuller's 1,000th Broadcast	Conference Room
11:00 am (10 min)	Phone Call to Bruce Levine	Office
11:10 am (50 min)	Personal Time	Office
12:00 m (60 min)	Lunch ❹	Office
1:00 pm (1 hr)	Personal Time ❺	Office
2:00 pm	Depart for Appointment with Dr. Bookman	Fox Plaza
2:15 pm (5 min)	Appointment with Dr. Bookman ❼	Dr. Bookman's Office
2:20 pm	Depart for haircut at Drucker's Barber Shop	Dr. Bookman's Office
2:30 pm (30 min)	Haircut ❽	Drucker's Barber Shop
3:00 pm	Depart for Residence	Drucker's Barber Shop
3:10 pm	Arrive Residence	Residence

REVISED
02/27/89
3:30 pm

"This is for the campless, not the homeless," he was saying.

The jokes fit right into the Grove's Ayn Rand R&R mood. "My grandmother always said, 'You can find sympathy in the dictionary,'" a guy with a cigar said, walking on the River Road. I'd made it in that day for breakfast at the Dining Circle, the most lavish meal of the Bohemian day, an experience redolent of moneyed western ease. The rough wooden tables were piled with perfect fruit. As I sat down a great glistening arc of melon was slid before me. Today they were offering Alaskan cod, sautéed lamb kidneys, eggs, French toast, bacon, sausages. The encampment's rules about dealing with waiters reinforce the heartless but egalitarian values of the Grove. Tipping the help is strictly forbidden, but so is reprimanding them. It's easy to imagine that many early Bohemians started out as laborers and had to remind more aristocratic visitors that social mobility was a cherished ideal. In the Grove's Club Med–like plan, the meals are covered in the fee for the encampment, which, judging from schedules I'd seen from two years back, ran about $850 on top of annual dues.

A waiter in a red jacket dropped an uneaten chunk of the bright red cod into a waste bin, and the Bohemians at my table talked about presidents.

It looked as though Richard Nixon would once again not show. One old-timer said that Nixon was feuding with the board of directors. He was waiting to be asked to give a Lakeside Talk, but the club wasn't going to invite

The dining circle: drinks and sautéed lamb kidneys all around!

him until he had shown them the respect of visiting Cave M[...] for a weekend or so. In my informant's opinion, there was b[...] blood; Nixon's resignation 15 years ago had offended the clu[...] honor—it had been so un-Bohemian. The feud was unf[...] tunate because Nixon and the club went back a long way. [...] 1953, when he was vice president, Nixon led a ceremo[...] honoring Herbert Hoover's 40th year as a Bohemian. It to[...] place at the Waldorf-Astoria, in a room piled with redwo[...] bark and branches shipped to Manhattan from the Grove. [...] 1971, when the press corps forced him to cancel his speech [...] the Grove, President Nixon had wired the club to say, "Anyo[...] can be president of the United States, but few have any hope [...] becoming president of the Bohemian Club."

Meanwhile, the Bohemians' new favorite son had arrived [...] camp the night before. One of the waiters had heard who[...] house piano music coming from Owl's Nest, and he sa[...] Ronald Reagan liked that kind of music. Rumor had it th[...] Reagan was going to give the next day's Lakeside Talk. Sor[...] said there were Secret Service men guarding the roads and t[...] perimeter. They'd built special platforms in the trees for m[...] with binoculars. I didn't want to disagree. On hikes I'd take[...] my impression had been that the on[...] people patrolling the ten miles [...] Grove perimeter were a guy at th[...] Guard House on Smith Creek Roa[...] who spent a lot of time whittling [...] walking stick and ancient Bohemia[...] taking the daily 10:00 a.m. ope[...]

backed bus tour. Rim rides, the tours were called. Two of the buses bore vanity license plates commemorating the '89 presidential inauguration—they had the words KINDER and GENTLER stamped on them.

In the afternoon I walked up Kitchen Hill Road to Owl's Nest. I wanted to visit the former president. Owl's Nest is sort of an old-Hollywood-corporatist camp. Eddie Albert is here, and United Technologies chieftain Harry Gray, who this year had brought along Union Carbide boss Robert D. Kennedy. The camp has a false outer door and two overlapping walls that form an S-shaped entry. Inside, a plump Secret Service guy in a Members Only jacket sat near a giant wooden owl. There were owl figures everywhere, notably a silver owl ice bucket on the bar whose head tilted off cleverly.

I walked over to the Secret Service guy and asked if it was okay to meet the president. He said Reagan would love it and motioned with an open hand toward the deck.

Reagan was mixing it up with a bunch of old-timers a few feet away. The first thing I noticed was that he had finally let his hair go gray. Also, he's not as tall as he looked in office. He wore western gear all the way, a gray-blue checked western shirt, a white braided western belt, cowboy boots and, in his left breast pocket, an Owl's Nest pin with an owl on it. The getup stood out because it was so fastidious among men who had let themselves go.

We shook hands firmly (his: small, bony) and chatted. Even one-on-one he has that habit of smiling and cocking his head and raising an eyebrow to encourage you. He projects an automatic, almost druggy congeniality. I worked hard to respond in kind (I invented an infant son named Ronald Wilson Weiss). We talked about his guest days at the Grove, before he became a member in 1975 (two months after he lost the California governorship, a week after George Shultz joined). I asked him whether it was true that it was at the

this year's surprise speaker: the former president

ground, they'd announced the next day's Lake-side Talk. The mystery was over. COMMENTS BY RONALD WILSON REAGAN, said placards on the wooden signboards. By the time the talk was over, the posters had all been lifted by souvenir-seeking Bohemians.

AS DINNER BEGAN THAT NIGHT, PEOPLE WERE already sitting down on the redwood benches at the main stage for the Grove play (despite the poster, a humorless enactment of the destruction of Pompeii). Everything felt peaceful and sweet, like death, the good things they say about it: the end to striving, the sunlight-dappled heavenliness. Music sounded softly. A bagpiper walked in the woods by himself squeezing out a melancholy song, a brass band played "Sweet Georgia Brown" in Cliffdwellers, and in Band camp a young guitarist and an old pianist experimented with the Isley Brothers' "It's Your Thing."

Nearby, a young member of the cast dressed as a woman pulled apart purplish gossamer robes to pee. The popular redwoods between the Dining and Camp Fire Circles now reeked of urine and wore what looked to be a permanent skirt of wet, blackened soil. For a while I thought the bar of salt bracketed on one tree by the lake was an experimental effort to neutralize uric acids before they hit the roots. It turned out to be only a deer lick.

Down by the lake I saw three men lying on the ground, talking. When they got up to go to dinner, one hugged another around the middle from behind and trudged up the bank with him that way, laughing.

"Honey, I lost my ring and I want to sell the house," the third one said, mocking a homecoming speech.

At dinner I sat across from a young broker who shared his wine with me and complained about his girlfriend. The meal (tournedos of beef) was festive and communal. The long ta-

Bohemians like their women stripped down: note Romany camp's headless, shirtless, legless lady in bronze.

AIDS HAS PUT A DAMPER ON THE GROVE'S RIVER ROAD

Grove in 1967 that he, then the new governor, had assured Nixon that he wouldn't challenge him outright for the Republican nomination in 1968.

Reagan didn't get the question the first time around. He pitched himself forward in his seat with a puzzled look, still trying to be genial. I repeated myself, and he said, "Yes, yes, that's true," in the famous furry voice. Then an old friend came up and snagged his attention.

By the time I got back into the central camp-

bles are lit by gas pipes that spring from the ears of wooden owl silhouettes three feet above the table, a half dozen of these per table. Wine gets passed around (though members must sign for the bottles on a chit). Old friends move among the tables, kissing one another, and a ruddy Bohemian gets up on a bench and, as his friends cheer him on, removes his cap and opens his mouth to sing. Great intimacy is achieved in song.

The physical aspect of Bohemian male bond-

PICKUP SCENE, BUT A MAN ON HIS OWN OFTEN GETS INVITED BACK TO CAMPS BY BROTHER BOHEMIANS

ing can't be overlooked. Even 100-year-old Grove annals have a homoerotic quality, with references to "slender, young Bohemians, clad in economical bathing suits." Nudity was more common then. Today AIDS has put a damper on the Grove's River Road pickup scene, which Herb Caen used to write about in his *San Francisco Chronicle* gossip column. Just the same, a man on his own often gets invited back to camps by gay Bohemians. The weirdest approach I experienced came from a tall redhead in western wear, a fourth-generation Californian. He wandered up with a beer in his hand as I sat reading on a bench and, pausing for emphasis, pronounced, "In the beginning the Lord created—cunts."

make the two-year congressman's term four years, to reduce the number of elections that we have, because I think that's one of the reasons that only about 53 percent of the people vote. We're just overdoing it. There's a kind of emotional experience with an election year, that between state elections, local elections—and besides, with a two-year term, a congressman gets elected and the next day he starts campaigning for the next election."

I wanted to ask Reagan about efforts to desegregate the club. It's only a matter of time before the club gets sued under either California's civil-rights act or San Francisco's civil-rights ordinance, both of which bar sex discrimination in business establishments. The Bohemians will be hard-pressed to prove that they are a purely private club that falls outside the legal definition of a business, when clearly so many members participate for business-related reasons. Some day the walls will fall, though it's hard to see why any woman would want to join a crowd of old Republicans chewing

WHEN RONALD REAGAN CAME TO THE GREEN

"I GOT TO TAKE
A S E C O N D
T O D O S O M E -
T H I N G
NAUGHTY HERE," REAGAN SAID, "SINCE THIS IS AN ALL-STAG ARRANGEMENT"

The Lamp of Fellowship warms Bohemians to new heights of brotherly love.

parasol the next day, the organ player broke into "California, Here I Come." Reagan said that it was good to be back. The Grove had been a major factor in his "homesickness...when you are forced to be away, as I was, for eight years."

The speech was canned and courtly. Though he cursed now and then, he seemed uncomfortable with the word *damn*, which he said almost sotto voce. He did take a crack at toilet humor:

"You know, I got to take a second to do something naughty here, since this is an all-stag arrangement. You know how many times we've been in someone's home and we've wanted to go to the powder room and we've maybe said, 'Excuse me, I've got to powder my nose.' Well, a man did that at a party, and his hostess said, when he came back, she said, 'You must have the longest nose in the world.' He said, 'What are you talking about?' She said, 'Your fly's open.'"

Polite laughter.

The only surprises came when he took questions. He got rousing applause when he called for greater regulation of the media. "You know, the press conferences were adversarial bouts—they were there to trap me in something or other."

Reagan also came out in favor of four-year terms for congressmen. "You know," he said, for he started every comment with that phrase, "I haven't said this publicly before. I would like to

cigars and reminiscing about potency.

I wrote "How do you feel about government and legal efforts to force the Club to admit women?" on a piece of Grove stationery and went up to the fellow taking questions from my section, by the giant owl. It was a risk, but then it was my last hour of my first and last Grove. My bags were packed—a camera in one pocket, a tape recorder in the other. Also, I'd tried to grab one of the free Bohemian Club walking sticks from the museum, something I could lean against my office wall with the B/C shield turned out to remind myself that this right-wing fantasia had not been just a dream. But there were none left; Bohemians had taken them all hiking.

The moderator studied the page and asked who I was and what camp I was in. We were a few feet from the Lamp of Fellowship, and after looking me over he said he didn't know, this was pushing it. He didn't ask Reagan my question, of course. The rest of the questions were about the world outside the Grove. Then the organist struck up "America the Beautiful" and Reagan left in a red truck, waving.

Later I heard a Bohemian on the River Road saying it had been brave of Reagan to take on all comers. But another Bohemian pointed out it really hadn't been a big risk. *Who was going to offend the president?* After all, this was Bohemia. ❥

BEST OF THE MAIL: PART THREE

David Halbfinger (see far right) wasn't more than 18 when he made the mistake of tangling with *Spy* in its own pages. Before long, his mother and sister had gotten involved, firing off epistolary gambits he says he had no advance knowledge of and that he viewed as "horning in" on his territory. Unpacking boxes not long ago in L.A.—where he had just been posted by his employer, *The New York Times*—Halbfinger came across his old *Spys*. "My wife didn't know about this," he says. "So I had to tell her."

October 1988

DEAR EDITORS A couple issues have really got me perplexed. Why is it that every time Ignatz's name appears in print, it seems to pick up an extra vowel or consonant along the way? (A simple issue, I know, but I have a low *Gaslight* threshold.) Also, the word *preternaturally* appeared no fewer than ten times in your November issue. Was this deliberate, or did one of your editorial staffers forget to change his word-a-day calendar? Straight answers are not expected but would be greatly appreciated. Aside from that, you guys make me scream.

Thérèse L. Hentz
Philadelphia, Pennsylvania

Although the word preternaturally *appears in every issue of SPY, it's possible that the November issue was preternaturally brimming. As for Ratzwizkiwzki's name changing its spelling, nonsense. Surely you're imagining*

things. Ratzwikzizwki's name has always been spelled the same in SPY—always. You're overtired. Get some rest, Ms. Hentz. See a movie. How about a good George Cukor film? Now that you mention it, Gaslight *would be an excellent* choice.

March 1989

---

of Hellman; she thought her a literary and political fraud. I was not jealous of Mailer; I thought him wrong on the sexual politics of women's liberation.

Final thought: the inability to tell good from bad, relevant from irrelevant, the joke (this is crucial) from the straight line, is true decadence. That's it, SPY.

See you in federal court. Have a nice pretrial deposition.

Gore Vidal
Hollywood, California

Shortly after Mr. Vidal sent this letter, he called SPY to find out if we'd received it. In the course of a discursive and wholly pleasant colloquy, Mr. Vidal, who once said, "As one gets older, litigation replaces sex," delivered a tongue-lashing for what he claimed were numerous errors, fundamental among them that he was not a recidivist litigator. Mr. Vidal claimed to have sued only one person in his life, and that was Truman Capote. "To say otherwise," he informed us solemnly, "would be actionable." SPY stands by its story.

SPY welcomes letters from its readers. Address correspondence to SPY, The Puck Building,

March 1989

From the SPY mailroom: The Halbfingers are back! Or rather, one lone Halbfinger is. Just as we had all but lost hope, the mail brought word. For the Halbfinger-ignorant among you, it's like this: exactly a year ago, a lethal mother-son combination (Andrea Kanner and David M. Halbfinger) ganged up on SPY in these very pages (Letters to SPY, November 1987). We won't go into the messy details, but suffice it to say that in such confrontations there are never winners, only losers. And now this third, previously undetected Halbfinger, Leona M., has written from Amherst, Massachusetts, to extend the olive branch. "Your loyal fan," in fact, is how she closes. Skeptics might doubt the note's authenticity—certainly "Leona M." suggests playful, Helmsley-related chicanery, and, more significantly, there are none of the telltale allusions to degrees, academic honors, archery awards or camper-of-the-week certificates following the name Halbfinger. *Very suspicious.* A phone call could have resolved this question, but we'd rather not know. We'd rather believe in miracles. *Halbfingers everywhere: all is forgiven.*

Noa A. Kaumeheiwa, of Marquette, Michigan, not to mention Ronald Gans, Maxim Engers, Jonathan Skinner, David Pittaway and Susan Barish, have written to correct something apparently called the "quadratic formula," as depicted in A. Silverberg's "Spot the College Graduate" cartoon (June). It is not

$$x = \frac{-b \pm \sqrt{4ac - b^2}}{2a}$$

but rather

$$x = \frac{-b \pm \sqrt{b^2 - 4ac}}{2a}$$

SPY regrets any anxiety we may have caused among the logarithm-and-slide-rule set. Ms. Kaumeheiwa, in a postscript, expresses concern that she may

November 1988

DEAR EDITORS A re you guys going soft on us? Over the years we've come to know and love the relentless sarcasm of SPY; then you hit us, in the November Webs column, with "Andy Lack, the executive producer of *Face to Face*, is...the creator of the not unwatchable *West 57th*." What kind of sycophantic pandering is this? *Has someone been paid off?*

McLean Brice, 06936-021
Federal Prison Camp
Maxwell Air Force Base
Montgomery, Alabama

You know, Mr. Brice, sometimes we attribute to others qualities we dislike in ourselves.

April 1991

DEAR EDITORS I thought the article about Judy Price ("Nightmare on Park Avenue," March) by Jennet Conant was right on target.

Sylvia Mitnick
Philadelphia, Pennsylvania

Mrs. Mitnick is Judy Price's mother.

April 1990

11

"Evil, but Kind of Innocent"

Spy vs. *New York*, and Other Sordid Tales from the End of the Decade

It was like an hour and a half out of my time, the round-trip to Secaucus. You know, it was a very comfortable limo—I appreciated that you didn't skimp on the limo.

—DAVID BLUM

YES, *SPY* BRIEFLY FOUND ITSELF in the livery business. But first:

The new issue is huge. It will be 160 pages and perfect bound. It includes five substantial features, a double-fold-out celebrity memoir chart, a thirty-two-page rock 'n' roll promotional supplement, an 8-page J&B supplement, and 65 pages of advertising.

—Staff memo, June 7, 1988

You and a guest are invited to dance the night away in celebration of Spy's second anniversary and the first Spy *book,* Separated at Birth?...*The Puck Ballroom...Black tie...Please present this invitation to the heavily armed security personnel at the door.*

—Invitation to *Spy*'s third annual party, October 1988

On Sunday, Separated at Birth? *becomes a* Times *bestseller, hitting the relevant list at #5 (and displacing, we are all especially happy to note, L. Ron Hubbard's* Dianetics*). And the following Sunday, we are told,* Separated at Birth? *will move up two slots to #3. Huzzah.*

—Staff memo, December 2, 1988

WHOA.

The magazine was thriving. With the ad-sales success first spearheaded by Anne Kreamer and the steady circulation growth and relentless fiscal discipline overseen by Tom Phillips, *Spy* began to break even month to month in 1989, only three years after it had started publishing. Newsstand sales, flat the first six months of *Spy*'s existence and still less than 10,000 in April 1987, doubled and then doubled again in two successive six-month periods; in mid-'88, they were past 42,000. The average newsstand sales rate for that entire period was an exceptionally high 72 percent. By 1989, *Spy*'s total circulation was approaching 200,000.

Opposite: A painter at rest during the "My Kid Could Do That" prank (June 1989). Many of the pint-size emerging artists showcased by *Spy* were moonlighting offspring of the editors and of the editors' friends.

It was just around then that Donald Trump put out the entirely false story that we were in financial trouble. More than anyone else, Trump really was *Spy*'s Professor Moriarty, looming large in the magazine's history from the very beginning to—as we'll see—the absolute end. In 1988 he predicted our imminent demise to Liz Smith. "Donald said that *Spy* magazine…is in trouble financially and will not be around much longer," Smith wrote. "I chided the handsome mogul, of whom I am very fond…that he should not indulge in wishful thinking. He said, 'No, you'll find this is true if you just investigate. I predict they won't even be around in a year.'" So we started running the prediction as a monthly countdown (Chronicle of Our Death Foretold [see page 238]), and a year later, in October 1989, when Trump was proved wrong, we started another countdown: *Spy* consulted an actuary and predicted that Trump "won't even be around in another 31.7 years." This ran under the rubric "Death Be Not Short-Fingered."*

The magazine was turning out some of its best cover stories, such as the Kurt Andersen–Paul Rudnick collaboration on the mass-market proliferation of irony (March 1989; see pages 164–70) and, at the other end of some sort of spectrum, the "Garbology" package, in which reporters in protective—or at any rate brilliantly white—gear rooted around celebrity trash and turned the results over to experts for analysis, though not before the trash had sat festering in the office for days, for fact-checking and photo-op purposes. (Chief researcher Carrie Weiner remembers, "John Brodie and Bob Mack would bring in these plastic bags full of stained and wrinkled electric bills. It was like a cat bringing a dead mouse to its master, they'd show them to Graydon and he'd say, 'Oh, this is great stuff!'")

The March issue is here. Due to the sensitivity of the Toback piece, please observe the following special precautions: 1. Take only one copy. 2. Don't show it to anyone. 3. Don't give it to anyone. 4. Don't leave it out on your desk. 5. Take it home and read it there.…The issue will reach subscribers on February 8th. It will be on newsstands beginning February 13th. Until then, these precautions should be followed. Seriously.

—Office memo, January 30, 1989

---

*Eerily, just as this was being written in 2005, *precisely half* of Trump's projected remaining life span as of 1989 had passed. —Eds.

Beefy guy we've hired is sitting outside our front door in anticipation of possible Toback visit.

—Journal entry, February 9, 1989

OUR GATEFOLD REPORT ON THE inspired dating habits of movie director James Toback (see pages 220–21) made us all a little nervous, particularly after an unnerving phone conversation he had with the piece's editor, Susan Morrison. "I am going to be dangerous," Toback warned her. "I don't care what the consequences are." In a subsequent conversation, says Morrison, he added that he knew where she lived. So our paranoia was perhaps understandable.

"YOU NEVER KNEW WHAT WAS GOING to happen when you got to the office," says Aimée Bell, who started as an editorial assistant in 1990. "You couldn't predict it."

Spy's peculiar needs were in abundant evidence around the increasingly overpopulated Puck loft. Here was the art department hitting the phones to hunt down obscure fonts to use in a multiple-magazine parody package. There was a reporter popping his head up to call out, "What do any of you guys know about [William F.] Buckley's silverware sets?" (Even that kind of question usually got some sort of response.) "It was like going to a clubhouse," says one reporter. "We were all together getting paid to make prank phone calls."

Some top editor would call out your name, and the games would begin. Among reporter Rachel Urquhart's impromptu undercover assignments—curious preparation for her subsequent decade writing for *Vogue*—were auditioning for the Vanna White role in a never-realized Donald Trump version of *Wheel of Fortune* and, along with Elissa Schappell, turning up at the office of that era's Dr. Feelgood with a litany of made-up ailments, in order to gauge the physician's level of quackery. "Susan [Morrison] would always make these things sound as if they were completely routine, just part of the job," says Urquhart.

"I was terrified doing reporting on the private lives of famous people," remembers Henry Alford. "Terrified. There was a threat, early on during my tenure, that all of us reporters and editorial assistants would be sent down to Harry Helmsley's trial with garage-door openers and answering-machine beepers in order to try to activate Mr. Helmsley's prosthetic penis. I had a nightmare about that. The name 'Harry Helmsley' is still inextricably linked

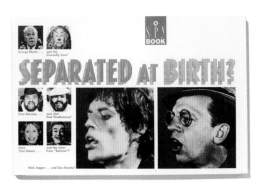

Spy High,
the book, 1991

Spy Notes,
1989

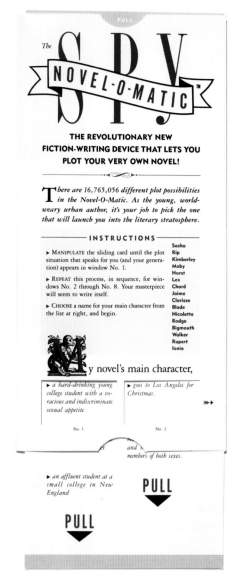

The Novel-O-Matic that came with *Spy Notes* really worked: Pulling the tabs yielded 16,765,056 plot possibilities. Optional extra steps included: "Publish. Attend lots of parties... Buy Italian wardrobe with royalties...Write second book (use the Novel-O-Matic again—there are still 16,765,055 possible plots left)...Gradually fade from public memory."

The best-seller,
Separated at Birth?
(1989) and its
sequel (1990)

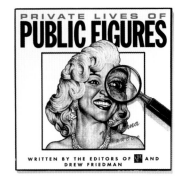

Drew Friedman's
Spy cartoons
collected, 1993

suring Toback that we were not interested in gambling with him but were intrigued by the journalistic possibilities of a polygraph exam concerning the substance of this article, we agreed to set up such a test for him alone with a polygrapher of our choosing. When scheduling the test and meeting Toback's many demands proved difficult, he made such remarks as "I hope you know what you're doing when you fuck with me." He went on, grimly, "If you print this piece, I promise it will be the single thing you regret most in your life." When pressed for details, he said, "Think of your very very worst nightmare. [Dramatic pause.] *It'll be worse than that.*" When we objected to these threats, Toback became flustered. "I didn't threaten you. Those were just forecasts," he said. "You're into slander. I'm into astrology."

After satisfying Toback's conditions, we agreed on a time and a place for the polygraph test. Toback stood us up, and SPY's editors have had no further contact with him except for a phone call and two letters from his lawyer. One letter indicated that after reneging on his agreement to take the polygraph test we had arranged, Toback went to his own polygrapher and "passed" a lie detector test based on a rough draft of questions we had sent him. Since we have no way of assessing the circumstances, particulars or results of this secret test, we can't consider it meaningful (let alone persuasive) information. Finally, in an effort to get Toback's side of things, we asked to interview him again. He has been unwilling.

Earlier, when asked to comment on his evidently abundant personal magnetism, Toback had told SPY that his ongoing search for future cast members entails approaching a great number of men as well as women. For the record, though, Toback boasted to *Interview* magazine recently, "I've been very lucky with women—even, if you'll forgive me, I would say blessed." We don't think *blessed* is precisely the word we'd use.

THE WOMEN,* THE PLACE, THE TIME	THE INTRODUCTION	THE CREDENTIALS	SETTING THE HOOK: FLATTERY	PITCHING THE PROJECT	"CALL ME"	THE ANSWERING SERVI
SARA **Movie Director** *outside Citicorp* *September 1985*	I was walking down the street and he pulled up alongside me and said, "Listen, **I'm a film director** and I've just finished making a film called *The Pick-Up Artist*. . . ."	He went on about *The Pick-Up Artist* and then started in with *Exposed*, starring **Nastassia Kinski**, using it all to the hilt.	"You're the **most beautiful** girl I've ever seen. . . ."		"I want to give you **my telephone number**." I said, "Forget it. I'm never going to use it, because I'm a film director, too." FINAL CONTACT	
VINCENZA **Writer** *Broadway and 69th Street* *March 1987*	Following me for two blocks up Broadway, he kept saying, "Excuse me, please! **This may sound strange, but I'm a movie director**, and I really want to talk to you for a second. . . ."	When I wouldn't stop, he said, "Jesus, you're really suspicious. By now, I'd said much more obscene things to **Nastassia Kinski**, and now we're best friends. You know who she is, don't you? I *made* her. Have you heard of *The Pick-Up Artist*? That's my film. Here, let me show you my **Directors Guild of America card**. . . . And here's my driver's license. If you don't believe me, go to Barnes & Noble and look up plate 88 in *Portraits* by Helmut Newton and you'll see me with **Nastassia**. . . ."	"You have such a **powerful beauty**. . . ."	"I want to talk to you about a **documentary film** I'm making involving five women and a man. I want to show how interesting the real lives of women are."	"Now, *don't* give me your phone number. Here, take mine, and after you've checked me out and trust that I am who I say I am, then you can **call me**. . . ."	I left a **message** on his home answering machine and within 30 minutes he called back from the street. "Can you **meet me** at my place at 10:30 tonight?" I said, "Those are strange office hours." "That's how I work." I said, "No thanks."
ALEXIA **Auction House Employee** *IRT No. 1 train* *February 1988*	He walked past me on the subway, stopped and then sat down opposite me and stared. "**You're going to think this is crazy, but I'm a director** and I have to use you in my next movie."	"I know you don't believe me," he said and then pulled his driver's license and **Directors Guild card** right out. He told me, "I'm responsible for **Nastassia Kinski**'s fame."	"I can't take my eyes off you. . . . You have a very **commanding stride**. . . ."		He wrote his number on a piece of newspaper. "Promise you'll **call me**," he said, and "I know you're suspicious, but after you check me out, give me a call." He kept saying over and over, "Check me out."	I left a **message** on his machine that I wasn't interested.
BETTINA **Chiropractor** *Third Avenue and 32nd Street* *May 1988*	This guy came up from behind me and said, "I really like your walk. I think you're really pretty, and I'd like to use you in a movie I'm making."	He showed me his driver's license and his **Directors Guild card**. He said he was on his way to Gamblers Anonymous. He also said he'd gone to Harvard and that he'd been married to one of the richest women in the world. "I've been a millionaire and a pauper," he said. He also told me to see *Exposed* that night.		He said he was making a **movie** about walking. I told him I wasn't an actress. He said that didn't matter, it was going to be a "natural" film, and that it wasn't about acting but would start production soon.	He wrote his number on a piece of newspaper. It was a studio number for *The Pick-Up Artist*. He said, "**Call me**, after you've seen *Exposed*."	I left **several messages**, and when I reached him, h put me on hold for 15 minutes. It took me several before we hooked up; he always seemed to be eatin into the phone. I kept asking, "Is this for real?" He "You have to **trust me**." I told him to call me if he was interested. He didn't.
ELAINE **Publicist** *West 3rd Street, L.A.* *January 1988*	He came running down the street behind me and said, "You're so beautiful, I want you to be in a movie. **I know this sounds ridiculous, but I am a producer**."	He offered to show me his **Directors Guild Card** and said he'd just finished making *The Pick-Up Artist*. He gave me a list of his movies and told me to see them all, especially *Exposed*. He said he had directed and known **Nastassia Kinski** in more than a professional sense.		He made it very clear that he was working on a project that he had directed, written and produced. He said the **movie** would be true to life—something about his story.		I called him three days later from L.A. and he w at a postproduction facility. "I'm so glad you call I didn't think you would." He said he'd have to **me back** when he got back to L.A. on a certain date. He didn't.
DANIELLE **Editor** *Toback's Upper West Side building* *December 1987*	This is the weirdest thing that ever happened to me. He was staring at me as I was going up in the elevator. Then I saw him again in the same elevator two hours later. He said, "Excuse me, can I talk to you? It's an omen we're in the same elevator again. My name is James Toback. I just made *The Pick-Up Artist*. **I'm a director**." He followed me out into the street. "I was going to talk to you. I was thinking about you in the shower, that I should have talked to you. These things aren't accidents."	He said, "I need to change my suede coat; come up to my apartment and we can talk. I want to tell you about my new project. You can stand outside." I thought, *Well, all right*. We went back up in the elevator. He told stories about **Nastassia Kinski** and said he wasn't a psycho. He showed me posters for *Exposed* and a book by Helmut Newton that had a photo of him and Nastassia.	"You've got this **vibrancy**. You have this **energy** emanating from you. I felt it in the elevator."	"I'm making a new, experimental **movie** with five unknown people and Mike Tyson. I'm putting people in a room to see how they interact and I need three more women."	We left his apartment. "I think this would be really cool. Think about it. **Call me**."	He called the next day. "Can you come to my apartment **at ten at night**?" My mom said no w wanted to meet at a restaurant for coffee. He sa "Okay, I'll call you back." He called once. I returned his call. He never called me back.
ELLA **Fashion Editor** *43rd Street and Fifth Avenue* *November 1987*	A man in a long black leather trench coat started following alongside me with a barrage of compliments like "I can't believe how great you look. **I don't know if you know me, but I'm a director**."	He pulled out **all these cards** and insinuated that I was his next **Nastassia Kinski**.	"You're so **unusual**."	He didn't mention a project, but he did ask me out to lunch.		
JENNY **Editor** *Balducci's* *May 1986*	"Excuse me, **I'm a film director**. Please stop. . . . Really I am. . . ."	"Please take my card. I made a film called *Exposed* with **Nastassia Kinski**."			He gave me his card and told me to **call**.	When I called, a secretary gave me a number at production office. He didn't seem to remember I was, but he said, "**Let's meet** later at the **Har Club**." I said, "How about next week?" But he really forceful and said it had to be that night.
GWEN **Production Assistant** *the Harvard Club* *October 1987*						A friend gave me **his numb** told me to call him because looking for a job in product
BETH **Model** *the Harvard Club* *April 1984*	We met through friends over drinks at the **Harvard Club**. He immediately started saying how easy it was for him to sleep with women.	He bragged about how he made **Nastassia Kinski**.	"Your **green eyes**!"	He wanted to discuss a **semidocumentary** about five different women. He said he wanted to elevate the female race in the film.		
KAY **Editor** *Second Avenue and 57th Street* *September 1986*	"Hi, I'm James Toback, the film director. . . . **I know you don't believe me, but I'm a well-known film director**."	He was carrying a whole portfolio of clips about himself, which he started to show off while rattling off the names of all his films.		He wanted-me to read for a part in *The Pick-Up Artist*.	"Here's **my number at Fox**. I want you to read with Robert Downey Jr."	When I called Fox, he took my call right away. "**When can you come up?**" I said I'd come by a five.
LYN **Dancer** *Lincoln Center subway station* *October 1987*	This guy started chasing me down the street; he was disheveled, in a raincoat, and carrying a Monet print. "**I know this sounds crazy, but I'm a big director**."	"You've seen *The Pick-Up Artist*; you've seen *Exposed*; you've seen . . ." Actually, I hadn't heard of any of them; but he went on. "I know you think I'm Charles Manson, but trust me, this is how I discovered **Nastassia Kinski**."	"I couldn't help noticing your presence and your **star quality**."	I told him I was a dancer and he said that he was just looking for a dancer in this **project** involving five women. He said I'd be perfect for it.	I told him I was in a hurry and gave him my number, or actually my boyfriend's number.	He called me at 12:30 that night and wasn't fa at all when my boyfriend answered. "**Can you c over** now?" No way, I said, and told him he cou meet me for lunch in a public place if he wante talk about a film project.
SANDRA **Writer** *Fairway Market, Broadway and 74th Street* *August 1988*	This guy with an unbuttoned shirt reached for my forearm at the peach stand at Fairway: "**I know this sounds ridiculous, but I'm a producer** and I'm making a movie and you'd be perfect for it." I told him to leave me alone.	"I lived with **Nastassia Kinski**, you can see our picture together on plate 88 of Helmut Newton's new book." He showed me his **DGA card** and his driver's license. He told me about *The Pick-Up Artist* and that *Fingers* had been singled out by Truffaut as one of the best American films. He also told me about being married to a British heiress.	"Your eyes! You're so **provocative**. You know that, don't you?"	He said the **film** was a new kind of film about astrology and the creation of the universe. There would be interviews with people talking about real experiences. He said it didn't matter that I wasn't an actress.	He left me **his number** on a corner of the Sunday *Times* and told me to **call** after I'd seen *Exposed*. He was with a woman that he'd left waiting with a bag of groceries; she was obviously getting impatient.	I ran into him at a party. He said he **had to see** the next day and that I should call. I left a **mess** on his machine and he called about 15 minutes later to make a date for that night at the **Harv Club**, to discuss the film he was making.
JAMES TOBACK'S POSTGAME INTERVIEW WITH SPY *on the telephone* *November 1988*	*After phoning female* SPY *editor, having been told about article:* "What I'd like to do is get together with you and discuss this."	"What do you say to a stranger you want to be in your films? You say, '**Hi, I'm Jim Toback, I'm a movie director.**'" (Asked about Nastassia Kinski, Toback insisted, "She scrupulously kept herself at arm's length from me.")	"Any one individual I would approach [in a manner] according to who that person is."	"I lead as work-oriented a life as anyone I know. I am completely and totally and wholeheartedly uninterested in meeting anyone at this point in my life who does not suggest some cinematic capacity—male or female, young or old."	*[Over two days, Toback left seven phone messages at the* SPY *offices.]*	*[Five phone messages were promptly left by* SPY.*]*

***not their real names**

THE DATE	TALKING DIRTY	A FASCINATION WITH NUMBERS	THE ALLURE OF DANGER	"TRUST ME"	LAST STRAWS
We walked down the street and he led me to the **Harvard Club**. He asked for his mail before we sat down.	It wasn't two minutes before he was talking about sex. I think he started by asking me, "**Do you like to fuck?**"	He told me how he'd first had sex at a very early age, **maybe 12**, when he hooked up with an older composer. Toward the end of lunch he said he found me incredibly attractive. "There are rooms here. **We could go upstairs.**" I said I'd already taken a long enough lunch. [FINAL CONTACT]			
I met him in the lobby of the **Harvard Club**; he looked disheveled. We went to the bar, where he started jamming gobs of nuts in his mouth. He didn't ask me anything about myself and told me a lot about his career in the movies.	He didn't waste any time getting disgusting, maybe 10 or 15 minutes. "I feel like we're old lovers. I feel like I've already **had sex with you** many times, that we have this special sexual rapport."	He said, "I have this physical need. I have to come **15 to 20 times a day.** Even my therapist says I have to have frequent sex." I stood up and demanded, *Do you relate everything to sex?* He said, "Yes!"	"I like to live on the edge," he said. "**I do dangerous things.**" He then went on to tell me about feeling violent when he was jealous over someone cheating on him. [FINAL CONTACT]		
He said he was staying at the **Harvard Club** and we were supposed to meet at 1:00 p.m. He left a note saying he wouldn't be back until 6:00, and when I showed up again, he said that we couldn't have a drink in the lobby because I was wearing jeans, so we went up to his room.	He jumped right in when I got to his room. And he kept getting calls from women and he'd say, "No, I **can't fuck you** again tonight."	He wanted to know **how many men** I'd made love to. I said, "That has nothing to do with my ability to be an assistant on a film." Later he called and said he had to explore my sexuality, that I needed a teacher and that he would teach me. Then he went on to say he had a large penis and asked me how much pubic hair I had.	He also got a call about gambling. He told me **he thought he had it in him to kill someone**, it would just be a little messy.	He said to do this film we would have to live together to get to know each other. I said, "No thanks." [FINAL CONTACT]	
We were all drinking and talking openly about sex. He gave his entire sexual history and then said we should all go up to his room at the **Harvard Club**.	When I told him I was probably more interested in other women than men, that only made him more interested.	No one was sacred: he bragged about sex with everyone, and then he claimed that even a **seven-year-old** was after him.			He tracked me down in Kyoto, Japan, where I was modeling. He wanted to fly me to his hotel in Santa Monica. I told him I wasn't as weird as on the first time we met at the Harvard Club. I also said I'd been a bulimic. He said, "You're wonderful, however you are!" I thought it might be my big break, but first I telegrammed the friend we'd had drinks with, asking if he thought Toback would expect me to have sex if I did go to Santa Monica. He wrote right back. *Of course!* [FINAL CONTACT]
When I got to his office at Fox, he told me all about his career and his credits as a director. He kept picking up the phone and calling his bookie to place huge bets. When he came back, he was getting calls from women, and he'd say, "Okay, honey, meet me at the **Harvard Club** at X time."	He started in with the gross stuff fairly quickly. "I'm a freak. Do you know what a freak is? It's someone who is totally into sex. Are you a freak, too?" When he said **he wanted to fuck me**, I told him I was married. He said, "Let me call your husband." I gave him the number, but he backed off.	He told me that when he wanted to be a concert pianist as a kid, he slept with a lot of people in the music business. That was when **he was 14**.	He claimed that his ass was on the line with this project and that the mob was on his tail. He even **tried to get me to believe that he could have had people killed** to get movies made in the past.	I told him he was scaring me with the dirty talk, so he changed the subject for a while but always worked back around by demanding, "Why don't you **trust me**? This is for the film. You'll have to use these words in the movie. What do you want me to say for *pussy*?" Then he went on, "How often do you masturbate? Do you enjoy sex during your period?" He wanted me to take off my shoes so he could massage my feet because he knew dancers like that. No way, I said. "I can't work with people who are afraid of me! Listen, I have an idea. Stand up. Come over here and **touch my nipples**. Come on, just touch them. **Then I'll come** and you can **trust me**, because you'll see that that's all I need to be really turned on. You don't have to do anything more!"	People kept coming into the office while we were talking. To one guy he said, "This is Kay; she's considering fucking me right now. She hasn't fucked anybody but her husband in seven years, but she's really tempted to fuck me." All these women were constantly calling. After one call he said, "I can't believe that was her! I was walking down Central Park West and this woman came out of the bushes and said, 'Come over here, I really want to fuck you.' She just dragged me into the bushes. So we fucked, and it was really great. And that was just her!" He gave me a safe-sex rap too: he said he gets every girl tested before he'll have sex with them. He said, "**Just touch my nipples and I'll come.**" I decided to leave; he said he still wanted me to read with Robert Downey Jr. [FINAL CONTACT]
We met at an Upper West Side health food restaurant. He was really interesting at first. We talked about film and philosophy. He was fascinated by my midwestern past. Toward the end of lunch it started getting weird, but it couldn't have been too bad yet because when he said, "Listen, I've got cassettes of my films right here, let's go to my place — it's just across the street — and you can see them for yourself," I called my boyfriend and told him exactly where I would be for the next two hours, and I went.	He made me some pasta, put on the films and left to do errands. The movies were pretty bad. When he came back, he sat on the couch and started talking and used words like *pussy, cunt* and *dick*.	"You don't love your boyfriend," he said. "You're so much more sensuous. I can tell you masturbate **three or four times a day.**" He said he has to come **14 times a day** and that he stops **100** women a week. Actually, he did smell like dried come.			He was calling me late at night for a while to tell me all about his exploits. My boyfriend got sick of the calls, so I blew him off. The next time he called, he said he had people over and I should come over to his house. I went and the phone kept ringing and Toback was making all these dates for later in the evening. And the doorbell was constantly ringing! He avoided those. When I left with the others, another woman, in a Wisconsin sweatshirt, was on her way in. The last time he called it was 1:00 a.m. His doorbell rang while we were talking. He went to get it and I heard a girl's voice. I heard him say, "Just get a Coke and sit on the couch. Sit on the couch!" I wanted to know if he had a girl there and what was she doing there at 1:00 a.m. I said she was this sexy little thing from the Bronx. I got really mad. He said, "Are you still going to be up in 45 minutes? **Let me just fuck this girl and I'll call you back.**" I said not to bother. [FINAL CONTACT]
We met outside the **Harvard Club** at 10:00 p.m. for dinner, but it was closed, so we went to the **Algonquin**.	He told me, "You need a father figure to unlock your sensuality. You haven't come to terms with your erotic side. You're a caldron of complexity. With you, I would deny you three times before **I had sex with you.** I'd play with you. I'd come but I wouldn't enter you. It has to be an obsession, and I would guess you've never really needed it before, have you? I would never enter a woman without her needing me."	He said, "I have approached **1,000** women. No, it's more like **500.** I've used **50** in my films."	"I like to constantly surprise myself. I go to sleep at 4:00 a.m. and I'm fascinated with the 2:00 a.m. creatures," he said. He talked about living with **Nastassia Kinski**, and how he tried to live beyond conventions and without domesticity in his life. When he asked me if I considered myself an artist, that somehow led to him saying that whether he has killed 40 people or none, he knows **he has a killer's instinct.**	He said, "I require **complete trust** and a jump of faith. I can see endlessly working with you, but I would need to know you like no one else has ever known you. And you would have to **trust me** more than you have ever trusted anyone."	"I would bring you to the point where you need me so badly **you would put a gun to your head.**" [FINAL CONTACT]
[Preferring to talk on the telephone, SPY didn't take Toback up on his offer to meet.]	"What I've sought to do is test people with a bold and aggressive approach, because . . . the easiest way you can tell if someone is going to be loose in front of a camera is just to lay it out, just put it all on the table, without sugarcoating, as boldly as possible."	"The number of people I approach on the street [about possible roles in movies] is about 65/35, male/female, not necessarily of any particular age. . . . The ratio of people I talk to in public to people I use in my movies is about **1 to 100,** which is about the same as other directors, I would say."	"I will do anything I can to get the cast I need."	"I immediately weed out people where there will be any offense or indignation, any barrier to being open. I'm interested in who has good stories to tell, the wildest person in his sexual openness."	"Yes, I run into my share of people who are not interested in working. But I have never talked to anyone where I haven't been open and honest and direct." ▣

A Word of Warning: This chart contains frank, explicit language, including the phrase, uttered by a man, "Just touch my nipples and I'll come." What follows is not for the squeamish.

From "The Pickup Artist's Guide to Picking Up Women," an exploration of the dating habits of filmmaker James Toback, March 1989

THE DEATH OF A SHOW BUSINESS LEGEND
Mr. Jack Fine (1990–91)

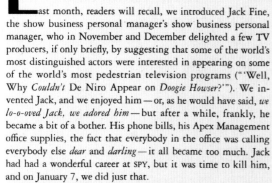

Last month, readers will recall, we introduced Jack Fine, the show business personal manager's show business personal manager, who in November and December delighted a few TV producers, if only briefly, by suggesting that some of the world's most distinguished actors were interested in appearing on some of the world's most pedestrian television programs ("'Well, Why *Couldn't* De Niro Appear on *Doogie Howser?*'"). We invented Jack, and we enjoyed him — or, as he would have said, *we lo-o-oved Jack, we adored him* — but after a while, frankly, he became a bit of a bother. His phone bills, his Apex Management office supplies, the fact that everybody in the office was calling everybody else *dear* and *darling* — it all became too much. Jack had had a wonderful career at SPY, but it was time to kill him, and on January 7, we did just that.

To inform the members of the entertainment community of our loss — and theirs — we paid for a death notice in *The New York Times*, which ran on page D20 on January 9, and an in-memoriam notice in *Variety*, which appeared on page 127 of the January 14 issue. *Variety* also published its own obituary of Fine, based on information in a press release we had sent. *Variety* runs its obituaries each week in rough order of importance

and celebrity — the week Jack Fine died, Richard Maibaum's obit came first (he wrote screenplays for 12 James Bond movies, after all), but Jack was no lower than twelfth place, ahead of 30 other, presumably real entertainment-industry figures who had passed away. Finally, we sent an item about Jack's passing to columnist Liz Smith, which she accepted as fact and reported.

We realized, however, that written words did not do justice to Jack, a man who was defined by his person-to-person skills. Only personal reminiscences could truly honor the memory of this truly great man and his truly remarkable accomplishments. Therefore, we ventured to the heart of Jack Fine's milieu, to a place where everybody would be a Jack Fine kind of guy, had Jack ever existed. On the evening of January 7, the very day of Jack's demise, we went to the New York Helmsley Hotel to attend the party that *New York Post* gossip columnist Cindy Adams threw for the 80th birthday of her husband, comedian Joey Adams. Some of the biggest names in the New York celebrity orbit had turned out for the occasion. With all that love in one room, we thought, surely some memories would start flowing. And they did. A transcript of part of the evening's conversation follows.

SPY: I'm wondering if you have any memories of Jack Fine?

Comedian Pat Cooper: No, I don't — uh, what was the name again?

SPY: Jack Fine.

Cooper: Oh, *Jack!* Are you kiddin' me? Yeah, what a nice man! One of the —

SPY: You knew Jack Fine?

Cooper: Oh, yes, *absolutely*. I didn't know him very… y'know, *intimately*, but I knew him — I knew *of* him. He was one of the finest men —

Comedian Freddie Roman: Who?

Cooper: Jack Fine.

Roman: Oh, *sure!*

Cooper: Y'know, he passed on….

Roman: [*Sadly*] I kno-o-ow, I know.

SPY: You knew him?

Roman: Absolutely. Sure.

SPY: And what remembrances of him do you have?

Roman: Fond.

SPY: He was with Apex Management —

Roman: I didn't realize that. Well, he was a lovely man.

Cooper: He *was* a lovely man. A good man. An honest man.

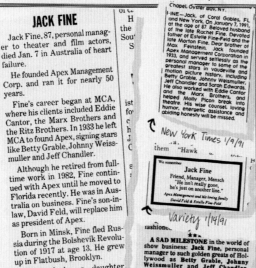

JACK FINE

Jack Fine, 87, personal manager to theater and film actors, died Jan. 7 in Australia of heart failure.

He founded Apex Management Corp. and ran it for nearly 50 years.

Fine's career began at MCA, where his clients included Eddie Cantor, the Marx Brothers and the Ritz Brothers. In 1933 he left MCA to found Apex, signing stars like Betty Grable, Johnny Weissmuller and Jeff Chandler.

Although he retired from full-time work in 1982, Fine continued with Apex until he moved to Florida on business. Fine's son-in-law, David Feld, will replace him as president of Apex.

Born in Minsk, Fine fled Russia during the Bolshevik Revolution of 1917 at age 13. He grew up in Flatbush, Brooklyn.

Survived by a daughter Estelle Fine-Feld, and a brother.

Variety 1/14/91 ↗

Liz Smith, Daily News 1/11/91

FINE—Jack, of Coral Gables, FL and New York, On January 7, 1991, at the age of 87. Beloved husband of the late Rachel Fine. Devoted father of Estelle Fine-Feld and the late Morton Fine. Dear brother of Max Feinstein. Jack founded Apex Management Corporation in 1933, and served selflessly as the personal manager to some of the greatest stars in vaudeville and motion picture history, including Betty Grable, Johnny Weissmuller, Jeff Chandler and Sarah Edwards. He also worked with Eddie Cantor and the Marx Brothers, and helped Molly Picon break into theatre. His wise counsel, loving humor, energetic assistance and abiding honesty will be missed.

New York Times 1/9/91

We remember
Jack Fine
Friend, Manager, Mensch
"He isn't really gone,
he's just on another line."
*Apex Management and his loving family
David Feld & Estelle Fine-Feld*

Variety 1/14/91

★★★
A SAD MILESTONE in the world of show business: **Jack Fine**, personal manager to such golden greats of Hollywood as **Betty Grable**, **Johnny Weissmuller** and **Jeff Chandler**, passed away recently in Australia, far from his beloved New York. Jack founded Apex Management and ran it for 50 years before retiring. Early in his amazing career, Jack represented such legends as the **Marx Brothers**, the **Ritz Brothers** and **Eddie Cantor**. He was known for his unflagging optimism, expressed in his famous signature line: "Smile darling — somewhere it's opening night!"

A fair man….Really, I'm not being funny. He was a really honest man.

Roman: Absolutely.

SPY: How did you know him?

Roman: Just in passing, but always kind and pleasant. And good.

As it turned out, the guest of honor, Joey Adams, also had warm memories of Jack.

SPY: I'm wondering if you remember Jack Fine; he passed away this morning.

Joey Adams: Who?

SPY: Jack Fine.

Adams: Oh, sure, yeah.

SPY: Do you remember much about him?

Adams: No, not too much, but I knew him very well.

SPY: How did you know him?

Adams: Well, in the business, y'know, same business.

SPY: How long have you known him?

Adams: Since I was a kid, I don't know — a long time.

SPY: He founded Apex Management, is that right?

Adams: I think so, yes. But, y'know, I — it's all a blur…. When I stop to reminisce, I'll be able to remember. ❂

---

in my mind with the phrase 'searing abdominal cramps.'"

"Once, I was helping Henry out with a phone prank where you misrepresent yourself and then see how long it takes to have the call returned," says *Spy*'s D.C. correspondent Andrea Rider (now Leidolf). "I was 'Emma Peel from William Rehnquist's office.' But Jack Kent Cooke, who owned the Redskins, and Rehnquist were apparently good friends—so instead of simply ignoring the call, Cooke called the FBI. And my phone was tapped for six weeks! One morning, I was going off to my job as a caterer on the Hill. It was early, like 6 a.m., and there were two FBI agents on my front step. They started asking me about the phone calls. One of the agents said, 'You don't like it and I don't like it, but there are a lot of people in this town who have more power than you do.' I admitted that I'd made the calls and said that they were pranks for *Spy*. There was a silence and then one of them said, 'Who is Emma Peel?' I laughed and said that she was the Diana Rigg character on *The Avengers*, the old British TV show about spies. More silence, and then the other agent told me that it was time that I 'grew up.' When I called Jamie Malanowski and told him, he laughed and said, 'Graydon is Rollerblading in the hall.'"

For that same prank, Rider phoned then–Secretary of Defense Dick Cheney.

"He was *relentless* about calling me back," she remembers. "Most people gave up after I told them they had the wrong number, but not Dick! At one point, I was on the phone with my sister and it was, like, 10 p.m., and I got the call-waiting click and crossed over. 'Hi! Dick Cheney here!' I couldn't take it anymore and had to explain the whole prank to him. He actually laughed and was very gracious about it."

Apart from gold-standard *Spy* hoaxes included or mentioned elsewhere herein—the zillionaire-check-cashing escapade (see pages 252–56), the sifting-through-waste of "Garbology," the Jack Fine saga (opposite), the "My Kid Could Do That" art show (see page 224), offering John Sununu a job (see page 250)— the magazine's pranks ranged from having Eric Kaplan test the limits of the citizen's arrest laws in 1987 to sending "casually schlumpy fashion rebel" Harry Shearer and photographer Sara Barrett to some of New York's stuffiest restaurants ("I'm Sorry, Mr. Shearer, Jacket Required") in 1988 to the *New York Times* parody (see pages 268–69) smuggled in to the Democratic National Convention in 1992.

"PARDONNEZ-MOI, OÙ EST UN PARISIEN AVEC HUMANITÉ OU COMPASSION?"

A SPY Pronunciation Gazetteer for the World Traveler

It is not uncommon for American tourists to find themselves in situations in which their grasp of the native language proves inadequate. Part of the problem is that traditional phrase books, so quick to inform us how to respond politely in situations involving cousins or gloves, are much less helpful when the tide of events turns to personal inconvenience and unpleasantness. Thus the visitor to Pamplona, equipped with scores of flowery phrases about *vino* and *arte*, finds himself ill equipped to impress upon others the fact that he has been gored by a bull and is unable to clot. Herewith, a brief guide to communicating abroad, with special emphasis on some of the phenomena the international traveler may actually encounter.

FRANCE	
We are confused by the telephone.	*Luh tay-lay-PHONE noo pah-RAY com-plee-KAY.*
Our waiter has abandoned us.	*NO-trrh sair-VOOR noo-ZAH ah-bon-do-NAY.*
Six thousand francs? Surely you are joking.	*See meel franhs? Voo duh-VAY sair-ten-MONH play-sonh-TAY.*

MEXICO	
We are sunburned and angry.	*Es-TAH-mos toe-STAH-dose pore el sole ee en-fah-DAH-dose.*
The younger of your two sons has urinated on our luggage.	*El may-NOR day soos dose EE-hoe ah oh-ree-NAH-doe en new-ace-tro eh-key-PAH-hay.*

—Henry Alford

ITALY	
Our luggage was sent to	*Lay NO-stray vah-LEE-jay*

August 1990

Michael Hainey was once sent out to test-drive celebrities' pickup lines. "I think it was Susan's idea," he says. "They'd collected a dozen lines that had been reported. 'Just go up to a bar on Columbus Avenue and start buying drinks.' It was Friday night, I went and circled around. The one that got the strongest reaction was from Schwarzenegger—it was something like 'Do you need someone to flip your mattress for you?' One woman slapped me."

Even the simple act of calling in photos for an article could be dicey. "What's it for? What's it for?" was the standard, terrified response when the *Spy* call came, remembers photo editor Nicki Gostin. "You could feel people's insides turn to jelly," she says.

Paul Simms came down for his job interview on what he remembers as the hottest day of the summer of '88, and it ended with Graydon saying, "You're hired, and your job now is to make yourself indispensable."* But Simms was, in his own estimation, "the world's worst reporter. I didn't have whatever Bob Mack and John Brodie had, a lack of laziness or something. I was always trying to sit at my desk and do funny stuff without having to call anyone." Simms cowrote *Spy*'s first TV show and was the main author of *Spy Notes*, the *Cliffs Notes* parody that

---

*This was our standard advice to new employees, and remains, in its tautological way, the only good advice for new employees anywhere. —Eds.

became the second *Spy* book. "I took it over and made it my own, mainly because it was such a good excuse to stay at the office all night, come in late, and avoid any other kind of work," he says. (Simms went on to write for *Letterman* and *The Larry Sanders Show*, and he created *NewsRadio*—in some measure basing his funny New York news radio station on his first job, working at a funny New York magazine.)

The posthumous publication of *The Andy Warhol Diaries* was a major pop-culture event in 1989, one of *the* publishing events of the '80s—the book was dishy, revealing, and deliciously crammed with names, but it was missing the one thing it needed: an index. It got a rigorous, useful, and funny 16-page one (see opposite), which was bound into an issue of *Spy* and fit right into the odd-size Warhol book as if it belonged there. It was one of *Spy*'s most public-spirited gestures, especially given how labor-intensive a project it was, even by the magazine's extreme stan-

dards. "This was done by fucking hand, with, like, candles and quill pens," says Graydon. Adds Kurt, "As with so much we did, it really sort of presaged the Web. (In fact, didn't we invent the Internet?)" This somewhat monkish, puckish will to utility was a constant: A few months later we started publishing an index to *Spy* itself on the last page of each issue, an innovation since adopted by *The Atlantic* and other magazines.

Graydon and Kurt were trailed by a white van this past week, and we think it's part of New York *magazine's "Spying on* Spy*" story. We have taken countermeasures.*

—Journal entry, February 24, 1989

THESE COUNTERMEASURES INCLUDED sending a letter to *New York*'s editor-in-chief, Ed Kosner, indicating what we already knew about the story, which was being reported by

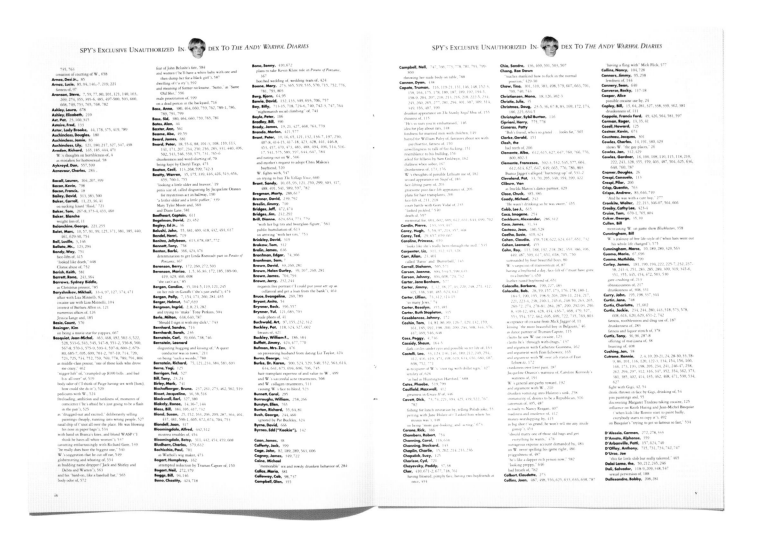

From
"Spy's Exclusive
Unauthorized
Index to *The Andy
Warhol Diaries*,"
August 1989

David Blum. Blum, the journalist who'd coined the term *Brat Pack* and helped popularize *yuppie*, knew Graydon and Kurt personally, and he and his wife, Terri Minsky, had both made early contributions to *Spy*—which made his transgression worse. The piece—a cover story, presented in *faux-Spy* style and featuring the earth-shattering "scoop" that Graydon had no college degree*— appeared in *New York* in April, and retaliatory arrangements were quickly in place. They involved pretending to book Blum to talk about his piece on a TV talk show, *People Are Talking*, which was taped at WOR-TV out in New Jersey, and thoughtfully providing a driver.

"We had to do something to get even with David—not because it was a bad piece, but just because somehow, you know, they'd

---

*Something he has never claimed to have; in fact, he talked often and proudly about having been thrown out of school. —Eds.

fired a shot across our bow," says Jamie Malanowski. "Carrie Weiner played the booker for the TV show—we had a phone line set up at *Spy* for such purposes. Geoff Reiss played the driver."

"The car was some kind of generic maroon four-door we rented," Reiss remembers. "The art department made us a little fake limousine sign that we could put in the window. And I still had some blazer I'd bought in high school that fit well, so I looked suitably shabby. I picked Blum up on the Upper West Side. And he just talked the whole time. I had a tape recorder. He explained how he'd written an article about these guys, really it was a morality tale. 'So you were out to get them?' 'Yeah. They definitely had it coming.' He was so excited, it was really kind of sad. I dropped him off in Secaucus and asked if it was okay if I went to the diner for a cup of coffee, and I'd come back for him. Then I went home."

Fifteen years after Blum finally made his way back from

THE SPY LIST

Cory

James

Pamela

Fred

Coretta

Jacqueline

Yoko

Isabel

Joan

Ian

Gayfryd

the Yuletide

FRIEDMAN

his supporters an
15 years
Noah Robinsc
Jackson's half bro
was convicted of l
witness to a slayir
Adolph Hitler
sought to exculpa
from murder char
ing he'd turned to
cause of his name
Joel Steinberg
Lisa Steinberg: 8 ¹
years and a $5,00
Mario Biaggi,
congressman con\
ing a Wedtech ra
8 years²
David Bloom,
Street whiz kid co
defrauding invest
company of almo:
lion: 8 years
**The Reverend
Streitferdt**, the H
tor convicted of s
attacking three pa
who had come to
counseling: 7 to 2
Stanley Friedr

¹ Three other PTL o
been convicted on v
of fraud. James Tag;
brother, got 17 years
plus a $500,000 fin
Dortch, a former P
dent, received 8 yea
$200,000 fine; and
Bakker got 45 years
$500,000 fine.
² His son, who was
fronting for his fath
two-year term and a

DECEMBER

Secaucus, I met him at a bar near Columbia University, where he was teaching a graduate course in journalism.

"As much as I loved *Spy*, I thought it would be fun to do to *Spy* what it was doing to others," he explained over a beer. "I hooked up with a photographer and we thought we would spy on Graydon with a telephoto lens. We stationed ourselves outside his apartment, followed him to the subway, looked through the office window, watched them go out to Buffa's for lunch. It was going to be a lighthearted thing."

And the subsequent day trip?

"It was a good idea for a prank, because it was a way to trap me in my own ego."

In the matter of *Spy* vs. Blum, only David Korzenik, *Spy*'s legal counsel, still needs to be heard from. So—honestly—did Geoff Reiss kidnap David Blum?

"I think that all happened before I was consulted," Korzenik replies carefully. "On the other hand, it was kind of an innocent prank. Evil, but kind of innocent."

SPY HAD ALWAYS BEEN A FUN PLACE to work, especially if you bought into "the nostalgia of the profession," as John Brodie puts it. "I really feel like there was this mass psychosis that we were in *The Front Page* or *His Girl Friday*," he says. "It was the sort of newsroom where you could say, 'Sweetheart, get me rewrite,' and not worry about being called into Human Resources." (Or Brodie could, anyway. More typically the cries emanating from Kurt's and Graydon's offices were, respectively, "Fuck!" and "What the *h-e-double-hockey-sticks*…?!")

The fun, in its most concentrated form, was best experienced at the formal weekly senior editorial meetings. For the (rare) expanded, ultra-democratic versions, *everyone* in editorial was encouraged to come and bring ideas, though the junior staff would often prefer to listen. "You said your bit very quickly," says one of them, "and then you'd just sit and watch everybody lob these little hand grenades back and forth.* It was like theater."

At the smaller weekly conclaves of the editorial cabal—usually six to eight people—the pace was breakneck. "Those meetings were fast, like basketball games," remembers Jamie Malanowski. "You had to keep up." Graydon and Kurt would sit at opposite ends of the long conference-room table and basically try to make each other laugh. Seemingly irrelevant digressions could turn into feature assignments; serious attempts to address specific topics could degenerate into anecdotes about Dean Martin or blunt discussions about why a certain starlet would never be a suitable cover model ("I've met her, and she looks like chicken that's been left out in the sun").

"For a while, on Fridays, we had to come in incredibly early—seven-thirty? eight?—and have all these ideas," says Tad Friend.

---

*By which trope—hand grenades—this former junior staff member surely means "impressively tossed-off bon mots and stunning insights," not "deadly anti-personnel devices." There was good-natured teasing, but deliberate public unkindness was virtually nonexistent at *Spy*. —Eds.

"And I remember Graydon expostulating once about how Kingsley Amis was a 'coaster' after *Lucky Jim*. I said, 'No, he's not,' and listed other funny books he'd written, and Graydon brushed his hair upward in that fake/real embarrassed manner, eyes darting, and said, 'Don't let facts get in the way, Tad.'"

As inherently competitive as these sessions were, they remained friendly. "What's almost startling to realize is that there was complete trust in that room," says Malanowski. "We were all possessive about the ideas we were working on, but we accepted that others could jump in and that the best ideas prevailed. So we all felt free to use our imaginations and think way out of the box."*

Working at *Spy* became still more fun once salaries had risen to the standard low-paying publishing-job level. But hiring people who fit in wasn't easy. Finding suitable editors—from *outside*—was especially problematic.

"In the beginning, it was an organic thing when the four of us got together, and it worked," says Susan Morrison. "But after that, the editors who worked most successfully were those who'd written for us—Tad and Bruce and Jamie, you could bring them right in as editors." Joanne Gruber, who was there nearly from the beginning, moved from copy editing and traffic-flow-managing to full-on editing as well. "But it was really hard to find somebody new who both could do the strenuous rewriting and who *got it*. I remember feeling like I was tapping people to be in a fraternity, because it really did bring out the worst in terms of our snobby exclusivity. When you found somebody who had it—Jim Collins, say—it was great. Walter Kirn had it, too, but he was never comfortable with it."

Kirn, a wonderful writer of fiction and nonfiction then and now, had a short tenure as a *Spy* editor, but one that both began and ended in memorable fashion. It concluded abruptly in the spring of 1990, when, having left a personal, handwritten note for each of the editorial staff late one night, he simply quit, for what he now describes as a combination of reasons: stress over navigating the conflicting wishes of writer Nicholas von Hoffman and of Graydon and Kurt concerning a profile of Richard Holbrooke; "queasiness" over an intrusive *Spy* cover story, just out, about Jay McInerney; and alarm over the effect it all might have on his nascent literary career (his first book was about to be published).

"It all came to a head when I went to a party for *Esquire*'s fiction issue, at '21'," Kirn says. "The moment I walked in, [writer and editor] Jim Atlas said, 'I can't believe what you guys did at *Spy* with that Jay McInerney thing.' He scolded me and tried to shame me about it. And I went home that night feeling like I had something to lose. Kurt had told me, 'You've got to be willing to burn some bridges,' and those words came back to haunt me: I had a picture of an island in the middle of the sea with four bridges basically collapsing.

"Now, I didn't know how to quit a job," Kirn continues. "I didn't realize you could go in and discuss it with people, or sit and think about it." So the next night he worked late at the office, then "left the notes and turned out the lights. I don't even think I picked up my last paycheck. It was a mixture of sudden morality, blind fear, craven self-interest, and the general willies."

> *"It was the sort of newsroom where you could say, 'Sweetheart, get me rewrite,' and not worry about being called to Human Resources."*

Only years later did he realize that Kurt and Graydon probably dealt with that kind of flak every day. "What was for me this gothic, shadowy moment, in which all the malignancies of the universe seemed to be converging, was for them another day at the fucking office," Kirn says, laughing. "I was like a Vietnam vet visiting someone who lives by an airport: I thought the bombers were coming, I run out of the house, and everybody looks at each other and goes, 'What the fuck?'*

"I can't imagine quitting a job in a more baffling and off-putting way, but Kurt and Graydon have, since, been nicer and more helpful to me than anybody in publishing. It made me think that *Spy* was a curious phenomenon all its own, that had really invented a kind of parallel universe, a place where there was all kinds of drama, and that once it was over everybody sort of got a general amnesty."

His hiring, just five months earlier, on the night of *Spy*'s fourth annual party, was equally dramatic. The search for a new senior editor had been going on for some time. "I was down at the Odeon

---

*Uttering the phrases "think out of the box" or "push the edge of the envelope," however, were grounds for dismissal. —Eds.

---

*Or maybe, rather, like a green recruit joining a somewhat battle-hardened platoon in a war zone and finding himself freaked out by routine small-arms fire. But whatever. —Eds.

at an after-party," Susan Morrison remembers, "awkwardly entertaining the two final candidates, who were both basically waiting to be told that they'd got the job."

Meanwhile, a little uptown at the Puck Building, among those attending the *Spy* party was Kirn, a young midwesterner who hadn't been in New York long and was the press critic at the new weekly *7 Days*.

"For a magazine that was done on a shoestring, it was a hell of a party," Kirn remembers. "All kinds of people were there, the drinking was definitely professional-level—mine was too, that night. And at some point, probably when Graydon and I had a harmonic convergence of intoxication, we started talking. And it was like something that happened in a musical. He sort of clapped me on the back and said, 'How'd you like to be an editor at *Spy*?' And I said, 'Boy, I don't know.' And within 30 seconds of making what was apparently an offer, and seeing that I didn't immediately say 'Sure,' he said, 'Well, you have until tomorrow morning. *The iron door is closing.*'"

The iron-door gambit (it's a John Barrymore line from Howard Hawks's *Twentieth Century*) was Graydon's ultimate threat.

"I didn't really know him, I was 26, but apparently he was a real editor at a real magazine and apparently a job had been offered to me—but now the iron door was already swinging shut!" Kirn continues. "And I was on the spot, half-drunk in the middle of this big crowd. So it was probably settled right there, but I didn't realize it. Then somehow the party spilled out into the street and we got into a limo."

That's where Kirn and I were first introduced. Piling into the limousine were a half-dozen of us, much the worse for wear. "George! Meet Walter Kirn, our new senior editor!" Graydon announced as the car screeched a left on Houston Street and we all shifted in the back seat. This was interesting news, and I wanted to hear more, but the topic was tabled because Graydon, awash in bonhomie, had elected to open the sunroof, stand up through it with Kirn at his side, and, waving around a champagne bottle, commence bellowing "My *man*!" at bewildered pedestrians.

"I had worked at *Vanity Fair*, where I remember feeling I was on the outside looking in," Kirn says. "And it dawned on me, in this limo, that I was now on the inside looking out, and whatever was inside should not have been permitted, and was actually the creation of people who just decided to make it up. That you could start a magazine, throw parties, be funny, create a sensation, and

act like you knew something nobody else did…I just thought, *Who are these characters?*"

In this manner we proceeded noisily to the Odeon, where Morrison was chatting with the two official candidates for the job.

There isn't much more to say.

"This limo pulls up," she remembers with a slight wince. "And Graydon barrels in there screaming, '*It's the Walter Kirn Decade!*' It was *really* awkward."

Graydon would insist that Kirn report to *Spy* the next morning. "I was told at the end of the evening that the iron door was still closing, so I showed up the next day and that was that," says Kirn. "It was a little bit like a beer commercial where a model comes up and kisses the 300-pound guy. I'm still waiting for the Walter Kirn Decade, by the way." (Both of the unilaterally and impulsively eliminated job candidates went on to extremely successful editorial careers, and both have held jobs at the tops of mastheads of major, still-extant magazines.)

Confined to more traditional job-interview settings, Graydon enjoyed improvising quizzes for entry-level employees: *Can you name Nick and Nora's dog in* The Thin Man*? What was Pete Maravich's nickname? How do you make an egg cream? What town do the Flintstones live in?* More than one flummoxed applicant would be escorted afterward, trembling, to the elevator, only to call out—desperately, too late, as the (possibly iron) door closed and the cage began its descent—"*Bed-rooooock!*"

"You'd bring these perfectly nice candidates in," Morrison says, "and they'd sit down and be kind of nervous. And the first thing Graydon would say was something like, 'Ah, I can see the hanger line on your pants. So that's your job-interview suit, huh? When's the last time you wore that, 18 months ago?' And just immediately made the poor guy feel like he wanted to climb out the window."

Had my annual review, with Kurt. Took us a while to find a secluded spot, the office has become so overcrowded. Walked this way and that, opening doors and looking down hallways, gravitating inevitably up to the Puck roof—where people were talking and smoking, and so we proceeded to the small, uppermost roof. Finally we stopped climbing and turned to face each other. "Everything's great," says Kurt. And so we head back downstairs.

— Journal entry, June 15, 1989

BUT NOT EVERYTHING WAS GREAT.

Spy grew extraordinarily quickly by every measure—circulation, advertising sales, attention, impact, and even editorial scope. Hollywood and, to a lesser extent, Washington had been in the *Spy* bailiwick almost from the beginning. And the embrace of the magazine by readers all over America had transformed our avowedly parochial New York publication into a national magazine.

"It's not like we pushed it onto a national distributor and spent lots of money in Chicago and L.A. and Austin or anything," says Kurt of circulation growth in 1987 and 1988. "It was local distributors in all those places calling and saying, 'Oh, we want to distribute your magazine.' So it organically became a national magazine over the first two years or so. And then we very consciously—month to month, as that happened—made it less of a strictly New York magazine."

If one wanted to pick a particular moment when *Spy* seriously "went national," a plausible choice would be September 1988, with the publication of an issue focused on Los Angeles. It was only our second perfect-bound issue; *Spy* was just starting to be designed with an almost-real-glossy-magazine art and production budget.

Yet as the magazine grew—the staff had gone from a dozen to more than 50 in just a couple of years—*Spy*'s ramshackle, amateurish charm proved less optimal on the business side.

"It was one step removed from 'I've got some old costumes, my dad has a garage we can use as a stage—let's put out a magazine,'" says Geoff Reiss, who apart from his prank-chauffeuring duties was by then *Spy*'s general manager. "Even as ad pages poured in, there was absolutely a naïveté to the way the whole thing was put together. It was learning on the job."

After three years of publishing, *Spy* was running six to 10 pages of media advertising in each issue—ads for magazines directed at advertising buyers. And despite huge circulation growth, Reiss argued for keeping ad rate increases modest. "I remember going to Tom and saying, 'Are we going to rate-protect these [media advertisers], or is their rate gonna be doubled like everybody else's?'" Reiss says. "And he said, 'No, we're going to double their rate, too.' So in one fell swoop we disenfranchised our second- or third-biggest advertising category. Tom said, 'We'll figure something out.' You wouldn't do that now. Maybe on a start-up, but at a grown-up magazine? This didn't allow us to be taken seriously by big-chip advertisers."

"We thought we could get away with doubling the rates," says Tom. "It was certainly justified by a circulation that had more than doubled and a layout that couldn't accommodate any more ad pages. And we *did* get away with it for a while."

Reiss acknowledges the "thought and sophistication" that went into the magazine's marketing and promotion. "We benefited from the exuberance that a bunch of neophytes were able to throw into a project like *Spy*—it was wonderful—but I think it ultimately hurt us some," he says. "The idea that you would not be aware that a feature on Michael Coady was going to completely destroy your relationship with your second-biggest advertiser, Guess—maybe first-biggest at the time—there's only one word for it: *naive*."

Coady was the head of the Fairchild Fashion Group, the publisher of *Women's Wear Daily*, and much reviled, according to a lot of the people *Spy* talked to for a December 1989 profile. Coady was also a close friend of Paul Marciano, one of the owners of Guess Jeans, whose ads then accounted for 4 percent of *Spy*'s total revenues. Immediately upon the article's publication, Mark Lasswell, who wrote the profile, received a four-page letter from an unhappy Marciano, who cc'd Tom and Kurt.

In his letter, Marciano reminded everyone that he had "been one of the very first supporters of *Spy* since the very first issue… and I never permitted myself to comment, criticize, or write any letter to *Spy* because of the respect I have for the freedom of the reporters." He described his and his brother's indebtedness to Coady and wrote that "the founders of *Spy* know specifically that I am a friend of Michael Coady and if they knew that you were working on such an article and I'm sure they knew, the least they could have done was to tell you to call me for a different sound to the story you seem to have in New York." (Lasswell stands by the Coady story and remembers in general how eager sources were to talk to a reporter about the monsters they worked for. "Writing about some of these awful people, you felt like you were fighting the good fight," he says.) Marciano concluded with: "I am extremely disappointed and sorry but I have to respect your right to report and print whatever you believe in and I do have the same right to advertise and support a magazine that I believe in, as I did with your first issue of *Spy*. I don't anymore."

And that was that, in terms of any Guess Jeans ads in *Spy*. Fast-forward two months.

*"You told me that if I left—
'my foot soldiers who go up
and down Wilshire Boulevard
each day will blow your
brains out.'…You said:
'If you make me eat shit, I'm
going to make you eat shit.'"*

ONE MAN AGAINST THE SYSTEM. IT IS A SHOPWORN BUT CROWD-PLEASING THEME THAT JOE ESZTERHAS, ONE OF HOLLYWOOD'S BEST-PAID SCREENWRITERS, HAS RECYCLED IN ONE MOVIE (*F.I.S.T.*) AFTER ANOTHER (*MUSIC BOX*). BUT WHEN HE WALKED INTO CREATIVE ARTISTS AGENCY HEADQUARTERS LAST FALL TO TELL MIKE OVITZ, THE MOST POWERFUL MAN IN THE MOVIE BUSINESS, THAT HE WAS LEAVING FOR A RIVAL TALENT AGENCY, ESZTERHAS FOUND HIMSELF IN AN IMPOSSIBLY MELODRAMATIC DAVID-AND-GOLIATH STRUGGLE THAT HAS FASCINATED AND SHOCKED EVEN JADED HOLLYWOOD. THE LETTERS BETWEEN THE TWO MEN, FAXED AND REFAXED FROM AGENTS TO PRODUCERS TO SCREENWRITERS COAST TO COAST BARELY MOMENTS AFTER THEIR AUTHORS HAD DISPATCHED THEM, PROVE THAT THE MOVIE INDUSTRY IS INDEED THE AMERICAN CENTER OF ROUTINE CRUELTY AND SLEEK CYNICISM, THAT EVERYTHING THEY SAY ABOUT HOLLYWOOD IS COR-RECT, THAT REALLY AND TRULY

THERE'S NO BUSINESS LIKE SHOW BUSINESS

THE CHILLING, UNABRIDGED MIKE OVITZ-JOE ESZTERHAS

It started, as so many things in Hollywood do, with four words: "Let's have a meeting." Joe Eszterhas, the 45-year-old former *Rolling Stone* star reporter turned star screenwriter, who had written the scripts for *Flashdance, Jagged Edge, F.I.S.T.* and *Betrayed*, wanted to end his professional relationship with his agent, Mike Ovitz, the driven overlord of the powerful Creative Artists Agency.

Since CAA's founding in 1975, Ovitz had got his fingers in more — and more important — film and television deals than any other agent. If he did not exactly create the concept of "packaging" — the monopolistic procedure whereby an agency lashes together a package of talent culled from its own stable of writers, stars, directors and producers for a particular film, regardless of the appropriateness of the fit, and then strong-arms a studio into accepting it as an all-or-nothing deal and charges it 15 percent for this service — he at least perfected it. It was often speculated, perhaps a bit hyperbolically, that after 1982 no major movie got made in Hollywood without Ovitz's approval. It's not difficult to see why. CAA's client list includes Sylvester Stallone, Bill Murray, Barbra Streisand, Robert Redford, Paul Newman, Kevin Costner, Dustin Hoffman, Robert De Niro, Jane Fonda, Al Pacino, Robin Williams, Billy Crystal, Michael Keaton, Chevy Chase, Sean Connery, Tom Cruise, Goldie Hawn, Gene Hackman, Bette Midler, Cher, S[...] ney Pollack, Martin Brest, John Hughes, Oli[...] Stone, Rob Reiner, Sidney Lumet, Bob Zemec[...] and Richard Donner, along with another 550 or [...] of the highest-paid writers, directors, produc[...] and performers in television, movies and p[...] music. By all accounts, Mike "the Manipulat[...] Ovitz really had become, by the mid-1980s, [...] most powerful man in Hollywood. And the l[...] year had been particularly sweet, personal-pow[...] wise. The agency's sleek, nameless I. M. Pei-[...] signed headquarters on Little Santa Monica Bou[...] vard had finally opened. Presidential candida[...] governors and senators came to Ovitz hoping [...] curry favor with him and, in turn, the money a[...] endorsements of his stars. Last fall he chaire[...] celebrity-clotted Los Angeles benefit for Sena[...] Bill Bradley that raised almost $750,000. A[...] puff pieces on Ovitz and CAA had appeared [...] *Time, New York* and *The New York Times Magaz*[...] And before Sony chose Peter Guber and Jon Pet[...] to run Columbia Pictures, it offered the chairm[...] ship to Ovitz and even offered to buy CAA if t[...] would permit him to accept the job. There w[...] even rumors that Ovitz might buy a bank in or[...] to finance the making of his own movies (and C[...] was said to have actually underwritten last su[...] mer's production of *Quick Change*, Bill Murray's torial debut). The high point of the year was most surely Oscar night, when neither the director of the award-winning *Rain Man* (Barry Levinson) nor the producer of *Rain Man* (Mark Johnson) nor the star of *Rain Man* (Dustin Hoffman) remembered to thank one another in their acceptance speeches. All three, however, thought to thank their agent—Mike Ovitz. The meeting that Ovitz had with his client Joe Eszterhas in late September managed to overshadow all the inexorable fabulousness that befell CAA last year. Although the meeting was private, the ensuing epistolary barrage between Eszterhas and Ovitz proved the movie business at its highest levels to be an uglier, even more hysterically dangerous milieu than any fiction had previously portrayed. Here, then, that fabled correspondence.

OCTOBER 3, 1989: JOE ESZTERHAS WRITES TO MIKE OVITZ

Two weeks ago I walked into your office and told you I was leaving CAA.[1] Not for any reason that had to do with CAA's performance on my behalf, I said: I was leaving because Guy McElwaine was back in the agency business and Guy was my oldest friend in town.[2] He was one of my first agents; he was responsible for the biggest breakthrough in my 13-year-career;[3] he and I continued our relationship while he was at Rastar,[4] Columbia[5] and Weintraub.[6] My decision, I told you, had to do with loyalty and friendship and nothing else.[7] I knew when I walked in that you wouldn't be happy[8]—no other writer at CAA makes $1.25 million a screenplay[9]—but I was unprepared for the crudity and severity of your response.[10] You told me that if I left—"my foot soldiers who go up and down Wilshire Boulevard each day will blow your brains out."[11] You said that you would sue me. "I don't care if I win or lose," you said, "but I'm going to tie you up with depositions and court dates so that you won't be able to spend any time at your typewriter." You said: "If you make me eat shit, I'm going to make you eat shit." When I said to you that I had no interest in being involved in a public spectacle, you said: "I don't care if everybody in town knows. I want them to know. I'm not worried about the press. All those guys want to write screenplays for Robert Redford."[12] You said: "If somebody came into the building and took my Lichtenstein off the wall, I'd go after them. I'm going to go after you the same way. You're one of this agency's biggest assets." You said: "This town is like a chess game. ICM isn't going after a pawn or a knight, they're going after a king. If the king goes, the knights and pawns will follow." You suggested facetiously that maybe you'd make a trade with ICM. You'd keep me and give ICM four or five clients. Almost as an aside, you threatened to damage my relationships with Irwin Winkler[13] and Barry Hirsch.[14] They are relationships you know I treasure: Irwin and I have done Betrayed and Music Box together and we are contracted to do four more movies; Barry has been my attorney for 13 years.[15] "Those guys are friends of mine," you said. "Do you think they'll still be good friends of yours if you ▸

stranger to high-pitched ... with the powers that be, ...rhas, the son of a Hungar...novelist, distinguished him...arly in his career by writing ...imed investigative stories. ...s a human-interest story, ...ver, that resulted in a suc...al invasion-of-privacy suit ...brought against his em...r, the Cleveland *Plain Dealer*. ...paper paid $60,000 in set...ent to an Ohio family that ...rhas had misrepresented in ...count of flood victims. (He ...visited the family home and ...ed the mother in his story, ...ugh she was not there when ...nducted the interview.) Be...e Eszterhas was in job arbi...on with *The Plain Dealer* at ...ime of the suit (the result ...s having written an article ...*ergreen Review* critical of the ...r's publisher), he was never ...sed at the libel hearing and ...fore never allowed to give ...ide of the story. (Many of ...details on Eszterhas's two-...des-old newspaper career ...ced in a report of the feud ...appeared in the *Los Angeles*

ONDENCE

; it is believed that CAA ...ed through the highest ech...at the *Times* to bring these ...ents to the reporter's atten...In 1971 he joined the staff ...*lling Stone* in San Francisco ...ecame the magazine's star ...tigative reporter (publisher-

...r Jann Wenner is the godfather of one of Eszterhas's children). He left *Rolling* ...sometime after his first screenplay, the awful labor-organizing melodrama ...*T.*, was produced in 1978.

...tall, silver-haired Beverly Hills fixture who has been married eight times, ...waine joined the International Creative Management talent agency in ...after a decade of running his own public-relations firm, which repre...d such clients as Judy Garland, Frank Sinatra and Warren Beatty. At ...his client list included the likes of Steven Spielberg, Aaron Spelling, Rich-

ard Pryor, Martin Ritt, Robert Wagner and Eszterhas. (McElwaine took a year and a half off during his time at ICM to serve as a senior vice president of Warner Bros., and helped bring *All the President's Men* and *Dog Day Afternoon* to the screen.) McElwaine subsequently headed up Rastar Films, the production company owned by Columbia Pictures strongman Ray Stark; then Columbia Pictures itself; then his own production company; and then the Weintraub Entertainment Group, where he produced a string of recent box office duds, including *My Stepmother Is an Alien*, *She's Out of Control* and *Troop Beverly Hills*. McElwaine fled Weintraub last summer to return to superagentry—during his eight-year absence, Ovitz had made the profession respectable, even glamorous—as ICM's vice-chairman.

3. Early in his career, Eszterhas (McElwaine's first writer client) wrote a script called *City Hall*, which the agent auctioned for $500,000, effectively dou-

bling Eszterhas's going price for a screenplay.

4. McElwaine worked for Stark from 1981 to 1982. One of the most powerful men in pre-Ovitz Hollywood, Stark was instrumental in brokering Columbia, the studio with which he has long been associated, to Coca-Cola, and in ensuring that during the David Begelman–Cliff Robertson check-forgery scandal the studio stood behind Begelman. He also helped orchestrate the departure of David Puttnam from Columbia in 1987, after Puttnam balked at the self-rewarding new deal that Stark had arranged for himself at the studio. When Dawn Steel succeeded

ANNOTATED BY CELIA BRADY

January 1990

Puttnam in the job, one of her first acts was to renew Stark's studio contract, a quid pro quo–ism that continued last year with Stark's dispatch of weekly gifts to Steel's child.

5. McElwaine was at Columbia for five years, during which time the studio produced Eszterhas's *Jagged Edge*.

6. McElwaine was at Weintraub from 1987 to August 1989.

7. The words *loyalty and friendship*, in Hollywood terms, roughly mean "We've made money together, and our current spouses like each other."

8. This is something of an understatement, as Ovitz's mania for loyalty is legendary. When Judy Hofflund and David Greenblatt defected from CAA in 1988 to form InterTalent, Ovitz not only threatened to use his power to ensure that no one signed with their new agency but fired another CAA agent, Tom Strickler, and had him escorted from the building by security personnel, because he had dared to have breakfast with the defector Greenblatt.

9. A somewhat self-serving figure. Under his current studio contract, Eszterhas receives $750,000 for the final draft and a $500,000 production bonus if the screenplay actually gets turned into a film.

10. Again, an understatement. Ovitz's possessiveness and hysterical reactions to client defections are well known. Even such embryonic assets as mailroom employees are told, "If you leave Creative Artists, we sit *shivah* for seven days...and then you die."

11. A reflection of CAA's new corporate address. Previous Ovitz threats must have been something like *My foot soldiers who go up and down Century Park East each day will blow your brains out*, proving that in top-echelon show business thuggery, as in real estate, location is everything.

do this?"[16] You said all these things in a friendly, avuncular way. "I like you," you said. "I like your closeness to your family. I like how hard you work. I like your positive outlook. I like the fact that you have no directing or producing ambitions.[17] You write original screenplays with star parts—your ideas are great and so are your scripts.[18] I like everything about you," you said, "except your shirt."[19] You said I reminded you of one of your children. The child would build these wooden blocks up-high and then would knock all the blocks down. "I'm not going to let you do this to yourself," you said. That night at dinner at Jimmy's,[20] Rand Holston was friendly, too, but he described the situation more specifically.[21] Rand said you were the best friend anyone could have and the worst enemy. What would happen, I asked Rand, if I left CAA? "Mike's going to put you into the fucking ground," Rand said. Rand listed the particulars: If I left CAA, Rand said, no CAA star would play in any of my scripts. "You write star vehicles," Rand said, "not ensemble pieces. This would be particularly damaging to you." In addition, Rand said, no CAA director would direct one of my scripts.[22] But perhaps most important, Rand said, is that you would go out of your way with studio executives and company executives "like Martin Davis,"[23] to use Rand's example, to speak about me unfavorably. What would you say to them? I asked Rand. You'd say that while I was a pretty good writer, Rand said, I was difficult and hard to work with. You'd say that I wrote too many scripts.[24] "There's no telling what Mike will say when he's angry," Rand said.[25] "When I saw him after the meeting with you, the veins were bulging out of his neck."[26] Even worse, Rand said, was that you would make sure the studio people knew that I was on "your shit list."[27] And since most studio executives anxiously wanted to use CAA's stars in their pictures, these executives would avoid me "like the plague" to curry favor with you and your stars. Rand added that since I was late turning in my latest script to United Artists, I was technically in breach of contract with U.A. on my overall deal[28] and said that if I left CAA, United Artists would sue me. To say that I was in shock after my meetings with you and Rand would be putting it mildly. What you ▶

play deals at Columbia and Warners; David Friendly left the *Los Angeles Times* work for Brian Grazer's Imagine Films, a major CAA client; Dean Valenti[ne] abandoned Time Inc. for executive jobs first at NBC and later at Disney; frien[d]less *New York* writer David Blum and his wife, Terri Minsky, a contributing edi[tor] at *Premiere*, pressured her uncle Norman Steinberg, the producer of the witless s[it]com *Doctor, Doctor*, into giving them jobs as story editors on the show.

13. Winkler was originally [a] partner in (Robert) Charto[ff-]Winkler Productions, which, [in] addition to the *Rocky* seri[es,] produced *The Right Stuff* and *T[he] Gang That Couldn't Shoot Straig[ht.]* On his own, Winkler has p[ro]duced, among other films, E[sz]terhas's *Betrayed* and *Music Bo[x.]*

14. A cofounder and partner [in] Armstrong, Hirsch & Levi[ne] and one of the highest-pa[id] entertainment lawyers in L[os] Angeles.

15. The length of this relatio[n]ship is not exceptional. Lawye[rs] often play a bigger role in th[e] most important clients' liv[es] than do agents—they negoti[ate] the final details of most contra[cts] and are likely to be far more in[ti]mately acquainted with the p[er]sonal life, financial shenaniga[ns,] wills and divorces of the art[ist] than the agent is. When a st[ar's] agent needs to be fired, mo[re] often than not it is the lawy[er] who delivers the bad new[s.] Hirsch, along with Johnny Bran[ca] (Michael Jackson's and Mick Ja[g]ger's lawyer) and Jake Bloo[m] (Sylvester Stallone's), is amo[ng] the most powerful entertai[n]ment attorneys in Los Ange[les] these days.

16. A pretty good question, a[c]tually. Hirsch, whose office w[as] just four floors from Ovitz's [be]fore CAA moved, represents [a] number of the agency's bigg[est] clients, including Robert R[ed]ford, Barbra Streisand, Sa[lly] Field, Sydney Pollack, Se[an] Penn, Kim Basinger, Barry L[ev]inson, Tom Cruise and Bill M[ur]ray. Indeed, Ovitz had a hand in the firm's very creation, having introduc[ed] Hirsch to his future partner Gary Hendler. And Winkler has used CAA clients [in] his most important films: Philip Kaufman (director, *The Right Stuff*), Stallone ([the] *Rocky* series, *F.I.S.T.*), Robert De Niro (*Raging Bull*) and Jessica Lange (*Music Bo[x]*).

17. Everybody in Hollywood wants to move to the next creative level. Scree[n]writers want to direct; television stars want to be in films; film stars want [to] produce and direct; and in the case of Don (*Top Gun*) Simpson, you have [a] producer who wants to be a director and a film star. Ovitz has facilitated [...]

12. Ovitz is right. Hollywood's impulse to co-opt journalists with implicit promises of production deals and studio jobs if they play the game is time-honored, but during the last decade more journalists than ever have gone over to the other side. Former journalist Tony Schwartz managed sufficient groveling-in-print to secure production deals from both Fox and NBC; Michael London, a talented reporter at the *Los Angeles Times*, left the paper to work first for Don Simpson and Jerry Bruckheimer at Paramount and then for Barry Diller at Fox; Bruce Feirstein, a former CAA client and *New York* (and SPY) contributor, won screen-

sitions of many CAA writer clients turned writer-director clients (Chris
[*Gremlins*] Columbus, Ovitz's close friend Barry Levinson, Cameron [*Fast Times
at Ridgemont High*] Crowe). Generally for CAA, though, it is simply not cost-
effective to indulge such ambitions. Writers are often obliged to take a pay
[cut] if they want to direct their own work — resulting in a smaller commission
[for] CAA. It also means one less screenplay available for one of Ovitz's many

[dir]ector clients — resulting in
[few]er commissions for CAA.
[An]d when a writer is directing,
[he] is not writing the kind of
[scri]pts that CAA stars can act
[in] — resulting in fewer commis-
[sio]ns for CAA. Maintaining the
[cre]ative status quo as much
[as] possible is very important
[to C]AA.

Beyond his impulse to
[eg]alitarianism, this is the real
[rea]son Ovitz so badly wanted to
[kee]p Eszterhas at CAA. "Star
[scr]ipts" — that is, screenplays
[with] the sort of large, glamorous,
[ego]-glorifying parts that attract
[big]-name stars — are a precious
[com]modity in Hollywood, be-
[cau]se stars are still what drive
[box] office receipts. The script to
[wh]ich Michael Douglas or Paul
[Ne]wman or Robert Redford will
[co]mmit is manifestly more im-
[po]rtant to a studio than the
[bit]tersweet little coming-of-age
[sto]ry that every screenwriter
[has] tucked away somewhere. A
[wr]iter who can consistently
[tu]rn out this kind of script, a
[wr]iter like Eszterhas — whose
[scr]eenplays have attracted Glenn
[Cl]ose, Jeff Bridges, Debra Winger
[an]d Jessica Lange (all of them
[C]AA clients) — is a writer an
[age]ncy cannot afford to lose.

[...] Eszterhas was wearing a
[sli]ghtly rumpled green-and-white
[ch]ecked shirt that he had bought
[in] Florida that summer, jeans
[an]d tennis shoes. Ovitz, who
[fav]ors the brown, soft-shoul-
[de]red, impeccably bland Valley
[loo]k, was wearing a white shirt,
[...] and suit pants. Most CAA

[cli]ents dress like Colombian agribusiness merchants — thin-soled leather pumps,
[...]s of Gianni Versace and nubby raw silk. At *Rolling Stone*, Eszterhas was fond of
[ac]cessorizing his fashion look by wearing on his belt a hunting knife that he used
[to] clean his pipe.

[...] Frou-fancy "continental" restaurant popular with CAA agents that is located
[on] the fringe of Century City, not far from Beverly Hills High. The agency has a
[ho]use account there.

[...] Holston, a CAA agent, is in his late thirties, drives a BMW 633CSI (no

were threatening me with was a twisted new version of the old-
fashioned blacklist. I felt like the character in Irwin's new script
whose career was destroyed because he refused to inform on
his friends.[29] You were threatening to destroy my career because
I was refusing to turn my back on a friend. I live in Marin
County; I spend my time with my family and with my work;
I've avoided industry power entanglements for 13 years. Now I
felt, as I told my wife when I came home to think all this over,
like an infant who wakes up in his crib with a 1,000 pound
gorilla screeching in his face. In the two weeks that have gone
by, I have thought about little else than the things you and Rand
said to me. Plain and simple, cutting out all the smiles and
friendliness, it's blackmail.[30] It's extortion, the street-hood protection racket we've seen too many times in bad gangster movies.
If you don't pay us the money, we'll burn your store down. Never
mind that in this case it wasn't even about money — not for a
while, anyway: I told you that ICM didn't even want us to split
the commissions with you on any of my existing deals — "Fuck
the commissions," you said, "I don't care about the commissions."[31] Even the dialogue, I reflected, was out of those bad gangster movies: "blow your brains out" and "put you into the fucking
ground" and "If you make me eat shit, I'm going to make you
eat shit."[32] As I thought about what happened, I continued, increasingly, to be horrified by it. You are agents. Your role is to
help and encourage my career and creativity. Your role is not
to place me in personal emotional turmoil. Your role is not to
threaten to destroy my family livelihood if I don't do your bidding. I am not an asset; I am a human being. I am not a painting
hung on a wall; I am not part of a chess set. I am not a piece of
meat to be "traded" for other pieces of meat. I am not a child
playing with blocks. This isn't a game. It's my life. What I have
decided, simply, after this period of time, is that I can not live
with myself and continue to be represented by you. I find the
threats you and Rand made to be morally repugnant. I simply
can't function on a day to day business basis with you and Rand
without feeling myself dirtied. Maybe you can beat the hell out of
some people and they will smile at you afterwards and make nice, ▸

CAA vanity plates) and uses a headset instead of a standard telephone (thought
to be the inspiration for Tom Cruise's telephonic apparatus in the CAA-pack-
aged *Rain Man*.) Less visible than such CAA agents as cofounders Ron Meyer
and Bill Haber or Rosalie Swedlin, Holston is a second-tier operative. In the CAA
universe, all clients are theoretically represented by Ovitz the shogun, but
each one also has a shadow warrior who takes care of the client's day-to-day
needs. Holston succeeded Swed-
lin in serving this function for
Eszterhas.

22. CAA client Costa-Gavras
directed *Betrayed* and *Music Box*.
Sidney Poitier (also a CAA
client) was set to direct Eszterhas's *Beat the Eagle* for Columbia
but withdrew from the film in
November, weeks after Eszterhas
left CAA.

23. The reed-thin New York–
based chairman of Paramount
Pictures.

24. A reference to William Goldman, a million-dollar-a-screen-
play writer, who in the eighties
turned out three such scripts in
one year, thereby saturating the
market for Goldman screenplays.
Eszterhas has written 16 screenplays over the last 13 years:
F.I.S.T., *Nark*, *Die Shot*, *City Hall*,
Platinum, *Flashdance* (co-written
with Tom Hedley), *Pals*, *Jagged
Edge*, *Magic Man*, *Big Shots*, *Checking Out*, *Hearts of Fire* (co-written
with Scott Richardson), *Betrayed*,
Music Box, *Beat the Eagle* and
Sacred Cows. What is interesting
here is Ovitz's tendency in battle
to turn an opponent's strength —
a writer's productivity — into
a weakness, or as Ovitz's own
aikido master might say, "Combine the opponent's strength
with your strength and then
make your move."

25. As Ovitz's own management
bible, *The Art of War*, by Sun Tzu,
puts it, "[When] on desperate
ground, fight."

26. A surprising depiction,
since Ovitz is notorious for displaying no emotion at all. The

bulge in his neck might not have been there had Ovitz not made his former personal trainer, Steve Seagal, a movie star. (Seagal's *Above the Law* [1988] was written
by CAA client Ronald Shusett.)

27. Not a list professional moviemakers want to find their name on. When
producer-manager Bernie Brillstein was on it (in the late eighties he ran Lorimar), the studio was effectively shut off from CAA's stars and directors. Jay
Weston, the producer of the hit *Lady Sings the Blues*, sued CAA over a rights dis-
pute in 1979. In the last eleven years, he has produced just three feature-length

"You can quote Rashomon as much as you like, but words like...'he'll put you into the fucking ground' leave little room for ambiguity."

movies — *Night of the Juggler, Buddy Buddy* and *Chu Chu and the Philly Flash.* "I regret more than anything else in my business life the mistake of suing CAA," Weston told the *Los Angeles Times* in 1988. "They are the best agency.... I have nothing but admiration for them." Yes, Master! When Tim McCanlies, who wrote *North Shore,* told CAA agent Richard Lovett that he was switching to InterTalent, he was informed that *a terrible accident* would befall his career. When word reached CAA that McCanlies had taped the conversation, the agency threatened to sue the writer. When Michael Dinner, who wrote *Miss Lonelyhearts* and *Heaven Help Us,* bolted from the agency to go to Sam Cohn at ICM, he too began suffering career difficulties. And in the weeks after Eszterhas's letter began making the rounds in Hollywood, the *Los Angeles Times* reported receiving six such complaints and SPY received equally as many. Such is the malignant influence of CAA that none of the callers wanted to be identified in print. Eszterhas himself reportedly received more than 100 letters of support, two dozen of which came from former CAA clients who had experienced similar horrors, which they recounted in graphic terrifying detail, when they tried to extricate themselves from the agency.

28. An agreement for a given number of scripts over a certain period of time that ties a writer exclusively to a studio. Eszterhas had a six-picture deal with United Artists that guaranteed him more than $5 million over five years. At the time of leaving CAA, he had completed half the scripts in the contract.

29. The movie is *Fear No Evil,* a drama about Hollywood blacklisting in the fifties directed and co-written by Winkler and starring Robert De Niro.

30. Although the Justice Department's antitrust division and the California Attorney General's Office are involved in no active proceedings against CAA,

but I can't do that.[33] I have always believed, both personally and in my scripts, in the triumph of the human spirit.[34] I have abhorred bullying of all kinds — by government, by police, by political extremism of the Left and the Right, by the rich — maybe it's because I came to this country as a child and was the victim of a lot of bullying when I was an adolescent. But I always fought back; I was bloodied a lot, but I fought back.[35] I know the risks I am taking; I am not doing this blithely. Yes, you might very well be able to hurt me with your stars, your directors and your friends on the executive level.[36] Yes, Irwin and Barry are friends of yours and maybe you will be able to damage my relationships with them — but as much as I treasure those relationships with them, if my decision to leave CAA affects them, then they're not worth it anyway. Yes you might sue me and convince U.A. and God knows who else to sue me. And yes, I know that you can play dirty — the things you said about Guy and Bob Towne in your meeting with me are nothing less than character assassination.[37] But I will risk all that. Rich or poor, successful or not, I have always been able to look myself in the mirror. I am not saying that I don't take your threats seriously; I take your threats very seriously indeed. But I have discussed all of this with my wife, with my 15-year-old boy and my 13-year-old girl, and they support my decision. After three years of searching, we bought a bigger and much more expensive house recently. We have decided, because of your threats and the uncertainty they cast on my future, to put the new house up for sale and stay in our old one.[38] You told me your feeling for your own family;[39] do you have any idea how much pain and turmoil you've caused mine? I think the biggest reason I can't stay with you has to do with my children. I have taught them to fight for what's right. What you did is wrong. I can't teach my children one thing and then, on the most elemental level, do another. I am not that kind of man. So do whatever you want to do, Mike, and fuck you. I have my family and I have my old manual imperfect typewriter and they have always been the things I've treasured the most. Barry Hirsch will officially notify you that I have left CAA and from this date on Guy McElwaine will represent me.[40]

Law" guarantees that any personal-service contract can be broken without pen on 60 days' notice.

31. When a client leaves an agency, the agency generally receives the commissi resulting from all deals that it negotiated for the client — several hundred th sand dollars, in this instance.

32. Eszterhas, of course, avoids such clichéd dialogue in his own work (see "Fr Eszterhas to Your House," p 96). His characters act in a m natural manner, preferring stalk human beings with MAC automatic rifles (*Betrayed*) a bring hunting knives wit perilous proximity to hum genitalia (*Jagged Edge*).

33–35. See "From Eszterhas Your House," page 96.

36. Almost everyone with last power in Hollywood: Mich Eisner at Disney, Barry Dille Fox, Peter Guber at Columb Barry Levinson, Steven Sp berg, Barbra Streisand and a one in the business who has L Lakers season tickets.

37. Towne is the writer *Chinatown* and *Greystoke: Legend of Tarzan. Lord of the A* and the writer and director *Tequila Sunrise.*

38. Eszterhas's old house orig ally cost $225,000 and is c rently valued at $650,000. October, Ray Stark called McElwaine and offered to the $2 million new house Eszterhas with "no strings tached." When word leaked the press, Stark downgraded gesture to just lending Eszter the money. The simplest exp nation for Stark's generosit discounting outright comp sion for another human be (this is Hollywood, after all) that he felt he wasn't gett enough press attention a wanted to reassert himself a Hollywood power broker. also reportedly hoped to end himself to Eszterhas so that might get a first look at his fut

Ovitz's attempt to "blackmail" Eszterhas might constitute a "predicate act" under the federal racketeering (RICO) statutes. If a litigant were able to prove that a pattern of extortion had been perpetrated by CAA agents, then Ovitz, Haber and Meyer — the three owners of the agency — might find themselves prosecuted under the same statute as Fat Tony Salerno. Were Eszterhas to prove that Ovitz actively conspired with others in the film business to thwart his career, the agent could be found in violation of the Sherman Antitrust Act, known in California as the Cartwright Act. Additionally in California, the "Bette Davis

screenplays. Stark's involvement is doubly curious given that he and Ovitz h previously been allies, having most recently worked in concert to purge Da Puttnam from Columbia.

39. Ovitz has three children and is married to his college sweetheart, Judy Rei

40. All this talk and in reality there was no contract to be broken, as I terhas's contract with CAA had lapsed more than a year earlier. He has a ha shake agreement with McElwaine. (Eszterhas cc'd this letter to Holston, Hirs Winkler and McElwaine.)

OCTOBER 3, 1989: OVITZ RESPONDS TO ESZTERHAS'S LETTER

When I received your letter this morning I was totally shocked since my recollection of our conversation bore no relationship to your recollection. Truly this appears to be one of those Rashomon situations,[1] and your letter simply makes little or no sense to me.[2]

As I explained to you when we were together, you are an important client of this company and all that I was trying to do is to keep you as a client. There was no other agenda. If you have to leave, you have to leave and so be it. I have talked to Guy and I have told him that whatever we can do to be helpful in his transition we will do. Of course, as you assured me, I am expecting that you will pay us whatever you owe us.

I am particularly sensitive when people bring families and children into business discussions. If someone said to me what you think I said to you, I would feel the same way as you expressed in your letter. I think that your letter was unfair and unfounded, but it does not change my respect for your talent. I only hope that in time you will reflect on the true spirit of what I was trying to communicate to you.

I want to make it eminently clear that in no way will I, Rand, or anyone else in this agency, stand in the way of your pursuing your career. So please, erase from your mind any of your erroneous anxieties or thoughts you may have to the contrary.

Best wishes and continued success.

OCTOBER 5, 1989: ESZTERHAS RESPONDS TO OVITZ'S RESPONSE

A brief response to your letter dated Oct. 3, 1989:

1. You can quote Rashomon as much as you like, but words like "my foot soldiers…will blow your brains out" and "he'll put you into the fucking ground" leave little room for ambiguity.

2. I am particularly sensitive when people bring their families and children into business discussions, too — and I hope that in the future you will reflect that keeping important clients isn't worth haunting families and children the way you haunt mine.

3. I understand very well "the true spirit" of what you were trying to communicate to me in the meeting and will live my life accordingly.

4. My "erroneous anxieties" notwithstanding, we are selling our new house anyway.[3]

5. Please understand that after the things you and Rand said to me, I can hardly take your "best wishes" for my "continued success" seriously.

[1]. A reference to Akira Kurosawa's 1951 Oscar-winning meditation on the meaning of truth, in which four characters relate wildly different versions of an event at which all were present. *You say "tomato" and I say "tomato." You say "extortion" and I say "career advice."*

[2]. See *Gaslight* (1944).   **3.** Eszterhas ultimately sold the house that he had bought and renovated but never moved into.

Few people in the movie industry doubt that Mike Ovitz threatened Joe Eszterhas. The everyday vocabulary of Hollywood is rife with images of violence and malediction, and the crude threat and the vulgar epithet have long been part of that language. There is an uninterrupted tradition of crass bravado among the rulers of the movie business from Harry Cohn to Dawn Steel.

Mike Ovitz, however, stepped over the line.

At any given time, there are a dozen or so men who truly run Hollywood. The club currently includes Lew Wasserman and Sidney Sheinberg at Universal, Thomas Murphy of ABC/Cap Cities, Laurence Tisch of CBS, Robert Wright of GE (owner of NBC), Steve Ross and Robert Daly of Warners, Disney's Michael Eisner and Jeffrey Katzenberg, Barry Diller at Fox, Sony dealmaker Michael Schulhof (a new member of the club, replacing Victor Kaufman) and Martin Davis of Paramount. They're the men who exercise real power in Hollywood — the ones who can order checks of sufficient size to get movies made. They socialize together and contribute to one another's charities; their wives serve on the same boards and hire the same cooks and caterers. Above all else — above all the glamour, the sequins, the plush seats in the studio Gulfstream and the inflated salaries and toadying underlings — they regard themselves as respectable corporate leaders. They aren't supposed to threaten to blow people's brains out. They aren't supposed to threaten to destroy people's livelihoods. They aren't supposed to talk like thugs, or at least not in the presence of onetime journalists.

And when they drive home at night to their houses in Bel Air or Beverly Hills, or their apartments on Park Avenue, they don't like having to explain to their mates (who also read the trades, and the Calendar Section of the *Los Angeles Times*) that one of their business associates — a man who might have come to dinner last week — threatened to grind some writer into the "fucking ground." It doesn't play on the Bel Air–Holmby Hills dinner circuit, or on the New York Stock Exchange.

When the Hollywood elders brought the banty, wheedling former LBJ aide Jack Valenti out from Washington a quarter century ago to head up the Motion Picture Association, they also wanted him to advance the notion that the film business was being run by upright businessmen with briefcases and lace-up shoes.

Eisner, Wasserman and Tisch may well threaten people — they're certainly familiar with the vocabulary — but they're clever enough to avoid actually bearing the message themselves; Ovitz, for all his maniacal self-control and planning, wasn't. He embarrassed the Old Guard — he brought up all the things they'd worked so hard to eradicate or disguise — and in doing so caused them to reassess his position in the Hollywood food chain.

The elders didn't enjoy reading that Ovitz — an *agent*, for

FROM ESZTERHAS TO YOUR HOUSE

HOW ONE BRAVE MAN'S LIFE IMITATES HIS SCREENPLAYS

In his now-legendary missive to Mike Ovitz, the Hollywood *capo di tutti capi*, screenwriter Joe Eszterhas wrote, "I have always believed, both personally and in my scripts, in the triumph of the human spirit." No truer words were ever spoken. Since the release of *F.I.S.T.* in 1978, Eszterhas has been rehearsing in his screenplays for a real-life, final-act showdown with a force of darkness of the sort embodied by Ovitz.

Scholars of this underdog laureate's work can glimpse in the highly autobiographical *F.I.S.T.* rare snatches of its author's personality. Sylvester Stallone, Eszterhas's first on-screen alter ego, portrays the incorruptible Johnny Kovak, who sees the powers of management conspiring against the humble lunchpail class. Kovak (like Eszterhas, a Hungarian immigrant) becomes a union organizer and transforms a ragtag band of menials from Ohio (Eszterhas's home state) into a cadre of national union officials.

Kovak inspires his men, and the audience, with rousing populist rhetoric. "No goddamn company bastard livin' up in the Heights is gonna walk over your life!" he pledges. When Kovak is cheated by a factory manager, he roars uncomprehendingly, "He shook my hand! The bastard said we have a deal!" Some Eszterhas scholars have argued that these two scenes are eerily prophetic of the Ovitz episode. Yet, in all fairness, the roughneck language of *F.I.S.T.* is a radical departure from the elegant prose of the letter, which includes such lines as "Maybe you can beat the hell out of some people and they will smile at you afterwards and make nice, but I can't do that."

Eszterhas's *Flashdance* (1983) centers on the heroic Alex, a gorgeous welder and pious Roman Catholic who dreams of becoming a ballerina. While working part-time as a peculiarly prissy stripper, Alex suffers the lewd taunts of a flesh peddler. In the end, she tells her would-be pimp to get lost, demonstrating her refusal to be turned into a piece of merchandise. In his own rebuke to Ovitz, Eszterhas wrote to his Hollywood nemesis, "I am not a piece of meat to be 'traded' for other pieces of meat."

In *Jagged Edge* (1985), Eszterhas slyly reverses his relationship with Ovitz, taking the part of lawyer (played by Glenn Close) for himself and assigning Ovitz the role

of her client (Jeff Bridges). Close eventually suspects that Bridges is not entirely trustworthy. When she complains of feeling dirty and attempts to sever her ties to him, Bridges coldly tells her, "You can't." (Eszterhas employed similar language in his letter to Ovitz, saying, "I simply can't function on a day to day business basis with you and Rand without feeling myself dir-

tied.") Later Close learns from the District Attorney that Bridges is "an ice man"—words that have often been used to describe the driven Ovitz. Spurned and furious, Bridges dresses up in a Ninja costume and finally resorts to actual Ninja-like violence—a reference by the screenwriter to Ovitz's own passion for martial-arts training and neo-Eastern management philosophies.

Eszterhas's disgust with CAA is further foreshadowed by Debra Winger's desire to leave the FBI in *Betrayed* (1988). Again, like

the Eszterhas who complains in his letter of feeling dirtied, Winger's character ultimately confronts her own control agent—who just happens to be named *Michael*—about quitting. Winger tells him, "Michael, you promised me that I wouldn't get dirty." Michael replies, giving what sounds very much like a CAA client-recruitment spiel: "We're your family. We protect you." Winger counters, "You betrayed me." Eventually she leaves the agency, and the movie closes on her as a lonely, forsaken barfly, crucified for her unyielding conscience.

In yet another variation on the theme of embattled Eszterhasian integrity, the author's latest film, *Music Box*, follows a crusading young attorney as she fights to clear the good name of her father. But it is *Beat the Eagle*, currently in pre-production, that is likely to stand as the most lasting allegory of Eszterhas's conflict with the omnipotent Ovitz and CAA: the film tells the story of one proud man who dares to take on the Internal Revenue Service—alone.

—*John Brodie*

Christ's sake!—was the most powerful man in Hollywood, and they didn't like their shareholders reading it either. But so long as Ovitz didn't misstep, there was not much they could do about it. The moment he delivered his assault on Eszterhas, Ovitz gave them an opening to begin reclaiming the empire. It was as if they suddenly woke up and said, "Wait a minute. Aren't *we* the ones writing the checks? Aren't *we* the ones who are supposed to be running Hollywood?"

Nothing will change immediately, of course—wives will be polite, if slightly cooler; surely some of the politicians may shy away; perhaps a client or two will leave the agency, and then a few more. Although now that Eszterhas has shown how difficult it is to leave CAA—*Look, Vito, sure I wanted to join the mob, but only*

for a week or so—the agency might have some difficulty recruiting fresh talent.

One might think the Eszterhas affair would cause Ovitz to realize that he had, Colonel Kurtz–like, gone too far this time, that he was operating in a world of his own conventions. One might think so, but one would be wrong. Ovitz has reportedly ordered his frothing troops in CAA's new fortress to be stronger and more aggressive than ever—after all, his management bible, *The Art of War*, advises taking the offensive at just such a moment as this. But that may be just a pose. With Stark, an elder in the movie establishment, having taken Eszterhas's side in this Manichaean Beverly Hills struggle, it is clear—surely even to Ovitz—that the balance of power in Hollywood has shifted. ∋

BEST OF THE USUAL SUSPECTS: PART ONE

Our gossip column: New Journalism meets popcorn (if not outright cheese). We were after gossip with a bite—more of a shock in those days than it is now. We also saw these as vignettes, even morality tales, and we buffed and polished them obsessively.

THIS IS NOT A a Polish joke. This is not a Los Angeles joke. This is not blasphemy. This is true. During his recent three-day visit to the Coast, after scolding **STEVEN SPIELBERG**, **DOM DE LUISE** and the rest of pagan Hollywood, after the nightly celebration of Mass, **POPE JOHN PAUL II** would head back to his room, get comfortable, kick back, then—we *swear*—pop open some beers. Yes: each night in L.A. (and, for all we know, in Miami and Phoenix and San Antonio as well), the Holy Father swigged a cold brewskie and, in his fashion, partied down.

November 1987

IIII

WHILE WE WERE AWARE OF OSTENSIBLY LOVABLE flesh-muppet **BILL COSBY**'s obsession with money, even we were impressed by the recent bean-counting advances he has made. It seems that some business associates of Cosby's were invited to his East Side townhouse for what they thought would be a genial lunch. Almost immediately after their arrival, however, a Cosby factotum began taking photos—making the baffled, uncomfortable visitors feel as if they had somehow stumbled onto a Carnival cruise ship. Of course, the Cos was up to something far more financial-planning-minded than snapping souvenir photos to sell back to his guests. (Although, if he had thought of it . . .) In fact, America's hardest-working professional dad admitted that he was stockpiling proof that the lunch was, indeed, a deductible business expense.

August 1989

George

At a recent sports benefit, **George Bush** and son-of-a-Nazi **Arnold Schwarzenegger** were teamed up to play indoor volleyball, and George, ever the frat boy, kept referring to Arnold as Terminator. "Come on, Terminator," he would say. "You can do it, Terminator....Nice try, Terminator." Despite the encouragement, Arnold played poorly. He spent more time ducking, bobbing and cringing than forcefully propelling the ball. As the defeated pair left the court, Bush mumbled to the victors, "Terminator's *Warren* kind of a *pussy*, isn't he?"

December 1991

1

Time: the present. Place: the White House. Matters of grave consequence were under discussion. **George Bush** passed a note to the vice president. "How do you titillate an ocelot?" the note read. "You oscillate her tit a lot!" Not quite stupid enough for you? Well, just a year after **Dan Quayle** purchased an anatomically exaggerated statuette in Chile, Bush now has his very own piece of smutty folk art. Bush's comes by way of a visiting Third World dignitary who, upon his arrival at the White House, gave the president a small wooden table whose base is a carved representation of a man with a large erect penis. At first Bush chose to display the gift in the Oval Office, but then he hit upon the *even funnier* idea of placing the table in his executive bathroom. Lately he has taken vast pleasure in ordering aides, particularly female ones, *Do me a favor and get those papers I left on the table in the bathroom.*

2

June 1991

THE SCENE IS AS FOLLOWS: Warner Bros. executives are in conference with **Jerry Lewis** and **Joe Piscopo** to discuss the sad state of a world hitherto deprived of a sequel to *The Nutty Professor*. When Lewis, who has made millions of Frenchmen laugh, quits the meeting, he neglects to take his briefcase with him. Those remaining regard the case much the way a London bobby would an unattended package; it is gingerly removed. Why? The multitalented writer–performer–director–comic genius apparently is notorious for leaving his briefcase behind at meetings and retrieving it later, and supposition has it that a tape recorder concealed within preserves whatever thoughts and feelings the assembled might have left unexpressed in Lewis's presence. (The *Son of Nutty Professor* project proceeds dangerously apace, but without the horrid Piscopo. Lewis, a devotee of the more-is-more school of comedy, will be playing *two* dual roles—four characters in all.)

▼ ▼ ▼

May 1987

THE RICH REALLY ARE different from you and me: *they're evil*—or, at least, they pay pious poor people to debase themselves amusingly at fancy private parties. Details of an extraordinary dinner conducted last Christmas are just now slithering into public view. The 20 revelers included, in fact, a solid plurality of usual suspects: eyeliner-and-comic-book mogul **RONALD PERELMAN**; his wife, **CLAUDIA COHEN**; **DONALD** and **IVANA TRUMP**; groceries commissar **HENRY KRAVIS** and his dress-designer wife, **CAROLYNE ROEHM**; and nonbillionaires **JANN** and **JANE WENNER**. For entertainment the Perelmans had ordered in a Salvation Army band—*how recherché!*—and, best of all, a sad, dumpling-cheeked Salvation Army Santa Claus. Wealthy guest after wealthy guest sat on the rented Santa's lap in turn, and each was given a personalized gift—tiny Henry Kravis, for instance, on the eve of his pointless $25 billion takeover of RJR Nabisco, got a giant Oreo cookie. Is that *cute*, or what? Is that *fun*, or what? Is this the twilight of the millennium, or what?

May 1989

IIII

TIME FOR AN UPDATE on **J. D. SALINGER**—still, of course, a *New Yorker* writer. (*Has today's mail arrived? Anything with a New Hampshire postmark? No?*) Salinger, who likes to divide his energies between not publishing his work, fending off earnest liberal arts majors, farming and suppressing biographies, apparently has always found time to watch a little prime-time television—enough, we are reliably told, to have once developed a crush on then *Dynasty* star and putative aristocrat **CATHERINE OXENBERG**. Before long, letters were exchanged, phone calls made, and eventually there was a flight to Los Angeles to visit the adored one on the show's set—where even famous, normally reclusive writers can become such obtrusive nuisances that they get the bum's rush from the starlet and are asked to leave.

December 1987

" . . . I ran into my pal **Donald Trump** at the lovely private dinner dance **Anne Bass** gave in her Fifth Ave. apartment . . . Anyway, Donald said that SPY magazine . . . is in trouble financially and will not be around much longer. I chided the handsome mogul, of whom I am very fond . . . that he should not indulge in wishful thinking. He said, 'No, you'll find this is true if you just investigate. **I predict they won't even be around in a year.**' "

—*Liz Smith in the* Daily News, *September 29, 1988*

SCENES FROM THE BIBLE BELT

GO, BOBBY, AND SIN NO MORE.

12

Spy, Unlimited?

Moving into Books, TV, Film, and Semi-Swank New Digs (Hubris Alert!)

Who knows what would have happened if we had said yes. Today, probably, Spy *would be a shopping and travel magazine for inquisitive single women over 40.*

—KURT ANDERSEN

EVERYONE LOVED THE PUCK BUILDING, but the office had taken on the aspect of a cattle car. Some people were tripling- and quadrupling-up at desks, and those were the lucky ones— at least they were *in* the office. Several additional desks had been set up on the landing, near the front elevator.

Sometime during the winter of '88–'89 the three founders, one of them reluctantly, had decided to look for a new space. They asked Geoff Reiss to be the point person.

"Graydon was terrified of the move," says Reiss. "He didn't want to go. He was convinced that we would lose our edge."

"I remember having arguments—I was very against it, for a number of reasons," Graydon says. "I thought, *Why spend the money?* And even though the new offices were beautiful and spacious and heavenly, the fact is, the *crammedness* of the Puck Building was a

metaphor of Manhattan. Being crowded: That's the way we live here. If we wanted to live in the suburbs with lots of space, then we'd live in the suburbs."

The move wasn't to the 'burbs, quite—we were headed less than a mile north to 5 Union Square West. So one Friday in August 1989, with a pang we didn't particularly want to acknowledge, we left the Puck Building and walked uptown to the new digs. *Spy* had taken the top floor, nearly 14,000 square feet—quadruple the size of the Puck space—of a nondescript old building we were permitted to rename The *Spy* Building. Each month, on the day the new issue appeared, the enormous yellow-and-black *Spy* flag would fly from the roof, "like a pirate ship sailing through lower Manhattan," remembers Michael Hainey, on whose first day the flag happened to be raised for the first time. The space itself was lovely and airy, designed by the same architects who had done the old offices. The walls and partitions were covered in rough blond wood, and wavy, '40s-*noir*–style glass separated the cubicles. There was a fish tank and, shockingly for a satirical magazine, something called "The

Opposite:
A running
countdown to our
own demise.
Trump was off
by nine years,
but still outlived us.
December 1988

us costs and
orney's fees.

se No. 3: One
-worker of a
male truck
iver proposi-
oned her over
s CB radio;
other tried to
ag her into
s truck; an-
her fondled
r breast; 37 of
em wagered
er who would
st have sex
th her. **Penal-**
: The compa-
' remitted
ck pay, *less* her
rnings from
bs held after
r departure.

se No. 4: An
ecutive asked
ecretary if she
oled around,"

Private Lives of Public Figures

Justice Clarence Thomas greets the day before heading off to work.

Illustration by Drew Friedman

script so som
else can read
and then und
stand whethe
were saying y
no....So, I m
from time to
stop you and
just answer it
yes or no....

Springsteen:
hmm.

**Compl
Senten
Crimin
Style**

In our zany, c
world, we son
times lose sig
the good thin
life: the laugh
a child, a rose
bloom, a park
place near the
restaurant, a
stiff sentence
meted out to
serving crimir

February 1992

Zen Room," with a little Japanese rock garden, the point of which seemed to escape everyone. It was incredibly nice, and a little cold. (The office is occupied today by the architect David Rockwell's firm; it is much more lived-in and densely packed but otherwise unchanged.)

"I remember there was some consternation, at the time, that Kurt and Graydon and Tom's offices were too grand," says Bruce Handy. "It felt like they were more removed. It sort of changed everything. I can totally understand why they wanted the offices like that, but there was an intimacy that was lacking after the move."

"It took us a while to grow into that space," says Reiss. "It wasn't as immediate as the Puck Building, where the editors-in-chief were right there. I remember one of my first days at the Puck Building, just hearing Graydon laugh from the back of the room, and it was the magazine equivalent of smelling good smells from the kitchen: *Something good is happening, because Graydon is laughing.* In the new space, if you were on the business side or in the back, you could go two weeks without *seeing* Graydon. And I

think it adversely affected us, this desire for grandeur."

We are talking about "grandeur" in relative terms, but Kurt admits "a certain amount of understandable hubris" on the part of a successful, expanding enterprise. We had been moving full-steam into books: Apart from *Spy Notes*, there was the year-book parody *Spy High*; a sequel to *Separated at Birth?*; and our never-completed *Who's Who* by way of *Brief Lives*, an end-of-the-analog-age project with a hopeless lead time—sentences would more or less become outdated as they were written. Television was next (an offer from HBO, a deal with NBC for specials; Fox came along later), and records (three jokey Rhino compilations that were given the *Spy* imprimatur). Even movies: Paramount proposed to pay us annual six-figure sums to develop comedies. "Tom had not implausible visions of a *Spy* multimedia empire," Kurt says. "We moved because we were bigger and more profitable. So it corresponded to a lot of other things that changed the nature of the *Spy* experience internally. I *don't* think the new office space is the cause of them. It can be, in people's memories, symbolic of them, or embody them—it does in mine—but I really don't think it was causal. I could be wrong."

Reiss cautions against overly romanticizing the Puck Building (too late!) because, as he points out, "I remember being able to see your breath in the winter, the electrical grid not being sufficient to allow more than two air conditioners at a time in the summer, and having to come in really early or stay really late just to use one of the computers on the business side."

More mixed feelings lay just ahead. There was, to start with, that hastily called staff meeting in February 1990 to confirm that *Spy* was in fact looking for a major investor or buyer, and had hired Morgan Stanley as its investment bank. The announcement was greeted mainly with trepidation and, eventually, an attempt at upbeat resignation.

What none of the staff knew was that *Spy* had come close to being sold a year and a half earlier—to Condé Nast.

The partners had been approached in the summer of 1988 by Condé Nast's chairman, S. I. Newhouse Jr., about buying a minority stake. "We'd been so incredibly lucky," Kurt says. "And I thought, *Our luck can't last.* I'm not pessimistic as a person, but I do habitually think of the reasonable bad-case scenarios. I'm not the sort who goes, 'I won five hands in a row! Let's go for six!'"

Kurt, Tom, Graydon, and Steven Schragis had a pleasant luncheon meeting with Newhouse and John Veronis, the media investment banker, in Veronis's Manhattan apartment. Afterward, Newhouse gave them a ride back—"To the Puck Building? To the subway stop? I don't know where," Kurt recalls, or rather, doesn't. "But I do remember talking to Si in his car about *October*, this completely eggheady intellectual art journal. I think I pretended to have read some recent issue; he definitely *had* read it. I had expected some other kind of person. And here was, you know, Susan Sontag's brother."

At lunch, Newhouse and Veronis floated the idea of buying a percentage of the magazine, at least 25 percent—Schragis's stake, in effect. "I don't think there was ever a dollar offer," says Kurt. "They were very sweet. And I assume they were just shocked that we said no." Tom Phillips, who believed that *Spy* still had plenty of room to grow as a stand-alone company, was adamantly opposed, and essentially vetoed the idea. No mention of price, no negotiation, just…no.

Suppose they had said yes? Suppose *Spy*, scarcely two years old, had been swallowed up by Condé Nast?

"Yeah…I don't know if that would have been more good or more bad," Kurt says. "Probably bad. I mean, talk about changing the nature of the thing. Today, probably, it would be a shopping and travel magazine for inquisitive single women over 40, you know?"

Still, despite the internal turmoil provoked by the prospect of an *owner*, for the magazine's readers the first half of 1990 was not different from what had come before.

Spy kept publishing good, and varied, stuff. Susan Orlean's account of the Manhattan mega-socialite Nan Kempner preparing for a dinner party appeared in February 1990. The July issue had the cover story "Every Man Has His Price, In Some Cases, 13 Cents: A Mortifying *Spy* Experiment in Comparative Chintziness, Featuring Real Checks for Teeny Sums Actually Cashed by Candice Bergen, Bill Blass, Cher, Michael Douglas, Henry Kravis, Rupert Murdoch, S. I. Newhouse, Donald Trump, Mort Zuckerman and Dozens More"* (see pages 252–56), as well as a serious investigation by Seth Roberts into the work and motivation of the celebrated early AIDS researcher Robert Gallo. A month later came an almost painfully revealing presentation of the Tina Brown–Michael Ovitz correspondence (see pages 178–79).

---

*This was engineered, under a pseudonym, by *Spy* reporter Eddie Stern, son of billionaire Leonard Stern. —Eds.

Graydon at *Spy*'s new offices, circa 1990

Spy also benefited from the addition of new staff, including a character in the mailroom named Ronin Ro (né Marc Flores), who would later become the most-published author of all *Spy* alumni, an expert on the world of hip-hop. ("*That's* the big *Spy* story," says Bob Mack, a big-time hip-hop journalist himself, who worked with Ronin both at the magazine and afterward. "He's like Salman Rushdie, he's undercover—he wrote the Suge Knight book.")

Charmingly, *Spy* became the subject of a master's thesis: "Satire and the Repairing of Social Reality: *Spy* Magazine as Ritual Communication," by Theodore Matula, Illinois State University ("APPENDIX A: Blurb-o-Mat").

AND *SPY* WAS GOING ON THE AIR.

"With advertising in the early days, and then later with both the books and the TV specials, what *Spy* benefited from tremendously was individuals—at the book publishers and at the network—who really *got* the magazine," Kurt says. "It wasn't just like, 'This is a trendy thing, let's try to exploit it.' Nancy Evans at Doubleday really loved *Spy*, and Brandon Tartikoff at NBC really loved *Spy*.

Town With Rex Reed for such unintentionally funny writing as the paragraph that began, "Visually, [the McGuire Sisters] defy the laws of gravity. Dorothy lives in Scottsdale, married to the same husband for 31 years...."

Not long ago Liz Smith wrote me a charming note (see Letters to SPY, August) in which she took exception to my characterizing some of her behavior as "erratic." In fact, I may have jumped the gun. My assessment, after all, came *before* her Memorial Day column, an instant classic if ever there was one. James Ledbetter of *The Village Voice* has already addressed this particular bit of Liziana, but at too little length; here is a more generous excerpt. The mise-en-scène: Smith, reacting to passing criticism of her in SPY and in the *Voice*, is defending her association with Republican media manipulator Roger Ailes. The donkey that Smith introduces has not previously been mentioned by anyone.

ROGER and Liz know we're on Spy's "hit parade" and that we won't please them if we ride the donkey, if Roger rides and I lead the donkey, if I lead and Roger rides the donkey, or if we carry and drop the donkey in the river, as in **AESOP'S** fable. And we don't care. But what did **WAYNE** [Newton], one of the most popular performers in showbiz, ever do to Spy? Working with Roger Ailes reminded me that if some had their way, there'd be no interaction at all between folks in this democracy. We'd all get in our slots and stay there; we'd never mix, mingle and learn....Races would never intermingle....The entire melting pot, the live-and-let-live aspect of democracy, would close up shop....Isn't this what **HITLER** wanted?...I believe separatism and dogged other "isms" will be the death of this country....This is why I would—as my critics have charged—sit down with Vlad the Impaler. I'm curious. I want to hear what he wants to say....I don't care to spend my time trying to satisfy somebody else's idea of whom to know, talk to and work with, and behaving in the way somebody else has decided I should. It's still a free country. Too bad so many people no longer understand that all-American fact.

Amen. Liz Smith and *Doonesbury* are the only reasons to buy the *Daily News*, and at this point Smith is the more reliably hilarious of the two. Just one nagging question: why wasn't *Vlad the Impaler* in boldface? ⬥

Henry "Dutch" Holland, September 1990

BEST OF REVIEW OF REVIEWERS

Taking on one's colleagues in the media is today a staple of bloggers, but 20 years ago no one else did this on a regular basis. *Spy's* critics' critics—there were several, in sequence—were pseudonymous, and Graydon had the enduring fantasy of hosting a party for all of the Reviewers of Reviewers, virtually none of whom would have known the others' secret identity.

We are distressed to note that *The Village Voice's* David Edelstein is a man obsessed. Reviewing *Vamp*, he describes Grace Jones as "lean as a phallus and considerably more lethal." Reviewing *Aliens* for *Rolling Stone*, he describes the monsters as "spidery wangdoodles with tongues like little phalli." Reviewing the original *Alien*, he describes its "intricately coded sexual imagery—from the womblike mother ship to the unmistakable vaginal openings of the alien craft to the beast itself." And what of the beast itself? It's "a shape-

Michèle Bennett, October 1986

Weaver's head before she opens fire." And so, with that "sad little cock" of her head, she blows away the phallic-tongued and spidery wangdoodles. "Mamma mia," Edelstein writes, bringing his review to a limp, exhausted close, "that's entertainment."

The big summer entertainment was, of course, *Heartburn*—if you discount *Howard*

The only pleasure in reading *Esquire* these days is in discovering anew why you don't read *Esquire* these days. Many of the most compelling reasons to be found in April's issue — the issue *before* the almost-too-embarrassing-to-carry-around SEX AND OTHER PLEASURES issue — were supplied by editor in chief Lee Eisenberg himself.

"Suddenly," writes Eisenberg in his Backstage column, "there is a near-consensus that the country's fragile place in the global market needs immediate, nonpartisan attention." I remember that morning well. It was early spring, and although the day was lovely, as I walked to the corner newsstand I felt somehow burdened, burdened by the lack of consensus regarding immediate, nonpartisan attention to the country's fragile place in the global market. But when I got back to my rooms— *everything had changed.*

H. "D." H., July 1989

suggest you stare through the sidewalk windows and save a heap of cash."

We are always indebted to *The Nation* without quite knowing why. So it seems only fair to pass on the recommendation of its reviewer, a Stuart Klawans, for the *New England Review and Bread Loaf Quarterly*, Vol. IX, No. 4 ($12 per year, c/o Middlebury College, Middlebury, Vt. 05753). According to Klawans, it features "a poem by Albert Goldbarth that somehow addresses the issues of torture, violence against women and mass murder in the context of the adventures of the Donald Duck family of Duckburg. The poem is called 'Donald Duck in Danish.' "

Last month I noted that John Ritter was compared to Cary Grant in the *Times*, Tom Hanks to Cary Grant in *Esquire*, and Jeff Daniels to Cary Grant in *GQ*. Here's the latest: Marcello Mastroianni is the "Continental Cary Grant"—from "Cary Grant, Italian Style," *Time* magazine.

New York Times book reviewer and bi-

M. B., February 1988

continued the barmy Barnes, "played on the black notes of nostalgia's piano."

Moving tactfully along, black filmmaker Spike Lee hit back at the *Times's* Janet Maslin (who gave a fair though not terribly favorable review to Lee's very bad second film, *School Daze*), possibly for being white. "Ms. Maslin says *School Daze's* musical numbers are beyond the range of my 'technical abilities,'" Spike wrote to the *Times*. "What does she base this on?...What does she know about song and dance? I bet she can't even dance, does she have rhythm?"

Moving tactfully along, the reconstructed extraterrestrial Michael Jackson, who almost certainly has more rhythm than Janet Maslin, did better in the *Times* than oversensitive Spike. "The show was an exercise in perception," wrote balletomane Anna Kisselgoff so...perceptively of Jackson's Madison Square Garden show. "To express approval, the audience responds with 'Woof woof.'"

The *Times's* almost always ecstatically happy Stephen Holden responded to Jackson with more than "Woof woof." Holden described him as "a shy misunderstood manchild with a martyr complex." Then he called the man-child martyr "a brave spiritual warrior bearing the torch of sweetness and joy in the face of ridicule, shame and rejection." But the brave spiritual warrior also became an "aggrieved sacrificial sufferer," who then became an "inspirational messenger of hope," which is certainly a lot of woof woof.

Meanwhile, *Newsday's* must-read report

Ignatz Ratzwikziwzki, June 1988

THE SPOILED BARNARD FRESHMAN who has a crush on Claus von Bülow—that is, *Vanity Fair*'s target reader—must be laughing her head off. Back in April, James "Moo Cow" Wolcott, literary America's number one couch potato, presented a bleak survey of modern humor. "Color me confused," Wolcott began, "but I don't quite get the *hang* of much of the new humor writing."

He did find some fairly neutral things to say about the late S. J. Perelman ("He called himself a feuilletonist, 'a writer of little

**I. R.,
October 1988**

leaves,' fer sure"), but for the most part Wolcott wasn't amused. Singled out for nasty comments were *The New Yorker* ("The humor writing has become hairier and weirder. More far-out, fer sure"), Philip Roth ("Phil is onto something, fer sure"), Roy Blount Jr. (a contributing editor of this magazine) and this magazine. For the really big laughs, of course, the reader should stick with *Vanity Fair.*

---

na Speaks, without the girlish modesty."

Woody Allen's latest Bergmanesque bust, *September*, is infused with Chekhovian flair. All his serious movies are, aren't they? "The humor of [the characters'] humorlessness is often Chekhovian" (Richard Schickel, *Time*). "If you think this sounds like a Chekhov play, you have a point" (Kathleen Carroll, the *Daily News*). "The [screen]play is Chekhovian" (Frank Rich, the *Times*). "Neo-Chekhovian" (Vincent Canby, the *Times*). "True to Chekhov, everyone (including the camera) is trapped in this house, in this country, on this planet" (Robin Flicker, *Downtown*). "A Chekhovian house party" (David Denby, *New York*). Marcelle Clements anticipated all this nonsense in *Premiere*: "You can bet your boots that the word 'Chekhovian' will be uttered at least once by everyone at the table." Whereupon she described *September* as "generated by para-Chekhovian intricacies of character." And Ralph Novak, para-intellectual movie critic of *People*, wrote, "To understand how heavy it is, imagine eating 14 peanut butter sandwiches."

Talking of *Premiere*, as few people are, the *L.A. Weekly* recently scored big points for objective journalism by sagely allowing Anne Thompson, a writer for *Premiere*, to review *Premiere*. "After only four issues," Thompson wrote, "Rupert Mur-

**M. B.,
March 1988**

In most reviews and magazine stories, a use of metaphor or figurative language in general is to good writing what wearing a tie clip or a tie stickpin or one of those odd looping tie chains is to being well dressed, so to speak. For example, here is an analogy from one of Jami Bernard's movie reviews in the *New York Post*: "Just as nature abhors a vacuum, society evidently abhors contrast." In fact, this is not evident to me. To me, *nature* is to *vacuum* as *society* is to *the peace and quiet I try to maintain in the evenings when I listen to my English as a Second Language tapes at home*—with English as both my first and second languages, I will have a spare—*while my neighbors hold raucous drinks parties that include something called a "conga line" snaking through my apartment after I politely answer a knock on the door.* But then, what do I know? I abhor nature.

In a *Mirabella* profile of Sean

**Humphrey
Greddon,
August 1991**

Atkinson. You would have to possess a third-former mentality to find Rowan Atkinson funny, but that isn't quite the point. "I beg your indulgence if I overuse words like 'adorable' in this review of *You Never Can Tell*," Simon writes in another critique. "Shaw numbered it among his Plays Pleasant, but this is an understatement; it is a Play Delicious, a Play Exquisite, a Play Adorable. (I won't say it again, I promise.)"

Brilliant mind? Simon is revealing an unexpected side of himself. He is a man with a juvenile sense of humor prone to attacks of the cutes. (I won't say it again, I promise.) But what he consistently takes pride in is his use of words. He is a Guardian of the English Language. Here he is, then, on the performers in *Mummenschanz*, whose fantastic abstract shapes, he observes in his brilliant way, are "filled with prankishly prancing life."

What kind of life? "They come to life variously: by meiosis or mitosis, parthenogenesis or copulation . . . animism or anthropomorphism. . . . Sometimes, conversely, it is a process of reification. . . ." All of which is phooey. I don't know about the readers of *New York*, but it certainly surprises me that the performers in *Mummenschanz* are, it seems, masters of meiosis ("a phase of nuclear change in germ cells," according to the *Oxford Concise Dictionary*), or mitosis (a "process of division of a cell into minute threads").

The reviewer's weighty words are inappropriate to the joyful little show being reviewed. They create the impression of writerly brilliance, but they are evidence only of a preten-

priate to the joyful little show being reviewed. They create the impression of writerly brilliance, but they are evidence only of a pretentious form of word flashing, or the obsessive use of a well-thumbed thesaurus. Little wonder Simon complains irritably that "every parent" watching the show could be heard explaining to "every child": "It is whatever your imagination tells you it is; if you think it's a spider, it's a spider." What would he have them say—"Shut up, child, and enjoy the meiosis and mitosis"?

"But, then," Simon adds, "I get impatient with much of our abstract art too." And that's the smoking gun. John Simon is not a "brilliant mind." He has an extremely limited mind. Whatever his flaws, glaring enough, he possesses a narrow, literal sensibility. He cannot respond genuinely to *Mummenschanz* because he cannot respond to "abstract art." It is why the whole of the modern movement in drama, from Peter Brook to Robert Wilson to Martha Clarke, is closed to him, and why the innovatory work of such directors is consistently dismissed by him. Because he is blinkered. It is not just that Simon reveals himself to be an unpleasant personality with an affected style. It is that at center he possesses the worst of all things for a critic—a closed mind.

Apart from that, it's been lively business as usual this month. Personality Tama Janowitz

THE BULLYING MALEVOLENCE of John Simon, *New York* magazine's theater critic, is well known. The unkind personal attacks on actors, the insulting attitude toward homosexuals, have revealed the character of the man. At times, too oftentimes, it is as if he hates theater, hates his job, hates everything, except himself. Yet the feeling persists that in spite of his flaws and moral lapses, Mr. Simon is still a brilliant mind. In his way, he is the Chief Justice Rehnquist of drama criticism.

Still, he has been in a charitable mood of late. "I laughed like a third-former," he writes of the English toilet-humor specialist Rowan

M. B.,

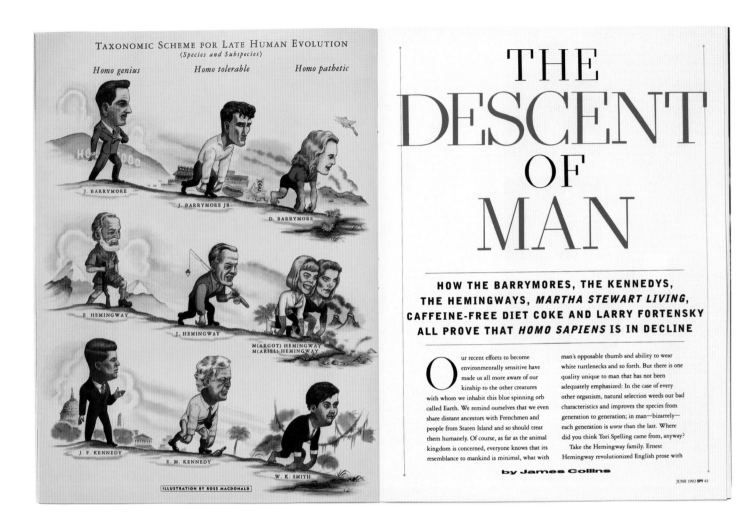

TAXONOMIC SCHEME FOR LATE HUMAN EVOLUTION
(Species and Subspecies)

Homo genius   Homo tolerable   Homo pathetic

J. BARRYMORE

J. BARRYMORE JR.

D. BARRYMORE

E. HEMINGWAY

J. HEMINGWAY

M(ARGOT) HEMINGWAY
M(ARIEL) HEMINGWAY

J. F. KENNEDY

E. M. KENNEDY

W. K. SMITH

ILLUSTRATION BY ROSS MACDONALD

THE DESCENT OF MAN

HOW THE BARRYMORES, THE KENNEDYS, THE HEMINGWAYS, *MARTHA STEWART LIVING*, CAFFEINE-FREE DIET COKE AND LARRY FORTENSKY ALL PROVE THAT *HOMO SAPIENS* IS IN DECLINE

Our recent efforts to become environmentally sensitive have made us all more aware of our kinship to the other creatures with whom we inhabit this blue spinning orb called Earth. We remind ourselves that we even share distant ancestors with Frenchmen and people from Staten Island and so should treat them humanely. Of course, as far as the animal kingdom is concerned, everyone knows that its resemblance to mankind is minimal, what with man's opposable thumb and ability to wear white turtlenecks and so forth. But there is one quality unique to man that has not been adequately emphasized: In the case of every other organism, natural selection weeds out bad characteristics and improves the species from generation to generation; in man—bizarrely— each generation is *worse* than the last. Where did you think Tori Spelling came from, anyway?

Take the Hemingway family. Ernest Hemingway revolutionized English prose with

by James Collins

And that's why those projects worked.

"We had terrific beginners' luck," he continues. "After we did a book of *Separated at Birth?*—and it was a best-seller—we went to HBO, in 1989. We had an idea to do a show basically making fun of the '70s—as we had done an issue about it. It seemed ridiculous at the time: We were still so close to the '70s, the instant ironic retrospective recycling machine didn't yet exist as it does today. I guess maybe we invented it. Anyhow, Michael Fuchs, who was head of HBO then, couldn't have been nicer, but my memory of that meeting was: 'I have no idea what you mean, but, yeah, sure, go ahead.' And then we got a better offer from NBC. At that point, HBO was not the cool HBO of *The Sopranos* and *Sex and the City*. The networks were still *the fucking networks*.

"So we went to NBC. We wanted to do a new kind of Sunday-morning show. Essentially *Politically Incorrect* once a week on Sunday was the idea. And Tartikoff said, 'Unfortunately, I don't control Sunday morning, that's the news division. But how'd you like to do prime-time specials?'"

And so the distant reaches at the back of the office turned into *Spy*-TV HQ, and a team of *Spy* staff members and regular contributors—Bruce Handy, Paul Simms, Andy Aaron, and others—were writing away, overseen by Kurt. In late January 1990, *Spy*'s first special, *How to Be Famous*, was taped over the course of a chaotic week at the offices, with the scarcely known comic Jerry Seinfeld as host.

"We were clearly people who hadn't done TV," says Handy. "Scripts were way too wordy. That first show, the voice-over was so *not* suited to Jerry Seinfeld, it was so not his voice. You can see his discomfort with the wordiness. That ultra-high-gloss, fine-tuned language of *Spy*—the complex sentences, almost like Henry James humor with sentences that turned back on themselves—trying to do that on TV just doesn't work. I remember being impressed that Seinfeld was just doing all the stuff the way we wrote it. Beforehand, a lot of us had been a little skeptical of him," continues Handy. "His show was in the can [*Seinfeld* premiered that May 31], but nobody had seen it and we regarded him as just another late-night-TV, run-of-the-mill, ha-ha comedian."

The shoots were exhausting, going till three, four, five in the morning. Seinfeld flirted with the female staff and was a complete trouper. The special aired in April 1990, with featured guests including Harry Shearer, Joe Namath, and the Smothers Brothers. One of the funniest bits involved Ricardo Montalban, a buffet, and a hidden camera: The idea was to determine scientifically whether people were more drawn to celebrities or to free food.

"A *Spy* TV show was a logical move on a business level," says Simms, "but it really wasn't that good of a show."

Still, it got a nine-plus Nielsen rating and an 18 share—a middling success at the time, but numbers that would make it a smash hit today.

NBC was pleased enough to order a second hour-long special and a pilot for a series—and, happily for *Spy* and the world, both were *much* better. Kurt oversaw these as well. The first, called *Hit List*, was a year-end most-appalling-people-and-trends countdown hosted by Julia Louis-Dreyfus. The show included at least two unquestionably inspired and hilarious segments—the *Brady Bunch* theme song and opening sequence rewritten and remade to satirize the season's Woody Allen–Mia Farrow–Soon-Yi Previn scandal, and a digitally simulated duet between Wayne Newton and the late Janis Joplin.

Despite having somewhat oafishly pioneered comedic reality TV—a decade before the genre was named—the NBC shows were most notably a kind of unintended outplacement service for two of the magazine's most talented writers: Handy and Simms got full-time TV jobs at salaries several hundred percent higher than they were being paid at *Spy*. And for all the new let's-put-on-a-show excitement the TV gambits provided, we all understood that the magazine remained our enterprise's raison d'être.

Ad for *Spy*'s first TV special, April 1990. "We were clearly people who hadn't done TV," says writer Bruce Handy.

In its March issue, Spy *does it again—to Judy Price, the president of New York's* Avenue *magazine....*Spy *calls the Prices' magazine a 'sycophantic wet kiss.' And that turns out to be about the nicest thing it has to say about the Prices, their business methods, their social aspirations, their religious practices and their personal appearance.*

—Cynthia Crossen in *The Wall Street Journal*, March 8, 1990

SUSAN MULCAHY, the former Page Six editor, had just become editor of *Avenue,* a magazine unabashedly for Manhattan's rich. "*Spy* trashed all the *Avenue* editors, they trashed me," she says. "I was sort of devastated by that, and I'm fairly thick-skinned."

"I had worked at *Avenue*, I knew Judy Price," says Michael Caruso, then a *Vanity Fair* editor and later editor-in-chief of *Men's Journal*. "I thought she came off *well* in that article. The truth was much worse."

Night of the Living Career-Dead
The SPY Celebrity-Delusion Index

Save your pity for someone other than Bob Goulet. Not only has a significant portion of his supper-club audience from the 1960s held fast, but he has an entirely new, paying audience of young fans who find humor in his straight-faced comic turns in films like *Beetlejuice*, *The Naked Gun 2½* and *Scrooged*—*and he's completely in on the joke!* Goulet stands at the pinnacle of healthy campiness: he *knows* he is ultracampy, and he exploits his ultracampiness to his financial and professional advantage. Sadly, the same cannot be said of the Judy Carnes and Herve Villechaizes of the world. Two factors separate their plight from Goulet's: the quality of the work they get, and the degree to which they understand their audience's perception of them. The graph below illustrates how these factors together determine the relative cultural savviness of American camp icons. George Hamilton, who gets reasonably good work (*The Godfather, Part III*; *Love at First Bite*; pre-Fortensky Liz escort) and is completely aware of his campiness, rates in the category of Healthily Campy. And Carne, who scrapes the bottom of the barrel for work and doesn't even realize it, is Just Pathetic. See where your favorite camp icon places!

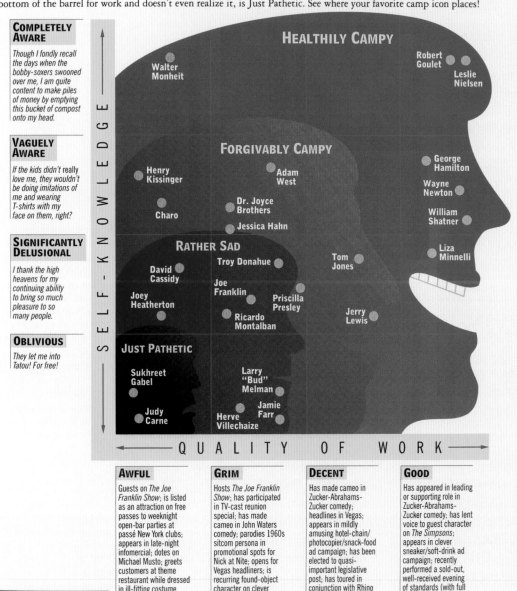

COMPLETELY AWARE

Though I fondly recall the days when the bobby-soxers swooned over me, I am quite content to make piles of money by emptying this bucket of compost onto my head.

VAGUELY AWARE

If the kids didn't really love me, they wouldn't be doing imitations of me and wearing T-shirts with my face on them, right?

SIGNIFICANTLY DELUSIONAL

I thank the high heavens for my continuing ability to bring so much pleasure to so many people.

OBLIVIOUS

They let me into Tatou! For free!

SELF-KNOWLEDGE

QUALITY OF WORK

HEALTHILY CAMPY — FORGIVABLY CAMPY — RATHER SAD — JUST PATHETIC

Walter Monheit · Robert Goulet · Leslie Nielsen · Henry Kissinger · Adam West · George Hamilton · Wayne Newton · Charo · Dr. Joyce Brothers · William Shatner · Jessica Hahn · David Cassidy · Troy Donahue · Tom Jones · Liza Minnelli · Joey Heatherton · Joe Franklin · Priscilla Presley · Jerry Lewis · Ricardo Montalban · Sukhreet Gabel · Larry "Bud" Melman · Jamie Farr · Judy Carne · Herve Villechaize

AWFUL

Guests on *The Joe Franklin Show*; is listed as an attraction on free passes to weeknight open-bar parties at passé New York clubs; appears in late-night infomercial; dotes on Michael Musto; greets customers at theme restaurant while dressed in ill-fitting costume from 1960s sitcom; is a client of agent Michael Levine

GRIM

Hosts *The Joe Franklin Show*; has participated in TV-cast reunion special; has made cameo in John Waters comedy; parodies 1960s sitcom persona in promotional spots for Nick at Nite; opens for Vegas headliners; is recurring found-object character on clever late-night talk show; has performed on Chabad telethon; has appeared in smarmy trash-metal rock video

DECENT

Has made cameo in Zucker-Abrahams-Zucker comedy; headlines in Vegas; appears in mildly amusing hotel-chain/photocopier/snack-food ad campaign; has been elected to quasi-important legislative post; has toured in conjunction with Rhino Records rerelease of oeuvre; has performed on Muscular Dystrophy telethon; has appeared in hip rock video

GOOD

Has appeared in leading or supporting role in Zucker-Abrahams-Zucker comedy; has lent voice to guest character on *The Simpsons*; appears in clever sneaker/soft-drink ad campaign; recently performed a sold-out, well-received evening of standards (with full orchestra) at Radio City; collects residuals from shrewd syndication/CD-reissue deal

The issue immediately flew off the newsstands, though not in the way we'd hoped. It was simply disappearing, bought up all over metropolitan New York, we assumed, by operatives employed by Price and her husband, Peter. *Spy*'s staff fanned out to question news dealers and post REWARD flyers. "If the Prices did do it—*and I would like to emphasize that I have no proof that they did*—but *if* they did do it, it backfired," says Mulcahy. "Because it became the most faxed piece in New York."

"They—or somebody—bought tens of thousands of copies," says Geoff Reiss. "We had 98 percent sell-through. Stuff like that you don't forget."

That same spring, the magazine published a Washington, D.C., issue, which provided an exuberantly low-point reportorial moment for *Spy* (and, perhaps, for all of magazine journalism). Having covertly reported the Ironman Nightlife Decathlon for several years, John Brodie and Bob Mack thought it might be interesting to do a D.C. version. The idea was to follow Ted Kennedy and Lee Atwater. (Atwater was Bush 41's Karl Rove, but more interesting.) "Kennedy proved very hard to tail," Brodie says. "We had an incident with the Capitol Hill police after stalking him for several days, and we were dissuaded from pursuing that element of the story.

"So we figured we had to get Atwater. We knew he'd be at this big Republican fundraiser at the Hilton. The women there were gorgeous, there was free prime rib and all you could drink—we were 25, so we thought this was just the best assignment ever. We saw Atwater and started chatting with him. He autographed our ties. And we decided we were going to follow him and see where he went that night.

"We saw where his Town Car was parked and decided it would be a good idea to put a potato in the tailpipe. We didn't realize it was a car with a dual exhaust, so the potato barely started baking. We were doing such a good job tailing him that he stopped the car, got out, walked over, and rapped on the glass: 'Are you guys following me, do you want something?' We said, 'Yeah, we're cub reporters from *Spy* magazine, we're trying to get an interview with you—we're big fans, big fans.' He proceeded to get into our car with us. 'I happen to have a bootleg of my upcoming album, you want to hear me jam with B. B. King?' He put in the tape and was accompanying himself and B. B. King on air guitar. He goes, 'Hey, I've got a better idea, let's not just drive around, why don't you guys come back to my house, we'll have a beer and you can ask

Maybe someday the world really will be kinder and gentler. Until then, there's *Spy*.

Smart. Funny. Fearless.

Changing times, changing *Spy*. Note the (possibly coincidental and not at all telling) omission of a particular word from the magazine's original motto, "Smart. Fun. Funny. Fearless."

▲▲▲

WHAT IF UNEMPLOYED ACTORS WORKED IN BANKS INSTEAD OF RESTAURANTS?

9:12 a.m. Loan officer confuses patron by asserting, "Less is more."

10:49 a.m. Ingenue teller decorates brass nameplate area with dreary Pierrot doll collection.

11:30 a.m. Branch manager fires singer-dancer-teller because she wasn't making interesting "choices."

12:09 p.m. Man in torn T-shirt and faded jeans enters bank: surly "Method teller" has finally arrived for work.

1:28 p.m. Competition among tellers to work at window closest to surveillance camera results in tears and vicious gossip.

2:59 p.m. Bank robber's forceful "Put your hands up!" unleashes frenzy of precision dancing.

— Henry Alford

me anything you want to ask me.' And we show up at the house, his wife answers the door literally barefoot and pregnant, and he says, 'Get these boys some beer, we're going down to the rec room.'

"We asked him questions about John Stuart Mill and the future of the Republican Party. Then he got a call from one of his aides saying to turn on the 11 o'clock news. And the lead story was that Mayor Marion Barry was busted smoking crack in a hotel in downtown Washington. And Bob and I looked at each other: 'That's *our* hotel.' And then they announced the room number that he had been caught smoking in: '*Holy shit, that's the room next to ours!*' And Atwater was laughing with glee—we're not sure whether it was because Barry was a Democrat or because we were such inept journalists that this had been going on in the room next door while we'd been eating prime rib at a benefit. He said,

'I'm out with the Katzenjammer Kids of American journalism.' At that point we decided we'd better get back to the hotel.

"There was FBI crime-scene tape in our hallway. The only person around to interview was our maid, in our worst high school Spanish. We really ended up with nothing. I was incredibly depressed."

The Washington issue, like the L.A. issue two years earlier, was not *Spy*'s strongest. "We didn't know what we were doing," Susan Morrison says. "And I know there was hand-wringing about becoming more national. But I don't think it really changed the character of the magazine."*

Kurt points out that the "final conscious change" came "when we dropped 'The New York Monthly' from the cover" in the summer of 1990.

"Spy High," a feature inspired by the old line about New York (or Hollywood or wherever) being "like high school with money," was later expanded into a book. May 1991

---

*Becoming more national was a gradual process that really had begun by the end of the first year and which we didn't talk about with the staff until almost a year after that. It did change the magazine some—a prank would be pulled on Reagan's chief of staff John Sununu, say, instead of on some known-only-in-Manhattan writer—but not its essential character. After all, even at the beginning it was national celebrities we recruited for the covers. —Eds.

OVERUSED WORDS WERE at that moment not the most acute of *Spy*'s problems.

"I remember very specifically," says Kurt, "Graydon and I had started to write memos back and forth in the fall of '89, the consensus of which were, *We should think about selling.* We had investors to think about, including my non-rich parents. Tom was still resistant—he really wanted to keep it as our independent thing.

"Over Thanksgiving, I remember writing a memo to Graydon about why I thought *this* was the time," Kurt continues. "We had been very lucky; the bull market was getting old and the two of us knew that *Spy* wasn't going to get any 'hotter.' We were breaking even, but we didn't have the capital to make the thing grow on our own."

John Sununu: What Color Is Your Parachute?

An Exclusive SPY Prank on an Unemployed Despot

In these hard economic times, it's incumbent upon all Americans to help the less fortunate. Here at SPY, that means we should come to the aid of, say, any once powerful, now unemployed bullies who have served as the butt of our jokes. Like John Sununu. Figuring that Sununu would probably need some practice retooling himself for the private sector, we decided to help him brush up. Pretending to be Nicholas J. Scott, the president of an imaginary executive-head-hunting firm, we called the White House, where Sununu was permitted to keep an office through March, and broached a job offer we had concocted.

John Sununu: Mr. Scott, how are you?

SPY: *I'll cut right to it, because I know you're busy—your name has been suggested in connection with a CEO position we're currently attempting to fill. To protect the stock price, we can't at this point reveal the name of the company to candidates. I can tell you that the position is CEO of a Fortune 200 company whose primary business is energy….Is this something that you could conceivably be interested in?*

Conceivably, yes, but I have to tell you, I just don't like operating on things as nebulous as that….How large a company is it? Can you give me an idea of what its sales are?

It's a $9 billion company, so it's right up there. But I wonder if I could just ask you a couple of questions very briefly.

What end of the business? Oil?

Yes.

Can you tell me where it's located?

Well, heh heh, now we're getting…

North, south, west, east?

Actually, there are several major offices. If you have a couple of minutes, I'd like to ask you a couple of questions….First, how would you rate your organizational skills?

The federal government's been ticking quite well….I have what I call the acorn theory of management. I know enough about the details so that if there's an acorn of a problem, I go solve it.

What do you think your subordinates think of you as a boss?

Contrary to what the press has said, they'd say this is the smoothest-running White House they've ever had.

Do you consider yourself a people person?

Yeah.

How would you rate your interpersonal skills?

Depends how badly the other guy's screwing up. If they've really screwed up, [my skills are] probably lousy.

Do you have any weak points?

Yeah. My impatience has always been a weak point, and I've mellowed and matured and gotten that more under control. And I really still naively expect people to do as much homework before they come into a meeting as I'm willing to do. And I'm discovering in life that that doesn't always happen.

As I mentioned earlier, the company has a lot of operations spread all over the globe. Do you mind traveling?

No, no.

Okay. Now, I'm not negotiating here…but the company anticipates offering a base salary in the high six figures with an incentive compensation potentially equal to the base, so we're talking about low seven figures here as a total package. Does that sound competitive?

Well, I can tell you that it enters the range….Most of what I've been putting together as packages start at three and a half million.

We realize that you might want to write memoirs or make speeches about {policy}. Would you agree to have them reviewed by someone in the company?

If they're related to the company, yes. I do want to make some speeches. To be honest with you, I just had a speech—um, whatever the right word is, these folks that line 'em up— and they're talking about a couple of million dollars in six months, and I do not want to give that up.* But I'm sure that can all be worked out.

Well, let me be more specific. If there would be something in your speech… that some of the folks at the company might say, "Let's take a little closer look at that"…

I don't have a problem with that. I don't, I don't, I don't, I'm not—I have no particular set of horses I'm riding.

Do you have aspirations for holding public office again?

No, I'm done.

*To earn that much within six months, Sununu would have to get $20,000 a speech and average four speeches a week. We called some speakers' bureaus and asked if that was possible. Most thought not. "Not only is that not in the ballpark," one said, "that's not even in the country." What would be more likely? "A *lot* fewer zeros."

March 1992

By the end of 1989, the two editors had persuaded their business partner of the virtues of finding a simpatico major investor or buyer—a case enhanced by their Morgan Stanley investment bankers' declaration that *Spy* was worth tens of millions of dollars.

Kurt's ire becomes audible when he describes that particular Wall Street experience. "Those fancy Morgan Stanley guys were just atrocious, smug but clueless. I remember *we* had to supply *them* with some of the correct names for their list of go-to guys at prospective buyers. I suppose it's perfect poetic justice that the founders of *Spy* were suckered by—*disappointed* by!—a bunch of slick investment bankers."*

It's all in the timing, poetically just or not. Unfortunately, at exactly the same time that a deal was being sought, the 1990 recession hit the media business early and hard. "And we," Kurt says, "were fucked."

Advertising accounted for about 60 percent of *Spy*'s revenue. When the recession hit, says Kurt, "we were the canary in the coal mine. We had a banner year in 1989, even made a little money, which was pretty unprecedented for a three-year-old start-up. But with the turn of the decade, the shit hit the fan. By June, our annualized ad revenues went from over $4 million down to $2 million. It was awful. Made it tough to be funny and fearless. So 1990 was kind of unpleasant, especially by the end of the year."

In addition, the magazine was no longer new: Cutting-edge coolness has a shelf life.

And there was one other thing.

"Remember 'kinder, gentler'?" Kurt says. "The first Bush administration's version of 'compassionate conservatism'? That was sort of being played against us, as a story, casting us as strident mischief-makers swimming against the new tide."

Steve Schragis, who owned the largest single share of *Spy* (but a minority share), had withdrawn from active involvement in 1989. "The meanness was starting to get to me, and the concept that I would be able to have everything I wanted—come in when I want, and people would have meetings when *I* wanted them to, and whatever I would say, people would say, 'Now,

---

*We might have done better had we turned instead to *Spy* investor Nancy Peretzman of Allen & Company, now perhaps the top media investment banker on Wall Street. —Eds.

that's a good idea!'" he says and trails off, laughing. Schragis estimates that he "roughly broke even" on his *Spy* investment.

As you all know, times are tough everywhere, and show no signs of improving soon. Laying off people was among the hardest things we have ever had to do here. To our departing colleagues, thank you and farewell.

Spy, the only truly independent general-interest magazine in America, has no deep-pocket sugar daddy, no foundation endowment, no bottomless corporate treasury. As ever, we must survive by our wits. And by eliminating these jobs, by instituting various other cost-cutting measures, by re-energizing our advertising sales effort, and by continuing to pursue non-magazine projects (some good news: NBC has just given the go-ahead to our new prime-time pilot), we can weather this difficult economic period.

The miraculous creation of Spy *has been the result of brilliant, enterprising people of good will and immense energy working together to make something delightful and singular and important. It is now time for all of us to call upon even greater reserves of brilliance, enterprise, goodwill and energy.*

—Staff memo, August 27, 1990

GRAYDON TOOK THE FLOOR at an all-staff meeting on September 5, fielding questions and doing his best to boost morale. He delivered his this-is-the-best-place-we'll-ever-work-and-these-are-the-good-old-days speech. Four independent investors were interested in *Spy*, he announced. A movie deal was imminent. That NBC series pilot, *Spy Pranks*, was happening.

At an editors' lunch the following week, gallows humor dominated. Kurt and Graydon defended their decision to have *Spy* collaborate on a fashion spread with the designer Paul Smith. "This is so *Spy* can be around in 50 years," Graydon said. "Or six," cracked Kurt.

As the year drew to a close and *Spy* shopped itself around during a deepening recession, there was little cheer. The staff approached the annual Christmas dinner with dampened enthusiasm. Worse, Graydon's father had passed away in early December, and Graydon was naturally not expected to attend the party. But he flew back from Canada on the night of the dinner—even stepped up and did his Santa routine—and there were moments when it almost felt like, well, 1989.

HOW CHEAP ARE THE RICH? AS CHEAP AS THE REST OF US? DO THEY SCOUR THE
NETHER REGIONS OF THEIR BARCALOUNGERS FOR LOOSE CHANGE? DO THEY STOCK UP WHEN
THEY SEE SLOAN'S HAS A SPECIAL ON CHARMIN? WOULD THEY SUFFER THE MODERATE INCONVENIENCE
INVOLVED IN DEPOSITING A CHECK FOR AN ALL-BUT-WORTHLESS SUM OF MONEY? WELL, WE CAN'T ANSWER
THE FIRST TWO QUESTIONS, BUT OUR ACCOUNTANCY CORRESPONDENT, **JULIUS LOWENTHAL**, EXAMINED THE THIRD.

every man has his
PRICE
IN SOME CASES, 13 CENTS

Yes, it is a mark
of immaturity
to disrespect the
value of a dollar, and while
money can't buy happi-
ness, all the people we know
tend to be happier when they
have money than when they
don't. Still, who can help but
look askance at the manic grab for
cash that we see all around us every
day, despite the nominal end of the
1980s: Ronald Reagan unembarrassedly
accepting $2 million to glad-hand Jap-
anese businessmen; Ed Koch discredit-
ing his own nascent reputation as a pundit by shilling for the *New York Post*'s
Second Chance Lotto; Tip O'Neill de-
basing himself after years of worthwhile
public service by turning huckster for
anyone willing to pay at least $50,000.
Everybody, it seems, has his price.

But just how money-loving are
America's rich and famous? Sure, the
megawealthy are forever doing unseemly things to make a buck: en-
gineering hostile takeovers that leave
companies hobbled with debt, for example, or erecting huge skyscrapers
that crowd and darken already shadowy city streets, or denying
their soon-to-be-ex-wives an equitable share of their assets. But
do they do the stupid, simple things that we regular folk do?

A MORTIFYING **SPY** EXPERIMENT
IN COMPARATIVE CHINTZINESS,
FEATURING REAL CHECKS FOR TEENY
SUMS ACTUALLY CASHED BY
CANDICE BERGEN, BILL BLASS, CHER,
MICHAEL DOUGLAS, HENRY KRAVIS,
RUPERT MURDOCH, S. I. NEWHOUSE,
DONALD TRUMP, MORT ZUCKERMAN
AND DOZENS MORE

Does your average swell
clip supermarket coupons?
Does he check the coin
slot when placing a call at
a pay phone? Does she pick
up loose change from the
street? We wondered: *If Cher,
Bill Cosby, Michael Douglas, Adnan Khashoggi, Shirley MacLaine,
Saul Steinberg or Donald Trump happened upon a penny on Fifth Avenue,
would he or she take the time to bend over
and soil a finger lifting the coin from the
street? Suppose it were a quarter? What if it
were a buck?* As much as these questions haunted us, we couldn't figure
out a way to reckon the answers. After
all, we couldn't exactly drop a couple of
pennies in front of the Four Seasons
and wait to see which prominent skil-
lionaires would stop and retrieve them.

We could, however, send them checks
for minuscule sums of money—sums
so small they couldn't fund as much as
a minute of the recipients' existence—
and see who would bother to bank
these teensy amounts of money.

Of course, we'd need a mechanism for
giving rich people money—they would
get suspicious if we just sent them official SPY checks out of the
apparent goodness of our hearts. No, some subterfuge was necessary. Therefore, to get the money into their hands, we created a

THE EVIDENCE

Some of the checks we sent, *below*, along with the signatures of the rich
and famous (but evidently parsimonious) who endorsed them

company, the National Refund Clearing-
house, which we fully and legally incorporated in New York State. This enabled us
to open a checking account. Thus armed
with a mechanism, we needed a pretext.
To that end, we drafted a cover letter.

> *Dear* [WEALTHY PERSON'S NAME HERE],
> *Our records show that you were over-*
> *charged $1.11 for services rendered in 1988*
> *due to a computer error. Enclosed is a check to*
> *make up the difference. We apologize for any*
> *inconvenience this may have caused you.*
> *Sincerely,*
> *Edward Topolansky*
> *Account Manager*

That accomplished, we ordered up some
suitably cheap stationery, had some suitably
unimpressive National Refund Clearing-
house letterhead and checks printed — several of the actual checks are reproduced on
these pages — and began giving away money
to 58 well-known, well-heeled Americans.
We sent these people checks for $1.11:

Woody Allen	Michael Korda
Richard Avedon	Henry Kravis
Candice Bergen	William Kunstler
Leonard Bernstein	Ralph Lauren
Bill Blass	Arthur Levitt
Tom Brokaw	Arthur Liman
William F. Buckley	Shirley MacLaine
Cher	David Mamet
Oscar de la Renta	John McEnroe
Philippe de Montebello	Zubin Mehta
Brian DePalma	Rupert Murdoch
Michael Douglas	S. I. Newhouse
Faye Dunaway	Mike Nichols
Ahmet Ertegun	William Paley
John Fairchild	Pete Peterson
Mia Farrow	Christopher Reeve
Richard Gere	Steve Ross
Bob Guccione	Francesco Scavullo
John Gutfreund	Arthur Schlesinger
Halston	Martin Scorsese
Harry Helmsley	Beverly Sills
Dustin Hoffman	Carly Simon
Thomas Hoving	Liz Smith
William Hurt	Saul Steinberg
Billy Joel	Arthur Ochs Sulzberger
Adnan Khashoggi	Donald Trump
Henry Kissinger	Kurt Vonnegut
John Kluge	Raquel Welch
Edward Koch	Mortimer Zuckerman

Let's see what happened.

I. SOME OF THEM DEPOSIT
THE FIRST PIDDLING CHECK
To make sure that the checks ac-
tually reached these people and

Murdoch

July 1990

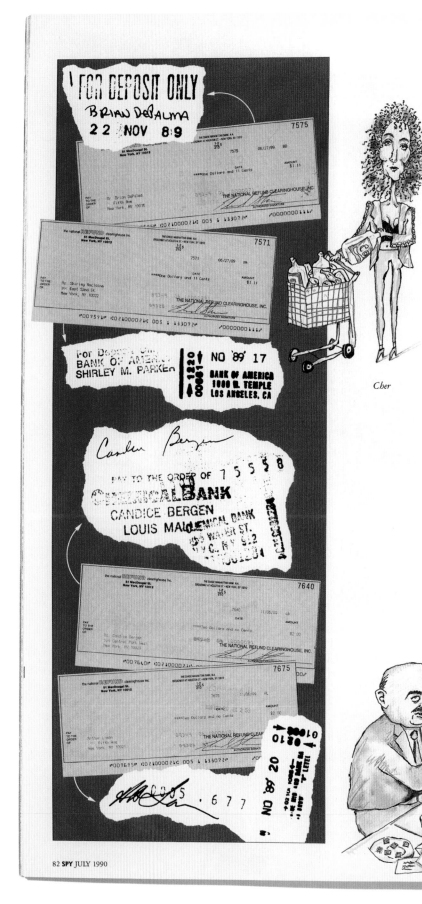

Over the next two months, 13 more people—including at least four billionaires—went to the trouble of depositing this measly 64-cent check.

Cher

not just their accountants, we sent the letters to their home addresses. Over the next two months, 26 of them—nearly half—deposited the checks. In other words, 26 of America's best-off (and *busiest*) citizens valued at no more than $1.11 the time and labor it took to consider the message, detach the check, endorse it—in some cases personally, by hand—put it in a safe place and deposit it. Those 26 were

Bill Blass	**William Kunstler**
Cher	**Shirley MacLaine**
Philippe de Montebello	**Rupert Murdoch**
Brian DePalma	**S. I. Newhouse**
Michael Douglas	**Mike Nichols**
Faye Dunaway	**Pete Peterson**
Ahmet Ertegun	**Steve Ross**
Mia Farrow	**Francesco Scavullo**
Harry Helmsley	**Arthur Schlesinger**
Thomas Hoving	**Arthur Ochs Sulzberger**
Adnan Khashoggi	**Donald Trump**
John Kluge	**Kurt Vonnegut**
Henry Kravis	**Mortimer Zuckerman**

II. WE RAISE THE ANTE

As pleased as we were to find 26 prominent people who'd pocket a gift $1.11 with no questions asked, we still wondered about the 32 recipients whose checks hadn't come back. We sweetened the deal by sending these people second checks, this time for $2, along with the following note:

> *Dear* [WEALTHY PERSON'S NAME HERE],
> *Our records show that we recently sent you a check for $1.11 to compensate for an overcharge on services rendered to you in 1988. Due to a computer error, we underpaid you $2.00, since you should, in fact, have received $3.11. The enclosed check for $2.00 should make up the difference. We apologize for any inconvenience this may have caused you.*
> *Sincerely,*
> *Edward Topolansky*
> *Account Manager*

Six of those who had turned up their noses at $1.11 jumped in when the offer reached $2:

Candice Bergen	**Carly Simon**
Richard Gere	**Liz Smith**
Arthur Liman	**Saul Steinberg**

So pleased were we by these results that we raised the stakes again and sent the 26 remaining ce-

Khashoggi

lebrities checks for $3.47. Only two additional people capitulated at that amount:

Halston

Beverly Sills

III. WE RETURN TO OUR ORIGINAL RESPONDENTS AND *LOWER* THE ANTE
Having discovered 26 nabobs who would take $1.11, we wondered, *Just how low would they go?* Accordingly, we had Mr. Topolansky's amanuensis draft another letter.

Dear [WEALTHY PERSON'S NAME HERE],
Our records show that you were recently sent a check for $1.11 in compensation for services that you were overcharged for in 1988. Due to a computer error, you were undercompensated by $0.64. The enclosed check should make up the difference. We apologize for any inconvenience this may have caused you.

Sincerely,
Edward Topolansky
Account Manager

Over the next two months, 13 more people — including at least four billionaires — went to the trouble of depositing this measly 64-cent check:

Cher	**William Kunstler**
Ahmet Ertegun	**Rupert Murdoch**
Harry Helmsley	**S. I. Newhouse**
Thomas Hoving	**Mike Nichols**
Adnan Khashoggi	**Francesco Scavullo**
John Kluge	**Donald Trump**
Henry Kravis	

Kravis

IV. GOING LOW, LOW, UNBELIEVABLY LOW
Pleased to find that 13 of these people would bother to deposit a 64-cent check, we decided to go back to the well one more time. This time we sent an amount so small that most New Yorkers routinely waste its equivalent many times over in a single day — by not bothering to return some soda cans, or to turn the heat down, or to make a lunch out of the leftovers — simply because none of them think it's worth the energy or the bother. Well, almost none of them.

Dear [WEALTHY PERSON'S NAME HERE],
Our records show that you were recently sent a check for $0.64 in compensation for services that you were overcharged for in 1988. In fact, you should have been sent $0.77. The enclosed check for $0.13 should make up the difference. We apologize

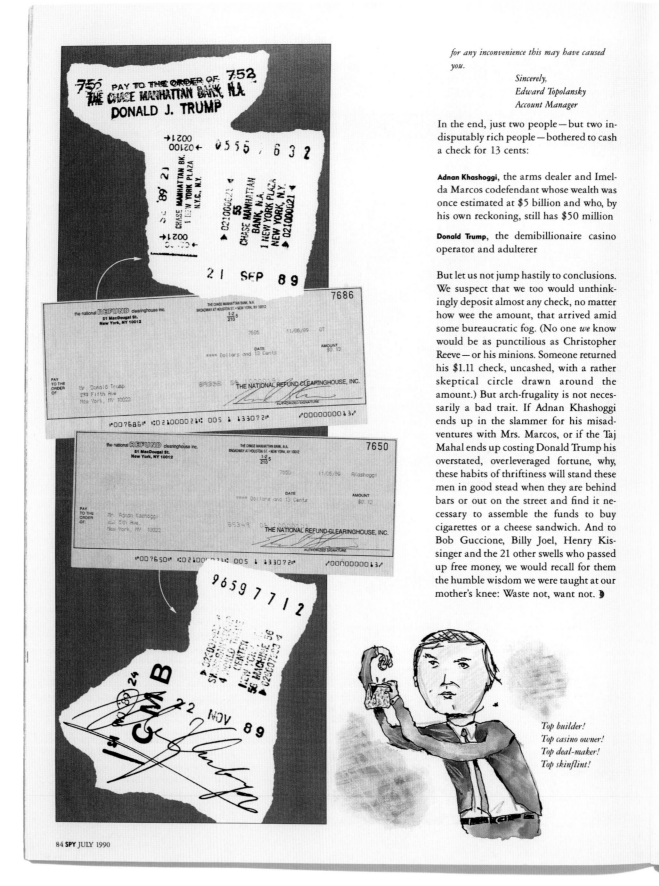

In the end, just two people — but two indisputably rich people — bothered to cash a check for 13 cents:

Adnan Khashoggi, the arms dealer and Imelda Marcos codefendant whose wealth was once estimated at $5 billion and who, by his own reckoning, still has $50 million

Donald Trump, the demibillionaire casino operator and adulterer

But let us not jump hastily to conclusions. We suspect that we too would unthinkingly deposit almost any check, no matter how wee the amount, that arrived amid some bureaucratic fog. (No one *we* know would be as punctilious as Christopher Reeve — or his minions. Someone returned his $1.11 check, uncashed, with a rather skeptical circle drawn around the amount.) But arch-frugality is not necessarily a bad trait. If Adnan Khashoggi ends up in the slammer for his misadventures with Mrs. Marcos, or if the Taj Mahal ends up costing Donald Trump his overstated, overleveraged fortune, why, these habits of thriftiness will stand these men in good stead when they are behind bars or out on the street and find it necessary to assemble the funds to buy cigarettes or a cheese sandwich. And to Bob Guccione, Billy Joel, Henry Kissinger and the 21 other swells who passed up free money, we would recall for them the humble wisdom we were taught at our mother's knee: Waste not, want not. ◗

Top builder!
Top casino owner!
Top deal-maker!
Top skinflint!

PEOPLE SAY THAT **GEORGE BUSH** is nothing but a get-along, go-along clubman, a blue-chip hack, a man without any real convictions at all. But it simply isn't so. Bush, SPY has learned, is like **MARIO CUOMO** and **RONALD REAGAN**—*a man of vision*. Not long ago a White House aide was detached to provide fresh oratory for the vice president's presidential campaign. The new speech writer took a meeting with Bush to find out just what kind of material would be required—something about family values, maybe, or prudence in foreign relations, or the fight against drugs? Nahhh. "Just put in some of that *vision* thing," Vice President Bush instructed. The new speech writer did not quite understand. "Which aspect of your vision do you want to convey, Mr. Vice President?" he or she asked. "You know," Bush said, as if trying to make a child or a servant understand something obvious simply by repeating it, "*that vision thing.*"

June 1988

How does socialite-novelist **Norman Mailer** keep his prose so fresh, tart and provocative? Why, by being fresh, tart and provocative himself! Not long ago, at a swank Manhattan literary salon that *wasn't* presided over by socialite–real estate broker **Alice Mason**, a tall, blond, jewelry-dripping Texas-oilwife type held Mailer's attention the entire evening. As the cocktails and canapés accumulated in the mailbox-shaped author's gut, his wit grew ever more rapier-sharp. *You are soooo funny*, the woman repeatedly responded to his bons mots. *You are soooo funny.* To which Mailer cleverly replied, in a similarly mantralike refrain, *You are a starfucker. I'm the star, you're the fucker. I'm the star, you're the fucker....*

2

September 1991

TINY EIGHTIES RELIC **HENRY KRAVIS** was dining calmly at an Upper East Side restaurant one evening last spring when something suddenly activated his internal social-climbing mechanism: **JESSYE NORMAN**, the jumbo-size soprano, was dining at a corner table not far from the one where Kravis and his wife, clothing designer **CAROLYNE ROEHM**, were picking at their meager portions. Eager to add Norman to his list of highbrow sort-of-acquaintances, Kravis begged the owner of the restaurant for an audience with the diva. The meeting was arranged, and the overleveraged buyout hustler was introduced to Norman. After they exchanged pleasantries, Kravis urged, in his inimitable bull-market style, "Please, sing one note—I'll pay you *anything.*" Needless to say, Norman politely declined.

August 1989

spoken, looked up, startled, and Mailer berated her. "It's a recycling day!" he cried. "Cans, bottles, papers! Anyone can see that!" And so, little by little, the planet is saved.

3

Busy bachelor dad **Jack Nicholson** is perhaps finally feeling his age. He was in Paris not long ago, promoting *Hoffa*, and his labors included being interviewed by a comely young *journaliste*. He answered questions for a while but then decided to remind the interviewer that he hadn't always been his current, slow-moving, Brando-size self. *You know*, he said, *in the old days, after 20 minutes of this, I would have tried to fuck you.* If Nicholson had hoped his line would be provocative—*Why, M. Nicholson, what do you mean, "zee old days"?*—he was disappointed. The reporter simply confirmed his intuition that he probably seemed fairly decrepit to her. She replied, *Oh, zat's funny—20 years ago you tried to fuck my mother.*

IIII

NINE YEARS OF PROFESSIONAL CYNICISM have apparently become something more than a comic mask for **DAVID LETTERMAN**. During commercial breaks on *Late Night*, his funny, once-revolutionary television program, Letterman does not, as one might suspect, engage in amusing repartee with his guests and audience or prepare for the next segment. Instead, he sits, head downward, pencil in hand, scribbling, like a disturbed child, "I hate myself" and "I hate my job" on a notepad on his desk.

March 1991

SPY

August 1991   Volume 5   Number 9

Hot Summer Number

Our
Completely Gratuitous
Swimsuit Issue

The Free-fallin' Bob Dylan
EXCLUSIVE INTERVIEW BY JOE QUEENAN

The President Who
Couldn't Say No BY PHILIP WEISS

Pack

Sharon Ston
That Cyni
Exploited Sex O

13

And Then There Were None

In Which *Spy* Is Sold, the Founders Bail, and Sharon Stone's Lips
Are Deemed to Be "Not in a Good Position"

The times changed, but we changed, too.
—Susan Morrison

IN LATE 1990, ONE SERIOUS BUYER remained in the picture—a group of rich Europeans who would have been called jet-setters by an earlier generation. "Originally," Graydon explains, "it was going to be Pigozzi, Saatchi, Jimmy Goldsmith, and Chris Blackwell." Jean "Johnny" Pigozzi is a Harvard-educated photographer, African-art collector, and heir to the Simca car fortune; it was in the latter capacity that he was in a position to buy a magazine. Charles Saatchi is a cofounder of the London-based ad agency Saatchi & Saatchi and one of the most significant collectors of contemporary art. Goldsmith was an Anglo-French wheeler-dealer who lived in Europe and Mexico. Blackwell is the legendary recording mogul (Island Records) and Caribbean hotelier. "But Goldsmith and Blackwell got cold feet," Graydon continues, "and in the end only Saatchi went in with Pigozzi. They flew us to London, and they said: *What we want to do is*—I can remember the expression Charles Saatchi used exactly—*we want*

to make Vanity Fair *look wet.* And I just thought, *You're going to need a lot more fucking money than you're spending right now.*"

That trip to the U.K., Kurt says, is his most vivid memory of the sale, "for better, and worse, and just metaphorical aptness." Tom had already met with Saatchi and Pigozzi in London. Then the other two were flown over on the Concorde. Graydon, famously, hated to fly, "and somewhere over the Atlantic," Kurt says, "it was like the thing hit a wall. There's only, I think, two engines on the Concorde, and one of them was gone. It was the most terrifying flight of my life. We landed in Ireland and ended up staying in Shannon Airport for hours and hours before they could get us a plane to London. We were given free beers and then later, in London, had this odd meeting with the very odd—charming and odd—Charles Saatchi, followed by dinner at his house. We weren't in Kansas anymore."

It was February 1991, and *Spy* had new owners—more precisely, *actual owners*, for the first time.

The agreement was announced in *The Wall Street Journal* and elsewhere. It was to be for $4 million—$3.5 million in capital

**Opposite:
Spy's new owner
hated this cover.
We disagreed,
but it didn't
matter: Tom and
then Graydon were
already headed
out the door.
August 1991**

8 212 721 0354 ENORME CORP

cc: KA, GC, SM, GR

JEAN PIGOZZI

JUNE 17, 1991

BY FAX

MR. B.W. HONEYCUTT
SPY

DEAR B.W.:

I JUST GOT THE JULY/AUGUST COVER SHOT AND I DON'T LIKE IT. AS I FAXED YOU SOME DAYS AGO, SHARON STONE'S FACE IS TOO SMALL COMPARED TO THE SPY LOGO. NOW THAT I SEE THE REAL COVER, I ALSO DISCOVER WITH HORROR THAT HER EYE MAKE-UP IS TOO DARK, HER LIPS ARE NOT IN A GOOD POSITION, THAT HER LIPSTICK IS HORRIBLE, THAT THERE IS NO LIGHT ON HER BREAST AND THAT HER HIPS LOOK VERY WIDE. THIS PHOTO IS ABSOLUTELY NOT SEXY. IT SIMPLY IS NOT A GOOD PHOTO OF SHARON STONE WHO IS A VERY PRETTY AND SEXY GIRL.

FROM NOW ON I WANT TO BE INVOLVED FROM THE BEGINNING, AND I WANT TO APPROVE ALL COVERS. I HOPE THIS IS CLEAR ENOUGH. PLEASE INFORM KURT AND GRAYDON.

HAVE A VERY GOOD WEEK,

JEAN

DICTATED BUT NOT
READ BY JEAN PIGOZZI

Fax from new *Spy* owner Jean Pigozzi to art director B. W. Honeycutt regarding the August 1991 cover

invested in the company, the rest distributed among the investors. Tom, Kurt, and Graydon didn't make any money on the deal. (Back in 1987, when they had each sold a quarter of their shares to Schragis, each had been paid a sum in the low six figures.)

The trip to London was the last time Kurt, Graydon, or anyone else at *Spy* communicated with Charles Saatchi about the magazine. Pigozzi, who divides his time among New York, London, Cap d'Antibes, and Panama, was the hands-on owner. Before long, *Spy*'s tiny mailroom would be filled with lists of fax numbers for him in his various homes around the world.

Jim Collins, a *Spy* editor and writer during this period, remembers Graydon giving Pigozzi an early tour of the office. "I had those In-box, Out-box trays, and there was a FedEx envelope sitting there. And Pigozzi saw it and said, 'Ah! See this? This is what we have to stop!' And Graydon said, 'Yeah, but…that's in the *In*-box.' I have no idea why Pigozzi bought the magazine. I have no idea what was on his mind."

"He does have a sense of humor and style," Kurt hazards, "and lots of fancy, glammy friends, so I think he thought that owning *Spy* would be a relatively inexpensive way to give himself a booster shot of glamour and big-boy stature."

Tom continued as publisher, but Pigozzi made it clear that he wanted to replace him. Kurt and Graydon, however, he intended to keep as editors.

"As Pigozzi said to us when he bought us, 'No—of course you stay on. What? You know, if I bought the Rolling Stones, I would get rid of Mick and Keith?'" says Kurt, laughing. Jagger, in fact, was one of Pigozzi's fancy friends. "We never talked about which one of us was Mick and which was Keith."

At last, after nearly a year of uncertainty, the deal is done. Charles Saatchi and Jean Pigozzi now own 87% of this magazine. And this magazine now has a good deal of money in the bank.

For any of you who would like to talk with us about the deal, the new proprietors and the implications of it all, we'll be in the back conference room this Friday at 11:30 a.m.

  Kurt, Graydon, Tom
  —Staff memo, February 19, 1991

THE FOLLOWING NIGHT AT A PARTY I asked Kurt about the sale. He told me how close we'd come to folding, how he'd thought that each of his last several Intros—the Great Expectations

editorial that kicked off every issue—might be the last he'd ever write. He mentioned that he felt "more sanguine than Graydon" about the new owners.

"Well, we might still manage to have some fun," I offered.

"Maybe six months of fun."

"I DON'T KNOW WHETHER JOHNNY KNEW what he was buying," says Graydon, "but it wasn't desks and computers. You're buying people when you buy a magazine, and I don't think he took proper care of those assets."

"Johnny basically had two classes of human beings he knew how to deal with: Mick Jagger and Barry Diller, to whom he was amusing and deferential…and his cooks and housekeepers," says Kurt. "We were something in between, which he wasn't used to. As the Newhouses and Grahams and others show, rich guys who really have their heart and soul in putting out magazines can be the best owners. But he really wasn't, in a grown-up way, prepared to put his heart and soul in it."

"Thank God for Pigozzi—hey, he paid my salary," says Jim Collins. "But like anyone who does that, you resent them more for paying your salary than if they didn't. And there was also this cloud of lost opportunity—even I was empathetically kicking Graydon and Kurt, or helping them kick themselves, for not having sold it earlier."

Things got pretty depressing at an editors' meeting. Kurt is away on vacation. Graydon left for maybe 20 minutes to take a call from Pigozzi, who apparently told him at length that the new issue (July/August) was "shit." It's probably our best in months. Gloom descends.

  —Journal entry, June 26, 1991

"I REMEMBER THAT MEETING," says Jamie Malanowski. "It was really terrific, we were all laughing, and right at the end of it Pigozzi called, and you could just see Graydon blanch."

Days later, Tom Phillips's not-unexpected departure was announced:

Spy managed to be born against long odds, to grow against long odds, and now to survive and renew itself against long odds. No one more determinedly, sincerely and tightfistedly fought those odds than Tom Phillips. Without Tom's heroic contributions over

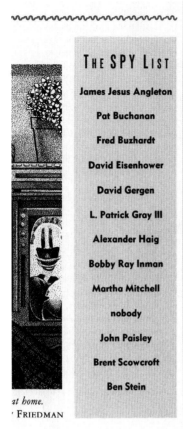

THE SPY LIST

James Jesus Angleton

Pat Buchanan

Fred Buzhardt

David Eisenhower

David Gergen

L. Patrick Gray III

Alexander Haig

Bobby Ray Inman

Martha Mitchell

nobody

John Paisley

Brent Scowcroft

Ben Stein

at home.
' FRIEDMAN

about $7,000
constituents h
him out. Ever
collects $553
for the six yea
terrorizing ne
one who cros:
path.

Perhaps th
this dole is th
convicted of t
of theft and o
yet *still* get th
check from th
Currently, 14
receiving ben
during their o
on Capitol Hi
are, along wit
of their montl
checks:

Ex-represer
Biaggi (D-N.Y
of taking payo

Ex-senator
ster (D-Md.),
no contest to
taking an illeg
ity: $915

Ex-represer
Diggs Jr. (D-N
took kickback
staff and misa
government fi
$4,139

Ex-represer
Dowdy (D-Tex
perjury: $5,0:

Ex-represer
Eilberg (D-Pa

May 1990

the last six years, all of us would probably be working at
Cooking Light, *Modern Podiatry,* or worse; *without Tom,*
Spy *wouldn't have been born, wouldn't have grown, wouldn't*
have survived....

KA/GC

—Staff memo, July 1, 1991

AND THEN THERE WERE TWO. *Spy*'s new publisher, Jerry
Taylor, a former publisher of the *National Lampoon* and a generation older than the oldest of us, would start in the fall.

On Wednesday, July 10, we had a particularly boisterous and
fun editorial brunch/meeting. But later in the day, a colleague
ran across a stray list among what appeared to be notes, in Kurt's
handwriting, about possible ways to cut costs: "Fire 2 editors,"
it read in part, "save $84,000."

Kurt was still away on vacation. I wandered into Graydon's
office and flopped into a chair.

"So," I said, casually. "What's new?"

"I'll tell you next week."

We didn't have to wait that long. A certain conversation was
overheard late Friday, the gist of which quickly spread among
the senior staff: Graydon was leaving for the then-very-sleepy
New York Observer, a one-time *Spy* target. The weekly's owner,
Arthur Carter, had offered him the top job.

> *Attached is a press release we're sending out tomorrow.*
>
> *As utterly friendly as this separation is—indeed, Graydon*
> *will continue to consult with me and contribute to Spy—it*
> *is nevertheless a sad moment. I have never had as fulfilling a*
> *professional relationship with anyone as I have had with*
> *Graydon for the last six years. He has been my partner and pal*
> *for the most remarkable adventure of our lives. And now the*
> *adventure continues, for Graydon and for the rest of us.*
>
> *KA*
>
> —Staff memo, July 15, 1991

THE PRESS RELEASE ANNOUNCED that Graydon would
become editor of the *Observer* on September 1. The day of Kurt's
memo we had our regular Monday-morning editors' meeting in
the conference room; Graydon was there. It took a little while to
get around to story ideas—Kurt talked for a bit about how "it's
like having a favorite brother move to another city"—but since the
announcement wasn't news at this point, we eventually slipped
into a normal, if slightly subdued meeting rhythm. But Graydon
noticed at one point that Kurt had tuned out the discussion and
was completely focused on trying to attach a pen and a pencil to
either end of a straw. Everyone gradually stopped talking.

"Uh, Kurt?" Graydon said, gently. "Are you going to be
all right?"

Much laughter, of course, but the meeting really broke up
(in every way) a few minutes later when Michael Lipscomb, the
receptionist, buzzed the conference room: "Graydon! Arthur's on
line four!" Graydon took the call.

It's not as if the signs hadn't been there. Although he hadn't
seriously begun thinking about starting a paper until *Spy* was
sold, Graydon was industrious and ambitious and always had a
few things percolating. As far back as 1989 he had taken me to

lunch—in midtown, a safe distance from the office—and told me about his eventual plan to start "the best small-town newspaper in America." It was going to be great. It would be called *The Sketch*. He wanted me to be editor and part-owner and—one minor detail—Rachel and I would have to move to Litchfield County, Connecticut. But we'd love it there! "Think about it, keep it in the back of your mind," he said, signaling for the check. "It'll be an adventure." Two years later, a whole new plan was brewing: This one was a magazine, called *Scout*. It, too, was going to be great. In this scenario, I'd been demoted to number-two editor (under Graydon), but at least I would be allowed to remain in New York.

"I think it was a little more painful the year *before* Graydon left, because there was just this sense that he was disengaged," says Susan Morrison. "It was like, 'Dad's having an affair.' You knew that he was pulling away."

"I've never talked to him about it," says Kurt. "I don't know when he started having serious conversations with Arthur Carter. But I think it was back into 1990. He was thinking about the next chapter. I wasn't. And then, as soon as he left it was clear that when we sold the magazine, he knew he was a very, very short-timer. Because the only time after the very beginning he ever expressed anger at me was over a provision in the deal about how long we had to stay at *Spy*."

In June, Graydon had phoned Kurt in Colorado, where Kurt was vacationing, to tell him he was leaving. "I was surprised to the degree that he had given me no inkling or indication that this was about to happen," he says. "Surprised, but not shocked."

"Leaving the magazine, and Kurt, was the most difficult professional move I have ever made, but I had three kids and a wife to look after," says Graydon. "You get a partnership like the one we had maybe once in a lifetime, if you're lucky. But being men, Kurt and I didn't talk about all of this much, and I know it did come as a surprise when I told him I was leaving. In hindsight, we should have talked it through."

"I think he was getting tired of being the bad guy," says Morrison. "It was a lot of work. He started going home earlier and earlier. I think he got a little weary of the meanness of *Spy*."

"Graydon helped create this great thing, and toward the end became more and more bored with it," says Jamie Malanowski. "And I think Pigozzi took all the wind out of his sails."

"When we began negotiating with Pigozzi, we were offended that he never asked us to sign 'employment contracts' that would have forced us to stick around after the sale for some period of time," Graydon says. "Then, as we got close to selling, and we realized what a change there would be in our daily lives, we prayed that he *wouldn't* realize what a foolish and arrogant thing that was, and ask us to sign contracts. He never did, though.

"I'm friends with Pigozzi now," he continues. "But after he bought the magazine, I really felt I didn't want to be an employee at a place I helped found. And I had this idea for a twice-weekly newspaper, so I was out raising money for that. I came to see Si Newhouse, and a bunch of other people, and I had about $8 million committed."

Would this be *Scout*? Or *The Sketch*?

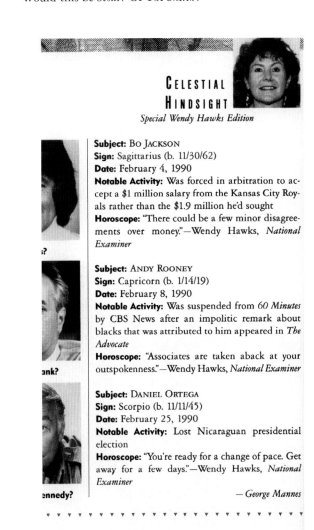

CELESTIAL HINDSIGHT
Special Wendy Hawks Edition

Subject: BO JACKSON
Sign: Sagittarius (b. 11/30/62)
Date: February 4, 1990
Notable Activity: Was forced in arbitration to accept a $1 million salary from the Kansas City Royals rather than the $1.9 million he'd sought
Horoscope: "There could be a few minor disagreements over money."—Wendy Hawks, *National Examiner*

Subject: ANDY ROONEY
Sign: Capricorn (b. 1/14/19)
Date: February 8, 1990
Notable Activity: Was suspended from *60 Minutes* by CBS News after an impolitic remark about blacks that was attributed to him appeared in *The Advocate*
Horoscope: "Associates are taken aback at your outspokenness."—Wendy Hawks, *National Examiner*

Subject: DANIEL ORTEGA
Sign: Scorpio (b. 11/11/45)
Date: February 25, 1990
Notable Activity: Lost Nicaraguan presidential election
Horoscope: "You're ready for a change of pace. Get away for a few days."—Wendy Hawks, *National Examiner*

— George Mannes

"No, this one was called *The Camera*—eventually we'd go daily, and then it would be *The Daily Camera*. I did drawings for it and everything. And it was going to be sort of a tabloid, but designed like a broadsheet. Then I ran into Arthur Carter at a cocktail party and asked him if he'd be interested in investing. And he said, 'Why don't you come over and do the *Observer?*'

"Nothing against Pigozzi, but I didn't want to work for him."

The farewell dinner for Graydon was held on August 22, Kurt's 37th birthday and a month after Graydon's 42nd, in a private upstairs room at the Landmark Tavern on 11th Avenue (the site, as it happened, of Kurt and Graydon's first, pre-startup fight). It is recalled by the dozen who attended as everything from "a perfect night" to "the drunkest I've ever been in my entire life." The evening was formal. A Frank Sinatra impersonator sang "*Spy* Way." There were stingers and toasts and reminiscences, sing-alongs and kick lines and conga lines until 3 a.m.

A week later I went in and told Kurt I thought it was time for me to leave. I'd been restless for quite a while—for the past year I hadn't done much beyond the Mailroom column and a fictional George Bush Diary, and I'd started writing more for other magazines. Kurt said he thought it was a good move. Then I mentioned

that Graydon had offered me a choice of columns at the *Observer*; that went over less well. I agreed to say nothing for the time being, stay on the *Spy* masthead for a few more issues, and continue to contribute occasionally.

Turned in my last (December) "Mailroom." Brought home my Rolodex, files, etc. Gave Joanne my folding fan.
—Final journal entry, October 7, 1991

That same autumn, B. W. Honeycutt also peeled off, for Condé Nast's relaunch of *Details*, "having designed 36 of the 55 issues of the greatest magazine on earth," as the staff announcement put it. His deputy, Christiaan Kuypers, became *Spy*'s art director.

But there was no time for Kurt or anyone else to catch their breath: *Spy*'s (latest) new era was very much in progress.

"EVERYONE WAS THINKING, *What's Kurt going to do next?*" says Jim Collins. "You just can't keep feeding people Mexican food constantly—the same dish, with the same seasoning, month after month after month. It becomes boring. So the question was how to evolve it."

Susan Morrison moved into Graydon's office and continued to be the editorial number two. "After Graydon left, it was really tough for Kurt," she says. "For months he would slip and call me 'honey' or 'sweetheart,' like I was Anne [Kreamer]. He was clearly used to having that kind of thing."*

Kurt doesn't recall his solo year and a half with much happiness,† but people who went through it with him describe it as a bittersweet but professionally satisfying phase of *Spy*'s history. Graydon's last issue had been the *Vanity Fair*–parodying, pregnant–Bruce Willis cover of September 1991, though his name was on the masthead for one more. The first just-Kurt *Spy* came in November, and in it was John Connolly's page-turning investigation of a Palm Beach society murder, which led directly to the killer's indictment and conviction.

"I think the magazine enjoyed a creative renaissance during

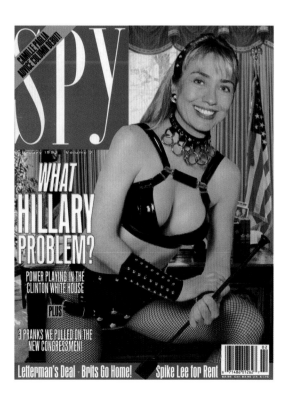

February 1993

---

*The founding coeditors, as far as they remember, never called each other by romantic endearments.

†Actually, he doesn't recall it much at all. –Eds.

Kurt's final year there," says Geoff Reiss. "Kurt was far more… I wouldn't say *extroverted*, but as the sole surviving partner, he played a significantly different role than he had before."

The magazine came up with some very memorable, acutely topical covers, such as Hillary Clinton as a dominatrix, Bill Clinton as Pinocchio, and Pee-wee Herman with Clarence Thomas. "That year, it seemed to me, there was the greatest amount of clarity in terms of editorial direction," says Reiss. "Kurt was very comfortable with what he wanted the magazine to be."

And there was Larry Doyle—"this strange little person who wore a trench coat indoors," says Lisa Birnbach—who joined the magazine during Kurt's last year there. "But what an incredible, integral, clever, modest, bizarre genius he was. His contribution was *enormous*."

"I pitched some ideas and they picked the most difficult one, which was '1000 Reasons Not to Vote for George Bush,'" says Doyle, whose office featured framed prints of dogs playing poker. "Then I had something like four weeks to come up with a thousand reasons. Jim Collins had the pleasure of cutting what was I think close to 50,000 words down to maybe 10,000. They went down to four-point type—it started in regular type and then got smaller and smaller as it went along."

That cover story, published the summer just before the Bush vs. Clinton election, received enormous publicity. Reason number one was "He Cheats on His Wife," an infamous, deeply reported story by Joe Conason that posited (but by no means proved) a certain moral equivalency between the Republican incumbent and his Democratic challenger. At a dinner at the Sheraton following Bill Clinton's acceptance speech at the Democratic convention, when John Connolly introduced himself to the nominee as "a reporter from *Spy*," Clinton *thanked* him— *for the Bush cover story* was the clear implication.

The advent of more serious investigative journalism—such as Lynda Edwards's disturbing account in March 1992 of whom the Senate Judiciary Committee could have called, but didn't, as witnesses during the Clarence Thomas confirmation hearings—in no way meant an end to the *Spy* pranks. A staffer posed as a representative of the Yankees and called mayors in various New Jersey backwaters to see what kind of relocation deal they could put together for the team. Jerry Taylor, the publisher, was recruited to pose as an executive headhunter and got John Sununu, who had just been fired as Bush's very powerful

Naked City

Meet the Nobelists!

This month's question: What is the best way to eat an Oreo cookie?

Dr. Daniel Nathans, 1978 Nobel Prize in Physiology/Medicine: "I haven't eaten Oreos for a while.…I eat *animal* cookies with my granddaughter. I generally bite off the head first, then proceed in a bit more random way to eat the rest.…Maybe that sort of, let's say, dehumanizes them.…But this is sort of ruminating without any conviction that I've got my finger on anything."

Dr. Hamilton O. Smith, 1978 Nobel Prize in Physiology/Medicine: "I love to take them apart; I don't know why. [Not] completely apart: I like to take one piece off and then the other, with the white filling still on it, [and] I eat that…then I eat the single side, separately. Lots of kids will take off the white stuff and flick it on their plate.…They collect it, then eat it last."

Dr. J. Michael Bishop, 1989 Nobel Prize in Physiology/Medicine: "Dunk it in tea. Dunking cookies is part of my heritage—central Pennsylvania. I think it's a way to revive stale baked goods. Oreos may not be stale, but they're certainly crunchy. You dunk them, and then they're nice and soft. I don't eat Oreos now, anyway. It's been years…much to my regret. You dunk it about halfway in and eat half the cookie, then dunk it a quarter, and so forth.…I hope none of my friends see this."

Dr. Rosalyn S. Yalow, 1977 Nobel Prize in Physiology/Medicine: "In general, I don't eat Oreos.…My mother weighed 118 when she got married, [and] when I was a child, she weighed over 200. That wasn't going to happen to me. In fact, the way I keep my figure is to get on a scale, and I lose my appetite if I've gained any weight. I do eat cookies, but I can't remember the last time I had an Oreo. It might be 50 years ago."

Dr. Baruj Benacerraf, 1980 Nobel Prize in Physiology/Medicine: "I have eaten an Oreo; apparently it is something which happens to one in one's life. My grandchildren love it, and it is put out by Nabisco, right? It is pleasant, but it certainly does not compare with better forms of food. I eat it with two fingers of one hand. Every time I eat a cookie like that, I take it out of the package and eat it, usually in a couple of swallows. I was very careful not to eat any more than that, because I tend to be chubby."

Dr. Gertrude B. Elion, 1988 Nobel Prize in Physiology/Medicine: "Oh, for heaven's sake, what kind of question is that?…I eat them straight out of the package." —*Gregg Stebben*

Illustration by Tim Gabor

February 1992

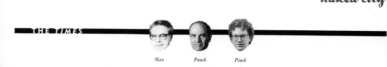
BEST OF THE *TIMES*

"There were, we thought, six or seven major sources for The *Times* column," says Graydon. "And one day I walk into a restaurant on the Upper East Side and every one of them, every fucking *Times* source, is there having lunch. And they all pretended they didn't know me. It was like their plastic surgeon had just walked in."

September 1990

The *Times*

Little Bi█

The same grit and determination that made his *7 Days* a favorite of New York's youngish would-be movers and shakers has made Adam Moss, New York's most huggable editor-for-hire, the *Times*'s most celebrated new employee.

positioning.

The hiring of Moss, who has never worked as either a magazine writer or a newspaper reporter, has triggered an unprecedented amount of resentment and indignation; never before have so many *Times* people been so eager to do in a new colleague. And he's not likely to get

Illustration by Barry Bli█

May 1991

much in the way of emotional support: the *Times*, a rough-and-tumble, quasi-macho outpost where men wear dark suits and conservative ties, is not known for its sensitivity.

The most significant factor in Moss's favor, aside from his not inconsiderable talents, is his cordial relationship with the intense, fiercely intelligent Lelyveld, who is generally considered to be the heir apparent to editor in chief Max Frankel. Lelyveld's influence is such that the Moss-ification of the *Times* is not as unlikely as the staff might like to think. Among the new boy's early major assignments was rethinking the paper's sports coverage. And in his first few days on the job, Moss nearly netted the *Times* one of journalism's megatalents: shortly before she signed on with *New York Newsday*, the gossip columnist Liz Smith telephoned a writer who had profiled her in *7 Days* and, virtually weeping, asked if he'd put in a good word for her with Mr. Moss. One can only imagine what Chronicle, the *Times*'s bone-dry gossip column, would have been like in Liz's hands:

The question of the moment is, What exactly has she been up to with *The New Columbia Encyclopedia*? Miller's tastes usually run toward middle-aged powerguys. But if a handsomely bound one-volume almanac of world knowledge can be of use—hell, why not?

That the encyclopedia is one of Miller's sources is not in doubt. She recently published a book on the Holocaust called *One, by One, by One*, and there, amid the references to Fritz Stern and Oliver Rathkolb (*Gesellschaft und Politik am Beginn der Zweiten Republik*), is a footnote citing *The New Columbia Encyclopedia* (New York and London, 1975). The last time I tried to support a statement in a research paper by referring to an encyclopedia, my social studies teacher told me she was not so much angry as, well, *disappointed*. The issue here, however, is not Miller's intellectual tackiness but rather her intellectual integrity. It's one thing to use an encyclopedia; it's another to *crib* from it.

The first to notice similarities between wording in *One, by One, by One* and Judy's research materials was David Walton, in his remarkable *Philadelphia Inquirer* review. He gives a number of examples of phrases and images that she employed without properly citing them. The review culminates in a comparison of an unfootnoted passage from Miller with a passage from *The New Columbia Encyclopedia*. Judy writes,

Although he was repeatedly humbled by

September 1990

Napoleon I, Hapsburg Emperor Francis managed to emerge, in part through skillful diplomacy, as one of the strongest monarchs at the Congress of Vienna in 1815. Austria gave up the Netherlands, but regained Dalmatia, Istria, and Tyrol.

The encyclopedia says,

Though repeatedly humbled by Napoleon I, Francis emerged at the Congress of Vienna (1815) as one of the most powerful European monarchs. Giving up the Austrian Netherlands, the Hapsburgs regained Dalmatia, Istria, and Tyrol.

Miller's "cut-and-stitch job" is lazy and a bit amateurish, but as Walton says, it is probably no more than that. Nevertheless,

▊THE *TIMES*

The departure of E. J. Dionne, the *Times*'s Pig-pen-like, pustle-gutted national political correspondent, rings down the curtain on the diverting ad hoc *Odd Couple* revival that Dionne and the paper's persnickety Washington bureau chief, Howell Raines, had been performing for their co-workers. It seems that Raines had grown displeased with Dionne's work following a period of allegedly lackluster presidential-campaign coverage, during which Raines, a southerner, felt Dionne, a Harvard-educated northerner, had made far too much of Jesse Jackson. A noisy shouting match

Senior editor Gerald Boyd was the first to approach Dionne with the news of Raines's displeasure. He suggested that a stint in the *Times*'s Budapest bureau just might salvage Dionne's flagging fortunes. When Boyd's overtures failed to produce the desired effect—groveling compliance— Raines was forced to issue the ultimatum himself. *We want you off politics*, he told Dionne, *because your stories lack sufficient conceptual sweep. And by the way, E.J.*, his boss said, getting to the heart of the matter, *you really should lose some weight.*

December 1989

chief of staff, to list his requirements for a corporate position. Sununu wanted his own jet—essentially the thing he'd been fired for.

And *Spy* had huge fun with the excellent *New York Times* parody (see pages 268–69) it distributed one July night (through the good offices of a well-placed friend at the NYPD) to media outlets and on delegates' seats all over the Democratic National Convention hall at Madison Square Garden—a thousand copies, smuggled in 15 at a time by a stream of dubiously credentialed *Spy* staff. The front sections of copies of the real *Times* were wrapped with *Spy*'s new pages one, two, op-ed, and back page. Ross Perot was running as a strong third-party candidate, so the lead front-page story was: PEROT SET TO PICK TV'S OPRAH WINFREY AS RUNNING MATE. For a few incredible seconds, democracy teetered. Then everyone laughed, and *Spy* once again made the national news—the parody was discussed on *The Tonight Show* by Tom Brokaw, reporting live from the convention floor, and by Ted Koppel as well, who fooled his wife with a copy.

Extremely funny young writers like Louis Theroux (who subsequently became a TV star in the U.K.) and Tim Long (originally hired as an intern—twice—while Graydon was still there, and who went on to become a *Letterman* and *Simpsons* writer and producer) joined the staff. "I don't think people felt the magazine was going downhill editorially," says Kurt's assistant at the time, Larissa MacFarquhar. "And it was a happy, functional office, because Kurt's authority was never questioned."

Interestingly, circulation was up—the magazine had a strong year in '92. The recession was winding down, and there was optimism that things might start to click again financially.

On joining as publisher, Jerry Taylor had negotiated an enviable salary for himself: $280,000, almost twice as much as Graydon and Kurt had been paying themselves. "I said to Pigozzi, 'You can't pay me that much through *Spy*, because people will find out, and that's too much for *Spy* to handle,'" Taylor says. "It was a lot more than Kurt was making. So I said, 'Pay me 180 at *Spy*, and you must have another company you can pay me the other hundred from.' And he said okay."*

Taylor sums up *Spy*'s advertising problems this way: "What

---

*This is the first Kurt has ever heard about this, and he is—no joke—chagrined. —Eds.

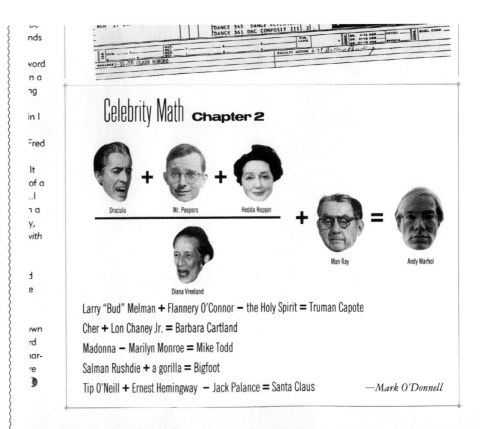

Celebrity Math Chapter 2

Dracula + Mr. Peepers + Hedda Hopper

Diana Vreeland + Man Ray = Andy Warhol

Larry "Bud" Melman + Flannery O'Connor − the Holy Spirit = Truman Capote

Cher + Lon Chaney Jr. = Barbara Cartland

Madonna − Marilyn Monroe = Mike Todd

Salman Rushdie + a gorilla = Bigfoot

Tip O'Neill + Ernest Hemingway − Jack Palance = Santa Claus

—*Mark O'Donnell*

we faced was, 'You were an ill-tempered magazine of the '80s.' Over and over and over again. So it was all about building back credibility for the magazine."

But Reiss feels that Taylor "struggled with the fact that we had moved into the 1990s, that this wasn't the *National Lampoon* in the 1970s, that 'chicks' didn't drink 'booze' and listen to 'the hi-fi.' There was a tough time relating to the contemporary ad vibe. But Jerry's instincts were generally pretty good, and he had to do something that Tom never had to do, which was to manage Johnny—that was really hard."

"Pigozzi kept saying to me, 'I'm a businessman'—the sure sign that someone is not a businessman," Taylor says.

"Johnny was, to put it kindly, pretty mercurial in terms of what he was interested in and how engaged he was," says Reiss. "You'd get these faxes from, you know, the South of France, and we wouldn't even know what they'd mean sometimes. And Jerry had to deal with that."

"All the News
That's Fit to Print"

The New York Times

Copyright © 1992 The New York Times

VOL. CXLI...No. 49,013

NEW YORK, WEDNESDAY, JULY 15, 1992

50 CENTS

PEROT SET TO PICK TV'S OPRAH WINFREY AS RUNNING MATE

Host of "Oprah" First of Her Race to Take Spot on Major Ticket

BREAKTHROUGH PICK

By R. W. APPLE, JR.
Special to The New York Times

CHICAGO, July 14 — Oprah Winfrey, the popular daytime talk show host, actress and businesswoman, has been tendered an offer by undeclared presidential candidate Ross Perot to run as Vice President on his ticket. Sources at the candidate's Dallas headquarters and among Ms. Winfrey's intimates in Chicago say she has flown to Dallas, and will announce her acceptance at an afternoon rally there Thursday.

Mr. Perot was unavailable for comment. Neither the White House nor the Clinton campaign would comment.

The decision caught other political professionals around the country flat-footed and elicited further, if grudging, respect for the banty Texarkanan.

"The boldness and brilliance of the decision are self-evident," said Norman Ornstein of the American Enterprise Institute. "She brings in the blacks. She brings in women. She charges up a whole segment of the electorate who are normally apolitical couch potatoes. Plus, she humanizes Perot. They're both self-made people, they're both straight talkers, but he doesn't look so paranoid with someone as warm as her around."

"Forget the presidency," said one Democratic Party official, who wished to remain anonymous. "We're just running to hold on to Congress now."

Academy Award Nominee

Oprah Winfrey is said to be Ross Perot's running mate.

Damon C. Torres

BUSH SON ARRAIGNED IN PENSACOLA AFTER HIGH-SPEED CHASE

FOUR POLICE HURT IN SCUFFLE

Andrew Bush, 37, Estranged from Family, Had Scrapes With Law, Never Liked Maine

By B. DRUMMOND AYRES, JR.
Special to The New York Times

PENSACOLA, FLORIDA, July 14 — In an incident that is certain to create more turmoil in an already bruising and volatile political year, President Bush's second-youngest son, Andrew E. Bush, 37, known as Trip, was arrested here today on charges of kidnapping, extortion, attempted murder, conspiracy to transport stolen goods across state lines, possession of burglary tools, auto theft, felonious assault, wire fraud and sexual battery of a minor. He was held without bail after his arraignment before Justice Daniel Burrows of the Santa Rosa County Superior Court.

The younger Mr. Bush has been estranged from his family for some time. He is seldom mentioned in family biographies. The last time he was seen in public with his father was in 1980, in Detroit, when Ronald Reagan offered the elder Mr. Bush the vice presidential nomination.

The White House Comments

The Pensacola police said that at 4:45 a.m., Mr. Bush's Camaro was stopped for running a red light. When the officer approached his car, Mr. Bush, who was being sought on several charges, sped away, police said.

Six radio cars joined in the ensuing chase, in which speeds reached more than 100 mph.

Mr. Bush eluded his pursuers, but was taken into custody about an hour later, when he stopped at the drive-

Perot Hid Mother in Attic Years After Her Death

By STEVEN A. HOLMES
Special to The New York Times

DALLAS, July 14 — Following his mother's death in 1980, Ross Perot kept her body in his attic for seven years, apparently believing that she was still alive, according to his neighbors here.

Mr. Perot's mother, Lulu May Perot, died of natural causes on May 5, 1980, at the age of 79. But in independent statements to The New York Times, sev-

COLUMBIA UNIVERSITY BOUGHT BY JAPANESE

Ivy League Institution Goes to Sony for $650 Million

By RONALD SMOTHERS

Sony, the giant Japanese consumer electronics and entertainment company, announced today that it had purchased financially troubled Columbia University for $650 million in cash and preferred stock. The company immedi-

Hillary Clinton's Big Day

By MAUREEN DOWD
Special to The New York Times

While her husband roamed the corridors of power—or as near an illusion of power—or as near an illusion of them as the grimy hallways of Madison Square Garden can provide—Hillary Clinton slipped away from the convention hubbub for some Big Apple sightseeing.

Accompanied by a handful of aides and a small horde of reporters, Mrs.

Taking advantage of a break in convention week activities, Gov. Bill Clinton entertains potential voters at the Union Square subway station.

ionable clothing of a kind that would be difficult to imagine a candidate's wife wearing. Fingering several silk dresses with price tags upwards of $1,000, Mrs. Clinton whistled softly.

"Do you sell headbands here?" she asked.

For the final stop of the day, Mrs.

Gregg Trueman for The New York Times

Despite Risks, Majority Finds Sexual Activity Pleasurable

By PHILLIP J. HILTS
Special to The New York Times

ATLANTA, July 14 — A massive five-year study by the National Institutes of Health has concluded that Americans engage in sexual activity on a regular basis, and that most enjoy themselves while doing so. The study warns that if current trends continue, future generations may be expected to engage in such activity as well. However, it also asserts that sexual activity, particularly when engaged in by adults in good health, is not necessarily a source of concern.

25,000 Subjects

"No one has ever tried to address these questions with the discipline and comprehensiveness that we have achieved," said Dr. William R. Bacon, who directed the study. "Basically, we wanted to know—are you, you know, engaging in coitus?

Overwhelmingly, the answer is yes.

The study was conducted through periodic interviews and questionnaires given to 25,000 subjects living in five geographically disparate cities: St. Paul, Minnesota; Chattanooga, Tennessee; Oakland, California; Kansas City, Missouri; and El Paso, Texas. Results for a sixth city, Brooklyn, New York, were thrown out after it was discovered that Brooklyn has not been a city since the early 1900's.

Experts warn that sexual participants face several dangers: contracting venereal disease or AIDS or developing serious psychological dependencies resulting from the physical or emotional attachment to another person. Despite these risks, the evidence indicates that Americans continue to be gratified by the stimulation of their sexual organs. Explanations vary, but the medical community has reached a consensus that

Continued on Page C14, Column 3

INSIDE

Associated Press

Paul McCartney Dead

The pop music legend was killed in a farm equipment accident on his estate in Somerset, England. He was 50. Page D18.

Charles, Wife Reconcile

Prince Charles and Princess Diana shook hands outside Buckingham Palace, ending rumors of marital unhappiness. Page A4.

Dan Quayle's Image

One month after the "potatoe" incident, the Vice President's advisers see new respect for Quayle. Page A13.

---

for some months.

Mr. Schmidt left his post as president of Yale University less than two months ago to join Knoxville entrepreneur Christopher Whittle in a for-profit educational venture. Sony will buy out Mr. Schmidt's contract for an undisclosed sum, said by sources close to the deal to be in the area of $20 million.

Yetnikoff Role

"We're thrilled," said Sony USA president Michael Schulhof at a press conference held at Sony's Manhattan headquarters. "Columbia is a distinguished institution, and we look forward to moving forward together. Benno is just the sort of leader who will make this partnership work." He also expressed gratitude to Walter Yetnikoff, the former chairman of CBS Records, for brokering the deal.

"I'm delighted," said Mr. Schmidt. "I had found myself already missing the university atmosphere."

Wall Street reacted favorably to the news. Arthur Ng, an entertainment industry analyst at Bear Stearns and Company, said, "This is another of Sony's hardware-software plays, sweetened by a move into the top end of the market. With Mariah Carey and Meyer Shapiro, Sony's product line is

Continued on Page D4, Column 1

Before the shopping, however, came a stop at a computer-equipped day care center for disadvantaged youth at the Harlem Assembly of God meeting hall on Lenox Avenue. Mrs. Clinton smiled as the wide-eyed pre-schoolers worked on letter identification as a 150-member letter-perfect media entourage looked on.

Then came dessert—a stop at Mrs. Field's Cookies. Choosing several varieties, all dripping with chocolate, Mrs. Clinton told reporters that she planned to take some back to her husband's suite at the Intercontinental Hotel. "He'll never forgive me if I don't," she said. "Of course," she laughed convincingly, "they're not as good as my homemade ones."

Asked in a decidedly offhand manner for the secret to her recipe, Mrs. Clinton's face for a moment paled. She jerked her head suddenly toward her aides, then muttered, "Oh, you know, flour. And how you sift it."

"Oh, look!" Mrs. Clinton interrupted herself. "We must keep moving." The entourage filed into Charivari, where Mrs. Clinton shook hands with the youthful employees, all dressed in fashionable

Sitting on the corner of 44th Street and Eighth Avenue, local denizen Manuel Ortiz sipped amber liquid from a paper bag and watched the crowds entering and leaving Madison Square Garden.

"Who's playing?" he wanted to know.

When informed that the Garden was being occupied by the Democrats, Mr. Ortiz responded, "Oh, yeah. Hockey, right?"

A companion of Mr. Ortiz's, who said he could not remember his name, approached a group of passing delegates. "You got a dollar?" he asked. Without taking their eyes off the Don't Walk sign, the group shook their heads nervously. Then one young man unpinned a Tsongas '92 button from his lapel and offered it with a shy smile.

Do You Like My Hat?

"How about this one?" asked Mayor David N. Dinkins, donning a Virginia Is For Lovers baseball cap. He has received

Continued on Page A12, Column 6

---

edly earns $60 million a year. Along the way, she has been a victim of child abuse, won the Miss Tennessee beauty pageant, been nominated for an Oscar for her role in Steven Spielberg's The Color Purple," and become a broadcaster. Her selection would add further proof that this is the year of the broadcaster in politics.

Perot's Strategy

By choosing Ms. Winfrey, Perot seems determined not merely to win the presidency but, in the process, to stand the political establishment on its ear. His predilection for the daring and the dramatic stands in marked contrast to the cautious, careful politics that have been practiced at the presidential campaign level for decades. By taking the offensive, by making his announcement in a way guaranteed to steal Governor Clinton's thunder during convention week, by leaving President Bush to be the guardian of politics-as-usual, Perot seems poised not merely to seize the leadership of the nation, but to take its breath away.

The major parties will face a formidable obstacle if they intend to run a campaign focusing on Ms. Winfrey's negatives. "Sure, you could say she doesn't have experience," said Stu Spencer, the veteran Republican strategist, "but that's precisely what people want this year. What's left to criticize? That her weight fluctuates?"

Mr. Perot's choice of running mate had been the subject of much speculation ever since the billionaire made his interest in the presidency known last spring. Speculation had centered on former U.N. Ambassador Jeane Kirkpatrick, Gen. Norman Schwarzkopf, Joint Chiefs

Continued on Page B8, Column 4

who occasionally discussed business at the Perot household. "He thought that she was still with us. He'd say that she was living upstairs, and he didn't mean in Heaven."

One woman who said Mr. Perot gave her a tour of his estate in 1984 recalled a more dramatic incident. Mary McCartney, a prison matron from Huntsville, recalled that when they reached the attic of Mr. Perot's house, "he knocked on the door real quiet like and whispered to me. 'Mother lives in here.' I don't like to judge, but it felt creepy."

Reached by phone at his office yesterday, Mr. Perot emphatically denied the accounts.

"Pure poppycock and bulldangle," he said. "Who said that? I'll bet those people never even knew my mother.

"Look," Mr. Perot continued, "this is a non-issue. I took this call because I thought you wanted to go into all the minutiae of how she was buried. You just want to say 'Gotcha.' This is all part of the Republican dirty-tricks campaign, isn't it?"

Mr. Perot said that he'd buried his mother within several days after her death. But handwritten instructions on a receipt from the Newport Brothers Funeral Home dated May 7, 1980, indicate that Mr. Perot requested the return of Mrs. Perot's remains to EDS headquarters in Dallas.

"He wanted her stuffed, like some old buck or something," said Jimmy Ray Noonan, 43, an undertaker at the home. "We don't usually do that, but we figured what the hey, he's doing"

Mr. Perot's press secretary, Sharon Hol-

Continued on Page A11, Column 4

---

ing statement: "President and Mrs. Bush have not been in contact with their son for many years, and probably would not know him if they saw him. They still love him and support him, and have every confidence in the fairness and objectivity of the criminal justice system."

The Perot campaign declined to comment. George Stephanopoulos, deputy campaign manager for Gov. Bill Clinton, said, "It's a tragedy, of course. The important thing to remember is that of all the candidates, only Bill Clinton has presented a detailed plan for prison reform."

Appearing before Justice Burrows, Mr. Bush wore dungarees, black motorcycle boots and a denim shirt cut off at the sleeves. His shoulder-length hair was disheveled, and it was evident that he had not shaved for several days.

Trailer In Hobe Sound

Trip Bush has always been a bit different, friends say, from his siblings. A cocky renegade with little use for the tennis games and genteel manners of the Bush clan, Mr. Bush never quite fit in. Officials at St. Paul's School, an elite preparatory school in New Hampshire that Mr. Bush attended in the 1970's, say that Mr. Bush was the only student they could recall who insisted on taking metal shop at a nearby high school. Mr. Bush was ultimately expelled from St. Paul's for dismantling stolen cars off-campus and selling their parts, which the school forbids.

Mr. Bush, who dropped out of Florida State University after one semester, has drifted in recent years, friends say, from Texas to Alaska, from Alabama to Flori-

Continued on Page A8, Column 6

Stamp Buyer's Pick: Young Eleanor or Old?

By HERBERT MITGANG
Special to The New York Times

WASHINGTON, July 14 — Eleanor Roosevelt, goodwill ambassador to the world? Or a younger, more fetching Eleanor, the one who caught the heart of the destiny-driven future president?

Encouraged by the reception to letting the mailing public vote on the design of the Elvis Presley stamp, the U.S. Postal Service has decided to do it again, this time with former First Lady Eleanor Roosevelt. Starting on August 1, post office patrons will be able to vote for their choice of designs of a new first-class postage stamp to honor Mrs. Roosevelt.

"You can't overestimate what the Presley thing meant to us," said Postmaster General Marvin Runyon at a news conference in Washington this morning. "After years and years of nothing but abuse and criticism, suddenly we did something that got people

Eleanor Roosevelt

Eleanor Roosevelt

excited—in a good way.

"I don't know about you," the Postmaster continued, "but when I've got a good thing going, I keep at it."

The designs, both by Vermont artist Alexander Kovalevov, show Mrs. Roosevelt's face. The image in one, showing an older Mrs. Roosevelt, circa 1950, should be recognizable to anyone familiar with Mrs. Roosevelt's place in history. The other wasn't even recognizable to Roosevelt biographer Joseph Lash.

Continued on Page A8, Column 3

Stamp Buyer's Pick: Young Eleanor or Old?

Young Eleanor or Old?

OUR BIENNIAL *WIGWAG* SCORECARD

Articles that have already appeared in *Wigwag*, the gentle magazine that bills itself as "A Picture of American Life":	Articles that have yet to appear in *Wigwag*:
A profile of Fred Rogers A report on various uses for soaps and lotions A chart showing the frequency of garbage collection in various municipalities A visit with a golf pro in New Jersey Ruminations on taking old clothes to a thrift shop An editor's note about how a neighborhood grocery smells An editor's note reflecting wistfully on the shortcomings of the new Mr. Potato Head as compared with the original Mr. Potato Head A look at stuttering David Updike regretting change in Cambridge, Massachusetts A poem about brooms A look at white bread	A profile of Gumby creator Art Clokey An illustrated history of male hosiery A look at clover A profile of *Family Circus* creator Bil Keane Reflections on cleaning out a basement and finding old cans from the 1940s Reminiscences about a memorable maiden aunt in Troy, New York A visit to *Yankee* magazine A photo essay on tractor-trailer mud flaps An editor's note about how a neighborhood hardware store smells A children's story by Louise Erdrich featuring characters from Native American mythology An account of getting one's shoes shined by an old black man in the lobby of a fading downtown hotel in Oklahoma City A visit with a guy who makes banjo strings A report on how dry cleaning works A look at bed-wetting A visit to a graham-cracker factory 🢒

Wigwag was a smart, short-lived, and— as the left-hand column attests— incredibly gentle magazine of the late '80s. June 1990

"All Pigozzi's faxes had a stamp: 'DICTATED BUT NOT READ,'" Jim Collins remembers. "Just in case...what? His secretary dropped a word or something? Another of his quirks was that in France he had a fax machine that had a continuous roll, so when you sent him a fax you had to tape the pages together. At one Christmas party, there was some joke picture-caption thing for the staff that Ted Heller did, and the one for Pigozzi was, 'He liked his women the same way he liked his faxes...long and all taped together!'"

When I contacted Pigozzi to talk to him for this book, he suggested I email him some questions. I did—a dozen pretty standard ones about what he enjoyed and didn't enjoy about *Spy*, why he got involved, how he worked with each of the editors, what kinds of difficulties the magazine faced. He replied almost immediately:

Dear George,
    Sadly I do not like any of your questions.
        Yours, Jean

SUSAN MORRISON LEFT after the October 1992 issue.

"There was a change in the air," she says. "During the Clarence Thomas hearings, I remember thinking that this was the most interesting thing that had come along in a few years. This kind of stuff was happening all the time. But there wasn't anything like the pure vanity of the high '80s."

Plus, she had a great job offer: editor of *The New York Observer*. The position was open because Graydon was leaving it to become editor of *Vanity Fair*. (Morrison later became articles editor at *The New Yorker*.) Still, she says, "it was the hardest decision I've ever had to make. Kurt said, 'I want you to stay and do *Spy* with me. If you want to run something, I'll go and you stay and run *Spy*.' I thought about it for weeks. It would have been fun, but it was time to do something different. And I think it would have been lonely to be at *Spy* without everyone else."

And so the three top editors of *Spy* during its heyday all found themselves, within a half-dozen years of the launch, editors-in-chief simultaneously—of *Spy*, the *Observer*, and *Vanity Fair*.

№ 948

Federal funds paid for *Sex Respect,* an anti-premarital-sex comic book for high schoolers, produced by a conservative religious organization.

1000 REASONS NOT TO VOTE FOR GEORGE BUSH

little bit of an extra dimension," said Sununu. **927** Beginning a tour of drug-exporting countries, he bumped his assistant secretary of State for International Narcotics Matters off the plane. **928** Sig Rogich came instead. **929** The president has involved the military in civilian drug-law enforcement. **930** In the drug war, tens of millions of dollars have gone to corrupt colonels in Bolivia. **931** The 900 Bolivian troops the Army is training will probably just be hired by drug lords. **932** In August 1989, after a meeting to plan drug-war strategy, he met with reporters and said, "Well, we had a—this is nothing other than your basic photo op." **933** The $2 billion the Pentagon has spent to fight drugs has "not had a significant impact" on the availability of cocaine in the U.S., says the General Accounting Office. **934** "I can't say I identify with any specific educational goal"—1988. **935** He watches five TV shows at a time. **936** In 1990 the *Houston Post* reported that the CIA had links to more than 20 failed S&Ls. **937** "We have a sluggish economy....That's why I favor this deficit so much"—October 1990. **938** "When you project income and it doesn't come in like you project, you have a revenue shortfall"—on his $300,000 1980 campaign debt. **939** He threatened to veto Daniel Patrick Moynihan's Social Security—tax cut, which primarily would have benefited working people. **940** To balance the budget by 1993 "without raising taxes," he kept the Social Security trust-fund surplus on budget. **941** Twice in 1991 he thwarted efforts to extend unemployment benefits. **942** HHS canceled a survey on teenage sexuality after the head of a conservative pressure group complained that "we already know teenagers have sex too early, too often and with too many people." **943** Teenage AIDS cases nearly doubled between 1989 and '91. **944** He doesn't mention AIDS much. **945** U.S. policy bars HIV-infected people from entering the country. **946** But when a beloved basketball star became infected, Bush invited him to the White House. **947** "I want him to stop dancing around the truth....If he's not going to do anything, I just want him to tell me, straight out"—Magic Johnson. **949** HHS blocked publication of an AIDS-education pamphlet because it explained how to use a condom. **950** HHS's AIDS-education campaign doesn't mention the word *sex* or *condom.* **951** He vetoed a bill that would have provided funds for the UN family-planning agency. **952** He feared the money might be used for forced contraception in China. **953** HHS refused to fund in vitro–fertilization research, because many fertilized eggs do not survive. **954** He favored the *Rust* v. *Sullivan* decision, which prohibits family-planning clinics from discussing abortion if they receive federal money. **955** He vetoed legislation that would

have limited *Rust.* **956** The White House sent copies of the *Rust* decision to judges hearing a case about government funding of leftist filmmakers. **957** He backed away from his earlier endorsement of a law to limit the size of ammo clips. **958** It "didn't meet with a lot of enthusiasm" from his friends, according to an aide. **959** He said he would back stronger penalties for people who buy large ammo clips and then kill people. **960** "Amending the Constitution to protect the flag is not a matter of partisan politics. It's an American issue"—holding a miniature version of the Iwo Jima Memorial, June 1990. **961** The Reporters Committee for Freedom of the Press lists 340 incidents in which he tried to keep information from the American people. **962** In a Florida school district, children must now get their parents' permission to check out *Snow White.* **963** The Justice Department went to court to defend the right of prolifers to interfere physically with women trying to get abortions. **964** The president wants to spend $1,000 per person for defense in fiscal 1993. **965** He supports the B-2 bomber, which was designed to elude Soviet radar and deliver nuclear bombs. **966** He supports Timberwind, an $8 billion nuclear-powered rocket engine. **967** He supports MILSTAR, a $40 billion network of space satellites and blast-hardened ground stations. **968**

He supports the National Program Office, which makes plans for keeping the White House functioning in case of nuclear war. **969** So far $7.5 billion has been spent. **970** As head of the National Program Office, the vice president has been compiling a list of people to take over the country if everybody mentioned in the 25th Amendment is killed. **971** You are not on this list. **972** We've heard too many tiresome puns when he hunts quail. **973** Even Margaret Thatcher is convinced that the world needs to cut carbon-dioxide emissions. **974** Nine out of ten middle-class Americans think it's more difficult to make ends meet now than it was a few years ago. **975** Maybe James Baker would go down with him. **976** Hobe Sound, the posh Florida resort where the Bush family has a house, is rife with anti-Semitism. **977** The Greenwich-country-club world in which he grew up, and of which he has remained a part, is rife with anti-Semitism. **978** Not to mention racism. **979** Not to mention the anti-Semitism and racism of Texas plutocrats. **980** Nixon, Ford, Reagan and he could play golf as a Republican ex-president foursome. **981** Chief of Staff Sam Skinner, who he thought was so brilliant, has made people miss Sununu. **982** "Thing." **983** In 1988 he said, "Watch my vice presidential decision, that will tell all." **984** "You have to stand between him and a window or he'll spend the whole time looking out the window daydreaming"—an aide. **985** He's actually made you feel guilty for despising Dukakis so much. **986** "Let's go...get a pineapple float and cool you off"—a boy to his overeager date in *Sex Respect.* **987** He makes Jack Kemp look like a subtle thinker. **988** He boasts that AIDS spending has increased 118 percent since he took office. This is because more people covered by Medicare and Medicaid are dying of AIDS. **989** A 1992 survey by the National Institute of Drug Abuse found that the same number of people are using cocaine weekly as in 1989. **990** The infant-mortality rate in the U.S. is higher than that in 23 other industrialized nations. **991** In 1980 he said, "You can have a winner [in a nuclear war]." **992** "I never said that," he insisted in 1984. The original interview had been tape-recorded. **993** If he loses, he might become interestingly embittered. **994** "He doesn't seem to stand for anything"—Ronald Reagan on Bush, March 1992. **995** "Unleash Chiang!"—a common Bush utterance during sporting contests. **996** "Those who say good field, no hit—I think it's a vicious assault not only on my baseball ability but on my character." **997** At Yale he was a good fielder and a mediocre hitter. **998** "It was Vic Damone on the links today." **999** "I'm not going to comment on the fishing—vicious assault on my ability." **1000** "If you're so damned smart, why are you doing what you're doing and I'm president of the United States?" ❱

From "1000 Reasons Not to Vote for George Bush," August 1992

That period of overlap was brief, however. *Spy* wasn't making money, and there were brutal cutbacks in the offing. Pigozzi had scaled back the budget, and in late 1992, Kurt holed up in Jerry Taylor's office along with Geoff Reiss over several days to figure out what to do.

"Jerry was chain-smoking," Reiss recalls. "Johnny wanted a 10 percent head-count reduction. We ran every scenario in terms of who would stay and who would go. Kurt would say, '*I'll* go—take me out of this one.' We, uh, didn't run any scenarios where Jerry left.

"It was horrible," continues Reiss. "The magazine was struggling because it didn't have enough revenue, not because its expenses were out of line. And it was too small a circulation to matter to big national advertisers in a meaningful way. We had so many ad directors and sales people go through, such turnover, that it was easy for them to cut *Spy* from their schedules—they weren't violating a long-standing relationship. Yet we were too *big* to recapture whatever New York–L.A. metro business we'd had. We were in a circulation no-man's-land."

Amid the layoffs, in the wake of Morrison's departure, Kurt nevertheless had to hire a number two.

Lisa Birnbach had done the profile of Wayne Newton for *Spy* a year earlier but, she says, "I was not a *Spy* person. I came to a Christmas party and felt like I really didn't fit in at all." Besides, she and her family were then living in L.A. But after Morrison left, Kurt called.

"I knew that Kurt wanted to hire a woman to replace Susan," Birnbach says. "He talked beautifully, eloquently, about our being a great team. And that was a big piece of it for me, because I wasn't really looking for a job. But Kurt talked about how we would be doing other TV projects and how we could come up with book ideas and so on."

Birnbach and her family moved back to New York, and she joined as deputy editor.

"There was a lot of talk about Graydon," she remembers. "A lot of the staff felt let down by him—like it was the Kurt 'n' Graydon ride that they'd bought tickets for, and the co-pilot was gone. It put a lot of pressure on Kurt, but he seemed to handle that. Kurt definitely had a vision for the magazine that protected it."

Birnbach, brought in as a high-ranking outsider, didn't have the easiest task. "People wanted Kurt's approval, not mine," she says. "There was some territorialism. Yet I had to be the warm, supportive person at the office—'Oh, no, no, you *are* a good writer! Why don't you come into my office and we'll talk about it.' Meanwhile, Kurt was, as we now know, negotiating for his exit." (They would, in their months working together, end up collaborating with Jamie Malanowski on *Loose Lips*, an eventual Off-Broadway revue that had six-month runs in New York and L.A. It was based on real transcripts and recordings—Prince Charles telling Camilla Parker Bowles he dreamed of being her tampon, Bill Clinton and Gennifer Flowers talking dirty, and dozens more—that had appeared in

Spy and elsewhere.)

Jerry Taylor remembers Kurt walking into his office one day and simply saying, "Hi. I'm leaving."

The official announcement came in February. Kurt would be returning to *Time* as one of its top editors and its first weekly cultural columnist. The May 1993 issue of *Spy* was his last.

"I knew that he was a charismatic editor, but even so, I was shocked—people were *weeping* when it was announced," remembers Larissa MacFarquhar. "It was very emotional. And then people started leaving as soon as they could."

Joanne Gruber took to standing in Kurt's doorway in his last weeks at *Spy* and singing him medleys of breakup songs. Jamie Malanowski regrets that they didn't all take the opportunity to go out with a bang.

"I really wish that Kurt hadn't kept it all inside, that he had come to us and said, 'Let's fight for our magazine,'" he says. "We should have done a Pigozzi issue and sent it to the printer and then quit. I once sat at a meeting with Johnny where he said, 'You notice how few women are giving blow jobs anymore?' I just wish we'd put 'THE STUPIDEST OWNER IN THE WORLD' on the cover and said goodbye."

Not long ago I asked Kurt why he left when he did.

"Ohhhh…because…you know."

Try again.

"Because as sweet as Jean Pigozzi was in many ways, it was just a constant struggle, really. We never yelled at each other—he was respectful and everything—but he always sort of had his finger on the pin of the grenade. And that's just not a pleasant way to live. Also, so many of my best friends had gone, so it was less fun on that level. And as so much of the rest of media began having bits of *Spy*-ishness, *Spy* became less singular and less unique and, therefore, inevitably, less interesting.

"And at that point, I'd been doing it six going on seven years. It kind of had its run for me personally—as if that book or movie or whatever was finished. There were still great moments, but my last year there was simply not nearly as fun as the previous five years."

In fact, Kurt says now, he found "the whole thing, all of the time doing *Spy*, insanely high-stress. As exciting as it was, as wonderful and as gratifying, it was also sapping, if not soul-draining. I literally had recurring dreamlike images of myself holding onto the wires of a giant turbine."

Kurt's farewell party was held at a now-defunct restaurant called Nosmoking in TriBeCa.

"I was very moved and a little shaken by how emotional that was for everyone," Birnbach remembers. Despite the obligatory heavy drinking, Kurt made an extemporaneous and more or less coherent, hour-long farewell speech, acknowledging every person in the room.

It felt like a wrap party. Surely *Spy* was finished now.

---

bags and
The pos-
yethylene
thinking
"Just to
hrough it
ne film."
have ben-
roduct as

on, might
, moving
mmunica-
lependent
working
stic inner

distinction now being that he is one of the town's few homeless people.   — *Rachel Urquhart*

WHAT IF JEAN-PAUL SARTRE HAD HAD A LITTLE IMAGINARY FRIEND NAMED SNEAKERS?

1956 Sartre scours Paris for a tiny beret.

1957 Sartre abandons Sneakers in a cardboard box on the *métro*.   — *Henry Alford*

June 1989

October 1992

Love forgives;
friendship prorates.
Love does not alter when it
alteration finds;
friendship sues.
Love invests;
friendship speculates.
Love is unconditional;
friendship has clauses.

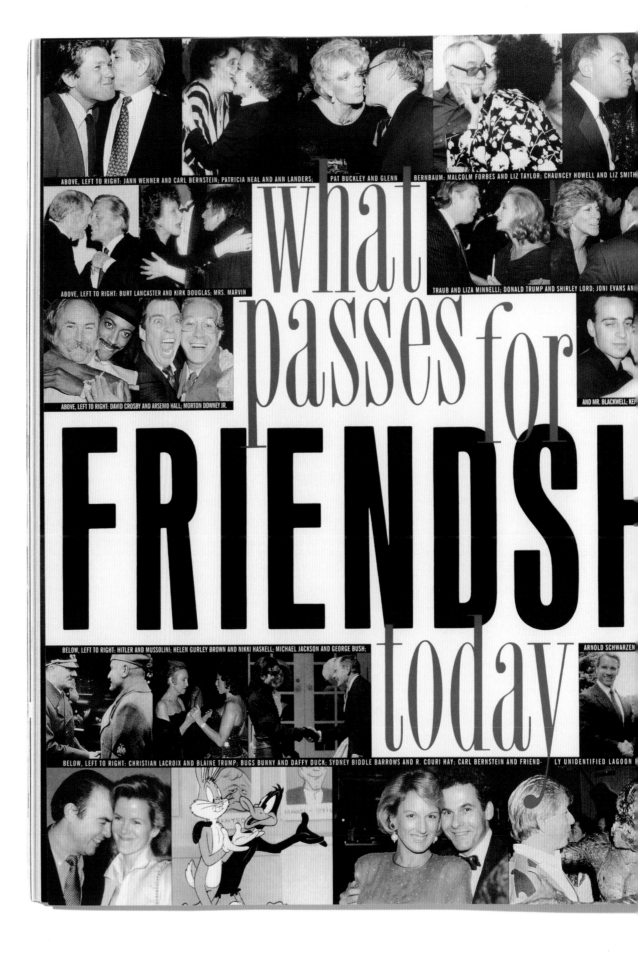

what passes for FRIENDSHIP today

ABOVE, LEFT TO RIGHT: JANN WENNER AND CARL BERNSTEIN; PATRICIA NEAL AND ANN LANDERS; PAT BUCKLEY AND GLENN BERNBAUM; MALCOLM FORBES AND LIZ TAYLOR; CHAUNCEY HOWELL AND LIZ SMITH

ABOVE, LEFT TO RIGHT: BURT LANCASTER AND KIRK DOUGLAS; MRS. MARVIN TRAUB AND LIZA MINNELLI; DONALD TRUMP AND SHIRLEY LORD; JONI EVANS AN

ABOVE, LEFT TO RIGHT: DAVID CROSBY AND ARSENIO HALL; MORTON DOWNEY JR. AND MR. BLACKWELL; KE

BELOW, LEFT TO RIGHT: HITLER AND MUSSOLINI; HELEN GURLEY BROWN AND NIKKI HASKELL; MICHAEL JACKSON AND GEORGE BUSH; ARNOLD SCHWARZEN

BELOW, LEFT TO RIGHT: CHRISTIAN LACROIX AND BLAINE TRUMP; BUGS BUNNY AND DAFFY DUCK; SYDNEY BIDDLE BARROWS AND R. COURI HAY; CARL BERNSTEIN AND FRIEND- LY UNIDENTIFIED LAGOON

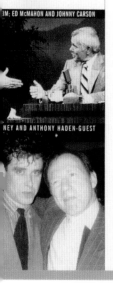

by James Collins

P

*a*t a cocktail party, two magazine editors are talking about one of their colleagues, a journalist who has just been publicly humiliated because of his involvement in a minor professional scandal. Editor No. 1 says to Editor No. 2, "I'm glad he finally got what's coming to him, the little weasel." Just then, the mortified journalist approaches to say goodnight. He places a hand on Editor No. 1's shoulder and says with emotion, "I just wanted to thank you again for your words of support earlier. They meant a lot to me."

This is a true story, witnessed last fall in New York City; the names have been omitted to spare feelings — the principals are friends of ours.

At a recent wedding of two quite successful professionals, a group of somewhat more successful professionals sat talking at their table. Slowly they discovered something they all had in common: none of them had any idea why they had been invited.

This is a true story, witnessed last year in New York City; the names have been omitted to spare feelings — the principals are friends of ours.

A flamboyant real estate mogul falls on hard times. Every day for three weeks the tabloids carry stories about how he is sure to go bankrupt. None of these stories contain comments from any of his many, many swell friends and associates, the ones he has entertained on his yacht time and again. Finally, one paper finds a friend willing to say a good word about the overleveraged businessman; that friend is his contractor.

This is a true story, collected this past summer in New York City; the names have been omitted for consistency's sake.

NOW COME THE LONG SHADOWS AND BURNISHED LEAVES AS AUTUMN, THE VIOLA IN OUR quartet of seasons, takes up nature's melody. The sunshiny days just past still caper in the mind, and yet, like fallen petals, they soon will lose their savor. Only one remembrance of those sweet weeks will never fade. It lingers. It is timeless. It is this: during the entire summer, exactly one friend invited you away for the weekend, *and that was a friend you despise.*

But then again, remember a few weeks ago, when you finally returned all those calls from your college roommate — the one now in public relations? He dropped by for a drink — fine, enjoyable really. Then the sun began to set, and you said to him, "Well, I wish you could stay for dinner, but I'm having some people over...."

As is well known, love is a gift, freely given. Friendship, however, is more like a lease. (People who fall out of love but then remain friends have a kind of sale-and-leaseback arrangement.)

Love forgives; friendship prorates.

Love does not alter when it alteration finds; friendship sues.

Love is blind; friendship is like a private eye.

Love invests; friendship speculates.

Love serves; friendship uses.

Love is Tristan and Isolde or Abélard and Héloïse or Bruce and Demi or Nick and Nora Charles; friendship is Malcolm and Liz.

Love is unconditional; friendship has clauses. Think you've been kicked out unfairly? Read your lease: no pets, no electronic instruments or horns, *no being sort of boring and less great than your friends' other friends.* Remember that wonderful cobbler around the corner? The Yugoslavian man who was always so eager and whom you could pay with English muffins? His store is

September 1990

now a swank bistro. Well, friends are always essentially saying to each other what his landlo said to him: "The neighborhood is changing, and you can no longer afford it."

This was not always so, but friendship, like every other fine thing in these sad times of ours—like wisdom and music and lunch—now always involves a deal. In another era, if yo asked a friend to loan you a fiver, he'd give you a twenty, no questions asked. Now he says, at least suggests, "What use do you intend to make of these funds?" The once-familiar word *Here, let me,* or *Please, I'll get this,* or *Forget about it,* sound a faint and almost poignant note; phrase *So—what do I owe?* has replaced them. Deal-making for these tiny stakes is just the beginning. These days the friendship market is huge. It trades actively; the bargaining take many forms. How much is your wit worth when offered in exchange for someone else's beauty? How much power can be brokered for how much coolness? If you bid so much loyalty, how much wealth is your friend required to have? What's the exchange rate between sympathy and excitement? How many lunches equal how many dinners?

The auditing, the calculations, the close rereading of codicils and subsections, are never-ending. Who are your friends, anyway, and why are they worth it?

"MY SOCIAL LIFE WAS PAYING OFF." THESE WORDS, TAKEN FROM THE JUST-PUBLISHED MEM of Bob Colacello, hired friend, portrait broker, society lapdog and longtime "editor" of *Interview,* could serve as Colacello's epitaph. His book is definitive. It is to contemporary friendship what Robert Caro is to LBJ, what Jack Nicklaus's *Golf My Way* is to golf.

Colacello is virtuosic. When an aging heiress invites him to Bermuda for the weekend, h

goes to work peddling his master's services subtly, with a surgeon's skill: never made sales pitches....People knew that Andy painted portraits. T also knew that I worked for Andy. I waited for them to put two and two together, although I wasn't above dropping a hint at the appropriate moment. [The modesty of genius.] When our conversation quite natura came round to Andy, I told Lily [Auchincloss] about his latest portraits.' Mrs. Auchincloss claims not to be the portrait type but would, she tells Colacello, like to buy something from Andy, "'so long,'" Colacello felt

compelled to include in his book, " *you* get the commission.'" So right th in her own home, on his weekend visit, Colacello sells her a Mick Jagg portfolio. Colacello does have one regret, though: "Shortly before Andy died, Lily sold [the portfolio] for th same price she paid for it, $16,000. now worth ten times that."

Yet by the end of his stor a story of redemption, really Bob Colacello is sick of it a he wants to breathe pure ai to feel clean. A friend repea to Colacello what Andy has said about him: "Doesn't he know that these rich people just see him because he pu their names in *my* magazine?" *How dare he!* "That did it," Colacello fumes. "I was going to show hin once and for all who my real friends were. I was sick of seeing the world the way Warhol saw it. S of assuming that all marriages were for money a that all friendships were based on business." *No,* *no, no!* Or, as Macbeth said, "Is this a dagger whi I see before me?" Colacello makes the momentous decision to leave *Interview* (but no before calling his agent—and, no doubt, friend—Mort Janklow, "to check my emotio and thereby prove his rich friends' loyalty. He triumphs. Today he can say to himself *So, Andy thought these rich people were my friends only because of his slick, gossipy magazine. How wrong I have proved him. They are still my friends. and now I work for* Vanity Fair!

CONTEMPORARY-FRIENDSHIP STANDARD-BEARERS, *clockwise from top:* Veronica and Betty; *thirtysomething*'s Miles Drentell and Michael Steadman; Michael Kinsley and Pat Buchanan; Andy Warhol and Bob Colacello. **BOUGHT FRIEND:** loathed superpublicist Peggy Siegal and business associate Sherry Lansing. **FIRST FRIEND:** Jilly Rizzo takes his orders from Frank.

The kind of people who Colacello thinks are his friends have a rather odd notion of how one exercises friendship. No staying up late talking about complicated aches or sharing confidences. They prefer to pay $1,000 a head to eat dinner together once a week in a shrine to a pair of minor Egyptian princes on upper Fifth Avenue. It's a strange choice of hangouts, but then teenage kids do love to smoke pot in cemeteries.

Did you know that muscleman Jim Robinson, for the moment the head of American Express, and his wife, Linda, a highly paid publicist, are close to Mr. and Mrs. Ronald Perelman? (Perelman, of course, is the proprietor of Revlon—he has old, eighties money.) The Robinsons are reportedly close also to the Henry Kissingers, to Frank and Barbara Sinatra (she the former Mrs. Zeppo Marx) and to the Tom Brokaws. As is fitting for a megastockbroker in this era of elaborate financing, Robinson's relationships represent complex bundles of junk, preferred stock, options, media coverage and cash. Business, fame, power and access are all swapped around so that everybody thinks he's coming out ahead. Jim puts Henry on Amex's board of directors; Ron puts Linda on the board of Revlon; then Linda convinces Henry to accept Ron's offer of a seat on the Revlon board. Linda's corporate public-relations business, Henry's ego and international corporate consultancy, and the legitimacy of Ron the takeover pirate are all served nicely by these arrangements. Jim, the stockbroker, stays close to Ron, who likes to play the market (buying companies, not odd lots); Jim, secretary of State for corporate America, can sit in on boring meetings with the former U. S. secretary of State and can familiarly poke Henry's stomach on social occasions. Sinatra provides some glitz and earns some respectability, a commodity of which he seems constantly in need. Brokaw, triply vulnerable as someone who must wonder whether he is vastly overpaid, whether he is still a real journalist and, if so, whether journalists are part of the real world anyway, surely gains a sense of substantiality and in return provides a pleasing combination of fame, charm and power. Of course, when all is said and done, there is still no reason to doubt that the members of this group also connect on a human level.

SOMEWHERE IN THE WORLD (ROCHESTER, NEW YORK, THE CONTROL TEST MARKET FOR our study), friendship works like this: two boys grow up side by side. They meet in the schoolyard, where one beats the other up. One—the beaten-up one—is bookish, the other more adventuresome, but they become friends. Together they explore the strange tunnels outside of town, lie to each other's parents and, as young men, try to sort out the mysteries of the world (that is, women). The studious one may go far, or he may founder, uncertain in action; the heedless friend may squander his fortunes, or his guile and pluck may bring him wonderful success. Or nothing much may happen to either of them. But regardless of who is up and who is down, who is having some tough luck and who is doing all right, when one of these two needs some advice or an attentive ear or just a familiar presence to set him straight, he knows where to turn. To his lawyer. Still, the old pair are friends, and they help each other out, and it would take something pretty serious to pull them apart.

Elsewhere (that is, in some big town where you don't trust anybody but your mother, and even her you're not so sure about) the story runs more this way: two men meet at the client-driven business they have both recently joined. They arrived in New York or Los Angeles or Chicago a few years earlier from ridiculous places like Tulsa and Canada. For a few months they pal around: one knows lots of chicks, the other used to do business for a couple of clubs and they still treat him right. Sold! Friends! But what if one is promoted to group VP? Or buys a house on the beach in the Malibu Colony? Or finds somebody with an extra seat in his Rangers sky box? All this as the other merely stays in place. Everything changes. From the sky box, the world looks quite different. He begins to reevaluate. Reading the fine print, he sees that these new circumstances release him from the obligations of his friendship—and, anyway, *it was only a rental.*

Friendship is…

…never having to say, "But I'm sure *he put my name on the list."*

A FRIEND IN NEED IS NOT AS GOOD AS A FRIEND WITH A HOUSE IN TUSCANY

SPY *Presents the Friendship Index*

Who's a close friend? Who's an acquaintance? Which person should you hang up on when a second call comes in on call waiting? We've invented a simple, user-friendly system — the Friendship Index — to help ease the worry and the confusion of deciding who's who, what's what and when to beg off where friendship is concerned.

Here's how it works: Choose the level of Desirability (left axis) that best describes what attracts you to your "friend." Then select the level of Actual Intimacy (right axis) that accurately reflects how well you really know this "friend." Plot the point on the graph below. The location will tell you whether you should refer to your "friend" as your *best friend*, a *close friend*, a *friend* and so on.

DESIRABILITY

This, of course, is the result of some combination of fame, wealth, genius, power, beauty and coolness. The categories below contain some examples of the attributes that would place potential friends at a particular level of Desirability. The lists are by no means exhaustive but should offer a good guide.

ACTUAL INTIMACY

This can be measured by duration and depth of acquaintance — two straightforward properties easy to quantify. The classifications below should cover the entire range of people with whom you might ever have any contact of any kind.

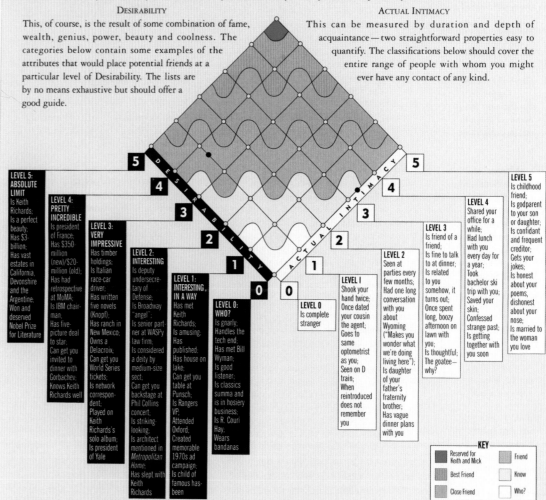

LEVEL 5: ABSOLUTE LIMIT
Is Keith Richards; Is a perfect beauty; Has $3-billion; Has vast estates in California, Devonshire and the Argentine; Won and deserved Nobel Prize for Literature

LEVEL 4: PRETTY INCREDIBLE
Is president of France; Has $350-million (new)/$20-million (old); Is Italian race-car driver; Has written five novels (Knopf); Has ranch in New Mexico; Owns a Delacroix; Can get you World Series tickets; Is network correspondent; Played on Keith Richards's solo album; Is president of Yale

LEVEL 3: VERY IMPRESSIVE
Has timber holdings; Is Italian race-car driver; Has written five novels (Knopf); Has ranch in New Mexico; Owns a Delacroix; Can get you World Series tickets; Is network correspondent; Played on Keith Richards's solo album; Is president of Yale

LEVEL 2: INTERESTING
Is deputy undersecretary of Defense; Is Broadway "angel"; Is senior partner at WASPy law firm; Is considered a deity by medium-size sect; Can get you backstage at Phil Collins concert; Is striking-looking; Is architect mentioned in *Metropolitan Home*; Has slept with Keith Richards

LEVEL 1: INTERESTING, IN A WAY
Has met Keith Richards; Is amusing; Has published; Has house on lake; Can get you table at Punsch; Is Rangers VP; Attended Oxford; Created memorable 1970s ad campaign; Is child of famous has-been

LEVEL 0: WHO?
Is gnarly; Handles the tech end; Has met Bill Wyman; Is good listener; Is classics summa and is in hosiery business; Is R. Couri Hay; Wears bandanas

LEVEL 0
Is complete stranger

LEVEL I
Shook your hand twice; Once dated your cousin the agent; Goes to same optometrist as you; Seen on D train; When reintroduced does not remember you

LEVEL 2
Seen at parties every few months; Had one long conversation with you about Wyoming ("Makes you wonder what we're doing living here"); Is daughter of your father's fraternity brother; Has vague dinner plans with you

LEVEL 3
Is friend of a friend; Is fine to talk to at dinner; Is related to you somehow, it turns out; Once spent long, boozy afternoon on lawn with you; Is thoughtful; The goatee — why?

LEVEL 4
Shared your office for a while; Had lunch with you every day for a year; Took bachelor ski trip with you; Saved your skin; Confessed strange past; Is getting together with you soon

LEVEL 5
Is childhood friend; Is godparent to your son or daughter; Is confidant and frequent creditor; Gets your jokes; Is honest about your poems, dishonest about your nose; Is married to the woman you love

KEY
- Reserved for Keith and Mick
- Best Friend
- Close Friend
- Friend
- Know
- Who?

Let's go for a test drive: A college pal of yours is seeing a hypothetical younger sister of Dennis Hopper's; on a trip to Los Angeles you talked with Hopper in a private home. Dennis Hopper has a Desirability factor of 3.6. The Actual Intimacy factor of your relationship weighs in at around 1. Plotting these two coordinates, we see that Dennis Hopper, whom you barely know, is nevertheless your *friend*. Let's take a different case. Your best friend in the tenth and eleventh grades (difficult, crucial years) has always kept up with you. She is coming to live in the large city to which you moved in order to escape the stifling hometown where you both grew up. She is planning to open a pet store. Her Desirability factor is 0; the Actual Intimacy factor is 3.3. The graph reveals that she is someone you *know*. —J.C.

CHART BY NIGEL HOLMES

In Rochester the nicest thing to say to a friend who has had good luck is "I'm so happy for you!" In New York the nicest thing to say to a friend who has had good luck is "I'm so envious!"

Sometimes the reasons behind the acquisition and sloughing off of friends aren't so obvious. Even in New York, remnants of the traditional friendship economy survive, but these forms of friendship just serve selfish ends indirectly. Tom Wolfe wrote a police procedural recently that received wide attention because of its wonderfully detailed social "atmosphere." One thing that rang particularly false, however, was the portrayal of the hero's friends. Sherman McCoy grows up in New York, where he attends a small boys' school, and goes on to boarding school and Yale, where undoubtedly he joins a secret society. Wolfe, who is from the South, presents Sherman as really having no friends, whereas under the circumstances he would of course have collected dozens of them—almost as an obligation. And when he gets into a scrape, would his tribal brothers from Buckley and St. Paul's abandon him? Certainly not. No, these Ridgeleys and Stuyvies would enjoy nothing more than the chance to cluster round and prove their steadfastness. Sherman, the missing chum! When Claus von Bülow had his little problem, the members of the Union Club were adamant that he should always feel welcome. Of course, the pleasure in this sort of constancy is not in helping an individual you care about (*Claus?*) but in making a show of your hearty, chivalric code. Indeed, on the principle that if you save someone's life, you are in his debt forever, Sherman's friends would be *grateful*.

What's a legitimate use of the term *friend*? If you have dinner at a restaurant with an important person in a small group *and* bump into her once at the movies, you are friends. Well, not *friends* exactly, but you know each other—no, really, you'd say you were friends, not *close* friends or anything, but friends. If a colleague marries the son of a famous painter, your colleague's husband is your friend; if your colleague marries someone kind of strange from Delaware, your colleague's husband is your colleague's husband. If your brilliant, funny, engaging friend calls you twice a year, the two of you are friends; if your boring, nice but sort-of-a-drag friend calls you every week, well, you *know* him. Your friend with the house in Italy has qualities of perception and wit and compassion that your friend who doesn't have a house in Italy in some measure lacks. The friend who got you out of that jam, the one who is in public relations, becomes a virtual stranger when, at a party, you run into your friend *the novelist*. (A great tradition exists for such betrayals. Peter's saying of Christ, "Who? I've never seen Him before in my life," is the most renowned example.)

Large social events always create fascinating crosscurrents and eddies of friendship and pseudofriendship. Sean Young is excruciatingly beautiful; she also demands that she be accorded the proper friendship status. She felt compelled simply to leave a recent big dinner in honor of her friend Martin "Marty" Scorsese when she learned she had not been seated at his table. Jann Wenner has his priorities straight. *Rolling Stone's* Christmas party is always a big event in the straitened, glamourless world of magazine publishing. Wenner, of course, is by tradition the Falstaffian host of the celebration. Last year, though, something really more important—considering the season and all—called him away at the very last minute. Playing Santa at an orphanage? No—hunting with John Kennedy Jr.

Like businessmen using shell corporations to hide from the IRS, some friends mask the real profits derived from their friendship by means of a clever subterfuge, the Unlikely Friend. *Surely*, an observer thinks, *these two people, who are so different, so at odds, must truly be friends, or else what could possibly unite them?* Simply this: having a friend from another social galaxy or ideology makes you seem so…complex. William F. Buckley Jr. and John Kenneth Galbraith are pleased as punch that they are great friends—who would have thought? Felix Rohatyn and Victor Gotbaum cannot contain their glee about their friendship, either. (An investment banker and a labor leader?!) The friendship between Bruce Wasserstein, the

Friendship is…

…never bowing out as a result of conflict of interest.

mergers-and-acquisitions illusionist, and Mark Green, a boring ex-radical now working with the system, follows the same plutocrat-lefty recipe. George Plimpton, skittish, white Harvard boy writer, befriends Muhammad Ali, black lethal weapon. Norman Mailer, skittish, white Harvard-boy writer, befriends Jack Henry Abbott, white-trash lethal weapon. Why would su different people be friends? Why, *because they're such different people.* It is morally and politicall reassuring to hedge your bets with a friend who is unlike you. (How greedy can I be if Marl Green is my friend?) How terrific, how absolutely great you must be to have such a friend— how interesting, how unexpected, you broad-minded, unpredictable jackanapes!

But for the most part the basis of the modern friendship nexus is *very* obvious. Forms of payment can be in kind—professional advancement, a few days at their place on Mustique, an invitation to a great party—or they can be in…cash. Take Johnny Carson and Ed McMahon, his $1-million-a-year "pal." Is that on-air bonhomie faked? The divorces, the drinking, the garrulous ex-wives—Johnny and Ed have endured them together. They've laughed, they've cried; but in all likelihood Ed has never been over to Johnny's house.

Some people simply put their old friends directly on the payroll. Prizefighters have continually refined the technique of finding jobs for their friends from the neighborhood, to the point that they now must have a levee like Louis XIV's—robe holders, boot lacers, towelers, drivers, runners, telephoners, bag carriers, conversation holders. Eddie Murphy employs such ever-present old friends and relations as Fed, Larry, Jerome, Rough House, Roy Fruity and Ray-Ray. Madonna made her best friend, Debi, her highly paid makeup artist. Peter Guber finds odd jobs for his friend Jon Peters. And certainly, even if they don't receive health benefits, some friends are easily purchased. Once the occasion for good talk among good people, a small dinner now approximates a low-budget horror movie: Night of the Living Checkbook Register. Around the table you find the hostess's lawyer, her hairdresser, he *faux-marbre* painter, her florist, the owner of her favorite restaurant, her trainer, her trust officer and her husband. Other friends for hire include decorators (like Liz Taylor's new best friend, Waldo Fernandez), fashion designers (like Blaine Trump's friend Christian Lacroix), psychiatrists (like Brian Wilson's friend Dr. Eugene Landy), English aristocrats (like any number of Mick Jagger's friends), children (like Warren Beatty's friend Molly Ringwald), publicists (like Sherry Lansing's friend Peggy Siegal), stockbrokers (like Bruce Springsteen's friend John Mulheren Jr.), real estate brokers (like every swell's friend Alice Mason) and the man with the squeegee at the entrance to the tunnel.

Still, there are those for whom the idea of receiving *payment* for their friendship is abhorrer They care about a friend as a *person.* A very famous person. This type of friend simply lives o and takes his whole identity from the reflected glory of a famous friend. This is a First Frien

FRIENDSHIP AS A STATUS SWAP MEET, *clockwise from top*: the pre-1987 Gary Hart and Warren Beatty (power traded for glamour); Mick Jagger and Princess Margaret (fame traded for breeding); Sylvester Stallone and Arnold Schwarzenegger (intellect traded for beauty); John Kenneth Galbraith and William F. Buckley Jr. (liberal credibility traded for conservative credibility)

Lem Billings's entire life was spent as…Jack Kennedy's *First Friend.* You recognize the name Jilly Rizzo. Why? Is h a businessman of some stature in your community? No. I he a former governor? No. He is Frank Sinatra's…*First Friend.* The First Friend has only his sycophancy to offer, but if his famous friend finds it worthy, the two can strike a bargain—slavish devotion in exchange for the right to b in every paparazzo picture, partially obscured.

Of course, like premodern sultans, some people are exempt from all this grubby, bourgeois haggling. For them friendship comes with the wave o a hand. These people are very, very famous people.

Isn't it strange that television and radio waves exist all around us all the time, yet we are unawar of them? At this moment electron signals carrying the voice and image of Sebastian Cabot are passing through you, yet you feel nothing. Turn on the television, though, and he appears. Interesting, isn't it? But is this seemingly marijuana-induced reverie related to the discussion? Yes. Similarly, famous people have friendships that are invisible but that can be activated at will. Is John McEnroe a friend of François Mitterand's? It is unlikely that the two hav ever met, but because they are both famous, they are bathed in immaterial rays of mutual friendship. Had President Bush ever spent any time with Michael Jackson and really *talked* before Jackson just dropped by the White House to hang out recently? Had Richard Nixon and Donald Trump ever met before the former president sent the sinking casino operator a recent note full of warm wishes? Do Faye Dunaway and Lee Iacocca speak? Do they know the birthdays of each other's children? Not likely. Yet even without knowing it, *they are friends* — if they encountered each other in an airport VIP lounge somewhere, they would probably engage in easy banter. Bo Jackson and Henry Kissinger; Oscar de la Renta and Bob Hope; Madonna and Prince Charles — all friends as if by magic, without meeting, without speaking, without any possible business connection. If sometime Bo does call Henry at

Friendship is...

...considering maybe returning his call even though he's dead in the ratings.

home, will the latter say, "I'm sorry, I do not speak to perfect strangers"? Absolutely not. "Bo, it's Henry...." If Bob asks to drop in on Oscar, will Oscar reply, "You mean now? Just like that?" *No, no.* "Certainly, terrific, what're you drinking?" Would you do the same if someone you had never met phoned? Of course not. That just proves that Bo and Henry and Bob and Oscar *have been friends all along*; the relationships simply haven't been consummated yet. (If Bo Jackson called you at home, would you say, "I'm sorry, I do not speak to perfect strangers"? Doubtful, but Bo Jackson would never call *you*. You aren't his friend.) Like ham-radio operators or people with a rare disease, all famous people are connected by an invisible web of loyalty and fellow feeling.

In one of his books about his life and the half bottles of Côte Rôtie he has with lunch, William F. Buckley tells a story that concerns himself and his friend Norman Mailer and his friend Pat Moynihan. Buckley and Mailer are standing on the corner when a station wagon narrowly misses them. Moynihan leans out of the passenger window and shouts, "Damn, I could have gotten both of you with one swipe!" In Rochester this sort of joshing occurs only between neighbors and buddies, guys whom you find playing hooky on the links on Wednesday afternoon. Buckley and Mailer and Moynihan? Have the three of them ever been alone in a room together? Has Bill or Pat ever lent Norman a car? Would he really care if they died? Yet — what great friends they are. "Get out of here, you nut!" you'd expect Buckley to yell back.

Lillian Hellman and John Belushi? What a witty and unlikely pairing. Friends. Actual friends and neighbors during their last years alive. Belushi's nuanced view of American communism (if only he had lived to see the changes in Eastern Europe!) could not have brought them together. Possibly their mutual friend Dan Aykroyd did? Both Hellman and Belushi had houses on Martha's Vineyard at the time, but so did your former boss at Shearson, and *he* didn't get to know them. Belushi and Hellman must somehow have just...*found* each other.

Most regular people, though, have to deal. You broker your classy managing partnership for a social superior's dinners; you know "interesting" people, your friend has got a house; you buy the paintings, the painter is a faithful party guest; you need a loan, your friend wants a toady; you are boring but nice, your friend is selfish but entertaining.

The problem with friendship, like the problem with New York real estate, is that there is at once too much and too little of it. Sure, there are plenty of your one-bedroom-condo friends, your West Side–rehab friends. There's a glut. They call you constantly; they want you to see them on the night you want to be alone; they impose their latest tedious discoveries on you (the music of the 1920s, the Hold Everything catalog, rice and beans). They are self-absorbed and dull and not even all that kind. You couldn't *give* these friends away. On the other hand, the top end of the market remains as firm as ever. The prewar friends with original moldings, the townhouse–in–the–East Sixties friends with the French windows. They are smart. They have a talent for sympathy. They always have something witty and unexpected to say. They have lives in which things happen. And, just as a quiet garden is nicer than a high-rise balcony, they are nicer than your other friends. But they cost. ⑤

14

Times to *Spy*: You Dropped Dead

Warm Beds and Cold Realities

Pigozzi once said to me, "With the money I invested in Spy, *I could have bought two pleasure boats!" And I remember thinking,* What's a pleasure boat?

—TONY HENDRA

"WE DIDN'T HAVE ANY STABBINGS or anything," says Larry Doyle. "But I guess everyone just got kind of depressed after Kurt left."

Kurt took a hand in trying to choose his successor. He lobbied Pigozzi for either Jim Collins (if he would stay) or Bruce Handy (if he would return). "I just didn't think I had the Graydon- or Kurt-like personality, the power or imagination or strength," Collins says. "I just imagined a great darkness, and Pigozzi, and what is this going to be about, and is anybody interested anymore?" He did stay on briefly as de facto "acting editor" before leaving for good.

Pigozzi had someone in mind, an established financial journalist whom Jerry Taylor interviewed and, claims the publisher, whose "idea of a great story was a wet-kiss feature on Gianni Versace's mansion in Florida!" Kurt, preparing to leave, wrote Pigozzi a long letter reminding the owner that "there are dozens of fine, intelligent, well-credentialed, respected, professional journalists around—people who would make *Spy* like *Esquire* or *Harper's*....What's far more rare in any potential editor is a confident, thoughtful sense of humor and fun; the ability to make weird, revealing, witty connections between facts; to walk close to the line of taste and respectability; to come up with and inspire others to come up with odd, only-in-*Spy* charts and sidebars...." It was as close to a job description as there would ever be for the position of "editor of *Spy*," and Kurt recommended Bruce Handy.

A week or so later, on March 4, 1993, Kurt faxed Pigozzi a very different sort of letter, in response to the owner's extreme unhappiness that his Mick and Keith would now both be gone. It began, "I probably ought to ignore your grousing and accusations of bad faith and betrayal. I probably should just pack up, leave, and forget about it," and concluded, several pages later, with the suggestion that the owner "*really listen* to people when they talk to you about *Spy*" and the reminder that "it's not widgets or soda pop you're making and selling."

**Opposite:
From "The End
of Innocence,"
November 1993**

The editor Adam Moss and writer Lynn Hirschberg, a *Spy* contributor, met with Pigozzi, proposing to take over the magazine and turn it into *The Industry*—the slick, smart media-and-entertainment-business publication that Moss had been trying to start. Pigozzi turned them down (and Moss shortly thereafter began his decade as a top editor at *The New York Times*).

The editor's chair was initially offered to Michael Caruso. Accounts differ on what happened next. Caruso, who says he would have made *Spy* "less broad and comic" and more of a magazine "for young, hip New Yorkers," either (a) turned the job down or (b) saw the offer almost instantly retracted by Pigozzi. In any event, instead of succeeding Kurt at *Spy*, Caruso stayed at *Vanity Fair*—working for Graydon.

Pigozzi decided he wanted Tony Hendra. The British-born satirist had written for *Spy* and was something of a comedy legend—a former editor of the *National Lampoon*, where he had worked with Taylor, and a performer (most famously the manager Ian Faith in *This Is Spinal Tap*).

Taylor contacted Hendra in Las Vegas, where he'd been helping George Carlin with his autobiography.

"I came back to New York, I met with Jerry, and he took me to see Jean," Hendra remembers. "I said I wanted to 'attack more aggressively the celebritocracy.' And Jean didn't seem to like that much. I also said that I wanted to be more satirical. And that he did seem to like."

Taylor, on the other hand, did not want Hendra. He thought he would be a bad manager and went so far as to prepare for Pigozzi a "Caruso vs. Hendra" comparison chart (how *Spy*-ish) to bolster his case.

In the end, it was Hendra. He started work in April 1993. (That June's *Spy* had his name on it, but August's—with the investigative story by John Connolly on Steven Seagal—was his proper debut.) It's a pity he didn't start a month sooner, because in that brief, editorless interregnum, *Spy* bobbled and dropped one of the biggest stories of the year.

Lisa Birnbach was still there. "I had a nodding acquaintance with Pigozzi, who liked my shoes and therefore spoke to me," she says. "Which was a *bad* thing, because people started to resent it. And I got nothing out of it—I didn't get a trip, a meal, anything; he'd just give me clippings of European magazines and say, 'Why don't we do more of this? Nude celebrities, everybody loves that!'" One day in March, her phone rang.

"I got a call from a woman named Heidi Fleiss," Birnbach says. "I had no idea who she was—this was *before*. And she tells me she's a madam in California, and that a producer owes her a few hundred dollars, and she's trying to humiliate him publicly. But in humiliating him, she can name all these public figures in Hollywood who use her services. She mentions people at Columbia Pictures.

"She faxes over an uncanceled check written to her by the producer, and it's on a check printed with his wife's name and his name. How stupid. So this is extremely exciting, who knows if it's real, but I go in to talk to Jerry. I say, 'Wow, this is unbelievable, what she's telling me!' Of course, no one knew who she was…it's almost too good to be true. Maybe she's got some grudge, she's an old girlfriend, maybe she's not responsible. So Jerry thinks about it, talks about it, and comes back to me and says, 'You can't run this article. Columbia Pictures is an advertiser.' I'm sure if Kurt had been there, or Graydon had been there, *Spy* would have had the Heidi Fleiss story."*

(Taylor says he doesn't remember any Heidi Fleiss episode. "To my recollection, I never killed a story because of an advertiser." Larry Doyle says there were also "doubts about the story, not just its veracity but whether we really wanted to go down that road—celebrity sleaze without the usual hubris or hypocrisy or other hallmarks of a *Spy* story." But it was still quite a story and, written by John Connolly, it ended up in *Us* magazine.)

"Almost immediately it was very clear that Kurt's leaving was an enormous blow to the staff," says Hendra. "It was more than just that they were used to doing it a certain way; it was also that Kurt had this mystique—quite deservedly—that he'd built up over the years."

Hendra might not have realized entirely what he'd gotten himself into. "Tony walked into this situation where everyone was trying to leave as fast as possible," says Larissa MacFarquhar. "And he didn't want to be a custodian; he wanted to find his own people and do his own thing. He was not given a chance, either financially or by the staff."

"I like Tony, he was just the wrong guy," says Geoff Reiss. "First thing he wanted was an elaborate set of bookshelves built in his office. He wanted a heavyweight training bag put in the back so he could box. And part of my job that last year was to ask for advances from the distributor on newsstand sales and negoti-

---

*Yes, indeed we would've. This is all news to us. —Eds.

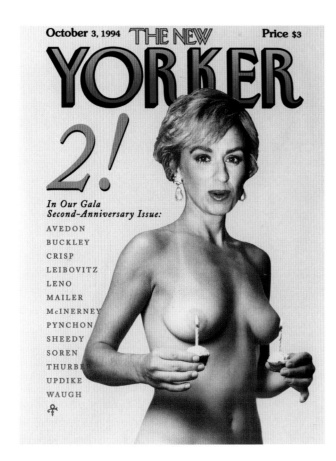

ANNALS OF ENTREPRENEURSHIP

THE MAN WHO *SIGNS* THE CHECKS

It is hard to say whether S. I. Newhouse is more J. P. Morgan or Lorenzo de' Medici. Perhaps the only person to exceed his contributions to the world of publishing is Tina Brown, whom he brought to this country to turn around not one but two flagging publications, Vanity Fair *and* The New Yorker. *He is a great man.*

BY *STEPHEN SCHIFF*

By 1985, S. I. Newhouse had bought so many things that it was only natural that he buy *The New Yorker.* The transaction became a showcase of his business acumen. For several months he assured Peter Fleischman, the then-owner, that he had no interest in owning that man's magazine, that he would limit himself to acquiring twenty-five percent of the company's stock. Then, in a move that showed Si's unutterable and unpredictable financial genius, he did just what he said he would not do: He bought more than twenty-five percent. In fact, he bought it all.

On that day not a newspaper in the country could deny that Si Newhouse was the Saladin of the publishing world.

Today, as I sit down with Si at 44, the restaurant of the Royalton Hotel, I see a different man: I am struck by how modest he is. Calvin Klein is here, as is Anna Wintour. But Si is not seeking their company. He is dressed simply, in a black turtleneck set off by a plain gold pin of some educational significance—a sign of solidarity with the world of higher learning. If he is Saladin, he is also Rousseau, never failing to donate to charities, responding to the needs of society in every business move he makes. It was Si who rejuvenated *Vanity Fair* and gave the country the

cult of celebrity it had—in its egalitarian wallow—long been missing. It was Si who gave stable, dependable homogeneity to the magazine world; it was Si who brought relevance and brevity and the British accent to the long-winded and all-too-American *New Yorker.*

S. I. Newhouse

Which says not a thing about the real Si Newhouse. He is blank. "I am blank—even blank—about blank," he says, and at that moment there is no doubt that it is true. There is, some say, a dark side to Si Newhouse, a surprisingly crude demeanor that cuts across the expanse of his more obvious virtues, turning him from a benevolent Rous-

seau into a vicious Ivan. In either case, you'd never be tempted to compare Si to anyone but a famous cultural or historical figure. He's that big. He is Bonaparte. As I look across the table at his wayward eye, he is Diaghilev to my Nijinsky. Jesus to my Matthew. Don Simpson to my Tom Cruise. Hansel to my Gretel.

Later we dance.

Samuel Irving Newhouse was born in 1927, the grandson of an immigrant. Life was hard, if not in a financial sense then in other ways, but then suddenly he was on top of the world, owning everyone, doing everything. Si is looking over my shoulder as I write this. He is breathing loudly through his nose, though he doesn't seem to realize it. Perhaps he does now. He shifts his breathing to his mouth, but it is still noisy; he is full of vitality, a man for whom breathing itself is a kind of music and a battle with the air. His eyes—eye-shaped, nearly oval—have a droopy quality that gives Si the appearance of a young Henry Kissinger, or an old Marlon Brando, or maybe John Belushi. His character is etched broadly across his face, which is bulbous and craggy, with the forlorn look of a man who has long had a mouth full of mashed potatoes.

Which is not to say simian. He is above all a man who redefined class in America. He is a man who by his very *Please turn to page 67*

A fake Tina Brown on the cover of *Spy's* parody of *The New Yorker,* September 1993

ate stretch payments. If we had a shitty cover, it meant somebody wasn't going to get paid—Jerry managed the cash tightly. So here's Tony coming in—'I have a carpenter ready'—and meanwhile we're firing people."

BIG PICTURE

Reinstate Back of Book, including one-time, experimental columns, perhaps by famous people like Rob Reiner?

Jettison "Reviewers"?

Run reviews, with twist TK?

Get Andrea Dworkin to respond to Camille {Paglia}

SAB {Separated at Birth?} getting boring: should only include funny pairings, not just people who look alike

Investigative reporting not taken seriously because: faked covers? too-smart-for-the-room? combo of humor and seriousness? crying wolf over Bush 41 mistress story?

—Tony Hendra's meeting notes, April 12, 1993

ACROSS THE TOP OF THAT PAGE, Hendra had written "How to Implement?"

A very good question. The new editor needed so many things, starting with an art director, because Christiaan Kuypers had given notice.

"I felt very strongly that people had got used to the *Spy* mix," Hendra says. "I wanted to open it up a bit and give it islands of more frankly visual stuff. In theory, Pigozzi was very pro-that, but he refused to spend any money on it. I actually lined up [graphic designer] Roger Black to 'consult' for us on a redesign. I can't remember what the consulting fee was, maybe $10,000, but Pigozzi said it was out of the question. He tied the purse strings from day one."

Hendra also needed writers, but the ones he wanted, like Bruce McCall, the artist and writer for *The New Yorker* and *Vanity Fair,* were also expensive. (McCall did contribute one piece.) Another problem was that when Kurt left, he took with

From
"Those Surprising
Gore Girls,"
November 1993

him any information about the true identity of the must-read Hollywood columnist Celia Brady. Hendra had no idea who Celia was, and Kurt wouldn't tell him (very few people know to this day—even Taylor, who signed every check, says, "I still don't know who was paying her, him, it"). Hendra started combing Kurt's old office-phone records for West Coast calls, hoping to track Celia down that way. He never did.

"Tony was fun, a blast to work with, but it was not going to work out," says MacFarquhar. "He was an old-school guy. We would go out to lunch, have several glasses of wine, have an *excellent* meal at the Union Square Cafe entertaining writers from out of town. But the magazine did not have the money to sustain the old style. Alas."

It didn't help that Hendra and Larry Doyle never clicked. Doyle wanted to bring back complicated, labor-intensive features and thought the magazine could be "nationalized" by choosing better-known, more political targets. "But Tony," Doyle says, "wanted to do the *National Lampoon*."

"He was difficult," Hendra says of Doyle. "He made it quite clear that he thought Kurt was the best editor he'd ever worked with, and I was a dim-bulb replacement, and besides, he hated the *Lampoon*. This was the opening conversation that we had. And he was expressing a sort of general feeling among the back-

office people who were devoted to Kurt.

"But it was also very much the case that Larry had a lot of ideas; he was a valuable member of the staff. So I had to decide whether to fire Larry or find a way to get along with him. I decided, probably foolishly, on the second course. And I could feel this revolt building. Almost everything I wanted to do, the staff didn't. I don't think Larry was an active campaigner against me—although when he left, he apologized for fomenting unrest in the rank and file."

Of course, it wasn't just the rank and file: Hendra's own publisher opposed his appointment, and today refers to the editor's arrival as "the day the music died."

This might be a good time to own up to the fact that *Spy* endured its share of intramural squabbling. There were unfortunate misunderstandings, breakdowns in communication, hurt feelings, lengthy estrangements—and that's just among the three authors of this book—but these upheavals were confined almost entirely to our post-*Spy* years. When we were all working on the magazine, with extraordinarily few exceptions, the *Spy* operation was genuinely harmonious (the coil of barbed wire that for a time separated two staffers' cubicles notwithstanding). When the magazine struggled to redefine itself after the founders had all gone, and was simultaneously faced with an inexperienced and temperamentally unsuitable owner, the office, by all accounts, became a far less happy place.

Still, the point of this volume is not to fan the flames of ancient grievances, but rather to lay the foundation for brand-new ones. And so we continue....

"I was always disappointed that the *National Lampoon* had never become the humor magazine of my generation," Hendra says. "So I thought it would be nice to give *The New Yorker* a run for its money, especially since *The New Yorker* under Tina Brown had no sense of humor whatsoever. There was a humor vacuum that could be usefully filled. *Spy* could have become a slightly different kind of magazine and taken up that slack. But the staff didn't want to do that. And I didn't have enough replacements—or young enough replacements—to deliver on my own promise."

Joanne Gruber was now the number two, keeping the editorial operation afloat. Collins, Malanowski, Birnbach, and others had by now left, and soon Doyle was gone, too. Hendra was able to bring in some new names (Eric Zicklin and Chris Kelly, both now successful television writers) and get some old names to write the occasional piece (Joe Queenan, Bruce Handy). The theater critic

Mimi Kramer, who hadn't written for *Spy* since the first issue, joined briefly as literary editor. Hendra is proud of *Spy's New Yorker* parody (see page 285), and also of the re-instituted *Spy* 100 with Jerry Seinfeld at number one.

"Six or seven years after this came out, at a private club function on the Upper East Side, Seinfeld was the guest of honor," Hendra says. "And we were introduced, and he said, 'Tony Hendra? Oh, you're the asshole who put me on the cover of *Spy*.' And he seemed really quite gleeful that he finally had the opportunity to call me an asshole."

Hendra had successfully sidestepped Pigozzi's attempts to keep his celebrity friends out of the magazine ("Mick. Bianca. There was a whole laundry list. I basically ignored it"), and circulation was still growing. But there was no getting around the paucity of advertising. And Hendra had another problem on his hands.

"Geoff Reiss began to warn me, about three months in, that I needed to clean house or there would be a lot of trouble," Hendra says. "I began to realize that there were people leaking stories—various poisonous stories being put out about me in the press."*

> *Dear Jerry,*
>
> *I hope you have had a good retreat.*
>
> *Every month someone at* Spy *sends me the letters to the editor by fax. {This} month I received 14 pages. This {is} completely ridiculous....This is a typical example that shows* Spy *is not run well....I am also extremely disappointed in the advertising in the December issue.*
>
> *The cover was horrible. Supposedly you approved it...how could this happen?*
>
> *You must not let go of the control of* Spy. *You are in charge of running this magazine.*
>
> —Fax from Jean Pigozzi to Jerry Taylor, November 12, 1993

IN THE TWENTY-ONE MONTHS he had owned *Spy*, Pigozzi had apparently spent something approaching $6 million on the magazine—more than twice as much as had been invested during its first five years. By Christmas, Pigozzi had begun to

---

*In retrospect it is astonishing (and deeply gratifying) that **never**, not once, in the nearly seven years we ran the magazine, did anything leak into the press from inside *Spy*. —Eds.

"make noises about selling the magazine," Hendra says. "And he clamped down more and more. He kept accusing me of upping the budget. And whatever I would say, it made no difference. He was obviously on the way out, too."

"When *Spy* was really having financial problems, a lot of people were getting hurt," John Connolly says. "Tony, to his credit, went to Jerry Taylor and he said, 'Jerry, let's show a little solidarity, let's you and I take a 10 percent salary cut so the staff will feel like we're all in the same boat.' Jerry's reply was, 'Tony, to me *Spy* is a warm bed.'"

Hendra says it happened, but Taylor denies it. "You have to be joking," he says. "Hendra never made that suggestion and I never said that."

Meanwhile, Pigozzi's personal business manager started showing up and going over the books: not a good sign.

"We knew it was coming for a long time," says Joanne Gruber. "Morale was so low, so many people were giving notice. It dragged on, but it felt inevitable."

> *After seven and a half years as the country's only magazine of satire, investigative journalism and establishment-bashing,* Spy *magazine went out of business today. The 78th and final issue will reach New York newsstands on March 1 and national stands on March 8....*
>
> —Press release from the staff of *Spy*, February 18, 1994

THAT STAFF WAS TO VACATE THE OFFICES immediately; a few days later they were allowed back in for an hour or so to get their things.

> SPY *MAGAZINE CAN'T FIND A BUYER, AND CLOSES*
>
> Spy, *the self-styled humor magazine that took aim at the Establishment and skewered many of its members, closed yesterday after months of futile efforts to find a buyer. Jean Pigozzi, the majority owner, was in Europe and could not be reached for comment....*
>
> *It was an ignominious end for the once-trendy magazine that mocked, reviled, savaged, but often titillated many movers and shakers of the 1980's....*
>
> —Deirdre Carmody in *The New York Times*, February 19, 1994

If only the *Times* had been right.

> *"As Santa continues on his mission—leaving deafening sonic booms in his wake—charred reindeer will constantly be sloughed off. All 214,200 reindeer will be dead within 4.26 thousandths of a second."*

NO, VIRGINIA, THERE *isn't* A SANTA CLAUS!

*D*o you believe in Santa Claus?

This is a complex theological question that each child must decide for him- or herself. Until now, that is. With the aid of computers, SPY JR. has conducted a rigorous **statistical** investigation into the question of Santa's existence. Be fore-warned: you may not like our conclusions....

We begin our investigation by assuming that Santa Claus really does exist. Now, if you've learned anything about human nature, you know it's highly unlikely that a normal man would choose, for no particular reason, to devote his life to making toys and deliv-ering them to boys and girls the world over. But this is an **objective** inquiry, and questions of motiva-tion aren't relevant. We want only to know whether such a man could accomplish his mission.

ANYBODY HOME? No toy-manufactur-ing facility or elf living quarters are visible in this aerial surveillance photo taken over the North Pole.

Santa's first obstacle is that *no known species of reindeer can fly*. However, scientists estimate that out of the earth's roughly 2 million species of living organisms, 300,000 or so have yet to be classified. So, even though most of these undiscovered species are insects and germs, we can't rule out the slight possibility that a species of flying reindeer does, in fact, exist. And that no one besides Santa has ever seen one.

A bigger obstacle for Santa is that there are 2 billion children under the age of 18 in the world. The good news is that he needs to deliver presents only to *Christian* children, of whom there are approximately 378 million (according to figures provided by the Population Reference Bureau). Let's assume that 15 percent of these Christian children have been

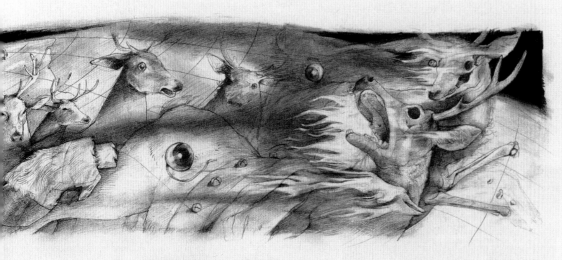

ON, DANCER, ON—*AIEEEEE!!!* Artist's rendition of Santa's hypersonic gift-delivery vehicle

ad and are thus—like Muslim, Hindu, Jewish
nd Buddhist children—ineligible for gift
etting. Still, at an average rate of 3.5 children
er household, Santa has a backbreaking
1.8 million homes to visit on any given
hristmas Eve.

Fortunately, Santa has 31 hours of Christmas
ve darkness to visit all these homes if he
avels from east to west, thanks to the rotation
the earth. Unfortunately, this still works
it to 822.6 visits per second. So, for each
hristian household with good children, Santa
as just over a thousandth of a second to land,
op out of his sleigh, jump down the chimney,
l the stockings, distribute the rest of the
resents under the tree, eat whatever snacks
ive been left out, get back up the chimney,
imb back into his sleigh, take off and fly to
e next house.

How fast is Santa moving? Assuming all
1.8 million stops are spread evenly over the
rth's landmass, Santa must travel 0.79 miles
er household—a total trip of 72,522,000
iles. (This is a conservative estimate. It doesn't

include trips across oceans, feeding stops for
the reindeer, etc.) Given the 31-hour time
period, Santa's sleigh must maintain an average
speed of 650 miles per second, or more than
3,000 times the speed of sound. To give you
an idea how fast that is, the fastest man-made
vehicle ever built, the *Ulysses* space probe,
travels at a relatively poky pace of 27.4 miles
per second, and conventional, land-bound
reindeer travel at a top speed of 15 miles per
hour. But let's just assume that Santa's flying
reindeer are somehow able to reach hypersonic
speeds—thanks, say, to the magical spirit of
Christmas giving.

Let's take a closer look at Santa's vehicle.
First of all, assuming a cheapo 2 pounds of
presents per child (that's like one crummy Lego
set), the sleigh must still be able to carry a load
of 321,300 tons—plus Santa, an overweight
man. On land, a reindeer can't pull more than
300 pounds of freight, and even assuming that
flying reindeer could pull ten times that amount,
Santa's massive sleigh has to be drawn by
214,200 beasts. They increase the weight of the

From the *Spy Jr.* magazine-within-a-magazine, February 1991. Thanks to its unauthorized appearance on the Internet a few years later, this is one of the most widely known *Spy* pieces of all.

overall Santa payload to 353,430 tons (not including the weight of the sleigh itself). This is more than four times the weight of the *Queen Elizabeth* ocean liner. Imagine: Santa skimming over rooftops in a gargantuan hypersonic aircraft with even less maneuverability than a Big Wheel.

of a second.

As for Santa, he will be subjected to centrifugal forces 17,500.06 times greater than gravity. A 250-pound Santa will be pinned to the back of his sleigh by 4,375,015 pounds of force (after we deduct his weight) This force will kill Santa instantly, crushing his bones, pulverizing his flesh turning him into pink goo

Here's where things get fun.

Three hundred fifty-three thousand tons of reindeer and presents are going to create an enormous amount of air resistance—especially at 650 miles per second. This air resistance will heat the reindeer in the same way that spaceships are heated up when they reenter the earth's atmosphere. According to our calculations, the lead pair of reindeer will absorb 14.3-quintillion joules of energy per second each. This means they will burst into spectacular, multicolored flames almost instantaneously, exposing the reindeer behind them. As Santa continues on his mission—leaving deafening sonic booms in his wake—charred reindeer will constantly be sloughed off. All 214,200 reindeer will be dead within 4.26 thousandths

PHOTOGRAPHIC EVIDENCE!
This sequence of snap-shots, taken by a SPY JR. reader in western Oregon, purports to show actual parents setting out presents and eating cookies left for "Santa."

In other words, if Santa tries to delive presents on Christmas Eve to every qualified boy and girl on the face of the earth, he will be liquefied.

If he even exists, he's already dead.

So where *do* the presents come from? Weirdl kindhearted intruders? Stupid robbers? Magic? Your parents, maybe?

We won't insult your intelligence with the answer. ▸

SPY JR. VOCABULARY BUILDERS

statistical: this is an almost always meaningless word that i frequently used when people want to make something tha is vague and haphazard sound authoritative and scientific

objective: see *statistical*.

FUN QUIZ!

How does Santa fit down a chimney if he's so fat?

How does Santa deliver presents to houses and apartments that don't have chimneys?

Assuming reindeer have aerodynamic lift, what is the minimum speed a reindeer would have to attain in order to become airborne?

Our Un-Adult Crossword Puzzle

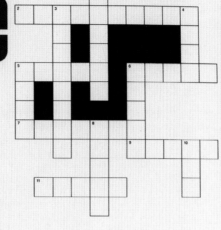

Down

1. *Prizzi's Honor* costar;
Sis's shame. (6)

3. Aftermath of 7
Across. (4,4)

4. Nice word for
retarded. (4)

5. Metropolitan
Museum o_ ___. (1,3)

6. Dumb mistake—
especially in swim
trunks. (5)

8. Mountain range
dividing Asia and
Europe. (5)

10. Gross stuff. (3)

Across

2. Grandpa's specialty.
(7,3)

5. ...round the corner
_____ is made. (5)

6. Amusing color. (5)

7. Wedgie, e.g. (7)

9. TV's porcelain-bus
driver? (5)

11. *Yellow River*
author. (5)

SPY JR. STAFF: *Edited by Bruce Handy. Written by Kurt Andersen, Josh Gillette,
Joanne Gruber, Bruce Handy, Jamie Malanowski, George Meyers, Susan Morrison,
Joel Potischman. Designed by Christiaan Kuypers. Educational consultant: the
Reverend Harry Powell, D.D., Ph.Ed.* ❱

In addition to
the investigative
tour de force
on Santa (mainly
the work of
Bruce Handy),
Spy Jr. featured
"Inside Your
Parents' Bedside
Drawer: A *Spy Jr.*
Annotation"
and an all-the-dirt
media column
about *MAD*
magazine.

om the

Vhite

etary

rice

peo-

del-

is

tion, v

grabs-

was,

in a

been

15

Unnoticed, Unwanted, Undead, and (Frequently) Unfunny

Spy's Endgame

*Would this be for "*Spy* The Funny Years"? So basically you want me to contribute to a book according to whose very title two whole years of my professional career were essentially a failure? The answer's yes, by the way, but I just want to clarify.*
—EMAIL RESPONSE FROM BRUNO MADDOX, SEPTEMBER 2004

"THE LIFE SPAN OF THE MAGAZINE was an organic thing," Susan Morrison suggests, "having as much to do with our own energies and talents and where we were in our lives, and also the economy and the people in New York." So February 1994—or, possibly, a much earlier date—should have been the end.

It wasn't.

*Who is **Owen Lipstein** and why is he trying to revive the defunct* Spy *magazine?…*

Since signing a letter of intent to buy the Spy *name from **Jean Pigozzi**, Lipstein has been meeting with virtually the entire* Spy *masthead. Word is that Lipstein is trying to get an editor and staff*

for the new bimonthly Spy, *which may hit the stands with a July/August issue.*

Problem is, the usual suspects from the Spy *masthead—former top editors **George Kalogerakis** (now with* Vanity Fair *and* Vogue), ***Bruce Handy** (*Time), ***Larry Doyle** (*New York), ***David Kamp** (*GQ) *and **Jamie Malanowski** (*Esquire), *as well as regular contributors like playwright **Paul Rudnick**—are just not interested in what Lipstein has to say.…*
—Page Six, *The New York Post*, May 7, 1994

"I LOVED THE *SPY* OF THE WONDER YEARS, and I thought it deserved a second chance as a title," says Owen Lipstein, an '80s magazine entrepreneur who had launched *American Health* and *SMART*, Terry McDonell's *Esquire*-style magazine. By the mid-'90s he was the very successful publisher and editor-in-chief of *Psychology Today* and *Mother Earth News*, which were owned by John ("Jo") Colman, a former banker. When Pigozzi put what was left of *Spy* on the block, Lipstein says, "I talked Jo into doing it, against his better judgment."

The New York Times

BOOK OF THE DEAD

Why Must We Suffer So?

Millions of Americans find life boring and depressing.

Is there an unworkable quick-fix solution, or with weekly lessons can we learn to wallow in our misery?
By Bruno Maddox and Jared Paul Stern

From the *New York Times Magazine* parody, September/ October 1997

"Owen is a very persuasive guy," says Colman.

And so Colman became *Spy*'s last owner and, to his considerable discomfort, *Spy*'s executioner.

Even though the magazine's influences live on in the media, nowhere does *Spy* survive more *tangibly* than in the East 23rd Street offices of *Psychology Today*, which Colman still owns.

He pushes aside some papers on his antique desk to reveal the initials "K.A." carved deep in the wood. "It's a bit haunting," he says. Best of all is the long oak table in his conference room, which is covered with initials, also deeply carved, from "E.G.C." to…well, most of them—most of us—are still there.

Touching, albeit a little gothic. Forget about all the *Spy*'s-memes-spreading-through-the-culture stuff. *How did this guy get our furniture?*

Colman had arrived in New York from London in 1987 and had even attended early *Spy* parties at the Puck Building. Six years later, he says, "when I first met Pigozzi, he would come into my office and moan about how much money he was losing on it and sniff around to see how things are done on a tighter scale. But I was in for business, he was in for prestige. There was a period of a few months when Johnny was winding it up and trying to sell it at the same time. Anyway, we bought it free and clear. We paid an upfront sum, which was probably insignificant compared to the operating losses I incurred."

Spy was relaunched as a bimonthly, overseen by Lipstein, with the July/August 1994 issue. The stripped-down magazine had a series of offices, sharing space—and non-editorial staff—with *Psychology Today* and *Mother Earth News*.

"Here's a difference between early and late *Spy*," says David Korzenik, the *Spy* lawyer, who continued to vet the magazine. "Owen—nice fellow—for a while he was doing a *Times* column. What was interesting about the original *Times* column, and about the original *Spy*, was that when it reported stuff from the inside, it was in the experienced voice of somebody who was senior. Part of it had to do with the fact that our sources were often top-down. But it was also a sophisticated, knowing voice, and Owen's shots at the *Times* were very mailroom-voice. I hate to say it, but that told me something."

This *Spy* became increasingly national—even international—in subject matter, and the comic strokes were much broader. "We were the link in the evolutionary chain from the old *Spy*, which was great, to the lad mags [such as *Maxim*]—not necessarily some-thing to be proud of," says Lance Gould, who was editor in 1996 and 1997. Even in this dismal era, the magazine continued to attract talent: Contributors included Alex Gregory and Peter Huyck, who went on to write for *Letterman*, *The Larry Sanders Show*, *Frasier*, and *King of the Hill*; film critic Richard Roeper; and future Pulitzer Prize winner Samantha Power. But it just wasn't the same *Spy*, and today Gould wonders whether they might have fared better had they taken that fact and run with it. "Maybe," he says, "it should have been called something else."

"It was very hard to live up to—I was aware of the long shadow that Kurt and Graydon cast," says Lipstein, who himself left the resurrected *Spy* after two years. "But there's a contradiction between the publishing success and the editorial success of that magazine. If you do your job as an editor, no advertiser can be entirely comfortable. If you do your job as a publisher, your editors are unhappy. You have to have editors who are completely subversive and adolescent in their state of mind."

"The other fundamental flaw in the publishing model of *Spy* was the timeliness issue," adds Colman. "The magazine was by its nature acerbic and media-driven and reactive to what was going on—but then it would take six weeks once it left your desk to appear on the newsstand. And with the Internet coming along, that became even more of an issue."

Few of the old *Spy* hands contributed. For us the magazine had become dreadful, unreadable.

"The *Spy* after *Spy* was as if your grandmother had died and they stuffed her and kept her in the living room," says Joanne Gruber. "It *kind* of looks like her. But it's not acting like her. And it's very unpleasant to have around."

Spy kept on not being what it used to be for another two dozen issues, right up through March 1998. And yet, toward the end, people noticed that it was getting…a little better. There was a *new* new editor, Bruno Maddox.

"You could only get a Graydon type *or* a Kurt type; you could never get both—that was the other thing about the early *Spy*, the hydra-headed sensibility," says Lipstein. "But Bruno was brilliant. He was funny, and he may well have found his own way to make it work."

> *"The* Spy *after* Spy *was as if your grandmother had died and they stuffed her and kept her in the living room."*

Spy: *Are you ticklish?*

HK: *Skip that one.*

"You Must Be Out of Your Mind"

A SPY Interview with Henry Kissinger

His soothingly phlegmatic monotone mumble is known the world over—from the inner sanctums of the White House, where he served as Secretary of State for eight years, to the rice paddies of Cambodia, where people still cheer the legacy of his delicate diplomacy. And while his days as a Cabinet member are long over, Nobel Peace Prize laureate Henry Kissinger remains a vital member of the global body politic, recently knighted by Queen Elizabeth and still powerful enough to publicly scold Newt Gingrich like a truant schoolboy.

As if being one of the most influential political advisers of the 20th century weren't enough, "Dr. K" (as those close to Kissinger call him) has also made a name for himself on the social circuit, engaging in an extended fling with busty Bond girl Jill St. John and partying with the likes of Hollywood player/coke addict Robert Evans.

So how does he wind down after all this action? We spent the last 10 months trying to find out.

Last September, SPY received a press release from the Ohashi Institute—a nonprofit worldwide organization dedicated to spreading a brand of shiatsu massage (which they do, for $65 a session) invented by a bespectacled elfin Japanese masseur named Ohashi. The release boasted that Dr. Henry Kissinger himself was giving a speech on behalf of the institute at an occasion entitled "Touch for Peace."

Posing as the editors of a well-known health magazine, we journeyed to a Las Vegas–style ethnic eatery in which 2-in-1-decorative-ceiling-ornament-security-camera-clusters did not seem out of place. In addition to the speech, the Institute was running a silent auction, with a signed copy of Kissinger's latest tome up for grabs—alongside sessions with a psychic whose press kit was, even for a psychic, downright weird.

What was Henry Kissinger doing here?

What did the institute have on him? Nude pictures in a Thai brothel? Plagiarism at Harvard? Could *he* have been Deep Throat?

As we were wondering where this trail might lead, some of the representatives of the Institute not-so-subtly hinted that in exchange for an article in our "magazine," they might be able to put us in touch with the great man himself.

Over a period of many months, we wheedled, cajoled, and outright lied to land a chat with Dr. K. We interviewed everyone but the janitor for our pending "article." We visited the Institute's New York branch, watched a few Ohashiatsu rubdown sessions, and even kept straight faces as the instructors earnestly explained that the human body is composed of energy zones called "meridians"—and that if you are in the midst of a cardiac arrest, the proper emergency procedure is to bite your fingertip.

And when our efforts didn't seem to be producing the results we wanted, we played hardball.

"In order for us to go through with this piece [on the Institute]," we claimed, "the 'money people' need something to sell this story—a hook." And the only hook that would suffice would be a Q & A session with Dr. Henry Kissinger, Nobel Prize–winning knight.

Eventually, we received word that Dr. K would be more than happy to talk to us about his hitherto unknown fascination with the art of massage.

Before we knew it, we were talking with that familiar voice, asking the burning questions of our time: about ticklishness, body oils, and thoroughly preposterous rumors of S&M orgies....

—*Peter Huyck and Alex Gregory*

SPY: *How did you get involved with the Ohashi Institute?*

DR. HENRY KISSINGER: To tell you the truth, I don't know how I got involved with Ohashi; somebody recommended him to me, but I forget who that was. It certainly was a very happy occasion.

SPY: *Do you know how long ago that was?*
HK: About eight years.

SPY: *Have you suffered any stress-related illnesses?*
HK: No.

SPY: *During which period in your life were you under the most stress? How did you deal with it?*
HK: When I was in government for eight years…and…uh…I don't think I had a particular way of dealing with it.

SPY: *So you didn't get massaged back then?*
HK: Uh…I got occasionally [a massage], but not regularly.

SPY: *Have you ever experimented with other New Age healing methods, like crystals, aromatherapy, or chanting?*
HK: No.

SPY: *When you're getting a massage, do you prefer it hard or soft?*
HK: Well, he doesn't really do a massage as such, he does shiatsu…. Generally, I prefer it hard, but that's irrelevant to him.

SPY: *Are you ticklish?*
HK: Skip that one.

SPY: *What part of your body needs the most massaging?*
HK: Lower back.

SPY: *Do you wear clothes during the massage sessions or do you do it* au naturel*?*
HK: I wear pajamas.

SPY: *Do they use any special oils or lotions?*
HK: None…no oils.

SPY: *Are you experienced enough with the Ohashiatsu technique to massage someone else?*
HK: No.

SPY: *Is it possible to massage yourself?*
HK: I doubt it.

SPY: *You've traveled all over the world to hundreds of exotic countries; where can you get the best rubdown?*
HK: Oh, there are a number of places….I'll confine myself to Ohashi.

SPY: *So you'd just recommend him and no one else?*
HK: No, I don't want to get into all these other questions.

SPY: *Is there a particular massage session or Ohashi session that stands out as the best you've ever had?*
HK: No, they're about all the same standard.

SPY: *Do you find it preferable to be massaged by a man or a woman?*
HK: I've never had shiatsu by a woman.

SPY: *Many men experience penile arousal during massage. How do you control it?*
HK: Many WHAT?!

SPY: *Many men experience penile arousal—that was something {an instructor} had told me about, and that it was a problem. Do you have any way of controlling that?*
HK: I-I-I-I don't want to answer these questions.

SPY: *Oh, okay—we often ask questions that sound kind of clinical, to get people interested.*
HK: Okay, ask one or two more, and then we'll cut it out.

SPY: *Is your life still stressful now that you're out of government? How do you deal with it?*
HK: My life is still stressful, and I get occasional shiatsu.

SPY: *How much of an impact has Ohashiatsu had on your life?*
HK: He's been very helpful, and I've been very grateful to him.

SPY: *There's a rumor going around that the Ohashi Institute has group S&M sex sessions at its retreats in upstate New York—how often did you take part in this?*
HK: I've never been at the Institute, so I don't know.

SPY: *Off the record, who was Deep Throat?*
HK: You must be out of your mind. {hangs up}

End of interview.

"Generally, I prefer it hard. But that's irrelevant to him."

"But by that stage the economics had resolved themselves," says Colman. "It was clear that it was an untenable position—advertising would never pick up, even though we could deliver the readership. You could just see from the numbers that this was not something that was ever going to make any money."

So Colman started thinking about closing it down—something he shuddered at doing for several reasons.

"I knew I was going to be remembered as the guy who killed *Spy*," he says. "But I was not going to run a charity, however noble the cause. So I built up this big thing in my mind, for months—and then it literally took five minutes. I told Bruno, I told the staff. And afterward, rather than the world collapsing, there was this huge sigh of relief. It was a beautiful sunny day, and I walked outside and thought, *Why didn't I do that months ago?*

"There was really nothing more to say. It was now just assumed *that anyone successful was a controlling psychopath."*

"I lost quite a few millions on *Spy*," Colman continues. "But it was entirely my fault, and a magical lesson. I often think that one day I'll put a screen print of the *Spy* logo—it's such a beautiful logo—above my fireplace. And people will say to me, 'Oh, why have you got that there?' And I'll say, 'Well, it's my Monet.' Because I paid the same amount."

And so, one day in January 1998, *Spy* was gone.

The fact that Bruno Maddox was The Last Editor of *Spy* seems reason enough to track him down. We meet for a drink at the Gramercy Park Hotel in Manhattan.

"I suppose it did get incrementally better," the genial, rumpled Maddox says. "We were getting good press, finally, which is obviously everything to a magazine like that. Most of the work at the end was done by myself and William Monahan, a novelist now and Hollywood's hottest screenwriter [*Kingdom of Heaven, The Departed*]. The writing was pretty good, the last couple of issues. Everything was very poorly conceived, and poorly executed, but there was some quality prose."

Maddox, like Colman, had come over from London, where he'd gone to school with old *Spy* writer Louis Theroux.

"But my education about *Spy* mainly came at the hands of people I'd meet at parties and bars," he says. "They'd tug me aside and be extremely obnoxious about how great *Spy* had been, and how far it had fallen, and what I needed to do, and could we

repeat the stunt of sending the checks to the billionaires? It was incredibly tedious.

"But to say we were a shell of our former selves is almost to understate the situation," he continues. "The early *Spy* was so effective at publicizing the human side of gargantuan celebrities that there was really nothing more to say—it was now just *assumed* that anyone successful was a controlling psychopath. And with a satirical magazine, you can't make many mistakes. If you ever lose your authority, all the people you victimized victimize you, and you're done. But Lipstein was a true believer. He was a great guy to work for. He's got a terrible reputation, but he knew what he wanted."

Still, there were surreal meetings in which Maddox would be encouraged to assign *Spy* stories that could piggyback photo shoots with *Psychology Today* stories. "Obviously these are the classic conditions under which true creativity happens," he says with a smirk. "Morale was extremely low all the time. We were sharing an office with these two really quite profitable magazines. And here we were, a bunch of young, drunk men. We really were a fraternity—the money-losing wastrel sons of the family."

Maddox cites a parody of *The New York Times Magazine* as a high point: "It was one of those rare days when I thought there was a way forward. I thought maybe there was a role for *Spy*."

"And the lows?"

"Oh, the brown-paper cover."

"That's one I missed."

"It's very rare, because no one bought it. The cover art was a piece of brown paper [see opposite]. Which sounds quite groovy in the recollection, but it was a very *cheap-looking* piece of brown paper. And, it covered the logo."

Maddox thinks for another moment.

"I might also have to point to the JFK Jr. story in the last issue—a fairly telling note to go out on," he continues. "We dug around, and there wasn't anything—anything *negative*—really to say about the guy. That piece was very much symptomatic of our general problem. People had become more discreet in their personality defects—they were no longer strutting around New York with girlfriends three feet taller than them and getting drunk. Everyone was sipping water and wearing baseball caps. It was a much subtler time for evil social excrescence. Also, the satirical takes that the early *Spy* pioneered had been so thoroughly incorporated into the general media. *Entertainment Weekly* was reading like the old *Spy* at that point. Then you had *The Daily Show* starting up. We didn't feel very needed, either in the marketplace or in the larger culture."

Fittingly, when the end came, Donald Trump was there.

"I was actually just talking to my therapist about this," Maddox says. "The day before the plug got pulled, there was an embarrassing incident with Trump. I had written a letter to him late one night, saying, 'Hey, Mr. Trump, it's me, I'm the editor of *Spy*, we haven't—or the man in my chair hasn't—spoken to you in years. What if we patched things up? What if you let me come and hang out with you for a day, and I wrote some sort of piece, and I gave you full approval over the final copy, and we can see what happens? It would be like Arafat and Rabin shaking hands on the White House lawn. Anyway, just some random thoughts, get back to me!'

"And rather than getting back to me, he released it to the press. Didn't contact me at all, just faxed it straight to the *Post*, which ran it under some horrible headline."

WHEN I SPOKE TO TRUMP for this book and said in passing that in the end he had outlasted *Spy*, he seized on it: "That's the most important thing!" Sadly, a long conversation was out of the question just then—Trump said he was too busy "working on a big deal," by which he may have meant the bankruptcy of his casinos, announced several days later—but he did confess (or purport) to have enjoyed the back-and-forth with *Spy*.

"It was fun even when *Spy* was knocking the crap out of me," Trump fairly shouted over the phone. "But it's more fun now that *I'm* on top and *Spy* is gone."

THE *SPY*-TRUMP PEACEMAKING STUNT that Bruno Maddox proposed in 1998 "was taken as a fatal symptom," says the editor. "I was called into Jo Colman's office. He sort of frowned at me and looked at the *Post* and back at me and said, 'Well, whatever.' And I walked out. The next day I was working at home, and Jo called and said, 'Bruno, I'm closing *Spy*.'

"I experienced a wave of mixed emotions. We were trying to do a hit piece on Oprah Winfrey, but it was the usual thing: We'd discovered that actually she was really nice, does a lot of charity work—so I was looking at a horrible day of spinning good into evil. And suddenly *I didn't have to do any work*. A PR friend of mine gave me some good advice—to call Kurt and

Graydon to try and get some sort of positive feedback. Which they were great about. So there was a very nice story the next day in the *Post* saying we'd done a great job, that things had been looking up editorially.

"And then the staff all went and got completely shitfaced. And we hatched a cunning plan to march into Colman's office the next day in suits—'Suits at dawn!' was the rallying cry—and buy the magazine from him with our savings and keep it going. Anyway. It fell victim to our hangovers. And that was the end of *Spy*.

"We felt like footnotes to the history of *Spy*," says the magazine's final editor, rising from his chair. "In fact, you can just use that as a *poignant last detail*."

Done. 🂡

A final *Spy* List, and for a change one that isn't utterly, utterly random. Herewith our attempt to list all of *Spy*'s editorial, art, business, and production staff, as well as regular contributors, culled from every masthead from The Funny Years straight through The Unfunny Years. We regret any misspellings. We apologize if your name isn't here and it should be. And we're sorry if your name is here and you'd rather it weren't.

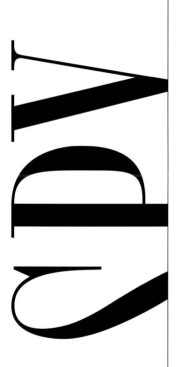

Andy Aaron
Salma Abdelnour
Josh Abrams
Stephen Abrams
Peter Ackerman
Allison Ackerman
Kathleen Adams
Devon Alexander
Henry Alford
Elaine Alimonti
Rodney Alvarado
Kurt Andersen
Misha Anderson
Sonda Andersson
Kimia Ansari
Michael Appelbaum
Jaime Arango
Miles Archer
Cindy Arlinsky
Lisa Auslander
John Baker
Tina Bakhtamian
Holly Barnett
Harriet Barovick
Lukas Barr
Jonathan Barrett
Sara Barrett
Jack Barth
C. C. Baxter
Laura Belgray
Aimée Bell
Michèle Bennett
Harry Benson
Phillip Berroll
Lisa Birnbach
Barry Blitt
Roy Blount, Jr.
Jillian Blume
Randy Blunk
Oleg Bogomolny
Lynn Bollmeyer

Chad Bonney
Ellen Bourdeaux
David Bourgeois
Dan Bova
Anne Bowen
Celia Brady
John Brink
John Brodie
Kathleen Brophy
Colin Brown
Holly Brubach
Bill Buchanan
Richard Bulman
Carter Burden III
Laura Burke
Kevin Burnett
Daniel Burrows
Susan Buttenwieser
Jillian Byck
Lorraine Cademartori
Virginia Cahill
Peter Callahan
Chris Callis
Catherine Cantieri
Amid Capeci
Wendi Carlock
Christopher Carroll
Daniel Carter
Graydon Carter
Christine Cauchon
George Cerezo
Christian Cervegnano
Ben Chase
Karen Cho
John Cienki
Cathy Clarke
James Clauss
Hal Cohen
Margaret Cohen
Meg Cohen
Santiago Cohen
James Collins
Michael Collins
John Colman
Yves Comeliau
John Connolly
Macaulay Connor
Amy B. Conway
Bill Cooley
Carrie Cooper
Ethan Cornell
Signe Corriere
Cynthia Cotts
Jane Craig
Sarah Crichton
Brian Cronin

Tom Cunningham
Bonnie Datt
Cara Joy David
Caldwell Davis
Meredith Davis
Lorri Day
Celeste de Brunhoff
Lisa Degliantoni
Kara Dellopoulos
Wendy Dembo
Eric Demby
Deborah DeStaffan
Elizabeth Devereaux
Jill Dickey
David Dircks
Adam Dolgins
Paul Donald
Andrew Dong
Alan Dorsey
David Doty
Michael Dougan
Joe Doughney
Larry Doyle
Stephen Doyle
Constance Drayton
William Drenttel
Alisha Drucks
Josh Dubler
Gina Duclayan
Stephen Dudley
Robert Dwek
Anna Dylan
Gregory Easley
Paula Eastwood
Mark Ebner
Chris Eboch
Sunny Edmunds
Andrea Egert
Lizabeth Einbinder
Emily Eldridge
Paul Elie
Edward Jay Epstein
Amy Erario
Julie Erlich
Blake Eskin
Jeffrey Estilo
Robinson Everett
Francis Evers
Ellen Falb
Linda Sue Farber
Mark Fefer
Bruce Feirstein
Amelia Felix
Samantha Fennell
Douglas Ferguson
Rosa Fernandez

Meredith Fiedler
Gaylord Fields
Linda Fischbach
Michael Fish
Nian Fish
Karin Fittante
Birgitte Fjord
Louis Flanigan
Marc Flores
Robyn Fontes
Jonathan Foreman
Murphy Freelen
Peter Frelinghuysen
Drew Friedman
Tad Friend
Scott Frommer
Laura Frost
Robert Frumkin
David Fuchs
Lisa Furlong
Steve Futterman
Irene Gallo
Phil Gammage
Andrew Gardner
Jane Garland Katz
Marina Garnier
Dave Garrett
Valerie Garrison
Francis Gasparini
Robert J. George
Suzanne Gerber
Mary Gilbert
Patrick Giles
Josh Gillette
Joe Gillis
Catherine Gilmore-Barnes
Lisa Giordani
Randi Glatzer
Laura Glenn
Timothy Godsall
Hilary Goins
Daniel Goldberg
Lauren Goldstein
Karen Gooby
Fred Goodman
Erwin Gorostiza
Nicki Gostin
Lance Gould
James Grant
L. P. Grant
Steve Grant
Susannah Grant
Humphrey Greddon
Joey Green
Josh Greenberg
Alex Gregory

Joanne Gruber
Steven Guarnaccia
Sean Gullette
Hadley Gustafson
Randi Hacker
Anthony Haden-Guest
Michael Hainey
Linda Hall
Sarah Hammond
Sallie Han
Lucy Handley
Bruce Handy
Armin Harris
John Hart
Huntley Haverstock
Audrey Hawkins
Charlotte Hays
Alex Heard
Jeff Hearn
Deanna Hearns
Peter Heffernan
John Heilpern
Ted Heller
Patrick Hemsworth
Tony Hendra
Beata Henrichs
Anna Herceg
Holly Hester
Lawrence Hettleman
Paul Hilts
Lynn Hirschberg
Laureen Hobbs
Drew Hodges
Ann Hodgman
Moira Hodgson
Michael Hofmann
Barbara Hofrenning
Henry "Dutch" Holland
Jana Hollingshead
David Hollingsworth
Eric Hollreiser
B. W. Honeycutt
Euny Hong
Susan Horner
Caroline Howard
Jennifer Hsu
Bridget Hughes
Troy Hughes
J. J. Hunsecker
Michael Hunter
Pam Hunter
Anna Husarka
Peter Huyck
David Hyatt
Brian Hyland
Catherine Iannone

Paul Iorio
T. W. Irwin
Alexander Isley
David Ives
A. J. Jacobs
Brian Jacobsmeyer
J. F. Jacobson
Chere Jalali
Peggy Jameson
Laurel Janensch
Emma Joels
Carrie Johnson
Carolyn Jones
Dafydd Jones
Donald Jones
Marian Jones
William Joyce
David Kaestie
Eve Kahn
Leah Kalatoy
George Kalogerakis
David Kamp
Richard Kanar
Eric Kaplan™
Howard Kaplan
Hjalti Karllson
Jackie Kaufman
Melik Kaylan
Nancy Keating
Chris Kelly
Pamela Keogh
Tad Kepley
Geof Kern
Jeff Kiddon
Nicholas Kierstead
Martin Kihn
Karina Kindler
Rachel King
Renee Kinsella
Walter Kirn
John Kirwan-Taylor
Matthew Klein
Alexander Knowlton
Alice Koh
Katherine Kohoe
David Korzenik
Frank Koughan
Mimi Kramer
Anne Kreamer
Gerry Kreger
Catherine Kruchko
Julie Krumholz
Sasha Kurtz
Christiaan Kuypers
Carlos Lamadrid
Lisa Lampugnale

David Lange
George Lange
Douglas Lansky
Mark Lasswell
Leslie Laufer
Mitchell Lavnick
Janet Lazarus
Michael Lee
Susan Lehman
Adam Lehner
Jamie Leo
John Leonard
Natasha Lessnik
Lawrence Levi
Art Levine
Mitchell Levine
Tajlei Levis
Wendy Levy
Robin Lewis
Steven Lighty
Kenneth Lin
Nicky Lindeman
Michael Lipscomb
Jennifer Lipshy
Alexis Lipsitz
Owen Lipstein
Karmen Lizzul
Bari Goodman Lloyd
Peter Lo
Andrea Lockett
Susan Lofgren
Dian Lofton
Timothy Long
Jane Loranger
T. S. Lord
Brant Louck
Caitlin Lovinger
Alison Clark Lowander
Peter Lubell
Ed Lucaire
Mike Luckovich
Holly Ludvigsen
Larissa MacFarquhar
Bob Mack
George Mackin
Suzanne MacNeille
Bruno Maddox
Monica Mahoney
Susan Mainzer
Maija-Lisa Makinen
Jamie Malanowski
Joseph Malgarini
Craig Malisow
Thomas Mara
Douglas Marolla
Delia Marshall

Anne Marie Martin
Guy Martin
Patty Marx
Leslie Maslow
Joseph Mastrianni
Ann C. Mathers
James Mauro
Rudy Maxa
Vincent McCann
Dana McDowell
Kate McDowell
Steve McMillan
Patrick McMullan
Denise Meenan
Candace Meighan
Giulia Melucci
Kirsten Menger-Anderson
Diane Mercer
Alfred Meyer
David Michaelis
Mark Michaelson
Deborah Michel
Julie Mihaly
Steven Mirkin
Christopher Mitchell
Susan Mitchell
William Monaghan
Dorothy Mongiello
Walter Monheit™
Dave Moore
Joe Moore
Susan Morrison
Anne Mortimer-Maddox
Jeanine Moss
Nat Moss
Karen Mui
Jarvis Murphy
Robert Nachman
Rita Nadler
Jonathan Napack
Patty Nasey
Galt Neiderhoffer
Guy Jeffery Nelson
Matthew Nelson
R. E. Neu
Liz Newkirk
Guy Nicolucci
Philip Nobile
John Norton
Don Novello
Melissa Nussbaum
Chris Nutter
Ric O'Brien
Lawrence O'Donnell
Mark O'Donnell
Jennifer Ogden

David Olivenbaum
Sana Olkovetsky
Christina O'Neil
David Onody
Jamey O'Quinn
Elizabeth Osborne
Rosie O'Shea
Sean O'Sullivan
David Owen
Camille Paglia
Julia Palmore
Jane Park
Luanne Parker
Tawan Parsons
Cleo Paskal
Mia Paterno
C.F. Payne
Barbara Peck
James Pendergast
Belinda Peres
Darrell Perry
Thomas Phillips, Jr.
Andrea Pinto
Denise Platkin
John Pollock
Charles Pooter
Jill Pope
Nessia Pope
Micaela Porta
Joel Potischman
David Potorti
Kate Pottinger
Ann Preisman
Suzy Preston
Martha Proctor
Nancy Puskuldjian
Joe Queenan
Tim Quirk
Steve Radlauer
Daniel Radosh
Ignatz Ratzwikziwzki
Kristen Rayner
Stefanie Rehder
Gabrielle Reiffel
Natasha Reilly
Geoffrey Reiss
Susan Relihan
Andre Ricciardi
Kristall Richardson
Andrea Rider
Robert Rifkin
Aimee Rinehart
Alexandra Ringe
Bryan Riss
Brian Ritt
Catherine Roach

Margaret Robbins
Howard Robbins
Dale Robbins
Ty Robertson
Stephen Robinson
Ricardo Robles
Edel Rodriguez
Robert Rooney
Lawrence Rose
Jack Rosenberger
Ellen Rosenbush
Hank Rosenfeld
Marion Rosenfeld
Ellen Rosenthal
James Rosenthal
Laurie Rosenwald
Marissa Rothkopf
Anne Rothschild
Debby Rovine
Chip Rowe
Jonathan Rowe
Paul Rudnick
Lori Ruicki
Kimberly Ruiz
David Runnion
James Sackel
Lori Salotto
Luc Sante
Dora Sarafini
Andrew Savulich
Elissa Schappell
Alyson Schenck
Gary Schrader
Steven Schragis
Kay Schuckhart
Karen Schwartz
Jessica Scofield
Cintra Scott
Nell Scovell
John Seabrook
Melissa Secondino
Jim Seibert
Will Self
John Sellers
Max Sentry
Rebecca Serksnys
Andreanna Seymore
Matthew Sharlot
Maura Shea
Harry Shearer
Anne Shearman
Maureen Shelly
David Shenk
Josh Shenk
Chuck Shepherd
Heidi Sherman

Rodrigo Shopis
Randall Short
Gary Shrader
Kay Shuckhart
Vernon Silver
Karin Silverstein
James Simmons
Judy Simms
Paul Simms
Tamara Sims
David Singer
Elisabeth Sinsabaugh
Paul Slansky
Caitlyn Slockbower
Wendell Smith
William Smith
Suliman Snipes
Lynn Snowden
Sheryl-Sue Sober
Deanne Sokolin
Cheryl Solimini
Elizabeth Soltis
Ilyssa Somer
Michael Sorkin
Michele Spane
Robert Spillman
Laura Spivak
Chris Spuches
Cristie Stanton
Randall Stanton
Amy Stark
Don Steinberg
Richard Stengel
Christopher Stern
Eddie Stern
Phil Stern
Brian Sternberg
Jeffery Stevens
Tod Stiles
Jo Stockton
Tracy Stora
David Stott
John Strapp III
Mark Strauss
Julia Strongson
Melissa Stubis
Barbara Sullivan
Eva Sullivan
Christine Summer
Benjamin Svetkey
Carl Swanson
Shari Syrkett
Taki
Frank Tantillo
Gerald Taylor
Rachel Telegen

Gwan Liong The
Louis Theroux
Dorrit Thomas
Rafael Thomas
Denis Timm
Terrence Tocantins
Atif Toor
Damon Torres
Lissa Townsend Rodgers
James Traub
Douglas Truppe
Liz Tuccillo
Matthew Tyrnauer
Rachel Urquhart
Hilary Van Kleeck
Tony Vanaria
E. L. Vandepaer
George Vernadakis
Gregory Villepique
Carol Vinzant
Laura Vogel
Nicholas von Hoffman
Ari Voukydis
Anna Walker
Alden Wallace
Jason Ward
Bret Watson
Caren Weiner
Ellis Weiner
Matthew Weingarden
Nicky Weinstock
Nina Weiss
Philip Weiss
Charles Welch
Jeff Wellington
Leah Welsh
Philippe Weisbecker
Sam Whitehead
Elaine Wilkins
Wendi Williams
Anne Williamson
Bill Wilson
Edward Winslow
Jennifer Winston
Michael Witte
Deirdre Cummins Wright
Lisa Wu
Scott Yates
Jonathan Yevin
Jonathan Zarov
Barry Zeger
Ned Zeman
Eric Zicklin
Edward Zuckerman
Heather Zullinger
Victoria Zurkan

This book was produced by

**MELCHER
MEDIA**

124 West 13th Street
New York, NY 10011
melcher.com

Publisher: Charles Melcher
Associate Publisher: Bonnie Eldon
Editor in Chief: Duncan Bock
Editor: David E. Brown
Production Director: Andrea Hirsh
Assistant Editor: Lindsey Stanberry

Spy *The Funny Years*
© 2006 Kurt Andersen, Graydon Carter, and George Kalogerakis

Published in 2006 by Miramax Books

For information address Hyperion,
77 West 66th St.
New York, NY 10023-6298

ISBN 1-4013-5239-1

Library of Congress Cataloging-in-Publication Data
is available upon request.

Designed by Alexander Isley Inc.

Printed in Malaysia

First Edition

2 4 6 8 10 9 7 5 3 1
08 07 06

*For Ash, Max, Kate, Spike, Lucy, Bronwen
and Theo—and all the other children
whose parents created Spy.*

ACKNOWLEDGMENTS

No one deserves more thanks than our
several hundred colleagues at *Spy*. We were
extraordinarily lucky, or blessed, which may
amount to the same thing.

But absolutely indispensable to the
present project have been three of those
beloved *Spy* alumni: Alex Isley, Joanne
Gruber, and Marissa Rothkopf Bates,
our art director, text editor, and executive
assistant, respectively, at *Spy* then and
of this book now. A special thanks also to
all the *Spy* alumni who were generous with
their memories, photos, commemorative
swizzle sticks, et cetera, and to *Spy*'s
lawyer, David Korzenik, for revisiting this
with a still-gimlet eye. And thank goodness
for the tough-ish love of David Brown,
our editor at Melcher Media, and assistant
editor Lindsey Stanberry, whom we hereby
declare honorary *Spy* veterans.

Nor could we have managed this without
the enthusiastic faith and support of Jim
Wiatt, Suzanne Gluck, and Erin Malone
at the William Morris Agency; David
McCormick; Harvey Weinstein, Jonathan
Burnham, Rob Weisbach, and Kristin
Powers at Miramax Books; Charles Melcher
at Melcher Media; and Heather Halberstadt
and Chris Mueller at *Vanity Fair*.

Melcher Media thanks Hayley Capodilupo,
Dave McAninch, Lauren Nathan, Jessie
Morgan Owens, Lia Ronnen, Holly Rothman,
Nathan Sayers, Alex Tart, Shoshana Thaler,
Emily Votruba, and Megan Worman.

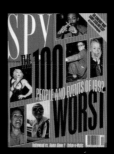